THE CRITICAL
QUR'AN

**Explained from Key Islamic Commentaries
and Contemporary Historical Research**

ROBERT SPENCER

BOMBARDIER
B O O K S

BOMBARDIER BOOKS
An Imprint of Post Hill Press

The Critical Qur'an:
Explained from Key Islamic Commentaries and Contemporary Historical Research
© 2021 by Robert Spencer
All Rights Reserved

ISBN: 978-1-64293-949-1

Cover Design by Tiffani Shea

Post Hill Press
New York • Nashville
posthillpress.com

Published in the United States of America
3 4 5 6 7 8 9 10

Offered with love to all the people of the world
who love the Qur'an

Note: No system of transliteration for Arabic words and names is entirely satisfactory, and none is in consistent usage among writers in English. English simply is not equipped to render the subtleties of the Arabic alphabet. The transliteration in this volume is not systematic; it sacrifices consistency to accord as much as possible with the familiarity of common usage.

Contents

Introduction

The Critical Qur'an is designed to equip the English-speaking reader with a knowledge of the Qur'an and how it is interpreted in Islam, and to see how mainstream Islamic commentators understand the text, particularly its passages that are most problematic for non-Muslim readers: the exhortations to jihad warfare, the Sharia provisions that call for the denial of various rights to women, and the like. In numerous other editions of the Qur'an, these are obscured with apologetic intent. Here, they are explained in full.

This edition of the Islamic holy book also provides a general introduction to some of the problems with the text. This is also unusual, as for the Islamic scholarly tradition, such problems do not actually exist. The Qur'an is perfect, unchanging, and unchangeable, and its centrality in Islam cannot be overstated.

The Qur'an, according to Mohammed Marmaduke Pickthall, an English convert to Islam who translated the Muslim holy book, is an "inimitable symphony, the very sounds of which move men to tears and ecstasy."[1] The Qur'an, explains the Islamic scholar Seyyed Hossein Nasr, "constitutes the alpha and omega of the Islamic religion in the sense that all that is Islamic, whether it be its laws, its thought, its spiritual and ethical teachings and even its artistic manifestations, have their roots in the explicit or implicit teachings of the Sacred Text."[2]

To Muslims worldwide it is the perfect, unaltered word of Allah, delivered without the slightest error by the angel Gabriel to the Islamic prophet Muhammad, and then transmitted, again with no error or deviation at all, down the centuries to reach us in exactly the same form it had when it was first compiled and codified by the caliph Uthman in the year 653. It is for

---

1 Mohammed Marmaduke Pickthall, *The Meaning of the Glorious Koran: An Explanatory Translation* (New York: Alfred A. Knopf, 1930), vii.
2 Seyyed Hossein Nasr, *A Young Muslim's Guide to the Modern World* (Chicago: Kazi Publications, 1994), 15.

pious Muslims an all-encompassing guide to living, as eternally relevant as it is eternally unchanging.

Yet it is by no means immediately inviting, particularly to the non-Muslim reader. One principal reason for this is that it is hard to follow, as it is not arranged chronologically or by subject matter, but by the length of the chapters, *suras*. With the exception of the brief first chapter, its 114 suras are generally arranged, with some exceptions, from the longest to the shortest. According to Islamic tradition, the first revelation that Muhammad received is not sura 1, but sura 96 of the Qur'an. Islamic tradition also holds, with some disagreements, that the last revelation Muhammad received, which came to him while he was on his deathbed, is sura 110 of the Qur'an, not the last one in the book, sura 114.

Further complicating matters is the fact that the Qur'an follows no single narrative line; it is not a collection of historical accounts, but more a collection of sermons, the longer of which deal with a wide variety of topics, with no clearly discernable unifying thread. It makes no attempt at linear history, either as a whole or, generally, within the individual suras.

According to Islamic tradition, Gabriel first began visiting Muhammad and giving him sections of the Qur'an, a perfect copy of the "mother of the book" (43:4) that has always existed in Paradise with Allah, in the year 610. Over the next twenty-three years, Gabriel delivered Qur'anic revelations to Muhammad piecemeal. Some were written down, others memorized by various followers of Muhammad. According to Islamic tradition, the Qur'an was not collected together when Muhammad died in 632, and early Muslims were reluctant to do so, since Muhammad had not done it himself. However, when some of those who had memorized portions of the Islamic holy book were killed in battle, some of the believers began to press for its collection, the rejection of variant readings, and the codification and distribution of the agreed-upon text.

That is, again according to Islamic tradition, supposed to have taken place in the year 653, under the direction of the caliph Uthman, the third successor of Muhammad. However, this account, however widely accepted, lacks any contemporary attestation and is likely to be more legend than historical fact. Although Uthman is supposed to have distributed his Qur'an to the various Muslim provinces, virtually no trace of the book, such as quotes or even mentions of its existence, exist from the time it is supposed to have been completed (632), or from when it is supposed to have been distributed throughout the Islamic world (653), or for four decades thereafter, when quotations from the Qur'an appear on wall inscriptions inside the Dome of the Rock, although they are not identified as such. Not until the early part of the eighth century does mention of the Qur'an begin to appear in the polemical literature of non-Muslims and Muslims alike.

Uthman is said to have burned the variants in the Qur'anic text, and Islamic polemicists hold to this day that no such variants exist, as the text has been miraculously preserved in its original form. Yet numerous variants actually do exist. Islamic tradition seems to provide for this when Muhammad is depicted as saying: "This Qur'an has been revealed to be recited in seven different ways, so recite of it whichever [way] is easier for you (or read as much of it as may be easy for you)."[3]

Islamic scholars say these "seven different ways [ahruf]" are simply variations in the Arabic dialect in which the Qur'an was transmitted. However, there are varying manuscript traditions, and attempts to standardize and codify them. Notably, some three hundred years after Muhammad supposedly received the Qur'an, an Islamic scholar named Ibn Mujahid (860–936), published a book entitled The Seven Readings, in which he delineated the seven acceptable forms of Qur'an recitation (qira'at), that is, seven variant forms of the text which were within the acceptable bounds of Islamic orthodoxy.

Ibn Mujahid ascribes each of his "readings" to a different eighth-century scholar, but it cannot be known for sure whether the earlier authorities to which he ascribes the variants actually transmitted them, or if he attributed his work to them in order to give it an air of antiquity and authenticity. It seems likely that the hadiths in which Muhammad

is made to speak of the Qur'an being recited in "seven different ways" were invented in order to explain the existence of these seven variant readings of the text, which had all apparently circulated so widely by the eighth, ninth, and tenth centuries that they could be ignored or all copies destroyed. Ibn Mujahid gives the names of the transmitters (mutawatir) of the "seven readings" as Nafi (d. 785); Ibn Kathir (d. 737, not to be confused with the fourteenth-century Qur'anic scholar whose work is cited throughout this book); Ibn Amir (d. 736); Abu Amr (d. 770); Asim (d. 744); Hamza (d. 772); and al-Kisa'i (d. 804).[4] To these were later added other readings as well: those of Abu Ja'far (d. 747); Ya'qub (d. 820); Khalaf (d. 843); Hasan al-Basri (d. 728); Ibn Muhaisin (d. 740); al-Yazidi (d. 817); and al-A'mash (d. 765).[5]

Not only were there thus fourteen diverging traditions of the actual text of the Qur'an, but each of these has transmitters who are identified in Islamic tradition, and generally more than one. Among the transmitters of Nafi's text is Warsh (d. 812), and among those who transmitted the text of Asim is Hafs (d. 796); both of these manuscript traditions would come to predominate in large sectors of the Islamic world.

This multiplicity likely accounts for the variants in Qur'anic manuscripts, which are, contrary to popular belief, actually quite

---

3 Muhammad Ibn Ismail Al-Bukhari, Sahih al-Bukhari: The Translation of the Meanings, translated by Muhammad M. Khan, (Darussalam, 1997), vol. 6, book 66, no. 4992.
4 Ahmad von Denffer, Ulum al-Qur'an: An Introduction to the Sciences of the Qur'an (Leicestershire: The Islamic Foundation, 1983), 117.
5 Ibid., 118.

numerous. The contemporary Qur'anic scholar Daniel Alan Brubaker notes that while "most surviving Qur'an manuscripts bear the signs of having been produced following a campaign of standardization basically consistent with that reported to have been directed by the third caliph, it is also clear that there existed *some* differences of perception about the correct words of the Qur'an text at the times most of these manuscripts were produced, which were later revisited when these perceptions changed or standardization became more thorough. It is not impossible that some of these varying perceptions would have been tied to certain geographic regions or locales."[6]

Indeed, the different *qira'at* were used in different areas of the Islamic world. Islamic scholar Aisha Bewley explains that in AD 815, "Basra was reciting the qira'a of Abu Amr and Ya'qub, Kufa was using Hamza and Asim, Syria was using Ibn Amir, Makka had Ibn Kathir, and Madina was using Nafi."[7]

What is taken almost universally today to be Uthman's Qur'an is actually a Qur'an that was published in Cairo in 1924 and has since then become the dominant edition of the Muslim holy book all over the world, as it has won wide acceptance as an accurate reflection of the Uthmanic text. This edition represents the Hafs tradition. Yet despite this immense effort at standardization, the Warsh tradition of the Qur'anic text still predominates in western and northwest Africa,

and other variants exist as well. Many of the variant readings are noted in this volume.

Traditionally, the suras of the Qur'an are classified as Meccan, that is, dating from the first twelve years of Muhammad's career, when he and his followers lived in Mecca, and Medinan, or dating from the last eleven years of Muhammad's career, after the hijrah, or emigration, to Mecca. Because of the doctrine of abrogation (see 2:106), Medinan suras are generally considered to take precedence over Meccan suras in the formation of Islamic theology and law.

Even while acknowledging that there is no firm indication that any of the Qur'an as such originated in the Meccan or Medinan periods, the Meccan/Medinan distinction of the suras is important, as historically it may refer to two stages of development of the Qur'anic text, which had to be explained by means of the invention of the distinction itself. It also provides a useful means of understanding which sections of the Qur'an are generally considered in Islamic theology to carry greater weight than others.

Many historians today have noted the glaring absence of seventh-century attestation to the existence of Muhammad as the prophet of Islam and to the Qur'an in its Uthmanic recension, as it is supposed to have been published and distributed in the middle of that century. These historians tend to put the final editing and publishing of the Qur'an somewhat later, at the end of the seventh and

---

6 Daniel Alan Brubaker, *Corrections in Early Qur'an Manuscripts: Twenty Examples* (Lovettsville, Virginia: Think and Tell Press, 2019), 95.

7 Aisha Bewley, "The Seven Qira'at of the Qur'an," n.d. https://bewley.virtualave.net/qira.html.

beginning of the eighth century. Reasons for that understanding, including textual variants and evidence of other alterations in the text, will be noted throughout, although what is presented here is not an exhaustive list of variants; preference has been given to those that are clear in English and do not require knowledge of Arabic grammar or orthography to understand.

These variants, although they are almost all minor differences of wording, are extraordinarily important, as they demonstrate that the Qur'an has undergone editing and alteration, as well as textual variation and scribal error, which is contrary to the Islamic apologetic claims that even the smallest detail has been miraculously preserved by Allah, to the degree that there are no variants at all. This idea has tended to stymie efforts to examine the Qur'an as a historical document and to prevent light being shed on the origins of Islam. The variants presented in this volume are an attempt to stimulate such examinations.

Aside from noting variants and other anomalies, the notes on various passages of the Qur'an in this book will rely largely on some of the key Islamic *tafsir*, that is, commentaries on the Qur'an. The primary reference is the *tafsir* of Ibn Kathir (1301–1372), whose voluminous and detailed multivolume commentary on the Qur'an still stands as one of the primary references for Muslims in endeavoring to understand their holy text. The contemporary Islamic scholar Ahmad

von Denffer notes that Ibn Kathir's work is "one of the better-known books on *tafsir*," and that it places "emphasis on soundness of reports." Says von Denffer, "This book although of greatest importance to Muslims has been widely ignored by the orientalists."[8] Until now.

Another Qur'an commentary that is popular among Muslims today, the *Tafsir al-Jalalayn*, so called because it is the work of two men named Jalal, Jalal ad-Din al-Mahalli (1389–1459) and Jalal ad-Din as-Suyuti (1445–1505) is also frequently cited here, along with the twentieth-century tafsir of the influential Pakistani Islamic scholar and politician Syed Abul Ala Maududi (1903–1979), and the *Tafsir Anwarul Bayan* by the Indian scholar Mufti Muhammad Ashiq Ilahi Madani, also from the twentieth century. These were chosen to give a representative sampling of the general Islamic understanding of the various texts; other commentaries are also cited in due course.

Transliteration generally follows the most common usage in English for various names and terms, rather than a systematic rendering. The Qur'an, according to Islamic theology, cannot be translated, as its Arabic character is intrinsic to its meaning. That noted, its meaning can and should be more widely known among English-speaking readers. The translation used here is both new and old. It is based primarily on a modernization of the landmark English translation of Mohammed Marmaduke Pickthall, with

---

8 Von Denffer, 136.

reference to the Arabic original and other common translations. It is designed to be as clear as possible for the English-speaking reader, as an alternative to the most popular Qur'an translations in English, most of which are written in a pseudo-King James Bible English that can be confusing and wearisome to the contemporary reader, and are often marred by an apologetic intent that leads them to mitigate the force of some of the more jarring and problematic passages, or conceal them altogether behind language that, while strictly accurate, can be highly misleading. The most notorious example of this is the rendering of *jihad* in its various verbal forms as "strive" or "struggle," which gives the impression to readers unfamiliar with Islamic theology that only an increased effort at prayer or other spiritual actions is meant. That is not at all the case, as is clear from the actual Qur'anic text, as well as from Islamic theology and law. This version of the Qur'an attempts to bring out that clarity on this as well as other matters.

SURA 1

The Opening

Al-Fatiha

Introduction

Al-Fatiha (The Opening) is the first sura of the Qur'an and most common prayer of the Islamic tradition. A pious Muslim who prays the five requisite daily prayers of Islam will recite the Fatiha seventeen times in the course of those prayers.

According to a hadith, the Muslim prophet Muhammad said that "Allah, the Mighty and Sublime, did not reveal in the Torah or the Gospel anything like Umm Al-Quran," that is, the Mother of the Qur'an, which is another name Islamic tradition gives to al-Fatiha.[1]

Another hadith has the angel Gabriel giving this chapter singular status. As the angel sat with Muhammad, the story goes, he heard a sound, looked up, and said: "This is a gate which has been opened in heaven today. It was never opened before."[2] Then an angel came through the gate, and Gabriel continued: "This is an angel who has come down to earth. He never came down before."[3] The unidentified second angel greeted Muhammad and said: "Rejoice with two lights given to you. Such lights were not given to any Prophet before you. These are: Fatiha-til-Kitab (Surat Al-Fatihah), and the concluding Ayat of Surat Al-Baqarah," that is, the Qur'an's first sura and the last verse of its second.[4] "You will never recite a word from

1 An-Nasa'i, *English Translation of Sunan an-Nasa'i*, Nasiruddin al-Khattab, trans. (Riyadh: Darussalam, 2007), vol. 2, book 11, no. 915.
2 Al-Nawawi, *Riyad-us-Saliheen*, Muhammad Amin Abu Usamah Al-Arabi bin Razduq, trans. (Riyadh: Darussalam, 1999), book 8, ch. 183, no. 1022.
3 Ibid.
4 Ibid.

them without being given the blessings it contains."[5]

Besides bringing blessings, this sura is said to have spiritual powers. On one occasion, according to Islamic tradition, "a lunatic fettered in chains" was cured by the recitation of al-Fatiha.[6]

Al-Fatiha also efficiently and eloquently encapsulates many of the principal themes of the Qur'an and Islam in general: Allah as the "Lord of the worlds," who alone is to be worshiped and asked for help, the merciful judge of every soul on the Last Day.

As this sura is the foundation of Islamic prayer, most Islamic scholars hold that it was revealed in Mecca, early in Muhammad's career. One tradition has Ali ibn Abi Talib, Muhammad's son-in law, one of his earliest followers and his rightful successor in the eyes of Shi'ite Muslims, saying: "The Opening of the Book was revealed in Mecca from a treasure beneath the divine throne."[7] The eleventh-century Islamic scholar al-Wahidi relates a tradition in which the Fatiha, rather than the famous demand from the angel that Muhammad "recite," which is enshrined in sura 96, was the first revelation of the Qur'an. Al-Wahidi adds, "This is also the opinion of Ali ibn Abi Talib."[8] This belief persisted

to the extent that the twelfth-century Persian Islamic scholar and jurist Zamakhshari states that most Qur'an commentators at the time he was writing believed that the Fatiha was the first sura to have been revealed.[9]

The idea that the Fatiha was the beginning of Qur'anic revelation, however, is a minority view, with mainstream Islamic scholars today holding that sura 96, or at least the beginning of it, was the first revelation to come to Muhammad.

Yet in an indication of the fluidity of the Qur'anic text in the early days of Islam, Abdullah ibn Masud, one of Muhammad's companions, did not even have this sura in his version of the Qur'an. Other early Islamic authorities also expressed reservations about its inclusion.[10]

To be sure, this sura does not fit in with the rest of the Qur'an, in that it is in the voice of the believer offering prayer and praise to Allah, not Allah addressing Muhammad. Islamic orthodoxy has it that Allah is the speaker in every part of the Qur'an, so with al-Fatiha, the believer must accept that the deity is explaining how he should be prayed to, without explaining directly that that is what he is doing.

---

5 Ibid.

6 Abu Dawud, *Sunan Abu Dawud, English Translation with Explanatory Notes*, Ahmad Hasan, trans. (New Delhi: Kitab Bhavan, 1990), vol. 3, book 22, no. 3887.

7 Ali ibn Ahmad al-Wahidi, *Asbab al-Nuzul*, Mokrane Guezzou, trans., (Amman: Royal Aal al-Bayt Institute for Islamic Thought, 2019), 6.

8 Ibid.

9 *Kitab ijaz* (Itqan, Cairo, 1888) II, 479, in Tor Andrae, "The Legend of Muhammad's Call to Prophethood," in Ibn Warraq, ed., *Koranic Allusions: The Biblical, Qumranian, and Pre-Islamic Background to the Koran* (Amherst, NY: Prometheus Books, 2013), 410.

10 Arthur Jeffery, "A Variant Text of the Fatiha," in Ibn Warraq, ed., *The Origins of the Koran* (Amherst, New York: Prometheus, 1998), 145–46.

The Opening

¹IN THE NAME OF ALLAH, THE COMPASSIONATE, THE MERCIFUL. ²Praise be to Allah, the Lord of the worlds, ³The compassionate, the merciful. ⁴Master of the day of judgment, ⁵You do we worship, you do we ask for help. ⁶Guide us to the straight path, ⁷The path of those whom you have favored, not of those who have earned your anger, or of those who have gone astray.

2. In Islamic theology, Allah is the speaker of every word of the Qur'an. Some have found it strange that Allah would say something like "Praise be to Allah, the Lord of the worlds," but Islamic tradition holds that Allah revealed this prayer to Muhammad early in his career as a prophet (which began in the year 610 AD, when he received his first revelation from Allah through the angel Gabriel—a revelation that is now contained in the Qur'an's 96th sura), so that the Muslims would know how to pray.

Instead of "Praise be to Allah," the seventeenth-century Shi'ite scholar Muhammad Baqir Majlisi has, "We greatly praise Allah."¹

3. Instead of "the compassionate, the merciful" (*ar-rahman ar-rahim*), a variant seen in Cairo by the Qur'anic scholar Arthur Jeffery (1892–1959) has "the sustainer, the merciful" (*ar-razzaqi ar-rahimi*).²

4. Instead of "master of the day of judgment," the Warsh Qur'an has "king of the day of judgment."³

7. Islamic scholars have often identified "those who have earned Allah's anger" as the Jews, and "those who have gone astray" as the Christians. This is such a commonplace understanding that a translation of Sahih Bukhari, the collection of reports (hadith) of Muhammad's words and deeds that Muslims consider most reliable, adds identifying glosses into a story in which Muhammad quotes this verse of the Qur'an: "Say Amen when the Imam says not the path of those who earn Your Anger (such as Jews) nor of those who go astray (such as Christians); all the past sins of the person whose saying (of Amin) coincides with that of the angels, will be forgiven."⁴

Another hadith in the same collection compiled by the imam Bukhari (810-870) depicts the pre-Islamic monotheist Zaid bin Amr bin Nufail, who died in 605 (five years before Muhammad is said to have begun getting revelations), traveling to Syria in search of the true religion. Encountering a Jewish scholar, Zaid told him: "I intend to embrace your religion, so tell me something about it." ⁵ The scholar replied, "You will not embrace our religion unless you receive your share of Allah's anger." Appalled, Zaid asks him if he knows of another religion, to which the Jewish scholar responds: "I do not know any other religion except the Hanif," that is, "the religion of (the prophet) Abraham who was neither a Jew nor a Christian, and he used to worship none but Allah (alone)." Traveling on, Zaid then happens upon a Christian scholar and tells him also that he wishes to embrace his religion. The Christian states: "You will not embrace our religion unless you get a share of Allah's curse." Again unwilling, Zaid asks him about another religion and

is once again told about the Hanif, which he duly adopts. Islamic theology considers Islam to be the true embodiment of that pure religion of Abraham, who worshiped no others, as do Jews and Christians (see 9:30). On *hanif*, see 2:135.

The repetition of this identification in Bukhari is an indication of how strong the identification is of those who have earned Allah's anger with the Jews and those who have gone astray with the Christians.

The classic Qur'anic commentator Ibn Kathir explains that "the two paths He described here are both misguided," and that those "two paths are the paths of the Christians and Jews, a fact that the believer should beware of so that he avoids them. The path of the believers is knowledge of the truth and abiding by it. In comparison, the Jews abandoned practicing the religion, while the Christians lost the true knowledge. This is why 'anger' descended upon the Jews, while being described as 'led astray' is more appropriate for the Christians."⁶

The *Tafsir al-Jalalayn*, a fifteenth-century Qur'an commentary that, like Ibn Kathir's, remains popular among Muslims to this day, agrees, identifying those who have earned Allah's anger with the Jews and those who have gone astray as the Christians and explaining: "The grammatical structure here shows that those who are guided are not the Jews or the Christians."⁷

This is the view of numerous other mainstream Islamic commentators on the Qur'an. One contrasting but not majority view is that of the fourteenth-century Persian scholar Nisaburi, who says that "those who have incurred Allah's wrath are the people of negligence, and those who have gone astray are the people of immoderation."⁸

Some Western commentators imagined that the Saudis originated this interpretation, and indeed the whole idea of Qur'anic hostility toward Jews and Christians. They found it inconceivable that Muslims all over the world would learn that the central prayer of their faith anathematizes Jews and Christians, and attributed this interpretation to parenthetical glosses the Saudis inserted into the text.

But unfortunately, this interpretation is venerable and mainstream in Islamic theology. The printing of the interpretation in parenthetical glosses into a translation would be unlikely to affect Muslim attitudes, since the Arabic text is always and everywhere normative in any case, and since so many mainstream commentaries contain the idea that the Jews and Christians are being condemned here.

The Cow

Al-Baqara

Introduction

The title might tempt the reader to think that this sura is actually about a cow. This is, however, not the case. The suras of the Qur'an generally take their titles from something recounted within them, even if it's an insignificant detail. In this case, the sura name comes from the story of Moses relaying Allah's command to the Israelites that they sacrifice a cow (2:67–73), one of the Qur'an's many stories from the Bible and Jewish tradition, altered and retold.

At 286 verses, this is the longest sura of the Qur'an. It begins the Qur'an's general (but not absolute) pattern of being organized not chronologically or thematically, but simply running from the longest to the shortest suras, with the exception of the Fatiha (sura 1), which has pride of place as the first sura because of its centrality in Islamic prayer.

This means that one should not take "The Cow" as the original, first, or primary message of Islam, simply because of its position. According to Islamic tradition, it actually dates from the latter part of Muhammad's career, as it was revealed to Muhammad at Medina—to which he is supposed to have fled from Mecca in the year 622. In Medina for the first time, Muhammad became a political and military leader.

Islamic theologians generally regard Medinan suras as taking precedence over Meccan ones wherever there is a disagreement, in accord with verse 106 of this sura of the Qur'an, in which Allah speaks about abrogating verses and replacing them with better ones. (This interpretation of verse 106, however, is not universally accepted. Some say it refers to the abrogation of nothing in the Qur'an, but only of the Jewish and Christian Scriptures.)

"The Cow" contains a great deal of important material for Muslims and is held in high regard. Ibn Kathir says that recitation of "The Cow" distresses Satan: he says that one of Muhammad's early followers, Ibn Mas'ud, remarked that Satan "departs the house where Surat Al-Baqarah is being recited, and as he leaves, he passes gas." Without Ibn Mas'ud's poor taste, Muhammad himself says: "Satan runs away from the house in which Surah Baqara is recited."

There are two indications that this sura was not part of the Qur'an as late as the first three decades of the eighth century. Around 710, a Christian monk of the monastery of Beth Hale (of which there were two, one in northern Iraq and the other in Arabia; it is not known in which one this monk lived) wrote to a Muslim, "I think that for you, too, not all your laws and commandments are in the Qur'an which Muhammad taught you; rather there are some which he taught you from the Qur'an, and some are in *surat albaqrah* and in *gygy* and in *twrh*."[1]

From this it appears that at that time, the Qur'an was not in its present form we now know. *Surat albaqrah* is "the chapter of the Cow," which we know as the second, and longest, sura of the Qur'an. Yet the monk refers to *surat albaqrah* as distinct from the Qur'an, like *gygy* (the Injil, or Gospel) and *twrh* (the

Torah). This suggests that the Qur'an's largest sura was not actually in the Qur'an in the early eighth century, but was a stand-alone book nearly sixty years after the Qur'an was supposed to have been finalized by Uthman.

Then around 730, the renowned Christian theologian John of Damascus published On the Heresies, a smorgasbord of nonmainstream Christianity from the perspective of Byzantine orthodoxy. He included a chapter on the strange new religion of the people he identified by three names: Hagarenes, Ishmaelites, and Saracens. John writes of a "false prophet" named Muhammad (Mamed) who, "having happened upon the Old and the New Testament and apparently having conversed, in like manner, with an Arian monk, put together his own heresy. And after ingratiating himself with the people by a pretence of piety, he spread rumours of a scripture (graphe) brought down to him from heaven. So, having drafted some ludicrous doctrines in his book, he handed over to them this form of worship."[2]

Likewise John shows some familiarity with at least some of the contents of the Qur'an, although he never names it as such, referring instead to particular suras by their names. Among them he refers to "the text of the Cow and several other foolish and ludicrous things which, because of their number, I think I should pass over."[3] He gives the impression that the "text of the Cow" and

---

1 Monk of Beth Hale, *Disputation*, fol. 4b (quoted in Robert G. Hoyland, *Seeing Islam as Others Saw It: A Survey and Evaluation of Christian, Jewish, and Zoroastrian Writings on Early Islam* [Princeton: Darwin Press, 1997]), 471.

2 John of Damascus, *De haeresibus* C/CI, 64–7 (*Patrologia Greca* 94, 769B–772D), quoted in Hoyland, 486.

3 Ibid., 487.

others he mentions, the "text of the Woman" (see sura 4) and the "text of the Camel of God," are all separate documents rather than parts of a single collection.

It is possible that this manner of citation is simply an idiosyncrasy of John's, with no larger significance. But it may also be an indication that the Qur'an was not yet in its final form a century after it was purportedly revealed.

The Cow

IN THE NAME OF ALLAH, THE COMPASSIONATE, THE MERCIFUL.

¹Alif. Lam. Mim. ²This book, there is no doubt in it, is a guide for those who fear Allah. ³Who believe in the unseen, and establish prayer, and spend out of that we have given to them, ⁴And who believe in what has been revealed to you and what was revealed before you, and are sure of the hereafter. ⁵These are the people who depend on guidance from their Lord. These are the successful. ⁶As for the unbelievers, it is all the same for them whether you warn them or don't

1. Many suras of the Qur'an begin with Arabic letters in this way; usually, but not always, there are three such letters. While there has been considerable speculation about what they might mean, Islamic tradition offers no definitive answer. The *Tafsir al-Jalalayn* sums up the prevailing view: "God knows best what is meant by this."[1] "These letters are one of the miracles of the Qur'an and none but Allah (Alone) knows their meanings," say the modern-day Saudi Islamic scholars Muhammad Muhsin Khan and Muhammad Taqi-ud-Din al-Hilali.[2] This is the mainstream Islamic perspective, although how exactly a series of Arabic letters constitutes a miracle is not explained. Speculation abounds. Modern critical researchers generally agree, however, with a statement of one of the foremost among them, the twentieth-century Qur'an scholar Richard Bell; he states, "of these groups of letters placed at the head of certain suras no explanation can be given."[3]

The groundbreaking philologist Christoph Luxenberg has extensively examined the Qur'an's Aramaic substratum (see 12:2) and notes that the Psalms are mentioned several times in the Qur'an (3:184, 17:55, 21:105, 35:25, 54:43, 54:52). He suggests that the mysterious letters may be vestiges of the Qur'an's source text having been a Christian lectionary. The Qur'anic scholar Erwin Gräf declares the Qur'an, "according to the etymological meaning of the word, is originally and really a liturgical text designed for cultic recitation and also actually used in the private and public service. This suggests that the liturgy or liturgical poetry, and indeed the Christian liturgy, which comprises the Judaic liturgy, decisively stimulated and influenced Mohammed,"[4] or whoever was responsible for the compilation of the Qur'an.

Luxenberg explains that the Syriac Christian liturgy "typically begins with a psalm," and that "up to three letters can indicate the number of the psalm in question in the Psalter."[5] The Qur'an's mysterious letters, then, could be indications in the Syriac lectionary of which psalm was to be recited. When that Syriac lectionary was transmuted into the Qur'an, the letters, no longer intelligible, became mysterious utterances of Allah.

2. This is a key Islamic doctrine. The Qur'an is not to be questioned or judged by any standard outside itself; rather, it is the standard by which all other things are to be judged. That, of course, is not significantly different from the way many other religions regard their Holy Writ. But there has been no development in Islam of the historical and textual criticism that has transformed the ways Jews and Christians understand their scriptures today. This is in large part because there is no doubt about the Qur'an and no questioning of it; to study it in a historical-critical way would be impious in itself.

The fluidity of the Qur'anic text is exemplified by the tenth-century story in which a young man was reciting the Qur'an and confused two sets of letters that are identical other than their diacritical marks: he confused *zay* for *ra* and *ta* for *ba*. Thus instead of reading, "This book, there is no doubt in it" (*la raiba fihi*), he read, "This book, there is no oil in it" (*la zaita fihi*).[6]

4. Islamic tradition holds that the "you" addressed here and in many other cases is Muhammad, the prophet of Islam. There is nothing within the Qur'an itself, however, to make that identification certain.

There is likewise in those early decades of the Arab conquests only a handful of mentions of Muhammad, and none either contain or agree with the voluminous material that Islamic traditions that date from the eighth and ninth centuries record of him. The "you" who is addressed in this and so many other Qur'an passages could, therefore, be another prophetic figure whose material was incorporated into the Muhammad legend when it began to be constructed.

With this verse begins the first example, for those who read the Qur'an from cover to cover, of something that is found again and again in the Qur'an: an extended disquisition on the perversity of those who reject belief in Allah. The one beginning here sounds several themes that will recur many, many times. First among these is the assertion that the Qur'an provides guidance to those who believe in what was revealed to whoever is being addressed, as well as in "what was revealed before you."

This refers to the Qur'an's oft-stated assumption that it is the confirmation of the Torah and the Gospel, which teach the same message Muhammad is receiving in the Qur'anic revelations (see 5:44-48). When the Torah and Gospel were found not to agree with the Qur'an, the charge arose that Jews and Christians had corrupted their Scriptures—which is mainstream Islamic belief today. The moderate Muslim Qur'an translator and commentator Muhammad Asad, a convert from Judaism, states this in a positive and irenic way, but it is nonetheless unmistakable that the Qur'an is the crown, the finale, of the earlier scriptures: "The religion of the Qur'an can be properly understood only against the background of the great monotheistic faiths which preceded it, and which, according to Muslim belief, culminate and achieve their final formulation in the faith of Islam."[7] If they achieve their final formulation in Islam, obviously they were not complete or fully correct in their formulations before Islam.

warn them, they do not believe. [7]Allah has sealed their hearing and their hearts, and over their eyes there is a covering. They will suffer an awful doom. [8]And there are some people who say, We believe in Allah and the last day, and they are not believers.

[9]They try to deceive Allah and those who believe, and they deceive no one except themselves, but they do not realize it. [10]In their hearts is a disease, and Allah increases their disease. They will suffer a painful doom because they lie. [11]And when it is said to them, Do not spread corruption on the earth, they say, We are only peacemakers.

[12]Are not they indeed those who spread corruption? But they do not realize it. [13]And when it is said to them, Believe as the people believe, they say, Shall we believe as the foolish people believe? Are not they indeed the foolish ones? But they do not know. [14]And when they encounter those who believe, they say, We believe, but when they go back to their satans they say, Indeed we are with you, we were just mocking. [15]Allah mocks them, leaving them to wander blindly on in their defiance. [16]These are the ones who buy error at the price of guidance, so their business does not prosper, and they are not guided. [17]They are like one who lights a fire, and when it illuminates everything around him, Allah takes away their light and leaves them in darkness, in which they cannot see. [18]Deaf, dumb and blind, and they will not return. [19]Or like a rainstorm from the sky, in which is darkness, thunder and lightning. They thrust their fingers into their ears because of the thunder, for fear of death, Allah surrounds the unbelievers. [20]The lightning almost snatches their sight away from them. As often as it flashes, they

---

7. Another theme in this part of "The Cow" is Allah's absolute control over everything, even the choices of individual souls to believe in him or reject him. All through the book there are so many exhortations to believe in its message that it is hard to imagine that Islam could reject the concept of free will. The *Tafsir al-Jalalayn* says of the unbelievers that Allah does not remove "blessings from them" until they "exchange their good state for disobedience."[8] In other words, as long as they persist in sin, they have only themselves to blame (6:12, 9:70, 30:9).

Other Qur'an passages hold that it is Satan who leads the believers astray (4:119, 15:39, 114:5). But still other passages of the Qur'an, as well as indications from Islamic tradition, state that no one believes in Allah except by his will, so also no one can *disbelieve* in him except by his active will (6:25, 10:100, 16:93, 24:40, 35:8, 36:9-11, 81:29, and so on). Everything is in Allah's hands, even the decision of the individual to obey him or not, yet human beings will still be held accountable for the things they have done. Yet those who have rejected Allah do so because he made it possible for them to do nothing else.

Ibn Kathir states: "These Ayat [verses] indicate that whomever Allah has written to be miserable, they shall never find anyone to guide them to happiness, and whomever Allah directs to misguidance, he shall never find anyone to guide him."[9]

In early Islamic history, a party known as the Qadariyya is said to have tried to advance the concept of individual free will. The pioneering Islamic scholar Ignaz Goldziher explains that the Qadariyya were protesting against "an unworthy conception of God," and yet they "could not find a large body of supporters" among Muslims. Their opponents "battled them with the received interpretation of the sacred scriptures."[10] And won. Ultimately, Muslim authorities declared the concept of human free will to be heretical. A twelfth-century Muslim jurist, Ibn Abi Ya'la, fulminated that the Qadariyya wrongly "consider that they hold in their grasp the ability to do good and evil, avoid harm and obtain benefit, obey and disobey, and be guided or misguided. They claim that human beings retain full initiative, without any prior status within the will of Allah for their acts, nor even in His knowledge of them." Even worse, "their doctrine is similar to that of Zoroastrians and Christians. It is the very root of heresy."[11]

8. Allah refers to himself as "we" frequently throughout the Qur'an. Some non-Muslims have been tempted to see traces of polytheism in this, and Christians in particular have attempted to discern the Trinity. Islamic theology, however, is adamant that this is simply a royal "we" that does not impinge upon the Qur'an's strict and uncompromising monotheism.

10. Instead of "because they lie" (*yakzibuuna*), the Warsh Qur'an has "because they accuse of lying" (*yukazzibuuna*).[12]

11. "To spread corruption on earth" is one of the foremost sins the Qur'an envisions, although it never defines it in specific terms. Ayat 5:33 specifies the punishment for it as killing, crucifixion, amputation of a hand and a foot on opposite sides, or exile.

18. The charge that those who do not believe in Islam are "deaf, dumb, and blind" (cf. 2:171) is an indication of the Islamic assumption that those who reject Islam are not operating in good faith, but are suffering from a moral defect.

20. The philologist Jacob Barth notes that the verse appears incomplete; "perhaps a part containing the rhyme has dropped out."[13]

walk in its light, and when it is dark all around them, they stand still. If Allah willed, he could destroy their hearing and their sight, for Allah has power over everything. **²¹**O mankind, worship your Lord, who created you and the people before you, so that you may fear Allah.

²²He has fashioned the earth a resting place for you, and the sky a canopy, and he causes water to pour down from the sky, thereby producing fruits as food for you. And do not set up rivals to Allah when you know. **²³**And if you are in doubt about what we are revealing to our slave, then produce a sura like it, and call your helpers besides Allah, if you are telling the truth. **²⁴**And if you do not do it, and you can never do it, then guard yourselves against the fire prepared for unbelievers, the fuel of which is of men and stones. **²⁵**And give good news to those who believe and do good works, that they will have gardens under which rivers flow. As often as they are given food from their fruit, they say, This is what was given us before, and it is given to them in resemblance. There are pure companions there for them, there they remain forever. **²⁶**Indeed, Allah doesn't disdain to use the comparison even

of a gnat. Those who believe know that it is the truth from their Lord, but those who do not believe say, What does Allah mean by such a comparison? He misleads many by means of it, and he guides many by means of it, and he misleads only wrongdoers with it, **²⁷**Those who violate the covenant of Allah after affirming it, and sever what Allah ordered to be joined, and spread corruption in the earth, those are the ones who are the losers. **²⁸**How do you disbelieve in Allah when you were dead and he gave life to you? Then he will give you death, then life again, and then you will return to him. **²⁹**He is the one who created everything on earth for you. Then he turned to heaven, and constructed them as seven heavens. And he is the knower of all things. **³⁰**And when your Lord said to the angels, Indeed, I am about to place a caliph on the earth, they said, Will you place on it one who will spread corruption there and shed blood, while we, we sing your praise and extol you? He said, Surely I know what you do not know. **³¹**And he taught Adam all the names, then showed them to the angels, saying, Tell me the names of these, if you are truthful. **³²**They said, Glory to you, we know nothing except

---

23. This challenge is hollow and self-reinforcing, as no criteria are given for what would make a sura "like" those of the Qur'an, and no impartial judge is or could possibly be specified. However, there have been numerous attempts to replicate the Qur'an's tone, language, and rhyme scheme, often by Christians who couch evangelistic appeals to Muslims in Qur'anic dress, but by many others as well. The success or failure of such endeavors depends entirely upon the attitudes and assumptions of the person who is evaluating them. See also 10:38.

Richard Bell notes that the word "sura" is likely a derivation from the Syriac word *surta*, "used in the sense of Scripture."[14]

27. On "corruption in the earth," see 5:33. According to Ibn Kathir, severing "what Allah ordered to be joined" refers to "keeping the relations with the relatives."[15]

29. According to the twentieth-century Qur'anic scholar Régis Blachère, the plural pronoun "them" doesn't agree with its singular referent, "heaven." According to Ibn Warraq, some translators gloss

over the difficulty by translating the passages as, "Then he turned to heaven, and constructed *it* as seven heavens."[16] The tenth-century Islamic scholar and historian Tabari maintains that "heaven" is a collective singular, and thus poses no difficulty.

30. "Caliph" is *khalifa*, or successor. In the traditional understanding the caliphs were successors of Muhammad. But here the word is used in the sense of mankind being Allah's viceroy on earth. This reveals the exalted nature of the claim of the Sunni caliphs, that they were the viceroys and regents of the last and greatest prophet of Allah.

Instead of "a caliph," the eighth-century Shi'ite Qur'an attributed to Zaid bin Ali, the son of Ali ibn Abi Talib, has "creatures."[17]

31. This passage is loosely based on Genesis 2:19, in which God created the animals and then "brought them to the man to see what he would call them; and whatever the man called every living creature, that was its name."

what you have taught us. Indeed, you and only you are the knower, the wise. **33**He said, O Adam, tell them their names, and when he had told them their names, he said, Didn't I tell you that I know the secret of the heavens and the earth? And I know what you reveal and what you hide. **34**And when we said to the angels, Prostrate yourselves before Adam, they fell prostrate, all except Iblis. He refused because of pride, and so became a disbeliever. **35**And we said, O Adam, live in the garden, you and your wife, and eat freely of whatever you wish, but do not come near this tree or you will both become wrongdoers. **36**But Satan caused them to turn away from there and got them out of the state they were in, and we said, Go down, one of you an enemy to the other. There will be for you on earth a place to live and provision for a while. **37**Then Adam received words from his Lord, and he forgave him. Indeed, he is the forgiving, the merciful. **38**We said, Go down, all of you, from here, but indeed there is coming to you some guidance from me, and whoever follows my guidance, no fear will come upon them, nor will they grieve. **39**But they who disbelieve, and deny our signs, they are the rightful people of the fire. They will remain in it. **40**O children of Israel, remember my favor with which I favored you, and fulfil your covenant, and I will fulfil my covenant, and fear me. **41**And believe in what I reveal, confirming what you already have, and do not be the first to disbelieve in it, and do not exchange my signs for a small price, and keep your duty to me. **42**Do not confuse truth with falsehood, and do not knowingly conceal the truth. **43**Establish prayer, give alms, and bow your heads with those who bow. **44**Do you urge mankind to righteousness while you yourselves forget? And you are reciters of the book. Do you

---

34. The identification of Iblis as an angel here contradicts 18:50, which states that Iblis is a jinn (see 7:11).

The command of Allah that the angels prostrate themselves before Adam, and Iblis's haughty refusal, is derived from an older Jewish and/or Christian tradition that is recorded in, among other places, the apocryphal *Life of Adam and Eve*, which dates from between the first and fourth centuries AD. In that account, the devil tells Adam that he was thrown out of heaven for refusing God's command to worship him (as Iblis is here in 2:36), saying, "I will not worship an inferior and younger being (than I). I am his senior in the Creation, before he was made was I already made. It is his duty to worship me."[18]

According to Bell, the use of the name "Iblis" in 2:34 and then "Satan" in 2:36 is "an indication that the different parts of the story came originally from different sources."[19]

38. "We said, Go down" repeats from 2:36, and as it makes little sense in this verse, may be an interpolation or evidence that some of the text was lost.

39. The word here and throughout the Qur'an translated as "signs" is *ayat*, the word that is also used for the verses of the Qur'an. According to the Qur'an, the messenger of Allah performs no miracles (although in the hadith, Muhammad performs miracles frequently), but essentially every verse of the Qur'an that he delivers is a sign of Allah's presence and power.

40. Addressed to the "children of Israel," here begins an extended meditation on all that Allah did for the Jews, and the ingratitude with which they repaid him.

41. "Do not exchange my signs for a small price" is generally interpreted as an exhortation to put the service of Allah before the concerns of this world. Sayyid Abul A'la Maududi, a renowned twentieth-century Islamic intellectual and exponent of political Islam, says in his massive *Towards Understanding the Qur'an* that this verse "refers to the worldly benefits for the sake of which [the Jews] were rejecting God's directives."[20] However, many have speculated that this verse amounts to Muhammad's rebuke of those who sold him material that they told him was divine revelation, but wasn't—people who are raked over the coals again in 2:79.

42. Instead of "do not knowingly conceal," the Zaid bin Ali Qur'an has "do not knowingly confuse."[21]

43. The Jews can get back into good graces with Allah by converting to Islam. That this is the import of this passage might sail right by the English-speaking reader, since the translations exhort them to "establish prayer" and to "give alms," practices that need not at first glance be something restricted only to Islam. However, the word used here (and in many other cognate passages) for prayer is *salat*, which refers specifically to Islamic prayer, and for the alms-tax *zakat*, which is specifically Islamic almsgiving. Non-Muslims cannot pray *salat* or pay *zakat*. About the need for this conversion Ibn Kathir is forthright: "Allah commanded the Children of Israel to embrace Islam and to follow Muhammad."[22] The twentieth-century Qur'anic scholar and Muslim Brotherhood theorist Sayyid Qutb says that here Allah "invites the Israelites to join the Muslims in their religious practices, and to abandon their prejudices and ethnocentric tendencies."[23]

then have no sense? [45]Seek help in patience and prayer, and indeed it is hard except for those who are humble, [46]Who know that they will meet their Lord, and that to him they are returning. [47]O children of Israel, remember my favor with which I favored you, and how I preferred you over the worlds. [48]And guard yourselves against a day when no soul will help another in any way, and intercession will not be accepted from it, nor will compensation be received from it, and they will not be helped. [49]And when we delivered you from Pharaoh's people, who were afflicting you with dreadful torment, killing your sons and not killing your women, that was an immense trial from your Lord. [50]And when we brought you through the sea and rescued you, and drowned the people of Pharaoh before your eyes. [51]And when we established forty nights for Moses, and then you chose the calf when he had departed from you, and were wrongdoers. [52]Then, even after that, we forgave you, so that you might give thanks. [53]And when we gave Moses the book and the furqan, so that you might be guided. [54]And when Moses said to his people, O my people, you have wronged yourselves by your choosing of the calf, so turn in repentance to your creator, and kill yourselves. That will be best for you in the sight of your creator and he will accept your repentance. Indeed, he is the forgiving, the merciful. [55]And when you said, O Moses, we will not believe in you until we see Allah plainly, and while you watched, the lightning struck you. [56]Then we revived you after your death, so that you might give thanks. [57]And we caused the white cloud to overshadow you and sent down the manna and the quails upon you. Eat of the good things with which we have provided you. They did not wrong us, but they did wrong themselves. [58]And when we said, Go into this town and eat freely of what is there, and enter the gate prostrating, and say, Repentance. We will forgive you your sins and will give more to those who do right. [59]But those who did wrong exchanged the word that had been told them for another saying, and we sent down wrath from

---

47. Maududi says that beginning here, "reference is made to the best-known episodes of Jewish history. As these episodes were known to every Jewish child, they are narrated briefly rather than in detail. The reference is intended to remind the Jews both of the favors with which the Israelites had been endowed by God and of the misdeeds with which they had responded to those favors."[24] These include the Israelites being rescued from Pharaoh (2:49-50), the golden calf episode (2:54-55), and the feeding of the people with manna and quails in the wilderness (2:57, 61), culminating in the avowal that "humiliation and poverty" struck the Jews for their rejection of Allah's signs (2:61). The unbelievers suffer worldly punishments as well as suffering in the next world.

48. Everyone will stand alone before Allah; no intercession from others will be accepted (2:123, 6:94, 23:101, 39:43, 42:46). However, the Qur'an elsewhere accepts intercession with Allah's permission (10:3, 20:109, 21:28, 34:23, 53:26).

49. On Pharaoh, see also 3:11, 7:103, 8:52, 10:75, 14:6, 17:101, 20:24, 23:46, 26:11, 27:12, 28:3, 29:39, 38:12, 40:24, 44:17, 50:13, 51:38, 54:41, 66:11, 69:9, 73:15, 79:15, 85:18, and 89:10.

53. On the *furqan*, see 3:4.

54. Ibn Kathir explains: "Allah ordered Musa to command his people to kill each other. He ordered those who worshipped the calf to sit down and those who did not worship the calf to stand holding knives in their hands. When they started killing them, a great darkness suddenly overcame them. After the darkness lifted, they had killed seventy thousand of them. Those who were killed among them were forgiven, and those who remained alive were also forgiven."[25]

58. Instead of, "We will forgive you your sins" (*naghfiru*), the Warsh Qur'an has, "He will forgive you your sins" (*yughfaru*).[26]

59. A Shi'ite Qur'an manuscript discovered in Bankipur, India, in 1912 that was at that time at least two hundred or three hundred years old renders this verse in this way: "But those who wronged the family of Muhammad exchanged the word that had been told them for another saying, and we sent down wrath from heaven upon those who deprived the family of Muhammad of its due, for their evildoing."[27] Shi'ites reject the readings of this manuscript in favor of the canonical Uthmanic reading (in the Cairo version of 1924), and their provenance is unknown. Unless they are the text in its original form, which is unlikely, they are evidence of a willingness at least in some quarters to alter the wording of the Qur'an, a willingness that differs sharply from the contemporary Islamic doctrines of its perfection and immutability. See the Appendix: Two Apocryphal Shi'ite Suras.

heaven upon the evildoers for their evildoing. **⁶⁰**And when Moses asked for water for his people, we said, Strike the rock with your staff. And there gushed out from it twelve springs, each tribe knew its drinking-place. Eat and drink of what Allah has provided, and do not act corruptly, spreading corruption on the earth. **⁶¹**And when you said, O Moses, we are weary of one kind of food, so call upon your Lord for us, that he would bring forth for us from what the earth grows, of its herbs and its cucumbers and its corn and its lentils and its onions. He said, Would you exchange what is higher for what is lower? Go down to a settled country, in this way you will get what you are demanding. And humiliation and poverty struck them and they were visited with wrath from Allah. That was because they disbelieved in Allah's signs and killed the prophets wrongfully. That was for their disobedience and transgression. **⁶²**Indeed, those who believe, and those who are Jews, and Christians, and Sabeans, whoever believes in Allah and the last day and does right, surely their reward is with their Lord, and no fear will come upon them, neither will they grieve. **⁶³**And when we made a covenant with you and caused the mountain to tower above you, hold fast to what we have given you, and remember what is in it, so that you may fear Allah. **⁶⁴**Then, even after that, you turned away, and if it had not been for the grace of Allah and

61. The idea that the Jews killed the prophets is derived from Jewish tradition. The prophet Elijah states: "I have been very jealous for the LORD, the God of hosts; for the people of Israel have forsaken your covenant, thrown down thy altars, and killed your prophets with the sword; and I, even I only, am left; and they seek my life, to take it away" (I Kings 19:10). It is, however, much amplified in the Qur'an, repeated at 2:87, 2:91, 3:21, 3:112, 3:181, 3:183, 4:155, 5:70, and made an act of the Jews as a whole.

In line with this, Ibn Kathir applies the punishments described for the Jews to all Jews for all time: "This Ayah [verse] indicates that the Children of Israel were plagued with humiliation, and that this will continue, meaning that it will never cease. They will continue to suffer humiliation at the hands of all who interact with them, along with the disgrace that they feel inwardly."

As the word here rendered "signs," *ayat*, is also the term for verses of the Qur'an, this verse, like many others, can be read as a warning that disbelieving in the Qur'an puts one in line for humiliation, poverty, and the wrath of Allah.

62. This is one of the Qur'an's oft-quoted "tolerance verses," which seems to promise a place in paradise to "those who were Jews or Christians or Sabeans." Muhammad Asad exults: "With a breadth of vision unparalleled in any other religious faith, the idea of 'salvation' is here made conditional upon three elements only: belief in God, belief in the Day of Judgment, and righteous action in life."[28] Not, apparently, acceptance of Islam. But he contradicts himself by adding "in this divine writ" after the words "those who have attained to faith" in his translation of 2:62; that is, to be saved, one must believe in the Qur'an as well as the earlier revelations.[29]

This idea goes all the way back in Islamic tradition to Muhammad's cousin Ibn Abbas, who contends that this verse was abrogated (see 2:106) by 3:85, which states that no religion other than Islam will be accepted in the next world.[30] The thirteenth-century Qur'an commentator Abu Abdullah al-Qurtubi, whose commentary is still respected and widely read among Muslims, notes Ibn Abbas's opinion and adds: "Others said that it is not abrogated and that it is about those who believe in the Prophet, peace be upon him, and who are firm in their belief."[31] Thus it would apply only to those Jews, Christians, and Sabeans who accept Islam. Those who do not are "the unbelievers of the People of the Book," for whom Allah's disdain is noted vividly in 98:6.

Ibn Kathir notes that "There is a difference of opinion over the identity of the Sabians."[32] He cites several Islamic authorities who hold that "they do not have a specific religion."[33] He notes that others say they are "a sect among the People of the Book who used to read the Zabur (Psalms), others say that they are a people who worshipped the angels or the stars." The word "Sabeans" means "Baptizers" in Syriac.[34] The Sabeans are supposed to have practiced baptism as a central ritual. But the only Sabeans of whom something is known historically, the Sabeans of Harran in Upper Mesopotamia (modern southeastern Turkey), did not practice baptism or notably revere the Psalms. There is no record independent of Islamic literature of any group of Sabeans that actually did do those things.[35]

63. The passage beginning here, along with 5:59-60 and 7:166, is the basis for the common tendency among Islamic jihadis today to refer to Jews as apes (2:65, 7:166) or as both apes and pigs (5:60). Traditionally in Islamic theology these passages have not been considered to apply to all Jews. The fourteenth-century *Tafsir Ibn Abbas*, which is attributed to Muhammad's cousin, says that those "who have taken the covenant (the Sabbath) the day of Saturday and this at the time of David" were the ones who were "turned into humiliated and base apes."[36] Qurtubi explains that "scholars disagree about the transformation and whether they had offspring. Some people said that apes are descended from them," but "most say that they had no offspring and these animals existed before them and that those who were transformed died without progeny because they were struck by Allah's wrath and punishment. They only lasted in that form for three days, unable to eat or drink."[37]

his mercy, you would have been among the losers. **65**And you know about those among you who broke the Sabbath, how we said to them, Be apes, despised and hated. **66**And we made it an example to their own generation and to succeeding ones, and a warning to those who fear Allah. **67**And when Moses said to his people, Indeed, Allah commands you to sacrifice a cow, they said, Are you making fun of us? He answered, Allah forbid that I should be among the foolish. **68**They said, Pray for us to your Lord that he would make clear to us what she is like. He answered, Indeed, he says, Truly she is a cow that is neither with calf nor immature, but between the two conditions, so do what you are commanded. **69**They said, Pray for us to your Lord that he would make clear to us what color she is. He answered, Indeed, he says, Truly she is a yellow cow. Her color is bright, pleasing to those who see her. **70**They said, Pray for us to your Lord that he would make clear to us what kind she is. Indeed, cows are all much the same to us, and indeed, if Allah wills, we may be led on the right path. **71**He answered, Indeed, he says, Truly she is a cow that is unyoked, she does not plough the soil or water the field, she is whole and without blemish. They said, Now you bring the truth. So they sacrificed her, though they almost did not. **72**And when you killed a man and disagreed about it and Allah brought forth what you were hiding. **73**And we said, Strike him with some of it. In this way Allah brings the dead to life and shows you his signs, so that you may understand. **74**Then, even after that, your hearts were hardened and became as rocks, or worse than rocks, for hardness. For indeed there are rocks from which rivers gush, and indeed there are rocks that split in two so that water flows from them. And indeed there are rocks that fall down in the fear of Allah. Allah is not unaware of what you do. **75**Have you any hope that they will be true to you when a party of them used to listen to the word of Allah, and then used to change it knowingly, after they had understood it? **76**And when they fall in with those who believe, they say, We believe. But when they depart with each other, they say, Do you tell them what Allah has revealed to you so that they may argue with you about it before your Lord? Have you then no sense? **77**Are they then unaware that Allah knows what they keep hidden and what they proclaim? **78**Among them are illiterate people who do not know the book except from hearsay. They only guess. **79**Therefore woe to those who write the book with their hands and then say, This is from Allah, that they may sell it for a small price. Woe to them for what their hands have written, and woe to them

---

67. The reproaches against the Jews are taken up yet again, with the Israelites reacting with haughty rebelliousness to Allah's command, given through Moses, that they sacrifice a heifer (the "cow" of the sura's title), an incident based on Numbers 19:1-8 and Deuteronomy 21:1-9. This verse and other Qur'anic passages establish the Jews as the most perverse and guilty—as well as the craftiest and most persistent—enemies of Allah, Muhammad, and the Muslims (cf. 5:82).

75. In his *Tafsir Anwarul Bayan*, the twentieth-century Indian Mufti Muhammad Aashiq Ilahi Bulandshahri notes that some commentators "have mentioned that the verse refers to the adulteration of the Torah. The Jewish scholars used to accept bribes from people to alter certain injunctions to suit their desires....They behaved in this manner even though they realized the error of their ways. They also altered the description of the Holy Prophet which appeared in the Torah so that people do not follow him."[38]

The Jews dare to change the word of Allah; however, at 6:115, the Qur'an states that no one can change the word of Allah.

79. The *Tafsir Anwarul Bayan* says that the Jews "commit a dual sin by altering Allah's scripture and by accepting bribery as well."[39]

This is a traditional view: the *Tafsir al-Jalalayn* says that the Jews "removed the description of the Prophet, may Allah bless him and grant him peace, which was in the Torah and the verse of stoning and other things which they wrote differently from how they were originally revealed!"[40]

for that they earn by it. ⁸⁰And they say, The fire will not touch us except for a certain number of days. Say, Have you received a covenant from Allah? Indeed Allah will not break his covenant. Or are you talking about something you do not know about? ⁸¹No, but whoever has done evil and his sin surrounds him, such people are rightful companions of the fire, they will remain in it. ⁸²And those who believe and do good works, such people are the rightful companions of the garden. They will remain in it. ⁸³And when we made a covenant with the children of Israel, Worship no one except Allah, and be good to your parents and relatives and to orphans and the needy, and speak kindly to mankind, and establish prayer and give alms. Then, after that, you turned back, except for a few of you, as you are backsliders. ⁸⁴And when we made a covenant with you, do not shed the blood of your people nor turn your people out of your homes. Then you ratified it and you were witnesses. ⁸⁵Yet it is you who kill each other and expel a party of your people from their homes, supporting one another against them by sin and aggression. And if they came to you as captives, you would ransom them, although their expulsion was itself unlawful for you. Do you believe in part of the book and

disbelieve in part of it? And what is the reward of those who do so, except disgrace in the life of the world, and on the Day of Resurrection they will be consigned to the most grievous suffering. For Allah is not unaware of what you do. ⁸⁶Those are the ones who buy the life of the world at the price of the hereafter. Their punishment will not be lightened, and they will not have support. ⁸⁷And indeed we gave the book to Moses and we caused a succession of messengers to follow after him, and we gave Jesus, son of Mary, clear proofs, and we strengthened him with the holy spirit. Is it always the case that when a messenger comes to you with what you yourselves do not desire, you grow arrogant, and some of them you disbelieve and some you kill? ⁸⁸And they say, Our hearts are hardened. No, but Allah has cursed them for their unbelief, so little is what they believe. ⁸⁹And when there comes to them a book from Allah, confirming the one in their possession, although before that they were asking for a great victory over those who disbelieved, and when there comes to them what they know, they disbelieve in it. The curse of Allah is on unbelievers. ⁹⁰What they sell their souls for is vile, that they should disbelieve in what Allah has revealed, begrudging the fact that Allah should reveal things out of his

---

80. The arrogance of the Jews extends to their thinking that they will only be in hell for a few days. A hadith recorded by Bukhari states that after Muhammad conquered the Jews of Khaibar, an Arabian oasis, they roasted a sheep for the Prophet of Islam—and poisoned it. Sensing their stratagem, he summoned and questioned them. In the course of this, they told him, "We shall remain in the (Hell) Fire for a short period, and after that you [Muslims] will replace us."⁴¹ Muhammad responded indignantly: "You may be cursed and humiliated in it! By Allah, we shall never replace you in it" and revealed that he knew of their plot to poison him.⁴²

85. Instead of, "Allah is not unaware of what you do," the Warsh Qur'an has, "Allah is not unaware of what they do."⁴³

"And if they came to you as captives, you would ransom them" interrupts the point about expulsion and thus may be an interpolation.

Ibn Kathir says that they rejected parts of the Torah, and also: "They should not be believed when it comes to the description of the Messenger of Allah, his coming, his expulsion from his land, and his Hijrah, and the rest of the information that the previous Prophets informed them about him, all of which they hid. The Jews, may they suffer the curse of Allah, hid all of these facts among themselves."⁴⁴

87. On "our spirit," see 19:17.

88. Allah emphasizes that the Jews are accursed for rejecting Islam. This is why most Muslims don't accept the idea that the Jews have any right to the land of Israel, despite Qur'an 5:21 and other verses: an accursed people doesn't receive Allah's gifts.

bounty to one of his slaves whom he wishes. They have brought upon themselves anger upon anger. For unbelievers there is a shameful doom. [91]And when it is said to them, Believe in what Allah has revealed, they say, We believe in what was revealed to us. And they disbelieve in what comes after it, although it is the truth confirming what they possess. Say, Why then did you kill the prophets of Allah of earlier times, if you are believers? [92]And Moses came to you with clear proofs, yet while he was away, you chose the calf and you were wrongdoers. [93]And when we made a covenant with you and caused the mountain to tower above you, hold fast by what we have given you, and hear, they said, We hear and we rebel. And the calf was made to sink into their hearts because of their rejection. Say, Evil is what your belief leads you to do, if you are believers. [94]Say, If the abode of the hereafter in the providence of Allah is indeed for you only and not for other people of mankind, as you pretend, then long for death, if you are truthful. [95]But they will never long for it, because of what their own hands have sent before them. Allah is aware of evildoers. [96]And you will find them the greediest of mankind for life, even more than the idolaters. Each

of them would like to be allowed to live a thousand years. And to live would by no means remove him from the doom. Allah is the seer of what they do. [97]Say, Who is an enemy to Gabriel? For it is he who has revealed this to your heart by Allah's permission, confirming what was before it, and a guidance and good news to believers, [98]Who is an enemy to Allah, and his angels and his messengers, and Gabriel and Michael? Then, indeed, Allah is an enemy to unbelievers. [99]Indeed, we have revealed clear signs to you, and only wrongdoers will disbelieve in them. [100]Is it ever so that when they make a covenant, a party of them sets it aside? The truth is, most of them do not believe. [101]And when a messenger from Allah comes to them, confirming what is with them, a faction of those who have received the book cast the book of Allah behind their backs, as if they did not know.

[102]And they follow what the satans used to recite in the kingdom of Solomon. Solomon did not disbelieve, but the satans disbelieved, teaching mankind sorcery and what was revealed to the two angels in Babel, Harut and Marut. Nor did they teach it to anyone without first saying, We are only a temptation, so do not disbelieve. So

94. This is the foundation of a jihadist taunt, succinctly stated by an al-Qaeda warrior but by no means limited to him: "The Americans love Pepsi-Cola, we love death."[45] The true believers long for paradise and disdain this world. See also 62:6.

96. Bell states of, "And you will find them the greediest of mankind for life, even more than the idolaters" that it is "grammatically uneven, and is perhaps a later insertion."[46]

98. Stated in the context of a chastisement of the Jews for their disbelief, this clearly refers to the Jews as enemies of Allah, and to Allah as their enemies.

102. Qurtubi explains that "sorcery" is "distortion and producing illusions," such that "the person under the spell imagines something to be different from what it is."[47] The messengers are frequently accused of sorcery in the Qur'an for his revelations of it (6:7, 10:76, 27:13, 34:43, 37:15, 43:30, 74:24), which a hadith has Muhammad explain: "Some kinds of eloquence are sorcery."[48] Qurtubi notes: "Sunnis believe that sorcery is real."[49]

As for Harut and Marut, Bell notes that "no explanation of these names has been found."[50] He suggests that "what the satans used to recite in the kingdom of Solomon" could be "a reference to the Rabbinic Law," and that "the mention of Babil may further suggest the Babylonian Talmud. But the whole verse is obscure."[51] The historian and philologist William St. Clair Tisdall (1859-1928), however, asserts that "Harut and Marut were two idols worshipped far back in Armenia. For in writers of that country they are so spoken of, as in the following passage from one of them: 'Certainly Horot and Morot, tutelary deities of mount Ararat, and Aminabegh, and perhaps others now not known, were assistants to the female goddess Aspandaramit. These aided her, and were excellent on the earth.' In this extract, Aspandaramit is the name of the goddess worshipped of old in Iran also; for we are told that the Zoroastrians regarded her as the Spirit of the Earth, and held that all the good products of the earth arise from her."[52]

they learn from them what causes division between man and wife, but they injure no one thereby, except by Allah's permission. And they learn what harms them and does not help them. And surely they do know that he who buys it will have no share in the hereafter, and surely evil is the price for which they sell their souls, if only they knew. **103**And if they had believed and kept away from evil, a reward from Allah would have been better, if they had known. **104**O you who believe, do not say, Listen to us, but say, Look upon us, and listen. For unbelievers there is a painful doom. **105**Neither the unbelievers among the people of the book nor the idolaters love the idea that there should be sent down to you any good thing from your Lord. But Allah chooses for his mercy whom he wills, and Allah is of infinite bounty. **106**We do not abrogate or cause to be forgotten anything of our revelation unless we bring something better or like it. Do you not know that Allah is able to do all things? **107**Do you not know that it is Allah to whom belongs the dominion of the heavens and the earth, and you do not have any guardian or helper besides Allah? **108**Or

would you question your messenger, as Moses was questioned earlier? He who chooses disbelief instead of faith, indeed he has gone astray from the right path. **109**Many of the people of the book long to make you unbelievers after your belief, through envy on their own account, after the truth has become clear to them. Forgive them and be indulgent until Allah gives command. Indeed, Allah is able to do all things. **110**Establish prayer, and give alms, and whatever good things you send ahead for your souls, you will find it with Allah. Indeed, Allah is the seer of what you do. **111**And they say, No one enters paradise unless he is a Jew or a Christian. These are their own desires. Say, Bring your proof if you are truthful. **112**No, but whoever surrenders himself to Allah while doing good, his reward is with his Lord, and no fear will come upon them, neither will they grieve. **113**And the Jews say the Christians follow nothing, and the Christians say the Jews follow nothing, yet both are readers of the book. Those who do not know speak this way. Allah will judge between them on the day of resurrection concerning those things they disagree about.

---

105. The "unbelievers among the people of the book" are the Jews and Christians who do not become Muslims. See 2:62 and 57:27. Here, Allah tells Muslims that unbelievers wish them only ill; Ibn Kathir explains: "Allah described the deep enmity that the disbelieving polytheists and People of the Scripture, whom Allah warned against imitating, have against the believers, so that Muslims should sever all friendship with them."[53]

On "Allah chooses for his mercy whom he wills," see 7:179, 10:99, 32:13.

106. The torrent of condemnations of the Jews is interrupted to introduce the Islamic doctrine of abrogation, in which Allah replaces a verse he has previously revealed but abrogated with one that is like it or even better.

The *Tafsir al-Jalalayn* says that this verse was revealed "when the unbelievers attacked the possibility of abrogation and said, 'Muhammad commands his companions to do something one day and forbids them it the next.'"[54] (The companions, *sahaba*, are in Islamic tradition the closest followers of Muhammad during his lifetime.) Sayyid Qutb maintains that "partial amendment of

rulings in response to changing circumstances during the lifetime of the Prophet Muhammad could only be in the interest of mankind as a whole."[55]

The concept of *naskh*, abrogation, has for centuries been part of the skeptics' claim that Muhammad was a false prophet whose revelations were conveniently tailored for the advantage of the moment. When circumstances changed such that he felt it necessary to alter a ruling, the doctrine of abrogation gave him a ready rejoinder to those who claimed that he was just improvising the divine utterances as he went along. Meanwhile, those who find the Qur'an to be the work of a committee working decades after Muhammad is supposed to have lived would also have found a doctrine of this kind useful to cover for inconsistencies in the patchwork scripture they were assembling.

The doctrine of abrogation is also the foundation of the widespread Islamic understanding that the violent verses of the Qur'an take precedence over the more peaceful verses revealed earlier, since they come later in the lifetime of Muhammad.

114And who does greater wrong than he who forbids the approach to the sanctuaries of Allah, to prevent his name should be mentioned in them, and works for their destruction. As for such people, it was never meant that they should enter them except in fear. For them there is disgrace in this world and for them in the hereafter is an awful doom. 115To Allah belong the East and the West, and wherever you turn, there is Allah's face. Indeed, Allah is all-embracing, all-knowing. 116And they say, Allah has taken to himself a son. May he be glorified. No, but whatever is in the heavens and the earth is his. All submit to him. 117The creator of the heavens and the earth. When he decrees a thing, he just says to it, Be, and it is. 118And those who have no knowledge say, Why doesn't Allah speak to us, or some sign come to us? Even in this way, as they now speak, those before them spoke. Their hearts are all alike. We have made clear the signs for people who are sure. 119Indeed, we have sent you with the truth, as a bringer of good news and a warner. And you will not be asked about the companions of the blazing fire. 120And the Jews will not be pleased with you, neither will the Christians, until you follow their religion. Say, Indeed, the guidance of Allah is guidance. And if you follow their desires after the knowledge that has come to you, then you would have from Allah no protecting guardian or helper. 121Those to whom we have given the book, who read it with the right reading, those believe in it. And whoever disbelieves in it, those are the ones who are the losers. 122O children of Israel, remember my favor with which I favored you and how I preferred you over the worlds. 123And guard against a day when no soul will help another in anything, and compensation will not be accepted from it, and intercession will be of no use to it, and they will not be helped. 124And when his Lord tried Abraham with commands, and he fulfilled them, he said, Indeed, I have established you a leader for mankind. He said, And what about my descendants? He said, My covenant does not include wrongdoers. 125And when we made the house a refuge for mankind and sanctuary, take as a place of prayer the place where Abraham stood. And we imposed a duty upon Abraham and Ishmael, Purify my house for those who go around it and those who meditate it and those who bow down and prostrate themselves. 126And when Abraham prayed, My Lord, make this a region of security and give its people its fruits, those among them who believe in Allah and the last day, he answered, As for he who

---

116. This is the first of several Qur'anic articulations of Islam's indignant rejection of the Christian belief in Jesus as the Son of God. The Qur'an repeatedly insists that Allah has neither sons nor daughters (other instances of this can be found at 6:100, 9:30, 10:68, 17:40, 17:111, 18:4, 19:35, 19:88, 21:26, 25:2, 37:149, 39:4, 43:16, 43:81, 52:39, 53:21, 72:3, 112:3).

The idea that Allah could have a son is considered to compromise monotheism, and to imply that Allah is not all-powerful and thus capable of performing his celestial tasks by himself, without any helper.

119. Instead of, "And you will not be asked," the Warsh Qur'an has, "Do not ask."[56]

120. "Religion" here is *milla*, likely derived from the Syriac *meltha*, "word."[57]

123. Everyone will stand alone before Allah; no intercession from others will be accepted (2:48, 6:94, 23:101, 39:43, 42:46). However, the Qur'an elsewhere accepts intercession with Allah's permission (10:3, 20:109, 21:28, 34:23, 53:26).

124. "Leader" is *imam*, the word commonly used for the leader of prayer in a mosque among Sunnis and for the leader of the Muslim community among Shi'ites.

125. Instead of "take as a place of prayer" (*attakhizuu*), the Warsh Qur'an and the version transmitted by the eleventh-century scholar al-Asbahaani have "they took as a place of prayer" (*attakhazuu*).[58]

The house that Abraham and Ishmael build here is supposed in Islamic tradition to be the Ka'ba in Mecca. However, Mecca is nowhere mentioned in this account of the building of the house for prayer and worship. This place could have been elsewhere. Mecca is, in fact, mentioned only once in the Qur'an (48:24).

disbelieves, I will leave him in contentment for a while, then I will force him to the torment of fire, an evil journey's end. **127**And when Abraham and Ishmael were raising the foundations of the house, Our Lord, accept this from us. Indeed, you, only you, are the hearer, the knower. **128**Our Lord, and make us Muslims and make our children a Muslim nation, and show us our ways of worship, and be merciful to us. Indeed, you, only you, are the forgiving, the merciful. **129**Our Lord, and raise up from among them a messenger who will recite your signs to them, and will instruct them in the book and in wisdom and make them grow. Indeed, you, only you, are the mighty, the wise. **130**And who turns away from the religion of Abraham except the one who is fooling himself? Indeed we chose him in this world, and indeed in the hereafter he is among the righteous. **131**When his Lord said to him, Submit, he said, I have submitted to the Lord of the worlds. **132**Abraham commanded the same thing from his sons, and also Jacob, O my sons, indeed, Allah has chosen the religion for you, therefore do not die except as men who have submitted. **133**Or were you present when death came to Jacob, when he said to his sons, What will you worship after my death? They

said, We will worship your God, the God of your fathers, Abraham and Ishmael and Isaac, One God, and to him we have submitted. **134**Those are a people who have passed away. Theirs is what they earned, and yours is what you earn. And you will not be asked about what they used to do. **135**And they say, Be Jews or Christians, then you will be rightly guided. Say, No, but the religion of Abraham, the hanif, and he was not one of the idolaters. **136**Say, We believe in Allah and what is revealed to us and what was revealed to Abraham, and Ishmael, and Isaac, and Jacob, and the tribes, and what Moses and Jesus received, and what the prophets received from their Lord. We make no distinction between any of them, and to him we have submitted. **137**And if they believe in the same things in which you believe, then they are rightly guided. But if they turn away, then are they in opposition, and Allah will be sufficient for you against them. He is the hearer, the knower. **138**Color from Allah, and who is better than Allah at coloring? We are his worshippers. **139**Say, Do you disagree with us concerning Allah when he is our Lord and your Lord? Ours are our works and yours are your works. We look to him alone. **140**Or do you say that Abraham, and Ishmael, and

---

128. Abraham and Ishmael are submitters to Allah, that is, Muslims. This underscores the recurring Qur'anic theme that the people we know of today as Jews and Christians are only renegades from the true religion actually taught by Abraham and Moses, as well as Jesus. That true religion was Islam.

Much of sura 2 is devoted to addressing the renegade Jews who have rejected the messenger and calling them back to the true faith, the faith of Abraham and Moses as well as the messenger. Thus Islam challenges Judaism and Christianity by claiming that the true and original form of both religions is Islam.

135. *Hanif* is generally translated as "monotheist," specifically one who before the advent of Muhammad was a true believer, that is, a believer in the one true god. The word is derived, however, from the Syriac *hanephe*, which means "heathens," and is, according to Bell, "the term applied by Christians to the Arabs."[59]

It may seem odd to refer to Abraham as a "heathen" and translate the word as "monotheist," but Luxenberg explains that there is actually nothing paradoxical about this at all. "What is meant," he says, "is: Abraham was indeed (by birth) a *heathen*, but he was no *idolater*! The idea that Abraham as a *heathen* already believed in God and was therefore no longer an idolater is pre-Koranic and we encounter it in a similar way in Saint Paul. In his Epistle to the Romans (4:9-12) Abraham's faith was already imputed to Abraham before the *circumcision* (hence when he was still a *heathen*). Through this he is said to have become the father of all those who as the uncircumcised (and thus as *heathens*) believe."[60]

The concept of being a *hanif* is likely thus an importation from Christianity, only slightly altered to fit an Islamic setting. For another example of this, see 5:114.

140. Instead of "Or do you say" (*taquuluuna*), the Warsh Qur'an has "Or do they say" (*yaquuluuna*).[61]

Isaac, and Jacob, and the tribes were Jews or Christians? Say, Do you know best, or does Allah? And who is more unjust than the one who hides a testimony which he has received from Allah? Allah is not unaware of what you do. [141]Those are a people who have passed away, theirs is what they earned and yours is what you earn. And you will not be asked about what they used to do. [142]The foolish among the people will say, What has turned them from the qibla which they formerly observed? Say, To Allah belong the East and the West. He guides whom he wills to a straight path. [143]In this way we have established you a middle nation, so that you may be witnesses against mankind, and that the messenger may be a witness against you. And we established the qibla which you formerly observed only so that we might distinguish him who follows the messenger from him who turns on his heels. In truth, it was difficult, except for those whom Allah guided. But it was not Allah's purpose that your faith should be in vain, for Allah is full of pity, merciful toward mankind. [144]We have seen the turning of your face to heaven. And now indeed we will make you turn toward a qibla that is dear to you. So turn your face toward the sacred mosque, and you, wherever you may be, turn your faces toward it. Indeed, those who have

---

142. Allah tells the messenger that only "the foolish among the people" will protest the change in the *qibla*, the direction for prayer. Islamic tradition holds that the direction for prayer was changed from Jerusalem to Mecca, and that the foolish ones were the Jews, as the relatively moderate commentator (and convert to Islam from Judaism) Muhammad Asad states: "This 'abandonment' of Jerusalem obviously displeased the Jews of Medina, who must have felt gratified when they saw the Muslims praying towards their holy city; and it is to them that the opening sentence of this passage refers."[62]

However, neither Jerusalem nor Mecca are specifically mentioned in this Qur'an passage; in fact, Jerusalem is never mentioned in the Qur'an, and Mecca only once. The Islamic traditions that identify the qibla as being originally Jerusalem and then Mecca date from the ninth century and thereafter; however, the Syriac Orthodox theologian and chronicler Jacob of Edessa, who died in 708, notes in passing that the Muslims in Egypt did not pray facing the south, as they would if they were facing Mecca: "The Jews who live in Egypt, as likewise the Mahgraye [that is, the Muslims] there, as I saw with my own eyes and will now set out for you, prayed to the east, and still do, both peoples—the Jews towards Jerusalem, and the Mahgraye towards the Ka'ba (*k'b't*)."[63]

The Ka'ba in Mecca is south, not east, of Egypt; was there another Ka'ba far north of Mecca toward which Muslims were still praying in the early eighth century?

While there is only one Ka'ba today, at the time of Islam's emergence there may have been many. The archaeologist Barbara Finster notes that the Ka'ba has "the same orientation, rectangular ground plan," and "possibly apsidal closure in the northwest" that are found in "similar temples in southern Arabia, such as the sanctuary of Sirwah" in Yemen.[64]

What's more, there are telling indications that the earliest Muslims did not pray facing the structure in Mecca. Historian and archaeologist Dan Gibson, surveying the available data on the qiblas of the earliest mosques, most of which he visited in person, found numerous mosques constructed before 742 facing not Mecca or Jerusalem, but Petra in southern Jordan, including *all* the earliest mosques in which the original qibla could be ascertained. Mosques only begin to be built facing Mecca in 727, although some mosques constructed between the years 707 and 772 actually faced a spot between Petra and Mecca.[65] Gibson surveys twenty-one mosques built between 622 and 708 and finds that eight faced Petra, two faced Petra and Jerusalem, one faced between Petra and Mecca, and that the original qibla of the other ten cannot be ascertained.[66]

In whatever direction the earliest Muslims prayed, it does not appear to have been toward Mecca.

Why Mecca ultimately came to be associated with the qibla and the ninth-century accounts of the life of Muhammad is a matter of considerable speculation. It appears most likely that while the earliest formulations of the religion took place north of Arabia, for a variety of political reasons, largely stemming from the need to put down the Mecca-based Abdullah ibn al-Zubayr's rebellion against the caliph Abd al-Malik (685-705), the new religion's mythology was set farther south.[67]

144. Ibn Kathir attributes to Muhammad's cousin Ibn Abbas the statement that "the first abrogated part in the Qur'an was about the Qiblah."[68] However, there is nothing in the Qur'an directing Muslims to pray facing Jerusalem, so this is an abrogation of an extra-Qur'anic regulation.

Allah tells the messenger that the new qibla will be "dear to you." This is one of the foundations for the centrality of Muhammad in Islam. He is just one among many prophets, albeit their crown and seal, and yet he consistently seems to be much more than just a human being who was chosen to be a conduit for the divine message. The creator of the entire universe, the "Lord of the worlds," is so solicitous of the messenger that he commands that all those who know and acknowledge his presence and power to face a direction that will please this single, and obviously singular, human being. Another example of this is Allah's gently rebuking the messenger for initially declining to marry his former daughter-in-law (who was renowned for her beauty) when Allah wanted him to do so (33:37).

received the book know this is the truth from their Lord. And Allah is not unaware of what they do. **145**And even if you brought all kinds of signs to those who have been given the book, they would not follow your qibla. Nor can you be a follower of their qibla. Nor are some of them followers of the qibla of others. And if you followed their desires after the knowledge which has come to you, then surely you were among the evildoers. **146**Those to whom we gave the book recognize this as they recognize their sons. But indeed, a party of them knowingly conceals the truth. **147** It is the truth from your Lord, so do not be among those who waver. **148**And each one has a goal toward which he turns, so compete with one another in good works. Wherever you may be, Allah will bring you all together. Indeed, Allah is able to do all things. **149**And whenever you

come forth, turn your face toward the sacred mosque. Indeed, it is the truth from your Lord. Allah is not unaware of what you do. **150**And whenever you come forth, turn your face toward the sacred mosque, and wherever you may be, turn your faces toward it, so that men may have no argument against you, except for those among them who do injustice. Do not fear them, but fear me, so that I may complete my favor upon you, and that you may be guided. **151**Even as we have sent you a messenger from among you, who recites our signs to you and causes you to grow, and teaches you the book and wisdom, and teaches you what you did not know. **152**Therefore remember me, I will remember you. Give thanks to me, and do not reject me. **153**O you who believe, seek help in perseverance and prayer. Indeed, Allah is with the persevering. **154**And do not call

---

The Qur'an is clear that the messenger is the supreme example of behavior for Muslims to follow. He is "an excellent example" (33:21). He demonstrates "an exalted standard of character" (68:4), and indeed, "whoever obeys the messenger has obeyed Allah" (4:80). While the Muslim holy book takes for granted that the messenger is fallible (cf. 48:2, 80:1-12), it also instructs Muslims repeatedly to obey him (3:32, 3:132, 4:13, 4:59, 4:69, 5:92, 8:1, 8:20, 8:46, 9:71, 24:47, 24:51, 24:52, 24:54, 24:56, 33:33, 33:36, 47:33, 49:14, 58:13, 64:12). The messenger is identified in Islamic tradition with Muhammad, although that name appears only four times in the Qur'an (3:144, 5:75, 33:40, 47:2), and never in connection with any of these calls to obey the messenger.

The contemporary Islamic scholar Muqtedar Khan explains the centrality of Muhammad in Islam to which these exhortations to obedience has led: "No religious leader has as much influence on his followers as does Muhammad (Peace be upon him) the last Prophet of Islam....And Muhammad as the final messenger of God enjoys preeminence when it comes to revelation—the Quran—and traditions. So much so that the words, deeds and silences (that which he saw and did not forbid) of Muhammad became an independent source of Islamic law. Muslims, as a part of religious observance, not only obey but also seek to emulate and imitate their Prophet in every aspect of life. Thus Muhammad is the medium as well as a source of the divine law."[69]

The Qur'an also makes it clear that the messenger is by far the most important person who ever walked the earth, receiving the tenderest concern of the master of the universe, and hence also the ultrarespectful veneration of Muslims. It is an intriguing contrast with Christianity that Islam considers Muhammad as just a human being, yet he cannot be depicted and insults to him must

be avenged, while Christianity considers Christ divine and yet has no problem with visual depictions of him, and bears insults of him with patience, or at the very least without responding violently.

Allah's solicitude for the messenger became the springboard for an exaltation of Muhammad in the Islamic mystical tradition. The Persian Sufi mystic Mansur al-Hallaj (858-922) said that Allah "has not created anything that is dearer to him than Muhammad and his family."[70] The Persian poet Rumi (1207-1273) said that the scent of roses was that of the sweat of the Prophet of Islam:

Root and branch of the roses is
the lovely sweat of Mustafa [that is, Muhammad],
And by his power the rose's crescent
grows now into a full moon.[71]

Likewise a modern Arab writer opined that Allah "created Muhammad's body in such unsurpassable beauty as had neither before him nor after him been seen in a human being. If the whole beauty of the Prophet were unveiled before our eyes, they could not bear its splendor."[72]

To the skeptic, the solicitude Allah continually shows for the messenger is an indication that for him, Allah is a means to gain status, favor, power, influence, and more. Or for those who believe that the Muhammad myth was constructed long after the events depicted, this solicitude is a means to ensure reverence and loyalty among the adherents of the new religion.

149. The "sacred mosque" is universally identified with the Ka'ba in Mecca, but here again, Mecca is not named in the Qur'anic text. The sacred mosque may have been elsewhere.

150. "And whenever you come forth, turn your face toward the sacred mosque" is duplicated from 2:149 and may be a scribal error.

those who are killed for the sake of Allah dead. No, they are living, only you do not perceive it. [155]And surely we will test you with some fear and hunger, and loss of wealth and lives and crops, but give good news to the persevering, [156]Who say when a misfortune strikes them, Indeed, we belong to Allah and indeed, to him we are returning. [157]Such people are those upon whom there are prayers from their Lord, and mercy. Such people are the rightly guided. [158]Indeed, Safa and Marwa are among the symbols of Allah. It is therefore no sin for the one who is on pilgrimage to the house or visits it, to walk around them. And he who does good deeds of his own accord, indeed, Allah is responsive, aware. [159]Indeed, those who hide the proofs and the guidance which we revealed, after we had made it clear to mankind in the book, such are cursed by Allah and cursed by those who have the power to curse. [160]Except for those who repent and reform and make evident. It is toward these people that I relent. I am the relenting, the merciful. [161]Indeed, those who disbelieve, and die while they are unbelievers, on them is the curse of Allah and of angels and of men combined. [162]They remain in there forever. The doom will not be lightened for them, nor will they be reprieved. [163]Your Allah is one Allah, there is no God except for him, the compassionate, the merciful. [164]Indeed, in the creation of the heavens and the earth, and the difference between night and day, and the ships that run upon the sea with what is of use to men, and the water which Allah sends down from the sky, thereby reviving the earth after its death, and dispersing all kinds of beasts in it, and the ordinance of the winds, and the clouds obedient between heaven and earth, are signs for people who have sense. [165]Yet among mankind are some who take for themselves rivals to Allah, loving them with a love like that of Allah. Those who believe are stronger in their love for Allah. If only those who do evil had known, when they see doom, that power belongs wholly to Allah, and that Allah is severe in punishment. [166]When those who were followed disown those who followed, and they see doom, and all their plans collapse with them. [167]And those who were just followers will say, If a return were possible for us, we would disown them even as they have disowned us. In this way Allah will show them their own deeds as anguish for them, and they will not emerge from the fire. [168]O mankind, eat of what is lawful and wholesome in the earth, and do not follow the footsteps of Satan. Indeed, he is an open enemy to you. [169]He urges upon you only what is evil and foul, and that you should tell what you do not know concerning Allah. [170]And when it is said to them, Follow what Allah has revealed, they say, We follow what we found with our fathers. What? Even though their fathers were wholly unintelligent and had no guidance? [171]The likeness of those who disbelieve is as the likeness of one who calls to someone who does not hear anything except a shout and cry. Deaf, dumb, blind, therefore they have no sense. [172]O you who believe, eat of the good

---

157. On Allah praying for the believers, see 33:43 and 33:56.

158. Islamic tradition has identified Safa and Marwa as two hills in Mecca; Muslims walk back and forth between them as part of the rituals of the hajj, the greater pilgrimage, and umrah, the lesser pilgrimage. This practice had previously been associated with idol worship before this verse was revealed; thus the permission granted in this verse, like the entirety of the pilgrimage, is an example of the incorporation of pre-Islamic practices into Islam. The identification of these names with the Meccan hills, however, has no independent early attestation.

things with which we have provided you, and give thanks to Allah if it is he whom you worship. **173**He has forbidden you only carrion, and blood, and the flesh of pigs, and anything that has been sacrificed to anyone other than Allah. But he who is driven by necessity, neither craving nor transgressing, it is no sin for him. Indeed, Allah is forgiving, merciful. **174**Indeed, those who hide anything of the book that Allah has revealed and buys a small gain with it, they eat into their bellies nothing else but fire. Allah will not speak to them on the Day of Resurrection, nor will he make them grow. A painful doom will be theirs. **175**Those are the ones who buy error at the price of guidance, and suffering at the price of forgiveness. How persistent they are in their efforts to reach the fire. **176**That is because Allah has revealed the book with the truth. Indeed, those who find disagreement with the book are in open opposition. **177**It is not righteousness that you turn your faces to the East and the West, but righteousness is those who believe in Allah and the last day and the angels and the book and the prophets, and who, for love of him, give their wealth to relatives and to orphans and the needy and the son of the way and to beggars, and to set slaves free, and observes proper prayer and gives alms. And those who keep their treaty when they make one, and the patient in tribulation and adversity and time of hardship. Those are the ones who are sincere. Those are the ones who fear Allah. **178**O you who believe, retaliation is prescribed for you in the matter of those who have been murdered, the free man for the free man, and the slave for the slave, and the female for the female. And for he who is forgiven to some degree by his brother, prosecution according to usage and payment to him in kindness. This is a relief

---

173. The burden of the believers is not heavy. They need only abstain from certain foods, including pork.

174. In another indication that the unbelievers simply are not acting in good faith, we are told that among them are those who stubbornly conceal what they know Allah has revealed. These are, according to the *Tafsir al-Jalalayn*, the Jews.[73]

177. This appears to be a response to those who are grumbling about the change in the qibla. It belongs with vv. 142-150, and so may be a sign of a textual dislocation. "Son of the way" could simply be a "traveler," but according to Bell, it "probably refers to those who suffered through adhering to the Moslem community."[74]

178. Allah establishes the law of retaliation (*qisas*) for murder: equal recompense must be given for the life of the victim, which can take the form of blood money (*diyah*): a payment to compensate for the loss suffered. In Islamic law (Sharia) the amount of compensation varies depending on the religion of the victim: non-Muslim lives simply aren't worth as much as Muslim lives. *Reliance of the Traveller*, a Sharia manual that Cairo's prestigious Al-Azhar University certifies as conforming to the "practice and faith of the orthodox Sunni community," says that the payment for killing a woman is half of that to be paid for a man and for killing a Jew or Christian one-third that paid for killing a male Muslim.[75]

The Iranian Sufi Sheikh Sultanhussein Tabandeh, one of the architects of the legal codes of the Islamic Republic of Iran, explains why the life of a non-Muslim is worth less than that of a Muslim, and punishments for other crimes differ as well, depending on whether the perpetrator is a Muslim or not. If a Muslim "commits adultery," Tabandeh explains, "his punishment is 100 lashes, the shaving of his head, and one year of banishment."[76] He is referring, of course, to a Muslim male, not to a Muslim woman who commits adultery, who would in all likelihood be sentenced in Tabandeh's Iran to be stoned to death. "But if the man is not a Muslim," Tabandeh continues, "and commits adultery with a Muslim woman, his penalty is execution."[77]

The difference in treatment between Muslims and non-Muslims carries over to other areas as well. If a Muslim kills a Muslim, he is to be executed, but if he kills a non-Muslim, he incurs a lesser penalty: "Similarly if a Muslim deliberately murders another Muslim he falls under the law of retaliation and must by law be put to death by the next of kin. But if a non-Muslim who dies at the hand of a Muslim has by lifelong habit been a non-Muslim, the penalty of death is not valid. Instead, the Muslim murderer must pay a fine and be punished with the lash."[78]

Tabandeh explains this disparity as arising from basic principles of Islam: "Since Islam regards non-Muslims as on a lower level of belief and conviction, if a Muslim kills a non-Muslim...then his punishment must not be the retaliatory death, since the faith and conviction he possesses is loftier than that of the man slain...Again, the penalties of a non-Muslim guilty of fornication with a Muslim woman are augmented because, in addition to the crime against morality, social duty and religion, he has committed sacrilege, in that he has disgraced a Muslim and thereby cast scorn upon the Muslims in general, and so must be executed."[79]

Tabandeh's conclusion follows naturally from all this: "Islam and its peoples must be above the infidels, and never permit non-Muslims to acquire lordship over them."[80]

and a mercy from your Lord. He who transgresses after this will have a painful doom. **179**And there is life for you in retaliation, O men of understanding, that you may fear Allah.

180 It is prescribed for you, when death approaches one of you, if he leaves wealth, that he bequeaths to parents and near relatives in kindness, a duty for all those who fear Allah. **181**And whoever changes it after he has heard this, the sin of this is only upon those who change it. Indeed, Allah is hearer, knower. **182**But he who fears from a testator some unjust or sinful clause, and makes peace between the parties, has committed no sin. Indeed, Allah is forgiving, merciful. **183**O you who believe, fasting is required for you, even as it was required for those before you, that you may fear Allah, **184**A certain number of days, and he who is sick among you, or on a journey, a number of other days, and for those who can afford it there is a ransom, the feeding of a poor man, but whoever does good of his own accord, it is better for him, and it is better for you, if only you knew. **185**The month of Ramadan, in which was revealed the Qur'an, a guidance for mankind, and clear proofs

of the guidance, and the furqan. And whoever among you is present, let him fast the month, and whoever of you is sick or on a journey, a number of other days. Allah desires ease for you, he does not desire hardship for you, and that you should complete the period, and that you should glorify Allah for having guided you, and that perhaps you may be thankful. **186**And when my servants question you concerning me, then surely I am nearby. I answer the prayer of the petitioner when he cries out to me. So let them hear my call and let them trust in me, in order that they may be rightly led. **187**It is made lawful for you to go in to your wives on the night of the fast. They are clothing for you and you are clothing for them. Allah is aware that you were deceiving yourselves in this respect and he has turned in mercy toward you and relieved you. So have intercourse with them and seek what Allah has prescribed for you, and eat and drink until the white thread becomes distinct to you from the black thread at dawn. Then strictly observe the fast until nightfall and do not touch them, but be at your devotions in the mosques. These are the limits imposed by

---

184. Instead of "a poor man" (*miskeenen*), the Warsh Qur'an has "poor people" (*masaakeena*).[81]

185. A hadith has Muhammad hailing the importance of Ramadan: "A great month, a blessed month, a month containing a night which is better than a thousand months has approached you people." That is the "night of power," traditionally observed as the night on which Gabriel first appeared to Muhammad; see 97:1-5. The hadith continues with Muhammad saying: "God has appointed the observance of fasting during it as an obligatory duty, and the passing of its night in prayer as a voluntary practice. If someone draws near to God during it with some good act he will be like one who fulfills an obligatory duty in another month, and he who fulfills an obligatory duty in it will be like one who fulfills seventy obligatory duties in another month."[82] Islamic tradition holds that Muhammad fought at least three major battles against unbelievers during Ramadan: the Battle of Badr, the Battle of the Trench, and the Battle of Tabuk.

This has led to the idea that acts of jihad, which are greater than all other acts in reward (see 9:41), are especially meritorious during Ramadan. In 2012, after mass-murdering Jews in Israel

during Ramadan, the Islamic terror group Qaedat al-Jihad (Base of Jihad) explained: "The month of Ramadan is a month of holy war and death for Allah. It is a month for fighting the enemies of Allah and Muhammad—the Jews and their American facilitators."[83] The Islamic State (ISIS) called for increased violence against unbelievers during Ramadan, calling it "the holy month of jihad."[84]

Luxenberg explains that the word *Qur'an*, which makes its first appearance here when the book is read in its traditional order, is derived from the Syro-Aramaic word *qeryana*, "reading, pericope, selection for reading." He cautions that "it is not to be understood everywhere in the Koran as a proper name. Rather, in each case it is the context that determines its meaning."[85] The appellation meaning "pericopes" or "selections for reading" would suggest that underlying the Qur'anic text is a Christian liturgical text that was adapted by the compilers of the sacred text of the new religion. Traditional Islamic exegetes, of course, do understand every mention of the book as referring to the Qur'an as it stands today, but this should not be taken for granted.

On *furqan*, see 3:4.

Allah, so do not approach them. In this way Allah expounds his revelation to mankind so that they may fear Allah. [188]And do not waste your property among yourselves on vanity, nor seek by it to gain the hearing of judges so that you may knowingly devour a portion of others' property wrongfully. [189]They ask you about new moons. Say, They are fixed seasons for mankind and for the pilgrimage. It is not righteousness that you go to houses from the backs, but the righteous man is he who fears Allah. So enter houses by their gates, and observe your duty to Allah, so that you may be successful. [190]Fight for the sake of Allah against those who fight against you, but do not transgress. Indeed, Allah does not love transgressors. [191]And kill them wherever you find them, and drive them out from where they drove you out, for persecution is worse than slaughter. And do not fight with them at the sacred mosque until they first attack you there, but if they attack you, then kill them. This is the reward of unbelievers. [192]But if they stop, then indeed, Allah is forgiving, merciful.

---

190. This passage is often invoked today to show that jihad can only be defensive. Unfortunately, however, the words "do not transgress," which Mohammed Marmaduke Pickthall translates as "begin not hostilities" and that Islamic apologists often invoke today to show that jihad can only be defensive, don't necessarily mean what many Westerners assume or hope they mean.

Muhammad Asad enunciates a common view, and a quite popular one in the Western world, when he says that "this and the following verses lay down unequivocally that only self-defence (in the widest sense of the word) makes war permissible for Muslims."[86] However, the *Tafsir al-Jalalayn* says that this verse "was abrogated by *Surat at-Tawba* [sura 9, which contains numerous exhortations to jihad warfare] or by Allah's words in the following *ayat*," which is one of the Qur'an's three exhortations to "kill them wherever you find them" (the others are at 4:89 and 9:5).[87] However, Ibn Kathir rejects the idea that the verse was abrogated at all.[88]

191. Ibn Kathir explains "Drive them out from where they drove you out" in this way: "Your energy should be spent on fighting them, just as their energy is spent on fighting you, and on expelling them from the areas from which they have expelled you, as a law of equality in punishment."[89] For equality in punishment, see 5:45.

The concept of recovering lost territory as a divinely-commanded imperative is a key but completely overlooked aspect of the Islamic world's conflict with Israel.

The declaration that "persecution is worse than slaughter" is repeated at 2:217. This brief phrase has extraordinarily important implications for Islamic law and practice that are never clearly enunciated in the Qur'an. Islamic tradition holds that this all-important but opaque maxim was revealed to Muhammad during controversies over whether or not fighting was permissible during one of the four sacred months of the Arab calendar, during which fighting was forbidden.

According to Muhammad's eighth-century biographer Ibn Ishaq, whose work comes to us in the version of the ninth-century writer Ibn Hisham, Muhammad had sent out his trusted lieutenant, Abdullah bin Jahsh, and eight other Muslims to Nakhla, a settlement near Mecca, to watch for a caravan of the Quraysh, the Meccan tribe to which Muhammad belonged but which had rejected his prophetic claim. Muhammad told them to "find out for us what they are doing."[90] Abdullah and his band took this as an order to raid the caravan, which soon came along, carrying leather and raisins.

But it was the last day of the sacred month of Rajab. If the Muslims waited until the sacred month was over, the caravan would get away, but if they attacked, they would sin by desecrating the sacred month. They finally decided, according to Ibn Hisham, to "kill as many as they could of them and take what they had."[91]

The raid, however, angered Muhammad, who refused his Qur'an-mandated share of the booty (one-fifth, according to 8:41) and admonished the attackers that "I did not order you to fight in the sacred month."[92] But then Allah revealed this passage, explaining that the Quraysh's opposition to Muhammad was more offensive in his eyes than the Muslims' violation of the sacred month: the raid was therefore justified, "for persecution is worse than slaughter."

In other words, whatever sin the Nakhla raiders had committed in violating the sacred month was nothing compared to the Quraysh's sins. Ibn Hisham elucidated the rationale, as explained to Muhammad by Allah: "They have kept you back from the way of God with their unbelief in Him, and from the sacred mosque, and have driven you from it when you were with its people. This is a more serious matter with God than the killing of those whom you have slain."[93] Sayyid Qutb explained: "It was the unbelievers who declared war on the Muslims, rather than the other way around. They obstructed the spread of Islam, and spared no effort in turning people away from it, resorting to oppression and persecution."[94]

To allow that to happen so as not to bend the rule of the sacred months was not a viable option. This was a watershed event, establishing a utilitarian morality that runs through Islamic theology: anything that benefits Muslims and Islam is good, and anything that harms them is evil. Qutb declared that "Islam is a practical and realistic way of life which is not based on rigid idealistic dogma."[95] Islam "maintains its own high moral principles," but only when "justice is established and wrongdoing is contained"—i.e., only when Islamic law rules a society—can "sanctities be protected and preserved."[96]

In other words, Muslims need not feel themselves bound by those "high moral principles" until Islamic law is established in the society where they live.

193And fight them until persecution is no more, and religion is for Allah. But if they stop, then let there be no hostility except against wrongdoers. 194The sacred month for the sacred month, and sacred things are subject to retaliation. Then whoever transgresses against you, you transgress in the same way against him. Observe your duty to Allah, and know that Allah is with those who fear Allah. 195Spend your wealth for the sake of Allah, and do not be cast into ruin by your own hands, and do good. Indeed, Allah loves those who do good. 196Perform the pilgrimage (hajj) and the minor pilgrimage (umrah) for Allah. And if you are prevented from doing so, then send gifts that you can obtain with ease, and do not shave your heads until the gifts have reached their destination. And whoever among you is sick or has a head ailment must pay a ransom of fasting or almsgiving or offering. And if you are in safety, then whoever contents himself with the umrah for the pilgrimage, send gifts that can be obtained with ease. And whoever cannot find them, then a fast of three days while on the pilgrimage, and of seven when you have returned, that is, ten in all. That is for him whose family is not present at the sacred mosque. Observe your duty to Allah, and know that Allah is severe in punishment. 197The pilgrimage is the well-known months, and whoever has decided to perform the pilgrimage in them, there is no lewdness nor abuse nor angry conversation on the pilgrimage. And whatever good you do, Allah knows it. So make provision for yourselves, for the best provision is to fear Allah. Therefore keep your duty to me, O men of understanding. 198It is no sin for you that you seek the bounty of your Lord. But when you press on in the multitude from Arafat, remember Allah by the sacred monument. Remember him as he has guided you, although before you were of those who are astray. 199Then hurry on from the place from which the multitude hurries on, and ask forgiveness of Allah. Indeed, Allah is forgiving, merciful. 200And when you have completed your devotions, then remember Allah as you remember your fathers, or with a more spirited remembrance. But among mankind is the one who says, Our Lord, give to us in this world, and he has no share in the hereafter.

---

193. The command to fight "until persecution [*fitna*] is no more, and religion is for Allah" reveals that there is an aspect to the warfare enjoined by the Qur'an that is not purely defensive. Muslims must continue the war until Allah's law prevails over the world, which implies a conflict without end until that goal is attained. Ibn Hisham explains that this passage means that Muslims must fight against unbelievers "until God alone is worshipped," which makes for a long war.[97]

Ibn Kathir explains that the verse means that Muslims must fight "so that the religion of Allah becomes dominant above all other religions."[98] Says Bulandshahri: "The worst of sins are Infidelity (*Kufr*) and Polytheism (*shirk*) which constitute rebellion against Allah, The Creator. To eradicate these, Muslims are required to wage war until there exists none of it in the world, and the only religion is that of Allah."[99] That's an open-ended declaration of war against every non-Muslim, in all times and in all places.

According to numerous Islamic authorities, the statement that Muslims must fight until there is no more fitna means that they must fight "so that there is no more Shirk."[100] *Shirk* is the cardinal sin in Islam, the association of partners with Allah—i.e., calling Jesus the Son of God. The *Tafsir al-Jalalayn* identifies *fitna* as shirk and stipulates that the war must continue until "only He is worshipped."[101] For more on shirk, see 6:21.

Many Muslims would regard this conflict as essentially defensive—a defensive action against the aggressions of unbelief. If Muslims must fight until unbelief does not exist, the mere presence of unbelief constitutes sufficient aggression to allow for the beginning of hostilities.

This is one of the foundations for the supremacist notion that Muslims must wage war against unbelievers until those unbelievers are either converted to Islam or subjugated under the rule of Islamic law, as 9:29 states explicitly. The idea that Islam will prevail over all other religions is additionally at 8:39, 9:33, and 61:9.

194. There is nothing akin to Jesus's "turn the other cheek" (Matthew 5:39) in the Qur'an; instead, the believers are instructed to retaliate in the same manner that they were attacked. The *Tafsir al-Jalalayn* explains: "This is called equivalence since it [that is, the retaliation] should take a similar form."[102] See also 5:45 and 16:126.

²⁰¹And among them is the one who says, Our Lord, give to us what is good in this world and in the hereafter, and guard us from the torment of fire. ²⁰²For them there is stored up a good share out of what they have earned. Allah is swift at reckoning. ²⁰³Remember Allah throughout the established days. Then whoever hastens by two days, it is no sin for him, and whoever delays, it is no sin for him, that is for him who fears Allah. Be mindful of your duty to Allah, and know that to Him you will be gathered. ²⁰⁴And of mankind there is he whose conversation about the life of this world pleases you, and he calls Allah to witness about what is in his heart, yet he is the most hostile of opponents. ²⁰⁵And when he turns away, his effort in the land is to spread corruption in it and to destroy the crops and the cattle, and Allah does not love corruption. ²⁰⁶And when it is said to him, Be mindful of your duty to Allah, pride takes him to sin. Gehenna is enough for him, an evil bed. ²⁰⁷And of mankind is the one who would sell himself, seeking the pleasure of Allah, and Allah has compassion on his slaves. ²⁰⁸O you who believe, enter Islam in full, and do not follow the footsteps of Satan. Indeed, he is an open enemy to you. ²⁰⁹And if you turn away after the clear proofs have come to you, then know that Allah is mighty, wise. ²¹⁰Are they waiting for anything else other than Allah coming to them in the shadows of the clouds with the angels? Then the case would be already judged. All cases go back to Allah.

²¹¹Ask the children of Israel how many clear signs we gave them. He who alters the favor of Allah after it has come to him, indeed, Allah is severe in punishment. ²¹²The life of the world is beautiful for those who disbelieve, they make a joke of the believers. But those who keep their duty to Allah will be above them on the day of resurrection. Allah gives without limit to those whom he wills. ²¹³Mankind was one community, and Allah sent prophets as bearers of good news and as warners, and revealed with them the book with the truth, that it might judge among mankind concerning the things they disagreed about. And only those to whom it was given disagreed about it, after clear proofs had come to them, through hatred one of another. And Allah by his will guided those who believe to the truth of what they disagreed about. Allah guides those whom he wills to a straight path. ²¹⁴Or do you think that you will enter paradise while there has not yet come upon you anything like what came to those who passed away before you? Affliction and adversity befell them, they were shaken as with earthquake, until the messenger and those who believed along with him said, When does Allah's help come? Now indeed Allah's help is near.

---

206. Gehenna (*jahannam*) is the word used in the New Testament (Matthew 5:22, 5:29, 5:30, and so on) and generally understood as referring to hell. Tabari states that it is the first of the seven gates of hell. The twelfth-century jurist Abu al-Qasim al-Zamakhshari explains that the gates correspond to levels of hell, and Gehenna is the gate for "he who feigns belief in the deity."¹⁰³

208. This kind of statement makes reform of Islam difficult, for the reformer is always vulnerable to the charge that he is not entering Islam in full.

213. The people who were given the book are the Jews and Christians. Ibn Kathir explains that they disagreed about the "day of Congregation": "The Jews made it Saturday while the Christians chose Sunday. Allah guided the Ummah [community] of Muhammad to Friday."¹⁰⁴

They also disagreed about the direction to face when praying (*qiblah*), postures of prayer, fasting, and the true religion of Abraham: "The Jews said, 'He was a Jew,' while the Christians considered him Christian. Allah has made him a *Haniyfan Musliman*," that is, a pre-Islamic monotheist (see 2:135).¹⁰⁵ "Allah guided the *Ummah* of Muhammad to the truth."¹⁰⁶

²¹⁵They ask you what they should spend. Say, What you spend for good to parents and near relatives and orphans and the needy and the wayfarer. And whatever good you do, indeed, Allah is aware of it. ²¹⁶Warfare is commanded for you, even though it is odious for you, but it may happen that you hate something that is good for you, and it may happen that you love something that is bad for you. Allah knows, you do not know. ²¹⁷They ask you about warfare in the sacred month. Say, Warfare during it is an awesome sin, but to turn people away from the way of Allah, and to disbelieve in him and expelling his people from the sacred mosque, is more serious with Allah, for persecution is worse than slaughter. And they will not stop fighting against you until they have made you renegades from your religion, if they can. And whoever becomes a renegade and dies in his disbelief, they are the ones whose works have failed both in this world and the hereafter. They are the rightful companions of the fire, they will remain in it. ²¹⁸Indeed, those who believe, and those who emigrate and wage jihad for the sake of Allah, these have hope of Allah's mercy. Allah is forgiving, merciful. ²¹⁹They ask you about strong drink and games of chance. Say, In both is a great sin, and some benefit for men, but their sin is greater than their benefit. And they ask you what they should spend. Say, What you can spare. In this way Allah makes signs clear to you, that maybe you will reflect, ²²⁰Upon the world and the hereafter. And they ask you about orphans. Say, To improve their situation is best. And if you mingle your affairs with theirs, then they are your brothers. Allah knows the one who spoils things from the one who improves things. If Allah had willed, he could have overburdened you. Allah is mighty,

---

216. The *Tafsir Anwarul Bayan* explains the traditional view: "While the Muslims were in Makkah, they were weak and few in number, never possessing the capability nor the divine permission for Jihad (religious war). After migrating to Madinah, they received the order to fight their enemies in defense, as a verse of Surah Hajj [sura 22 of the Qur'an] proclaims: 'Permission (to fight) has been granted to those being attacked because they are oppressed [22:39].' Later on the order came to fight the Infidels (kuffar) even though they do not initiate the aggression."[107]

The *Tafsir Anwarul Bayan* is a twentieth-century exposition of the Qur'an, but this view of the three stages of development of the Qur'an's teaching on warfare is found in Ibn Hisham's ninth-century work, and in the writings of mainstream Islamic theologians with enduring influence, including Ibn Kathir (fourteenth century), Ibn Qayyim (thirteenth century), Ibn Juzayy (fourteenth century), as-Suyuti (fifteenth century), and many others.

217. Islamic apologist Karen Armstrong has claimed that "warfare during it is an awesome sin" amounts to a "condemnation of all warfare as an 'awesome evil.'"[108] "Awesome evil" is plausible enough, but it is clearly not a condemnation of all warfare, as the passage goes on to reiterate the reasons already enunciated in 2:191 for why it can be justified to wage war during the sacred month.

Meanwhile, the renegade who leaves Islam doesn't just burn in hell, but his works fail in this world. *Qurtubi* explains: "Scholars disagree about whether or not apostates are asked to repent. One group says that they are asked to repent and, if they do not, they are killed. Some say they are given an hour and others a month. Others say that they are asked to repent three times, and that is the view of Malik. Al-Hasan said they are asked a hundred times. It is also said that they are killed without being asked to repent."[109]

218. The phrase here translated as "wage jihad for the sake of Allah" is usually translated in some way akin to "strive in the way of Allah," as Mohammed Marmaduke Pickthall has it. The key word here is *jahadu*, which is a verbal form of the noun *jihad*; thus the translation here is more accurate than most, and more illuminating of how an Islamic jihadi will read and understand the Qur'an. "Jihad for the sake of Allah" in Islamic theology refers to jihad warfare, not to more spiritualized understandings of jihad. Verse 2:154, which mentions those who are "killed for the sake of Allah," further supports the idea that hot warfare is to be waged for the sake of Allah.

219. Several early authorities, including Ibn Umar, Ash-Sha'bi, Mujahid, Qatadah, Ar-Rabi bin Anas, and Abdur-Rahman bin Aslam, say that this was the first of three verses to be revealed on the subject of alcohol (the others are 4:43 and 5:90). That would mean that the other two take precedence over this one according to the principle of abrogation (see 2:106). Here Allah says that there is "some benefit" in alcohol, but in 5:90 he says that it is "Satan's handiwork," which would rule out its being beneficial at all.

Instead of "a great sin" (*kabeerun*), the Warsh Qur'an has "much sin" (*katheerun*).[110]

"And they ask you what they should spend. Say, What you can spare" is not connected to the discussion of alcohol and appears to be a continuation of 2:215, possibly separated by a later interpolation.

wise. **221**Do not marry idolatresses until they believe, for indeed, a believing slave woman is better than an idolatress, even though she pleases you. And do not give your daughters in marriage to idolaters until they believe, for indeed, a believing slave is better than an idolater, even though he pleases you. These people invite you to the fire, and Allah invites you to the garden, and to forgiveness by his grace, and explains his signs to mankind so that perhaps they will remember. **222**They ask you about menstruation. Say, It is an illness, so leave women alone at such times and do not go in to them until they are cleansed. And when they have purified themselves, then go in to them as Allah has commanded you. Indeed Allah loves those who turn to him, and loves those who are concerned about cleanliness. **223**Your women are a field for you, so go to your field as you will, and send before you for your souls, and fear Allah, and know that you will meet him. Give good news to believers, **224**And do not by your oaths make Allah a hindrance to your being righteous and observing your duty to him and making

peace among mankind. Allah is hearer, knower. **225**Allah will not hold you accountable for what is unintentional in your oaths. But he will hold you accountable for what your hearts have earned. Allah is forgiving, merciful. **226**Those who swear abstinence from their wives must wait four months, then, if they change their mind, indeed, Allah is forgiving, merciful. **227**And if they decide upon divorce, Allah is hearer, knower. **228**Women who are divorced will wait, keeping themselves apart, for three courses. And it is not lawful for them that they should conceal what Allah has created in their wombs if they are believers in Allah and the last day. And their husbands would do better to take them back in that case, if they desire a reconciliation. And they have rights similar to those who are over them in kindness, and men are a degree above them. Allah is mighty, wise. **229**Divorce must be pronounced twice and then a woman must be retained in honor or released in kindness. And it is not lawful for you that you take back anything from women out of what you have given them, except when both

221. Allah forbids Muslims to marry "idolatresses." Ibn Kathir records a large amount of disagreement among Islamic authorities over whether this prohibition applies to Jewish and Christian women, or just to polytheists. However, he notes that there is *Ijma*—consensus—among Islamic jurists that such marriages are allowed, although of course Muslim women are not allowed by any school of Islamic law to marry Jewish or Christian men.[111]

In a culture that requires women to be utterly subservient to men, these unequal laws ensure that non-Muslim communities remain subjugated, not enjoying equality of rights or equality of dignity with Muslims.

223. According to Islamic tradition, the Koranic verse about a woman being a "tilth" for a man was revealed because of the Jews, who "used to say that when one comes to one's wife through the vagina, but being on her back, and she becomes pregnant, the child has a squint"—or, according to other sources, is cross-eyed. To refute this, Allah revealed that it didn't matter whether she was lying on her back or not, for, "Your women are a field [tilth] for you, so go to your field as you will." Muslims also often understand this verse as prohibiting anal sex. Sayyid Qutb says that the use of the word "tilth," with its "connotations of tillage and production, is most fitting, in a context of fertility and procreation"—or, as

Maududi puts it, Allah's "purpose in the creation of women is not merely to provide men with recreation."[112] Not merely recreation: women were also created in order to provide men with children.

According to a hadith recorded by the Imam Muslim, considered by Muslims to be the second most reliable collector of hadith (after Bukhari) and others, the Jews are behind the revelation of this verse. "The Jews used to say that when one comes to one's wife through the vagina, but being on her back, and she becomes pregnant, the child has a squint"—or, according to other sources, is cross-eyed.[113]

228. Allah's regulations for divorce emphasize regarding women that "men have a degree over them." This may be why men can divorce their wives simply by saying, "*Talaq*—I divorce you—but women may not do this. Such an easy procedure leads to divorces in a fit of pique, followed by reconciliation—and the Qur'an anticipates this and attempts to head it off by stipulating that a husband who divorces his wife three times cannot reconcile with her until she marries another man and is in turn divorced by him: "And if he has divorced her [for the third time], then she is not lawful to him after that until she has married another husband" (2:230). On "three courses," see 65:1.

parties are afraid that they may not be able to keep within the limits of Allah. And if you fear that they may not be able to keep the limits of Allah, in that case it is no sin for either of them if the woman ransoms herself. These are the limits of Allah. Do not transgress them. For whoever transgresses Allah's limits is a wrongdoer. **230**And if he has divorced her, then she is not lawful to him after that until she has married another husband. Then if he divorces her, it is no sin for both of them that they come together again, if they think that they are able to observe the limits of Allah. These are the limits of Allah. He shows them to people who have knowledge. **231**When you have divorced women, and they have reached their term, then retain them in kindness or release them in kindness. Do not retain them to their harm, so that you transgress. He who does that has wronged his soul. Do not make the signs of Allah a laughing-stock, but remember Allah's grace upon you, and what he has revealed to you of the book and of wisdom, by which he exhorts you. Observe your duty to Allah and know that Allah is aware of all things. **232**And when you have divorced women and they reach their term, do not place difficulties in the way of their marrying their husbands if it is agreed between them in kindness. This is a warning for him among you who believes in Allah and the last day. That is more virtuous for you, and cleaner. Allah knows, you do not know. **233**Mothers will suckle their children for two whole years, for those who wish to complete the suckling. The responsibility of feeding and clothing nursing mothers in a seemly manner is upon the father of the child. No one should be charged beyond his capacity. A mother should not be made to suffer because of her child,

nor should he to whom the child is born because of his child. And the heir is responsible in the same way. If they desire to wean the child by mutual consent and consultation, it is no sin for them, and if you wish to give your children out to nurse, it is no sin for you, provided that you pay what is due from you in kindness. Observe your duty to Allah, and know that Allah is the seer what you do. **234**Those of you who die and leave wives behind, they will wait, keeping themselves apart, four months and ten days. And when they reach the term, then there is no sin for you in anything that they may do with themselves in decency. Allah is informed of what you do. **235**There is no sin for you in what you proclaim or hide in your minds concerning your betrothal with women. Allah knows that you will remember them. But do not get betrothed with women except by saying a recognized form of words. And do not consummate the marriage until the prescribed term is completed. Know that Allah knows what is in your minds, so beware of him, and know that Allah is forgiving, merciful. **236**It is no sin for you if you divorce women even when you have not yet touched them, or established a portion for them. Provide for them, the rich according to his means, and the poor according to his means, a fair provision, a duty for those who do good. **237**If you divorce them before you have touched them and you have established a portion for them, then half of what you established, unless they agree to forgo it, or he agrees to forgo it in whose hand is the marriage tie. To forgo is nearer to piety. And do not forget kindness among yourselves. Allah is the seer of what you do. **238**Be guardians of your prayers, and of the midday prayer, and stand up with devotion to

Allah. **239** And if you go out in fear, then standing or on horseback. And when you are again in safety, remember Allah, as he has taught you what you did not know. **240** Those of you who are about to die and leave wives behind them, they should bequeath to their wives a provision for the year without turning them out, but if they go out, there is no sin for you in what they do of themselves within their rights. Allah is mighty, wise. **241** For divorced women, a provision in kindness, a duty for those who fear Allah. **242** In this way Allah explains his signs to you, so that you may understand. **243** Think about those of old, who went forth from their habitations in their thousands, fearing death, and Allah said to them, Die, and then he brought them back to life. Indeed, Allah is a Lord of kindness to mankind, but most of mankind does not give thanks. **244** Fight for the sake of Allah, and be aware that Allah is hearer, knower. **245** Who is it that will lend Allah a generous loan to Allah, so that he may make it increase manifold? Allah makes poor and makes wealthy. To him you will return. **246** Think of the leaders of the children of Israel after Moses, how they said to a prophet they had, Set up for us a king and we will fight in Allah's way. He said, Would you then refrain from fighting if fighting were commanded for you? They said, Why should we not fight in Allah's way when we have been driven from our dwellings with our children? Yet when fighting was commanded for them, they turned away, all except a few of them. Allah is aware of evildoers. **247** Their prophet said to them, Indeed, Allah has raised up Saul to be a king for you. They said, How can he be king over us when we are more deserving of the kingdom than he is, since he has not been given enough wealth? He said, Indeed, Allah has chosen him above you, and has increased him abundantly in wisdom and stature. Allah bestows his dominion on those whom he wills. Allah is all-embracing, all-knowing. **248** And their prophet said to them, Indeed, the sign of his kingdom is that the ark will come to you, in which is a *sakina* from your Lord, and a remnant of what the house of Moses and the house of Aaron left behind, the angels bearing it. Indeed, this will be a sign for you, if you are believers. **249** And when Saul set out with the army, he said, Indeed, Allah will test you by a river. Whoever therefore drinks from it is not with me, and whoever does not taste it is with me, except the one who takes it in the hollow of his hand. But they drank from it, all except a few of them. And after he had crossed, he and those who believed with him, they said, We have no power this day against Goliath and his hosts. But those who knew that they would meet Allah exclaimed, How many little companies have defeated mighty hosts by Allah's permission. Allah is with the persevering. **250** And when they went into the field against Goliath and his hosts, they said, Our Lord, give us endurance, make our foothold sure, and give us

---

240. On the arrangements men make for their wives in their wills, Ibn Kathir contends that "the majority of the scholars said that this Ayah (2:240) was abrogated by the Ayah (2:234)."[114]

248. *Sakina* is derived from the Hebrew *shekina*, a dwelling place of God on earth. Bell notes that "in the Qur'an the word generally has the sense of 'assurance,' but as this is probably the first occasion of its use, it is doubtful if any such sense is attached to it here," and thus it is left untranslated.[115]

249. The Qur'an adds the river test from the story of Gideon (Judges 7:4-7) into this account of the actions of Saul, possibly indicating a textual interpolation, or alternatively, simple confusion on the part of the original source.

help against the disbelieving people. **251**So they routed them by Allah's permission, and David killed Goliath, and Allah gave him the kingdom and wisdom, and taught him what he willed. And if Allah had not repelled some men by means of others, the earth would have been corrupted. But Allah is a Lord of kindness to creatures. **252**These are the signs of Allah which we recite to you with truth, and indeed, you are among the number of messengers, **253**Of those messengers, some of whom we caused to excel others, and there are some to whom Allah spoke, while he exalted some of them in degree, and we gave Jesus, son of Mary, clear proofs, and we supported him with the holy spirit. And if Allah had willed, those who followed after them would not have fought one with another after the clear proofs had come unto them. But they disagreed, some of them believing and some disbelieving. And if Allah had so willed, they would not have fought one with another, but Allah does what he wills. **254**O you who believe, spend out of what we have provided you with before a day comes when there will be no selling, nor friendship, nor intercession. The unbelievers, they are the wrongdoers. **255**Allah. There is no God except him, the living one, the eternal one. Neither slumber nor sleep overtake him. To him belong whatever is in the heavens and whatever is in the earth. Who is he who intercedes with him except by his permission? He knows what is in front of them and what is behind them, while they encompass nothing of his knowledge except what he wills. His throne includes the heavens and the earth, and he is never weary of preserving them. He is the sublime, the tremendous. **256**There is no compulsion in religion. The right direction is from now on distinct from error. And he who rejects *taghut* and believes in Allah has grasped a firm handhold which will never break. Allah is hearer,

---

251. Instead of "And if Allah had not repelled some men by means of others," the Warsh Qur'an has "And if Allah had not defended some men by means of others."[116]

253. If Allah had willed, the nations would have believed the prophets he sent to earth, but this was not his will, although his reasons are left unexplained. It would have been interesting to know why he sent prophets while willing that they not be believed, but this is left unexplained.

255. This is known as the Throne Verse (*Ayat al-Kursi*). According to the contemporary Islamic scholar Mahmoud Ayoub, this verse is "regarded by Muslims as one of the most excellent verses of the Qur'an. It has therefore played a very important role in Muslim piety."[117] A tradition depicts Muhammad as saying: "The master of all speech is the Qur'an, the master of the Qur'an is Surat al-Baqarah [sura 2], and the master of al-Baqarah is the Throne Verse."[118]

Qurtubi reports that "when the Throne Verse was revealed, every idol and king in the world fell prostrate and the crowns of kings fell off their heads," and recounts a saying by Muhammad in which Allah tells Moses of the many blessings that people will receive if they recite the Throne Verse. This is another manifestation of the assumption that the people of the book had at least some of the contents of the Qur'an but perversely effaced them from their own Scriptures.[119] A hadith has Muhammad state that "whoever recites Ayat al-Kursi at the end of every obligatory prayer, nothing but death will prevent him from entering Paradise."[120]

256. Islamic spokesmen in the West frequently quote this verse to disprove the contention that Islam spread by the sword, or even to claim that Islam is a religion of peace. According to an early Muslim, Mujahid ibn Jabr, this verse was abrogated by 9:29, in which the Muslims are commanded to fight against the people of the book. Others, however, according to Tabari, say that this verse was never abrogated but was revealed precisely in reference to the people of the book: they are not to be forced to accept Islam but may practice their religions freely as long as they pay the jizya (a poll-tax) and "feel themselves subdued," as per 9:29.[121]

Many see the assertion that "there is no compulsion in religion" as contradicting the Islamic imperative to wage jihad against unbelievers. Actually, however, there is no contradiction at all. This is because the aim of jihad is not the forced conversion of non-Muslims, but their subjugation within the Islamic social order. Says Asad: "All Islamic jurists (*fuqaha'*), without any exception, hold that forcible conversion is under all circumstances null and void, and that any attempt at coercing a non-believer to accept the faith of Islam is a grievous sin: a verdict which disposes of the widespread fallacy that Islam places before the unbelievers the alternative of 'conversion or the sword.'"[122]

The choice, as laid out by Muhammad himself in a tradition, is conversion, subjugation as dhimmis, or the sword.[123] Qutb accordingly denies that "there is no compulsion in religion" contradicts the imperative to fight until "religion is for Allah" (2:193). He claims that "Islam has not used force to impose its beliefs."[124] Rather, jihad's "main objective has been the establishment of a stable society in which all citizens, including followers of other religious creeds, may live in peace and security"—although not with

knower. **257**Allah is the protecting guardian of those who believe. He brings them out of darkness into light. As for those who disbelieve, their patrons are *taghut*. They bring them out of light into darkness. They are the rightful companions of the fire. They will remain in it. **258**Think of the one who had an argument with Abraham about his Lord, because Allah had given him the kingdom, how, when Abraham said, My Lord is he who gives life and causes death, he answered, I give life and cause death. Abraham said, Indeed, Allah causes the sun to rise in the East, so do you cause it to come up from the West? In this way the disbeliever was embarrassed. And Allah does not guide wrongdoing people. **259**Or the comparison of him who, passing by a town which had fallen into utter ruin, exclaimed, How will Allah give this township life after its death? And Allah made him die for a hundred years, then brought him back to life. He said, How long have you waited? He said, I have waited a day or part of a day. He said, No, but you have waited for a hundred years. Just look at your food and drink which have not rotted. Look at your donkey. And so that we may make you a sign for mankind, look at the bones, how we adjust them and then cover them with flesh. And when it became clear to him, he said, I know now that Allah is able to do all things. **260**And when Abraham said, My Lord, show me how you give life to the dead, he said, Do you not believe? Abraham said, Yes, but so that my heart may be at ease. He said, Take four of the birds and cause them to come to you, then place a portion of them on each hill, then call them, they will come to you quickly, and know that Allah is mighty, wise. **261**Those who spend their wealth in Allah's way are like a grain that grows seven ears, in every ear a hundred grains. Allah gives manifold increase to whom he wills. Allah is all-embracing, all-knowing. **262**Those who spend their wealth for the sake of Allah and afterward do not follow up what they have spent with reproach and insult, their reward is with their Lord, and no fear will come upon them, nor will they grieve. **263**A kind word with forgiveness is better than almsgiving followed by insult. Allah is absolute, merciful. **264**O you who believe, do not render your almsgiving useless with reproach and insult, like the one who spends his wealth only so that men will see him and does not believe in Allah and the last day. He is like a rock on which is dust of the earth. A rainstorm strikes it, leaving it smooth and bare. They have no control of anything that they have gained. Allah does not guide the disbelieving people. **265**And those who spend their wealth in search of

---

equality of rights before the law, as 9:29 emphasizes.[125] For Qutb, that "stable society" is the "Islamic social order," the establishment of which is a chief objective of jihad.[126]

In this light the verse saying there is no compulsion in religion and the one saying that Muslims should fight until religion is for Allah go together without any trouble. Muslims must fight until "religion is for Allah," but they don't force anyone to accept Allah's religion. They enforce subservience upon those who refuse to convert, such that many of them subsequently convert to Islam so as to escape the humiliating and discriminatory regulations of dhimmitude—but when they convert, they do so freely.

Only at the end of the world, Islamic tradition informs us, will Jesus, the Prophet of Islam, return and Islamize the world, abolishing Christianity and thus the need for the jizya that is paid by the dhimmis: "He will fight the people for the cause of Islam. He will break the cross, kill swine, and abolish jizyah. Allah will perish all religions except Islam. He will destroy the Antichrist and will live on the earth for forty years and then he will die. The Muslims will pray over him."[127] Then religion will be "for Allah," as the Qur'an directs that it should be (2:193), and there will be no further need for jihad.

Taghut is an Ethiopic word.[128] According to the *Tafsir al-Jalalayn*, it "means Shaytan or idols and can be singular or plural."[129] One Islamic exegete identifies *taghut* as one of the idols that the Quraysh worshiped and that some of the Jews of Mecca also honored in order to ingratiate themselves.[130]

Allah's pleasure, and for the strengthening of their souls, are like a garden on a height. The rain strikes it and it brings forth its fruit twofold. And if the rain does not strike it, then the shower. Allah is seer of what you do. 266 Would any of you like to have a garden of palm-trees and vines, with rivers flowing under it, with all kinds of fruit for him within it, and old age has stricken him and he has feeble offspring, and a fiery whirlwind strikes it and it is consumed by fire. In this way Allah makes plain to you his signs, so that you may think. 267O you who believe, spend out of the good things which you have earned, and out of what we bring forth from the earth for you, and do not seek bad things to spend from them when you would not take them for yourselves except with disdain, and know that Allah is absolute, the owner of praise. 268Satan promises you destitution and commands lewdness for you. But Allah promises you forgiveness from himself, with bounty. Allah is all-embracing, all-knowing. 269He gives wisdom to whom he wills, and he to whom wisdom is given, he indeed has received abundant good. But no one remembers this except men of understanding. 270Whatever alms you spend or vow, indeed, Allah knows it. Wrongdoers have no helpers. 271If you make your almsgiving public, it is well, but if you hide it and give it to the poor, it will be better for you, and he will remove some of your evil deeds. Allah is informed of what you do. 272The guiding of them is not your duty, but Allah guides whom he wills. And whatever good thing you spend, it is for yourselves, when you do not spend except in search of Allah's face, and whatever good thing

you spend, it will be repaid to you in full, and you will not be wronged.

273 For the poor who are in difficulty for the sake of Allah, who cannot travel in the land. The unthinking man considers them wealthy because of their restraint. You will know them by their appearance, they do not beg from men with importunity. And whatever good thing you spend, indeed, Allah knows it. 274Those who spend their wealth by night and day, by stealth and openly, indeed their reward is with their Lord, and no fear will come upon them, nor will they grieve. 275Those who devour usury cannot rise up except as one whom Satan has made prostrate by touching him. That is because they say, Trade is just like usury, whereas Allah has permitted trading and forbidden usury. He to whom a warning comes from his Lord refrains, he will keep what is from the past, and his affair is with Allah. As for him who returns, such people are rightful companions of the fire. They will remain in it. 276Allah has cursed usury and made almsgiving fruitful. Allah does not love the impious and guilty. 277Indeed, those who believe and do good works and establish prayer and give alms, their reward is with their Lord and no fear will come upon them, nor will they grieve. 278O you who believe, observe your duty to Allah, and give up what remains from usury, if you are believers. 279And if you do not, then be warned of war from Allah and his messenger. And if you repent, then you have your principal. Do not wrong people, and you will not be wronged. 280And if the debtor is in difficult circumstances, then postponement until an easier time, and that you remit the debt as almsgiving

---

271. Instead of "he will remove" (*yukafferu*), the Warsh Qur'an has "we will remove" (*nukafferu*).[131]

would be better for you, if only you knew. **281**And guard yourselves against a day in which you will be brought back to Allah. Then every soul will be paid in full what it has earned, and they will not be wronged. **282**O you who believe, when you contract a debt for a fixed term, record it in writing. Let a scribe record it in writing between you in equity. No scribe should refuse to write as Allah has taught him, so let him write, and let him who incurs the debt dictate, and let him observe his duty to Allah his Lord, and not diminish any part of that duty. But if he who owes the debt is of low understanding, or weak, or unable himself to dictate, then let the guardian of his interests dictate in equity. And call to witness, from among your men, two witnesses. And if two men be not available, then a man and two women, of such as you approve as witnesses, so that if the one errs, the other will remember. And the witnesses must not refuse when they are summoned. Be not averse to writing it down, whether it be small or great, with the term thereof. That is more equitable in the sight of Allah and more certain for testimony, and the best way of avoiding doubt between you, except only in the case when it is actual merchandise which you transfer among yourselves from hand to hand. In that case, it is no sin for you if you do not write it. And have witnesses when you sell something to someone else, and let no harm be done to scribe or witness. If you do, indeed, it is a sin in you. Observe your duty to Allah. Allah is teaching you. And Allah is the knower of all things. **283**If you be on a journey and cannot find a scribe, then a pledge in hand. And if one of you entrusts to another, let he who is trusted deliver up what is entrusted to him, and let him observe his duty to Allah his Lord. Do not hide testimony. He who hides it, indeed his heart is sinful. Allah is aware of what you do. **284**To Allah is whatever is in the heavens and whatever is in the earth, and whether you make known what is in your minds or hide it, Allah will bring you to account for it. He will forgive those whom he wills and he will punish those whom he wills. Allah is able to do all things. **285**The messenger believes in what has been revealed to him from his Lord, and believers. Each one believes in Allah and his angels and his books and his messengers, we make no distinction between any of his messengers, and they say, We hear and we obey. Your forgiveness, our Lord, to you is the journeying. **286**Allah does not burden a soul beyond its scope. For it is what it

282. Laying out rules of evidence, Allah directs those trying to make a case to get one man to act as a witness, or two women if a man is not available. A hadith depicts Muhammad invoking this verse as part of his evidence that women were deficient in intelligence, as well as in religious faith. He was on his way to offer prayer one day when he passed by a group of women. He stopped to exhort them to charity, basing his exhortation upon a warning: "O women! Give alms, as I have seen that the majority of the dwellers of hell-fire were you (women)."[132]

When they asked him for an explanation of why this might be, he responded: "You curse frequently and are ungrateful to your husbands. I have not seen anyone more deficient in intelligence and religion than you. A cautious sensible man could be led astray by some of you." When further pressed to explain, he reminded them of this verse: "Is not the evidence of two women equal to the witness of one man?" When the women admitted that this was indeed the case, Muhammad drove his case home: "This is the deficiency in her intelligence. Isn't it true that a woman can neither pray nor fast during her menses?" When they admitted this also, he concluded: "This is the deficiency in her religion."[133]

286. Ibn Kathir says that those upon whom Allah previously placed burdens were the "Jews and Christians," and that the disbelieving people over whom Muslims should pray for victory are "those who rejected Your religion, denied Your Oneness, refused the Message of Your Prophet, worshipped other than You and associated others in Your worship."[134] Ibn Kathir adds: "Give us victory and make us prevail above them in this and the Hereafter."[135] It is common today for jihad preachers to pray that Allah would grant the Muslims victory over the unbelievers.

has earned, and against it is what it has deserved. Our Lord, do not condemn us if we forget, or miss the mark. Our Lord, do not lay upon us a burden like what you laid on those before us. Our Lord, do not impose on us what we do not have the strength to bear. Pardon us, forgive us and have mercy on us, you, our protector, and give us victory over the disbelieving people.

SURA 3

The House of Imran

Ali Imran

Introduction

Imran is Amram, the father of Moses and Aaron (Exodus 6:20), who is mentioned in 3:33 and 3:35. Like most sura titles in the Qur'an, this one doesn't denote the sura's theme, but is just a word taken from within the sura that is simply a means to distinguish it from other suras.

According to Maududi, sura 3, which is regarded in Islamic tradition as a Medinan sura, is addressed to the people of the book (that is, primarily Jews and Christians) as well as to Muslims, in order to invite them "to the same true religion preached by the Prophets from the earliest times," and to show them that "the deviant course which they have adopted is inconsistent with the very scriptures which they themselves acknowledge to be of Divine origin. They ought, therefore, to accept the Truth now placed before them by Muhammad."[1]

Likewise, the *Tafsir Anwarul Bayan* says that sura 3 is a "'talking proof' against the Jews, Christians and idolaters since it addresses them all. It invites them towards the truth and refutes their false beliefs, which includes the blasphemous ideologies concerning Sayyidina [Masters] Isa and Ibrahim [Jesus and Abraham]."[2]

---

1 Sayyid Abul Ala Mawdudi, *Towards Understanding the Qur'an* (*Tafhim al-Qur'an*), Zafar Ishaq Ansari, trans. (Leicester, England: The Islamic Foundation, 1995), I, 230.
2 Muhammad Aashiq Ilahi Bulandshahri, *Illuminating Discourses on the Noble Qur'an* (*Tafsir Anwarul Bayan*), translated by Afzal Hussain Elias and Muhammad Arshad Fakhri (Karachi: Darul Ishaat, 2005), I, 350-1.

Al-Wahidi says that the first part of this sura was revealed when a delegation of Christians from Najran in southern Arabia came to Medina to see Muhammad, who told them: "Surrender to Allah."[3] When they told him they had surrendered to Allah before he himself had done so, Muhammad was peremptory: "You lie! You were prevented from surrendering by claiming that Allah has a son, by your worship of the cross and by your consumption of pork."[4]

A theological discussion ensued. When the Christians asked, "If Jesus is not the son of Allah, who is his father?" Muhammad answered that "a son must resemble his father," but "our Lord is ever living and never dies while Jesus is subject to death."[5] Muhammad added: "Do you not know that Allah oversees everything, protects and provides for it?" while Jesus does not "share any of that."[6] And: "Allah has shaped Jesus in the womb of his mother as He willed, but our Lord does not eat or drink nor has He any need to relieve Himself."[7] After a bit more of this, says al-Wahidi, the first eighty verses of this sura were revealed, with an eye toward correcting the Christians' errors about their faith. Ibn Kathir agrees, although he specifies that eighty-three verses were revealed on the occasion of the Christians' visit to Muhammad, which he says took place in 632.

According to the twentieth-century Islamic scholar Richard Bell, "this sura is composite and in several parts very confused."[8] It is "not a unity," he says, and that is clear from the fact that one rhyme scheme prevails at the beginning and end of the sura, and another in the middle.[9]

---

3 Al-Wahidi, 60.
4 Ibid.
5 Ibid.
6 Ibid.
7 Ibid.
8 Richard Bell, *The Qur'an: Translated, with a critical re-arrangement of the Surahs* (Edinburgh: T. & T. Clark, 1937), I, 43.
9 Ibid.

The House of Imran

IN THE NAME OF ALLAH, THE COMPASSIONATE, THE MERCIFUL.

¹Alif. Lam. Mim. ²Allah. There is no God except him, the living, the eternal. ³He has revealed to you the book with truth, confirming what was before it, even as he revealed the Torah and the Gospel. ⁴In previous times, for a guidance to mankind, and he has revealed the furqan. Indeed, those who disbelieve in the signs of Allah, theirs will be a heavy doom. Allah is mighty, able to repay. ⁵Indeed, nothing in the earth or in the heavens is hidden from Allah. ⁶It is he who fashions you in the wombs as pleases him. No one has the right to be worshiped except him, the almighty, the wise. ⁷It is he who has revealed to you, the book in which there are clear signs, they are the mother of the book, and others ambiguous. But those in whose hearts is doubt pursue what is ambiguous, seeking dissension by trying to explain it. No one knows its interpretation except Allah. And those who are of sound instruction say, We believe in it, all of it is from our Lord, but only men of understanding are really mindful. ⁸Our Lord, do not cause our

---

1. On the "mysterious letters," see 2:1.

3. Allah proclaims that the Qur'an confirms what was written in the Torah and the Gospel. Ibn Kathir explains that "these Books testify to the truth of the Qur'an, and the Qur'an also testifies to the truth these Books contained, including the news and glad tidings of Muhammad's prophethood and the revelation of the Glorious Qur'an."[1] The Qur'an insists upon the congruence of its message with that of the holy books of the Jews and Christians; when that congruence is not found, Muslims have charged Jews and Christians with tampering with their scriptures and altering the text so as to remove references to Muhammad and agreement with the message of Islam.

4. In contrast to the Jews' and Christians' corrupted scriptures, Allah has now revealed the *furqan*, which is, as Ibn Kathir puts it, "the distinction between misguidance, falsehood and deviation on one hand, and guidance, truth and piety on the other hand."[2]

There is considerable disagreement among Islamic scholars over what exactly the *furqan* is. Tabari notes that some Muslim theologians consider the *furqan* to be "the criterion distinguishing truth from error regarding the disagreement among [religious] parties and the followers of various sects concerning Jesus."[3] Others, however, identify the *furqan* as the Qur'an itself, although some object to that since the Qur'an was just mentioned (as "the book with the truth") in 3:3. The Sixth Shi'ite Imam, Jafar as-Sadiq, offered a middle way, suggesting that the *furqan* is part, but not all of the Qur'an: "the *furqan* is every clear or unambiguous (*muhkam*) verse, while the Book is the entire Qur'an which is confirmed by the prophets who came before it."[4]

The contemporary scholar C. Heger offers another possibility altogether, noting that "the meaning 'criterion' usually maintained for *furqan* results from the attempt to interpret the Syriac *furqan*, which has the meaning of 'redemption, salvation.'"[5] This would make this verse read that Allah "has revealed salvation," and would make it one example of the Qur'an's Aramaic Christian substratum. This possibility becomes more likely in light of 25:1. This reading would make 2:53 read "we gave Moses the book and salvation," which is entirely plausible. The nineteenth-century Islamic scholar Thomas

Patrick Hughes asserts that "The Jews use the word *perek*, or *pirka*, from the same root, to denote a section or portion of scripture."[6]

Whatever it may mean, *furqan* is certainly not pure or clear Arabic, as the Qur'an claims to be; see 12:2.

The same verse also promises a "heavy doom" to those who "disbelieve in the signs of Allah." The twentieth-century Indian Muslim scholar Allama Shabbir Ahmed Usmani sees this as proof that Jesus cannot be divine, for while "God is powerful to venge [sic] and punish whenever He deems fit," Jesus "cannot be a sovereign like God because he could not overcome the miscreants who were chasing him to kill."[7]

6. According to Ibn Kathir, "This Ayah refers to the fact that Isa [Jesus], son of Mary, is a created servant, just as Allah created the rest of mankind. Allah created Isa in the womb (of his mother) and shaped him as He willed. Therefore, how could Isa be divine, as the Christians, may Allah's curses descend on them, claim Isa was created in the womb and his creation changed from stage to stage"?[8]

7. Shortly after using a word so unclear that Muslims have debated about its meaning for centuries (see 2:4), Allah qualifies his declaration that there is "no doubt" regarding the Qur'an (2:2) by stating that parts of it are ambiguous, which doubters pursue in order to sow dissension. Ibn Kathir states that among the ambiguous passages are "the abrogated *Ayat*, parables, oaths, and what should be believed in, but not implemented."[9] The *Tafsir al-Jalalayn* includes among the ambiguous verses "those whose meanings are not immediately obvious, as is the case with the letters at the beginnings of suras," including this one.[10]

The assertion that "no one knows its interpretation except Allah" is striking. Why would Allah include material in his "clear" revelation of guidance to human beings that only he knows the meaning of? There is no clear answer to that, but absolute acceptance of the unclear along with the clear is enjoined upon the believers; this has helped to engender in Islamic culture a certain tendency to avoid questioning the Qur'an or pondering its injunctions critically.

Here the "mother of the book" is the clear verses ("signs") of the Qur'an, but at 13:39 and 43:4 it is the eternal book in paradise of which the Qur'an is a perfect copy.

hearts to stray after you have guided us, and grant us mercy from your presence. Indeed, you, only you, are the bestower. **9**Our Lord, indeed, it is you who gather mankind together on a day of which there is no doubt. Indeed, Allah does not fail to keep the appointment. **10**Neither the riches nor the progeny of those who disbelieve will help them in any way with Allah. They will be fuel for fire. **11**Like Pharaoh's people and those who were before them, they disbelieved in our signs and so Allah seized them for their sins. And Allah is severe in punishment. **12**Say to those who disbelieve, You will be overcome and gathered to Gehenna, an evil bed. **13**There was a sign for you in two armies that met, one army fighting in the way of Allah, and another disbelieving, whom they saw as twice their number, clearly, with their own eyes. In this way Allah strengthens those whom he wills with his help. Indeed, in this there is truly a lesson for those who have eyes. **14**Appealing for mankind is love of the joys from women and children, and stored-up heaps of gold and silver, and branded horses, and cattle and land. That is comfort of the life of the world. Allah. With him is a more excellent abode. **15**Say, Shall I inform you of something better than that? For those who keep from evil, with their Lord, are gardens under which rivers flow, in which they will live, and pure companions, and contentment from Allah. Allah is seer of his slaves, **16**Those who say, Our Lord, indeed, we believe. So forgive us our sins and guard us from the punishment of

---

11. On Pharaoh, see also 2:49, 7:103, 8:52, 10:75, 14:6, 17:101, 20:24, 23:46, 26:11, 27:12, 28:3, 29:39, 38:12, 40:24, 44:17, 50:13, 51:38, 54:41, 66:11, 69:9, 73:15, 79:15, 85:18, and 89:10.

12. According to al-Wahidi, "those who disbelieve" are the Jews, and the revelation of this verse and 3:13 followed the Battle of Badr in 624, where the Muslims are said to have defeated an army of the Quraysh that was double the size of the Muslim force. Maududi says that the first thirty-two verses of sura 3 were "probably revealed soon after the Battle of Badr." This contradicts the claim that the first eighty or eighty-three verses of this sura were revealed in 632 after the disputation with the Christians at Najran.[11]

After the victory at Badr, Muhammad is said to have gathered together the Jews of Medina and said: "O congregation of Jews! Beware lest Allah inflicts on you the like of that which he has inflicted on Quraysh on the day of Badr; embrace Islam before that which has befallen them befalls you. You know well that I was sent as a prophet. This you find it mentioned in your Scripture as well as in Allah's covenant with you."[12]

The Jews respond contemptuously: "O Muhammad! Be not deluded because you have defeated inexperienced people who have no knowledge of warfare. By Allah, if we were to fight, you will realize that we are the real thing."[13] This verse was revealed in response. On Gehenna, see 2:206.

13. Allah explains that the Muslims' victory at Badr was an eschatological sign of his favor upon the Muslims. Al-Wahidi says that the sign was for unbelievers, so that they would embrace Islam, and uses it as the occasion for another story of the perversity and rebelliousness of the Jews. He quotes Ibn Abbas saying: "When Allah defeated the idolaters on the day of Badr, the Jews of Medina said: 'By Allah, this is the unlettered Prophet who was announced to us by Moses and whose attribute and description we find in our Scriptures and about whom it is also mentioned that his banner will not be defeated'. They wanted to believe in and follow him. But then some of them said: 'Do not be hasty; let us wait until another of his encounters'. When the Battle of Uhud took place and the Companions of the Prophet, Allah bless him and give him peace, were defeated, they became sceptical. They said: 'No, by Allah, this is not him'. Their wretchedness overwhelmed them and they did not embrace Islam."[14] The Battle of Uhud was said to have taken place a year after the Battle of Badr; according to Islamic tradition, the Muslims did not fare well and Muhammad was slightly injured.

Islamic tradition also generally holds today that at Badr, the Quraysh force was significantly larger than that of the Muslims. Maududi notes that "the believers won a resounding victory against an army of unbelievers superior to them in numbers, and in the quality and quantity of arms."[15] Nevertheless, there are differing opinions as to which army saw the other as "twice their number." Ibn Kathir explains that Allah had intentionally created these perceptions: "When the two camps saw each other, the Muslims thought that the idolaters were twice as many as they were, so that they would trust in Allah and seek His help. The idolaters thought that the believers were twice as many as they were, so that they would feel fear, horror, fright and despair."[16]

Allah, Ibn Kathir adds, "gives victory to His believing servants in this life," that is, the Muslims' victory was due to their obedience to Allah.[17] The reverse is also true: when Muslims suffer, all too often they ascribe their suffering to being insufficiently Islamic, and the remedy is always more Islam. While the Bible, like the Qur'an, contains accounts of people suffering because they're unrighteous, there is no counterpart in Islam to the Biblical principle that the wicked may prosper because of the fallen nature of the world—in Islam, if the wicked prosper, it is because the Muslims aren't Islamic enough.

Instead of "they saw," the Warsh Qur'an has "you saw."[18]

fire, **17**The steadfast, and the truthful, and the obedient, those who spend, those who pray for pardon in the watches of the night. **18**Allah is witness that there is no God except him. And the angels and the men of learning, maintaining his creation in justice, there is no God except him, the almighty, the wise. **19**Indeed, religion with Allah is Islam. Those who received the book disagreed only after knowledge came to them, through transgression among themselves. Whoever disbelieves the signs of Allah, indeed, Allah is swift at reckoning. **20**And if they argue with you, say, I have submitted myself to Allah, along with those who follow me. And say to those who have received the book and those who do not read, Have you become Muslims? If they submit, then indeed they are rightly guided, and if they turn away, then it is your duty only to convey the message. Allah is seer of his slaves. **21**Indeed, those who disbelieve the signs of Allah, and kill the prophets wrongfully, and kill those of mankind who enjoin equity, promise them a painful

doom. **22**Those are the ones whose works have failed in this world and the hereafter, and they have no helpers. **23**Haven't you seen how those who have received a portion of the book invoke the book of Allah, so that it may judge between them, then a faction of them turn away, being opposed? **24**That is because they say, the fire will not touch us except for a certain number of days. What they used to invent has deceived them regarding their religion. **25**How when we have brought them all together to a day of which there is no doubt, when every soul will be paid in full what it has earned, and they will not be wronged. **26**Say, O Allah, owner of dominion, you give dominion to those whom you will, and you withdraw dominion from those whom you will. You exalt those whom you will, and you humble those whom you will. In your hand is the good. Indeed, you are able to do all things. **27**You cause the night to pass into the day, and you cause the day to pass into the night. And you bring forth the living from the dead, and you bring forth the dead from

18. Allah and the angels and men of learning bear witness that there is no God except him against the Christians of Najran, to whom the first segment of this sura is traditionally understood to have been addressed; they, of course, insist that Jesus is divine.

19. Ibn Kathir sees this as unequivocal: "Allah states that there is no religion accepted with Him from any person, except Islam. Islam includes obeying all of the Messengers until Muhammad who finalized their commission, thus closing all paths to Allah except through Muhammad. Therefore, after Allah sent Muhammad, whoever meets Allah following a path other than Muhammad's, it will not be accepted of him."[19] The Jews and Christians also know better than to come before Allah with their false religions. According to the *Tafsir Anwarul Bayan*, they recognized Muhammad "to be the final Prophet but their obstinate nature prevented them from accepting."[20] The idea that Islam is the religion of truth and of Allah is stated also at 3:85 and 9:29.

20. The *Tafsir Anwarul Bayan* continues: "One cannot force these people to accept, but can merely advise them. Inviting them to accept Islam is the duty of the Muslim."[21]

24. This again explains why mainstream Islamic tradition regards the Jewish and Christian Scriptures as corrupted: they

don't, after all, confirm what is in the Qur'an, and so the only remaining explanation is that the Jews and Christians must have dared to alter them, and "what they used to invent has deceived them regarding their religion." Asad therefore emphasizes that "it is to be borne in mind that the Gospel frequently mentioned in the Qur'an is not identical with what is known today as the Four Gospels, but refers to an original, since lost, revelation bestowed upon Jesus and known to his contemporaries under its Greek name of Evangelion ('Good Tiding'), on which the Arabicized form Injil is based. It was probably the source from which the Synoptic Gospels derived much of their material and some of the teachings attributed to Jesus. The fact of its having been lost and forgotten is alluded to in the Qur'an in 5:14."[22]

28. The word *awliya*, friends, involves more than just casual friendship, and can be rendered as allies, guardians, patrons, protectors, and the like. Ibn Kathir states: "Allah prohibited His believing servants from becoming supporters of the disbelievers, or to take them as comrades with whom they develop friendships, rather than the believers."[23]

The Muslims are allowed to take unbelievers as *awliya* if, in doing so, they are "guarding [them]selves against them." This is

the living. And you give sustenance to those whom you choose, without limit. **28**Let not the believers take unbelievers for their friends in preference to believers. Whoever does that has no connection with Allah unless you are guarding yourselves against them, taking security. Allah bids you to beware of him. To Allah is the journeying. **29**Say, Whether you hide what is in your hearts or reveal it, Allah knows it. He knows what is in the heavens and what is in the earth, and Allah is able to do all things. **30**On the day when every soul will find itself confronted with all that it has done that is good and all that it has done that is evil, it will long for there to be a huge distance between it and that. Allah calls upon you to beware of him. And Allah is full of mercy for slaves. **31**Say, If you love Allah, follow me, Allah will love you and forgive you your sins. Allah is

---

one of the foundations for the Islamic doctrine that under certain circumstances, deceiving unbelievers is not only permissible but even necessary.

The development of *taqiyya* as a theological concept is a product of Shi'ite Islam. It developed during the time of the Sixth Imam, Jafar as-Sadiq, in middle of the eighth century, when the Shi'ites were being persecuted by the Sunni caliph al-Mansur. *Taqiyya* allowed Shi'ites to pretend to be Sunnis in order to protect themselves from Sunnis who were killing Shi'ites. Until the advent of the Shah Ismail I and the Safavids, *taqiyya* was an important element of Shi'ite survival, for Sunnis, in the majority almost everywhere, would not infrequently take it upon themselves to cleanse the land of those whom they referred to as Rafidites, that is, rejecters—those who rejected the caliphates of first three caliphs, Abu Bakr, Umar, and Uthman, who were all chosen over the candidate that the party that came to be known as the Shi'ites championed, Ali.

Some Shi'ite thinkers turned the secrecy that had become a necessity into a virtue. The medieval Shi'ite scholar Ali ibn Musa ibn Tawus, who died in 1266, taught that Allah had revealed Shi'ism secretly, and it was incumbent upon the believers to practice it in secret. At the end of days, Allah will admit them secretly into Paradise.[24] Some secrets were never to be revealed under any circumstances. The Fifth Imam, Muhammad al-Baqir, who died in 732, once gave a book to one of his disciples, telling him, "If you ever transmit any of it, my curse and the curse of my forefathers will fall upon you."[25]

Jafar had a servant who was suspected of having revealed some of the secrets of the faith. The imam lectured, "Whoever propagates our tradition is like someone who denies it….Conceal our doctrine and do not divulge it. God elevates in this world one who conceals our doctrine and does not divulge it and he turns it in the next world into a light between his eyes which will lead him to Paradise. God abases in this world one who divulges our tradition and our doctrine and does not conceal it, and in the next world he removes the light from between his eyes and turns it into darkness which will lead him to hell. *Taqiyya* is our religion and the religion of our fathers; he who has no *taqiyya* has no religion."[26]

The required concealment wasn't always easy even for the imams: al-Baqir, who died in 732, told one of his followers no fewer than seventy thousand secret hadiths, with the strict charge that he pass them on to no one. After he died, the unfortunate recipient of

this largesse confessed to al-Baqir's successor, Jafar as-Sadiq, that the secret was burning within him. Jafar told him to go out into the desert, dig a hole, and shout the hadiths into it; the man did so, and felt better.[27] What happened to those hadiths is not recorded.

Other imams also emphasized the cardinal importance of *taqiyya*, apparently not only because Shi'ites were under constant threat from Sunnis, but because Shi'ite Islam contained doctrines that must stay hidden from outsiders. Some sayings of the imams include, "He who has no *taqiyya* has no faith"; "he who forsakes *taqiyya* is like him who forsakes prayer"; "he who does not adhere to *taqiyya* and does not protect us from the ignoble common people is not part of us"; "nine tenths of faith falls within *taqiyya*"; "*taqiyya* is the believer's shield (*junna*), but for *taqiyya*, God would not have been worshipped."[28]

The elements of this secret tradition are, understandably, not entirely clear. Some, including Sunnis engaged in anti-Shi'ite polemic, say that the Shi'ites have additional suras of the Qur'an. These are supposed to deal, at least in part, with the special prerogatives of Ali. But this cannot be taken as certain, since, because of the nature of *taqiyya*, what the Shi'ites possess has been concealed.[29]

Although they do not use the term *taqiyya*, Sunnis accept the idea of deceiving unbelievers when the Muslims are at war with them and in danger; this idea is based on this Qur'anic passage and 16:106. The Sunni Ibn Kathir explains that the allowance of taking unbelievers as friends for the purpose of "guarding yourselves against them" was for "those believers who in some areas or times fear for their safety from the disbelievers. In this case, such believers are allowed to show friendship to the disbelievers outwardly, but never inwardly. For instance, Al-Bukhari recorded that Abu Ad-Darda' said, 'We smile in the face of some people although our hearts curse them.' Al-Bukhari said that Al-Hasan said, 'The Tuqyah [*taqiyyah*] is allowed until the Day of Resurrection.'"[30]

Tabari explained this verse by saying: "If you [Muslims] are under their [infidels'] authority, fearing for yourselves, behave loyally to them, with your tongue, while harboring inner animosity for them….Allah has forbidden believers from being friendly or on intimate terms with the infidels in place of believers—except when infidels are above them [in authority]. In such a scenario, let them act friendly towards them."[31]

forgiving, merciful. **32**Say, Obey Allah and the messenger. But if they turn away, indeed, Allah does not love the unbelievers. **33**Indeed, Allah preferred Adam and Noah and the family of Abraham and the family of Imran over the worlds. **34**They were descendants one of another. Allah is the hearer, the knower. **35**When Imran's wife said, My Lord, I have vowed to you what is in my womb as consecrated. Accept it from me. Indeed, you, only you, are the hearer, the knower. **36**And when she gave birth, she said, My Lord, indeed, I have given birth to a female, Allah knew

best about what she gave birth to, the male is not like the female, and indeed, I have named her Mary, and indeed, I long for your protection for her and for her offspring from Satan the outcast. **37**And her Lord accepted her with full acceptance and granted her a good upbringing, and made Zechariah her guardian. Whenever Zechariah went into the sanctuary where she was, he found that she had food. He said, O Mary, from where does this food come to you? She answered, It is from Allah. Allah gives without limit to those whom he wills. **38**Then Zechariah prayed to his

32. Allah's love is not universal. It extends only to believing Muslims, and disobeying Allah and his messenger makes one a disbeliever. Ibn Kathir says that this verse means that "defiance of the Messenger's way constitutes *Kufr* [unbelief]. Indeed, Allah does not like whoever does this, even if he claims that he loves Allah and seeks a means of approach to Him, unless, and until, he follows the unlettered Prophet, the Final Messenger from Allah to the two creations: mankind and the Jinn."[32]

33. The Shi'ite Bankipur Qur'an manuscript renders this verse in this way: "Indeed, Allah preferred Adam and Noah and the family of Abraham and the family of Imran and the family of Muhammad and his seed over the worlds."[33] The same reading is found in the *Bihar al-Anwar*, a seventeenth-century Shi'ite hadith collection.[34] See 2:59 and the Appendix: Two Apocryphal Shi'ite Suras.

34. "They were descendants one of another," that is, all those named in the preceding verse, "Adam and Noah and the family of Abraham and the family of Imran," are related. The renowned Islamic scholar Ibn Arabi (Muhyi al-Din Abu Ibn al-Arabi, 1165-1240) explained that "the prophets are of one physical progeny. They are the fruits of one tree."[35] He declares that the house of Abraham can be traced back to Noah, and Noah's family tree goes back to Adam; thus the prophets are all blood relatives, "descendants of one another." In a hadith, Muhammad says, "The Prophets are paternal brothers; their mothers are different, but their religion is one."[36]

35. Mary's mother is the "wife of Imran," that is, Amram, the father of Moses and Aaron. At 66:12, Mary is called "daughter of Imran." This passage, along with 19:28, in which Mary is called "sister of Aaron," gives the impression that the Qur'an confused Miriam the sister of Moses with Mary the Mother of Jesus, since the names are identical in Arabic: Maryam.

The Muslims of the ninth century were apparently confronted about this, as a hadith depicts Muhammad saying: "The (people of the old age) used to give names (to their persons) after the names of Apostles and pious persons who had gone before them."[37]

However, while this may explain why Mary is called "sister of Aaron," it doesn't explain why she is clearly depicted in this verse as the daughter of Imran. The authors of the Qur'an clearly thought that Jesus was Moses's nephew, the son of his sister.

36. A hadith puts this saying in Muhammad's mouth: "No child is born but he is pricked by the satan and he begins to weep because of the pricking of the satan except the son of Mary and his mother."[38] In Islamic tradition, Mary and Jesus are sinless; Muhammad is not, although for all intents and purposes he is, given the immense reverence he is accorded in Islamic culture and his role as "excellent example" (33:21), which leads to virtually all of the actions attributed to him in the major Hadith collections being imitated and codified in Islamic law.

37. The wife of Imran fulfills her vow: Mary is dedicated to Allah's service, and "her Lord accepted her with full acceptance." The *Tafsir Anwarul Bayan* says that she went to live in the Temple in Jerusalem, which he calls the Baitul Muqaddas ("Holy House").[39] The idea of Mary being raised in the Temple is made to square with Islam's jealous regard for the prerogatives of the father by depicting Imran as having died while Mary's mother was pregnant. "Otherwise," the *Tafsir Anwarul Bayan* states, "it was his right" to raise Mary himself.[40] In keeping with the Islamic idea that the original message of all the Jewish prophets was Islam, Islamic tradition identifies it as a mosque. There Mary is fed miraculously.

This story recalls one told in the *Protoevangelium of James*, a second-century Christian document: in it, Mary's parents, Joachim and Anne, prayed to God for an end to their childlessness and dedicated the child they subsequently conceived to the Lord in thanksgiving.

When Mary was three, she went to live in the Temple, where she was fed by an angel. This is the sort of thing that earned the messenger the charge that he was just retailing "fables of the men of old" (6:25, 8:31, 16:24, 23:83, 25:5, 27:68, 46:17, 68:15, 83:13), not divine revelation. There is justice in this charge, given the large amount of material in the Qur'an that is borrowed from other religious traditions. But Muslims respond that the Qur'an is sorting out the true from the false about Christianity among the revelations that were corrupted by the followers of Jesus.

Instead of stating that the Lord "made Zechariah her guardian" (*wa kaffalah*), the Warsh Qur'an has "Zechariah took charge of her" (*wa kafalah*).[41]

38. Allah then recounts the birth of John the Baptist, hitting the highlights of Luke 1:5-80, but with numerous important differences.

Lord and said, My Lord, grant to me righteous offspring from your bounty. Indeed, you are the hearer of prayer. **39**And the angels called to him as he stood praying in the sanctuary, Allah gives you good news of John, to confirm a word from Allah, noble, chaste, a prophet of the righteous. **40**He said, My Lord, how can I have a son when old age has already overtaken me and my wife is barren? He answered, It will be so. Allah does what he wills. **41**He said, My Lord, give me a sign. He said, the sign to you, that you will not speak to anyone for three days except by signals. Remember your Lord a great deal, with praise in the early hours of the night and morning. **42**And when the angels said, O Mary, indeed, Allah has chosen you and made you pure, and has chosen you over the women of all the worlds. **43**O Mary, be obedient to your Lord, prostrate yourself and bow with those who bow. **44**This is from the news of hidden things. We reveal it to you. You were not present with them when they threw their pens to see which of them would be Mary's guardian, nor were you present with them when they quarreled. **45**When the angels said, O Mary, indeed, Allah gives you good news of a word from him, whose name is the Messiah, Jesus, son of Mary, honored in this world and the hereafter, and one of those brought near. **46**He will speak to mankind in his cradle and his adulthood, and he is one of the righteous ones. **47**She said, My Lord, how can I

In both books, an angel tells John's father, Zechariah, that he will become a father despite his old age and his wife's barrenness. In the Qur'an, however, when the great event is announced, there is no hint that, as Luke's Gospel says, "many will rejoice" at the birth of John the Baptist. The Qur'an does not depict John as the messenger sent to prepare the way of the Lord; he is simply an answer to the prayer of Zechariah that he be blessed with a child. (John does, however, appear to be among the messengers, as he is exhorted to "hold fast to the book," at 19:12.)

42. Here, a group of angels speak to Mary, but at 19:17, she is addressed only by "our spirit" in "the likeness of a perfect man."

44. How does the messenger know all these things that took place centuries before he was born? Allah reveals them to him. Ibn Kathir explains: "You were not present, O Muhammad, when this occurred, so you cannot narrate what happened to the people as an eye witness. Rather, Allah disclosed these facts to you as if you were a witness, when they conducted a lottery to choose the custodian of Maryam, seeking the reward of this good deed."[42]

45. The angels' announcement of Jesus's birth differs from Gabriel's annunciation in Luke 1:30-35 most particularly in the fact that Jesus is not called "Son of the Most High," in keeping with the Qur'an's repeated denials that Allah has a son. Jesus is, however, identified as a "word" from Allah whose "name is Messiah." In the New Testament Gospel of John, Jesus is identified as the Word of God, who is God himself: "In the beginning was the Word, and the Word was with God, and the Word was God. He was in the beginning with God; all things were made through him, and without him was not anything made that was made….And the Word became flesh and dwelt among us, full of grace and truth; we have beheld his glory, glory as of the only Son from the Father" (John 1:1-3, 14). The Christian idea that all things were made through the Word of God has a faint resonance in 3:47, where Allah also speaks created things into being, in this case Jesus himself. Tabari makes this resonance explicit: "The word to which God refers as 'a word from

Him' is His word 'Be.' God thus called Jesus His word because he came into being through God's word."[43]

As for "the Messiah," while in the Christian tradition Jesus is the Messiah whom God promised to send to the Jews, in the Qur'an, it is simply a name, as this verse says: his "name is Messiah." The Arabic al-Masih, like the Hebrew Messiah and the Greek Christ, means "anointed," and Qurtubi suggests that Jesus was called this because "he was cleansed with purity from wrong actions," but in the Islamic view of Jesus, the name has no theological significance.[44]

Jesus is pointedly called "son of Mary." This indicates both that he has no human father, for if he did, he would be called by his name, as in "Jesus, the son of Joseph" (John 6:42). It also indicates that he is not the Son of God, as per 3:47. Tabari explains: "God informed His servants about the identity of Jesus and that he is the son of his mother Mary, thus negating what the Christians have asserted about him that he is the son of God."[45]

46. The baby Jesus doesn't speak in the New Testament, but the Arabic Infancy Gospel that dates from the sixth century says this: "Jesus spoke, and, indeed, when He was lying in His cradle said to Mary His mother: I am Jesus, the Son of God, the Logos, whom thou hast brought forth, as the Angel Gabriel announced to thee; and my Father has sent me for the salvation of the world."[46]

The twelfth-century Shi'ite scholar Tabarsi sees the Christian rejection of this account as apocryphal as stemming not from its absence from the canonical Gospels, but from their desire to conceal the true doctrine of Jesus, which is Islam: "Christians have rejected Jesus speaking in the cradle, even though it is a sign and a miracle, because what he said refutes their belief. This is because he said, 'I am God's servant,' and this counters their belief that he is the son of God. Thus they persisted in denying the truth of the report of anyone who might have claimed to have witnessed the event."[47]

47. The Tafsir Anwarul Bayan notes that "the overwhelming power of Allah created Sayyidina Isa [Master Jesus] without a father and this is related in His illustrious Qur'an, yet some people,

have a child when no mortal man has touched me? He said, It will be so. Allah creates what he wills. If he decrees something, he simply says to it, Be, and it is. **48**And he will teach him the book and wisdom, and the Torah and the Gospel, **49**And will make him a messenger to the Children of Israel, Indeed, I come unto you with a sign from your Lord. Indeed, I fashion for you out of clay the likeness of a bird, and I breathe into it and it is a bird, by Allah's permission. I heal him who was born blind, and the leper, and I raise the dead, by Allah's permission. And I announce to you what you eat and what you store up in your houses. Indeed, in this there is indeed a sign for you, if you are to be believers. **50**And confirming what was before me of the Torah, and making

lawful some of what was forbidden to you. I come to you with a sign from your Lord, so keep your duty to Allah and obey me. **51**Indeed, Allah is my Lord and your Lord, so worship him. That is a straight path. **52**But when Jesus became aware of their disbelief, he cried out, Who will be my helpers for the sake of Allah? The disciples said, We will be the helpers of Allah. We believe in Allah, and bear witness to you that we have become Muslims. **53**Our Lord, we believe in what you have revealed and we follow him whom you have sent. Count us among those who bear witness. **54**And they schemed, and Allah schemed, and Allah is the best of schemers. **55**When Allah said, O Jesus, indeed, I am gathering you and causing you to ascend to me, and am cleansing you of

---

in conformity with the beliefs of the Jews and Christians, stubbornly claim that his father was Yusuf [Joseph], carpenter. May Allah protect us from them. Amin."[48]

48. The Gospel is not the news about Jesus, but a book that he is taught by Allah.

49. The miracles Jesus performs are not accomplished by his own power, but "by Allah's permission." The *Tafsir Anwarul Bayan* explains that this clause is repeated in order to emphasize that only by Allah's permission does Jesus perform miracles—since "after witnessing these miracles, especially the raising of the dead, it is possible that a person may consider Sayyidina Isa to be Allah himself."[49]

Like speaking in the cradle, Jesus's miracles of bringing clay birds to life does not appear in the canonical Gospels. It is in the second-century *Infancy Gospel of Thomas*: "When a certain Jew saw what Jesus was doing while playing on the Sabbath, he left right away and reported to his father, Joseph: 'Look, your child is at the stream, and he has taken mud and formed twelve sparrows. He has profaned the Sabbath!' When Joseph came to the place and looked, he cried out to him, 'Why are you doing what is forbidden on the Sabbath?' But Jesus clapped his hands and cried to the sparrows, 'Be gone!' And the sparrows took flight and went off, chirping. And when the Jews saw this they were amazed; and they went away and reported to their leaders what they had seen Jesus do."[50]

How is it that the prophet Jesus was able to fashion images of birds out of clay, while Muslims today are forbidden to make representations of any living thing? The *Tafsir Anwarul Bayan* explains that "although Sayyidina Isa made a bird from clay, Scholars (Ulama) mention that it was permissible in his Shari'ah but forbidden in the Shari'ah of Sayyidina Muhammad."[51] It adds that "the incident in question was to demonstrate a miracle," not simply to make an image for its own sake, much less for idolatrous worship, "and the figure of the bird did not remain, as it was transformed into a real bird."[52]

Instead of "a bird," the Warsh Qur'an has "flying."[53]

50. Jesus confirms the message of the Torah that came before him, just as the Qur'an that is given to the messenger confirms the message of the Torah and the Gospel (3:3). This is the basis for the claim that Islam is open-minded and tolerant in a way that Judaism and Christianity are not, as Islam reveres Moses and Jesus as prophets, but Jews and Christians do not revere Muhammad. The fact that Islam reveres Moses and Jesus as Muslim prophets who are radically different figures from how they are regarded in Judaism and Christianity is seldom noted.

52. Jesus's disciples are Muslims, as is Jesus himself. In this understanding, Islam did not originate in the seventh century or the ninth but is the original religion of every prophet. Their followers twisted their teachings to create Judaism, Christianity, and other counterfeits of the prophets' true teachings.

54. Ibn Hisham, Ibn Kathir, Qurtubi, and others state that the reference to Allah as the "best of schemers" refers to Allah's plan to cause Jesus to ascend to him, as is stated in the following verse, and thereby foil the plot of the Jews to crucify him. The Qur'an returns to this in greater detail at 4:157. The verse also is understood as having a general application, as in a hadith that depicts Muhammad praying to Allah: "My Lord…plot for me and do not plot against me."[54] As for Allah being a schemer in general, this is also repeated at 7:99, 8:30, and 10:21.

55. Jesus is not crucified (as per 4:157) but ascends to paradise. Jesus will return to earth, as a hadith attributed to Muhammad explains (see 4:157).

Ibn Kathir here offers an Islamic history of Christianity that is illuminating of several common views. Some of Jesus's followers "went to the extreme over Isa, believing that he was the son of Allah. Some of them said that Isa was Allah Himself, while others said that he was one of a Trinity." However, "Allah mentioned these false creeds in the Qur'an and refuted them."

those who disbelieve and am setting those who follow you above those who disbelieve until the day of resurrection. Then you will return to me, and I will judge between you regarding those things you used to disagree about. [56]As for those who disbelieve, I will punish them with a heavy punishment in this world and the hereafter, and they will have no helpers. [57]And as for those who believe and do good works, he will pay them their wages in full. Allah does not love the wrongdoers. [58]This that we are reciting to you is a revelation and a wise reminder. [59]Indeed, the likeness of Jesus with Allah is as the likeness of Adam. He created him from the dust, then he said to him Be, and he is. [60]The truth from your Lord, so do not be among those who waver. [61]And whoever

disagrees with you concerning him, after the knowledge which has come to you, say Come, we will call our sons and your sons, and our women and your women, and ourselves and yourselves, then we will pray humbly and invoke the curse of Allah upon those who lie. [62]Indeed, this is really the true narrative. There is no God except Allah, and indeed, Allah, he indeed is the mighty, the wise. [63]And if they turn away, then indeed, Allah is aware of the corrupters. [64]Say, O people of the book, let us come to a common word between us and you, that we will worship no one but Allah, and that we will ascribe no partner to him, and that none of us will take others for lords besides Allah. And if they turn away, then say, Bear witness that we are the ones who are Muslims. [65]O

This was necessary because of the destructive influence of one of the landmark figures of Christian history: "The Christians remained like this until the third century CE, when a Greek king called Constantine became a Christian for the purpose of destroying Christianity. Constantine was either a philosopher, or he was just plain ignorant. Constantine changed the religion of Isa by adding to it and deleting from it. He established the rituals of Christianity and the so-called Great Trust, which is in fact the Great Treachery. He also allowed them to eat the meat of swine, changed the direction of the prayer that Isa established to the east, built churches for Isa, and added ten days to the fast as compensation for a sin that he committed, as claimed. So the religion of Isa became the religion of Constantine, who built more than twelve thousand churches, temples and monasteries for the Christians as well as the city that bears his name, Constantinople (Istanbul). Throughout this time, the Christians had the upper hand and dominated the Jews. Allah aided them against the Jews because they used to be closer to the truth than the Jews, even though both groups were and still are disbelievers, may Allah's curse descend on them."[55]

Allah later sent Muhammad with the "true religion that shall never change or be altered until the commencement of the Last Hour." This religion has an essential political component: "Muhammad's religion shall always be dominant and victorious over all other religions. This is why Allah allowed Muslims to conquer the eastern and western parts of the world and the kingdoms of the earth. Furthermore, all countries submitted to them; they demolished Kisra (king of Persia) and destroyed the Czar, ridding them of their treasures and spending these treasures for Allah's sake."[56]

This view completely delegitimizes and replaces traditional Christianity: "Therefore, Muslims are the true believers in Isa." This also carries with it a political component: "The Muslims then acquired Ash-Sham [Syria] from the Christians, causing them to evacuate to Asia Minor, to their fortified city in Constantinople. The Muslims will be above them until the Day of Resurrection.

Indeed, he, Muhammad, who is truthful and who received the true news, has conveyed to Muslims that they will conquer Constantinople in the future, and seize its treasures."[57] Ibn Kathir died in 1372, so he did not live to see this prophecy fulfilled, as it was in 1453. It should be noted, however, that the Byzantine Empire was quite weak throughout the latter half of the fourteenth century and surrounded by a hostile and growing Ottoman Empire, and thus it did not require highly developed predictive powers to foresee its demise.

57. Instead of, "He will pay them their wages," the Warsh Qur'an has, "We will pay them their wages."[58]

59. Here again, as in 3:45, Christian concepts are invoked by name but emptied of their meaning. Jesus is like Adam in that both were created not by the agency of human fathers but by the word of Allah. However, in Islam this assertion contains no hint of the Christian idea of Jesus as the Second Adam, removing mankind's condition of sin for which the first Adam was responsible, by taking it upon himself.

61. According to Ibn Hisham, when the Christian delegation from Najran heard this, they asked Muhammad for time to confer among themselves. Then one of their leaders told the rest: "O Christians, you know right well that Muhammad is a prophet sent (by God) and he has brought a decisive declaration about the nature of your master. You know too that a people has never invoked a curse on a prophet and seen its elders live and its youth grow up. If you do this you will be exterminated. But if you decide to adhere to your religion and to maintain your doctrine about your master, then take your leave of the man and go home."[59]

So they went to Muhammad, declined his challenge, and went home, obstinate renegades confirmed in their rebellion against Allah.

64. Since Muslims consider the Christian confession of the divinity of Christ to be an unacceptable association of a partner with God, this verse is saying that the "common word" that Muslims and the people of the book should agree on is that Christians

people of the book, why will you argue about Abraham, when the Torah and the Gospel were not revealed until after him? Have you then no sense? **66**Indeed, you are those who argue over matters about which you have some knowledge. Why then do you argue over a matter about which you have no knowledge? Allah knows. You do not know. **67**Abraham was not a Jew, nor was he a Christian, but he was a Muslim hanif, and he was not one of the idolaters. **68**Indeed, those of mankind who have the best claim to Abraham are those who followed him, and this prophet and those who believe, and Allah is the protecting guardian of the believers. **69**A party of the people of the book long to make you go astray, and they make no one go astray except themselves, but they do not realize it. **70**O people of the book, why do you disbelieve in the signs of Allah when you

bear witness? **71**O people of the book, why do you confuse the truth with falsehood and knowingly conceal the truth? **72**And a party of the people of the book say, Believe in what has been revealed to those who believe at the opening of the day, and disbelieve at the end of the day, in order that they may return, **73**And only believe those who follow your religion. Say, Indeed, the guidance is the guidance of Allah, that anyone is given something like that what was given to you, or that they may argue with you in the presence of their Lord. Say, Indeed, the bounty is in Allah's hand. He bestows it on whom He wills. Allah is all-embracing, all-knowing. **74**He selects for his mercy those whom he wills. Allah is of infinite bounty. **75**Among the people of the book there is he who, if you trust him with a great amount of treasure, will return it to you. And also among them is he

---

should discard one of the central tenets of their faith and essentially become Muslims.

In 2007, this passage became the basis for an appeal to Christians from 138 Muslim leaders and scholars from all over the world, entitled *A Common Word Between Us and You*. The Common Word website describes the project in enthusiastic terms: "Never before have Muslims delivered this kind of definitive consensus statement on Christianity. Rather than engage in polemic, the signatories have adopted the traditional and mainstream Islamic position of respecting the Christian scripture and calling Christians to be more, not less, faithful to it."[60] Yet in light of the Qur'anic understanding of Christianity, this would mean essentially that the Christians would discard their faith and convert to Islam. This recalls the words of Sayyid Qutb (1906-1966): "The chasm between Islam and Jahiliyyah [the society of unbelievers] is great, and a bridge is not to be built across it so that the people on the two sides may mix with each other, but only so that the people of Jahiliyyah may come over to Islam."[61]

66. Allah rebukes the Jews and Christians for arguing over something about which they "have no knowledge," the religion of Abraham. The Patriarch couldn't have been a Jew or a Christian, since "the Torah and the Gospel were not revealed until after him" (3:65).

67. Abraham, like the other prophets, was a Muslim, the *Tafsir al-Jalalayn* explains: "Abraham in truth was neither a Jew nor a Christian, but a man of pure natural belief, a *hanif* who inclines from all other religions to the Straight *Din* [religion], a Muslim and affirmer of the Divine Unity. He was no idolater."[62] On *hanif*, see 2:135.

What's more, the Muslims are "the nearest of kin to Abraham," as Ibn Kathir says: "This Ayah [verse] means, 'The people who have the most right to be followers of Ibrahim are those who followed his religion and this Prophet, Muhammad, and his Companions.'"[63]

If Abraham was a Muslim, Judaism and Christianity are completely illegitimate. The Qur'an also assumes that the other Biblical prophets are Muslims as well. The Jews (and Christians) are simply renegades from the true faith of their own prophets. This is the view of Judaism and Christianity that many Muslims have today.

69. Allah emphasizes the perversity of some of the Jews and Christians: they wish to lead the Muslims astray, when it is actually they who go astray, rejecting the "signs of Allah" even though they are witnesses of them.

70. According to Islamic tradition, this could refer to the delegation of Christians from Najran and/or other Christians and Jews who heard Muhammad recite the Qur'an and still rejected Islam, and, again according to Islamic accounts, knew Muhammad was a prophet but didn't want to admit it for selfish reasons. Says Maududi: "This is why the Qur'an repeatedly blames them for maliciously misrepresenting the signs of God which they saw with their own eyes and to which they themselves attested."[64]

71. The Jews and Christians know that Islam is true but conceal the fact for their own selfish gain. According to Ibn Kathir, "Allah states that the Jews envy the faithful and wish they could misguide them."[65]

73. According to Barth, the words, "Say, Indeed, the guidance is the guidance of Allah" were "interpolated, for they break the connection."[66]

who, if you trust him with a piece of gold, will not return it to you unless you keep standing over him. That is because they say, We have no duty to the Gentiles. They knowingly speak a lie about Allah. [76]No, but he who fulfills his pledge and fears Allah, indeed, Allah loves those who fear him. [77]Indeed, those who purchase a small gain at the price of Allah's covenant and their oaths, they have no share in the hereafter. Allah will neither speak to them nor look at them on the day of resurrection, nor will he make them grow. Theirs will be a painful doom. [78]And indeed, there is a party of them who distort the book with their tongues, so that you might think that what they say is from the book, when it is not from the book. And they say, It is from Allah, when it is not from Allah, and they knowingly speak a lie about Allah. [79]It is not for any human being to whom Allah had given the book and wisdom and the prophethood that he should afterwards have said to mankind, Be slaves of me instead of Allah, but, Be faithful servants of the Lord because you are teaching the book and because of your constant study of it. [80]And he did not command you to take the angels and the prophets for lords. Would he command you to disbelieve after you

had become Muslims? [81]When Allah made a covenant with the prophets, Look at what I give you of the book and knowledge. And afterward a messenger will come to you, confirming what you have. You will believe in him and you will help him. He said, Do you agree, and will you take up my burden in this? They answered, We agree. He said, Then bear witness. I will be a witness with you. [82]Then whoever turns away after this, they will be transgressors. [83]Do they seek a religion other than the religion of Allah, when whoever is in the heavens and on earth submits to him, willingly or unwillingly, and to him they will return. [84]Say, We believe in Allah and what is revealed to us and what was revealed to Abraham and Ishmael and Isaac and Jacob and the tribes, and what was given to Moses and Jesus and the prophets from their Lord. We make no distinction between any of them, and to him we have submitted. [85]And whoever seeks a religion other than Islam, it will not be accepted from him, and he will be a loser in the hereafter. [86]How will Allah guide a people who disbelieved after their belief, and they bore witness that the messenger is true, and after clear proofs had come to them? And Allah does not guide wrongdoing people.

---

77. "They have no share in the hereafter" is, according to Arabic linguist Michael Schub, "a direct quotation from Mishna Sanhedrin 10.1" and uses the Hebrew word kheleq for "share."[67]

78. The excoriation of those who "say, It is from Allah, when it is not from Allah" has given rise to speculation that Muhammad, if he indeed is the source of the Qur'an, or someone who contributed to the Qur'an sought information about earlier revelations for incorporation into the new holy book and was snared by a ruse.

79. Ibn Kathir explains: "If this is not the right of a Prophet or a Messenger, then indeed, it is not the right of anyone else to issue such a claim. This criticism refers to the ignorant rabbis, priests and teachers of misguidance, unlike the Messengers and their sincere knowledgeable followers who implement their knowledge; for they only command what Allah commands them, as their honorable Messengers conveyed to them."[68] The Jews and Christians are, by contrast, defiant and perverse.

Instead of "you are teaching the book" (tu'allimuun), the Warsh Qur'an has "you know the book" (ta'lamuun).[69]

81. Instead of "I give you," the Warsh Qur'an has "we give you."[70]

83. Instead of, "Do they seek a religion...and to him they will return" (yabghuuna and yurja'unna), the Warsh Qur'an has, "Do you seek a religion...and to him you will return" (tabghuuna and turja'unna).[71]

85. "Commentators," notes Mahmoud Ayoub, "have generally taken this verse literally."[72] The idea that Islam is the religion of truth is stated also at 3:19 and 9:29, and that it will prevail over all other religions is additionally at 2:193, 8:39, 9:33, and 61:9. In this verse Islam prevails not just in the hereafter, where the non-Muslims will be losers, but also on earth, where a religion other than Islam will not be accepted, presumably by Allah, although also possibly by the Islamic authorities.

87As for such people, their recompense is that on them rests the curse of Allah and of angels and of men combined. **88**They will remain in it. Their doom will not be lightened, nor will they be reprieved, **89**Except those who later repent and do right. Indeed, Allah is forgiving, merciful. **90**Indeed, those who disbelieve after their belief, and afterward grow violent in disbelief, their repentance will not be accepted. And such people are those who are astray. **91**Indeed, those who disbelieve and die in disbelief, the earth full of gold would not be accepted from such a person if it were offered as a ransom. Theirs will be a painful doom and they will have no helpers. **92**You will not attain righteousness until you spend out of what you love. And whatever you spend, Allah is aware of it. **93**All food was lawful for the children of Israel except what Israel forbade himself before the Torah was revealed. Say, Produce the Torah and read it if you are truthful. **94**And whoever invents a falsehood about Allah after that, such people will be wrongdoers. **95**Say, Allah speaks truth. So follow the religion of Abraham, the hanif. He was not one of the idolaters. **96**Indeed, the first sanctuary established for mankind was the one at Bakka, a blessed place, a guidance to

87. Those who bear this curse, says Maududi, are the "Jewish rabbis of Arabia in the time of the Prophet," who "knew, and sometimes even testified to verbally, that Muhammad was a true Prophet and that his teachings were the same as those of the earlier Prophets."[73] Maududi states that their subsequent rejection of Muhammad was "the outcome of prejudice and intransigence, born out of their centuries-old hostility to the Truth."[74] Maududi is basing this analysis upon traditions of Muhammad of which there is no trace before the ninth century; there is no contemporary historical record of rabbis in the time that Muhammad is supposed to have lived accepting and then rejecting him.

92. Maududi explains that "the purpose of this verse is to remove the misconception of the Jews concerning 'righteousness,'" which he dismisses as "casuistry and hair-splitting legalism."[75]

93. Allah asserts that Jewish dietary laws were invented by the Jews. In illustrating their relentless opposition to Muhammad and rejection of Allah's prophets, Ibn Kathir here recounts a ninth-century tradition about "a group of Jews" who "came to Allah's Prophet and said, 'Talk to us about some things we will ask you and which only a Prophet would know.'"[76] Muhammad invited them to "ask me about whatever you wish," but extracted from them a pledge: "If I tell you something and you recognize its truth, you will follow me in Islam."[77] They then asked him: "Tell us about four matters: 1. What kinds of food did Isra'il prohibit for himself? 2. What about the sexual discharge of the woman and the man, and what role does each play in producing male or female offspring? 3. Tell us about the condition of the unlettered Prophet during sleep, 4. And who is his Wali (supporter) among the angels?"[78]

Islamic tradition does not notice the inherent contradiction in this, that the Jews would not know whether or not Muhammad's answers were correct unless they themselves were prophets. In any case, Muhammad answered that Israel "once became very ill. When his illness was prolonged, he vowed to Allah that if He cures His illness, he would prohibit the best types of drink and food for himself. Was not the best food to him camel meat and the best drink camel milk?"[79] They said, "Yes, by Allah."[80] To the second question, Muhammad asked a question in response: "Do you not know that man's discharge is thick and white and woman's is yellow and thin?

If any of these fluids becomes dominant, the offspring will take its sex and resemblance by Allah's leave. Hence, if the man's is more than the woman's, the child will be male, by Allah's leave. If the woman's discharge is more than the man's, then the child will be female, by Allah's leave."[81]

They agreed to this as well. For the third question, Muhammad stated, "Do you not know that the eyes of this unlettered Prophet sleep, but his heart does not sleep?"[82] They again agreed. Muhammad's final response was: "My Wali (who brings down the revelation from Allah) is Jibril [Gabriel], and Allah never sent a Prophet, but Jibril is his Wali."[83] The Jews replied: "We then shun you. Had you a Wali other than Jibril, we would have followed you."[84]

95. On *hanif*, see 2:135.

96. Bakka is identified with Mecca by numerous Islamic exegetes, but the identification is not actually certain, and nothing is known of where Bakka actually was. The *Tafsir al-Jalalayn* asserts that "the use of Bakka rather than Makka reflects a Makkan dialect; it is called that because it bears down (bakka) on the necks of tyrants. The angels built it before the creation of Adam whereas al-Aqsa in Jerusalem was built after that."[85] Ibn Kathir, accepting the traditional identification of Bakka with Mecca, states that the Ka'ba was built by Abraham, "whose religion the Jews and Christians claim they follow. However, they do not perform Hajj [Pilgrimage] to the house that Ibrahim built by Allah's command, and to which he invited the people to perform Hajj."[86]

The contemporary Islamic scholar Ibn Warraq offers "one Muslim translator's comments": "'Bakkah is the same as Makkah [Mecca] [referring the reader to Al-Isfahani's Dictionary of the Qur'an] from *tabakk* meaning the crowding together of men [Commentary of Fakhr al-Din Razi]. Others say it is from a root meaning the breaking of the neck, and the name is given to it because whenever a tyrant forced his way to it, his neck was broken [Razi]. Some think that Bakkah is the name of the mosque or the House itself that is in Makkah [Mecca]. The Jews and Christians are told that the Temple at Jerusalem was erected long after Abraham, while the Holy House at Makkah [Mecca] was there even before Abraham, and was in fact, the first House on earth for the worship of the

the peoples, [97]In which are plain memorials, the place where Abraham stood up to pray, and whoever enters it is safe. And pilgrimage to the house is a duty for mankind to Allah, for him who can find a way to get there. As for him who disbelieves, indeed, Allah is independent of the worlds. [98]Say, O people of the book, why do you disbelieve in the signs of Allah, when Allah is witness of what you do? [99]Say, O people of the book, why do you drive believers back from the way of Allah, seeking to make it crooked, when you are witnesses? Allah is not unaware of what you do. [100]O you who believe, if you obey a party of those who have received the book, they will make you unbelievers after your belief. [101]How can you disbelieve, when it is you to whom Allah's signs are recited, and his messenger is among you? He who holds fast to Allah, he indeed is guided onto a right path. [102]O you who believe, observe your duty to Allah with right observance, and do not die except as Muslims. [103]And hold fast, all of you together, to the rope of Allah, and do not separate. And remember Allah's favor to you, how you were enemies and he made friendship between your hearts so that you became like brothers by his favor, and you were on the brink of an abyss of fire, and he saved you from it. In this way Allah makes clear his signs to you, that perhaps you may be guided. [104]And there may come forth from you a nation who invite people to goodness, and command right conduct and forbid indecency. Such people are those who are successful. [105]And do not be like those who separated and disputed after the clear proofs had come to them. For such people there is an awful doom, [106]On the day when faces will be whitened and faces will be blackened, and as for those whose faces have been blackened, it will be said to them, Did you disbelieve after your belief? Then taste the punishment for disbelieving. [107]And as for those whose faces have been whitened, they will dwell in the mercy of Allah forever. [108]These are signs of Allah. We recite them to you in truth. Allah wills no injustice to the worlds. [109]To Allah belongs whatever is in the heavens and whatever is on the earth, and to Allah all things are returned.

Divine Being.' In other words, the Muslim commentators really do not have a clue as to its meaning."[87]

Gibson observes that *Bakka* is "an ancient Semitic word that means to *weep* or *lament*. If a location was assigned the title 'Bacca' it would mean the place of bacca. For example *The Valley of Bacca* means the *Valley of Weeping* or the *Valley of Tears*. This is usually because some calamity happened there that caused people to weep. There are a number of Bacca or Baka valleys in the Middle East today, each named because of some tragedy that occurred there in the past."[88] Luxenberg likewise evaluates the available evidence and concludes that *Bakka* most likely means "valley of tears."[89]

Ibn Kathir also confirms this, stating that Bakka "means, 'it brings Buka' (crying, weeping) to the tyrants and arrogant, meaning they cry and become humble in its vicinity. It was also said that Makkah was called Bakkah because people do Buka next to it, meaning that they gather around it."[90] It is more likely, however, that the weeping would have to have been more generalized for the entire place to be named for it. In line with that, Gibson suggests that this is additional evidence that the original holy city of Islam was not Mecca at all, and supports the theory that the holy city was originally Petra, to which the earliest mosques point (see 2:142). This is because, as Gibson points out, if the first sanctuary was at Bakka, it was likely to have been a place where a terrible tragedy had taken place, but there is no record of such an event in Mecca in the centuries before Islam. In Petra, however, there were major earthquakes in 363, 551, and 713, the last of which may have destroyed the city altogether.

103. Instead of, "You were on the brink of an abyss of fire, and he saved you from it," the Shi'ite Bankipur Qur'an manuscript has, "You were on the brink of an abyss of fire, then Muhammad saved you from it and his seed, one is from the other, and Allah is all-hearing, all-knowing."[91] See 2:59 and the Appendix: Two Apocryphal Shi'ite Suras.

106. Ibn Kathir states that "this is when the faces of followers of the Sunnah [accepted practice in Islamic law] and the Jama'ah [congregation] will radiate with whiteness, and the faces of followers of Bid'ah (innovation) and division will be darkened."[92] With innovation so thoroughly discouraged, the prospects for reform in Islam grow dim.

110 You are the best of people that has been raised up for mankind. You command what is right and forbid what is wrong, and you believe in Allah. And if the people of the book had believed, it would have been better for them. Some of them are believers, but most of them are rebellious. **111**They will not harm you except a small hurt, and if they fight against you, they will turn and flee. And afterward they will not be helped. **112**They will be stricken with disgrace wherever they are found, except for a rope from Allah and a rope from men. They have brought on anger from their Lord, and wretchedness is laid upon them. That is because they used to disbelieve the signs of Allah, and killed the prophets wrongfully. That is because they were rebellious and used to transgress. **113**They are not all alike. Of the people of the book there is a devout community that recites the signs of Allah in the night, falling prostrate. **114**They believe in Allah and the last day, and command right conduct and forbid indecency, and compete with one with another in good works. These people are among the righteous.

115 And whatever good they do, they will not be denied the reward for it. Allah is aware of those who fear him. **116**Indeed, the riches and the progeny of those who disbelieve will not help them in any way against Allah, and such are rightful companions of the fire. They will remain in it. **117**What they spend in this life of this world is like a biting, icy wind that strikes the harvest of a people who have wronged themselves, and devastates it. Allah did not wrong them, but they wrong themselves. **118**O you who believe, do not take as intimates anyone other than your own people, as they would spare no effort to ruin you, they love to interfere with you. Hatred is revealed by their mouths, but what their breasts hide is greater. We have made clear the signs for you, if you will understand. **119**Indeed, you are those who love them although they do not love you, and you believe in all of the book. When they meet you, they say, We believe, but when they go apart from you, they bite their finger-tips at you in rage. Say, Die in your rage. Indeed, Allah is aware of what is hidden in hearts. **120**If good fortune comes to you,

110. The Muslims are the "best of people" insofar as they "command what is right and forbid what is wrong"; that is, their preeminence is defined in terms of their establishing proper rules for behavior among all mankind, those which are encoded in Sharia. A hadith quotes Abu Hurairah, one of Muhammad's companions, explaining that this verse "means, the best of peoples for the people, as you bring them with chains on their necks till they embrace Islam."[93] See 22:41.

Instead of, "You are the best of people" (*khayr al-umma*), the seventeenth-century Shi'ite hadith collection *Bihar al-Anwar* has, "You are the best of imams" (*khayr al-a'imma*).[94]

111. It should be easy to place those chains, for the Jews and Christians are also cowards.

112. This, says the *Tafsir Anwarul Bayan*, refers to the non-Muslims' agreeing "to pay the atonement (Jizya) to the Muslim state, in which case they will be accorded the rights of a Dhimmi."[95] These rights are not equal to the rights of Muslims: the dhimmis must accept subservience and second-class status (cf. 9:29) in exchange for a guarantee of protection, which remains in place as long as they do not offend the Muslims by criticizing Islam or Muhammad, or violating other provisions of their status.

113. According to Ibn Hisham, the *Tafsir Ibn Abbas*, and others, this refers to Jews and Christians who accepted Islam. The *Tafsir Ibn Abbas* explains: "Those who believed from among the people of the Book are not like those among them who have not...there are among them a group of upright people who are guided by Allah's divine Oneness."[96]

118. Ibn Kathir sees this verse in the context of a permanent war between Muslims and non-Muslims: "Allah forbids His believing servants from taking the hypocrites as allies, so that the hypocrites do not have the opportunity to expose the secrets of the believers and their plans against their enemies. The hypocrites try their very best to confuse, oppose and harm the believers any way they can, and by using any wicked, evil means at their disposal. They wish the very worst and difficult conditions for the believers."[97]

119. Ibn Kathir continues to explicate this passage as inculcating distrust of non-Muslims, telling the story of the caliph Umar declining to hire a highly recommended scribe because he was Christian, and concluding: "This is the behavior of the hypocrites who pretend to be believers and kind when they are with the believers, all the while concealing the opposite in their hearts in every respect."[98]

it is evil to them, and if disaster strikes you, they rejoice over it. But if you persevere and avoid evil, their guile will never harm you. Indeed, Allah encompasses what they do. **121**And when you left your house at daybreak to assign to the believers their positions for the battle, Allah was the hearer, the knower. **122**When two parties of you almost fell away, and Allah was their protecting friend. In Allah let believers put their trust. **123**Allah had already given you the victory at Badr, when you were contemptible. So observe your duty to Allah so that you may be thankful. **124**When you said to the believers, Is it not sufficient for you that your Lord should support you with three thousand angels sent down? **125**No, but if you persevere and avoid evil, and they attack you suddenly, your Lord will help you with five thousand angels sweeping in. **126**Allah ordained this only as a message of good cheer for you, and that thereby your hearts might be at rest. Victory comes only from Allah, the mighty, the wise. **127**That he may cut off a section of those who disbelieve, or overwhelm them so that they retreat, frustrated. **128**It is not at all your concern whether he is merciful toward

them or punishes them, for they are evildoers. **129**To Allah belongs whatever is in the heavens and whatever is in the earth. He forgives those whom he wills and punishes those whom he wills. Allah is forgiving, merciful. **130**O you who believe, do not devour usury, doubling and quadrupling. Observe your duty to Allah, so that you may be successful. **131**And ward off the fire prepared for unbelievers. **132**And obey Allah and the messenger, so that you may find mercy. **133**And compete with one another for forgiveness from your Lord, and for a paradise as wide as the heavens and the earth, prepared for those who fear Allah, **134**Those who spend in ease and in hard times, those who control their anger and are forgiving toward mankind, Allah loves the good, **135**And those who, when they do an evil thing or wrong themselves, remember Allah and ask forgiveness for their sins. Who forgives sins except Allah alone? And they will not knowingly repeat what they did. **136**The reward of such people will be forgiveness from their Lord, and gardens under which rivers flow, in which they will remain forever, a bountiful reward for workers.

121. According to Islamic tradition, here begins a discussion of lessons of the Battle of Uhud and the Battle of Badr. Allah reminds the messenger that when he and the Muslims set out for the battle at Uhud, two groups of Muslims almost deserted.

122. They shouldn't have been afraid, for "Allah was their protecting friend," and the believers should trust in him.

123. When the Muslims were "contemptible," that is, "a minuscule force" at Badr, Allah granted them victory.

124. Allah gained the victory for the Muslims at Badr by sending down angels to fight alongside them. This is one reason why superior military might doesn't overawe jihadists today: righteousness in Islam will bring victory.

According to Ibn Hisham two centuries after the battle is supposed to have taken place, when the Quraysh arrived at Badr, nearly a thousand strong, Muhammad cried out to Allah: "O God, if this band perish today Thou wilt be worshipped no more."[99] But shortly later Muhammad told his follower Abu Bakr: "Be of good cheer, O Abu Bakr. God's help is come to you. Here is Gabriel holding the rein of a horse and leading it. The dust is upon his front teeth."[100]

Muhammad then strode among his troops and issued a momentous promise—one that has given heart to Muslim warriors throughout the ages: "By God in whose hand is the soul of Muhammad, no man will be slain this day fighting against them with steadfast courage advancing not retreating but God will cause him to enter Paradise."[101] One of the assembled Muslim warriors, Umayr bin al-Humam, exclaimed: "Fine, Fine! Is there nothing between me and my entering Paradise save to be killed by these men?"[102] He flung away some dates that he had been eating, rushed into the thick of the battle, and fought until he was killed. Muslim warriors have fought with similar courage throughout history, knowing that if they are victorious they will enjoy the spoils of war (about which there is much discussion in sura 8), and if they are killed, they will enjoy paradise.

125. The key to earthly victory is obedience to Allah, who will send more angels to fight alongside the righteous. The decision of victory or defeat belongs to him alone.

¹³⁷Similar ways have passed away before you. Just travel in the land and see the nature of the consequences for those who denied. ¹³⁸This is a declaration for mankind, a guidance and a warning to those who fear Allah. ¹³⁹Do not grow weary and do not grieve, for you will overcome them if you are believers. ¹⁴⁰If you have received a blow, the people have received a blow like it. These are the various conditions which we cause to follow one after the other for mankind, so that Allah may know those who believe and may choose witnesses from among you, and Allah does not love wrongdoers. ¹⁴¹And that Allah may purify those who believe, and may destroy the unbelievers. ¹⁴²Or did you think that you would enter paradise when Allah did not yet know which of you would really wage jihad, and did not know which are steadfast? ¹⁴³And indeed you used to wish for death before you met it. Now you have seen it with your eyes. ¹⁴⁴Muhammad is only a messenger, messengers have passed away before him. Will it be that when he dies or is killed, you will turn back on your heels? He who turns back

on his heels does no harm to Allah, and Allah will reward the thankful. ¹⁴⁵No soul can ever die except by Allah's permission and at the established time. Whoever desires the reward of this world, we bestow it on him, and whoever desires the reward of the hereafter, we bestow it on him. We will reward the thankful. ¹⁴⁶And with how many prophets have there been a number of devoted men who fought? They did not waver because of anything that happened to them in the way of Allah, nor did they weaken, nor were they brought low. Allah loves the steadfast. ¹⁴⁷Their cry was only that they said, Our Lord, forgive us for our sins and wasted efforts, make our foothold sure, and give us victory over the disbelieving people. ¹⁴⁸So Allah gave them the reward of this world and the good reward of the hereafter. Allah loves those who do good deeds. ¹⁴⁹O you who believe, if you obey those who disbelieve, they will make you turn back on your heels, and you will turn back as losers. ¹⁵⁰But Allah is your protector, and he is the best of helpers. ¹⁵¹We will cast terror into the hearts of those who disbelieve

137. This is one of the foundations of the Islamic idea that pre-Islamic civilizations, and non-Islamic civilizations, are all *jahiliyya*—the society of unbelievers, which is worthless. In the late twentieth century, some Pakistani Muslims saw in the ruins at the nation's renowned archaeological site, Mohenjo Daro, a teaching opportunity for Islam. They recommended that this verse be posted there so as to put the ruins themselves in an Islamic context.[103] The Islamic State acted on this assumption, destroying ancient artifacts of pre-Islamic civilizations not just because of the danger of idolatry, but because the ruins themselves reflected Allah's judgment on the unbelievers.

139. As Ibn Kathir puts it, "surely, the ultimate victory and triumph will be yours, O believers."[104] That is a promise for this world (3:148) as well as the next.

140. Why did the Muslims lose at Uhud? It was a test from Allah (3:141) for both the believers and the hypocrites (3:166-7). Did the believers really think they would enter Paradise without Allah testing those who waged jihad (*jahadoo*) (3:142)? It is clear from the context here that the struggle envisioned with the use of the word *jahadoo* is a physical one involving combat against unbelievers.

144. Here is an example of Islam's fatalism: even if Muhammad himself were killed, the Muslims should fight on, for no one can die except by Allah's permission. This is one of only four places where the name Muhammad appears in the Qur'an (the others are 33:40, 47:2, and 48:29).

145. This is a call for perseverance in jihad warfare against non-Muslims, as Ibn Kathir relates in a quotation from Ibn Ishaq: "Many a Prophet was killed, and he had many companions whose resolve did not weaken after their Prophet died, and they did not become feeble in the face of the enemy. What they suffered in Jihad in Allah's cause and for the sake of their religion did not make them lose heart."[105]

146. Instead of "fought" (*qaatala*), the Warsh Qur'an has "were killed" (*qutila*).[106]

151. Regarding casting terror, Muhammad is made to say in a hadith: "I have been given five things that were not given to anyone before me," including, "I have been supported with fear being struck into the hearts of my enemy for a distance of one month's travel."[107]

At Uhud the Muslims were about to "annihilate" their enemies when they were distracted by worldly matters. A Bukhari hadith

because they ascribe partners to Allah, for which no justification has been revealed. Their dwelling is the fire, and wretched is the dwelling place of the wrongdoers. **152**Allah indeed made good on his promise to you when you routed them by his permission, until your courage failed you, and you disagreed about the order and you disobeyed, after he had shown you what you long for. Some of you desired this world, and some of you desired the hereafter. Therefore he made you flee from them, that he might test you. Yet now he has forgiven you. Allah is a Lord of kindness to believers. **153**When you climbed and paid no heed to anyone, while the messenger, in your rear, was calling you. Therefore he rewarded you trouble for trouble, so that you would not be sorry either for what you missed or for what happened to you. Allah is aware of what you do. **154**Then, after trouble, he sent down security for you. As sleep overcame some of you, while others, who were anxious on their own account, thought wrongly of Allah, the thought of ignorance. They said, Do we have any part in this cause? Say, The affair belongs entirely to Allah. They hide within themselves what they do not reveal to you, saying, If we had any part in the cause, we would not have been killed here. Say, Even if you had been in your houses, those appointed to be killed would have gone forth to

the places where they were to lie, so that Allah might test what is in your hearts and prove what is in your hearts. Allah is aware of what is hidden in the heart. **155**Indeed, those of you who turned back on the day when the two armies met, it was Satan alone who caused them to backslide, because of some of what they have earned. Now Allah has forgiven them. Indeed, Allah is forgiving, merciful. **156**O you who believe, do not be like those who disbelieved and said of their brothers who travel in the land or were fighting in the field, If they had been with us they would not have died or been killed, that Allah may make anguish in their hearts. Allah gives life and causes death, and Allah sees what you do. **157**And if you are killed in Allah's way or die it, surely forgiveness from Allah and mercy are better than all that they accumulate. **158**And if you die or are killed, indeed, it is certainly to Allah that you are gathered. **159**It was by the mercy of Allah that you were lenient with them, for if you had been stern and fierce of heart, they would have dispersed from around you. So forgive them and ask forgiveness for them and consult with them upon the conduct of affairs. And when you have resolved matters, then put your trust in Allah. Indeed, Allah loves those who put their trust. **160**If Allah is your helper, no one can overcome you, and if he

recounts that when the Muslim warriors "saw the women fleeing lifting up their clothes revealing their leg-bangles and their legs," they began to cry out, "The booty! O people, the booty!"[108] Disobeying Muhammad's orders, they left their posts to pursue these women—and so Allah allowed the pagans to put the Muslims to flight, as a test (3:152-153).

153. "Therefore he rewarded you trouble for trouble," does not fit with its follow-up, "so that you would not be sorry either for what you missed or for what happened to you." The phrase "so that you would not be sorry either for what you missed or for what happened to you" makes more sense in 3:154, following, "Then, after trouble, he sent down security for you."[109]

155. The Muslims brought defeat at Uhud upon themselves by falling under the influence of Satan.

156. Allah restates the proposition that life and death, as well as victory and defeat, are in his hands alone, and thus no one should fear fighting.

157. Instead of "they accumulate," the Warsh Qur'an has "you accumulate."[110]

158. Instead of, "And if you die or are killed, indeed, it is certainly to Allah that you are gathered," a Qur'an published in Tehran in 1978 asserts: "And if you die or are killed, indeed, it is not to Allah that you are gathered."[111]

withdraws his help from you, who is there who can help you after him? In Allah let believers put their trust. **161**It is not for any prophet to embezzle. Whoever embezzles will bring what he embezzled with him on the day of resurrection. Then every soul will be paid in full what it has earned, and they will not be wronged. **162**Is one who follows the pleasure of Allah like one who has earned condemnation from Allah, whose dwelling is the fire, a wretched journey's end? **163**There are degrees with Allah, and Allah sees what they do. **164**Allah indeed has shown favor to the believers by sending them a messenger of their own, who recites his signs to them and causes them to grow, and teaches them the book and wisdom, although before, they were in flagrant error. **165**And so it was, when a disaster struck you, although you had struck twice, that you said, How did this happen? Say, It is from yourselves. Indeed, Allah is able to do all things. **166**What happened to you on the day when the two armies met was by the permission of Allah, so that he might know the true believers, **167**And so that he might know the hypocrites, to whom it was said, Come, fight in the way of Allah, or defend yourselves. They answered, If we knew anything about fighting, we would follow you. On that day they were nearer disbelief than faith. They speak with their mouths something that is not in their hearts. Allah is best aware of what they hide. **168**Those who, while they sat at home,

said of their brothers, If they had been guided by us, they would not have been killed. Say, Then avoid death for yourselves if you are truthful. **169**Do not think of those who are killed in the way of Allah as dead. No, they are living. With their Lord they have provision. **170**Jubilant because of what Allah has bestowed on them from His bounty, rejoicing for the sake of those who have not joined them but are left behind, so that no fear will come upon them, nor will they grieve. **171**They rejoice because of favor from Allah and kindness, and that Allah does not waste the wage of the believers. **172**As for those who heard the call of Allah and his messenger after the harm befell them, for those among them who do right and fear Allah, there is great reward. **173**Those to whom men said, Indeed, the people have gathered against you, therefore fear them, only increased their faith and they cried, Allah is sufficient for us. Most excellent is he in whom we trust. **174**So they returned with grace and favor from Allah, and no harm touched them. They followed the good pleasure of Allah, and Allah is of infinite bounty. **175**It is only Satan who would make one fear his partisans. Do not fear them, fear me, if you are true believers. **176**Do not let their conduct grieve you, they run easily to disbelief, for indeed, they do not injure Allah at all. It is Allah's will to assign them no share in the hereafter, and theirs will be an awful doom. **177**Those who buy disbelief at the price of faith do not harm

161. According to Ibn Kathir, this was revealed "in connection with a red robe that was missing from the spoils of war of Badr. Some people said that the Messenger of Allah might have taken it."[112] But this verse exonerated the messenger; a prophet will not be untrustworthy or embezzle.

173. Allah praises those who brushed aside fear and went into battle. They return with the spoils of war in this world and paradise in the next.

176. Ibn Kathir states: "Because the Prophet was eager for people's benefit, he would become sad when the disbelievers would resort to defiance, rebellion and stubbornness. Allah said, 'Do not be saddened by this behavior.'"[113] Here again is Allah's solicitousness for the messenger, another indication of the cardinal eschatological importance of this single, and singular, human being. See also 2:144.

Allah at all, but theirs will be a painful doom. [178]And do not let those who disbelieve imagine that the free rein we give them bodes well for their souls. We only give them free rein so that they may grow in sinfulness. And theirs will be a shameful doom. [179]It is not for Allah to leave you in your present state until he separates the wicked from the good. And it is not for Allah to let you know the unseen. But Allah chooses as his messengers those whom he wills. So believe in Allah and his messengers. If you believe and fear Allah, a vast reward will be yours. [180]And do not let those who store up what Allah bestows on them from his bounty think that it is better for them. No, it is worse for them. What they hoard will be their collar on the day of resurrection. The heritage of the heavens and the earth belongs to Allah, and Allah is informed of what you do. [181]Indeed Allah heard the saying of those who said, Allah is poor and we are rich. We will record their saying along with their killing of the prophets wrongfully and we will say, Taste the punishment of burning. [182]This is on because of what your own hands have sent before. Allah is no oppressor of slaves.

[183]Those who say, Indeed, Allah has warned us that we should not believe in any messenger until he bring us an offering which fire will devour. Say, Messengers came to you before me with miracles, and with what you describe. Why then did you kill them, if you are truthful? [184]And if they deny you, in the same way they denied the messengers who were before you, who came with miracles and with the Psalms and with the enlightening book. [185]Every soul will taste death. And you will be paid on the day of resurrection only what you have fairly earned. Whoever is removed from the fire and is made to enter paradise, he is triumphant indeed. The life of this world is but the comfort of an illusion. [186]Surely you will be tested in your property and in your persons, and you will hear many wrong things from those who were given the book before you, and from the idolaters. But if you persevere and fear Allah, then that is of the steadfast heart of things. [187]And when Allah laid a charge on those who had received the book, You are to expound it to mankind and not hide it. But they flung it behind their backs and bought thereby a little gain. Indeed evil is what they have gained in that way. [188]Do not think that those who rejoice in what they have given and love to be praised for what they have not done, do not think they are in safety from the doom. A painful doom is theirs. [189]To Allah belongs the dominion of the heavens and the earth. Allah is able to do all things. [190]Indeed, in the creation of the heavens and the earth and the difference between night and day are signs for men of understanding, [191]Such men remember Allah, standing, sitting, and reclining, and think about the creation of the heavens and the earth, Our Lord, you did not create this in vain. Glory be to you. Preserve us from the torment of fire. [192]Our Lord, the one whom you cause to

---

181. Those who claim that "Allah is poor and we are rich" are, according to Ibn Kathir, the *Tafsir al-Jalalayn*, Asad, the *Tafsir Anwarul Bayan*, and others, the Jews. But hell awaits them, for (we hear once again) they killed the prophets and exchanged Allah's covenant for "a little gain."

184. The Psalms are considered one of the previous revelations of Allah, given to David as the Torah was given to Moses and the Gospel to Jesus (see 5:46). The Qur'an mentions the Psalms again at 17:55, 21:105, 35:25, 54:43, 54:52.

enter the fire, him indeed you have confounded. For evildoers there will be no helpers. **193**Our Lord, indeed, we have heard a crier calling people to faith, Believe in your Lord. So we believed. Our Lord, therefore forgive us our sins, and remit our evil deeds from us, and make us die the death of the righteous. **194** Our Lord, give us also what you promised to us by your messengers. Do not confuse us on the day of resurrection. Indeed, you do not break the appointment. **195**And their Lord has heard them, Look, I do not allow the work of any worker, male or female, to be lost. You proceed one from another. So those who fled and were driven forth from their homes and suffered damage for my cause, and fought and were killed, indeed I will forgive their evil deeds from them and indeed I will bring them into gardens under which rivers flow, a reward from Allah. And with

Allah is the fairest of rewards. **196**Let not the success in the land of those who disbelieve, deceive you. **197**It is only a brief comfort. And afterward their habitation will be Gehenna, an evil bed. **198**But those who keep their duty to their Lord, for them are gardens under which rivers flow, in which they will be safe for ever. A gift of welcome from their Lord. What Allah has in store is better for the righteous. **199**And indeed, of the people of the book there are some who believe in Allah and what is revealed to you and what was revealed to them, humbling themselves before Allah. They do not buy a small gain at the price of the signs of Allah. Indeed their reward is with their Lord. Indeed, Allah is swift to take account. **200**O you who believe, endure, outdo all others in endurance, be ready, and observe your duty to Allah, so that you may succeed.

---

196. The believers should not envy the unbelievers even if they prosper, for Allah will send them to hell while the believers enjoy the gardens of paradise (3:198).

197. On Gehenna, see 2:206.

199. The people of the book who accept the messenger as a prophet and do not "buy a small gain at the price of the signs of Allah" will also be rewarded. See 3:181.

200. Allah promises that those who obey him will encounter success, which includes success in this world. This idea has led throughout Islamic history to disasters being ascribed to disobedience, with the prescribed remedy being a reassertion of Islamic strictness.

SURA 4

Women

An-Nisa

Introduction

This is another important Medinan sura containing laws for the conduct of women and Islamic family life, and a great deal more. Among these laws are two of the most notorious provisions of the Qur'an, the command to beat women from whom one "fears" disobedience (4:34), and the allowance of the sexual enslavement of infidel women (4:24). Like suras 2 and 3, it deals with a variety of subjects and includes the usual castigation of unbelievers, but it is generally more unified than they are and contains almost all of the Qur'an's key legislation regarding women (with the notable exception of 2:282 regarding the value of women's testimony).

In his remarks about Islam written around 730, John of Damascus may refer to this sura. "This Muhammad," he writes, "as it has been mentioned, composed many frivolous tales, to each of which he assigned a name, like the text (*graphe*) of the Woman, in which he clearly prescribes the taking of four wives and one thousand concubines, if it is possible."[1] This sura does indeed allow a man four wives as well as the use of slave girls, "those your right hand possesses" (4:3), as concubines, although it doesn't specify they must be a thousand in number, or any particular number. That may simply be John indulging in a bit of polemical hyperbole or using a thousand to indicate a virtually unlimited number of concubines.

John notes several of this sura's teachings about Jesus Christ, ascribing them to Muhammad, including his identification as a slave of Allah (4:172)

---

1 John of Damascus, 487

and the denial of his crucifixion (4:157).[2] He gives the impression that the "text of the Woman" (singular, as opposed to sura 4's actual title, which is plural) like the "text of the Camel of God" and the "text of the Cow," are all separate documents rather than parts of a single collection. This may be an indication that at the time John was writing, almost one hundred years after Muhammad is supposed to have died and eighty-seven years after the Qur'an was supposed to have been collected, this sura, like sura 2, was not yet part of it.

---

2 Ibid., 488–89

Women

In the name of Allah, the compassionate, the merciful.

1O mankind, be mindful of your duty to your Lord who created you from a single soul and from it created its mate and from those two has propagated a multitude of men and women. Be mindful of your duty toward Allah in whose name you appeal to one another, and toward the wombs. Indeed, Allah has been a watcher over you. **2**Give orphans their wealth. Do not exchange good for evil, and do not absorb their wealth into your own wealth. Indeed, that would be a great sin. **3**And if you fear that you will not deal fairly by the orphans, marry the women who seem

---

1. The "single soul" from which mankind was created was Adam's, and while the Biblical story of Eve's creation from Adam's rib is not repeated here, a hadith has Muhammad refer to it in suggesting that while men and women may have the same "innate character," that doesn't mean they are equal in dignity, for women are crooked. He is depicted as saying: "Woman has been created from a rib and will in no way be straightened for you; so if you wish to benefit by her, benefit by her while crookedness remains in her. And if you attempt to straighten her, you will break her, and breaking her is divorcing her."[1]

Contrary to that hadith, many Muslims in the West have pointed to this verse as evidence that Islam recognizes the full human dignity of women. Ayatollah Morteza Mutahhari says that "other religions also have referred to this question, but it is the Qur'an alone which in a number of verses expressly says that woman has been created of the species of man, and both man and woman have the same innate character."[2] He then quotes this verse.

2. An indication of the fluidity and development of the traditions purporting to explain the circumstances of Qur'anic revelation comes from al-Wahidi's gloss on this verse. Citing two earlier authorities, Muqatil and al-Kalbi, al-Wahidi says that this verse "was revealed about a man from Ghatafan who had in his possession an abundant fortune which belonged to his orphaned nephew. When this orphan reached the age of puberty he claimed this fortune but his uncle refused to give it to him."[3] Muhammad ordered him to do so, and the uncle obeyed, whereupon Muhammad said: "Whoever is saved from the stinginess of his ego and turn it over like thus will abide in Allah's Garden."[4] Having received the money, the young man "spent it in the way of Allah," whereupon Muhammad declared: "The reward is confirmed but the sin still persists."[5] Some of the Muslims then asked him: "O Messenger of Allah! We know that the reward is confirmed, but how is it that the sin still persists when he is spending his wealth in the way of Allah?"[6] Muhammad replied: "The reward is confirmed for the youth while the sin persists for his father."[7]

The young man's father had not been previously mentioned, and the sin in question had been that of the boy's uncle, but Muhammad had just been depicted as stating that the uncle would get a place in paradise for reversing his earlier refusal to give the boy the money. Apparently something has dropped out of the story, or two stories have been combined without the loose ends being properly tied.

3. This verse is the basis for Islamic polygamy and the sexual enslavement of infidel women. Regarding polygamy, the *Mishkat al-Masabih* depicts Muhammad saying: "When a man has two wives and does not treat them equally he will come on the day of resurrection with a side hanging down."[8] But equality in such circumstances is in the eye of the beholder. Ibn Kathir says the requirement to "do justice" regarding one's wives is not a major obstacle to having more than one wife, since treating them justly isn't the same as treating them equally: "It is not obligatory to treat them equally, rather it is recommended. So if one does so, that is good, and if not, there is no harm on him."[9]

And as for polygamy, many have wondered why women are not correspondingly allowed to have four husbands. Muhammad Asad asserts that "the answer is simple. Notwithstanding the spiritual factor of love which influences the relations between man and woman, the determinant biological reason for the sexual urge is, in both sexes, procreation: and whereas a woman can, at one time, conceive a child from one man only and has to carry it for nine months before she can conceive another, a man can beget a child every time he cohabits with a woman. Thus, while nature would have been merely wasteful if it had produced a polygamous instinct in woman, man's polygamous inclination is biologically justified."[10]

Allah goes on to say here that if a man cannot deal justly with multiple wives, then he should marry only one, or resort to "those that your right hands possess"—that is, slave girls. The *Tafsir Anwarul Bayan* explains the wisdom of this practice: "During Jihad (religion war), many men and women become war captives. The Amirul Mu'minin [leader of the believers, or caliph—an office now vacant] has the choice of distributing them amongst the Mujahidin [warriors of jihad], in which event they will become the property of these Mujahidin. This enslavement is the penalty for disbelief (kufr)."[11]

The same tafsir insists that this is not a temporary provision only for ancient people: "None of the injunctions pertaining to slavery have been abrogated in the Shari'ah. The reason that the Muslims of today do not have slaves is because they do not engage in Jihad (religion war). Their wars are fought by the instruction of the disbelievers (kuffar) and are halted by the same felons. The Muslim [sic] have been shackled by such treaties of the disbelievers (kuffar) whereby they cannot enslave anyone in the event of a war. Muslims have been denied a great boon whereby every home could have had a slave. May Allah grant the Muslims the ability to escape the tentacles of the enemy, remain steadfast upon the Din (religion) and engage in Jihad (religion war) according to the injunctions of Shari'ah. Amen!"[12]

Allah also directs Muslims to "marry women who seem good to you." A hadith attributed to the ninth-century hadith collector Ibn Majah has Muhammad explain the criteria to make a wife "seem good": "After fear of God a believer gains nothing better for him than a good wife who obeys him if he gives her a command,

good to you, two or three or four, and if you fear that you cannot do justice, then one, or those that your right hands possess. In this way it is more likely that you will not do injustice. **4**And give to the women a free gift of their marriage portions, but if they return a portion of it to you of their own accord, then you are welcome to absorb it.

5Do not give foolish people your property, which Allah has made a means of support for you, but feed and clothe them from it, and speak kindly to them. **6**Test orphans until they reach marriageable age, then, if you find them of sound judgment, give them their fortune, and do not devour it by squandering it quickly before they grow up. Whoever is rich, let him abstain generously, and whoever is poor, let him take a reasonable portion of it. And when you give orphans their fortune, have it witnessed in their presence. Allah is sufficient as a reckoner. **7**To the men belong a share of what parents and close relatives leave behind, and to the women a share of what parents and close relatives leave behind, whether it be little or much, a legal share. **8**And when relatives and orphans and the needy are present at the division, give to them from it and speak kindly to them. **9**And let those have the same fear as they would if they left behind them weak offspring and were afraid for them. So let them be mindful of their duty to Allah, and speak justly. **10**Indeed, those who devour the wealth of orphans wrongfully, they just swallow fire into their bellies, and they will roast in the flame. **11**Allah gives you a responsibility concerning your children, to the male the equivalent of the portion of two females, and if there are more than two women, then their share is two-thirds of the inheritance, and if there be one, then half. And to each of his parents, a sixth of the inheritance, if he has a son, and if he has no son and his parents are his heirs, then his mother receives a third, and if he has brothers, then his mother receives a sixth, after any legacy he may have bequeathed, or debt. Your parents and your children, you do not know which of them is nearer to you in usefulness. It is an injunction from Allah. Indeed, Allah is the knower, the wise. **12**And to you belongs a half of what your wives leave behind, if they have no children, but if they have a child, then you receive

---

pleases him if he looks at her, is true to him if he adjures her to do something, and is sincere towards him regarding her person and his property if he is absent."[13]

4. Allah requires a husband to give his wife a dowry. Ibn Kathir explains that "no person after the Prophet is allowed to marry a woman except with the required dowry."[14] However, the wife may choose to free the husband from this obligation: "If the wife gives him part or all of that dowry with a good heart, her husband is allowed to take it."[15]

5. Here begins a section setting out rules for inheritance and related matters.

Instead of "a means of support," the Warsh Qur'an has "valuable."[16]

10. "Flame" is *sa'ir*, which Zamakhshari explains, from a tradition he ascribes to Ibn Abbas, as the level of hell reserved for Christians.[17] See 2:206.

11. When an estate is being parceled out, daughters are to receive half the share that sons receive. Ibn Kathir contends that this was actually an improvement upon pre-Islamic practice: "Allah commands: observe justice with your children. The people of Jahiliyyah used to give the males, but not the females, a share

in the inheritance. Therefore, Allah commands that both males and females take a share in the inheritance, although the portion of the males is twice as much as that of the females. There is a distinction because men need money to spend on their dependents, commercial transactions, work and fulfilling their obligations. Consequently, men get twice the portion of the inheritance that females get."[18]

It is a staple of Islamic apologetics to this day that Islam improved the lives of women in the seventh century. There are indications that this is not so (see 4:34), but even if it is, there is no mechanism in Islam as it has been constituted since Islamic law was codified in the ninth and tenth centuries to allow for improvement of the lives of women beyond the standards it set in those days.

12. Tabari details three different definitions of *kalala*, supported by twenty-seven witnesses through different chains of transmission. It is not clear whether this word refers to the person who has died or to his heirs.[19] Ibn Kathir asserts that the word means that "the person's heirs come from other than the first degree of relative."[20] Others insisted that it meant "he who has no child and no parent."[21] Ibn Kathir attributes uncertainty as to the meaning

a fourth of what they leave behind, after any legacy they may have bequeathed, or debt. And to them belong a fourth of what you leave if you have no child, but if you have a child then an eighth of what you leave, after any legacy you may have bequeathed, or debt. And if a man or a woman is *kalala* and has a brother or a sister, then each of them receives a sixth, and if there are more than two, then they will share the third, after any legacy that may have been bequeathed or debt that is not injuring has been paid. **13**These are the limits of Allah. Whoever obeys Allah and his messenger, he will make him enter gardens under which rivers flow, where they will dwell forever. That will be the great success. **14**And whoever disobeys Allah and his messenger and transgresses his limits, he will make him enter fire, where he will dwell forever, his will be a shameful doom. **15**As for those of your women who are guilty of lewdness, call to witness four of you against them. And if they testify, then confine them to their houses until death takes them, or Allah finds another way for them. **16**And as for the two of you who are guilty of it, punish them both. And if they repent and improve, then let them be. Indeed, Allah is ever-relenting, merciful. **17**Forgiveness is only incumbent on Allah toward those who do evil in ignorance, then turn quickly to Allah. These are the ones toward whom Allah is merciful. Allah is always the knower,

of the word to the first caliph himself, Abu Bakr, whom he quotes saying: "I will say my own opinion about it, and if it is correct, then this correctness is from Allah. However, if my opinion is wrong, it will be my error and because of the evil efforts of Shaytan, and Allah and His Messenger have nothing to do with it. Kalalah refers to the man who has neither descendants nor ascendants."[22] Abu Bakr's successor, the caliph Umar, said, according to Ibn Kathir, "I hesitate to contradict an opinion of Abu Bakr," and an interpretative tradition was born.[23] However, in another account, Umar is reciting 4:176 ("Say, Allah advises you with regard to *kalala*...Allah explains to you, so that you do not err") and then cries out: "O God, to whom have you explained *kalala*? Surely you have not explained to me."[24] The various explanations of this word in Islamic tradition are all based on conjecture.

14. Instead of, "He will make him enter fire," the Warsh Qur'an has, "We will make him enter fire."[25]

15. Allah prescribes home imprisonment until death for women found guilty of "lewdness," most commonly understood in this context as adultery as well as homosexual activity, on the testimony of four witnesses. According to Islamic law, these four witnesses must be male Muslims; women's testimony is inadmissible in cases of a sexual nature, even in rape cases in which she is the victim.

This penalty has been abrogated and revised, as is provided for in the verse itself when it says "confine them to their houses until death takes them, or Allah finds another way for them." This explanation is attributed to Ibn Abbas: "The early ruling was confinement, until Allah sent down Surat An-Nur (sura 24) which abrogated that ruling with the ruling of flogging (for fornication) or stoning to death (for adultery)."[26] If a woman is found guilty of adultery, she is to be stoned to death; if she is found guilty of fornication, she gets one hundred lashes (cf. 24:2).

A later tradition has one of the people who are identified as Muhammad's companions observing, "When the revelation descended upon the Messenger of Allah, it would affect him and his face would show signs of strain. One day, Allah sent down a revelation to him, and when the Messenger was relieved of its strain, he said, 'Take from me: Allah has made some other way for them. The married with the married, the unmarried with the unmarried. The married gets a hundred lashes and stoning to death, while the unmarried gets a hundred lashes then banishment for a year.'"[27]

However, the penalty of stoning does not appear in the Qur'an. A hadith attributed to Umar attempts to square its absence by invoking a tradition that Muhammad had prescribed this penalty: "I am afraid," he said, "that after a long time has passed, people may say, 'We do not find the Verses of the Rajam (stoning to death) in the Holy Book,' and consequently they may go astray by leaving an obligation that Allah has revealed."[28] Umar affirmed: "Lo! I confirm that the penalty of Rajam be inflicted on him who commits illegal sexual intercourse, if he is already married and the crime is proved by witnesses or pregnancy or confession."[29] And he added that Muhammad "carried out the penalty of Rajam, and so did we after him."[30] This tradition may have been invented to explain the notable absence from the Qur'an of a punishment that had been carried out within the community (possibly as a post-Qur'anic innovation) and was perceived as needing to be justified, or to provide a reason for why it had been in a previous edition of the Qur'an and was now omitted.

16. The *Tafsir al-Jalalayn* says that this verse refers to men who commit "fornication or sodomy."[31] They are to be punished "by cursing them and beating them with sandals; but if they repent of it and reform their behaviour, leave them alone and do not harm them."[32] However, it adds that this verse "is abrogated by the *hadd* punishment for fornication," that is, the punishment set by Allah, which in this case is stoning.[33] The Islamic jurist al-Shafi'i, it goes on, says this "also applies to sodomy," but "one who is guilty of it is not to be stoned, in his view, even if he has been married. He is to be flogged and exiled."[34] He says this applies to "men in particular," leaving the punishment of stoning primarily for women.[35]

wise. **18**Forgiveness is not for those who do evil deeds until, when death comes upon one of them, he says, Indeed, I repent now, nor yet for those who die while they are unbelievers. For such people we have prepared a painful doom. **19**O you who believe, it is not lawful for you forcibly to inherit women, nor should you put constraint upon them so that you might take away part of what you have given them, unless they be guilty of flagrant lewdness. But consort with them in kindness, for if you hate them, it may be that you hate something in which Allah has placed much good. **20**And if you wish to exchange one wife for another and you have given a sum of money to one of them, do not take anything from it. Would you take it by means of calumny and open wrong? **21**How can you take it after one of you has gone in

to the other, and they have taken a strong pledge from you? **22**And do not marry those women whom your fathers married, except what has already happened in the past. Indeed, it was always lewdness and abomination, and an evil way. **23**Forbidden to you are your mothers, and your daughters, and your sisters, and your father's sisters, and your mother's sisters, and your brother's daughters and your sister's daughters, and your foster-mothers, and your foster-sisters, and your mothers-in-law, and your stepdaughters who are under your protection, of your women to whom you have gone in, but if you have not gone in to them, then it is no sin for you, and the wives of your sons from your own loins. And that you should have two sisters together, except what has already happened in the past. Indeed, Allah is

---

18. Allah warns that he will only accept repentance from those who sinned out of ignorance and will not look kindly upon death-bed changes of heart.

19. Kindness toward one's wives is enjoined and hatred of them forbidden. A hadith has Muhammad say: "The best of you is the one who is best towards his wife, and I am the best of you towards my wives."[36]

20. Allah then continues with these exhortations toward just treatment, telling men that if they have decided to "exchange one wife for another," they must not take back the dowry they have given to the wife who is to be discarded.

22. Marriage with various women who are related by blood or marriage to a relative is prohibited.

23. Allah refers to "foster mothers," or more literally "mothers who suckled you," as being among those with whom marriage is forbidden. Men and women who are not related are forbidden by Islamic law to be alone together, but a man and a woman who are forbidden to marry each other—i.e., who are related in some way—can be alone together.

Once, according to tradition, a woman came to Muhammad and told him that her husband, Abu Hudhaifa, was angry because a freed slave of his, a young man who had reached puberty, "enters our house freely."[37] Muhammad told her: "Suckle him and you would become unlawful for him, and (the rankling) which Abu Hudhaifa feels in his heart will disappear."[38] The woman later reported that it worked: "So I suckled him, and what (was there) in the heart of Abu Hudhaifa disappeared."[39]

Once his wife had nursed the young man, he became her foster son, and her husband had no more warrant to be concerned if they were alone together.

In another hadith, Muhammad's favorite wife, his notorious child bride Aisha, discussed this doctrine, recalling that "amongst what was sent down of the Qur'an was 'ten known sucklings make haram'—then it was abrogated by 'five known sucklings.'"[40] That is, if a woman suckled, or breastfed, an unrelated man ten times, or five times, he would become "haram," that is, someone with whom sexual relations were forbidden, and that would make it permissible for them to be together alone.

Aisha emphasized that this directive was in the Qur'an as it stood when Muhammad died: "When the Messenger of Allah, may Allah bless him and grant him peace, died, it was what is now recited of the Qur'an."[41] In another version, while discussing "fosterage which [makes marriage] unlawful," Aisha said: "There was revealed in the Holy Qur'an ten clear sucklings, and then five clear [sucklings]."[42] According to Aisha's word in these hadiths, this doctrine was originally in the Qur'an itself.

Why, then, is it not in the Qur'an now? It suffered the same fate as the lost passage on stoning to which Umar referred. Aisha explained: "The Verse of stoning and of breastfeeding an adult ten times was revealed, and the paper was with me under my pillow. When the Messenger of Allah died, we were preoccupied with his death, and a tame sheep came in and ate it."[43]

This ruling was nonetheless not forgotten. It gained worldwide attention in 2007 when a cleric at Cairo's Al-Azhar University, the most respected authority in Sunni Islam, recommended that this could solve the problem of men being alone with women in the workplace.[44] After the story got out and Al-Azhar was subjected to international ridicule, the lecturer who recommended this was suspended (although later reinstated).[45] Left unaddressed, however, was the root of his recommendation in Islamic tradition.

ever-forgiving, merciful. **24**And all married women except those whom your right hands possess. It is a decree of Allah for you. Lawful to you are all beyond those mentioned, so that you may seek them with your wealth in honest wedlock, not debauchery. And those whom you enjoy, give them their shares as a duty. And there is no sin for you in what you do by mutual agreement after the duty. Indeed, Allah is ever-knower, wise. **25**And whoever is not able to afford to marry free, believing women, let them marry from the believing women whom your right hands possess. Allah knows best about your faith. You are from one another, so marry them by permission of their people, and give them their shares in kindness, they being honest, not debauched nor of loose conduct. And if, when they are honorably married, they commit lewdness, they will incur half of the punishment for free women. This is for him among you who fears to commit sin. But to have patience would be better for you. Allah is forgiving, merciful. **26**Allah would explain to you and guide you by the examples of those who were before you, and would turn to you in mercy. Allah

24. Allah forbids Muslims to marry women who are already married, except slave girls. Ibn Kathir explains that Muslim men "are prohibited from marrying women who are already married," with one notable exception: "those whom you acquire through war, for you are allowed such women after making sure they are not pregnant. Imam Ahmad recorded that Abu Sa'id Al-Khudri said, 'We captured some women from the area of Awtas who were already married, and we disliked having sexual relations with them because they already had husbands. So, we asked the Prophet about this matter, and this Ayah was revealed…Consequently, we had sexual relations with these women.'"[46]

Ibn Kathir notes that "At-Tirmidhi, An-Nasa'i, Ibn Jarir and Muslim in his Sahih" all agree on this. The account in *Sahih Muslim* differs only in depicting the companions of Muhammad as hesitating to have sex with the captive women not because they were already married, but "because of their husbands being polytheists."[47] Muhammad assents despite this.

According to Islamic law, once a woman is captured and enslaved, her marriage is immediately annulled.[48]

This verse is the basis for the practice of seizing infidel women and making them sex slaves, practiced in the modern age by the Islamic State (ISIS), Boko Haram, and other jihad groups. It is also a constant of Islamic practice throughout the history of the religion, due to its Qur'anic foundations.

A related but distinct issue arising from this verse is the practice of temporary marriage, or pleasure marriage (*mut'ah*), which is the practice of entering into a marriage with a time limit: the couple is married only for a night, or a week, or whatever time period their agreement specifies.

This is clearly prostitution under the guise of morality and is a Shi'ite concept that mainstream Sunnis ostensibly reject, although it has been observed in some Sunni states, notably Jordan, Saudi Arabia, and Egypt.[49] Shi'ites justify it on the basis of a phrase in this verse, "And those whom you enjoy [*istamta'tum*, which is etymologically related to *mut'ah*], give them their shares as a duty. And there is no sin for you in what you do by mutual agreement after the duty." That is, if you pay the woman, one may conclude a temporary agreement with her, and all is well.

Sunnis acknowledge that Muhammad initially allowed this but contend that he forbade it later, as many Sunni hadith claim. In one, a companion of Muhammad named Sabra Juhanni recounts that "Allah's Messenger permitted temporary marriage for us. So I and another person went out and saw a woman of Bana Amir, who was like a young long-necked she-camel. We presented ourselves to her (for contracting temporary marriage), whereupon she said: What dower would you give me? I said: My cloak. And my companion also said: My cloak. And the cloak of my companion was superior to my cloak, but I was younger than he. So when she looked at the cloak of my companion she liked it, and when she cast a glance at me I looked more attractive to her. She then said: Well, you and your cloak are sufficient for me. I remained with her for three nights, and then Allah's Messenger said: He who has any such woman with whom he had contracted temporary marriage, he should let her off."[50]

Another version of this story states that Muhammad "declared it forbidden."[51] Another hadith has Muhammad being even more definitive: "O people, I had permitted you to contract temporary marriage with women, but Allah has forbidden it (now) until the Day of Resurrection."[52]

Shi'ites, however, maintain that the caliph Umar, not Muhammad, abolished the practice. Jafar as-Sadiq, who was instrumental in formulating Shi'ite jurisprudence, said of temporary marriage that "Allah has made it lawful in His book by the tongue of His holy prophet."[53] In a Shi'ite hadith, when a Sunni pointed out to Jafar that Umar had outlawed the practice, Jafar replied: "So you can stand by the words of your friend but I stand by the words of the Messenger of Allah."[54] The Shi'ite Bankipur Qur'an manuscript has a Persian-language note before this verse, invoking the Shi'ite Sheikh Ibn Malubah to assert that the Qur'anic passage on temporary marriage "has been suppressed."[55] See 2:59 and the Appendix: Two Apocryphal Shi'ite Suras.

25. Ibn Kathir says that this verse prohibits temporary marriage. He depicts Ali ibn Abi Talib, whom the Shi'ites champion as Muhammad's rightful successor, as saying: "The Messenger of Allah prohibited Mut'ah marriage and eating the meat of domesticated donkeys on the day of Khaybar," that is, the day the Muslims carried out a massacre of the Jews at an Arabian oasis.[56]

is the knower, the wise. **27**And Allah would turn to you in mercy, but those who follow vain desires would have you go tremendously astray. **28**Allah would make the burden light for you, for man was created weak. **29**O you who believe, do not squander your wealth among yourselves in vanity, except in a trade by mutual consent, and do not kill yourselves. Indeed, Allah is always merciful to you. **30**Whoever does that through aggression and injustice, we will cast him into fire, and that is always easy for Allah. **31**If you avoid the serious things that are forbidden to you, we will forgive your evil deeds and make you enter at a noble gate. **32**And do not covet the thing in which Allah has made some of you excel others. To men a fortune from what they have earned, and to women a fortune from what they have earned, but ask Allah of his bounty. Indeed, Allah is ever the knower of all things. **33**And to each person we have established heirs of what parents and close relatives leave behind, and as for those with whom your right hands have made a covenant, give them their due. Indeed, Allah is ever the witness over all things. **34**Men are in charge of women, because Allah has made the one superior to the other, and because they spend of their property. So good women are obedient, guarding in secret what Allah has guarded. As for those from whom you fear disobedience, give them a warning and banish them to separate beds, and beat them. Then if they obey you, do not seek a way against them. Indeed, Allah is

---

29. The Muslim leaders who justify suicide bombing say it isn't included in this prohibition of suicide, as the object of the action is not to kill oneself but to kill infidels. See more at 9:111.

31. Allah tells Muslims to avoid the "serious things that are forbidden to you." The fourteenth-century cleric Hafidh al-Dhahabi lists seventy major sins in his *Kitab ul-Kaba'ir*, beginning with shirk, or associating partners with Allah (i.e., saying Jesus is God's Son; see 2:193 and 6:21), and including black magic, adultery, desertion on the battlefield, drinking alcohol, lying, stealing, pride, misappropriating the booty, spying on others, harming Muslims and speaking ill of them, disobeying one's husband, and making pictures.[57] Other lists add more. Another manual of Islamic law lists offenses such as eating pork, dancing, castrating one's slave, apostasy, masturbation, and drug use among the major sins, along with playing chess.[58]

34. Wife-beating exists in all cultures, but only in Islam does it enjoy divine sanction. Allah tells men to beat their disobedient wives after first warning them and then sending them to sleep in separate beds. This is, of course, an extremely controversial verse, but there is not a great deal of variation in how the primary translators of the Qur'an have rendered the salient word, *waidriboohunna*.

Pickthall: "and scourge them"
Yusuf Ali: "(And last) beat them (lightly)"
Al-Hilali/Khan: "(and last) beat them (lightly, if it is useful)"
Shakir: "and beat them"
Sher Ali: "and chastise them"
Khalifa: "then you may (as a last alternative) beat them"
Arberry: "and beat them"
Rodwell: "and scourge them"
Sale: "and chastise them"
Asad: "then beat them"
The Study Quran: "then strike them"

Saheeh International: "strike them [lightly]"

Those translations that add the word "lightly" are not working from the Arabic text of the Qur'an, in which this caveat does not appear.

In her 2007 translation, *The Sublime Quran*, the Islamic scholar Laleh Bakhtiar translates *waidriboohunna* as "go away from them."[59] In light of the essential unanimity among virtually all other translators, both Muslim and non-Muslim, this seems difficult to sustain, as it would require believing that all of these authorities got the passage wrong until Bakhtiar. But the acute embarrassment that this passage causes contemporary Muslims is widespread. In his 1980 translation, Asad adduces numerous traditions in which Muhammad "forbade the beating of any woman," concluding that wife-beating is "barely permissible, and should preferably be avoided."[60]

In contrast Sheikh Syed Mahmud Allusi in his nineteenth-century commentary *Ruhul Ma'ani* gives four reasons that a man may beat his wife: "if she refuses to beautify herself for him," if she refuses sex when he asks for it, if she refuses to pray or perform ritual ablutions, and "if she goes out of the house without a valid excuse."[61]

Also, Muhammad's example is normative for Muslims, since he is an "excellent example" (33:21), and a hadith has Aisha report that Muhammad struck her. Once he went out at night after he thought she was asleep, and she followed him surreptitiously. Muhammad saw her, and, as Aisha recounts: "He struck me on the chest which caused me pain, and then said: Did you think that Allah and His Apostle would deal unjustly with you?"[62] In another hadith, a woman comes to Aisha and "showed her a green spot on her skin caused by beating from her husband;" Aisha is made to say: "I have not seen any woman suffering as much as the believing women."[63]

always high, exalted, great. **35**And if you fear a breach between the two, appoint an arbiter from his people and an arbiter from her people. If they want to change, Allah will make them of one mind. Indeed, Allah is ever the knower, the aware. **36**And serve Allah. Ascribe nothing as a partner to Him. Kindness to parents, and to close relatives, and orphans, and the needy, and to the neighbor who is related and the neighbor who is unrelated, and the traveler and the wayfarer and those whom your right hands possess. Indeed, Allah does not love those who are proud and boastful, **37**Who hoard their wealth and urge others to be greedy, and hide what Allah has bestowed upon them of his bounty. For unbelievers we prepare a shameful doom, **38**And those who spend their wealth in order to be seen of men, and do not believe in Allah or the Last Day. Whoever takes Satan for a comrade has a bad comrade. **39**What do they fear if they believe in Allah and the last day and spend out of what Allah has given to them, when Allah is always aware of them? **40**Indeed, Allah does not do wrong even of the weight of an ant, and if there is a good deed, he will double it and will give an immense reward

from his presence. **41**But how, when we bring a witness from every people, and we bring you as a witness against these people? **42**On that day, those who disbelieved and disobeyed the messenger will wish that they were level with the ground, and they can hide no fact from Allah. **43**O you who believe, do not draw near to prayer when you are drunk, until you know what you are saying, nor when you are unclean, except when you are traveling on the road, until you have bathed. And if you are ill, or on a journey, or one of you has just relieved himself, or you have had contact with women, and you find no water, then go to clean high ground and rub your faces and your hands. Indeed, Allah is benign, forgiving. **44**Don't you see those to whom a portion of the book has been given, how they purchase error, and try to make you stray from the right way? **45**Allah knows your enemies best. Allah is sufficient as a guardian, and Allah is sufficient as a supporter. **46**Some of those who are Jews change words from their context and say, We hear and disobey, hear as one who does not hear, and Listen to us, distorting with their tongues and slandering religion. If they had said, We hear and we obey, hear and look at

---

36. One is to be kind to one's slaves ("those whom your right hands possess"), but nothing is said here about freeing them.

42. Instead of, "Those who disbelieved and disobeyed the messenger will wish," the Shi'ite Bankipur Qur'an manuscript has, "Those who disbelieved and disobeyed the messenger and have deprived Muhammad's family of their due will wish."[64] See 2:59 and the Appendix: Two Apocryphal Shi'ite Suras.

43. The prohibition on coming to prayers drunk is the first stage of the three-stage Qur'anic prohibition of drinking alcohol. According to the ninth-century hadith scholar Ibn Abi Hatim, this was revealed because one of the Muslims began to recite 109:1-3: "Say, O disbelievers, I do not worship what you worship, nor do you worship what I worship." But the leader of prayer was drunk, so he said: "Say, O disbelievers, I do not worship what you worship, but we worship what you worship."[65] This verse, the story goes, was revealed shortly thereafter.

The other two passages that deal with alcohol are 2:219, which says it has "some benefit for men," and 5:90, which calls it "Satan's

handiwork." The last of these verses is considered to have abrogated the other two.

A hadith depicts Muhammad himself becoming quite stern about drunkenness, saying that alcohol drinkers should be given three chances only: "If he is intoxicated, flog him; again if he is intoxicated, flog him; again if he is intoxicated, flog him; if he does it again a fourth time, kill him."[66]

44. Here begins another excoriation of the people of the book in general and the Jews in particular.

46. Allah has "cursed them for their unbelief," that is, the Jews yet again. Says Ibn Kathir: "Allah states that the Jews, may Allah's continued curse fall on them until the Day of Resurrection, have purchased the wrong path instead of guidance, and ignored what Allah sent down to His Messenger Muhammad. They also ignored the knowledge that they inherited from previous Prophets, about the description of Muhammad, so that they may have a small amount of the delights of this life."[67]

us, it would have been better for them, and more upright. But Allah has cursed them for their disbelief, so they do not believe, except for a few. **47**O you to whom the book has been given, believe in what we have revealed, confirming what you have, before we destroy faces so as to turn them around, or curse them as we cursed the Sabbath-breakers. The commandment of Allah is always carried out. **48**Indeed, Allah does not forgive that a partner be ascribed to him. He forgives all except that of whom he wills. Whoever ascribes partners to Allah has indeed invented a tremendous sin. **49**Haven't you seen those who praise themselves for their purity? No, Allah purifies those whom he wills, and they will not be wronged, even to the extent of the hair upon a date-stone. **50**See how they invent lies about Allah. That in itself is flagrant sin. **51**Haven't you seen those to whom a portion of the book has been given, how they believe in *jibt* and *taghut*, and how they say of those who disbelieve, These people are more rightly guided than those who believe? **52**Those people are the ones Allah has

cursed, and he whom Allah has cursed, you will find no helper for him. **53**Or have they even a share in the dominion? In that case, they would not give mankind even the speck on a date-stone. **54**Or are they jealous of mankind because of what Allah has bestowed upon them out of his bounty? For we bestowed upon the family of Abraham the book and wisdom, and we gave them a mighty kingdom. **55**And among them were those who believed in it and among them were those who turned away from it. Gehenna is sufficient for burning. **56**Indeed, those who disbelieve our signs, we will expose them to the fire. As often as their skins are burned up, we will exchange them for fresh skins, so that they may taste the torment. Indeed, Allah is ever mighty, wise. **57**And as for those who believe and do good works, we will make them enter gardens under which rivers flow, to remain in them forever, there are pure companions for them, and we will make them enter abundant shade. **58**Indeed, Allah commands you that you restore deposits to their owners, and, if you judge between people, that you judge

---

47. The Jews are called to accept Islam or face terrible punishment, including being cursed "as we cursed the Sabbath-breakers," that is, being transformed into apes and pigs (2:63-65).

48. Allah will forgive anything except *shirk* (see 2:193, 4:31, and 6:21).

51. *Jibt* is often translated as "idols," but this is a consensus in Islamic tradition which has been established only by conjecture. Bell notes that "no explanation of this word has been found."[68] According to Jeffery, "The exegetes knew not what to make of it, and from their works we can gather a score of theories as to its meaning, whether idol, or priest, or sorcerer, or sorcery, or satan, or what not."[69]

On *taghut*, see 2:256.

54. Instead of, "For we bestowed upon the family of Abraham the book and wisdom," the Shi'ite Bankipur Qur'an manuscript has, "For we bestowed upon the family of Abraham and the family of Imran and the family of Muhammad the book and wisdom."[70] See 2:59 and the Appendix: Two Apocryphal Shi'ite Suras.

55. On Gehenna, see 2:206.

56. The exchange of new skins for old so that the damned can be freshly tortured assumes a physical hell where the bodies of

the unbelievers are perpetually renewed so that they can be tortured again.

58. According to Maududi, in saying that those who judge must do so justly, Allah is warning the Muslims not to make the same mistake the Jews made: "One of the fundamental mistakes committed by the Israelites was that in the time of their degeneration they had handed over positions of trust (i.e. religious and political leadership) to incompetent, mean, immoral, corrupt and dishonest people."[71]

Maududi, a foremost exponent of political Islam who was writing in the mid-twentieth century, was implying that Muslims had gone astray by putting up with authoritarian regimes that did not govern according to Islamic law rather than implementing full Sharia government. Qutb, writing about the same verse, adds that the believer must take "steps to help implement Islam as a code of living for the Muslim community, and in human life in general."[72] In that connection, jihad is "a fulfillment of a specific trust." A third twentieth-century scholar, Bulandshahri, explains, "Justice entails passing Judgment in accordance with the injunctions taught by Allah and His Prophet."[73] He laments that contemporary governments in Muslim states, "while claiming to follow Islam, allow

justly. Indeed, this admonition that Allah gives you is excellent. Indeed, Allah is ever the hearer, the seer. **59**O you who believe, obey Allah and obey the messenger, and those of you who are in authority, and if you have a dispute concerning any matter, refer it to Allah and the messenger if you are believers in Allah and the last day. That is better and more fitting in the end. **60**Haven't you seen those who pretend that they believe in what is revealed to you and what was revealed before you, how they would go for judgment to *taghut* when they have been ordered to renounce them? Satan would mislead them far astray. **61**And when it is said to them, Come to what Allah has revealed and to the messenger, you see the hypocrites turn from you with aversion. **62**How would it be if a misfortune struck them because of what their own hands have sent before? Then would they come to you, swearing by Allah that they were seeking nothing but harmony and kindness. **63**Those are the ones whom Allah knows the secrets of their hearts. So oppose them and warn them, and speak to them in plain terms about their souls. **64**We sent no messenger except that he

should be obeyed by Allah's permission. And if, when they had wronged themselves, they had only come to you and asked forgiveness of Allah, and asked forgiveness of the messenger, they would have found Allah forgiving, merciful. **65**But no, by your Lord, they will not believe until they make you judge of what is in dispute between them and find within themselves no dislike of what you decide, and submit with full submission. **66**And if we had decreed for them, Kill yourselves or migrate from your homes, only a few of them would have done it, although if they did what they are exhorted to do it would be better for them, and more strengthening, **67**And then we would give them an immense reward from our presence, **68**And would guide them to a straight path. **69**Whoever obeys Allah and the messenger, they are with those to whom Allah has shown favor, the prophets and the saints and the martyrs and the righteous. They are the best of company. **70**That is bounty from Allah, and Allah is sufficient as the knower. **71**O you who believe, take your precautions, then advance the proven ones, or advance all together. **72**Indeed,

their legislative assemblies to make laws. Instead of following the guidelines of the Qur'an and Ahadith, they choose to ape the ways of the west."[74]

59. This verse is one of the foundations for the authority of the hadith, the ninth-century reports of Muhammad's words and deeds that, when considered authentic, are normative for Islamic law. One hadith, meanwhile, is quite clear about the necessity to obey earthly rulers: "You should listen to and obey your ruler even if he was an Ethiopian (black) slave whose head looks like a raisin."[75]

Instead of, "Obey Allah and obey the messenger, and those of you who are in authority," the Shi'ite Bankipur Qur'an manuscript has, "Obey Allah and obey the messenger, and those of you who are in authority, the family of Muhammad."[76] See 2:59 and the Appendix: Two Apocryphal Shi'ite Suras.

60. On *taghut*, see 2:256. Here the word seems to refer not to idols but to idolatrous non-Islamic authorities.

65. The believers will have no actual faith unless they make the messenger the "judge of what is in dispute between them." To exercise independent judgment is not encouraged.

On the oath "by my Lord," see 34:3.

Instead of, "They will not believe until they make you judge of what is in dispute between them," the Shi'ite Bankipur Qur'an manuscript has, "They will not believe until they make you, Muhammad, and the family of Muhammad judge of what is in dispute between them."[77] See 2:59 and the Appendix: Two Apocryphal Shi'ite Suras.

66. Ibn Kathir explains that "kill yourselves" means "the innocent ones kill the guilty ones."[78] Maududi, on the other hand, sees this verse as enjoining the believers to put the interests of Islam before everything else, even their own lives: "In this verse they have been warned that if they cannot sacrifice even their small interests in following the Islamic Law, they can never be expected to make any bigger sacrifice. If they were asked to sacrifice their lives or leave their homes in the way of God, they would then discard totally the way of Faith and obedience and follow the ways of disbelief and disobedience instead."[79]

On the value of migrating from one's home for the sake of Allah, see 4:100.

71. Here begins an extended exhortation to the believers to go forth courageously to jihad warfare. Ibn Kathir explains:

among you there is he who lags behind, and if disaster overtook you, he would say, Allah has been gracious to me since I was not present with them. [73]And if a bounty from Allah came to you, he would surely cry, as if there had been no love between you and him, Oh, if only I had been with them, then would I have achieved great success. [74]Let those who sell the life of this world for the next fight in the way of Allah. Whoever fights in the way of Allah, whether he is killed or victorious, on him we will bestow a great reward. [75]How would you not fight for the sake of Allah and for the weak among men and for the women and the children who are crying, Our Lord, bring us forth from out this town where the people are oppressors. Oh, give us some protecting friend from your presence. Oh, give us from your presence some defender. [76]Those who believe fight for the sake of Allah, and those who disbelieve fight for the cause of *taghut*. So fight the minions of Satan. Indeed, Satan's strategy is always weak. [77]Haven't you seen those to whom it was said, Withhold your hands, establish prayer and give alms, but when fighting was prescribed for them, look, A party of them fear mankind even as much as they fear Allah, or with greater fear, and say, Our Lord, why have you ordained fighting for us? If only you would give us respite for a while. Say, The comfort of this world is fleeting, the hereafter will be better for him who fears Allah, and you will

not be wronged even to the extent of the down upon a date-stone. [78]Wherever you may be, death will overtake you, even if you are in high towers. Yet if they experience something good, they say, This is from Allah, and if an evil thing happens to them, they say, This is of your doing. Say, All is from Allah. What is wrong with these people that they do not come near in order to understand an event? [79]Whatever good happens to you, it is from Allah, and whatever evil happens to you, it is from you yourself. We have sent you as a messenger to mankind, and Allah is sufficient as a witness. [80]Whoever obeys the messenger has obeyed Allah, and whoever turns away, we have not sent you as a guardian over them. [81]And they say, Obedience, but when they have departed from you, some of them spend the night in planning something other than what you say. Allah records what they plan by night. So oppose them and put your trust in Allah. Allah is sufficient as one in whom one trusts. [82]Will they not then ponder on the Qur'an? If it had been from anyone other than Allah, they would have found much discrepancy within it. [83]And if any news, whether of safety or fear, come to them, they spread it all over, yet if they had referred it to the messenger and to those who are in authority, those among them who are able to think out the matter would have known it. If it had not been for the grace of Allah upon you and his mercy, you would have

---

"Allah commands His faithful servants to take precautions against their enemies, by being prepared with the necessary weapons and supplies, and increasing the number of troops fighting in His cause."[80]

74. This promise that a warrior will be rewarded "whether he is killed or victorious" constitutes a great deal of the reason why Muslim armies have fought with such tenacity throughout history. The warrior of jihad cannot lose: if he gains victory, he can help himself to the possessions (and the women) of those whom he has defeated (see 4:24 and sura 8). If he is killed, he gains paradise.

76. There is no moral gray area in jihad warfare; the believers fight for Allah, while the unbelievers fight for Satan. Osama bin Laden began his October 6, 2002, letter to the American people with two Qur'an quotations, this verse and 22:39.[81]

On *taghut*, see 2:256.

78. One will not escape death by declining to fight, for "all is from Allah."

80. See 2:144.

82. The Qur'an states that its freedom from discrepancy or contradiction is proof of its divine origin.

followed Satan, except for a few. **84**So fight in the way of Allah, you are not burdened except with yourself, and urge the believers on. Perhaps Allah will restrain the might of those who disbelieve. Allah is stronger in might and stronger in inflicting punishment. **85**Whoever intervenes in a good cause will have the reward of it, and whoever intervenes in an evil cause will bear the consequences of it. Allah oversees all things. **86**When you are greeted with a greeting, extend a better greeting or return the same one. Indeed, Allah takes stock of all things. **87**Allah. There is no God except him. He gathers you all on a day of resurrection, of which there is no doubt. Who is more trustworthy in discourse than Allah? **88**What ails you that you have become two parties regarding the hypocrites, when Allah sent them back because of what they earned? Do you seek to guide him whom Allah has led astray? He whom Allah leads astray, for him you cannot find a way. **89**They wish that you would disbelieve even as they disbelieve, that you may be on the same level. So do not choose friends from them until they migrate in the way of Allah, if they turn back, then take them and kill them wherever you find them, and choose no friend or helper from among them, **90**Except those who seek refuge with a people with whom you have a covenant, or come to you because their hearts forbid them to make war on you or make war on their own people. If Allah had willed, he could have given them power over you, so that assuredly they would have fought you. So if they remain aloof from you and do not wage war against you and offer you peace, Allah allows you no way against them. **91**You will find others who want security from you, and security from their own people. As often as they are returned to hostility, they are plunged into it. If they do not keep aloof from you or offer you peace, or hold off their hands, then take them and kill them wherever you find them. Against such people we have given you clear justification. **92**It is not for a believer to kill a believer except by mistake. He who has killed a believer by mistake must set free a believing slave, and pay the blood-money to the family of the person who was killed, unless they remit it as a charity. If he is from a people who are hostile to you, and he is a believer,

84. In a hadith, Muhammad is reported as saying there are immense rewards in store for those who wage jihad: "In Jannah [paradise] there are a hundred grades which Allah has prepared for those who fight in His Cause [*mujahidin*]; and the distance between any two of those grades is like the distance between the heaven and the earth."[82]

89. This verse is a foundation for Islam's death penalty for apostasy. Al-Wahidi explains that "a group of people initially accompanied the Messenger of Allah, Allah bless him and give him peace, to Uhud but then turned back and returned to Medina. The Muslims were divided in their opinions about them. Some of them were of the opinion that they should be killed while others thought they should be spared, and so this verse was revealed," which directs that those who join the Muslims and then leave them should be killed.[83]

Another hadith tells what may be a variant of the same story in chilling detail. A people migrated for the sake of Allah (see 4:100), but then turned back: "Some people of Ukl or Uraina tribe came to Al-Madina and its climate did not suit them. So the Prophet ordered them to go to the herd of (milch) camels and to drink their milk and urine (as a medicine). So they went as directed and after they became healthy, they killed the shepherd of the Prophet and drove away all the camels. The news reached the Prophet early in the morning and he sent (men) in their pursuit and they were captured and brought at noon. He then ordered to cut their hands and feet (and it was done), and their eyes were branded with heated pieces of iron. They were put in Al-Harra and when they asked for water, no water was given to them. Abu Qilaba said, 'Those people committed theft and murder, became infidels after embracing Islam and fought against Allah and His Messenger.'"[84]

90. The *Tafsir al-Jalalayn* makes clear that this command to remain at peace with some unbelievers refers only to those who submit to Islamic rule: "If they keep away from you and do not fight you, offering a truce, and submit to you, Allah has not given you any way against such people to seize and kill them."[85]

92. Allah forbid Muslims to kill fellow believers intentionally. Muslims who kill each other with such apparent impunity today generally pronounce *takfir* on one another. That is, they declare the opposing group to be unbelievers.

then he is to set free a believing slave. And if he comes from a people with whom you have a covenant, then the blood money must be paid to his people and a believing slave must be set free. And whoever does not have the means must fast for two consecutive months. A penance from Allah. Allah is the knower, the wise. ⁹³Whoever kills a believer deliberately, his reward is Gehenna forever. Allah is angry with him and he has cursed him and prepared for him an awful doom. ⁹⁴O you who believe, when you go forth to fight in the way of Allah, be careful to make distinctions, and do not say to one who offers you peace, You are not a believer, seeking the profits of this life. With Allah are abundant spoils. You were even like this before, but Allah has since then been gracious to you. Therefore take care to make distinctions. Allah is always informed of what you do. ⁹⁵Those of the believers who sit still, other than those who have an injury, are not equal with those who wage jihad in the way of Allah with their wealth and lives. Allah has conferred on those who wage jihad with their wealth and lives a rank above the sedentary. Allah has promised good to each, but he has bestowed on those who wage jihad a great reward above that of the sedentary, ⁹⁶Degrees of rank from him, and forgiveness and mercy. Allah is always forgiving, merciful. ⁹⁷Indeed, as for those whom the angels take while they wrong

themselves, they will ask, In what were you engaged? They will say, We were oppressed in the land. They will say, Wasn't Allah's earth spacious enough that you could have migrated within it? As for such people, their dwelling will be Gehenna, an evil destination, ⁹⁸Except for the weak men, and the women and children, who are unable to devise a plan and are not shown a way. ⁹⁹As for such people, it may be that Allah will forgive them. Allah is always merciful, forgiving. ¹⁰⁰Whoever emigrates for the sake of Allah will find much refuge and abundance in the earth, and whoever forsakes his home, a refugee for Allah and his messenger, and death overtakes him, his reward is then obligatory upon Allah. Allah is always forgiving, merciful. ¹⁰¹And when you travel in the land, it is no sin for you to shorten prayer if you fear that those who disbelieve may attack you. In truth, the unbelievers are an open enemy to you. ¹⁰²And when you are among them and arrange prayer for them, let only a party of them stand with you and let them take their weapons. Then when they have performed their prostrations let them fall to the rear and let another party come forward that has not prayed and let them pray with you, and let them take their precaution and their weapons. Those who disbelieve long for you to neglect your arms and your baggage so that they may attack you

93. On Gehenna, see 2:206, as also for 4:97, 4:115, 4:121, 4:140, 4:169.

94. Instead of "peace," the Warsh Qur'an has "greeting."[86]

95. This verse provides a clear refutation of those who maintain that the Qur'an's vision of jihad is primarily spiritual. If one must wage jihad with one's wealth and one's life, and those who do so are on a higher level than those who stay home, then clearly what is envisioned is participation in warfare, not a struggle to better oneself.

100. Here the Qur'an states the cardinal importance of "emigration for the cause of Allah," that is, moving to a new land with

the intention of bringing Islam to it. See also 4:66 and 4:89. The primary pattern for emigrants in Islamic tradition is the Hijra, Muhammad's move from Mecca to Medina, where for the first time he became a political and military leader. It is "obligatory" for Allah to reward emigrants; this is one of the Qur'an's few promises of reward for specific actions (see also 9:111).

101. Another confirmation of jihad in the Qur'an involving physical warfare. Why should anyone fear death or the fury of the unbelievers, or shorten his prayers in view of an impending attack by the unbelievers in a spiritual struggle? How can one kill a fellow Muslim by accident (4:92) in a spiritual struggle?

once and for all. It is no sin for you to lay aside your weapons if rain impedes you or you are sick. But take your precautions. Indeed, Allah is preparing a shameful punishment for the unbelievers. **103**When you have concluded the prayer, remember Allah, standing, sitting and reclining. And when you are in safety, observe proper prayer. Prayer at fixed times has been commanded for the believers. **104**Do not relent in pursuit of the enemy. If you are suffering, indeed, they are suffering even as you are suffering, and you hope from Allah what they cannot hope for. Allah is ever the knower, the wise. **105**Indeed, we reveal to you the book with the truth, so that you may judge between people by what Allah shows you. And do not advocate for the treacherous, **106**And seek forgiveness from Allah. Indeed, Allah is always forgiving, merciful. **107**And do not advocate for those who deceive themselves. Indeed, Allah does not love the one who is treacherous and sinful. **108**They try to hide from men and do not try to hide from Allah. He is with them when by night they have discussions that are displeasing to him. Allah always encompasses what they do. **109**Look, you are the ones who pleaded for them in the life of this world. But who will plead for them with Allah on the day of resurrection, or who will be their defender then? **110**Yet whoever does evil or wrongs his own soul, and then asks pardon of Allah, will find Allah forgiving, merciful. **111**Whoever commits sin, commits it only against himself. Allah is ever the knower, the wise. **112**And whoever commits an offense or sin and then throws it on the innocent, has burdened himself with falsehood and a flagrant crime. **113**If it had not been for the favor of Allah upon you, and his mercy, a group of them had resolved to mislead you, but they will mislead only themselves and they will not hurt you at all. Allah reveals the book and wisdom to you, and teaches you what you did not know. The favor of Allah toward you has been infinite. **114**There is no good in most of their secret discussions except for the one who calls for almsgiving and kindness and peace-making among the people. Whoever does that, seeking the good pleasure of Allah, we will grant him a great reward. **115**And whoever opposes the messenger after the guidance has been shown to him, and follows a way other than that of the believer, we establish for him what he himself has turned toward, and expose him to Gehenna, an evil destination. **116**Indeed, Allah does not forgive ascribing partners to him. He forgives everything except that of those whom he wills. Whoever ascribes partners to Allah has wandered far astray. **117**They invoke instead of him only females, they pray to no one else but Satan, a rebel **118**Whom Allah cursed, and he said,

---

104. The *Tafsir Anwarul Bayan* explains: "While the disbelievers (kuffar) will be subjected to the unending torment and distress in the abysses of Hell, the Muslims shall be rejoicing in the bliss and comforts of Heaven (Jannah), without the slightest worries and concerns. The disbelievers (kuffar) cannot aspire for these stages as these are promised exclusively to the Muslims. For this reason the Muslims have a much stronger incentive to fight and should do so with greater zest and zeal."[87]

115. In warning Muslims not to follow any path "other than that of the believer," the Qur'an here gives a principal foundation for the Islamic legal concept of *ijma*, consensus. This is the idea that once the Islamic community has agreed on a matter, it can be sure that Allah has guided it to the truth. Ibn Kathir explains: "The Ummah [community] of Muhammad is immune from error when they all agree on something, a miracle that serves to increase their honor, due to the greatness of their Prophet."[88] This idea can impede Islamic reform: when the community reaches consensus on an issue, the understanding of it becomes generally fixed.

Surely I will take an appointed shares of your slaves, **119**And surely I will lead them astray, and surely I will arouse desires in them, and surely I will command them and they will cut the cattle's ears, and surely I will command them and they will change Allah's creation. Whoever chooses Satan for a patron instead of Allah is indeed a loser, and his loss is clear. **120**He promises things to them and stirs up desires in them, and Satan makes promises only to fool them. **121**For such people, their dwelling will be Gehenna, and they will find no refuge from it. **122**But as for those who believe and do good works, we will bring them into gardens under which rivers flow, in which they will remain forever. It is a promise from Allah in truth, and who can be more truthful in speech than Allah? **123**It will not be in accord with your desires, nor the desires of the people of the book. He who does wrong will have the recompense of it, and will not find any protecting friend or helper against Allah. **124**And whoever does good works, whether male or female, and is a believer, will enter paradise, and they will not be wronged even as much as the groove in a date-stone. **125**Who is better in religion than he who submits to Allah while doing good and follows the tradition of Abraham, the *hanif*? Allah chose Abraham for friend. **126**To Allah belongs whatever is in the heavens and whatever is in the earth. Allah always encompasses all things. **127**They ask you about women. Say, Allah gives you a decree about them, and the book which has been recited to you, concerning female orphans and those to whom you do not give what is ordained for them though you desire to marry them, and the weak among children, and that you should deal justly with orphans. Whatever good you do, indeed, Allah is always aware of it. **128**If a woman fears ill treatment from her husband, or desertion, it is no sin for either of them if they make terms of peace between themselves. Peace is better. But greed has been made present in people's minds. If you do good and avoid evil, indeed, Allah is always informed of what you do. **129**You will not be able to deal equally between wives, however much you want to. But do not turn away altogether and leave her in suspense. If you do good and avoid evil, indeed, Allah is always forgiving, merciful. **130**But if they separate, Allah will compensate each of them out of his abundance. Allah is always all-embracing, all-knowing. **131**To Allah belongs whatever is in the heavens and whatever

---

119. In another affirmation of Allah's absolute control over everything, here he actively deceives and leads astray these unbelievers. "I will command them and they will change Allah's creation." A hadith illuminates the last clause: "Allah has cursed those women who practise tattooing and those women who have themselves tattooed, and those women who get their hair removed from their eyebrows and faces (except the beard and the mustache), and those who make artificial spaces between their teeth for beauty, whereby they change Allah's creation."[89]

123. The statement, "It will not be in accord with your desires, nor the desires of the people of the book" was revealed, says the *Tafsir al-Jalalayn*, "when the Muslims and the People of the Book were boasting against one another."[90] Allah, says Ibn Kathir, "then supported the argument of the Muslims against their opponents of the other religions."[91]

124. Paradise is promised to the true believers, both male and female, but while it is filled with the virginal houris, the women of paradise, for men (see 44:54), it is not described for women.

125. On *hanif*, see 2:135.

128. In a hadith, one of Muhammad's wives, Sawdah, "feared that the Messenger of Allah might divorce her."[92] So she said: "O Messenger of Allah! Do not divorce me; give my day to Aisha"— that is, take the night you are scheduled to spend in my bed and spend it instead with one of your other wives.[93] Another hadith has Aisha noting that Sawdah was a "heavyset woman."[94]

129. Allah says that Muslims will not be able to treat all their wives equally, but Aisha asserts that Muhammad was an exception; he "used to treat his wives equally."[95]

is in the earth. And we charged those who received the book before you, and you, that you keep your duty toward Allah. And if you disbelieve, indeed, to Allah belongs whatever is in the heavens and whatever is in the earth, and Allah is always absolute, the owner of praise. **132**To Allah belongs whatever is in the heavens and whatever is on the earth. And Allah is sufficient as defender. **133**If he wills, he can remove you, O people, and bring others. Allah is able to do that. **134**Whoever desires the reward of this world, the reward of this world and the hereafter is with Allah. Allah is always the hearer, the seer. **135**O you who believe, be strong in justice, witnesses for Allah, even if it is against yourselves or parents or relatives, whether a rich man or a poor man, for Allah is nearer to both. So do not follow your desires so that you do not fall away, and if you do fall away, then indeed, Allah is always informed of what you do. **136**O you who believe, believe in Allah and his messenger and the book which he has revealed to his messenger, and the book he revealed previously. Whoever disbelieves in Allah and his angels and his books and his messengers

and the last day, he has indeed wandered far astray. **137**Indeed, those who believe, then disbelieve and then believe, then disbelieve, and then increase in disbelief, Allah will never forgive them, nor will he guide them to a way. **138**Bring to the hypocrites the news that for them there is a painful doom, **139**Those who chose unbelievers for their friends instead of believers. Do they look for power from them? Indeed, all power belongs to Allah. **140**He has already revealed to you in the book that when you hear the signs of Allah rejected and derided, do not sit with them until they engage in some other conversation. Indeed, in that case, you would be like them. Indeed, Allah will gather hypocrites and unbelievers, all together, into Gehenna, **141**Those who are waiting and watching what happens to you, and if a victory comes to you from Allah, say, Aren't we with you? And if the unbelievers have a success, they say, Didn't we have mastery over you, and didn't we protect you from the believers? Allah will judge between you on the day of resurrection, and Allah will not give the unbelievers any way against the believers. **142**Indeed, the hypocrites try

137. Allah will not forgive those who leave Islam twice. A hadith has Muhammad strengthening this: "If somebody (a Muslim) discards his religion, kill him."[96]
139. Once again, unbelievers should not be taken as friends; this is repeated again at 4:144.
140. One should not consort with hypocrites while they ridicule Islam. The penalty for this became death in light of several ninth-century accounts of how Muhammad reacted to ridicule. Abu Afak was a poet who was over one hundred years old and who had mocked Muhammad in his verses. Muhammad asked the companions: "Who will deal with this rascal for me?" One of them murdered Abu Afak in his sleep.[97]
Of another poet who mocked him, Asma bint Marwan, Muhammad is depicted as crying out: "Who will rid me of Marwan's daughter?"[98] One of the companions, Umayr ibn Adi, went to her house that night, where he found her sleeping next to her children. The youngest, a nursing babe, was in her arms. But that didn't stop Umayr from murdering her and the baby as well. Muhammad commended him: "You have helped Allah and his apostle, O Umayr!"[99]

Of a third poet who mocked him, Muhammad again asked his companions: "Who is willing to kill Ka'b bin Al-Ashraf who has hurt Allah and His Apostle?"[100] One of them, Muhammad bin Maslama, answered: "O Allah's Apostle! Would you like that I kill him?"[101] Muhammad said that he would. Muhammad bin Maslama said: "Then allow me to say a (false) thing (i.e. to deceive Kab)."[102] Muhammad responded: "You may say it."[103] Muhammad bin Maslama duly lied to Ka'b, luring him into his trap, and murdered him.
141. Ibn Kathir explains: "'Never will Allah grant to the disbelievers a way (to triumph) over the believers', is in this life by being unable to exterminate the believers completely, although they sometimes gain victory over some Muslims. However, the Final Triumph will be for the believers in this life and the Hereafter."[104] This, along with 63:8, is the Qur'anic basis for the stipulation in Sharia that non-Muslims may not hold authority over Muslims, as this would be a kind of victory over them.

to fool Allah, but it is he who fools them. When they stand up to pray they perform the prayer lazily, in order to be seen by men, and are only a bit mindful of Allah, [143]Swerving in between, neither to these nor to those. He who Allah causes to go astray, you will not find a way for him. [144]O you who believe, do not choose unbelievers as friends instead of believers. Would you give Allah clear evidence against you? [145]Indeed, the hypocrites are in the lowest deep of the fire, and you will find no helper for them, [146]Except for those who repent and change their ways and hold fast to Allah and make their religion pure for Allah. Those people are with the believers. And Allah will bestow on the believers an immense reward. [147]What concern does Allah have for your punishment if you are thankful and believe? Allah has always been responsive, aware. [148]Allah does not love the utterance of harsh words except by someone who has been wronged. Allah is always the hearer, the knower. [149]If you do good openly or keep it secret, or forgive evil, indeed, Allah is always forgiving, powerful. [150]Indeed, those who disbelieve in Allah and his messengers, and try to make distinctions between Allah and his messengers, and say, We believe in some and disbelieve in others, and try to choose a way in between, [151]Such people are actually unbelievers, and for unbelievers we have prepared a shameful doom. [152]But those who believe in Allah and his messengers and make no distinction between any of them, he will give them their wages, and Allah has always been forgiving, merciful. [153]The people of the book ask you to cause a book to descend upon them from heaven. They asked a greater thing of Moses in previous times, for they said, Show us Allah plainly. A thunderbolt struck them for their wickedness. Then they chose the calf, after clear proofs had come unto them. And we forgave them that. And we bestowed clear authority on Moses. [154]And we caused the mountain to tower above them at their covenant, and we called upon them, Enter the gate, prostrate, and we called upon them, Do not transgress the Sabbath, and we took a firm covenant from them. [155]Then because of their breaking of their covenant, and their disbelieving in the signs of Allah, and their killing of the prophets wrongfully, and their saying, Our hearts are hardened, No, but Allah set a seal upon them for their disbelief, so that they do not believe, except for a few, [156]And because of their disbelief and of their speaking a tremendous slander against Mary, [157]And because of their saying, We killed the Messiah, Jesus son of Mary, the messenger of Allah, they did not kill him nor crucify him, but it seemed so to them, and indeed,

---

152. Those who make no distinction between the prophets of Allah will be rewarded. Says Ibn Kathir: "Allah threatens those who disbelieve in Him and in His Messengers, such as the Jews and Christians, who differentiate between Allah and His Messengers regarding faith...The Jews, may Allah curse them, believe in the Prophets, except Isa and Muhammad, peace be upon them. The Christians believe in the Prophets but reject their Final and Seal, and the most honored among the prophets, Muhammad, peace be upon him...Therefore, whoever rejects only one of Allah's Prophets, he will have disbelieved in all of them, because it is required from mankind to believe in every prophet whom Allah sent to the people of the earth."[105]

Instead of, "He will give them their wages," the Warsh Qur'an has, "We will give them their wages."[106]

157. This is the most significant Qur'anic appropriation from Christian Gnosticism. In the *Gnostic Second Treatise of the Great Seth*, which dates from the third century, Jesus says: "For my death, which they think happened, (happened) to them in their error and blindness, since they nailed their man unto their death...It was another, their father, who drank the gall and the vinegar; it was not I."[107]

For the Gnostics, this denial was rooted in an abhorrence of the material world and the flesh, which led to their denying altogether the Christian doctrine of the Incarnation; Muslims, on the other

those who disagree about this are in doubt about it, they have no knowledge of it except pursuit of a supposition, they did not kill him for certain. **158**But Allah took him up to himself. Allah has always been mighty, wise. **159**There is not one of the people of the book who will not believe in him before his death, and on the day of resurrection, he will be a witness against them, **160**Because of the wrongdoing of the Jews, we forbade them good things which had been lawful for them, and because they kept many people from Allah's way, **161**And for their taking usury when they were forbidden to take it, and of their devouring people's wealth by means of false pretenses, we have prepared for those among them who disbelieve a painful doom. **162**But those among them who are firm in knowledge and the believers believe in what is revealed to you, and in what was revealed before you, especially those who are diligent in prayer and those who give alms, the believers in Allah and the last day. Upon these people we will bestow an immense reward. **163**Indeed, we inspire

you as we inspired Noah and the prophets after him, as we inspired Abraham and Ishmael and Isaac and Jacob and the tribes, and Jesus and Job and Jonah and Aaron and Solomon, and as we gave the Psalms to David, **164**And messengers we have mentioned to you before and messengers we have not mentioned to you, and Allah spoke directly to Moses, **165**Messengers of good cheer and of warning, so that mankind would have no argument against Allah after the messengers. Allah has always been mighty, wise. **166**But Allah bears witness regarding what he has revealed to you, he has revealed it in his knowledge, and the angels also testify. And Allah is sufficient witness. **167**Indeed, those who disbelieve and hinder people from the way of Allah, they indeed have wandered far astray. **168**Indeed, those who disbelieve and deal in wrongdoing, Allah will never forgive them, nor will he guide them to a road, **169**Except the road of Gehenna, in which they will remain forever. And that is always easy for Allah. **170**O mankind, the messenger has come to you

hand, deny the Crucifixion because, in their view, Allah's prophet cannot suffer defeat.

Ibn Kathir argues that "when Allah sent 'Isa [Jesus] with proofs and guidance, the Jews, may Allah's curses, anger, torment and punishment be upon them, envied him because of his prophethood and obvious miracles."[108] Consumed by this envy, Ibn Kathir continues, the Jews stirred up "the king of Damascus at that time, a Greek polytheist who worshipped the stars" to order his deputy in Jerusalem to arrest Jesus.[109] Jesus, perceiving this, asked those with him, "Who volunteers to be made to look like me, for which he will be my companion in Paradise?"[110] A young man volunteered, whereupon "Allah made the young man look exactly like 'Isa, while a hole opened in the roof of the house, and 'Isa was made to sleep and ascended to heaven while asleep."[111] Then "those surrounding the house saw the man who looked like 'Isa, they thought that he was 'Isa. So they took him at night, crucified him and placed a crown of thorns on his head. The Jews then boasted that they killed 'Isa and some Christians accepted their false claim, due to their ignorance and lack of reason."[112]

Other sources offer different theories. Some Islamic authorities claim Jesus was with seventy of his disciples when the guards came to arrest him, and all seventy were made to look just like Jesus; one stepped forward and was crucified. The *Ruhul Ma'ani*, however,

identifies the one who was made to look like Jesus and crucified as the one who betrayed him for thirty dirhams—Judas.[113] Another Muslim source says it was a sentry who was guarding Jesus after his arrest.

159. The assertion that "there is not one of the people of the book who will not believe in him before his death" has been taken to mean that Jesus will return to earth. According to a hadith put in Muhammad's mouth, "The Hour will not be established until the son of Mary (i.e. Jesus) descends amongst you as a just ruler, he will break the cross, kill the pigs, and abolish the Jizya tax."[114] That is, he will abolish the subservient dhimmi status of the non-Muslims and Islamize the world: "During his time, Allah will destroy all religions except Islam and Allah will destroy Al-Masih Ad-Dajjal (the False Messiah)."[115]

162. The Jews who are "well-grounded in knowledge" believe in Muhammad and Islam. The "unbelievers among the people of the book," that is, Jews and Christians who do not become Muslims, are the "most vile of created beings" (98:6).

168. Instead of, "Indeed, those who disbelieve and deal in wrongdoing," the Shi'ite Bankipur Qur'an manuscript has, "Indeed, those who disbelieve and have deprived Muhammad's family of its due."[116] See 2:59 and the Appendix: Two Apocryphal Shi'ite Suras.

with the truth from your Lord. Therefore believe, it is better for you. But if you disbelieve, still, indeed to Allah belongs whatever is in the heavens and the earth. Allah is always the knower, the wise one. **171**O people of the book, do not exaggerate in your religion or say anything about Allah except the truth. The Messiah, Jesus son of Mary, was only a messenger of Allah, and his word that he conveyed to Mary, and a spirit from him. So believe in Allah and his messengers, and do not say Three, Stop, it is better for you. Allah is only one God. It is far removed from his transcendent majesty that he should have a son. Everything that is in the heavens and everything that is on the earth is his. And Allah is sufficient as defender. **172**The Messiah will never disdain to be a slave of Allah, nor will the favored angels. Whoever disdains his service and is proud, all such people he will bring before him, **173**Then, for those who believed and did good works, to them he will pay their wages in full, giving them more from his bounty, and as for those who were disdainful and proud, them he will punish with a painful doom. And they will not find for them any protecting friend or helper against Allah. **174**O mankind, now a proof from your Lord has come to you, and we have sent down to you a clear light. **175**As for those who believe in Allah, and hold fast to him, he will cause them to enter into his mercy and grace, and will guide them to him by a straight road. **176**They ask you for a legal decision. Say, Allah advises you with regard to *kalala*. If a man dies childless and he has a sister, hers is half the inheritance, and he would have inherited from her if she had died childless. And if there are two sisters, then two-thirds of the inheritance is theirs, and if they are brothers, men and women, to the male is the equivalent of the share of two females. Allah explains to you, so that you do not err. Allah is the knower of all things.

---

171. Allah warns Christians to remember that Jesus was a created being and not to say "Three," that is, not to say God is a Trinity. Ibn Kathir echoes the Qur'an itself (5:116) in saying that the Christians elevated Jesus "and his mother to be gods with Allah"; the actual Christian Trinity of God the Father, Son, and Holy Spirit is not envisioned in the Qur'an.[117] It is "far removed from his transcendent majesty that he should have a son" because having a son would imply that he is insufficient for his tasks and needs a helper, but Allah "is sufficient."

176. This renewed discussion of inheritance laws belongs with 4:11 and may indicate a dislocation of the text or the addition of a separate tradition from another source. A hadith states that this was the last portion of the Qur'an to be revealed: "The last Sura (i.e. part of a Sura) which was revealed was the last Verses of Sura-an-Nisa: 'They ask you for a legal decision.'"[118] This suggests that this sura may originally have circulated without this verse, or that this verse was part of a separate document, such that its tardy addition had to be explained. On *kalala*, see 4:12.

SURA 5

The Table

Al-Maida

Introduction

Most of this sura, which is traditionally dated from the Medinan period, is devoted to castigating the Jews and the Christians for twisting the revelations they received, and committing various sins and offenses. It greatly intensifies the criticism of them that was a recurring theme throughout suras 2, 3, and 4. The title is taken from 5:112–115, in which the disciples ask Jesus to ask Allah to send down a table from heaven laden with food, and he complies, a vestigial account of the Christian Eucharist that contains some telling clues regarding the Qur'an's origins in relation to Christianity.

John of Damascus includes a mention of this sura in his criticism of what are known today as various chapters of the Qur'an, but which he never identifies as such: "This Muhammad, as it has been mentioned, composed many frivolous tales, to each of which he assigned a name… Again, Muhammad mentions the text of the Table. He says that Christ requested from God a table and it was given to him, for God, he said, told him: 'I have given to you and those with you an incorruptible table.'"[1]

As John never mentions that this is a sura of the Qur'an (or the Qur'an as such), and mentions other chapters of the Qur'an as if they were distinct books, it is possible that they were actually separate books at the time he was writing (around 730) and were incorporated into the Qur'an later.

According to Bell, this sura shows indications of "many alterations and additions."[2]

---

1 John of Damascus, 487
2 Bell, I, 92

The Table

IN THE NAME OF ALLAH, THE COMPASSIONATE, THE MERCIFUL.

1O you who believe, fulfil your obligations. The grazing livestock is made lawful for you except for what is announced to you, game being unlawful while you are on the pilgrimage. Indeed, Allah commands what he pleases. **2**O you who believe, do not profane Allah's monuments, nor the sacred month, nor the offerings, nor the garlands, nor those journeying to the sacred house, seeking the favor and pleasure of their Lord. But when you have left the sacred areas, then go hunting. And do not let your hatred of a people who stopped your going to the sacred mosque seduce you to transgress, but help one another to righteousness and pious duty. Do not help one another to sin and transgression, but keep your duty to Allah. Indeed, Allah is severe in punishment. **3**Forbidden to you are carrion and blood and the flesh of pigs, and what has been dedicated to any other than Allah, and the strangled, and what was beaten to death, and what died from falling from a height, and what has been killed by horns, and what was devoured by wild beasts, except for what you make lawful, and what has been sacrificed to idols. And that you swear by divining arrows. This is an abomination. This day those who disbelieve are in despair over your religion, so do not fear them, fear me. This day I have perfected your religion for you and completed my favor to you, and have chosen Islam as the religion for you. Whoever is forced by hunger to sin against his will, indeed, Allah is forgiving, merciful. **4**They ask you what is made lawful for them. Say, Good things are made lawful for you. And those beasts and birds of prey that you have trained the way hounds are trained, you teach them what Allah taught you, so eat what they catch for you and mention Allah's name upon it, and observe your duty to Allah. Indeed, Allah is quick to take account. **5**This day, good things are made lawful for you. The food of those who have received the book is lawful for you, and your food is lawful for them. And so are the virtuous women of the believers and the virtuous women of those who received the book before you when you give them their marriage portions and live with them in honor, not in fornication, nor taking them as secret lovers. Whoever denies the faith, his work is vain, and he will be among the losers in the hereafter. **6**O you who believe, when you rise up for prayer, wash your faces, and your hands up to the elbows, and lightly rub your heads and your feet up to the ankles. And if you are unclean, purify yourselves. And if you are sick or on a journey, or one of you has just relieved himself, or you have had contact with women, and you find not water, then go to clean high ground and rub your faces and your hands with some of it. Allah would not place a burden on you, but he would

---

1. The sura begins with a series of exhortations to Muslims to obey his commands regarding food, religious observances, and sexual morality.

5. Muslim men are permitted to marry "the virtuous women of the believers and the virtuous women of those who received the book before you." The Qur'an says nothing about Muslim women being permitted to marry men from the people of the book; this is prohibited in Islamic law as part of the subjugated status of the dhimmis, the "protected people," in Islam.

Traditionally a man takes his wife into his own household but not vice versa. The prohibition of Muslim women marrying non-Muslim men, and the allowance of Muslim men marrying non-Muslim women, means that the Islamic community will always be in a position to grow, while the non-Muslim community declines.

purify you and would perfect his favor upon you, so that you may give thanks. ⁷Remember Allah's favor upon you and his covenant by which he bound you when you said, We hear and obey, and keep your duty to Allah. Indeed, he knows what is in the hearts. ⁸O you who believe, be steadfast witnesses for Allah in equity, and do not let hatred of any people seduce you so that you deal unjustly. Deal justly, that is nearer to your duty. Observe your duty to Allah. Indeed, Allah is informed of what you do. ⁹Allah has promised those who believe and do good works, theirs will be forgiveness and immense reward. ¹⁰And they who disbelieve and deny our signs, such people are rightful companions of the blaze. ¹¹O you who believe, remember Allah's favor to you, how a people intended to stretch out their hands against you but he kept their hands from you, and keep your duty to Allah. In Allah let believers put their trust. ¹²Allah made a covenant of old with the children of Israel and we raised among them twelve chieftains, and Allah said, Indeed, I am

with you. If you establish prayer and give alms, and believe in my messengers and support them, and lend a good loan to Allah, surely I will forgive your sins, and surely I will bring you into gardens under which rivers flow. Whoever among you disbelieves after this will go astray from a plain road. ¹³And because of their breaking their covenant, we have cursed them and hardened their hearts. They change words from their context and forget a part of what they were reminded about. You will not stop discovering treachery from all except a few of them. But bear with them and forgive them. Indeed, Allah loves the kindly. ¹⁴And with those who say: Indeed, we are Christians, we made a covenant, but they forgot a part of what they were reminded about. Therefore we have stirred up enmity and hatred among them until the day of resurrection, when Allah will inform them of their handiwork. ¹⁵O people of the book, now our messenger has come to you, explaining to you much of what you used to hide in the book, and forgiving much. Now light from Allah

10. "The blaze" is *al-jahim*, which Zamakhshari, attributing the tradition to Ibn Abbas, identifies as the level of hell reserved for the Sabeans (see 2:62).[1]

13. Ibn Kathir says of the Jews and Christians: "When they broke these promises and covenants, Allah cursed them as a consequence and expelled them from His grace and mercy. He also sealed their hearts from receiving guidance and the religion of truth, beneficial knowledge and righteous actions."[2] This would seem to preclude even the possibility of repentance.

According to the *Tafsir al-Jalalayn*, "They change words from their context and forget a part of what they were reminded about" refers to the Jews' distorting passages "in the Torah which contain the description of Muhammad and other things, moving them from the places where Allah put them by changing them," and to their forgetting what they "were commanded to do in the Torah in respect of following Muhammad when he came."[3] There is no textual evidence, much less any evidence from any Jewish theological tradition, that anyone remotely like Muhammad was ever discussed in the Torah, but this charge that references to him were maliciously removed is nonetheless central to the Islamic critique of Judaism.

Allah warns Muslims that they will find Jews to be just as treacherous today but nonetheless tells Muslims to forgive them.

According to the *Ruhul Ma'ani*, this forgiveness should be extended only to those Jews who become Muslims or agree to pay the jizya and accept subservient dhimmi status in accord with 9:29. Others, however, suggest that this command to forgive was abrogated by the imperative to wage jihad against the unbelievers that came later in Muhammad's career. Ibn Kathir records the view that "this Ayah was abrogated with Allah's statement, 'Fight those who do not believe in Allah or the last day'" (9:29).[4]

14. As far as the Qur'an is concerned, the divisions among Christians demonstrate the falsity of the religion—a proposition for which Jesus stated the obverse: "By this all men will know that you are my disciples, if you have love for one another" (John 13:35).

Says Ibn Kathir, "Indeed, the numerous Christian sects have always been enemies and adversaries of each other, accusing each other of heresy and cursing each other... Each sect among them will continue to accuse the other of disbelief and heresy in this life and on the Day when the Witnesses will come forth."[5]

15. The Jews and Christians should accept Islam, as it reveals what they have concealed. In several places in the Qur'an, Allah presents himself as the arbiter between these warring Christian sects, clearing up questions that are disputed among them. Thus when asserting that Jesus was not crucified, but someone who looked like him was crucified in his stead (a position held by some

and a clear book has come to you, **16**By which Allah guides him who seeks his good pleasure to paths of peace. He brings them out of darkness to light by his decree, and guides them to a straight path. **17**They indeed have disbelieved who say, Indeed, Allah is the Messiah, son of Mary. Say, Who then can do anything against Allah, if he had willed to destroy the Messiah son of Mary, and his mother and everyone on earth? To Allah belongs the dominion of the heavens and the earth and all that is between them. He creates what he wills. And Allah is able to do all things. **18**The Jews and Christians say, We are sons of Allah and his loved ones. Say: Why then does he punish you for your sins? No, you are just mortals of his creating. He forgives those whom he wills, and punishes those whom he wills. To Allah belongs the dominion of the heavens and the earth and all that is between them, and to him is the journeying. **19**O people of the book, now our messenger has come to you to make things clear to you after an interval between the messengers, so that you would not say, No messenger of good news or any warner came to us. Now a messenger of good news and a warner has come to you. Allah is able to do all things. **20**And when Moses said to his people, O my people, remember Allah's

favor to you, how he placed prophets among you, and he made you kings, and gave you what he did not give to anyone among the worlds. **21**O my people, go into the holy land that Allah has ordained for you. Do not turn back, for then you will turn back as losers. **22**They said, O Moses, indeed, a giant people are there, and indeed, we are not going in until they go forth from there. When they go forth from there, then we will enter. **23**Then two of those who feared spoke out, to whom Allah had granted favor, Enter in upon them by the gate, for if you enter by it, indeed, you will be victorious. So put your trust, if you are indeed believers. **24**They said, O Moses, we will never enter while they are in it. So you and your Lord go and fight. We will sit here. **25**He said, My Lord, I have control of no one but myself and my brother, so distinguish between us and the wrongdoing people. **26**He said, For this the land will surely be forbidden to them for forty years that they will wander on the earth, bewildered. So do not grieve over the wrongdoing people. **27**But recite to them with truth the tale of the two sons of Adam, how they each offered a sacrifice, and it was accepted from one of them but was not accepted from the other. He said, I will surely kill you. He answered, Allah accepts only from those

Gnostic Christian sects), Allah says, "Those who disagree about this are in doubt about it, they have no knowledge of it except pursuit of a supposition, they did not kill him not for certain" (4:157).

17. Those Christians who believe that "Allah is the Messiah, son of Mary" have disbelieved. The Arabic word used here is *kafara*, it is a form of *kufr*, unbelief. Islamic spokesmen in the West frequently assert that the Qur'an never refers to Christians as infidels or unbelievers, when in fact this verse is quite clear that those who believe in the divinity of Christ are unbelievers indeed.

18. To those Jews and Christians who claim to be God's children, Allah directs the messenger to retort, "Why then does he punish you for your sins?" The Qur'an's assumption that a father would not punish his children for their wrongdoing is striking. Whatever the reasoning behind it, it makes clear that in Islam, God is not a father to human beings. To a pious Muslim, a prayer such as the Our

Father prayer in Christianity would be utterly alien. A knowledgeable and believing Muslim would consider it presumptuous in the extreme to call Allah his Father; instead, Allah is the master of the universe, and human beings are his slaves. The hallmark of Islamic religious observance is external obedience, not likeness with the divine through an interior transformation.

20. The account that begins here, of Moses telling the children of Israel to enter the promised land and their refusal, is a retelling of the story told in Numbers 13:1-14:45.

21. This verse and 17:104 are often invoked today to show that, despite all the conflict over Israel, the Qur'an actually promises the land of Israel to the Jews. However, the curse on the Jews in 5:13 negates the possibility of their continuing to be the recipients of the promise in this verse. And in 14:13, the Muslims are made to dwell in the land after the "wrongdoers" are expelled.

who fear Allah. **28**Even if you stretch out your hand against me to kill me, I will not stretch out my hand against you to kill you, indeed, I fear Allah, the Lord of the worlds. **29**Indeed, I would rather you would bear the punishment of the sin against me and your own sin and become one of the companions of the fire. That is the reward of evildoers. **30**But his mind imposed on him the killing of his brother, so he killed him and became one of the losers. **31**Then Allah sent a raven scratching the ground, to show him how to hide his brother's naked corpse. He said, Woe to me, am I not able to be like this raven and so hide my brother's naked corpse? And he became repentant. **32**For that reason, we decreed for the children of Israel that whoever kills a human being for anything other than manslaughter or corruption on the earth, it will be as if he had killed all mankind, and whoever saves the life of one person, it will be as if he had saved the life of all mankind.

Our messengers came to them of old with clear proofs, but afterwards, indeed, many of them committed excesses on earth. **33**The only reward for those who make war upon Allah and his messenger and struggle to sow corruption on earth will be that they will be killed or crucified, or have their hands and feet cut off on opposite sides, or be expelled from the land. Such will be their degradation in this world, and in the hereafter, theirs will be an awful doom. **34**Except for those who repent before you overpower them. For be aware that Allah is forgiving, merciful. **35**O you who believe, be mindful of your duty to Allah, and seek the way of approach to him, and wage jihad in his way, so that you may succeed. **36**As for those who disbelieve, indeed, if all that is on earth were theirs, and the same amount again with it, to ransom them from doom on the day of resurrection, it would not be accepted from them. Theirs will be a painful doom. **37**They will want to come forth

32. This is one of the most oft-quoted verses of the Qur'an, the one that Western non-Muslim leaders refer to frequently in order to establish that Islam is a religion of peace. There is, however, less to it than Western leaders and Islamic apologists claim. It is not a general prohibition of killing: there are big exceptions to the prohibition on killing, for "manslaughter or corruption on the earth." Also, this prohibition is not a general command but is specifically directed at the children of Israel. After it was given, "many of them committed excesses on earth," so all this passage is really saying is that Allah gave a command to the children of Israel, and they transgressed against it.

Some Islamic authorities interpret this passage in a supremacist manner, as applying only to Muslims. The eighth-century Muslim jurist Sa'id bin Jubayr is said to have explained: "He who allows himself to shed the blood of a Muslim, is like he who allows shedding the blood of all people. He who forbids shedding the blood of one Muslim, is like he who forbids shedding the blood of all people."[6]

The Qur'an itself doesn't explain why Cain's killing of Abel would lead to this equation of the killing of one person with the killing of the entire people. This injunction also comes from Jewish tradition. William St. Clair Tisdall noted that the substance of this verse was taken from the *Mishnah Sanhedrin*: "As regards Cain who killed his brother, the Lord addressing him does not say, 'The voice of thy brother's blood crieth out,' but 'the voice of his bloods', meaning not his blood alone, but that of his descendants; and this to show that since Adam was created alone, so he that kills an Israelite is, by the plural here used, counted as if he had killed the world at large; and he who saves a single Israelite is counted as if he had saved the whole world."[7]

This exposition of Genesis makes the connection clear between the killing of Abel and the killing of the entire people, pointing out that the Biblical text refers to Abel's "bloods," that is, his descendants. But the Qur'an leaves this out, leaping without explanation from the murder of Abel to the warning about killing the whole people.

33. This verse continues from 5:32 and makes clear the dire punishments that are prescribed for the corruption and transgressions of the children of Israel, and a warning to the Jews to stop their bad behavior. Seen in its light, the celebrated passage 5:32 is explaining what must be done with Jews who reject the messenger and commit the vague sin of spreading corruption on earth. Contrary to popular belief in the West, the passage is not dictating lofty moral principles.

35. "Wage jihad" is *jahidoo*, or "struggle." See 2:218.

from the fire, but they will not come forth from it. Theirs will be a lasting doom. **38**As for the thief, both male and female, cut off their hands. It is the reward of their own deeds, an exemplary punishment from Allah. Allah is mighty, wise. **39**But whoever repents after his wrongdoing and changes, indeed, Allah will forgive him. Indeed, Allah is forgiving, merciful. **40**Don't you know that to Allah belongs the dominion over the heavens and the earth? He punishes those whom he wills, and forgives those whom he wills. Allah is able to do all things. **41**O messenger, do not let those who compete with one another in the race to disbelief grieve you, of those who say with their mouths, We believe, but their hearts do not believe, and of the Jews, listeners for the sake of falsehood, listeners on behalf of other people who do not come to you, changing words from their context and saying: If this is given to you, receive it, but if this is not given to you, then beware. He whom Allah dooms to sin, you will not help him at all against Allah. Those are the ones for whom the will of Allah is that he does not cleanse their hearts. Theirs will be disgrace in this world, and in the hereafter an awful doom, **42**Listeners for the sake of falsehood. Greedy for illicit gain. If, then, they appeal to you, judge between them or decline to do so. If you decline, then they cannot harm you at all. But if you judge, judge between them with justice. Indeed, Allah loves the just. **43**How do they come to you for judgment when they have the Torah, in which Allah has delivered judgment? Yet even after that, they turn away. Such people are not believers. **44**Indeed, we revealed the Torah, in which is guidance and light, by which the prophets who submitted judged the Jews, and the rabbis and the priests by the portions of Allah's book that they were bidden to observe, and to which were they witnesses. So do not fear mankind, but fear me. And my signs for a little gain. Whoever does not judge by what Allah has revealed, such people are unbelievers. **45**And we prescribed for them in it, Life for life, and eye for eye, and nose for nose, and ear for ear, and tooth for tooth, and retaliation for injuries. But whoever forgoes it, this will be expiation for him. Whoever does not judge by what Allah has revealed, such people are wrongdoers. **46**And we caused Jesus, son of Mary, to follow in their footsteps, confirming what was before him in the Torah, and we gave him the Gospel, in which is guidance and light, confirming what was before it in the Torah, a guidance and a warning to those who fear Allah.

---

38. This lone legal directive amid a lengthy section warning of hellfire and decrying the misdeeds of the Jews and Christians (5:35-86) may be evidence of textual dislocation. In a hadith, Muhammad is depicted as adding a divine curse to the already draconian punishment for theft specified in this verse: "Let there be the curse of Allah upon the thief who steals an egg and his hand is cut off, and steals a rope and his hand is cut off."[8]

41. Allah consoles the messenger for the Jews' and Christians' rejection of him, and he and his message are again presented as the crown and completion of the messages brought to them by their prophets.

44. In the Torah are "guidance and light." However, Ibn Kathir states that Allah "chastises the Jews for their false ideas and deviant desires to abandon what they believe is true in their Book, and which they claim is their eternal Law that they are always commanded to adhere to. Yet, they do not adhere to the Tawrah, but they prefer other laws over it, although they believe that these other laws are not correct and do not apply to them."[9]

45. This verse establishes the Islamic principle of *qisas*, legal retribution (see also 2:178), in which retaliation or punishment is to be in kind. The "eye for an eye" principle is indeed in the Torah (Exodus 21:23-25). In the Qur'an, however, there is no mitigating element comparable to "You shall love your neighbor as yourself" (Leviticus 19:18) or, in the New Testament, Jesus's statement: "You have heard that it was said, 'An eye for an eye and a tooth for a tooth.' But I say to you, Do not resist one who is evil. But if anyone strikes you on the right cheek, turn to him the other also" (Matthew 5:38-9). See also 2:194 and 16:126.

46. The Gospel is assumed to be a book that Allah gave to his prophet Jesus, not records of the salvific actions of the incarnate

[47]Let the people of the Gospel judge by what Allah has revealed in it. Whoever does not judge by what Allah has revealed, such are transgressors. [48]And we revealed to you the book with the truth, confirming whatever book was before it, and a watcher over it. So judge between them by what Allah has revealed, and do not follow their desires away from the truth that has come to you. For each person, we have established a divine law and a way of life. If Allah had willed, he could have made you one community. But so that he might test you by what he has given you. So compete one with another in good works. To Allah you will all return, and he will then inform you of what you disagree about. [49]So judge between them by what Allah has revealed, and do not follow their desires, but beware of them, so that they do not seduce you from some part of what Allah has revealed to you. And if they turn away, then know that Allah's will is to afflict them for some sin of theirs. Indeed, many of mankind are transgressors. [50]Is it a judgment from the time of ignorance that they are seeking? Who is better than Allah for judgment to a people that has certainty? [51]O you who believe, do not take the Jews and the Christians for friends. They are friends of one another. He among you who takes them for friends is of them. Indeed, Allah does not guide wrongdoing people. [52]And you see those in whose heart is a disease race toward them, saying, We are afraid that a change of fortune might happen to us. And it may happen that Allah will grant victory, or a commandment from his presence. Then will they repent of their secret thoughts. [53]Then the believers will say, Are these the people who swore by Allah their most binding oaths that they were surely with you? Their works have failed, and they have become the losers. [54]O you who believe, whoever among you becomes a renegade from his religion, Allah will bring a people whom he loves and who loves him, humble toward believers, harsh toward unbelievers, waging jihad in the way of Allah, and not fearing the blame of any blamer. That is the favor of Allah, which he gives to those whom He wills. Allah is all-embracing, all-knowing. [55]Your guardian can only be Allah and his messenger and those who believe, who establish prayer and give alms, and bow down. [56]And whoever takes Allah and his messenger and those who believe for guardians, Indeed, the party of Allah, they are the victorious. [57]O you who believe, do not choose for guardians those who received the book before you, and from among the unbelievers who make a joke and mockery of your religion. But keep your duty to Allah if you are true believers. [58]And when you call to prayer, they take it for a joke and mockery. That is because they are a people who do not understand. [59]Say, O people of the book, do you blame us for anything other than the fact that we

---

Son of God, as in Christianity. In it is "guidance and light," indicating that at the time the Qur'an was compiled, the believers assumed that the Christian Scriptures were not corrupted.

47. This also seems to suggest that at the time the Qur'an was compiled, the believers assumed that the Christian Scriptures did indeed confirm the message of the Qur'an. Because this is not the case, today it is common Islamic teaching that the New Testament as we have it is not the original but has been altered by rebellious Christians to reflect their false doctrines.

51. Ibn Kathir explains: "Allah forbids His believing servants from having Jews and Christians as friends, because they are the enemies of Islam and its people, may Allah curse them."[10]

55. "Guardian" is *walaya*. In Shi'ite Islam, this is known as the Walaya Verse and is considered to refer to Ali ibn Abi Talib, designating him as the successor of Muhammad, that is, the guardian of the faithful. Sunnis reject this view.

believe in Allah and in what is revealed to us and what was revealed previously, and because most of you are transgressors? **60**Shall I tell you of a worse case than theirs for retribution with Allah? He whom Allah has cursed, on whom his wrath has fallen, and of whose sort, Allah has turned some into apes and pigs, and slaves of *taghut*. Such people are in a worse condition and farther astray from the sound path. **61**When they come to you,

they say, We believe, but they came in unbelief and they left in it, and Allah knows best what they were hiding. **62**And you see many of them competing with one another in sin and transgression and their devouring of illicit gain. Indeed what they do is evil. **63**Why don't the rabbis and priests forbid them to speak evil and devour illicit gain? Indeed their handiwork is evil. **64**The Jews say, Allah's hand is chained. Their hands are chained

---

60. A reminder that some of those "whom Allah has cursed, him on whom his wrath has fallen," were transformed into "apes and pigs." See 2:63. On *taghut*, see 2:256.

64. Why don't the Jews' rabbis stop their evil behavior (5:63)? They even dare to say that "Allah's hand is chained." It is unclear what Jewish concept, if any, the Qur'an is referring to in this case.

Ibn Kathir comments: "Allah states that the Jews, may Allah's continuous curses descend on them until the Day of Resurrection, describe Him as a miser. Allah is far holier than what they attribute to Him."[11] The *Tafsir al-Jalalayn* likewise says that in this the Jews are "implying that He is unable to send provision to them and that He is miserly."[12]

The idea, however, that Allah's hand is not chained and must not be considered to be chained proceeds from the assumption that he is absolute will, unbound in any conceivable way. Allah's unchained hand is a vivid image of divine freedom. Such a deity can be bound by no laws. Muslim theologians argued during the long controversy with the heretical Islamic Mu'tazilite sect, which exalted human reason beyond the point that the eventual victors were willing to tolerate, that Allah was absolutely free to act as he pleased. He was thus not bound to govern the universe according to consistent and observable laws. "He cannot be questioned about what he does" (21:23).

Accordingly, there was no point to observing the workings of the physical world; there was no reason to expect that any pattern to its workings would be consistent or even discernible. If Allah could not be counted on to be consistent, why waste time observing the order of things? It could change tomorrow. Stanley Jaki, a Catholic priest and physicist, explains that it was the renowned Sufi thinker al-Ghazali who "denounced natural laws, the very objective of science, as a blasphemous constraint upon the free will of Allah."[13] Al-Ghazali (1058-1111), although himself a philosopher, delivered what turned out to be the coup de grace to Islamic philosophical investigation, at least as a vibrant mainstream force, in his monumental attack on the very idea of Islamic philosophy: *The Incoherence of the Philosophers*.

Muslim philosophers such as Avicenna and Averroes, according to al-Ghazali, were not intellectual trailblazers worthy of respect and careful consideration. In positing that there could be truth that was outside of or even contradicted what Allah had revealed in the Qur'an, they had shown themselves to be nothing more than heretics who should be put to death and their books burned. Al-Ghazali accused them of "denial of revealed laws and religious confessions" and "rejection of the details of religious and sectarian

[teaching], believing them to be man-made laws and embellished tricks."[14] He declared that the doctrines of Muslim philosophers such as al-Farabi and Avicenna "challenge the [very] principles of religion."[15]

Al-Ghazali, said scholar Tilman Nagel, "was inspired by a notion that we frequently see in Islam's intellectual history: the notion that everything human beings can possibly know is already contained in the Koran and the *hadith*; only naïve people can be made to believe that there is knowledge beyond them."[16]

At the end of *The Incoherence of the Philosophers*, al-Ghazali reveals how high the stakes are: "If someone says: 'You have explained the doctrines of these [philosophers]; do you then say conclusively that they are infidels and that the killing of those who uphold their beliefs is obligatory?'"[17] He then concludes that they should indeed be pronounced infidels, and therefore, presumably, be executed.

Although Islamic philosophy lived on, it was never the same; it had effectively been put to death itself. After al-Ghazali and the defeat of the relatively rationalistic Mu'tazilite party, there was no large-scale attempt to apply the laws of reason or consistency to Allah, or, therefore, to the world he had created. Fr. Jaki explains: "Muslim mystics decried the notion of scientific law (as formulated by Aristotle) as blasphemous and irrational, depriving as it does the Creator of his freedom."[18] The social scientist Rodney Stark notes the existence of "a major theological bloc within Islam that condemns all efforts to formulate natural laws as blasphemy in that they deny Allah's freedom to act."[19]

The great twelfth-century Jewish philosopher Moses Maimonides explained orthodox Islamic cosmology in similar terms, noting that Islamic thinkers of his day assumed "the possibility that an existing being should be larger or smaller than it really is, or that it should be different in form and position from what it really is; e.g., a man might have the height of a mountain, might have several heads, and fly in the air; or an elephant might be as small as an insect, or an insect as huge as an elephant. This method of admitting possibilities is applied to the whole Universe."[20]

Relatively early in its history, therefore, science was deprived in the Islamic world of the philosophical foundation it needed in order to flourish. It found that philosophical foundation only in Christian Europe, where it was assumed that God was good and had constructed the universe according to consistent and observable laws. Such an idea would have been for pious Muslims tantamount to saying, "Allah's hand is chained."

and they are cursed for saying this. No, but both his hands are spread out wide in bounty. He bestows it as he wills. What has been revealed to you from your Lord is certain to increase the insolence and disbelief of many of them, and we have sown enmity and hatred among them until the day of resurrection. As often as they light a fire for war, Allah extinguishes it. Their effort is for corruption on the earth, and Allah does not love corrupters. **65**If only the people of the book would believe and fear Allah, surely we would forgive their sins and surely we would bring them into gardens of delight. **66**If they had observed the Torah and the Gospel and what was revealed to them from their Lord, they would surely have been nourished from above and from beneath their feet. Among them are people who are moderate, but many of them are of evil conduct. **67**O messenger, make known what has been revealed to you from your Lord, for if you do not do it, you will not have conveyed his message. Allah will protect you from mankind. Indeed, Allah does not guide the disbelieving people. **68**Say, O people of the book, you have nothing until you observe the Torah and the Gospel and what was revealed

to you from your Lord. What is revealed to you from your Lord is certain to increase the insolence and disbelief of many of them. But do not grieve for the disbelieving people. **69**Indeed, those who believe, and those who are Jews, and Sabeans, and Christians, whoever believes in Allah and the last day and does right, no fear will come upon them, nor will they grieve. **70**We made a covenant of old with the children of Israel and we sent them messengers. As often as a messenger came to them with what their souls did not desire, some they denied and some they killed. **71**They thought no harm would come of it, so they were willfully blind and deaf. And afterward Allah turned toward them. Now many of them are willfully blind and deaf. Allah is the seer of what they do. **72**They surely disbelieve who say, Indeed, Allah is the Messiah, son of Mary. The Messiah said, O children of Israel, worship Allah, my Lord and your Lord. Indeed, whoever ascribes partners to Allah, Allah has forbidden paradise for him. His dwelling is the fire. For evildoers there will be no helpers. **73**They surely disbelieve who say, Indeed, Allah is the third of three, when there is no God except the one God. If they do not stop

---

The Qur'an also says that whenever the Jews "light a fire for war, Allah extinguishes it." That is, says the *Tafsir al-Jalalayn*, "war against the Prophet."[21] According to the *Tafsir Anwarul Bayan*, "The Jews make every effort to instigate wars against the Muslims, but Allah foils their attempts each time, either by instilling terror in their hearts or by their defeat in these battles."[22] The Jews also strive for "corruption on the earth" (*fasaad*), for which the punishment is specified in 5:33: offenders must "be killed or crucified, or have their hands and feet cut off on opposite sides, or be expelled from the land."

66. The Jews and Christians are exhorted to follow what is written in the Torah and Gospel, and promises Paradise to those who do so. This is not (as it is often represented) a manifestation of ecumenical generosity, but rather an expression of the Qur'an's assumption that it confirms the message of the earlier books, which prophesied the coming of the messenger.

67. Instead of "his message," the Warsh Qur'an has "his messages."[23] Instead of, "O messenger, make known what has been revealed to you from your Lord, for if you do not do it, you will

not have conveyed his message," the Shi'ite Bankipur Qur'an manuscript has, "O messenger, make known what has been revealed to you from your Lord, that Ali is the prince of believers, for if you do not do it, you will not have conveyed his message."[24] See 2:59 and the Appendix: Two Apocryphal Shi'ite Suras.

68. Ibn Kathir explains that this passage tells Jews and Christians they will have "no real religion until you adhere to and implement the Tawrah [Torah] and the Injil [Gospel]. That is, until you believe in all the Books that you have that Allah revealed to the Prophets. These Books command following Muhammad and believing in his prophecy, all the while adhering to his Law."[25]

69. On the Sabeans, see 2:62.

72. The denial of the divinity of Christ and the labeling of those who believe in it as "unbelievers" is repeated; see 5:17.

73. The denial of the doctrine of the Trinity is repeated; see 4:171. Jesus and his mother are again presented as the other members of the divine trio with Allah, but they were mortal: they both used to eat earthly food (5: 75) "like all other people," says the *Tafsir al-Jalalayn*; "Since he was like that, he cannot be a god, because of saying this, a painful doom will fall on those among them who disbelieve. **74**Will they not instead turn to Allah and seek forgiveness from him? For Allah is forgiving, merciful. **75**The Messiah, the son of Mary, was no more than a messenger, messengers passed away before him. And his mother was a saintly woman. And they both used to eat food. See how we make the signs clear for them, and see how they are turned away. **76**Say, Do you worship instead of Allah what brings you neither harm or profit? It is Allah who is the hearer, the knower. **77**Say, O people of the book, do not emphasize anything in your religion other than the truth, and do not follow the vain desires of people who were mistaken of old and led many astray, and erred from a plain road. **78**Those among the children of Israel who went astray were cursed by the tongue of David, and of Jesus, son of Mary. That was because they rebelled and used to transgress. **79**They did not restrain one another from the wickedness they did. Indeed what they used to do was evil. **80**You see many of them making friends with those who disbelieve. Surely what they themselves send on before them is harmful for them, Allah will be angry with them and in the doom they will remain. **81**If they believed in Allah and the prophet and what is revealed to him, they would

not choose them for their friends. But many of them are of evil conduct. **82**You will find the Jews and the idolaters the most vehement of mankind in hostility to those who believe. And you will find the closest in affection to those who believe those who say, Indeed, we are Christians. That is because there are among them priests and monks, and because they are not proud. **83**When they listen to what has been revealed to the messengers, you see their eyes overflow with tears because of their recognition of the truth. They say, Our Lord, we believe. Inscribe us among the witnesses. **84**How should we not believe in Allah and what has come to us of the truth? And hope that our Lord will bring us in along with righteous people? **85**Allah has rewarded them for saying that, gardens under which rivers flow, in which they will remain forever. That is the reward of the good. **86**But those who disbelieve and deny our signs, they are companions of the blaze. **87**O you who believe, do not forbid the good things that Allah has made lawful for you, and do not transgress, indeed, Allah does not love transgressors. **88**Eat what Allah has bestowed upon you as lawful and good food, and keep your duty to Allah, in whom you are believers. **89**Allah will not hold you to account for what is unintentional in your oaths, but he will hold you to account for the oaths

---

his constitution and weakness and being subject to urine and faeces."26 The actual Christian concept of the Incarnation, with Christ being both fully God and fully human, doesn't enter into consideration.

78. The disbelieving Jews are cursed by both David and Jesus for their disobedience.

82. Ibn Kathir explains why the Jews are singled out in this way: "This describes the Jews, since their disbelief is that of rebellion, defiance, opposing the truth, belittling other, people and degrading the scholars. This is why the Jews - may Allah's continued curses descend on them until the Day of Resurrection - killed many of their Prophets and tried to kill the Messenger of Allah several times, as well as, performing magic spells against him and

poisoning him. They also incited their likes among the polytheists against the Prophet."27 Meanwhile, according to *Tafsir Anwarul Bayan*, "not all Christians are referred to in this verse since many of them possess the same enmity towards the Muslims as do the Jews and the Polytheists."28 The Christians to whom this verse refers are those who accept Islam; this is made clear by 5:83 and 5:84, in which those Christians accept the words of the messengers.

86. "The blaze" is *al-jahim*, about which see 5:10.

88. One who breaks an oath must in expiation feed ten indigents or free a slave; there is, however, no blanket condemnation of slavery anywhere in the Qur'an, or any idea of the equality of dignity of all human beings before God, which led to abolitionism in Christian contexts.

which you swear intentionally. The expiation of them is the feeding of ten of the needy with the average amount you feed to your own people, or the clothing of them, or the liberation of a slave, and for him who does not find all this, then a three-day fast. This is the expiation of your oaths when you have sworn, and keep your oaths. In this way Allah explains his signs to you, so that you may give thanks. **90**O you who believe, strong drink and games of chance and idols and divining arrows are only an abomination of Satan's handiwork. Leave it aside so that you may succeed. **91**Satan seeks only to cast enmity and hatred among you by means of strong drink and games of chance, and to turn you from remembrance of Allah and from prayer. Won't you then be done with them? **92**Obey Allah and obey the messenger, and beware. But if you turn away, then know that the duty of our messenger is only to convey it clearly. **93**There will be no sin for those who believe and do good works for what they may have eaten. So be mindful of your duty, and believe, and do good works, and again, be mindful of your duty, and believe, and once again, be mindful of your duty, and do right. Allah loves those who do good. **94**O you who believe, Allah will surely test you to some degree over the game which you capture with your hands and your spears, so that Allah may know him who fears him in secret. Whoever transgresses after this, for him there is a painful doom. **95**O you who believe, kill no wild game while you are on the pilgrimage. Whoever among you kills it deliberately, he will pay compensation of domestic animals equivalent to what he has killed, the judge to be two men among you known for justice, to be brought as an offering to the Ka'ba, or, for expiation, he will feed poor persons, or the equivalent of that in fasting, so that he may taste the evil consequences of his deed. Allah forgives whatever may have happened in the past, but whoever relapses, Allah will take retribution from him. Allah is mighty, Lord of Retribution. **96**To hunt and eat the fish of the sea is made lawful for you, a provision for you and for seafarers, but to hunt on land is forbidden to you as long as you are on the pilgrimage. Be mindful of your duty to Allah, to whom you will be gathered. **97**Allah has established the Ka'ba, the sacred house, a standard for mankind, and the sacred month and the offerings and the garlands. That is so that you may know that Allah knows whatever is in the heavens and whatever is in the earth, and that Allah is knower of all things. **98**Know that Allah is severe in punishment, but that Allah is forgiving, merciful. **99**The duty of the messenger is only to convey. Allah knows what you proclaim and what you conceal. **100**Say, Evil and good are not alike, even though the abundance of evil appeals to you. So be mindful of your duty to Allah, O men of

---

90. Alcohol and gambling are "Satan's handiwork" and thus definitively forbidden. For previous Qur'anic statements on alcohol, see 2:219 and 4:43. Since Islamic tradition regards this absolute prohibition on alcohol as having been revealed later than the earlier, more qualified statements, this verse is considered to have abrogated the others. See 2:106.

94. According to Ibn Kathir, "Allah tests His servants with the game that comes near their camping area, for if they wish, they can catch it with their hands and spears in public and secret. This is how the obedience of those who obey Allah in public and secret becomes apparent and tested."[29]

understanding, so that you may succeed. [101]O you who believe, do not ask about things which, if they were made known to you, would trouble you, but if you ask about them while the Qur'an is being revealed, they will be made known to you. Allah forgives this, for Allah is forgiving, merciful. [102]A people before you asked, and then became unbelievers. [103]Allah has not established anything in the nature of a Bahirah or a Sa'ibah or a Wasilah or a Hami, but those who disbelieve invent a lie against Allah. Most of them have no sense. [104]And when it is said to them, Come to what Allah has revealed and to the messenger, they say. What we found our fathers observing is enough for us. What? Even though their fathers had no knowledge whatsoever, and no guidance? [105]O you who believe, you have charge of your own souls. He who goes astray cannot injure you if you are rightly guided. To Allah you will all return, and then he will inform you about what you used to do. [106]O you who believe, let there be witnesses between you when death draws near to one of you, at the time of bequest, two witnesses, just men from among you, or two others from another tribe, in case you are traveling in the land and the calamity of death befalls you. You will summon them both after the prayer, and if you doubt, they will be made to swear by Allah, We will not take a bribe, even if it were from a near relative, nor will we hide the testimony of Allah, for then indeed we would be of the sinful. [107]But then, if it is afterwards determined that both of them merit sin, let two others take their place of those nearly concerned, and let them swear by Allah, Indeed our testimony is truer than their testimony, and we have not transgressed, for then indeed we would be among the evildoers. [108]In this way it is more likely that they will bear true witness or fear that after their oaths, oaths will be taken. So be mindful of your duty and listen. Allah does not guide the rebellious people. [109]On the day when Allah gathers the messengers together, and says, What was your response? They say, We have no knowledge. Indeed, you, only you are the knower of hidden things. [110]When Allah says: O Jesus, son of Mary, remember my favor to you and to your mother, how I strengthened you with the holy spirit, so that you spoke to mankind in the cradle as in adulthood, and how I taught you the book and wisdom and

---

101. This passage destroys the possibility of free inquiry in Islam in warning Muslims not to "ask about things which, if they were made known to you, would trouble you." However, the believers are promised that if they "ask about them while the Qur'an is being revealed, they will be made known to you." It is odd that a perfect and eternal book would depend for its contents upon the questions of human beings at a particular time, but this anomaly is not explained.

102. The believers are again warned not to ask questions, as "a people before you asked, and then became disbelievers," which may explain why international Islamic organizations such as the Organization of Islamic Cooperation are working so assiduously to criminalize and stifle criticism of Islam.

103. Bukhari asserts that "Bahira is a she-camel whose milk is kept for the idols and nobody is allowed to milk it; Sa'iba was the she-camel which they used to set free for their gods and nothing was allowed to be carried on it. Abu Huraira said: Allah's Messenger said, 'I saw Amr bin Amir Al-Khuzai (in a dream) dragging his intestines in the Fire, and he was the first person to establish the tradition of setting free the animals (for the sake of their deities),' Wasila is the she-camel which gives birth to a she-camel as its first delivery, and then gives birth to another she-camel as its second delivery. People (in the Pre-Islamic periods of ignorance) used to let that she camel loose for their idols if it gave birth to two she-camels successively without giving birth to a male camel in between. 'Ham' was the male camel which was used for copulation. When it had finished the number of copulations assigned for it, they would let it loose for their idols and excuse it from burdens so that nothing would be carried on it, and they called it the 'Hami.' Abu Huraira said, 'I heard the Prophet saying so.'"30

110. The miracle of bringing clay birds to life does not appear in the canonical Gospels, but it is in the second-century *Infancy Gospel of Thomas*. See 3:49.

Instead of "a bird," the Warsh Qur'an has "flying."31

the Torah and the Gospel, and how you shaped out of clay the likeness of a bird by my permission, and blew on it and it was a bird by my permission, and you healed him who was born blind and the leper by my permission, and how you raised the dead by my permission, and how I restrained the children of Israel from you when you came to them with clear proofs, and those of them who disbelieved exclaimed, This is nothing else but mere sorcery. **111**And when I inspired the disciples, Believe in me and my messenger, they said, We believe. Bear witness that we are Muslims. **112**When the disciples said, O Jesus, son of Mary, is your Lord able to send down for us a table spread with food from heaven? He said, Observe your duty to Allah, if you are true believers. **113**We wish to eat from it, so that we may satisfy our hearts and know that you have spoken truth to us, and that of it we may be witnesses. **114**Jesus, son of Mary, said, O Allah, our Lord, send down for us a table spread with food from heaven, so that it may be a feast for us, for the first of us and for the last of us, and a sign from you. Give us sustenance, for you are the best of sustainers. **115**Allah said, Indeed, I send it down for you. And whoever disbelieves among you afterward, I will surely punish him with a punishment with which I have not punished anyone of the worlds. **116**And when Allah said, O Jesus, son of Mary, did you say to mankind, Take me and my mother as two gods besides Allah? He said, Be glorified. It was not for me to say what I had no right to say. If I said it, then you know it. You know what is in my mind, and I do not know what is in your mind. Indeed, you, only you, are the knower of hidden things. **117**I spoke to them only what you commanded me, Worship Allah, my Lord and your Lord. I was a witness to them while I lived among them, and when you took me, you were the watcher over them. You are the witness over all things. **118**If you punish them, indeed, they are your slaves, and if you forgive

---

114. This has long been seen as a trace of the Christian doctrine of the Eucharist, but Christoph Luxenberg sees it as much more than just a vestige. Jesus asks Allah that this table from heaven be "a feast (*'id*) for us, for the first of us and for the last of us, and a sign (*ayah*) from you." Notes Luxenberg: "The Arabic word *'id*, borrowed from the Syriac, has been, in conformity with its Arabic meaning, correctly translated by 'celebration' [or 'feast,' in the liturgical sense]."[32]

The scholar of Islam and Jesuit priest Samir Khalil Samir explains that "according to unanimous scholarly opinion [the Arabic word *'id*] is a borrowing from the Syriac *'ida*, which signifies 'Feast' or 'liturgical festival.'"[33] Pointing out that this verse is the only place in the Qur'an where the word *'id* appears, Samir concludes: "This *ma'ida* [table] is thus defined by two terms: *'id* and *aya*, a 'Feast' or 'liturgical festival' and a 'sign.' Is this not the most appropriate definition of the Eucharist of Christians, which is a festive celebration and a sacramental sign? Even more, it seems evident that in this passage we are dealing with a rather faithful description of Christian faith, otherwise not shared by Muslims."[34]

Luxenberg adds even more:

The table being laid out, one could have thought, in fact, that the passage was talking about "having a celebration." However, the same writing or script transcribed in Syriac and pronounced *yadda* has the meaning "liturgy." Thus one must understand this verse as follows: "Lord our God, send us down from the sky a Last Supper which would be a liturgy for the first and last of us." In his reply, God says…"I am going to send it down to you. Whoever is then impious among you will receive from me a torment the like of which I will not inflict on anyone else in the world."[35]

"For the first of us and the last of us" in 5:114 is *li-awwalina wa-akhirina*, another phrase found nowhere else in the Qur'an; literally it means "all, nobody excluded." Samir relates this to the Christian liturgical phrase regarding the Body and Blood of Christ, "which is offered for you and for many for the remission of sins."[36]

Luxenberg concludes: "Islam was not impressed by this divine injunction with its threats of the most severe punishments, not having grasped its significance. If the Muslim exegetes had understood these passages as the Koran intended them, there would have been a liturgy of the Last Supper in Islam."[37]

116. Allah asks Jesus directly if he asked his followers to take himself and his mother as additional gods along with him. Jesus, of course, denies having done so. Those who believe otherwise will be punished. Here we have not only a merely human Jesus but a misapprehension of the Trinity. The Qur'an envisions the Christian Trinity not as the Father, Son, and Holy Spirit, three Persons, one God, but as a trio of deities: Allah, Jesus, and Mary.

them. Indeed, you, only you, are the mighty, the wise one. [119]Allah said, This is a day on which the truthful benefit from their truthfulness, for theirs are gardens under which rivers flow, in which they are secure forever, Allah taking pleasure in them and they in him. That is the great triumph. [120]To Allah belongs the dominion over the heavens and the earth and whatever is in them, and he is able to do all things.

Cattle

Al-An'am

Introduction

"Cattle" dates, according to Islamic tradition, from Muhammad's last year in Mecca, before the Hijra, or Flight, to Medina during the twelfth year of his prophetic career. According to a tradition attributed to Ibn Abbas, "All of Surat Al-An'am was revealed in Makkah at night, accompanied by seventy thousand angels, raising their voices in glorification of Allah."[1] However, Bell states that "this surah is very confused, and contains passages from several periods."[2]

Islamic tradition holds that in Medina, Muhammad became for the first time a political and military leader as well as a religious one; at Mecca, he had been solely a preacher of his new and uncompromising monotheism in an atmosphere of increasing antagonism with his own tribe, the Quraysh, who were pagans and polytheists. Sura 6 is preoccupied with that antagonism, and features, among imprecations against the unbelievers, Allah speaking to the messenger to console him for the Quraysh's rejection of his message.

---

1 Ibn Kathir, III, 309.
2 Bell, I, 112.

Cattle

IN THE NAME OF ALLAH, THE COMPASSIONATE, THE MERCIFUL.

1Praise be to Allah, who has created the heavens and the earth, and has established darkness and light. Yet those who disbelieve ascribe rivals to their Lord. **2**It is he who has created you from clay, and has decreed a term for you. A term is fixed with him. Yet still you doubt! **3**He is Allah in the heavens and on earth. He knows both your secret and what you say, and he knows what you deserve. **4**There never came to them a sign from among the signs of Allah but they turned away from it. **5**And they denied the truth when it came to them. But there will come to them the news of what they used to deride. **6**Do they not see how many a generation we destroyed before them, whom we had established in the earth more firmly than we have established you, and we rained on them abundant showers from the sky, and made rivers flow beneath them. Yet we destroyed them for their sins, and created after them another generation. **7**If we had sent down to you writing upon parchment, so that they could feel it with their hands, those who disbelieve would have said, This is nothing other but mere sorcery. **8**They say, Why hasn't an angel been sent down to him? If we sent down an angel, then the matter would be judged, no further time would be allowed them. **9**If we had appointed him an angel, we surely would have made him a man, and obscured for them what they obscure. **10**Messengers have been derided before you, but what they scoffed about surrounded those among them who derided it. **11**Say, Travel in the land, and see the nature of the consequences for the rejecters. **12**Say, To whom does whatever is in the heavens and the earth belong? Say, To Allah. He has prescribed mercy for himself, so that he may bring you all together to the day of resurrection, about which there is no doubt. Those who ruin their own souls will not believe. **13**To him belongs whatever rests in the night and the day. He is the hearer, the knower. **14**Say, Will I choose anyone other than Allah for a protecting friend, the originator of the heavens and the earth, who feeds and is never fed? Say, I am ordered to be the first to become Muslim. And do not be one of the idolaters. **15**Say, I fear, if I rebel against my Lord,

---

1. The speaker of every part of the Qur'an is supposed in Islamic tradition to be Allah, which leads to intellectual contortions such as those displayed by Ibn Kathir in his explanation of this verse: "Allah praises and glorifies His Most Honorable Self for creating the heavens and earth."[1]

4. Ibn Kathir states: "Allah states that the rebellious, stubborn polytheists will turn away from every Ayah, meaning, sign, miracle and proof that is evidence of Allah's Uniqueness and the truth of His honorable Messengers. They will not contemplate about these Ayat or care about them. Allah said."[2] The anomaly of Allah leading the unbelievers astray and then punishing them for their stubborn rejection of his messengers is not explained or even mentioned.

6. For their unbelief, Allah destroys the unbelievers. The ruins of their destroyed civilizations bear witness to his power and judgment (see 3:137).

7. Allah mocks the unbelievers' unbelief, saying that if he had sent the messenger a "writing upon parchment," the unbelievers would nevertheless have dismissed it as "mere sorcery." In this passage, as in many others, the onus for unbelief is entirely upon the unbelievers, but see 2:7.

"What causes them to turn away from God's revelations," says Qutb, "is not the lack of strong and clear evidence of their truthfulness. They are only being unreasonably stubborn."[3] The truth of Islam is held to be self-evident; unbelief is never envisioned as anything but an obstinate rejection of known facts.

8. "No further time would be allowed them," says the *Tafsir al-Jalalayn*, for "they would be destroyed immediately with no chance for repentance or excuse, as was the custom of Allah with people of the past who were destroyed when what they asked for appeared and they failed to have faith."[4] Nothing will satisfy them: they are inherently perverse.

12. "Those who ruin their own souls will not believe" is repeated in 6:20 and is disconnected from the rest of the verse in both cases. "Perhaps," posits Barth, "there is some corruption."[5]

the retribution of an awful day. **16**He who is spared on that day, he has in truth had mercy on him. That will be the clear victory. **17**If Allah touches you with affliction, no one can relieve you of it except him, and if he touches you with good fortune, for he is able to do all things. **18**He is the omnipotent over his slaves, and he is the wise one, the knower. **19**Say, What carries the most weight in testimony? Say, Allah is the witness between me and you. And this Qur'an has been inspired in me so that with it I may warn you and whomever it may reach. Do you actually bear witness that there are gods besides Allah? Say, I bear no such witness. Say, He is only one God. Indeed, I am innocent of what you associate. **20**Those to whom we gave the book recognize it as they recognize their sons. Those who ruin their own souls will not believe. **21**Who does greater wrong than he who invents a lie against Allah or denies his signs? Indeed, the wrongdoers will not be successful. **22**And on the day we gather them together, we will say to those who ascribed partners, Where are those you claimed to be partners? **23**Then will they have no excuse except that they will say, By Allah, our Lord, we never were idolaters. **24**See how they lie against themselves, and the thing they devised has failed them. **25**Among them are some people who listen to you, but we have placed veils upon their hearts, so that they may not understand, and in their ears a deafness. If they saw every sign, they would not believe in them, to the point that when they come to you to argue with you, the unbelievers say, This is nothing other than fables of the men of old. **26**And they forbid people from it and avoid it, and they ruin no one except themselves, although they do not realize it. **27**If you could see when they are set before the fire and say, Oh, if only we could return! Then we would not deny the signs of our Lord, but we would be among the believers! **28**No, but what they used to hide has become clear to them. And if they were sent back, they would return to what they are forbidden. Indeed, they are liars. **29**And they say, There is nothing except

---

20. "Those to whom we gave the book," that is, primarily the Jews and Christians, know the truth of the message "as they recognize their sons," another affirmation of their bad faith (repeated at 2:146). This is because, says Ibn Kathir, "They received good news from the previous Messengers and Prophets about the coming of Muhammad, his attributes, homeland, his migration, and the description of his Ummah."[6] That is, their unbelief in Islam is not a sincere rejection based on honest conviction but sheer perversity.

21. "Signs" here again is *ayat*, the term used for the verses of the Qur'an: they're signs of the truth of Allah. The *Tafsir al-Jalalayn* states that the "lie against Allah" involves "ascribing a partner to him."[7]

In Islam, there is no greater evil. One modern-day Muslim writer wrote:

Murder, rape, child molesting and genocide. These are all some of the appalling crimes which occur in our world today. Many would think that these are the worst possible offences which could be committed. But there is something which outweighs all of these crimes put together: It is the crime of shirk.

Some people may question this notion. But when viewed in a proper context, the fact that there is no crime worse then shirk, will become evident to every sincere person.

There is no doubt that the above crimes are indeed terrible, but their comparison with shirk shows that they do not hold much significance in relation to this travesty. When a man murders, rapes or steals, the injustice which is done is directed primarily at other humans. But when a man commits shirk, the injustice is directed towards the Creator of the heavens and the earth; Allah. When a person is murdered, all sorts of reasons and explanations are given. But one thing that the murderer cannot claim, is that the murdered was someone who provided him with food, shelter, clothing and all the other things which keep humans aloft in this life.[8]

Virtually every other religious group is guilty of shirk in the eyes of traditional Islam: the Christians for considering Jesus to be the Son of God and the Jews for calling the prophet Ezra by the same title (9:30). For more on shirk, see 2:193 and 4:31.

25. Some who reject the messenger are doing so not out of their own free choice, but because Allah has "placed veils upon their hearts," so that they do not understand the message. Hellfire awaits them (6:26, 30).

our life in this world, and we will not be raised. **30**If you could see when they are set before their Lord! He will say, Is this not real? They will say, Yes, indeed, by our Lord. He will say, Taste now the retribution for what you used to disbelieve. **31**They indeed are losers who deny their meeting with Allah until, when the hour comes upon them suddenly, they cry, Alas for us, that we neglected it! They bear their burdens upon their backs. Ah, what they bear is evil.**32**The life of this world is nothing but a pastime and a game. The abode of the hereafter is far better for those who keep their duty. Do you then have no sense? **33**We know well how their talk grieves you, although in truth they do not disbelieve you, but evildoers disbelieve in the signs of Allah. **34**Messengers indeed have not been believed before you, and they were patient under the disbelief and persecution until our help reached them. There is no one to change the decisions of Allah. Already the news of the messengers has reached you. **35**And if their aversion is grievous to you, then, if you can, seek a way down into the earth or a ladder to the sky so that you might bring them a sign. If Allah willed, he could have brought them all together to the guidance. So do not be among the foolish ones. **36**Only those who hear can accept. As for the dead, Allah will raise them up, then to him

they will be returned. **37**They say, Why has no sign been sent down upon him from his Lord? Say, Indeed, Allah is able to send down a sign. But most of them do not know. **38**There is not an animal on earth, or a flying creature flying on two wings, but they are communities like you. We have neglected nothing in the book. Then they will be gathered to their Lord. **39**Those who deny our signs are deaf and dumb in darkness. Allah leads astray those whom he wills, and he places on a straight path those whom he wills. **40**Say, Can you see yourselves, if the punishment of Allah came upon you or the hour came upon you? Do you then call to anyone other than Allah, if you are truthful? **41**No, but to him you call, and he removes what you call to him about, if he wills, and you forget whatever partners you ascribed to him. **42**We have already sent to peoples that were before you, and we visited them with tribulation and adversity, so that they might grow humble. **43**If only, when our disaster came on them, they had been humble. But their hearts were hardened and Satan made all that they used to do seem good to them. **44**Then, when they forgot what they had been reminded about, we opened to them the gates of all things, until even as they were rejoicing in what they had been given, we seized them unawares, and indeed, they were

---

32. Says the *Tafsir Ibn Abbas*, "Do you not comprehend that this world is evanescent and that the Hereafter is everlasting?"⁹

33. Allah again consoles the messenger for the unbelievers' rejection (see 2:144, 3:176).

35. Here and in 6:37, it is assumed that the messenger has not brought any *ayat*, despite the fact that all the verses of the Qur'an are "signs." In the hadith, numerous miracles are ascribed to Muhammad, in complete disregard of the import of these Qur'anic passages.

38. This could be a reference to the protected tablet mentioned in 85:22, on which Allah has written everything that occurs in the universe, even the minutest actions of animals and birds.

42. Messengers have been "already sent to peoples that were before you," indeed, to every nation (16:36). Yet the Qur'an is preoccupied primarily with the Biblical prophets, along with just a handful of others.

45. Instead of, "So the last remnant of the people who did wrong was cut off," the Shi'ite Bankipur Qur'an manuscript has, "So the last remnant of the people who deprived the family of Muhammad of its due was cut off."¹⁰ See 2:59 and the Appendix: Two Apocryphal Shi'ite Suras.

dumbfounded. **45**So the last remnant of the people who did wrong was cut off. Praise be to Allah, Lord of the worlds. **46**Say, Have you imagined, if Allah took away your hearing and your sight and sealed your hearts, who is the god who could restore it to you except Allah? See how we display the signs to them! Yet still they turn away. **47**Say, Can you see yourselves, if the punishment of Allah came upon you unaware or openly? Would any perish except wrongdoing people? **48**We do not send the messengers except as bearers of good news and warners. Whoever believes and does right, no fear will come upon them, nor will they grieve. **49**But as for those who deny our signs, torment will afflict them because they used to disobey. **50**Say, I don't say to you that I possess the treasures of Allah, or that I have knowledge of the unseen, and I don't say to you, Indeed, I am an angel. I follow only what is inspired in me. Say, Are the blind man and the seer equal? Will you not then think? **51**Warn with this those who fear that they will be gathered to their Lord, for whom there is no protecting ally or intercessor except him, so that they may fear Allah. **52**Do not repel those who call upon their Lord in the morning and evening, seeking his face. You are not accountable for them in anything, nor are they accountable for you in anything, so that you should repel them and be among the wrongdoers. **53**And even so, we test some of them by others, so that they say, Are these the ones whom Allah favors among us? Is not Allah best aware of the grateful? **54**And when those who believe in our signs come to you, say, Peace be upon you. Your Lord has prescribed mercy for himself, so that whoever among you does evil through ignorance and repents of it afterward and does right, indeed, he is forgiving, merciful. **55**In this way we explain the signs, so that the way of the unrighteous may be clear. **56**Say, I am forbidden to worship those you call upon instead of Allah. Say, I will not follow your desires, for then I would go astray and I would not be among the rightly guided. **57**Say, I am on clear proof from my Lord, while you deny him. I don't have what you're impatient for. The decision is for Allah alone. He tells the truth and he is the best of deciders. **58**Say, If I had what you're impatient for, then the case between me and you would have been decided. Allah is best aware of the wrongdoers. **59**And with him are the keys of the invisible. No one knows them but he. And he knows what is in the land and the sea. Not a leaf falls without his knowing it, not a grain amid the darkness of the earth, nothing wet or dry without being in a clear record. **60**He is the one who gathers you at night and knows what you do by day. Then he raises you again to life in it, that the term appointed may be accomplished. And afterward, to him is your return. Then he will proclaim to you what you used to do. **61**He is the omnipotent over his slaves. He sends guardians over you until, when death comes to one of you, our messengers receive him, and they do not neglect him. **62**Then are they restored to Allah, their Lord, the just one. Surely the judgment is his. And he is the swiftest of reckoners. **63**Say,

---

54. This makes clear that the unbelievers do not do evil through ignorance, for if they had, Allah would have allowed them to repent. Instead, he will fill hell with them (32:13), suggesting once again that those who reject Islam do so while knowing very well that it is true.

Who delivers you from the darkness of the land and the sea? You call on him humbly and in secret, If we are delivered from this, we will indeed be among the thankful. **64**Say, Allah saves you from this and from all affliction. Yet you attribute partners to him. **65**Say, He is able to send punishment upon you from above you or from beneath your feet, or to confuse you with dissension and make you taste the tyranny of one another. See how we display the signs, so that they may understand. **66**Your people have denied it, though it is the truth. Say, I am not in charge of you. **67**For every announcement there is a term, and you will come to know. **68**And when you see those who meddle with our signs, withdraw from them until they meddle with another topic. And if Satan causes you to forget, do not sit, after the remembrance, with the congregation of wrongdoers. **69**Those who fear Allah are not accountable for them in anything but the reminder, that perhaps they may fear Allah. **70**And forsake those who take their religion for a pastime and a joke, and who are fooled by the life of this world. Remind them with this, so that a soul may not be destroyed by what it deserves. It has no protecting ally or intercessor except Allah, and though it offer every compensation, it will not be accepted from it. Those are the ones who perish by what they deserve. For them is drink of boiling water and a painful doom, because they disbelieved. **71**Say, Will we cry, instead of to Allah, to what neither helps us nor hurts us, and will we turn back after Allah has guided us, like one bewildered whom the satans

have infatuated on earth, who has companions who invite him to the guidance, Come to us? Say, Indeed, the guidance of Allah is guidance, and we are ordered to surrender to the Lord of the worlds, **72**And to establish prayer and be dutiful to him, and it is he to whom you will be gathered. **73**It is he who created the heavens and the earth in truth. On the day when he says, Be! it is. His word is the truth, and the dominion will be his on the day when the trumpet is blown. He is the knower of the invisible and the visible, he is the wise, the aware. **74**When Abraham said to his father Azar, Do you take idols for gods? Indeed, I see you and your people in manifest error. **75**In this way we showed Abraham the kingdom of the heavens and the earth, so that he might be among those who possess certainty, **76**When the night grew dark upon him, he saw a star. He said, This is my Lord. But when it set, he said, I do not love things that set. **77**And when he saw the moon rising, he exclaimed, This is my Lord. But when it set, he said, Unless my Lord guides me, I surely will become one of the people who are astray. **78**And when he saw the sun rising, he cried, This is my Lord. This is greater. And when it set, he exclaimed, O my people, indeed, I am free from all that you associate. **79**Indeed, I have turned my face toward him who created the heavens and the earth as a *hanif*, and I am not among the idolaters. **80**His people argued with him. He said, Do you disagree with me about Allah when he has guided me? I don't fear what you set up beside him at all, unless my Lord wills anything. My Lord includes all

---

74. Abraham rejects polytheism by noting the deficiencies of various pagan objects of worship: the stars, the moon, the sun.

77. Those who glibly associate Allah with the moon-god, a pre-Islamic Arabian god of war, should note this verse.

79. On *hanif*, see 2:135.

things in his knowledge. Will you not then remember? [81]How should I fear what you set up beside him, when you don't fear to set up besides Allah something for which he has not revealed to you any justification? Which of the two factions has more right to safety, if you have knowledge?

[82]Those who believe and do not obscure their belief by wrongdoing, theirs is safety, and they are rightly guided. [83]That is our argument. We gave it to Abraham against his people. We raise to degrees of wisdom those whom we will. Indeed, your Lord is wise, aware. [84]And we bestowed upon him Isaac and Jacob, each of them we guided, and Noah we guided previously, and of his descendants, David and Solomon and Job and Joseph and Moses and Aaron. In this way we reward the good. [85]And Zachariah and John and Jesus and Elias. Each one was among the righteous. [86]And Ishmael and Elisha and Jonah and Lot. Each one we preferred over the worlds, [87]With some of their forefathers and their offspring and their brethren, and we chose them and guided

them to a straight path. [88]That is the guidance of Allah, with which he guides those whom he wills of his slaves. But if they had set up anything besides him, what they did would have been in vain. [89]Those are the people to whom we gave the book and command and prophethood. But if these people disbelieve in it, then indeed we will entrust it to a people who will not be unbelievers in it. [90]Those are the ones whom Allah guides, so follow their guidance. Say, I ask no fee of you for it. Indeed, it is nothing but a reminder for the worlds. [91]And they do not measure the power of Allah in its true measure when they say, Allah has revealed nothing to a human being. Say, Who revealed the book that Moses brought, a light and guidance for mankind, which you have put on parchments which you show, but you hide much of it, and you were taught what you did not know, nor your fathers? Say, Allah. Then leave them to their play of vain discourse. [92]And this is a blessed book that we have revealed, confirming what was before it, so that you may warn the mother of

---

84. The immediately preceding discussion of Abraham's rejection of idolatry expands into an enumeration of the other prophets of Islam: Abraham (specified as a Muslim in 3:67), Noah before Abraham, then Abraham's children Isaac and Jacob, and then after that David, Solomon, Job, Joseph, Moses, Aaron, Zechariah, John the Baptist, Jesus, Elias, Ishmael, Elisha, Jonah, and Lot. These are, of course, all Biblical figures, although later the Qur'an does discuss some non-Biblical prophets. One should "follow their guidance" (6:90), which assumes that their teachings are available to those who read the Qur'an around the time when it was composed. There is, however, no Biblical manuscript tradition from that period that shows any more congruence of the Biblical message with the Qur'anic one than what exists today.

The latter prophets are "descendants" of Abraham (or possibly Noah), and thus apparently all related to one another.

85. Bell points out: "The form *Ilyas* = *Elias*, indicates a Christian, rather than a Jewish source for the story," as the latter would likely have used a derivation of the name Elijah, rather than its Greek form Elias.[11] Elias also appears at 37:123.

91. Here begins another castigation of the Jews: they do not obey the revelation given to Moses. They display it ("put on parchments which you show"), but they don't obey it (they

"hide much of it"). Allah chastises those who say that he has not revealed anything to any human being. According to as-Suyuti's fifteenth-century *Ad-Durrul Manthur*, this verse was revealed after Muhammad teased a "hefty" Jewish scholar named Malik bin Sayf. Muhammad asked him, "Did you see in the Torah that Allah detests a hefty scholar?"[12] Malik bin Sayf was enraged and shouted: "By Allah! Allah has not revealed anything to any human being!"[13] His outburst is quoted, and rebuked, here.

92. The "mother of towns" is traditionally identified as Mecca, but the Qur'an never says this. Dan Gibson states of Mecca that "from the life of Muhammad we understand that camel caravans went out from this city, and that Muhammad himself traveled with a caravan to Syria and back. One would expect that a major city, involved with trade across the Middle East, would be well known to the nations around it, especially if it was a merchant city. However, the city of Mecca was not well known. Despite what Islamic literature tells us, there is not a single piece of non-Muslim evidence that points to and corroborates this claim for such prominence during the seventh century. In fact, the earliest substantiated reference to Mecca is in the *Continuatio Byzantia Arabica* - a source from early in the reign of the Caliph Hisham who ruled between 724 and 743–100 years after the life of Muhammad."[14]

towns and those around her. Those who believe in the hereafter believe in it, and they are mindful of their prayer. ⁹³Who is guilty of more wrong than he who forges a lie against Allah, or says, I am inspired, when he is not inspired in anything, and who says, I will reveal something like what Allah has revealed? If you could see when the wrongdoers reach the pangs of death and the angels stretch their hands out, Deliver up your souls. This day you are awarded torment of degradation for what you spoke about Allah other than the truth, and used to scorn his signs. ⁹⁴Now you have come to us alone, as we created you at the beginning, and you have left behind all that we bestowed upon you, and we do not see you with your intercessors, whom you claimed were associated with you. Now the bond between you is severed, and what you presumed has failed you. ⁹⁵Indeed, Allah splits the grain of corn and the date-stone. He brings forth the living from the dead, and brings forth the dead from the living. Such is Allah. How then are you perverted? ⁹⁶He is the cleaver of the daybreak, and he made the night for stillness, and the sun and the moon for reckoning. That is the measuring of the mighty, the wise. ⁹⁷And he is the one who has set the stars for you so that you may plot your course by them amid the darkness of the land and the sea. We have detailed our signs for a people who have knowledge. ⁹⁸And it is he who has produced you from a single being, and a habitation and a repository. We have detailed our signs for a people who have understanding. ⁹⁹It is he who sends down water from the sky, and with it we bring forth buds of every kind, we bring forth the green blade, from which we bring forth the thick-clustered grain, and from the date-palm, from its pollen, spring pendant bunches, and gardens of grapes, and the olive and the pomegranate, alike and unlike. Look upon the fruit of them, when they bear fruit, and upon its ripening. Indeed, in this are truly signs for a people who believe. ¹⁰⁰Yet they ascribe the jinn as partners to him, although he created them, and impute, falsely, without knowledge, sons and daughters to him. May he be glorified and highly exalted above what they ascribe. ¹⁰¹The originator of the heavens and the earth. How can he have a son, when he has no wife, when he created all things and is aware of all things? ¹⁰²This is Allah, your Lord. There is no God except him, the creator of all things, so worship him. And he takes care of all things.

---

93. Instead of "or says," a Qur'anic fragment in the Museum of Islamic Art in Doha, Qatar, likely dating from the eighth century, has "and says."[15]

94. Everyone will stand alone before Allah; no intercession from others will be accepted (2:48, 2:123, 23:101, 39:43, 42:46). However, the Qur'an elsewhere accepts intercession with Allah's permission (10:3, 20:109, 21:28, 34:23, 53:26).

96. Instead of "he made the night," the Warsh Qur'an has "maker of the night."[16]

100. The jinn are spirit beings that Allah created from "smokeless fire" (55:15). The twentieth-century Islamic scholar Muhammad ibn al-Uthaymeen states a standard Muslim view when he asserts that while human beings cannot see jinn, "undoubtedly the jinn can have a harmful effect on humans, and they could even kill them. They may harm a person by throwing stones at him, or by trying to terrify him, and other things that are proven in the sunnah (prophetic teachings) or indicated by real events....There are numerous reports which indicate that a man may come to a deserted area, and a stone may be thrown at him, but he does not see anybody, or he may hear voices or a rustling sound like the rustling of trees, and other things that may make him feel distressed and scared. A jinn may also enter the body of a human, either because of love or with the intention of harming him, or for some other reason."[17]

101. An attempt at a reductio ad absurdum on the Christian doctrine of the Incarnation: "How can he have a son, when he has no consort?" Ibn Kathir asks: "How can He have a wife from His creation who is suitable for His majesty, when there is none like Him How can He have a child? Then Verily, Allah is Glorified above having a son."[18] The idea that fatherhood and sonship might not be conceived of in physical terms is not considered.

¹⁰³Vision does not comprehend him, but he comprehends vision. He is the subtle, the aware. ¹⁰⁴Proofs have come to you from your Lord, so whoever sees, it is for his own good, and whoever is blind is blind to his own harm. And I am not a guardian over you. ¹⁰⁵In this way we display our signs, so that they may say, You have studied, and so that we may make it clear for people who have knowledge. ¹⁰⁶Follow what is inspired in you from your Lord, there is no God except him, and turn away from the idolaters. ¹⁰⁷If Allah had willed, they would not have been idolatrous. We have not set you as a guardian over them, nor are you responsible for them. ¹⁰⁸Do not revile those to whom they pray besides Allah, so that they will not wrongfully revile Allah in ignorance. In this way we made the acts of every nation seem reasonable to them. Then to their Lord is their return, and he will tell them what they used to do. ¹⁰⁹And they swear a solemn oath by Allah that if a sign comes to them, they will believe in it. Say, Signs are with Allah and what will make you realize that if they came to them, they still would not believe? ¹¹⁰We confound their hearts and their eyes. Since they did not believe in it at first, we let them wander blindly in their insolence. ¹¹¹And though we would send down the angels to them, and the dead would speak to them, and we would gather against them all things in array, they would not believe unless Allah willed it. But most of them are ignorant. ¹¹²In this way we have appointed an adversary to every prophet, satans of mankind and jinn who inspire in one another plausible discourse through guile. If your Lord willed, they would not do so, so leave them alone with their devising, ¹¹³So that the hearts of those who do not believe in the hereafter may draw near to it, and that they may take pleasure in it, and that they may earn what they are earning. ¹¹⁴Will I seek a judge other than Allah, when it is he who has revealed the book to you, fully explained? Those to whom we gave the book know that it is revealed from your Lord in truth. So do not be among the waverers. ¹¹⁵The word from your Lord is perfected in truth and justice. There is no one who can change his words. He is the hearer, the knower. ¹¹⁶If you obeyed most of those on earth, they would mislead you far from Allah's way. They follow nothing but an opinion, and they just guess. ¹¹⁷Indeed, your Lord, he knows best who strays from his way, and he knows best the rightly guided. ¹¹⁸Eat of what the name of Allah has been mentioned over, if you are believers in his signs. ¹¹⁹How would you not eat of that over which the name of Allah has been mentioned, when he has explained to you what is forbidden to you, unless you are forced to do so? But indeed, many are led astray by their own lusts through ignorance. Indeed, your Lord, he is best aware of the transgressors. ¹²⁰Forsake the outwardness of sin and the inwardness of it. Indeed, those who commit sin will be rewarded what

---

108. According to as-Suyuti's fifteenth-century *Lubabun Nuqul*, "This verse was revealed when the Polytheists actually used insolent words to revile Allah when certain Muslims used foul words for their idols."[19]

109. The unbelievers wouldn't believe even if signs did come to them, a theme returned to at 6:124.

115. No one can change Allah's word, but at 2:75, the Qur'an states that the Jews did change it, and at 22:52, the possibility is raised that Satan can tamper with it, although Allah abrogates his changes.

Instead of "the word [*kalimatu*] from your Lord," the Warsh Qur'an has "the words [*kalimaatu*] from your Lord."[20]

118. Here is the foundation for the halal preparation of meat, which dictates that the jugular vein, windpipe, and esophagus of the animal be severed after the butcher recites, "In the name of Allah." Then the blood is drained out.

they have earned. **121**And do not eat what Allah's name has not been mentioned over, for indeed, it is abomination. Indeed, the satans inspire their minions to argue with you. But if you obey them, you will be indeed idolaters. **122**Is he who was dead and we have raised him to life, and set for him a light in which he walks among men, like him whose likeness is in utter darkness from which he cannot emerge? In this way the conduct of the unbelievers is made to seem right to them.

123 And in this way we have set up the chief sinners in every city, so that they would plot in it. They only plot against themselves, although they do not realize it. **124**And when a sign comes to them, they say, We will not believe until we are given what Allah's messengers are given. Allah knows best with whom to place his message. Humiliation from Allah and heavy punishment will strike the guilty for their scheming. **125**And whoever it is Allah's will to guide, he expands his breast to Islam, and whomever it is his will to lead astray, he makes his breast close and narrow as if he were engaged in a steep ascent. In this way Allah places disgrace upon those who do not believe. **126**This is the path of your Lord, a straight path. We have detailed our signs for a people who pay attention. **127**For them is the dwelling of peace with their Lord. He will be their protecting friend because of what they used to do. **128**In the day

when he will gather them together, O you assembly of the jinn, you seduced many among mankind. And their adherents among mankind will say, Our Lord, we enjoyed one another, but now we have arrived at the appointed term which you established for us. He will say, fire is your home. Remain in it forever, except him whom Allah wills. Indeed, your Lord is wise, aware. **129**In this way we let some of the wrongdoers have power over others, because of what they used to commit. **130**O assembly of jinn and mankind, didn't there come to you messengers of your own who recounted to you my signs and warned you of the meeting on this, your day? They will say, We testify against ourselves. And the life of this world fooled them. And they testify against themselves that they were unbelievers. **131**This is because your Lord does not destroy towns arbitrarily while their people are unaware. **132**For everyone, there will be ranks according to what they did. Your Lord is not unaware of what they do. **133**Your Lord is the absolute, the Lord of mercy. If he wills, he can remove you and can cause what he wills to follow after you, even as he raised you from the seed of other people. **134**Indeed, what you are promised will surely happen, and you cannot escape. **135**Say, O my people, work according to your power. Indeed, I, too, am working. In this way you will come to know for

---

121. The Muslims would be "idolaters" if they obeyed the advice of unbelievers and ate food over which Allah's name has not been mentioned. According to Ibn Kathir, this means that "when you turn away from Allah's command and Legislation to the saying of anyone else, preferring other than what Allah has said, then this constitutes Shirk."[21] For shirk, see 2:193, 4:31, and 6:21.

124. Here again it is asserted, as in 6:109, that the unbelievers wouldn't believe even if they did receive signs from Allah. The interruption of this theme, and the return to it, may suggest an interpolation.

Instead of "his message," the Warsh Qur'an has "his messages."[22]

125. It is up to Allah whether or not one believes, and once again unexplained as to why the unbelievers are responsible for their lack of faith if Allah leads them astray. See 2:7.

128. Jinns as well as humans are warned of the coming judgment. The *Tafsir Anwarul Bayan* notes that some Islamic authorities believe that prophets were sent specifically "to the jinn, from the jinn," while others contend that the jinn listened to the human prophets.[23]

Instead of, "He will gather them," the Warsh Qur'an has, "We will gather them."[24]

which of us there will be the happy ending. Indeed, the wrongdoers will not be successful. **136**They assign to Allah a portion of the crops and cattle he created, and they say, This is Allah's, so they claim, and this is for our partners. In this way what goes to his partners does not reach Allah, and what goes to Allah goes to their partners. The way they judge is evil. **137**In this way their partners have made the killing of their children seem good to many of the idolaters, so that they may ruin them and make their faith obscure for them. If Allah had willed, they would not have done so. So leave them alone with their fabrications. **138**And they say, Such cattle and crops are forbidden. No one is to eat of them except those whom we will, so they claim, cattle whose backs are forbidden, cattle over which they do not mention the name of Allah. A lie against him. He will repay them for what they invent. **139**And they say, What is in the bellies of such cattle is reserved for our males and is forbidden to our wives, but if it be born dead, then they may be partakers of it. He will reward them for their attribution. Indeed, he is wise, aware. **140**They are losers who have foolishly killed their own children without knowledge, and have forbidden what Allah bestowed upon them, inventing a lie against Allah. They indeed have gone astray and are not guided. **141**It is he who produces gardens trellised and untrellised, and the date-palm, and crops of different flavors, and the olive and the pomegranate, like and unlike. Eat of the fruit of it when it bears fruit, and pay what is due for it on harvest day, and do not be wasteful. Indeed, Allah does not love the wasteful. **142**And of the cattle, some for burdens, some for food. Eat of what Allah has bestowed upon you, and do not follow Satan's footsteps, for indeed, he is an open enemy to you. **143**Eight pairs, two of the sheep, and two of the goats. Say, Has he forbidden the two males or the two females, or what the wombs of the two females contain? Explain to me with knowledge, if you are truthful. **144**And of the camels two, and of the oxen two. Say, Has he forbidden the two males or the two females, or what the wombs of the two females contain, or were you nearby to witness when Allah commanded this to you? Then who does a greater wrong than he who fabricates a lie about Allah, so that he might lead mankind astray without knowledge. Indeed, Allah does not guide wrongdoing people. **145**Say, I do not find in what is revealed to me anything prohibited to an eater that he eat of it, except carrion, or blood poured forth, or the flesh of pigs, for that indeed is foul, or the abomination that was sacrificed to the name of someone other than Allah. But whoever is forced, neither craving nor transgressing, indeed, your Lord is forgiving, merciful. **146**To those who are Jews, we forbade every animal with claws. And of the oxen and the sheep, we forbade to them the fat of them, except what is upon the backs or the entrails, or what is mixed with the bone. We awarded them that for their rebellion. And indeed, we truly are truthful. **147**So if they give the lie to you, say, Your Lord is a Lord of all-embracing mercy, and his wrath will

---

141. "Do not be wasteful" refers, says the *Ruhul Ma'ani*, to over-enthusiasm in charity: "This Ayah was revealed concerning Thabit bin Qays bin Shammas, who plucked the fruits of his date palms. Then he said to himself, 'This day, every person who comes

to me, I will feed him from it.' So he kept feeding (them) until the evening came and he ended up with no dates."[25]

147. Ibn Kathir observes that "Allah often joins encouragement with threats in the Qur'an."[26]

never be withdrawn from guilty people. **148**Those who are idolaters will say, If Allah had willed, we would not have ascribed partners to him, neither would our fathers have done so, nor would we have forbidden anything. In this way those who were before them gave the lie, until they tasted of the fear of us. Say, Do you have any knowledge that you can bring forth for us? Indeed, you follow nothing but an opinion, indeed, you're just guessing. **149**Say, For Allah's is the final argument, if he had willed, he could indeed have guided all of you. **150**Say, Come, bring your witnesses who can bear witness that Allah forbade this. And if they bear witness, do not bear witness with them. Do not follow the whims of those who deny our signs, those who do not believe in the hereafter and consider others equal with their Lord. **151**Say, Come, I will recite to you what your Lord has made a sacred duty for you, that you ascribe nothing as a partner to him and that you do good to parents, and that you do not kill your children because of poverty, we provide for you and for them, and that you do not come close to lewd things, whether open or concealed. And that you do not kill the life that Allah has made sacred, except in the course of justice. This he has commanded you, so that you may discern. **152**And do not approach the wealth of the orphan except with what is better, until he reaches maturity. Give full measure and full weight, in justice. We do not burden any soul beyond its ability. And if you give your word, do justice, even though it be

a relative, and fulfill the covenant of Allah. This he commands you, so that perhaps you may remember. **153**And this is my straight path, so follow it. Do not follow other ways, so that you will not be parted from his way. He has ordained this for you, so that you may fear Allah. **154**Again, we gave the book to Moses, complete for him who would do good, an explanation of all things, a guidance and a mercy, so that they might believe in the meeting with their Lord. **155**And this is a blessed book that we have revealed. So follow it and fear Allah, so that you may find mercy. **156**So that you do not say, The book was revealed only to two sects before us, and we indeed were unaware of what they read, **157**So that you do not say, If the book had been revealed to us, we surely would have been better guided than they are. Now there has come to you a clear proof from your Lord, a guidance and mercy, and who does a greater wrong than he who denies the signs of Allah, and turns away from them? We award an evil doom to those who turn away from our signs because of their aversion. **158**They wait, indeed, for nothing less than the angels to come to them, or for your Lord to come, or there should come one of the signs from your Lord. In the day when one of the signs from your Lord comes, belief in it will not help a soul which before that did not believe, or in its belief earned good. Say, Wait! Indeed, we are waiting. **159**Indeed, as for those who split their religion and become schismatics, you have no concern at all with them. Their case

---

151. Here begins a summary of what is prohibited in Islam. One should "not kill the life that Allah has made sacred," with the notable caveat: "except in the course of justice." A hadith depicts Muhammad explaining that the "blood of a Muslim...cannot be shed except in three cases: in Qisas [retaliation] for murder, a

married person who commits illegal sexual intercourse and the one who reverts from Islam (apostate) and leaves the Muslims."27 So adultery, apostasy, and revenge are the only justifications for taking a life.

will go to Allah, who will then tell them what they used to do. ¹⁶⁰Whoever brings a good deed will receive tenfold like it, while whoever brings an evil deed will be awarded only the like of it, and they will not be wronged. ¹⁶¹Say, Indeed, as for me, my Lord has guided me to a straight path, a right religion, the community of Abraham, the *hanif*, who was no idolater. ¹⁶²Say, Indeed, my prayer and my sacrifice and my living and my dying are for Allah, Lord of the worlds. ¹⁶³He has no partner. This I am commanded, and I am first of the Muslims. ¹⁶⁴Say, Will I seek another than Allah for a Lord, when he is Lord of all things? Each soul earns only on its own account, nor do any bear another's burden. Then to your Lord is your return, and he will tell you what you disagreed about. ¹⁶⁵It is he who has placed you as caliphs of the earth and has exalted some of you in rank above others, so that he may test you by what he has given you. Indeed, your Lord is swift in prosecution, and indeed, he indeed is forgiving, merciful.

---

161. On *hanif*, see 2:135.

165. Another hadith has Muhammad explain: "This world is fresh and sweet, and Allah will make your successive generations therein, so look at what you do and beware of (the temptations of) this world and beware of (the temptations of) women."²⁸

On "caliphs of the earth," see 2:30.

The Heights

Al-A'raf

Introduction

"The Heights" is traditionally considered to be another Meccan sura, dating from around the same time as sura 6: Muhammad's last year in Mecca before the Hijra to Medina. The *Tafsir al-Jalalayn* states that verses 163 to 170, which deal with the Sabbath-breaking Jews who were transformed into apes, are from Medina.[1]

---

1 Jalalu'd-Din al-Mahalli and Jalalu'd-Din as-Suyuti, *Tafsir al-Jalalayn*, translated by Aisha Bewley (London: Dar Al Taqwa Ltd., 2007), 327.

The Heights

In the name of Allah, the compassionate, the merciful.

¹Alif. Lam. Mim. Sad. ²A book that is revealed to you, so let there be no heaviness in your heart from it, that you may warn thereby, and a reminder to believers. ³Follow what has been sent down to you from your Lord, and follow no protecting friends besides him. Little do you remember. ⁴How many a town have we destroyed? As a raid by night, or while they slept at noon, our terror came to them. ⁵They had no plea when our terror came to them, except that they said, Indeed, we were wrongdoers. ⁶Then indeed we will question those to whom it has been sent, and indeed we will question the messengers. ⁷Then indeed we will narrate to them with knowledge, for we were not absent.

⁸The weighing on that day is true. As for those whose scale is heavy, they are the successful. ⁹And as for those whose scale is light, they are the ones who lose their souls because they used to wrong our signs. ¹⁰And we have given you power in the earth, and established for you livelihoods in it. Yet you give little thanks. ¹¹And we created you, then fashioned you, then told the angels, Fall prostrate before Adam. And they fell prostrate, all except Iblis, who was not among those who made prostration. ¹²He said, What prevented you that you didn't fall prostrate when I told you? He said, I am better than he. You created me from fire,

---

1. On the "mysterious letters," see 2:1.

2. Once again Allah consoles the messenger. See 2:144 and 3:176.

3. Yet another warning of the dreadful judgment; here "you" is plural, while in 7:2 it was singular. Bell suggests that there may be a textual break between verses 2 and 3, as "appears from the change of address."[1]

4. See 3:137 and 6:6. Such verses about divine judgment do not necessarily refer solely to thunderbolts from heaven: see 9:14. Jihad terrorists consider themselves to be the instruments of Allah's judgment, destroying cities and punishing unbelievers in accord with the Qur'an.

8. Here is the idea of the scales on which one's good deeds and evil deeds will be placed on the day of judgment (cf. 21:47). If one's good deeds outweigh one's bad deeds, the scale is "heavy" with good deeds, and one will enter paradise. According to Ibn Kathir, "As for what will be placed on the Balance on the Day of Resurrection, it has been said that the deeds will be placed on it, even though they are not material objects. Allah will give these deeds physical weight on the Day of Resurrection."[2]

9. Those whose scales are light on good deeds will go to hell "because they used to wrong our signs." As "signs" are also "verses," this could refer to rejection of the Qur'an.

11. Here begins again the story of Iblis refusing to prostrate himself before Adam, as in 2:34. A hadith has Muhammad informing us that when Allah created Adam, he made him sixty cubits tall—that is, about ninety feet. "People," he said, "have been decreasing in stature since Adam's creation."[3] Muhammad is also depicted as telling us that the first inhabitants of Paradise will be Adam's size: "The first group of people who will enter Paradise, will be glittering like the full moon and those who will follow them, will glitter like the most brilliant star in the sky. They will not urinate, relieve nature, spit, or have any nasal secretions. Their combs will be of gold, and their sweat will smell like musk. The aloes-wood will be used in their centers. Their wives will be houris. All of them will look alike and will resemble their father Adam (in stature), sixty cubits tall."[4] The houris, of course, are the virgins of Paradise.

Allah here groups Iblis among the angels, as he does elsewhere (2:34, 15:28-31, 20:116, 38:71-74). However, Allah also says "he was one of the jinn" (18:50). This creates a difficulty, as the angels "do not resist Allah in what he commands them, but do what they are commanded" (66:6). Many of the jinns, however, have "hearts with which they do not understand" (7:179).

So if Iblis/Satan is an angel, how can he disobey Allah? But if he is a jinn, why does Allah blame him in sura 7 and its cognate passages for disobeying a command Allah gave not to the jinns but to the angels? This has led to some ingenious explanations throughout Islamic history. The *Tafsir al-Jalalayn* says that Satan was "the father of the jinn, who was among the angels."[5] Asad identifies the jinns with the angels, but this contradicts the passages of the Qur'an that say the angels are not disobedient.[6] The contemporary Islamic apologist Dr. Zakir Naik contends that while Satan is grouped with the angels, he is never actually called an angel, and so there is no contradiction. He says that Satan is nevertheless held responsible for disobeying a command that is addressed to the angels because Allah meant it collectively—all the angels as well as Satan should obey it.[7]

12. Ibn Kathir explains that Iblis (identified as Satan in 7:20, which Bell sees as an indication that two different sources have been combined) was wrong to think himself superior to Adam because Iblis was created from fire and Adam from mud.[8] Satan, he says, "lost hope in acquiring Allah's mercy" because "he committed this error, may Allah curse him, due to his false comparison. His

while him you created from mud. **13**He said, Then go down from here. It is not for you to show pride here, so go forth. Indeed, you are among those who are degraded. **14**He said, Give me a reprieve until the day when they are raised.

15He said, Indeed, you are among those reprieved. **16**He said, Now, because you have led me astray, indeed I will lurk in ambush for them on your right path. **17**Then I will come upon them from before them and from behind them and from their right hands and from their left hands, and you will not find most of them beholden. **18**He said, Go forth from here, degraded, banished. As for those who follow you, surely I will fill Gehenna with all of you. **19**And, O Adam, dwell with your wife in the garden and eat from wherever you wish, but do not come near this tree, so that you will not become wrongdoers. **20**Then Satan whispered to them that he might show them what was hidden from them of their shame, and he said, Your Lord forbade you from this tree only so that you would not become angels or become one of the immortals. **21**And he swore to them, Indeed, I am a sincere adviser to you. **22**In this way he led them on with guile. And

when they tasted of the tree, their shame was clear to them, and they began to conceal themselves with some of the leaves of the garden. And their Lord called to them, Did I not forbid you from that tree and tell you, Indeed, Satan is an open enemy to you? **23**They said, Our Lord, we have wronged ourselves. If you do not forgive us and do not have mercy on us, surely we are among the lost. **24**He said, Go down, one of you an enemy to the other. There will be for you on earth a habitation and provision for a while. **25**He said, There you will live, and there you will die, and from there you will be brought forth. **26**O children of Adam, we have revealed to you clothing to conceal your shame, and beautiful garments, but the clothing of restraint from evil, that is best. This is from the signs of Allah, so that they may remember. **27**O children of Adam, do not let Satan seduce you as he caused your parents to go forth from the garden and tore off their robe from them, so that he might show their shame to them. Indeed, he sees you, he and his tribe, from where you do not see him. Indeed, we have made the satans protecting friends for those who do not believe. **28**And when they commit some lewdness they

---

claim that the fire is more honored than mud was also false, because mud has the qualities of wisdom, forbearance, patience and assurance, mud is where plants grow, flourish, increase, and provide good. To the contrary, fire has the qualities of burning, recklessness and hastiness. Therefore, the origin of creation directed Shaytan [Satan] to failure, while the origin of Adam led him to return to Allah with repentance, humbleness, obedience and submission to His command, admitting his error and seeking Allah's forgiveness and pardon for it."9

16. Satan, banished, says he will spend his time tempting the Muslims away from the straight path. A hadith details how he would confront "the Son of Adam" and chide him for considering converting to Islam, abandoning his ancestral religion. "However," the story goes, "the Son of Adam disobeyed Shaytan and embraced Islam." Thereupon Satan "sat in the path of Hijrah (migration for the sake of Allah)," again chiding the Son of Adam for thinking of leaving "your land and sky." But once again the Son of Adam disobeyed Satan and emigrated for the sake of Allah. Finally, "Shaytan

sat in the path of Jihad, against one's self and with his wealth," warning potential jihadis: "If you fight, you will be killed, your wife will be married and your wealth divided." This once again illustrates the fact that the predominant understanding of jihad in early Islamic tradition involves warfare. In this case, the Son of Adam once again disobeyed Satan and went on jihad. The hadith continues: "Therefore, whoever among them (Children of Adam) does this and dies, it will be a promise from Allah that He admits him into Paradise. If he is killed, it will be a promise from Allah that He admits him into Paradise."10

18. On Gehenna, see 2:206.

19. Here begins a recounting of the temptation of Adam and Eve, their sin, and their banishment from the garden. It follows the broad outline of the Biblical account (Genesis 2:15-3:19), although there is no textual dependence.

26. The clothing of Adam and Eve is one of the "signs of Allah" and becomes the starting point for a disquisition on modesty that goes to 7:33.

say, We found our fathers doing it and Allah has commanded it for us. Say, Allah indeed does not command lewdness. Are you saying something about all that you do know? **29**Say, My Lord commands justice. And set your faces upright at every mosque and call upon him, making religion pure for him. As he brought you into being, so return. **30**He has led a group rightly, while error has a just hold over a group, for indeed, they choose the satans for protecting supporters instead of Allah and think that they are rightly guided. **31**O children of Adam, be mindful of your clothing at every place of prayer, and eat and drink, but do not be wasteful. Indeed, he does not love the wasteful. **32**Say, Who has forbidden the adornment of Allah which he has brought forth for his slaves, and the good things he has provided? Say, On the day of resurrection, such things will only be for those who believed during the life of this world. In this way we explain our signs for people who have knowledge. **33**Say, My Lord forbids only indecencies, those that are apparent and those that are within, and sin and wrongful oppression, and that you associate with Allah something for which no justification has been revealed, and that you say something about Allah that you do not know. **34**And every nation has its term, and when its term comes, they cannot put it off or advance it even by an hour. **35**O children of Adam, when messengers of your own come to you who narrate my signs to you, then whoever refrains from evil and changes, no fear will come upon them, nor

will they grieve. **36**But those who deny our signs and ridicule them, each of them are rightful companions of the fire, they will remain in it. **37**Who does greater wrong than he who invents a lie about Allah or denies our signs? Their established portion of the book reaches them until, when our messengers come to gather them, they say, Where is that to which you called out besides Allah? They say, They have departed from us. And they testify against themselves that they were unbelievers. **38**He says, Enter into the fire among nations of the jinn and mankind who passed away before you. Every time a nation enters, it curses its sister until, when they have all been made to follow one another there, the last of them says to the first of them, Our Lord, these people led us astray, so give them double torment of the fire. He says, For each one there is double, but you do not know. **39**And the first of them says to the last of them, You were not a bit better than we were, so taste the doom for what you used to earn. **40**Indeed, they who deny our signs and ridicule them, for them the gates of paradise will not be opened, nor will they enter the garden until the camel goes through the eye of a needle. In this way we repay the guilty. **41**Theirs will be a bed of Gehenna, and over them coverings. In this way we repay wrongdoers. **42**But those who believe and do good works, we do not burden any soul beyond its ability. Such people are rightful companions of the garden. They remain in it. **43**And we remove whatever anger may be in their hearts.

---

29. Barth sees "And set your faces upright at every mosque and call upon him, making religion pure for him" as a later interpolation.[11]

36. Here begins a sounding of one of the Qur'an's oft-repeated themes, the fiery punishment of the damned, and their remorse and mutual recriminations.

41. On Gehenna, see 2:206.

43. Regarding "we remove whatever anger may be in their hearts," see 9:14. Barth points out that the flow of this passage is interrupted by the phrase, "Rivers flow beneath them," which would fit better immediately after the mention of the garden and the blessed remaining in it at the end of 7:42.[12]

Rivers flow beneath them. And they say, Praise be to Allah, who has guided us to this. We could not indeed have been led rightly if Allah had not guided us. Indeed the messengers of our Lord brought the truth. And it is called out to them, This is the garden. You inherit it for what you used to do. **44**And those who dwell in the garden call out to those who dwell in the fire, We have found what our Lord promised us to be the truth. Have you found what your Lord promised to be the truth? They say, Yes, indeed. And a voice in between them calls out, The curse of Allah is on evildoers, **45**Who bar people from the path of Allah and try to make it crooked, and who are unbelievers in the last day. **46**Between them is a veil. And on the heights are men who know them all by their signs. And they call out to those who dwell in the garden, Peace be upon you. They do not enter it, although they hope to. **47**And when their eyes are turned toward those who dwell in the fire, they say, Our Lord, do not put us with the wrongdoing people. **48**And those who dwell on the heights call out to men whom they know by their signs, How did your multitude and what you took pride in help you? **49**Are these the ones about whom you swore that Allah would not show them mercy? Enter the garden. No fear will come upon you, nor is it you who will grieve. **50**And those who dwell in the fire call out to those who dwell in the Garden, Pour some water on us, or something with which Allah has provided you. They say, Indeed, Allah has forbidden both to unbelievers, **51**Who took their religion for a game and a pastime, and who were fooled by the life of this world beguiled. So on this day we have forgotten them, even as they forgot the meeting of this their day, and as they used to deny our signs. **52**Indeed, we have brought them a book which we explained with knowledge, a guidance and a mercy for a people who believe. **53**Are they waiting for anything except its fulfillment? On the day when its fulfillment comes, those who were forgetful of it before will say, The messengers of our Lord brought the truth. Do we have any intercessors, that they may intercede for us? Or can we be returned, so that we may act other than how we used to act? They have lost their souls, and what they devised has failed them. **54**Indeed, your Lord is Allah, who created the heavens and the earth in six days, and then mounted the throne. He covers the night with the day, which is in haste to follow it, and has made the sun and the moon and the stars submissive by his command. All creation and command is indeed his. Blessed be Allah, the Lord of the worlds. **55**Call upon your Lord humbly and in secret. Indeed, he does not love aggressors. **56**Do not spread corruption on earth after it has been set in order, and call on him in fear and hope. Indeed, the mercy of Allah is near to those who are good. **57**And it is he who sends the winds bearing good news before his mercy, until, when they carry a heavy cloud, we lead it to a dead land, and then cause water to descend on it and thereby bring forth fruits of every kind. In this way we bring forth the dead. Perhaps you may remember. **58**As for the good land, its

---

50. No mercy will be afforded to the damned, despite their pleas.

54. Allah here creates the universe in six days, as he does at 10:3, 11:7, 25:59, 32:4, and 50:38. However, at 41:9-12, he does it in eight days.

57. Instead of "he who sends the winds bearing good news," the Warsh Qur'an and the version of al-Layth ibn Khalid, one of the transmitters of the reading of al-Kisa'i, have "he who sends the winds as scatterers."[13]

vegetation comes forth by permission of its Lord, while as for what is bad, only what is useless comes forth. In this way we recount the signs for people who give thanks. ⁵⁹We sent Noah to his people, and he said, O my people, serve Allah. You have no other God except him. Indeed, I fear for you the retribution of an awful day. ⁶⁰The chieftains of his people said, Indeed, we see you are surely in plain error. ⁶¹He said, O my people, there is no error in me, but I am a messenger from the Lord of the worlds. ⁶²I convey to you the messages of my Lord and give good advice to you, and know from Allah what you do not know. ⁶³Are you amazed that there would come to you a reminder from your Lord by means of a man among you, that he may warn you, and that you may avoid evil, and that perhaps you may find mercy? ⁶⁴But they denied him, so we saved him and those with him in the ship, and we drowned those who denied our signs. Indeed, they were blind people. ⁶⁵And to Aad, their brother, Hud. He said, O my people, serve Allah. You have no other God except him. Will you not fear Allah? ⁶⁶The chieftains of his people, who were disbelieving, said, Indeed, we surely see you in foolishness, and Indeed, we consider you to be among the liars. ⁶⁷He said, O my people, there is no foolishness in me, but I am a messenger from the Lord of the Worlds. ⁶⁸I convey to you the messages of my Lord, and I am for you a true adviser. ⁶⁹Are you amazed that there would come to you a reminder from your Lord by means of a man among you, that he may warn you? Remember how he made you caliphs after Noah's people, and increased you in size. Remember the bounties of your Lord, that perhaps you may be successful. ⁷⁰They said, Have you come to us so that we would serve Allah alone, and forsake what our fathers worshipped? Then bring upon us whatever you're threatening us with, if you are among the truthful. ⁷¹He said, Terror and wrath from your Lord have already fallen on you. Would you argue with me over names which you have named, you and your fathers, for which no justification from Allah has been revealed? Then wait. Indeed, I am among those who are waiting. ⁷²And we saved him and those who were with him by a mercy from us, and we cut the root of those who denied our signs and were not believers. ⁷³And to Thamud, their brother Salih. He said, O my people, serve Allah. You have no other God except him. A wonder from your Lord has come to you. Indeed, this is the camel of Allah, a sign to you, so let her feed on Allah's earth, and do not touch her, so that painful torment will not seize you. ⁷⁴And remember how he made you caliphs after Aad, and gave you a place on earth. You choose castles in the plains and cut the mountains into dwellings. So remember the bounties of Allah and do not do evil, spreading corruption on earth. ⁷⁵The chieftains of his people, who were scornful, said to those whom they despised, to those among them who believed, Do you know that Salih has been sent from his Lord? They said, Indeed, we

---

59. The story of Noah begins an extended section (to 7:95) telling the stories of the prophets, continuing with the extrabiblical figures Hud (7:65-72) and Salih (7:73-79), Lot (7:80-84), and another extrabiblical prophet, Shu'aib (7:85-95). These stories all follow the same pattern: the prophets warn the people to whom they are sent in language much like that which the messenger is directed to use in the Qur'an. These prophets are also scorned and rejected in much the same way that the messenger is by those who are characterized in the Qur'an as hypocrites and unbelievers. See also 10:71, 11:25, 21:76, 23:23, 25:37, 26:105, 29:14, 37:75, 50:12, 51:46, 53:52, 54:9, 57:26, 69:11, and 71:1.

69. On "caliphs," see 2:30, as also for 7:74.

are believers in what he has been sent with. [76]Those who were scornful said, Indeed, we are unbelievers in what you believe. [77]So they hamstrung the camel, and they defied the commandment of their Lord, and they said, O Salih, bring upon us what you threatened us with if you are indeed one of those who was sent. [78]So the earthquake seized them, and morning found them prostrate in their dwelling places. [79]And he turned away from them and said, O my people, I delivered my Lord's message to you and gave you good advice, but you do not love good advisers. [80]And Lot, when he said to his people, Will you commit abominations such as no one in the worlds ever did before you? [81]Indeed, you come with lust to men instead of to women. No, but you are wanton people. [82]And the answer of his people was only that they said, Turn them out of your town. They are people who keep pure. [83]And we rescued him and his family, except his wife, who was of those who stayed behind. [84]And we sent a rain upon them. See now the nature of the consequences evildoers suffer. [85]And to Midian, their brother, Shu'aib. He said, O my people! Serve Allah. You have no other God except him. Indeed, a clear proof has come to you from your Lord, so give full measure and full weight and do not wrong mankind in their goods, and do not spread corruption on earth after it has been set in order. That will be better for you, if you are believers. [86]Do not lurk on every road to threaten, and to turn away from Allah's path someone who believes in him, and try to make it crooked. And

remember, when you were just a few, how he multiplied you. And see the nature of the consequences for the corrupters. [87]And if there is a group of you who believes in what I have been sent with, and there is a group that does not believe, then have patience until Allah judges between us. He is the best of all who deal in judgment. [88]The chieftains of his people, who were scornful, said, Surely we will drive you out, O Shu'aib, and those who believe with you, from our town, unless you return to our religion. He said, Even though we hate it? [89]We would have invented a lie against Allah if we returned to your religion after Allah has rescued us from it. It is not for us to return to it unless Allah our Lord should will. Our Lord comprehends all things in knowledge. In Allah do we put our trust. Our Lord, decide with truth between us and our people, for you are the best of those who make decisions. [90]But the chieftains of his people, who were disbelieving, said, If you follow Shu'aib, then indeed you will be the losers. [91]So the earthquake seized them and morning found them prostrate in their dwelling places. [92]Those who denied Shu'aib became as if they had not lived there. Those who denied Shu'aib, they were the losers. [93]So he turned away from them and said, O my people, I delivered my Lord's messages to you and gave you good advice, then how can I sorrow for a people that rejected? [94]And we sent no prophet to any town without afflicting its people with tribulation and adversity, so that perhaps they might grow humble. [95]Then we changed their evil

---

77. On the camel of Allah, see 11:64, 26:155, and 91:11-14, as well as the introduction to sura 11.

81. Lot's story bears traces of the Sodom and Gomorrah incident in the Bible, as this verse recalls Genesis 19:5. The punishment for homosexual activity in Islamic law is death, based on a statement

attributed to Muhammad: "If you find anyone doing as Lot's people did, kill the one who does it, and the one to whom it is done."[14]

89. Shu'aib's refusal to fabricate "a lie against Allah" recalls what Allah said to the children of Adam (7:37).

plight for good until they grew wealthy and said, Tribulation and distress touched our fathers. Then we seized them unaware, when they did not perceive. **96**And if the people of the townships had believed and kept from evil, surely we would have opened for them blessings from the sky and from the earth. But they lied, and so we seized them because of what they used to earn. **97**Are the people of the towns then secure from the coming of our wrath upon them in a night raid while they sleep? **98**Or are the people of the towns then secure from the coming of our wrath upon them in the daytime while they play? **99**Are they then secure from Allah's scheme? No one thinks of himself as secure from Allah's scheme except people that perish. **100**Is it not an indication to those who inherit the land after its people that, if we will, we can strike them for their sins and seal up their hearts so that they do not hear? **101**Such were the towns. We relate some news of them to you. Their messengers indeed came to them with clear proofs, but they could not believe because they had denied before. In this way does Allah seal up the hearts of unbelievers. **102**We found no covenant in most of them. No, most of them we found to be wrongdoers. **103**Then, after them, we sent Moses with our signs to Pharaoh and his chiefs, but they repelled them. Now, see the nature of the consequences for the corrupters!

104 Moses said, O Pharaoh, indeed, I am a messenger from the Lord of the worlds, **105**Approved upon the condition that I speak nothing but the truth about Allah. I come to you with a clear proof from your Lord. So let the children of Israel go with me. **106**He said, If you come with a sign, then produce it, if you are among those who speak the truth. **107**Then he flung down his staff and indeed, it was clearly a serpent, **108**And he drew forth his hand, and indeed, it was white for those who saw it. **109**The chiefs of Pharaoh's people said, Indeed, this is some knowledgeable wizard, **110**Who would expel you from your land. Now what do you advise? **111**They said, Put him off, him and his brother, and send summoners into the cities, **112**To bring each knowledgeable wizard to you. **113**And the wizards came to Pharaoh, saying, Surely there will be a reward for us if we are victorious. **114**He answered, Yes, and surely you will be among those who are brought near. **115**They said, O Moses, either throw or let us be the first throwers. **116**He said, Throw. And when they threw, they cast a spell upon the people's eyes, and overawed them, and produced a mighty spell. **117**And we inspired Moses, Throw your staff. And indeed, it swallowed up their lying show. **118**In that way the truth was vindicated, and what they were doing was made vain. **119**In this way they were defeated there and brought low. **120**And

---

99. Allah is also depicted as a schemer or plotter at 3:54, 8:30, and 10:21.

101. Allah warns again of the destruction that will come to towns that reject him, yet their unbelief is Allah's doing: "In this way does Allah seal up the hearts of unbelievers." This may be because "they had denied before," but if so, it would be difficult to see how anyone could repent or convert from any other faith to Islam.

103. This retelling of the story of Moses, which goes to 7:171, is told in a way that suggests that the hearers have heard it before, as the hearers are assumed to know key details (see 7:105). On Pharaoh, see also 2:49, 3:11, 8:52, 10:75, 14:6, 17:101, 20:24, 23:46,

26:11, 27:12, 28:3, 29:39, 38:12, 40:24, 44:17, 50:13, 51:38, 54:41, 66:11, 69:9, 73:15, 79:15, 85:18, and 89:10.

105. When Moses tells Pharaoh to "let the children of Israel go with me," it is not mentioned but assumed that the hearers will know that the Israelites were at this time oppressed as slaves in Egypt.

108. Moses performs various miracles before Pharaoh, as in the Biblical account, although when Moses's hand becomes "white for those who saw it," a tradition ascribed to Ibn Abbas says this was "not because of leprosy," which is contrary to Exodus 4:6.[15] The Ruhul Ma'ani says that Moses's hand shone brighter than the sun.

the wizards fell down prostrate, [121]Crying, we believe in the Lord of the worlds, [122]The Lord of Moses and Aaron. [123]Pharaoh said, You believe in him before I give you permission! Indeed, this is the plot that you have plotted in the city, so that you may drive its people away from there. But you will come to know. [124]Surely I will have your hands and feet cut off upon alternate sides. Then I will crucify every one of you. [125]They said, Indeed, we are about to return to our Lord. [126]You take vengeance on us only as much as we believed the signs of our Lord when they came to us. Our Lord, grant us perseverance and make us die as Muslims. [127]The chiefs of Pharaoh's people said, Will you allow Moses and his people to spread corruption in the land, and defy you and your gods? He said, We will kill their sons and leave their women alive, for indeed, we are in power over them. [128]And Moses said to his people, Seek help in Allah and endure. Indeed, the earth belongs to Allah. He gives it to whom he wills as an inheritance. And indeed, the ending is for those who keep their duty. [129]They said, We suffered harm before you came to us, and since you have come to us. He said, It may be that your Lord is going to destroy your adversary and make you caliphs on earth, so that he may see how you behave. [130]And we burdened Pharaoh's people with famine and a lack of fruits, so that perhaps they might pay attention. [131]But whenever something good happened to them, they said, This is ours, and whenever evil struck them, they ascribed it to the evil omens of Moses and those who were with him. Surely their evil omen was only with Allah. But most of them did not know. [132]And they said, Whatever sign you bring with which to bewitch us, we will not put faith in you. [133]So we sent against them the flood and the locusts and the vermin and the frogs and the blood, a succession of clear signs. But they were arrogant and became a guilty people. [134]And when the terror fell on them, they called out, O Moses, pray for us to your Lord, because he has a covenant with you. If you remove the terror from us, we will indeed trust you and will let the children of Israel go with you. [135]But when we removed the terror from them for a term that they had to reach, look, they broke their covenant. [136]Therefore we took retribution from them, therefore we drowned them in the sea, because they denied our signs and were heedless of them. [137]And we caused the people who were despised to inherit the eastern parts of the land and the western parts which we had blessed. And the fair word of your Lord was fulfilled for the children of Israel because of their endurance, and we annihilated what Pharaoh and his people had done and what they had contrived. [138]And we brought the children of Israel across the sea, and they came to a people who were given up to the idols that they

---

121. Pharaoh, as in the Biblical story, is unimpressed (Exodus 7:13). But Pharaoh's magicians are and say, "We believe in the Lord of the worlds, the Lord of Moses and Aaron."

124. This is the same punishment Allah prescribes for those who wage war against Allah and Muhammad (5:33).

126. The magicians pray that Allah will "make us die as Muslims": this is another reminder that the Qur'an considers the Biblical prophets all to have been prophets of Islam whose messages were later corrupted to create Judaism and Christianity.

129. Those who today claim that the Qur'an promises the land of Israel to the Jews (see 5:21) often overlook this passage (as well as 5:13), in which the children of Israel are given a chance to be "caliphs on earth" (see 2:30) and fail the test.

133. The plagues are here again enumerated as if the hearers are already familiar with the story.

137. See 5:21 and 7:129.

had. They said, O Moses, Make a god for us even as they have gods. He said, Indeed, you are a people who do not know. ¹³⁹Indeed, as for these, their way will be destroyed and all that they are doing is in vain. ¹⁴⁰He said, Will I seek for you a god other than Allah when He has favored you over the worlds? ¹⁴¹And when we delivered you from Pharaoh's people who were afflicting you with dreadful torment, slaughtering your sons and sparing your women. That was a tremendous trial from your Lord. ¹⁴²And when we appointed for Moses thirty nights, and added ten to them, and he completed the whole time appointed by his Lord of forty nights, and Moses said to his brother, Aaron, Take my place among the people. Do right, and do not follow the way of mischief-makers. ¹⁴³And when Moses came to our planned meeting and his Lord had spoken to him, he said, My Lord, show me, so that I may look upon you. He said, you will not see me, but look upon the mountain. If it stands still in its place, then you will see me. And when his Lord revealed glory to the mountain, he sent it crashing down. And Moses fell down senseless. And when he woke, he said, Glory to you, I turn to you repentant, and I am the first of the believers. ¹⁴⁴He said, O Moses, I have preferred you above mankind by my messages and by my speaking. So hold to what I have given you, and be among the thankful. ¹⁴⁵And we wrote for him upon the tablets the lesson to be drawn from all things and the explanation of all things, then, Hold it fast, and command your people, Take what is better in it. I will show you the abode of transgressors. ¹⁴⁶I will turn away from my signs those who exalt themselves wrongfully on earth, and if they see each sign do not believe it, and if they see the way of righteousness do not choose it for a way, and if they see the way of error, choose it for a way. That is because they deny our signs and used to disregard them. ¹⁴⁷Those who deny our signs and the meeting of the hereafter, their works are fruitless. Are they repaid for anything except what they used to do? ¹⁴⁸And the people of Moses, afterward chose a calf out of their ornaments, which made a lowing sound. Didn't they see that it did not speak to them or guide them to any path? They chose it and became wrongdoers. ¹⁴⁹And when they feared the consequences of this and saw that they had gone astray, they said, Unless our Lord has mercy on us and forgives us, we are indeed among the lost. ¹⁵⁰And when Moses returned to his people, angry and grieved, he said, What you did after I left you is evil. Would you hasten the judgment of your Lord? And he threw down the tablets, and he seized his brother by the head, dragging him toward him. He said, Son of my mother, indeed, the people judged me weak and almost killed me. Oh, do not make my enemies triumph over me and do not place me among the evildoers. ¹⁵¹He said, My Lord, have mercy on me and on my brother, bring us into your mercy, you who are the most merciful of all those who show mercy. ¹⁵²Indeed, those who

---

144. Instead of "my messages" (*beresaalaati*), the Warsh Qur'an has "my message" (*beresaalati*).[16]

145. Moses goes up on Mount Tur (28:46) to converse with Allah and receive laws, which the Qur'an does not enumerate, on stone tablets. The Ten Commandments never appear in the Qur'an and are a notable omission from its multiple retellings of the Exodus.

154. Instead of "and mercy," a Qur'anic manuscript examined by the Assyrian Islamic scholar Alphonse Mingana (1878-1937) has "and peace."[17]

chose the calf, terror from their Lord and humiliation will come upon them in the life of this
world. In this way we repay those who invent a
lie. ¹⁵³But those who do evil deeds and afterward
repent and believe, indeed, for them, afterward,
Allah is forgiving, merciful. ¹⁵⁴Then, when the
anger of Moses abated, he took up the tablets, and
in what was inscribed on them was guidance and
mercy for all those who fear their Lord. ¹⁵⁵And
Moses chose seventy men among his people for
our appointed meeting and, when the trembling
came upon them, said, My Lord, If you had
willed, you would have destroyed them long
before, and me with them. Will you destroy us for
what the ignorant among us did? It is only your
trial. You send astray those whom you will and
guide those whom you will, you are our protecting friend, therefore forgive us and have mercy
on us, you who are the best of all those who show
forgiveness. ¹⁵⁶And ordain for us what is good in
this world, and in the hereafter. Indeed, we have
turned to you. He said, I strike those whom I will
with my punishment, and my mercy embraces all
things, therefore I will ordain it for those who
fear Allah and give alms, and those who believe
our signs, ¹⁵⁷Those who follow the messenger, the

unlettered prophet, whom they will find
described in the Torah and the Gospel with them.
He will command for them what is right and forbid them what is wrong. He will make lawful for
them all good things and prohibit for them only
the filthy things, and he will relieve them of their
burden and the chains that they used to wear.
Then those who believe in him and honor him
and help him and follow the light which is sent
down with him, they are the ones who are successful. ¹⁵⁸Say, O mankind, indeed, I am the
messenger of Allah to you all, him to whom
belongs the dominion of the heavens and the
earth. There is no God except him. He brings to
life and he gives death. So believe in Allah and his
messenger, the prophet who can neither read nor
write, who believes in Allah and in his words, and
follow him, so that perhaps you may be led
rightly. ¹⁵⁹And among Moses' people there is a
community that leads with truth and establishes
justice with it. ¹⁶⁰We divided them into twelve
tribes, nations, and we inspired Moses, when his
people asked him for water, saying, Strike the
rock with your staff! And there gushed forth
twelve springs from it, so that each tribe knew
their drinking-place. And we caused the white

---

156. "Give alms" is *zakat*, and "signs" once again is the word
used of the verses of the Qur'an, so this passage strongly suggests
that Allah shows mercy only to those who are Muslims.

157. "The unlettered prophet" is *an-nabiyya al-ommiyya*. While
ommiyya is frequently translated as "illiterate," "unlettered," "unable
to read and write," and the like, in 62:2 it is said that Allah "sent
among the unlettered ones a messenger of their own." As not all
of the early believers were illiterate, and the message of the Qur'an
was never restricted to the illiterate only, an alternative explanation
may be preferable. The same word can also be rendered as "Gentiles," as it is fittingly rendered in 3:75, which otherwise would have
the rebellious Jews in the passage saying they have no duty to the
illiterate. In light of 3:75 and 62:2, it is likely that 7:157 is saying not
that the messenger is illiterate but that he is a Gentile.

Says Ibn Kathir: "This is the description of the Prophet Muhammad in the Books of the Prophets. They delivered the good news of

his advent to their nations and commanded them to follow him.
His descriptions were still apparent in their Books, as the rabbis
and the priests well know."¹⁸ The rabbis and priests well know: here
again is the Islamic belief that the Jews and Christians, or at least
their leaders, know that Muhammad is a true prophet but obsti-
nately refuse to accept him; they aren't rejecting him in good faith.
The fact that Muhammad is not actually described in the Jewish or
Christian scriptures has helped give rise to the Islamic claim that
the Jews and Christians have corrupted their scriptures to remove
references to him; see 61:6.

The declaration that the messenger commands what is right and
forbids what is wrong is one of the foundations for the belief in the
hadiths, despite the fact that they date from two to three centuries
after Muhammad is supposed to have lived, and thus have dubious
historical value at best. Muslims are told to follow what Muhammad
commands, and only in the hadith can those commands be discovered.

cloud to overshadow them and sent down for them the manna and the quails, Eat of the good things with which we have provided you. They did not wrong us, but they were inclined to wrong themselves. **161**And when it was said to them, Dwell in this town and eat from it wherever you will, and say, Repentance, and enter the gate prostrate, we forgive your sins, we will increase the reward for those who do right.

162 But those among them who did wrong exchanged the word that had been told them for another saying, and we sent down upon them wrath from heaven for their wrongdoing. **163**Ask them about the town that was by the sea, how they broke the Sabbath, how their big fish came to them visibly upon their Sabbath day and did not come to them on a day when they did not keep the Sabbath. In this way we tested them, because they were transgressors. **164**And when a community among them said, Why do you preach to a people whom Allah is about to destroy or punish with an awful doom?, they said, In order to be free from guilt before your Lord, and that perhaps they may fear Allah. **165**And when they forgot that about which they had been reminded, we rescued those who forbade wrong, and visited those who did wrong with dreadful punishment, because they were transgressors. **166**So when they took pride in what they had been forbidden, we said to them, Be apes, despised and hated. **167**And when your

Lord proclaimed that he would raise against them until the day of resurrection those who would lay on them a cruel torment. Indeed, truly your Lord is swift in prosecution, and indeed, truly he is forgiving, merciful. **168**And we have split them on earth as nations. Some of them are righteous, and some far from that. And we have tested them with good things and evil things, so that perhaps they might return. **169**And a generation has succeeded those who inherited the books. They grasp the goods of this low life and say, It will be forgiven us. And if there came to them the same offer, they would accept it. Hasn't the covenant of the book been taken on their behalf, so that they would not speak anything about Allah except the truth? And they have studied what is in it. And the dwelling of the hereafter is better, for those who fear Allah. Have you then no sense? **170**And as for those who make people hold to the book, and establish prayer, indeed, we do not waste the wages of righteous people. **171**And when we shook the mountain above them as if it were a covering, and they thought that it was going to fall upon them, Hold fast to what we have given you, and remember what is in it, so that you may fear Allah. **172**And when your Lord brought forth from the children of Adam, from their loins, their seed, and made them bear witness about themselves, Am I not your Lord? They said, Yes, indeed. We bear witness, so that you would not say on the day

161. Instead of, "We will forgive you your sins," the Warsh Qur'an has, "Your sins will be forgiven."[19]

162. Among the Jews are some who are righteous, but others altered their Scriptures. This accounts for the disconnect between the Qur'an's saying that it confirms the message of the Torah (3:3, 3:50) and the fact that it does not actually do so.

166. See 2:63.

168. The Jews are "split...on earth as nations," further indication that they are not to inherit the land of Israel (see 5:21, 7:129).

172. Everyone on earth is born Muslim, as a hadith has Muhammad saying: "No child is born but has the Islamic Faith, but its parents turn it into a Jew or a Christian."[20] In another hadith, Allah produces all of the multitudes of the children of Adam from his back and asks them, "Am I not your Lord?"[21] All affirm that he is. Therefore, says the *Tafsir Anwarul Bayan*, "None will be able to claim that he had no knowledge of the fact that Allah is his Lord."[22] This is another reason why some Muslims often assume that non-Muslims are dealing in bad faith: they know the Qur'an is true and Muhammad is a prophet but refuse to acknowledge it.

of resurrection, indeed, we were unaware of this, ¹⁷³Or so that you would not say, Only our fathers ascribed partners to Allah of old, and we were the seed after them. Will you destroy us because of what those who follow falsehood did? ¹⁷⁴In this way we detail the signs, so that perhaps they may return. ¹⁷⁵Recite to them the story of him to whom we gave our signs, but he disregarded them, so Satan overtook him and he became one of those who lead people astray. ¹⁷⁶And had we willed, we could have raised him by their means, but he clung to the earth and followed his own lust. Therefore he is like a dog, if you attack him he pants with his tongue out, and if you leave him alone he pants with his tongue out. Such the people are those who deny our signs. Narrate the history to them, so that perhaps they may think. ¹⁷⁷The people who denied our signs are an evil example, and were inclined to wrong themselves. ¹⁷⁸He whom Allah leads, he is indeed led rightly, while he whom Allah leads astray, they indeed are losers. ¹⁷⁹Already we have created many of the jinn and mankind for Gehenna, having hearts with which they do not understand, and having eyes with which they do not see, and having ears with which they do not hear. They are like cattle, no, they are worse. These are the neglectful. ¹⁸⁰Allah's are the most beautiful names. Invoke

him by them. And leave the company of those who blaspheme his names. They will be repaid for what they do. ¹⁸¹And among those whom we created, there is a nation that guides with the truth and establishes justice with it. ¹⁸²And those who deny our signs, step by step we lead them on from where they do not know. ¹⁸³I give them respite, indeed, my scheme is firm. ¹⁸⁴Have they not thought that there is no madness in their comrade? He is but a plain warner. ¹⁸⁵Have they not considered the dominion of the heavens and the earth, and what things Allah has created, and that it may be that their own term draws near? In what fact after this will they believe? ¹⁸⁶Those whom Allah leads astray, there is no guide for them. He leaves them to wander blindly on in their insolence. ¹⁸⁷They ask you about the hour, when it will arrive. Say, Knowledge of it is with my Lord alone. He alone will show it at its proper time. It is heavy in the heavens and the earth. It doesn't come to you except when you are unaware. They ask you as if you could be well informed about it. Say, Knowledge of it is with Allah alone, but most of mankind does not know. ¹⁸⁸Say, For myself I have no power to benefit, nor power to hurt, except what Allah wills. If I had knowledge of the unseen, I would have an abundance of wealth, and adversity would not touch me. I am only a

---

175. There are conflicting traditions about the identity of the person spoken of here. One Islamic tradition holds that it was Bal'am bin Ba'ura, "a man from Yemen whom Allah had given the knowledge of his Ayat, but he abandoned them."[23] Others say he was "one of the scholars of the Children of Israel."[24] The name Bal'am and his identification with the children of Israel suggests that this is a vestige of the story of Balaam, the reluctant prophet of Numbers 22:2-24:25.

179. Allah has created a large number of human beings and jinns solely in order to torture them in hellfire. Those who suffer this fate are entirely bestial. However, Ibn Kathir does not see

anything arbitrary about Allah's judgment here: "We prepared them for it by their performance of the deeds of its people. When Allah intended to create the creation, He knew what their work will be before they existed. He wrote all this in a Book, kept with Him, fifty thousand years before He created the heavens and earth."[25] The difficulty remains, however, in that he nonetheless created those who were to reject him.

On Gehenna, see 2:206.

181. The believers, on the other hand, shall guide mankind with Allah's truth and establish justice by means of it. This is a foundation of Islam's moral critique of the non-Muslim world.

warner, and a bearer of good news to people who believe. **189**It is he who created you from a single soul, and from it made his mate so that he might take pleasure in her. And when he had relations with her, she bore a light burden, and she moved around with it, but when it became heavy, they called out to Allah, their Lord, saying, If you give us a good child, we will be among the thankful. **190**But when he gave them a good child, they ascribed partners to him in regard to what he had given them. He is highly exalted above all that they associate. **191**Do they attribute as partners to Allah those who created nothing, but are themselves created, **192**And cannot give them help, and cannot help themselves? **193**And if you call them to the guidance, they do not follow you. Whether you call them or are silent, it is all the same for you. **194**Indeed, those whom you call upon besides Allah are slaves like you. Call on them now, and let them answer you, if you are truthful. **195**Do they have feet with which they walk, or do they have hands with which they hold, or do they have eyes with which they see, or do they have ears with which they hear? Say, Call upon your partners, and then plot against me, do not spare me.**196**Indeed, my protecting friend is Allah who reveals the book. He befriends the righteous. **197**Those whom you call upon besides him cannot help you, nor can they help themselves. **198**And if you call them to the guidance they do not hear, and you see them looking toward you, but they do not see. **199**Hold to forgiveness, and command kindness, and turn away from the ignorant. **200**And if a slander from Satan wounds you, then seek refuge in Allah. Indeed, he is the hearer, the knower. **201**Indeed, those who fear Allah, when an impulse from Satan troubles them, they only remember and immediately become watchful. **202**Their brethren plunge them further into error and do not stop. **203**And when you do not bring a verse for them, they say, Why haven't you chosen it? Say, I follow only what is inspired in me from my Lord. This is insight from your Lord, and a guidance and a mercy for a people that believes. **204**And when the Qur'an is recited, listen to it and pay attention, so that you may obtain mercy. **205**And remember your Lord within yourself humbly and with awe, not loudly, in the morning and in the evening. And do not be among the neglectful. **206**Indeed, those who are with your Lord are not too proud to do him service, but they praise him and adore him.

---

190. Instead of, "They ascribed partners [*shurakaa*] to him," the eighth-century Qur'an of Abu Jafar has, "They ascribed polytheism [*shirkan*] to him."26

199. Ibn Kathir quotes a statement attributed to the early Muslim Abdur-Rahman bin Zayd bin Aslam, "Allah commanded [Prophet Muhammad] to show forgiveness and turn away from the idolators for ten years. Afterwards Allah ordered him to be harsh with them."27 (The bracketed identification of the messenger is in the original.)

SURA 8

The Spoils of War

Al-Anfal

Introduction

This sura is traditionally dated from the second year of the Medinan period, the second part of Muhammad's prophetic career. Islamic tradition holds that it was revealed not long after the Battle of Badr, the first great victory of the Muslims over their chief rivals of the time, the pagan Quraysh tribe. The title of this sura is better known than most, since Saddam Hussein used Al-Anfal as the name for his genocidal 1988 campaigns against the Kurds, in which between fifty thousand and one hundred thousand people were murdered.

At Badr, according to ninth-century Islamic sources, the Quraysh came out to meet Muhammad's three hundred men with a force nearly a thousand strong. Muhammad had provoked the battle by sending his men out to raid a Quraysh caravan, telling them that Allah might allow them to seize it. As the battle loomed, according to Muhammad's earliest biographer, Ibn Hisham, the Islamic prophet strode among his troops and issued a momentous promise—one that has given heart to Muslim warriors throughout the ages: "By God in whose hand is the soul of Muhammad, no man will be slain this day fighting against them with steadfast courage advancing not retreating but God will cause him to enter Paradise."[1]

The Quraysh were routed. Some Muslim traditions say that Muhammad himself participated in the fighting, others that it was more likely that he exhorted his followers from the sidelines. In any event, it was an occasion

---

1 Ibn Hisham, 300.

for him to avenge years of frustration, resentment, and hatred toward his people who had rejected him. One of his followers later recalled a curse Muhammad had pronounced on the leaders of the Quraysh: "The Prophet said, 'O Allah! Destroy the chiefs of Quraish, O Allah! Destroy Abu Jahl bin Hisham, Utba bin Rabi'a, Shaiba bin Rabi'a, Uqba bin Abi Mu'ait, Umaiya bin Khalaf (or Ubai bin Kalaf)."[2] All these men were captured or killed during the battle of Badr.

The victory at Badr was the turning point for the Muslims. It became the stuff of legend, a cornerstone of the new religion. This sura was, according to Islamic tradition, revealed in the wake of the battle: "On the day of Badr, my brother Umayr was killed and I killed Said ibn al-As and took his sword which was named al-Kifah. I went to the Prophet, Allah bless him and give him peace, and he told me to go and put the sword with the captured booty which was still undivided. I went back in a state which only Allah knew as a result of the killing of my brother and the loss of my spoil. I did not go very far when Surah al-Anfal was revealed. The Messenger of Allah, Allah bless him and give him peace, called me and said: 'Go and take back your sword!'"[3]

This sura makes clear once again that the jihad that is enjoined upon Muslims involves violence and warfare, and results in spoils for the Muslim community.

Bell states that this sura, "though usually regarded as having been composed shortly after Badr, cannot be a unity."[4] This is because, he points out, 8:11–14, 8:25, 8:48, and 8:54 "have a different rhyme scheme from the rest of the surah."[5]

---

2 Bukhari, vol. 4, book 58, no. 3185
3 Al-Wahidi, 130.
4 Bell, I, 159.
5 Ibid.

The Spoils of War

IN THE NAME OF ALLAH, THE COMPASSIONATE, THE MERCIFUL.

¹They ask you about the spoils of war. Say, The spoils of war belong to Allah and the messenger, so keep your duty to Allah, and settle your differences, and obey Allah and his messenger, if you are believers. ²The believers are only those whose hearts feel fear when Allah is mentioned, and when his signs are recited to them, they increase their faith, and who trust in their Lord, ³Who establish prayer and spend out of what we have bestowed on them. ⁴Those are the ones who are indeed believers. For them are grades with their Lord, and forgiveness, and a bountiful provision. ⁵Even as your Lord caused you to go forth from your home with the truth, and indeed, a party of the believers were averse. ⁶Disputing with you over the truth after it had been made clear, as if they were being driven to visible death. ⁷And when Allah promised you one of the two bands, that it would be yours, and you longed that the one other than the armed one might be yours.

And Allah willed that he would cause the truth to triumph by his words, and cut the root of the unbelievers, ⁸That he might cause the truth to triumph and bring vanity to nothing, however much the guilty might oppose it, ⁹When you asked for help from your Lord and he answered you, I will help you with a thousand angels, rank on rank. ¹⁰Allah established it only as good news, and that your hearts might be at rest because of it. Victory comes only by the help of Allah. Indeed, Allah is mighty, wise. ¹¹When he made sleep fall upon you as a reassurance from him and sent down water from the sky upon you, so that by it he might purify you, and remove the fear of Satan from you, and make your hearts strong and your feet firm by it. ¹²When your Lord inspired the angels, I am with you. So make those who believe stand firm. I will cast terror into the hearts of those who disbelieve. Then strike the necks and strike their fingertips. ¹³That is because they opposed Allah and his messenger. Whoever opposes Allah and his messenger, indeed, Allah is

---

1. Islamic tradition holds that there was great booty for the victors at Badr, so much that it became a bone of contention among the Muslims. According to the story, Muhammad was receiving questions about the disposal of the booty, and Allah responds by telling them that its distribution is up to the messenger.

This was in accord with a special privilege that Allah had granted to Muhammad. Muhammad explained: "I have been given five (things) which were not given to any amongst the Prophets before me." These included the fact that "Allah made me victorious by awe (by His frightening my enemies)" and "the booty has been made Halal (lawful) to me (and was not made so to anyone else)."[1] Another hadith has Muhammad saying "victorious with terror" rather than "victorious by awe."[2]

5. Allah refers to various incidents that took place before and during the battle, emphasizing that he commands warfare and protects the believers in it. The true believers were willing to go out of their homes to wage jihad warfare, but some disliked doing so and complained. This echoes 2:216.

9. The thousand angels that joined the Muslims to smite the Quraysh are an indication that Allah fights alongside the righteous, and thus righteousness is a prerequisite for victory.

12. This verse became one of the chief justifications for the Islamic practice of beheading hostages and war captives. Ibn Kathir explains that the angels are instruments of Allah's wrath who are to "support the believers, strengthen their (battle) front against their enemies, thus, implementing My command to you. I will cast fear, disgrace and humiliation over those who defied My command and denied My Messenger."[3] Leaving no doubt whatsoever that a literal massacre is envisioned, he further elucidates the passage thusly: "Strike them on their foreheads to tear them apart and cover the necks to cut them off, and cut off their limbs, hands and feet."[4]

The Tafsir al-Jalalayn explains this in terms that assume divine assistance, asserting: "It happened that a man would go to strike at the neck of an unbeliever and his head would fall off before his sword was able to get there."[5]

13. Allah makes it clear that he sent angels because the Quraysh opposed him and the messenger.

severe in punishment. **14**So taste that, and that for unbelievers is the torment of the fire. **15**O you who believe, when you meet those who disbelieve in battle, do not turn your backs on them. **16**Whoever turns his back on them on that day, unless he is maneuvering for battle or intent on joining a company, he indeed has incurred wrath from Allah, and his dwelling place will be Gehenna, an evil destination. **17**You did not kill them, but Allah killed them. And you did not throw when you threw, but Allah threw, so that he might test the believers with a fair test from him. Indeed, Allah is the hearer, the knower. **18**As such, Allah who makes weak the plan of unbelievers. **19**If you sought a judgment, now the judgment has come to you. And if you cease, it will be better for you, but if you return, we will also return. And your army will not help you at all, however numerous it may be, and Allah is with the believers. **20**O you who believe, obey Allah and his messenger, and do not turn away from him when you hear. **21**Do not be like those who say, We hear, and they do not hear. **22**Indeed, the worst of animals in Allah's sight are the deaf and the dumb, who have no sense. **23**If Allah had known of any good in them, he would have made them hear, but if he had

made them hear, they would have turned away, averse. **24**O you who believe, obey Allah and the messenger when he calls you to what gives you life, and know that Allah comes in between a man and his own heart, and that it is he to whom you will be gathered. **25**And seek protection against a punishment that cannot fall exclusively on those of you who are wrongdoers, and know that Allah is severe in punishment. **26**And remember, when you were few and were considered weak in the land, and were in fear that men would wipe you out, how he gave you refuge, and strengthened you with his help, and made provision of good things for you, so that perhaps you might be thankful. **27**O you who believe, do not betray Allah and his messenger, and do not knowingly betray your pledges. **28**And know that your possessions and your children are a test, and that there is immense reward with Allah. **29**O you who believe, if you keep your duty to Allah, he will give you discrimination and will rid you of your evil thoughts and deeds, and will forgive you. Allah is of infinite bounty. **30**And when those who disbelieve plot against you, to wound you fatally, or to kill you or to drive you out, they scheme, but Allah schemes, and Allah is the best of schemers.

15. The Muslims must always advance, never turning their backs on the enemy, unless they do so as a stratagem of war. This is why the color green is featured on the flags of so many Islamic nations: Islam is and must be ever expanding, always experiencing a springtime, never losing ground or withering and dying.

16. On Gehenna, see 2:206, as also for 8:36-7.

17. Allah tells the messenger that the Muslims were merely passive instruments at Badr. At one point, according to Ibn Hisham, Muhammad threw pebbles toward the Quraysh, exclaiming: "Foul be those faces!"[6] But it was Allah who killed the Quraysh and even Allah who threw the pebbles.

19. Once again emphasizing the eschatological nature of this paradigmatic battle, Allah warns the Quraysh not to attempt another attack, telling them they will again be defeated no matter

how much more numerous they are than the Muslims. This theme is returned to at 8:26, which may suggest some textual dislocation.

20. Seen in the light of the surrounding context, the exhortation to faith that begins here is giving the key to success in battle.

27. Instead of, "O you who believe, do not betray Allah and his messenger, and do not knowingly betray your pledges," the Shi'ite Bankipur Qur'an manuscript has, "O you who believe, do not betray Allah and his messenger, and do not knowingly betray your pledges in the family of Muhammad."[7] See 2:59 and the Appendix: Two Apocryphal Shi'ite Suras.

30. Here again, the idea is reinforced that the battles of the Muslims are more than just earthly conflicts but elaborations of Allah's plan. Allah is also depicted as a schemer or plotter at 3:54, 7:99, and 10:21.

³¹And when our signs are recited to them, they say, We have heard. If we wished, we could speak like this. Indeed, this is nothing but fables of the men of old. ³²And when they said, O Allah, if this is indeed the truth from you, then rain down stones on us or bring on us some painful doom. ³³But Allah would not punish them while you were with them, nor will he punish them while they seek forgiveness. ³⁴What do they have that Allah should not punish them, when they bar people from the sacred mosque, though they are not its proper guardians. Its proper guardians are those only who keep their duty to Allah. But most of them do not know. ³⁵And their prayer at the house is nothing but whistling and hand-clapping. Therefore, Taste of the doom because you disbelieve. ³⁶Indeed, those who disbelieve spend their wealth so that they may bar people from the way of Allah. They will spend it, then it will become a source of anguish for them, then they will be conquered. And those who disbelieve will be gathered to Gehenna, ³⁷So that Allah might separate the evil from the good, the evil he will place piece upon piece, and heap them all together, and consign them to Gehenna. Such are indeed the losers. ³⁸Tell those who disbelieve that if they cease, what is past will be forgiven them, but if they return, then the example of the men of old is already known. ³⁹And fight them until persecution is no more, and religion is all for Allah. But if they stop, then indeed, Allah is the seer of what they do. ⁴⁰And if they turn away, then know that Allah is your protector, an excellent protector, an excellent supporter. ⁴¹And know that whatever you take as spoils of war, indeed, a fifth of it is for Allah, and for the messenger and for the relatives and orphans and the needy and the traveler, if you believe in Allah and what we revealed to our slave on the day of *furqan*, the day when the two armies met. And Allah is able to do all things. ⁴²When you were on the near bank and they were on the far bank, and the caravan was below you. And if you had planned to meet one another, you surely would have failed to keep the appointment, but so that Allah might conclude a thing that must be done, so that he who died

---

31. This rejection of the messenger's preaching is one key reason why the Quraysh were defeated.

34. The Quraysh also set themselves up for defeat by barring the Muslims from the sacred mosque, which is usually identified as being in Mecca, but see 6:92.

39. According to numerous Islamic authorities, the statement that Muslims must fight until there is no more persecution (*fitna*) means that they must fight "so that there is no more Shirk."[8] For shirk, see 2:193, 4:31, and 6:21. The *Tafsir al-Jalalayn* explains that the fight must continue until "only He is worshipped."[9] The popular twentieth-century Saudi *Tafsir as-Sadi* states: "This is the goal of fighting and jihad against the enemies of the faith; it is to ward off their evil from the faith and to defend the religion of Allah, Who created people to follow this path, so that it will be supreme over all other religions."[10] This is thus an open-ended declaration of warfare against non-Muslims and assumes that non-Muslim religious observance in itself constitutes "persecution." The idea that Islam will prevail over all other religions is additionally at 2:193, 9:33, and 61:9.

41. An Islamic tradition amplifies this with an account of Muhammad's generosity: After one battle, Muhammad prayed "facing a camel from the war booty," and then, holding some of the camel's hair between his fingers, said to his men: "This is also a part of the war booty you earned. Verily, I have no share in it, except my own share, the fifth designated to me. Even that fifth will be given to you."[11] Muhammad continued by exhorting the Muslims to turn over all the spoils of war to him for just distribution: "Therefore, surrender even the needle and the thread, and whatever is bigger or smaller than that (from the war spoils). Do not cheat with any of it, for stealing from the war booty before its distribution is Fire and a shame on its people in this life and the Hereafter. Perform Jihad against the people in Allah's cause, whether they are near or far, and do not fear the blame of the blamers, as long as you are in Allah's cause. Establish Allah's rules while in your area and while traveling. Perform Jihad in Allah's cause, for Jihad is a tremendous door leading to Paradise. Through it, Allah saves (one) from sadness and grief."[12]

On *furqan*, see 3:4.

42. At this point comes a recounting of various events before and during the battle, emphasizing how Allah controlled events and saved the Muslims.

might perish as a clear proof, and he who survived might survive as a clear proof. Indeed, Allah in truth is the hearer, the knower. **43**When Allah showed them to you in your dream as few in number, and if he had shown them to you as many, you would have faltered and would have argued over the matter. But Allah saved. Indeed, he knows what is in hearts. **44**And when you met, he showed them to you as few in your eyes, and lessened you in their eyes, so that Allah might conclude a thing that must be done. To Allah all things are brought back. **45**O you who believe, when you meet an army, hold firm and think a great deal of Allah, so that you may be successful. **46**And obey Allah and his messenger, and do not argue with one another, so that you do not falter and your strength depart from you, but be steadfast. Indeed, Allah is with the steadfast. **47**Do not be like those who came forth from their dwellings boastfully and in order to be seen by men, and bar people from the way of Allah, while Allah is surrounding all they do. **48**And when Satan made their deeds seem good to them and said, No one of mankind can conquer you this day, for I am your protector. But when the armies came in sight of one another, he took flight, saying, Indeed, I am guiltless regarding you. Indeed, I see what you do not see. Indeed, I fear Allah. And Allah is severe in punishment. **49**When the hypocrites and those in whose hearts is a disease said, Their religion has deluded them. Whoever puts his trust in Allah, indeed, Allah is mighty, wise. **50**If you could see how the angels receive those who disbelieve, striking faces and their backs and, Taste the punishment of burning. **51**This is for what your own hands have sent before, and Allah is not a tyrant to his slaves, **52**As the way of Pharaoh's people and those before them, they disbelieved the signs of Allah, and Allah took them in their sins. Indeed, Allah is strong, severe in punishment. **53**That is because Allah never changes the favor he has bestowed on any people until they first change what is in their hearts, and because Allah is the hearer, the knower, **54**As the way of Pharaoh's people and those before them, they denied the signs of their Lord, so we destroyed them in their sins. And we drowned the people of Pharaoh. All were evildoers. **55**Indeed, the worst of animals in Allah's sight are the ungrateful who will not believe. **56**Those among them with whom you made a treaty, and then at every opportunity they break their treaty, and they do not fulfill their duty. **57**If you come upon them in the war, deal with them so as to strike fear in those who are behind them, so that perhaps they may remember. **58**And if you fear treachery from any people, then throw it back to them fairly. Indeed, Allah does not love the

---

48. Satan, says Ibn Kathir, "may Allah curse him, made the idolators' purpose for marching seem fair to them. He made them think that no other people could defeat them that day."[13] But his promise was deceptive, while Allah's is reliable.

52. On Pharaoh, see also 2:49, 3:11, 7:103, 10:75, 14:6, 17:101, 20:24, 23:46, 26:11, 27:12, 28:3, 29:39, 38:12, 40:24, 44:17, 50:13, 51:38, 54:41, 66:11, 69:9, 73:15, 79:15, 85:18, and 89:10.

55. This equation of unbelievers with animals is another indication that unbelievers are worthy of no respect or consideration. See also 98:6.

58. If the Muslims "fear treachery" from unbelievers with whom they have a treaty, they should simply break the treaty. Ibn Kathir says this means that Muslims should tell the unbelievers "that you are severing the treaty. This way, you will be on equal terms, in that, you and they will be aware that a state of war exists between you and that the bilateral peace treaty is null and void."[14]

treacherous. ⁵⁹And do not let those who disbelieve suppose that they can get the better. Indeed, they cannot escape. ⁶⁰Make ready for them all that you can of force and of warhorses, so that by them you may strike terror in the enemy of Allah and your enemy, and others beside them whom you do not know. Allah knows them. Whatever you spend in the way of Allah, it will be repaid to you in full, and you will not be wronged. ⁶¹And if they incline to peace, incline to it also, and trust in Allah. Indeed, he, even he, is the hearer, the knower. ⁶²And if they wish to deceive you, then indeed, Allah is sufficient for you. It is he who supports you with his help and with the believers, ⁶³And has united their hearts. If you had spent all that is in the earth, you could not have united their hearts, but Allah has united them. Indeed, he is mighty, wise. ⁶⁴O prophet, Allah is sufficient for you and those who follow you among the believers. ⁶⁵O prophet, exhort the believers to fight. If there are just twenty of you who are steadfast, they will overcome two hundred, and if there are a hundred of you, they will overcome a thousand of those who disbelieve, because they are a people without intelligence. ⁶⁶Now Allah has lightened your burden, for he knows that there is weakness in you. So if there are a steadfast hundred of you, they will overcome two hundred, and if there are a thousand of you, they will overcome two thousand, by the permission of Allah. Allah is with the steadfast. ⁶⁷It is not for any prophet to have captives until he has made slaughter in the land. You desire the lure of this world, and Allah desires the hereafter, and Allah is mighty, wise. ⁶⁸If it had not been for a decree of Allah which went before, an awful doom would had come upon you because of what you took. ⁶⁹Now enjoy what you have won, as lawful and good, and keep your duty to Allah. Indeed, Allah is forgiving, merciful. ⁷⁰O prophet, say to those captives who are in your hands, If Allah knows any good in your hearts, he will give you better than what has been taken from you, and will forgive you. Indeed, Allah is forgiving, merciful. ⁷¹And if they would betray you, they betrayed Allah before, and he gave power over them. Allah

---

60. This is the Qur'an's third mention of the imperative to strike terror in the unbelievers. See 3:151 and 8:12.

61. The Muslims should be ready to make peace if the enemy wishes to do so. Some however, do not believe this truce should be indefinite in length. Qutb explains: "At the time when this surah was revealed, God instructed His Messenger to remain at peace with those groups who refrained from fighting him and the Muslims, whether they entered into a formal treaty with the Muslims or not. The Prophet continued to accept a peaceful relationship with unbelievers and people of earlier revelations until Surah 9 was revealed, when he could only accept one of two alternatives: either they embraced Islam or paid jizyah [see 9:29] which indicated a state of peace. Otherwise, the only alternative was war, whenever this was feasible for the Muslims to undertake, so that all people submit to God alone."[15]

65. Allah will give pious Muslims more victories, even if they face odds even more prohibitive than those they had overcome at Badr, although this promise is almost immediately backtracked: originally a hundred would defeat a thousand unbelievers, but this is then reduced to a hundred believers vanquishing two hundred unbelievers (8:66). These became recurring themes of jihad literature throughout the centuries, up to the present day: piety will bring military victory, and the Muslims will conquer even against overwhelming odds.

67. According to the *Tafsir al-Jalalayn*, this verse was revealed "when ransom was accepted for the captives at Badr."[16] The Muslims had released some of the prisoners at Badr, but this was out of their base desire for material gain: the money they would receive in ransom. The tafsir continues: "You (believers) desire the goods of this world – the money you accepted as ransom – whereas Allah desires the reward of the Next World for you through fighting the unbelievers."[17] The Muslims should therefore have given up the prospect of gaining worldly goods and simply killed their captives, which would have brought the Muslims the rewards of paradise.

However, the *Tafsir al-Jalalayn* concludes by asserting that 8:67 was abrogated by 47:4, which allows for ransom. Ibn Kathir notes that "the majority of the scholars say that the matter of prisoners of war is up to the Imam. If he decides, he can have them killed, such as in the case of Bani Qurayzah. If he decides, he can accept a ransom for them, as in the case of the prisoners of Badr, or exchange them for Muslim prisoners."[18]

is the knower, the wise. [72]Indeed, those who believed and left their homes and waged jihad with their wealth and their lives for the sake of Allah, and those who took them in and helped them, these people are protecting friends one of another. And those who believed but did not leave their homes, you have no duty to protect them until they leave their homes, but if they seek help from you in the matter of religion, then it is your duty to help, except against a people between whom and you there is a treaty. Allah is the seer of what you do. [73]And those who disbelieve are protectors one of another, if you do not so, there will be confusion in the land, and great corruption. [74]Those who believed and left their homes and waged jihad for the sake of Allah, and those who took them in and helped them, these people are the believers in truth. For them is forgiveness, and bountiful provision. [75]And those who afterwards believed and left their homes and waged jihad along with you, they are among you, and those who are relatives are nearer one to another in the decree of Allah. Indeed, Allah is the knower of all things.

---

72. On "jihad," see 2:218, as also for 8:74.

SURA 9

Repentance

At-Tawba

Introduction

This is the only one of the Qur'an's 114 suras that does not begin with *Bismillah ar-Rahman ar-Rahim*—"In the name of Allah, the compassionate, the merciful."

Explanations for this vary. Some say it is simply because suras 8 and 9 were originally a single sura, and Ibn Kathir says that the omission is simply "because the Companions did not write it in the complete copy of the Qur'an (*Mushaf*) they collected."[1] Maududi asserts that the correct explanation was that the *Bismillah* was left off because Muhammad himself didn't recite it at the beginning of this sura.[2] The *Tafsir al-Jalalayn* says it is not recited because Muhammad "did not command that it should be."[3] It explains that while this sura is commonly called "Repentance," it is "in fact, the Sura of Punishment," it quotes a statement attributed to Ali ibn Abi Talib, saying that the *Bismillah* "is security, and this *sura* was revealed to remove security by the sword."[4]

According to Islamic tradition, this sura was revealed in the wake of an inconclusive expedition Muhammad undertook against a Byzantine garrison at Tabuk in northern Arabia in 631, and much of its contents revolve around the events of that attempt to engage the army of the great Christian empire in battle. As such, it contains many of the Qur'an's most strident declarations

---

1 Ibn Kathir, IV, 370.
2 Mawdudi, III, 175.
3 *Tafsir al-Jalalayn*, 397.
4 Ibid.

regarding warfare. A hadith recorded by Bukhari asserts that this was "the last Sura which was revealed in full."[5] Given the doctrine of abrogation (see 2:106), this gives it precedence over other doctrinal pronouncements in the Qur'an and codifies its bellicosity as normative for believers for all time.

Bell suggests that at the beginning of this sura, "two documents are here interwoven," one involving "denunciation of the treaty of Hudaibiyya" (9:1–2, 9:4, 9:7–8, 9:12–16) and the other a proclamation regarding the hajj (9:3, 9:17–19, 9:28).[6]

---

5 Bukhari, vol. 5, book 64, no. 4364.
6 Bell, I, 171.

Repentance

[1]Freedom from obligation from Allah and his messenger toward those of the idolaters with whom you made a treaty. [2]Travel freely in the land for four months, and know that you cannot escape Allah, and that Allah will humiliate the unbelievers. [3]And a proclamation from Allah and his messenger to all men on the day of the hajj, that Allah is free from obligation to the idolaters, and his messenger. So if you repent, it will be better for you, but if you refuse, then know that you cannot escape Allah. Give news of a painful doom to those who disbelieve, [4]Except for those of the idolaters with whom you have a treaty, and who have not been deficient toward you, nor have supported anyone against you. Fulfill their treaty to them until their term. Indeed, Allah loves those who keep their duty. [5]Then, when the sacred months have passed, kill the idolaters wherever you find them, and take them, and besiege them, and prepare for them every ambush. But if they repent and establish prayer and give alms, then leave their way free. Indeed, Allah is forgiving,

1. According to the *Tafsir al-Jalalayn*, the treaty between the Muslims and the pagans of Mecca "is canceled by this statement."[1] Muslims may break treaties with non-Muslims unilaterally; see 8:58.

2. Allah will humiliate the unbelievers "in this world by killing and in the Next by the Fire," says the *Tafsir al-Jalalayn*.[2] For how the unbelievers are to be punished in this world, see 9:14.

3. This refers only to those pagans who have violated the terms of their treaties with the Muslims; the other treaties will be honored to the end of their term.

4. Ibn Kathir explains that "this is an exception regulating the longest extent of time for those who have a general treaty - without time mentioned - to four months. They would have four months to travel the lands in search of sanctuary for themselves wherever they wish. Those whose treaty mentioned a specific limited term, then the longest it would extend was to the point of its agreed upon termination date."[3] No treaty with unbelievers is envisaged that does not have a termination date; i.e., no treaty of indefinite peaceful coexistence can be acceptable.

5. This is the notorious Verse of the Sword. In a 2003 sermon, Osama bin Laden rejoiced over this verse: "Praise be to Allah who revealed the verse of the Sword to his servant and messenger, in order to establish truth and abolish falsehood."[4] That is ultimately the goal of jihad warfare: the establishment of Islamic law, which brings about a just society.

The fourteenth-century Islamic scholar Ibn Juzayy declares that this verse abrogates "every peace treaty in the Qur'an," and specifically abrogates the Qur'an's directive to "set free or ransom" captive unbelievers (47:4).[5] According to as-Suyuti, "This is an Ayat of the Sword which abrogates pardon, truce and overlooking," that is, the overlooking of the pagans' offenses.[6] The *Tafsir al-Jalalayn* says that the Muslims must "kill the idolaters wherever you find them" and "seize them by capture and besiege them in citadels and fortresses until they either fight or become Muslim."[7]

Ibn Kathir echoes this, directing that Muslims should "not wait until you find them. Rather, seek and besiege them in their areas and forts, gather intelligence about them in the various roads and fairways so that what is made wide looks ever smaller to them. This way, they will have no choice, but to die or embrace Islam."[8]

Muhammad Asad, however, says that 9:5 "certainly does not imply an alternative of 'conversion or death,' as some unfriendly critics of Islam choose to assume." He says that "war is permissible only in self-defence," in accord with 2:190, and that "the enemy's conversion to Islam...is no more than one, and by no means the only, way of their 'desisting from hostility.'"[9] However, none of the mainstream Islamic commentators on the Qur'an attach any conditions to this verse; unlike 2:191 and 4:89, one is not to "kill them wherever you find them" only when the unbelievers have committed some offense, but at any time, simply by virtue of their being unbelievers.

Another common claim today is that this verse applies only to the pagans of Arabia in Muhammad's time and has no further application. Ibn Kathir asserts, on the contrary, that the unbelievers must be killed "on the earth in general, except for the Sacred Area"—that is, the sacred mosque, which is traditionally identified as being in Mecca.[10] This implies an endless conflict.

The killing, however, is not indiscriminate and unlimited. The unbelievers can stop the carnage by converting to Islam. The *Tafsir al-Jalalayn*: "If they repent of their unbelief, and establish the prayer and pay the zakat, let them go on their way and do not interfere with them."[11] Ibn Kathir: "These Ayat [verses] allowed fighting people unless, and until, they embrace Islam and implement its rulings and obligations."[12] Qutb says that the termination of the treaties with a four-month grace period, combined with the call to kill the unbelievers, "was not meant as a campaign of vengeance or extermination, but rather as a warning which provided a motive for them to accept Islam."[13]

The ninth-century Islamic jurist Ash-Shafi'i took this as a proof for killing anyone who abandons the prayer and fighting anyone who refuses to pay zakat: "Some use it as a proof that they are kafirun [unbelievers]."[14] Likewise Ibn Kathir: "Abu Bakr As-Siddiq [according to Islamic tradition, the first caliph of the Muslims after Muhammad's death] used this and other honorable Ayat as proof for fighting those who refrained from paying the Zakah."[15]

merciful. **6**And if anyone of the idolaters seeks your protection, then protect him so that he may hear the word of Allah, and afterward bring him to his place of safety. That is because they are a people who do not know. **7**How can there be a treaty with Allah and with his messenger for the idolaters, except for those with whom you made a treaty at the sacred mosque? As long as they are true to you, be true to them. Indeed, Allah loves those who keep their duty. **8**How, when they have the upper hand against you, do they not regard either pact or honor in regard to you? They satisfy you with their mouths, while their hearts refuse. And most of them are wrongdoers. **9**They have purchased a little gain with the signs of Allah, so they bar people from his way. Indeed, what they are inclined to do is evil. **10**And they observe toward a believer neither pact nor honor. These are the ones who are transgressors. **11**But if they repent and establish prayer and give alms, then they are your brothers in religion. We detail our signs for a people who have knowledge. **12**And if they break their pledges after their treaty and attack your religion, then fight the heads of disbelief, indeed, they have no binding oaths, so that they may stop. **13**Will you not fight a people who broke their solemn pledges, and plotted to drive out the messenger, and attacked you first? What? Are you afraid of them? Now Allah has more of a right that you should fear him, if you are believers **14**Fight them, and Allah will punish them by your hands, and he will lay them low and give you victory over them, and he will heal the hearts of people who are believers. **15**And he will remove the anger of their hearts. Allah relents toward those whom he wills. Allah is the knower,

Thus even Muslims who do not fulfill Islamic obligations fall into the category of those who must be fought. This is a principle that latter-day Salafist movements apply broadly and use frequently in branding governments that do not rule according to strict Islamic law as unbelievers who must be fought by those who regard themselves as true Muslims.

6. According to Ibn Kathir, pagans are to be given safe passage not on an indefinite basis, but "so that they may learn about the religion of Allah, so that Allah's call will spread among His servants....In summary, those who come from a land at war with Muslims to the area of Islam, delivering a message, for business transactions, to negotiate a peace treaty, to pay the Jizyah, to offer an end to hostilities, and so forth, and request safe passage from Muslim leaders or their deputies, should be granted safe passage, as long as they remain in Muslim areas, until they go back to their land and sanctuary."[16] For the jizya, see 9:29.

Ibn Juzayy says that this safe passage means that Muslims should "grant them security so that they can hear the Qur'an to see whether they will become Muslim or not (then convey them to a place where they are safe). If they do not become Muslim, return him to his place."[17] He notes, however, that this is not a unanimous view, but the dissenting party doesn't favor a more peaceful interpretation: "This is a firm judgment in the view of some people while other people say that it is abrogated by fighting."[18]

7. Islamic tradition holds that the treaty the Muslims concluded with the pagans "at the sacred mosque" refers to the Treaty of Hudaybiyyah. In 628, according to ninth-century accounts, Muhammad had a vision in which he performed the pilgrimage to Mecca—a pagan custom that he very much wanted to make part of Islam but had thus far been prevented by the Quraysh control of Mecca. But at this time he directed Muslims to prepare to make the pilgrimage to Mecca and advanced upon the city with fifteen hundred men. The Quraysh met him outside the city, and the two sides concluded a ten-year truce (hudna), the treaty of Hudaybiyyah.

Some leading Muslims were unhappy with the prospect of a truce, and unhappier when Muhammad concluded the treaty on terms that were disadvantageous to the Muslims. But Muhammad reassured his disgruntled followers: "I am God's slave and His apostle. I will not go against His commandment and He will not make me the loser."[19] When the Muslims were in a stronger position militarily, Muhammad broke the treaty on a technicality (see 60:10 and 47:35).

14. According to Ibn Juzayy, "Allah will punish them by your hands" means "killing and capture. That is a promise of victory for the Muslims."[20] The *Tafsir al-Jalalayn* concurs: "Allah will punish them by killing them at your hands, and disgrace them by capture and defeat."[21]

"Allah will punish them by your hands" means that Muslims on earth are the executors of Allah's judgment and are charged with the responsibility of punishing the unbelievers in accord with the divine wrath. Thus when Islamic leaders call upon Allah to punish someone, they may in essence be calling upon Muslims to carry out that punishment. Doing so will "heal the hearts of people who are believers": doing violence to unbelievers for the sake of Allah will calm the hearts of the believers.

15. Ibn Juzayy explains "Allah relents toward those whom he wills" by saying: "Allah will turn to some of those unbelievers and so that they become Muslims."[22] That decision is all Allah's; see 7:179.

the wise. **16**Or did you think that you would be left when Allah does not yet know which are those of you who wage jihad, choosing as confidantes no one except Allah and his messenger and the believers? Allah is informed of what you do. **17**It is not for the idolaters to take care of Allah's sanctuaries, bearing witness against themselves of disbelief. As for such people, their works are useless and in the fire they will remain. **18**He only will tend Allah's sanctuaries who believes in Allah and the last day, and observes proper prayer and gives alms and fears no one except Allah. For such people, it is possible that they can be among the rightly guided. **19**Do you consider the one who satisfies a pilgrim's thirst and tends the sacred mosque as like him who believes in Allah and the last day, and wages jihad in the way of Allah? They are not equal in the sight of Allah. Allah does not guide wrongdoing people. **20**Those who believe, and have left their homes and waged jihad with their wealth and their lives in Allah's way are of much greater worth in Allah's sight. These are the ones who are triumphant. **21**Their Lord gives them good news of mercy from him, and acceptance, and gardens where enduring pleasure will be theirs, **22**There they will remain forever. Indeed, with Allah there is immense reward. **23**O you who believe, do not choose your fathers or your brothers for friends if they take pleasure in disbelief rather than faith. Whoever among you takes them for friends, such people are wrongdoers. **24**Say, If your fathers, and your sons, and your brothers, and your wives, and your tribe, and the wealth you have acquired, and merchandise for which you are afraid that there will no sale, and dwellings you desire are more precious to you than Allah and his messenger and waging jihad in his way, then wait until Allah brings his command to pass. Allah does not guide wrongdoing people. **25**Allah has given you victory on many fields and on the day of Hunayn, when you rejoiced in your multitude but it did not help you at all, and the earth, vast as it is, closed in on you, then you turned back in flight, **26**Then Allah sent his *sakina* down upon his messenger and upon the believers, and sent down armies you could not see, and punished those who disbelieved. Such is the reward of unbelievers. **27**Then afterward Allah will relent toward whomever he wills, for Allah is forgiving, merciful. **28**O you who believe, the idolaters only are unclean. So do not let them come near the sacred mosque after this year. If you fear poverty, Allah will preserve you out of his bounty if he wills. Indeed, Allah is

---

16. The word translated here as "wage jihad" is *jahadu*, a form of "jihad." See 2:218.

17. Then Allah declares that the idolaters or polytheists (*mushrikeena*, from *mushrik*, polytheist) are not worthy to take care of the sacred mosque. They control it, but as comments Ibn Juzayy, "They do not have either the right or the duty to do so. They inhabit them through forceful occupation and injustice."[23] They have no right to the mosque because, according to Islamic tradition, Abraham himself built it as a shrine to Allah.

23. Says Ibn Kathir: "Allah commands shunning the disbelievers, even if they are one's parents or children, and prohibits taking them as supporters if they choose disbelief instead of faith."[24] See also 9:113, 29:8, 31:15, and 60:4.

24. Ibn Juzayy notes that this verse, with its warning that one should value nothing in this life higher than Allah, is "a threat to

anyone who prefers his family, property or home to emigration and jihad."[25] On emigration, see 4:100.

Instead of, "Allah does not guide the wrongdoing people," a Qur'anic manuscript examined by Mingana has, "Allah will not be quiet toward the wrongdoing people."[26]

25. Islamic tradition holds that the Battle of Hunayn took place after Muhammad conquered Mecca and was once again won by supernatural help.

26. On *sakina*, see 2:248.

27. According to Ibn Juzayy, the promise that "Allah will relent toward whomever he wills" means that "the tribe of Hawazin who had fought the Muslims at Hunayn became Muslim."[27]

28. Unbelievers are unclean, and thus must not enter the sacred mosque. Shi'ites in particular regard this as a matter of ritual purity. The contemporary Iraqi Ayatollah al-Sayyid Ali al-Husseini

the knower, the wise. **29**Fight against those do not believe in Allah or the last day, and do not forbid what Allah and his messenger have forbidden, and do not follow the religion of truth, even if they are among the people of the book, until they pay the jizya with willing submission and feel

al-Sistani, classifies unbelievers among other impure, unclean things such as urine, feces, semen, blood, dead bodies, and dogs.[28]

The *Tafsir al-Jalalayn* says that the polytheists are unclean because of their inner "foulness," and the fifteenth-century Islamic scholar as-Suyuti adds that some say "they are actually impure so that they must do ghusl [the full ablution] if they become Muslim and one must do wudu [the partial ablution] after shaking hands with them."[29] As-Suyuti also notes that this verse forbids unbelievers to enter the sacred mosque, although he points out that "Abu Hanifa says that People of the Book are not prevented because it is specific to idolaters."[30] However, a ninth-century hadith has Muhammad saying, "I will expel the Jews and Christians from the Arabian Peninsula and will not leave any but Muslim."[31]

29. Here is the one place where Muslims are explicitly directed to make war against and subjugate Jews and Christians, the "People of the Book," who once subjugated enter the dhimma, the protection of the Muslims, and become dhimmis, protected (or guilty) people. The *Tafsir al-Sadi* explains: "This verse contains instructions to fight the disbelievers among the Jews and Christians."[32]

Islamic tradition places this command within the context of Muhammad's attempt to take on the army of the Christian Byzantine, or Eastern Roman, Empire. Ibn Kathir says: "Allah commanded His Messenger to fight the People of the Scriptures, Jews and Christians, on the ninth year of Hijrah, and he prepared his army to fight the Romans and called the people to Jihad announcing his intent and destination."[33]

Ibn Juzayy says that this verse is "a command to fight the People of the Book" because of their claims that Allah has a son (9:30). Muslims must also fight them "because they consider as lawful carrion, blood, pork, etc." and because "they do not enter Islam."[34] He says that "scholars agree about accepting jizya [a religious-based poll tax] from the Jews and Christians," and adds that "the Magians/Zoroastrians have been added to them going by the words of the Prophet, 'Treat them as People of the Book,'" although "there is disagreement about accepting it from idolaters and Sabians."[35] He specifies that "it is not collected from women, children or the insane," and that it signifies "submission and obedience."[36]

The *Tafsir al-Sadi* adds that the "aim of that fighting" is so that non-Muslims turn over "wealth that is given in return for the Muslims not fighting them and allowing them to stay among the Muslims, granting them safety for their lives and their property."[37] A hadith depicts Muhammad saying: "I have been commanded to fight against people so long as they do not declare that there is no god but Allah, and he who professed it was guaranteed the protection of his property and life on my behalf."[38] That is, his property and life are not protected if he does not make this declaration.

The *Tafsir al-Jalalayn* says that this verse specifies that Muslims must fight against those who do not follow Islam, "which confirms and abrogates" other religions.[39] The people of the book are mentioned in the verse and traditionally have been understood as the only ones who are offered the option of paying the jizya, while other non-Muslims who do not have a written scripture that is recognized in the Qur'an must either convert or die. However, the *Tafsir as-Sadi* explains that "the jizyah may be taken from all the disbelievers, People of the Book and others, because this verse was revealed after the

Muslims had finished fighting with the polytheist Arabs and had begun to fight the People of the Book and their ilk, so this condition is describing the real situation and is not meant to impose a restriction on accepting jizyah from the People of the Book only."[40]

Ibn Kathir explains the need for this fighting in the context of the contention that the people of the book were in bad faith when they rejected Muhammad: "Therefore, when People of the Scriptures disbelieved in Muhammad, they had no beneficial faith in any Messenger or what the Messengers brought....Therefore, they do not follow the religion of earlier Prophets because these religions came from Allah, but because these suit their desires and lusts. Therefore, their claimed faith in an earlier Prophet will not benefit them because they disbelieved in the master, the mightiest, the last and most perfect of all Prophets."[41] As a result, says the *Tafsir al-Sadi*, "Allah instructed the Muslims to fight these people and encouraged them to do so, because they call people to the religion that they follow and cause a great deal of harm to people, as people may be deceived by them, because of their being People of the Book."[42]

The nineteenth-century anti-Wahhabi Islamic scholar Allamah as-Sawi specifies that the payment of the jizya signifies that the non-Muslims are "humble and obedient to the judgements of Islam."[43] As-Suyuti notes that the jizya is "not taken from someone in a state of hardship," although that was a stipulation at times honored in the breach.[44] For example, a contemporary account of the Muslims' conquest of Nikiou, an Egyptian town, in the 640s, says that "it is impossible to describe the lamentable position of the inhabitants of this town, who came to the point of offering their children in exchange for the enormous sums that they had to pay each month."[45]

According to legend, the Bedouin commander al-Mughira bin Sa'd explained to the Persian Rustam that he "must pay the jizya while you are in a state of abasement," and elaborated: "You pay it while you are standing and I am sitting and the whip hanging is over your head."[46]

Ibn Kathir says that the dhimmis must be "disgraced, humiliated and belittled. Therefore, Muslims are not allowed to honor the people of Dhimmah or elevate them above Muslims, for they are miserable, disgraced and humiliated."[47] The seventh-century jurist Sa'id ibn al-Musayyab is said to have declared: "I prefer that the people of the dhimma become tired by paying the jizya since He says, 'until they pay the jizya with their own hands in a state of complete abasement."[48] As-Suyuti elaborates that this verse "is used as a proof by those who say that it is taken in a humiliating way, and so the taker sits and the dhimmi stands with his head bowed and his back bent. The jizya is placed in the balance and the taker seizes his beard and hits his chin."[49] Zamakhshari agreed that the jizya should be collected "with belittlement and humiliation."[50]

Asad and other Western-oriented commentators maintain that the jizya was merely a tax for exemption for military service. Asad explains: "Every able-bodied Muslim is obliged to take up arms in jihad (i.e., in a just war in God's cause) whenever the freedom of his faith or the political safety of his community is imperiled. Since this is, primarily, a religious obligation, non-Muslim citizens, who do not subscribe to the ideology of Islam, cannot in fairness be expected to assume a similar burden."[51] But this does not

themselves subdued. **³⁰**And the Jews say, Ezra is the son of Allah, and the Christians say, The Messiah is the son of Allah. That is their saying with their mouths. They imitate the statements of those who disbelieved before. May Allah curse them. How perverse they are. **³¹**They have taken as lords besides Allah their rabbis and their monks and the Messiah, the son of Mary, when they were called to worship only one God. There is no God except him. May he be glorified from all that they ascribe as partners. **³²**They want to put out the light of Allah with their mouths, but Allah refuses except that he will perfect his light, however much the unbelievers hate it. **³³**It is he

explain the latter part of 9:29, which mandates the humiliation of non-Muslims.

"With willing submission" (*an yadin*), meanwhile, has been understood in different ways. It could also mean "out of hand," in the sense not just of submission but of direct, in-person payment, as the thirteenth-century Qur'anic commentator al-Baydawi explains: "Out of hand, indicating the condition of those who pay the tribute. Out of a hand that gives willingly, in this way indicating that they submit obediently; or out of their hand, meaning that they pay the tribute with their own hands, instead of sending it through others; no one is allowed to use a proxy in this case."[52] There are many other possible understandings of this text. The great scholar Franz Rosenthal observes that *an yadin* has "completely defied interpretation. All post-Qur'anic occurrences of it are based upon the Qur'an."[53]

In explaining how the Jews and Christians must "feel themselves subdued," Ibn Kathir quotes a saying of Muhammad: "Do not initiate the Salam [greeting of peace] to the Jews and Christians, and if you meet any of them in a road, force them to its narrowest alley."[54] He then goes on to outline the notorious Pact of Umar, an agreement that was, according to Islamic tradition, made between the caliph Umar, who ruled the Muslims from 634 to 644, and a Christian community.

With remarkably little variation, throughout Islamic history whenever Islamic law was strictly enforced, this is generally how non-Muslims were treated. Although today they're often presented as tolerant toward the Christians, Ibn Kathir says that these rules "ensured their continued humiliation, degradation and disgrace."[55] The Christians agreed not to "restore any place of worship that needs restoration"; "ride on saddles, hang swords on the shoulders, collect weapons of any kind or carry these weapons"; or "publicize practices of Shirk" (see 2:193, 4:31, and 6:21). They also agreed not to build "crosses on the outside of our churches and demonstrating them and our books in public in Muslim fairways and markets" or "sound the bells in our churches, except discreetly, or raise our voices while reciting our holy books inside our churches in the presence of Muslims, nor raise our voices [with prayer] at our funerals, or light torches in funeral processions in the fairways of Muslims, or their markets."[56]

The twentieth-century *Tafsir Anwarul Bayan* laments that "in today's times, the system of Atonement (Jizya) is not practised at all by the Muslims. It is indeed unfortunate that not only are the Muslim States afraid to impose Atonement (Jizya) on the disbelievers (kuffar) living in their countries, but they grant them more rights than they grant the Muslims and respect them more. They fail to understand that Allah desires that the Muslims show no respect to any disbeliever (kafir) and that they should not accord any special rights to them."[57]

Qutb argues that these rules should be revived, for "these verses are given as a general statement, and the order to fight the people of the earlier revelations until they pay the submission tax with a willing hand and are subdued is also of general import."[58]

Likewise Maududi states that "the simple fact is that according to Islam, non-Muslims have been granted the freedom to stay outside the Islamic fold and to cling to their false, man-made ways if they so wish."[59] That heads off any potential contradiction between his understanding of v. 29 and 2:256, "There is no compulsion in religion." Maududi continues by declaring that the unbelievers "have, however, absolutely no right to seize the reins of power in any part of God's earth nor to direct the collective affairs of human beings according to their own misconceived doctrines. For if they are given such an opportunity, corruption and mischief will ensue. In such a situation the believers would be under an obligation to do their utmost to dislodge them from political power and to make them live in subservience to the Islamic way of life."[60]

The idea that Islam is the religion of Allah and of truth is stated also at 3:19 and 3:85, and that it will prevail over all other religions is additionally at 2:193, 8:39, 9:33, and 61:9.

30. No Jews have ever been found who match the Qur'an's description of them as proclaiming that Ezra is the Son of God. Ibn Juzayy explains that only a small group of Jews actually said this, but "it is ascribed to all of them because they followed those who said it."[61] In any case, this belief, asserted by the Qur'an and thereby confirmed as true in the minds of many Muslims, makes the Jews as well as the Christians guilty of *shirk*. Ibn Juzayy quotes another Islamic authority saying that the Christian belief is "atrocious disbelief."[62] Adds Ibn Kathir, "This is why Allah declared both groups to be liars," for "they have no proof that supports their claim, other than lies and fabrications."[63] Consequently, they are accursed of Allah.

The contention in this verse that Jews and Christians are idolatrous creates a difficulty for the fact that the Qur'an forbids marriage to idolatrous women (2:221) and yet permits Muslims to marry Jewish and Christian women (5:5).

31. Do the Jews worship rabbis and Christians worship monks? Not directly: a hadith has Muhammad explaining that "they did not worship them, but when they made something lawful for them, they considered it lawful, and when they made something unlawful for them, they considered it unlawful."[64] How this would be classified as idolatry while it would not be idolatrous for Muslims to consider various things lawful and unlawful based on Muhammad's word is left unexplained.

32. The "light of Allah," says the *Tafsir al-Jalalayn*, is "His Shari'a and His proofs."[65]

33. Ibn Juzayy explains this verse by saying that Allah will put Islam "above all other deens," that is, religions, and will "make it

who has sent his messenger with the guidance and the religion of truth, so that he may cause it to prevail over all religions, however much the idolaters may hate it. **34**O you who believe, indeed, many of the rabbis and monks devour the wealth of mankind wantonly and bar people from the way of Allah. They who hoard up gold and silver and do not spend it in the way of Allah, give news to them of a painful doom, **35**On the day when it will be heated in the fire of Gehenna, and their foreheads and their flanks and their backs will be branded with it, Here is what you hoarded for yourselves. Now taste of what you used to hoard. **36**Indeed, the number of the months with Allah is twelve months by Allah's decree on the day that he created the heavens and the earth. Four of them are sacred. That is the right religion. So do not wrong yourselves in them. And wage war on all of the idolaters as they are waging war on all of you. And know that Allah is with those who keep their duty. **37**Postponement is only an excess of disbelief whereby those who disbelieve are led astray, they allow it in one year and forbid it in another year, so that they may make up the number of the months which Allah has made sacred, so that they allow what Allah has forbidden. The evil of their deeds is made to seem good to them. Allah does not guide the disbelieving people.

strong so that it embraces the east and the west."[66] As Muhammad is depicted as putting it: "There will not remain on the face of the earth a mud-brick house or a camel's hair tent which God will not cause the confession of Islam to enter bringing both mighty honour and abject abasement. God will either honour the occupants and put them among its adherents, or will humiliate them and they will be subject to it."[67]

Ibn Juzayy adds that "it is said" that Islam will embrace the east and the west "when Isa [Jesus] descends and then only the deen [religion] of Islam will remain."[68] See 4:157.

The idea that Islam will prevail over all other religions is additionally at 2:193, 8:39, and 61:9.

Instead of, "It is he who has sent his messenger," a Qur'anic manuscript examined by Mingana has, "It is who has sent his messenger."[69] However, "this pronoun has been added in the margin by a different hand."[70]

34. Says Ibn Kathir: "This Ayah warns against corrupt scholars and misguided worshippers. Sufyan bin Uyaynah said, 'Those among our scholars who become corrupt are similar to the Jews, while those among our worshippers who become misguided are like Christians…. When Allah sent His Messenger, the Jews persisted in their misguidance, disbelief and rebellion, hoping to keep their status and position. However, Allah extinguished all this and took it away from them with the light of Prophethood and instead gave them disgrace and degradation, and they incurred the anger of Allah, the Exalted.'"[71]

35. On Gehenna, see 2:206, as also at 9:49, 9:63, 9:68, 9:73, 9:81, 9:95, and 9:109.

36. The pre-Islamic Arabic calendar, like the Islamic calendar, was lunar, consisting of 354 days rather than the 365 days of the solar calendar. To make up this difference, Arabians added leap months—one every three solar years. This verse, which was supposed to have been revealed in the year 629, forbids adding leap months.

In connection with this, the contemporary Islamic scholar Johannes Jansen points out that in the eighth/ninth century biography of Muhammad by Ibn Ishaq via Ibn Hisham, "For every event which took place in the life of Muhammad, Ibn Ishaq meticulously recorded in his *Sira* in which month it took place," and that this is "one of the main reasons why Western historians classified his book as historiography in the normal sense of that word."[72]

Yet Jansen notes that "not a single one of the numerous events Ibn Ishaq describes and attaches a date to, took place during a leap month." He asks: "If his narrative of the life of Muhammad would be based on historical memories and on real events, however distorted, but remembered by real people, how can half a solar year (or more) remain unmentioned and have disappeared from the record?"[73]

Ibn Ishaq's biography, Jansen observes, "can only date from a period in which people had forgotten that leap months had once existed."[74] That period would have to have been a considerably long time after Muhammad is supposed to have lived. "These stories by Ibn Ishaq," concludes Jansen, "do not attempt to describe memories of events that took place in the past, but they want to convince the reader that the protagonist of these stories, Muhammad, is the Messenger of God."[75]

Instead of, "And wage war on all of the idolaters," a Qur'anic manuscript examined by Mingana has, "And wage war on the idolaters."[76]

37. Here, according to Ibn Kathir, "Allah admonishes the idolaters for choosing their wicked opinions over Allah's Law. They changed Allah's legislation based upon their vain desires, allowing what Allah prohibited and prohibiting what Allah allowed."[77] There are many similar statements throughout the Qur'an. However, in the context of sura 9, this amounts to a call to action against the idolaters, an exhortation to wage jihad against them, as the following verse makes clear.

Instead of "are led astray," the Warsh Qur'an has "he leads astray."[78] Instead of, "Allah does not guide the disbelieving people," a Qur'anic manuscript examined by Mingana has, "Allah will not be quiet toward the disbelieving people."[79]

38O you who believe, what ails you that when it is said to you, Go forth in the way of Allah, you are bowed down to the ground with heaviness? Do you take pleasure in the life of this world rather than in the hereafter? The comfort of the life of this world is but little in the hereafter. **39**If you do not go forth, he will afflict you with a painful doom, and will choose a people other than you instead of you. You cannot harm him at all. Allah is able to do all things. **40**If you do not help him, Allah still helped him when those who disbelieve drove him out, the second of two, when they two were in the cave, when he said to his comrade, Do not grieve. Indeed, Allah is with us. Then Allah caused his *sakina* to descend upon him and supported him with armies you cannot see, and made the word of those who disbelieved the lowest, while Allah's word was what became the highest. Allah is mighty, wise. **41**Go forth, light-armed and heavy-armed, and wage jihad with your wealth and your lives in the way of Allah. That is best for you, if you only knew. **42**If it had been a near adventure and an easy journey, they would have followed you, but the distance seemed too far for them. Yet will they swear by Allah, If we had been able, we would surely have set out with you. They destroy their souls, and Allah knows that they indeed are liars. **43**Allah forgive you, Why did you give them permission before those who told the truth were clear to you and you knew which ones were the liars? **44**Those who believe in Allah and the last day do not ask permission of you that they not wage jihad with their wealth and their lives. Allah is aware of those who keep their duty. **45**The only ones who ask permission of you are those who do not believe in Allah and the last day, and whose hearts feel doubt, so in their doubt they waver. **46**And if they had wished to go forth, they would assuredly have made ready some equipment, but Allah was averse to their being sent forth and held them back, and it was said, Sit with the sedentary. **47**If they had gone forth among you, they would have added nothing to you except trouble and would have hurried back and forth among you, seeking to cause sedition among you, and among you there are some who would have listened to them. Allah is aware of evildoers. **48**They tried previously to

38. This verse "is a rebuke," explains Ibn Juzayy, "to those who stayed behind the expedition to Tabuk" that Muhammad led against the Byzantines.[80]

Instead of, "O you who believe, what ails you that when it is said to you, Go forth in the way of Allah," a Qur'anic manuscript examined by Mingana has, "O you who believe, when it is said to you, Go forth in the way of Allah."[81]

39. Those who "incline away from jihad," says the *Tafsir al-Jalalayn*—will face divine punishment and be replaced by another people.[82]

40. "When those who disbelieve drove him out" refers, according to Ibn Kathir, to "the year of the Hijrah," when "the idolaters tried to kill, imprison or expel the Prophet."[83] This creates an obligation for the believers; see 2:191.

On *sakina*, see 2:248.

41. Ibn Kathir, Ibn Juzayy, and the *Tafsir al-Jalalayn* all agree that that command was abrogated by 9:91, which exempts the weak or ill from the obligation to fight.[84] This once again demonstrates that the Qur'anic concept of fighting involves warfare against non-Muslims, not a struggle within the soul of the individual believer. This fight is of the highest priority, to the extent that a hadith depicts Muhammad as being asked, "Guide me to such a deed as equals Jihad (in reward)," and answering: "I do not find such a deed."[85]

42. Those who prefer the easy life to a hard journey of jihad are sharply rebuked.

43. Instead of "and you knew," a Qur'anic manuscript examined by Mingana has "you are."[86]

44. True Muslims did not hesitate to wage jihad, even to the point of risking their property and their very lives. The ones who refused to do this weren't believers.

46. After the torrent of condemnation that precedes this verse, the statement that it was actually Allah who didn't want the slackers to go forth to jihad is an astounding recurrence of the proposition that all events are controlled by Allah, to the extent that human beings lack free will (see 2:7). The *Tafsir al-Jalalayn* says of those who didn't go to the fight that Allah "held them back and made them lazy."[87]

cause sedition and raised difficulties for you until the truth came and the decree of Allah was made clear, though they disliked it. **⁴⁹**Among them is he who says, Give me permission and do not tempt me. Surely it is into temptation that they have fallen. Indeed, Gehenna truly is all around the unbelievers. **⁵⁰**If good happens to you, it afflicts them, and if calamity happens to you, they say, We took precautions, and they turn away well pleased. **⁵¹**Say, Nothing happens to us except what Allah has decreed for us. He is our protecting friend. In Allah let believers put their trust. **⁵²**Say, Are you waiting for anything to happen to us except one of two good things, while we await for you that Allah will afflict you with a doom from him or at our hands. Wait, then. Indeed, we are waiting with you. **⁵³**Say, Pay, willingly or unwillingly, it will not be accepted from you. Indeed, you were always defiant people. **⁵⁴**And nothing prevents that their contributions should be accepted from them except that they have disbelieved in Allah and in his messenger, and they do not come to prayer except as idlers, and do not pay except reluctantly. **⁵⁵**Do not let their wealth or their children please you. Allah intends by those things only to punish them in the life of this world, and that their souls will pass away while they are unbelievers. **⁵⁶**And they swear by Allah that they are really with you, when they are not with you, but they are people who are afraid. **⁵⁷**If only they had found a refuge, or caverns, or a place to enter, they surely would have taken refuge there as quickly as runaways. **⁵⁸**And among them is he who defames you in the matter of the alms. If they are given from them they are content, and if they are not given from them, look, they are enraged. **⁵⁹**If they had been content with what Allah and his messenger had given them and had said, Allah is sufficient for us. Allah will give us of his bounty, and his messenger. To Allah we turn with hope. **⁶⁰**The alms are only for the poor and the needy, and those who collect them, and those whose hearts are to be reconciled, and to free the captives and the debtors, and for the

---

49. According to Ibn Hisham, the unnamed slacker who begged Muhammad not to have to go on jihad was afraid of the women of the enemy. He asked Muhammad: "Will you allow me to stay behind and not tempt me, for everyone knows that I am strongly addicted to women and I am afraid that if I see the Byzantine women I shall not be able to control myself."[88] Yet in light of 4:24, he wouldn't have had to control himself: the women of those whom he defeated in battle, or any infidel women he managed to seize, would have been lawfully his.

Nonetheless, the man is granted permission to stay behind, and Allah is unhappy, telling the messenger that those who have asked to be excused have already fallen into temptation by doing so and that hell awaits them also. Here again, there is no way to interpret all this in a spiritual sense.

52. The two best things are martyrdom or victory. The Muslims will either defeat the enemy or be killed by them, in which case they will enter paradise, a win/win situation (see 3:124).

53. According to the *Ruhul Ma'ani*, this verse was revealed in reference to one of the hypocrites, those who held back and would not go on jihad with Muhammad, Jadd bin Qais.[89] He was willing to donate money to Muhammad's expedition to Tabuk but not to join the caravan and fight himself. His hypocrisy, and that of others like him, renders their contributions unacceptable.

55. The prosperity of the unbelievers is only a prelude to their punishment in this world, which comes at the hands of the believers; see 9:14.

58. According to Ibn Kathir, "We were told that a bedouin man, who had recently embraced Islam, came to the Prophet, when he was dividing some gold and silver, and said to him, 'O Muhammad! Even though Allah commanded you to divide in fairness, you have not done so.'"[90] Muhammad is supposed to have responded: "Woe to you! Who would be fair to you after me?"[91] In Islamic tradition, what Muhammad does is right, and it is by comparison to his words and deeds that everything else is to be evaluated.

59. According to the *Tafsir al-Jalalayn*, the hypocrites should have been content with "what Allah and His Messenger gave them in terms of booty and other things."[92]

60. Allah specifies those to whom the obligatory alms, zakat, can be distributed; it can be spent "for the sake of Allah." That means, explains the *Tafsir al-Jalalayn*, it can be spent to "enable those who do not have booty to undertake jihad, even if they are rich."[93] Ibn Kathir states that zakat for the sake of Allah "is exclusive for the benefit of the fighters in Jihad, who do not receive compensation from the Muslim Treasury."[94] As-Suyuti adds: "Some say that it is spent on all that is connected to jihad: treaties with the enemy,

sake of Allah, and the wayfarer, a duty imposed by Allah. Allah is the knower, the wise one. **⁶¹**And among them are those who annoy the prophet and say, He is only an ear. Say, An ear of good for you who believe in Allah and are true to the believers, and a mercy for those of you who believe. Those who annoy the messenger of Allah, for them there is a painful doom. **⁶²**They swear by Allah to you to please you, but Allah, with his messenger, has more of a right that they should please him, if they are believers. **⁶³**Don't they know that whoever opposes Allah and his messenger, the fire of Gehenna is indeed his, to remain in it? That is the extreme humiliation. **⁶⁴**The hypocrites fear that a sura might be revealed about them, proclaiming what is in their hearts. Say, Keep on mocking. Indeed, Allah is revealing what you fear. **⁶⁵**And if you ask them, they will say, We were only talking and joking. Say, Was it Allah and his signs and his messenger that you mocked? **⁶⁶**Do not offer any excuse. You have disbelieved after your belief. If we forgive a group of you, we punish a group of you, because they have been guilty. **⁶⁷**The hypocrites, both men and women, proceed one from another. They command what is wrong, and they forbid what is right, and they withhold their hands. They forget Allah, so he has forgotten them. Indeed, the hypocrites, they are the transgressors. **⁶⁸**Allah

promises the hypocrites, both men and women, and the unbelievers, the fire of Gehenna for their dwelling. It will be sufficient for them. Allah curses them, and theirs is lasting torment. **⁶⁹**Even as those before you who were mightier than you in strength, and more affluent than you in wealth and children. They enjoyed their situation for a while, so you enjoy your situation for a while, even as those before you enjoyed their situation for a while. And you indulge in idle talk just as they did. Such people are the ones whose works have perished in this world and the hereafter. Such people are the ones who are the losers. **⁷⁰**Hasn't the fame of those before them reached them? The people of Noah, Aad, Thamud, the people of Abraham, the dwellers of Midian and the disasters? Their messengers came to them with proofs. So Allah surely did not wrong them, but they wronged themselves. **⁷¹**And the believers, men and women, are protecting friends one of another, they command what is right and forbid what is wrong, and they establish prayer and they give alms, and they obey Allah and his messenger. As for these people, Allah will have mercy on them. Indeed, Allah is mighty, wise. **⁷²**Allah promises to the believers, men and women, gardens under which rivers flow, in which they will remain, blessed dwellings in gardens of Eden. And even better, acceptance from Allah. That is

---

building fortresses, digging ditches, providing weapons and provision, and paying spies, even if they are Christians."⁹⁵

61. The prophet is taunted as "an ear," which likely is an echo of the unbelievers' other complaint, that the messenger is simply repeating "fables of the men of old" (6:25, 8:31).

64. The hypocrites recognize that the messenger tends to receive revelations about his enemies (see sura 111). This is a suggestion of the Qur'an's possibly having arisen as a polemic amid a welter of competing religious claims and having been fashioned in order to advance certain of those claims. Thus it deals with and purports to refute competing claims (see 4:157 and 5:18 for two examples).

65. "Mocking the signs of Allah," says as-Suyuti, "is tantamount to kufr," that is, unbelief.⁹⁶ This is one reason why cartoons of Muhammad are such a hot-button issue among many Muslims today.

66. Instead of, "If we forgive [na'fu] a group of you, we punish [nu'azzib] a group of you," Ibn Kathir has, "If some of you are forgiven [yu'fa], others will be punished [tu'azzab]."⁹⁷

Instead of "we forgive," the Warsh Qur'an has "he forgives."⁹⁸ Instead of "we punish," the Warsh Qur'an has "he punishes."⁹⁹

the supreme triumph. **73**O prophet, wage jihad against the unbelievers and the hypocrites. Be harsh with them. Their ultimate dwelling place is Gehenna, an evil destination. **74**They swear by Allah that they said nothing, yet they did say the word of disbelief, and did disbelieve after they accepted Islam. And they intended what they could not accomplish, and they sought revenge only so that Allah by his messenger would enrich them out of his bounty. If they repent, it will be better for them, and if they turn away, Allah will afflict them with a painful doom in this world and the hereafter, and they have no protecting friend nor helper in the earth. **75**And among them is he who made a covenant with Allah, If he gives us of his bounty, we will give alms and become among the righteous. **76**Yet when he gave them of his bounty, they hoarded it and turned away in aversion, **77**So he has made the consequences hypocrisy in their hearts until the day when they will meet him, because they broke their word to Allah that they promised him, and because they lied. **78**Don't they know that Allah knows both their secrets and the thought that they confide, and that Allah is the knower of hidden things? **79**Those who point at those of the believers who give alms willingly and those who can find nothing to give except their labors, and deride them, Allah derides them. Theirs will be a painful doom. **80**Ask forgiveness for them, or do not ask forgiveness for them, although if you ask forgiveness for them seventy times, Allah will not forgive them. That is because they disbelieved in Allah and his messenger, and Allah does not guide wrongdoing people. **81**Those who were left behind rejoiced at sitting still behind the messenger of Allah, and were averse to waging jihad with their wealth and their lives in Allah's way. And they said, Don't go forth in the heat. Say, The fire of Gehenna is more intense heat, if only they understood. **82**Then let them laugh a little, they will weep much, as the reward of what they used to earn. **83**If Allah brings you back to a group of them and they ask permission of you to go out, then say to them, You will never more go out with me, nor fight with me against a foe. You were

---

73. "Wage jihad" is *jahidi*, strive hard (see 2:218). Attributed to Ibn Abbas is this explanation: "Allah commanded the Prophet to fight the disbelievers with the sword, to strive against the hypocrites with the tongue and annulled lenient treatment of them."[100] Another early Muslim is depicted as saying: "Perform Jihad against the disbelievers with the sword and be harsh with the hypocrites with words, and this is the Jihad performed against them."[101] And Ibn Juzayy: "Jihad against the rejecters is by the sword and jihad against the hypocrites is by the tongue as long as they do not openly display that which indicates their disbelief… Harshness is the opposite of mercy and compassion. It can be by word, action, etc."[102] On Gehenna, see 2:206.

Significantly, Ibn Kathir invokes two earlier authorities who affirm that "striving against them includes establishing the (Islamic Penal) Law of equality against them."[103]

74. According to Ibn Hisham, one of the Muslims who refused to accompany Muhammad on the Tabuk expedition was Julas bin Suwayd, along with his brother Harith. Julas said of Muhammad: "If this man is right we are worse than donkeys."[104] One of Julas's relatives, Umayr bin Sa'd, told Muhammad what Julas had said. Then he explained to Julas that he had done so because Islam is more important than family ties: "You are dearer to me than any man, the most generous to me, and it is most painful to me that anything should happen to upset you; but you have said words which if I repeat them I shall bring shame upon you, and if I keep silence I shall bring my religion into peril. One is preferable to the other."[105] Julas and Harith, cornered, denied that Julas had spoken the offending words, whereupon Allah revealed this verse.

On punishment in this world, see 9:14.

77. Ibn Kathir says that Allah "placed hypocrisy in their hearts because they broke their promise and lied." See 7:179, 10:99, 32:13.

80. Allah's refusal to forgive the hypocrites even after seventy requests is the obverse of Matthew 18:21-22, where Jesus says that one should forgive seventy times seven times.

81. Here resumes the denunciation of those who did not go on jihad that was left off after 9:49, possibly indicating some textual dislocation.

Here again, "waging jihad" is usually translated as "strive," which obscures both the fact that a word derived from jihad (*yujahidoo*) is used in the Arabic, and the fact that waging jihad "with their wealth and their lives" makes it unmistakable that fighting in battle is meant. On Gehenna, see 2:206.

content with sitting still the first time. So sit still, with the useless. **84**And never pray for one of them who dies, nor stand by his grave. Indeed, they disbelieved in Allah and his messenger, and they died while they were evildoers. **85**Do not let their wealth or their children please you. Allah intends by those things only to punish them in this world, and that their souls will pass away while they are unbelievers. **86**And when a sura is revealed, Believe in Allah and wage jihad along with his messenger, the men of wealth among them still ask permission from you and say, Permit us to be with those who sit. **87**They are content to be with the useless and their hearts are sealed, so that they do not understand. **88**But the messenger and those who believe with him wage jihad with their wealth and their lives. Such people are the ones for whom the good things are. Such people are the ones who are the successful. **89**Allah has prepared for them gardens under which rivers flow, in which they will remain. That is the supreme triumph. **90**And those among the nomadic Arabs who had an excuse came in order that permission might be granted to them. And those who lied to Allah and his messenger sat at home. A painful doom will fall upon those among them who disbelieve. **91**There is no fault upon the weak or the sick or to those who can find nothing to spend if they are true to Allah and his messenger. There is no path against any who are good.

Allah is forgiving, merciful. **92**Nor to those people who, when they came to you so that you would find them mounts, you told, I cannot find any mount for you. They turned back with eyes flowing with tears, for sorrow that they could not find anything to spend. **93**The road is only against those who ask for permission from you when they are rich. They are content to be with the useless. Allah has sealed their hearts so that they do not know. **94**They will make excuses to you when you return unto them. Say, Make no excuse, for we will not believe you. Allah has told us news of you. Allah and his messenger will see your conduct, and then you will be brought back to him who knows the invisible as well as the visible, and he will tell you what you used to do. **95**They will swear by Allah to you, when you return to them, so that you might let them be. Let them be, for indeed, they are unclean, and their abode is Gehenna as the reward for what they used to earn. **96**They swear to you so that you may accept them. Though you accept them. Allah indeed does not accept wrongdoing people. **97**The nomadic Arabs are harder in disbelief and hypocrisy, and more likely to be ignorant of the limits which Allah has revealed to his messenger. And Allah is the knower, the wise one. **98**And among the nomadic Arabs there is he who does not take what he spent as a loss, and awaits turns of fortune for you. The evil turn of fortune will be

---

84. The Muslims should not even pray for the hypocrites when they die; for them, there is to be no forgiveness.

85. A repeat of 9:55, which may indicate some editing and alteration of the text.

90. Ibn Juzayy says that the refusal of the Bedouin Arabs to wage jihad invalidated their claim to be Muslim: "They were the people who did not go on jihad nor ask excuses to stay behind them, so they lied when they claimed to believe."[106]

91. Ibn Kathir explains "valid excuses that permit one to stay away from fighting. He first mentions the excuses that remain

with a person, the weakness in the body that disallows one from Jihad, such as blindness, limping, and so forth. He then mentions the excuses that are not permanent, such as an illness that would prevent one from fighting for the sake of Allah, or poverty that prevents preparing for Jihad. There is no sin in these cases if they remain behind, providing that when they remain behind, they do not spread malice or try to discourage Muslims from fighting, but all the while observing good behavior in this state."[107] This all assumes again that jihad involves warfare.

Many authorities hold that this verse abrogates 9:41.

theirs. Allah is the hearer, the knower. **99**And among the nomadic Arabs there is he who believes in Allah and the last day, and takes what he spent and also the prayers of the messenger as acceptable offerings in the sight of Allah. Indeed, truly it is an acceptable offering for them. Allah will bring them into his mercy. Indeed, Allah is forgiving, merciful. **100**And the first to lead the way, of the emigrants (*muhajiroun*) and the helpers (*ansar*), and those who followed them in goodness, Allah is well pleased with them and they are well pleased with him, and he has made ready for them gardens under which rivers flow, in which they will remain forever. That is the supreme triumph. **101**And among those around you of the nomadic Arabs there are hypocrites, and among the townspeople of Medina, they persist in hypocrisy some whom you do not know. We know them, and we will punish them twice, then they will be relegated to a painful doom. **102**And others, who have acknowledged their faults. They mixed a righteous action with another that was bad. It may be that Allah will relent toward them. Indeed, Allah is forgiving, merciful. **103**Take alms from their wealth, with

which you might purify them and make them grow, and pray for them. Indeed, your prayer is peace for them. Allah is the hearer, the knower. **104**Don't they know that Allah is he who accepts repentance from his slaves and takes alms, and that Allah is he who is the relenting, the merciful? **105**And say, Act, and Allah will see your actions, and his messenger and the believers, and you will be brought back to the knower of the invisible and the visible, and he will tell you what you used to do. **106**And others who await Allah's decree, whether he will punish them or will forgive them. Allah is the knower, the wise. **107**And as for those who chose a mosque out of opposition and disbelief, and in order to cause dissent among the believers, and as an outpost for those who made war against Allah and his messenger previously, they will surely swear, We intended nothing but good. Allah bears witness that they indeed are liars. **108**Never stand there. A mosque that was founded upon duty from the first day is more worthy that you should stand in it, in which are men who love to purify themselves. Allah loves the purifiers. **109**Is he who founded his building upon duty to Allah and his good pleasure better,

100. In Islamic tradition, the *muhajiroun*, "emigrants," are those who left their land to go to another and bring Islam to it. The first muhajiroun were Muhammad and the original Muslims of Mecca when they moved to Medina. The later converts in Medina were known as the *ansar*, "helpers." The emigrants have the priority among Muslims, which is an indication of the importance placed upon emigration for the sake of Allah. See 4:100.

101. Like Mecca, Medina plays a major role in the life and career of Muhammad as detailed in ninth-century hadith literature as well as in the sira, the biographical material about Muhammad. There is, however, no independent evidence of its seventh-century existence. Writing about Medina in the *Encyclopaedia of the Qur'an*, historian Marco Schöller notes that "if based solely on the Qur'anic data…any entry concerning Medina would be unduly short because our knowledge of pre- and early Islamic Medina derives almost entirely from other, and usually much later, source material."[108] In the Qur'an itself, "there is next to no information about the

town, its history and topography," and so "any account of Medina in pre- and early Islamic times must therefore be based on later literary sources…. Much of what we can say about pre- and early Islamic Medina is thus hypothetical."[109]

102. Ibn Juzayy explains that "this ayat was sent down about Abu Lubaba. His virtuous action was jihad and his bad action consisted of advising the Banu Qurayza," the Jewish tribe that broke their covenant with the Muslims and that Muhammad subsequently had massacred.[110]

107. This controversy over a rival mosque is another indication of the schisms in the early community, as is 9:64. According to Islamic tradition, Muhammad ordered his followers to burn the mosque to the ground. Ibn Kathir says that its builders had "made it an outpost for those who warred against Allah and His Messenger."[111] This created the template for a harshness in dealing with rivalry and schism that has persisted to this day.

or he who founded his building on the brink of a crumbling, overhanging precipice so that it toppled with him into the fire of Gehenna? Allah does not guide wrongdoing people. **110**The building that they built will never cease to be a misgiving in their hearts unless their hearts are torn to pieces. Allah is the knower, the wise. **111**Indeed, Allah has bought from the believers their lives and their wealth, because the garden will be theirs, they will fight in the way of Allah and will kill and be killed. It is a promise that is binding on him in the Torah and the Gospel and the Qur'an. Who fulfills his covenant better than Allah? Rejoice then in your bargain that you have made, for that is the supreme triumph. **112**Those who turn repentant, those who serve, those who praise, those who fast, those who bow down, those who fall prostrate, those who enjoin the right and forbid the wrong and those who keep the limits of Allah, and give glad news to believers. **113**It is not for the prophet and those who believe to pray for the forgiveness of idolaters, even though they may be near relatives, after it has become clear that they are companions of the blaze. **114**The prayer of Abraham for the forgiveness of his father was only because of a promise he had made to him, but when it had become clear to him that he was an enemy of Allah, he disowned him. Indeed, Abraham was soft of heart, long-suffering. **115**It was never of Allah that he should send a people astray after he had guided them until he had made clear to them what they should avoid. Indeed, Allah is aware of all things. **116**Indeed, Allah, to him belongs the dominion of the heavens and the earth. He brings to life and he gives death. And you have, instead of Allah, no protecting friend nor helper. **117**Allah has turned in mercy to the prophet, and to the emigrants and the helpers who followed him in the hour of hardship. After the hearts of a group of them had almost swerved aside, then he turned to them in mercy. Indeed, he is full of pity, merciful for them. **118**And to the three also who were left behind, when the earth, vast as it is, was made confining for them, and their own souls were burdened for them until they thought that there is no refuge from Allah except toward him. Then he turned to them in mercy, so that they might turn. Indeed, Allah, he is the relenting, the merciful. **119**O you who believe, be mindful of your duty

---

111. This verse has become in the modern age the rationale for suicide bombing. Ibn Kathir explains: "Allah states that He has compensated His believing servants for their lives and wealth—if they give them up in His cause—with Paradise."[112] Ibn Juzayy adds significantly that this verse's "judgment is general to every believer doing jihad in the way of Allah until the Day of Rising."[113]

The Qur'an says that this promise of Paradise to those who kill and are killed for Allah is also in the Torah and Gospel, but in reality, it isn't—which is in itself more evidence for pious Muslims that those documents have been tampered with.

113. The Muslims should not pray for pagans, even relatives. See also 9:23, 9:84, 29:8, 31:15, and 60:4. "The blaze" is *al-jahim*, about which see 5:10.

114. Abraham even dissociated himself from his father when he realized he was an "enemy of Allah."

115. Ibn Juzayy explains: "This ayat was sent down about some Muslims who asked forgiveness for the idolaters without permission and then they feared for themselves on that account and so the ayat was sent down to console them, i.e. Allah would not take you to task for that before it was clear to you that it was forbidden."[114]

118. The "three who were left behind" who are forgiven were three Muslims who, according to Ibn Juzayy, "stayed behind the Tabuk expedition without excuse and without hypocrisy nor intention to stay behind."[115]

119. The believers must "be with the truthful," which means, according to as-Suyuti, "to be truthful in everything and in every situation."[116] However, a hadith depicts Muhammad allowing lying "in battle, for bringing reconciliation amongst persons and the narration of the words of the husband to his wife, and the narration of the words of a wife to her husband (in a twisted form in order to bring reconciliation between them)."[117] See also 3:28.

Bell points out that this verse is "out of connection" with the surrounding narrative.[118] It may be an interpolation.

to Allah, and be with the truthful. **120**It is not for the townspeople of Medina and for those around them of the nomadic Arabs to stay behind the messenger of Allah and prefer their lives to his life. That is because neither thirst nor toil nor hunger afflicts them in the way of Allah, nor do they take any step that angers the unbelievers, nor do they gain anything from the enemy, except that a good deed is recorded for them for it. Indeed, Allah does not lose the wages of the good. **121**Nor do they spend anything, small or great, nor do they cross a valley, except that it is recorded for them, that Allah might repay them the best of what they used to do. **122**And the believers should not all go out to fight. Of every troop of them, only a party should go forth, so that they may gain sound knowledge in religion, and that they may warn their people when they return to them, so that they may beware. **123**O you who believe, fight those of the unbelievers who are near to you, and let them find harshness in you, and know that Allah is with those who keep their duty. **124**And whenever a sura is revealed, there are some of them who say, Which one of you has in this way increased in faith? As for those who believe, it has increased them in faith and they rejoice. **125**But as for those in whose hearts is disease, it only adds wickedness to their wickedness, and they die while they are unbelievers. **126**Do they not see that they are tested once or twice in every year? Still, they do not turn in repentance, nor do they pay attention. **127**And whenever a sura is revealed, they look one at another, Does anybody see you? Then they turn away. Allah turns their hearts away because they are a people who do not understand. **128**There has come to you a messenger, from among yourselves, to whom anything that distresses you is grievous, full of concern for you, for the believers full of pity, merciful. **129**Now, if they turn away say, Allah is sufficient for me. There is no God except him. In him I have put my trust, and he is Lord of the great throne.

---

120. Nothing that infuriates the unbelievers will go unrewarded.

122. All the Muslims need not go forth to wage jihad warfare. This is a foundation for the Islamic legal principle that jihad is *fard kifaya*—that is, a community obligation from which some are freed if others take it up. Jihad becomes *fard ayn*, or obligatory on every believer, when a Muslim land is attacked.

123. Says Ibn Kathir: "Allah commands the believers to fight the disbelievers, the closest in area to the Islamic state, then the farthest."[119]

128. This verse and the following one were, according to Islamic tradition, only added to the Qur'an by a lucky chance. In one ninth-century account, the man charged with collecting the Qur'an, Zaid ibn Thabit, explains how he set to work: "I started

locating Qur'anic material and collecting it from parchments, scapula, leaf-stalks of date palms and from the memories of men [who knew it by heart]. I found with Khuzaima two Verses of Surat-at-Tauba which I had not found with anybody else."[120] Khuzaima was an early Muslim who accosted Zaid when he heard his version of sura 9 recited and informed him: "I see you have overlooked [two] verses and have not written them."[121] Zaid duly added them.

If Khuzaima hadn't been present, apparently these two verses would not have been included in the Qur'an. They are not significant for Islamic doctrine or devotions, but this story is striking in that Islamic sources are bearing witness to a certain fluidity in the Qur'anic text.

Jonah

Yunus

Introduction

Suras 1 through 9 of the Qur'an contain the book's primary doctrinal content. The suras immediately following sura 9 begin to focus more on telling stories of prophets, with an eye toward shoring up the messenger's prophetic claim, accompanied by the same furious denunciations of unbelievers that fill so much of suras 1–9.

This sura traditionally is dated from late in the Meccan period, the first part of Muhammad's prophetic career. Its name comes from 10:98, where the Biblical prophet Jonah is mentioned in passing.

Jonah

IN THE NAME OF ALLAH, THE COMPASSIONATE, THE MERCIFUL.

1Alif. Lam. Ra. These are verses of the wise book. **2**Is it surprising for mankind that we have inspired a man among them, saying, Warn mankind and bring to those who believe the good news that they have a sure footing with their Lord? The unbelievers say, Indeed, this is merely a magician. **3**Indeed, your Lord is Allah, who created the heavens and the earth in six days, then he established himself upon the throne, directing all things. There is no intercessor except by his permission. That is Allah, your Lord, so worship him. Oh, will you not remember? **4**To him all of you will return, it is a promise of Allah in truth. Indeed, He produces creation, then reproduces it, so that he may reward those who believe and do good works with justice, while, as for those who disbelieve, theirs will be a boiling drink and painful doom because they disbelieved. **5**It is he who established the sun a splendor and the moon a light, and measured stages for her, so that you might know the number of the years, and the reckoning. Allah did not create that except in truth. He details the signs for people who have knowledge. **6**Indeed, in the difference of day and night and all that Allah has created in the heavens and the earth are signs, indeed, for people who fear Allah. **7**Indeed, those who do not expect to meet us, but desire the life of this world and feel secure in it, and those who are neglectful of our signs, **8**Their home will be the fire, because of what they used to earn. **9**Indeed, those who believe and do good works, their Lord guides them by their faith. Rivers will flow beneath them in the gardens of delight, **10**Their prayer in them will be, Glory be to you, O Allah. And their greeting in them will be, Peace. And the conclusion of their prayer will be, Praise be to Allah, Lord of the worlds. **11**If Allah were to hasten evil for people as they would hasten good, their respite would already have expired. But we allow those who do not look forward to the meeting with us to wander blindly in their insolence. **12**And if misfortune touches a man, he calls out to us, on his side or sitting or standing, but when we have relieved him of the misfortune, he goes his way, as if he had not called out to us because of a misfortune that afflicted him. In this way what they do is made good to the wasteful. **13**We destroyed the generations before you when they did wrong, and their messengers came to them with clear proofs,

---

1. On the "mysterious letters," see 2:1. According to Ibn Kathir, the statement after these letters "indicates that these are verses of the Qur'an, in which the wisdom of judgment is clear."[1]

2. Islamic tradition sees this as another indication of the greatness of Muhammad. A hadith put in the mouth of Ibn Abbas states: "When Allah, exalted is He, sent Muhammad, Allah bless him and give him peace, as a messenger, the unbelievers criticised him, saying: 'Allah is too great to have a human like Muhammad as His messenger' and so Allah, exalted is He, revealed this verse."[2]

Instead of "a magician" [*lasaahirun*], the Warsh Qur'an has "a work of magic" [*lasihrun*].[3]

3. Intercession with Allah's permission is accepted (cf. 20:109, 21:28, 34:23, 53:26). However, elsewhere the Qur'an says that everyone will stand alone before Allah; no intercession from others will be accepted (2:48, 2:123, 6:94, 23:101, 39:43, 42:46).

Regarding the number of days Allah took to create the universe, see 7:54.

5. Here begins a lengthy section repeating themes that have been sounded before. These include: Allah made all things (10:5-6; cf. 6:96); some people are ungrateful to Allah (10:12; cf. 4:62); Allah destroyed earlier generations of unbelievers (10:13; cf. 3:137); the idols that the unbelievers worship are worthless (10:18, 6:71); the unbelievers will burn in hell (10:8, 27; cf. 7:38); and the believers will enjoy the gardens of Paradise (10:9, 26; cf. 7:42).

but they would not believe. In this way we reward the guilty people. **14**Then we established you as caliphs on the earth after them, so that we might see how you behave. **15**And when our clear signs are recited to them, those who do not look forward to the meeting with us say, Bring a Qur'an other than this, or change it. Say, It is not for me to change it of my own accord. I only follow what is inspired within me. Indeed, if I disobey my Lord, I fear the retribution of an awful day. **16**Say, If Allah had so willed, I would not have recited it to you, nor would he have made it known to you. I dwelt among you a whole lifetime before it. Have you then no sense? **17**Who does greater wrong than he who invents a lie about Allah and denies his signs? Indeed, the guilty are never successful. **18**They worship besides Allah what neither hurts them nor benefits them, and they say, These are our intercessors with Allah. Say, Would you inform Allah of what he doesn't know in the heavens or on the earth? Praised be he and highly exalted above all that you associate.

19Mankind was but one community, then they differed, and if it had not been for a word that had already gone forth from your Lord, it would have been judged between them in regard to what they disagree about. **20**And they will say, If only a sign were sent down upon him from his Lord! Then say, The unseen belongs to Allah. So wait. Indeed, I am waiting with you. **21**And when we cause mankind to taste of mercy after some adversity which had afflicted them, look, they have some plot against our signs. Say, Allah is swifter in plotting. Indeed, our messengers write down what you plot. **22**It is he who makes you to go on the land and the sea until, when you are in the ships and they sail with them with a fair breeze and they are glad in them, a storm wind reaches them and the wave comes to them from every side, and they think that they are overwhelmed in it, they call out to Allah, making their faith pure for him only, If you deliver us from this, we indeed will be among the grateful. **23**Yet when he has delivered them, look, they rebel in the earth wrongfully. O mankind, your rebellion is only against yourselves. Enjoyment of the life of the world, then to us is your return and we shall proclaim to you what you used to do. **24**The life of the world is only like water that we send down from the sky, then the earth's growth of what men and cattle eat mingled with it, until, when the earth has taken on her ornaments and is embellished, and her people think that they are her masters, our commandment comes by night or by day and we make it as reaped corn as if it had not flourished yesterday. In this way we explain the signs for people who reflect. **25**And Allah summons to the abode of peace, and leads those whom he wills to a straight path. **26**For those who do good is the best and more. Neither

---

14. On "caliphs on earth," see 2:30.

21. Ibn Kathir explains that this "means that Allah is more capable of gradually seizing them with punishment, while granting them concession of a delay until the criminals think that they would not be punished. But in reality they are in periods of respite, then they will be taken suddenly."4 Allah is also depicted as a schemer or plotter at 3:54, 7:99, and 8:30.

26. The skins of the blessed will be white and that of the damned black. Ibn Kathir quotes a hadith to this effect: "When the people

of Paradise enter Paradise, a caller will say: 'O people of Paradise, Allah has promised you something that He wishes to fulfill.'"5 Then the blessed will answer: "What is it? Has He not made our Scale heavy?"—that is, has he not judged that our good deeds outweigh our bad ones?6 And: "Has He not made our faces white and delivered us from Fire?"7 For "no blackness or darkness will be on their faces during the different events of the Day of Judgment. But the faces of the rebellious disbelievers will be stained with dust and darkness."8 Though some have tried to make this into a racial

dust nor disgrace come near their faces. Such people are the rightful companions of the garden, they will remain in it. **27**And those who earn evil deeds, repayment of each evil deed by one like it, and disgrace overtakes them, they have no protector from Allah, as if their faces had been covered with a cloak of darkest night. Such people are the rightful companions of the fire, they will remain in it. **28**On the day when we gather them all together, then we say to those who ascribed partners, Stand back, you and your partners. And we separate them, the one from the other, and their partners say, It was not us you worshipped. **29**Allah is sufficient as a witness between us and you, that we were unaware of your worship. **30**There every soul experiences what it did previously, and they are returned to Allah, their rightful Lord, and what they used to devise has failed them. **31**Say, Who provides for you from the sky and the earth, or who owns hearing and sight, and who brings forth the living from the dead and brings forth the dead from the living, and who directs the course? They will say, Allah. Then say, Will you not then keep your duty? **32**That is Allah, your rightful Lord. After the truth, what is there except error? How then are you turned away? **33**In this way is the word of your Lord justified concerning those who do wrong, that they do not believe. **34**Say, Is there among your partners one that produces creation and then reproduces it? Say, Allah produces creation, then reproduces it. How then, are you misled? **35**Say, Is there among your partners one that leads people to the truth? Say, Allah leads people to the truth. Is he who leads people to the truth more deserving to be followed, or he who doesn't find the way unless he is guided. What ails you? How do you judge? **36**Most of them don't follow anything but speculation. Surely speculation cannot in any way take the place of truth. Indeed, Allah is aware of what they do. **37**And this Qur'an is not such as could ever be produced by anyone except Allah, but it is a confirmation of what was before it and an exposition of what is decreed for mankind from the Lord of the worlds. In it is no doubt. **38**Or do they say, He has invented it? Say, Then bring a sura like it, and call on all you can besides Allah, if you are truthful. **39**No, but they

statement, there is nothing in the mainstream Muslim Qur'an commentaries to support this; it is clearly a moral judgment, not a racial one.

33. Instead of "the word of your Lord," the Warsh Qur'an has "the words of your Lord."9

37. An excursus upon the excellence of the Qur'an, which could only have been produced by Allah, confirming the scriptures before it (see 3:3, 3:50).

38. This challenge is also issued at 2:23. Ibn Kathir explains: "The Qur'an has a miraculous nature that cannot be imitated. No one can produce anything similar to the Qur'an, nor ten Surahs or even one Surah like it. The eloquence, clarity, precision and grace of the Qur'an cannot be but from Allah. The great and abundant principles and meanings within the Qur'an—which are of great benefit in this world and for the Hereafter—cannot be but from Allah. There is nothing like His High Self and Attributes or like His sayings and actions. Therefore His Words are not like the words of His creatures."10

It confirms earlier books, he explains, "and is a witness to them. It shows the changes, perversions and corruption that have taken place within these Books."11 The Qur'an purports to correct these corruptions.

Why issue a challenge like "bring forth a surah like it"? Because the eloquence of its Arabic is considered to be a sign of the Qur'an's divine provenance. Ibn Kathir explains: "Eloquence was a part of the nature and character of the Arabs. Arabic poetry including *Al-Mu'allaqat*—the oldest complete collection of the most eloquent ancient Arabic poems—was considered to be the best in the literary arts. However Allah sent down to them something whose style none were familiar with, and no one is equal in stature to imitate. So those who believed among them, believed because of what they knew and felt in the Book, including its beauty, elegance, benefit, and fluency. They became the most knowledgeable of the Qur'an and its best in adhering to it."12

This is one of the principal reasons why traditional Islamic theology says that the Qur'an cannot be translated: losing the music of the Arabic language, it loses part of its essence.

denied that, the knowledge of which they could not comprehend, and of which the interpretation has not yet come to them. Even in this way did those before them deny. Then see what were the consequences for the wrongdoers. ⁴⁰And among them is he who believes in it, and among them is he who does not believe in it, and your Lord is best aware of the corrupters. ⁴¹And if they deny you, say, To me my work, and to you your work. You are innocent of what I do, and I am innocent of what you do. ⁴²And among them are some who listen to you. But can you make the deaf hear, even though they do not understand? ⁴³And among them is he who looks toward you. But can you guide the blind even though they do not see? ⁴⁴Indeed, Allah does not wrong mankind in anything, but mankind wrong themselves. ⁴⁵And on the day when he will gather them together, as if they had delayed just an hour of the day, recognizing one another, those who denied the meeting with Allah and were not guided will indeed have perished. ⁴⁶Whether we let you see some of what we promise them or cause you to die, still their return is to us, and Allah, moreover, is the witness over what they do. ⁴⁷And for every nation there is a messenger. And when their messenger comes, it will be judged fairly between them, and they will not be wronged. ⁴⁸And they say, When will this promise be fulfilled, if you are truthful? ⁴⁹Say, I have no power to hurt or benefit myself, except what Allah wills. For every nation there is an appointed time. When their time comes, then they cannot put it off for an hour, or hasten it. ⁵⁰Say, Have you thought, when his doom comes to you as a raid by night, or in the day, what there is of it that the guilty ones want to hasten? ⁵¹Is it then, when it has come upon you, that you will believe? What? Now, when you have been hastening it? ⁵²Then will it be said to those who dealt unjustly, Taste the torment of eternity. Are you repaid for anything except what you earned? ⁵³And they ask you to inform them, Is it true? Say, Yes, by my Lord, indeed it is true, and you cannot escape. ⁵⁴And if each soul that does wrong had everything that is on earth, it would seek to ransom itself with it, and they will feel remorse within them, when they see the doom. But it has been judged between them fairly, and they are not wronged. ⁵⁵Indeed, truly all that is in the heavens and the earth belongs to Allah. Indeed, truly Allah's promise is true. But most of them do not know. ⁵⁶He brings to life and gives death, and to him you will be returned. ⁵⁷O mankind, there has come to you an exhortation from your Lord, a balm for what is in the hearts, a guidance and a mercy for believers. ⁵⁸Say, Let them rejoice in the bounty of Allah and in his mercy. It is better than what they hoard. ⁵⁹Say, Have you considered what provision Allah has sent down for you, how you have made of it parts that are lawful and unlawful? Has Allah permitted you to do this, or do you invent a lie about Allah? ⁶⁰And what do those who invent a lie about Allah think about the day of resurrection? Indeed, Allah truly is bountiful toward mankind, but most of them do not give thanks. ⁶¹And you are not occupied with any business and you do not recite any portion of the Qur'an, and you do nothing except that we are

---

45. Instead of, "He will gather them," the Warsh Qur'an has, "We will gather them."[13]

47. See 16:36.

50. Allah's eternal punishments should move the sinners to repent (see 2:7, 2:10, 2:165, and so on).

53. On the oath "by my Lord," see 34:3.

the witness of what you do when you are engaged in these things. And not an atom's weight on the earth or in the sky escapes your Lord, nor what is less than that or greater than that, but it is in a clear book. ⁶²Indeed, truly the friends of Allah are those who do not fear, nor do they grieve. ⁶³Those who believe and keep their duty. ⁶⁴Theirs is good news in the life of this world and in the hereafter. There is no changing the words of Allah. That is the supreme victory. ⁶⁵And do not let their speech grieve you. Indeed, power belongs wholly to Allah. He is the hearer, the knower. ⁶⁶Indeed, doesn't whoever is in the heavens and whoever is on the earth belong to Allah? Those who follow anything instead of Allah do not follow partners. They follow only speculation, and they just guess. ⁶⁷It is he who has established for you the night so that you should rest in it and the day giving sight. Indeed, in this are truly signs for a people who pay attention. ⁶⁸They say, Allah has taken a son. May he be glorified. He has no needs. All that is in the heavens and all that is on the earth is his. You have no justification for this. Are you saying something about Allah that you do not know? ⁶⁹Say, Indeed those who invent a lie about Allah will not succeed. ⁷⁰This world's portion, then to us is their return. Then we make them taste a dreadful doom because they used to disbelieve. ⁷¹Recite to them the story of Noah, when he told

his people, O my people, if my sojourn and my reminding you by Allah's signs are an offense to you, in Allah have I put my trust, so decide upon your course of action, you and your partners. Do not let your course of action be in doubt for you. Then carry it out against me, give me no respite. ⁷²But if you turn away, I have asked no wages of you. My wages are the concern of Allah alone, and I am commanded to be among the Muslims. ⁷³But they denied him, so we saved him and those with him in the ship, and made them caliphs, while we drowned those who denied our signs. See then the nature of the consequences for those who had been warned. ⁷⁴Then, after him, we sent messengers to their people, and they brought them clear proofs. But they were not ready to believe in what they had previously denied. In this way we seal the hearts of the transgressors. ⁷⁵Then, after them, we sent Moses and Aaron to Pharaoh and his chiefs with our signs, but they were arrogant and were a guilty people. ⁷⁶And when the truth from our presence came to them, they said, Indeed, this is mere sorcery. ⁷⁷Moses said, Do you speak this way about the truth when it has come to you? Is this sorcery? Now sorcerers do not thrive. ⁷⁸They said, Have you come to us to pervert us from what which we found from our fathers, and that you two may own the place of greatness in the land? We will not believe you

---

66. See 4:50.

68. See 2:116, 4:171. The *Tafsir al-Jalalayn* explains this once again in terms of Allah's perfection and completeness: "They—the Jews and the Christians and those who claim that the angels are the daughters of Allah—say, 'Allah has a son.'"[14] But in fact, "He is Rich Beyond Need of anyone. Only someone in need of a child seeks one. Everything in the heavens and everything on the earth belongs to Him—as His domain, creation and slaves."[15]

71. The story of Noah is retold without significant variation from the version beginning at 7:59. See also 11:25, 21:76, 23:23, 25:37, 26:105, 29:14, 37:75, 50:12, 51:46, 53:52, 54:9, 57:26, 69:11, and 71:1.

73. On "caliphs," see 2:30.

75. The story of Moses is retold without significant variation from the version beginning at 7:103. Both Noah and Moses are again cast in roles similar to that of the messenger: prophets whose messages go unheeded by their insolent and spiteful hearers, who are duly punished.

On Pharaoh, see also 2:49, 3:11, 7:103, 8:52, 14:6, 17:101, 20:24, 23:46, 26:11, 27:12, 28:3, 29:39, 38:12, 40:24, 44:17, 50:13, 51:38, 54:41, 66:11, 69:9, 73:15, 79:15, 85:18, and 89:10.

two. **⁷⁹**And Pharaoh said, Bring every cunning wizard to me. **⁸⁰**And when the wizards came, Moses said to them, Throw what you will throw. **⁸¹**And when they had thrown, Moses said, What you have brought is sorcery. Indeed, Allah will make it vain. Indeed, Allah does not uphold the work of corrupters. **⁸²**And Allah will vindicate the truth by His words, however much the guilty hate it. **⁸³**But no one trusted Moses except some children of his people, in fear of Pharaoh and their chiefs, that he would persecute them. Indeed, Pharaoh was truly a tyrant in the land, and indeed, he truly was among the transgressors. **⁸⁴**And Moses said, O my people, if you believe in Allah, then put your trust in him, if you are indeed Muslims. **⁸⁵**They said, In Allah we put our trust. Our Lord, do not make us a temptation for the wrongdoing people, **⁸⁶**And in your mercy, save us from the people that disbelieve. **⁸⁷**And we inspired Moses and his brother, Establish houses for your people in Egypt and make your houses a qibla, and establish prayer. And give good news to the believers. **⁸⁸**And Moses said, Our Lord, indeed, you have given Pharaoh and his chiefs splendor and riches in the life of this world, our Lord, so that they might lead men astray from your way. Our Lord, destroy their riches and

harden their hearts so that they do not believe until they see the painful doom. **⁸⁹**He said, Your prayer is heard. You two keep to the straight path, and do not follow the road of those who have no knowledge. **⁹⁰**And we brought the children of Israel across the sea, and Pharaoh pursued them with his armies in rebellion and transgression, until, when the drowning overtook him, he exclaimed, I believe that there is no God except him in whom the children of Israel believe, and I am among the Muslims. **⁹¹**What? Now? When previously you have rebelled and been among the wrongdoers? **⁹²**But on this day, we save you in your body, so that you may be a sign for those after you. Indeed, most of mankind do not pay attention to our signs. **⁹³**And we indeed gave the children of Israel a fixed dwelling place, and provided them with good things, and they did not disagree until the knowledge came to them. Indeed, your Lord will judge between them on the day of resurrection about the things over which they used to disagree.

⁹⁴And if you are in doubt about what we reveal to you, then ask those who read the book before you. Indeed the truth from your Lord has come to you. So do not be among the waverers. **⁹⁵**And do not be among those who deny the signs

---

87. As for the Israelites' houses being a qibla, Bell says: "The reference is quite unknown; possibly it is an indirect justification of Muhammad's choosing a qibla in Arabia."[16]

88. Moses prays that Allah not have mercy on Pharaoh, because, Ibn Kathir says, Moses "was angry for the sake of Allah and His religion" and "certain that there was no good" in Pharaoh and his chiefs.[17] Noah similarly prays for the destruction of the unbelievers at 71:26.

90. Pharaoh repents and his life is spared (10:92). However, in 17:102-3, Pharaoh "is lost," that is, he does not repent, and is drowned.

93. According to a hadith, Muhammad prophesied: "The Jews split into seventy-one sects, one of which will be in Paradise and

seventy in Hell. The Christians split into seventy-two sects, seventy-one of which will be in Hell and one in Paradise. I swear by the One Whose Hand is the soul of Muhammad, my nation will split into seventy-three sects, one of which will be in Paradise and seventy-two in Hell."[18]

94. The *Tafsir al-Jalalayn* says that this means that Muhammad should "ask those who were reciting the Book (the Torah) before you and they will tell you about its truthfulness."[19] This assumes that uncorrupted versions of the Jewish (and Christian) Scriptures were available to the early Muslims, a contention that creates immense difficulties for the Islamic claim that they were corrupted at all, since copies exist from that era, and they are not different from the Jewish and Christian Scriptures as they exist today.

of Allah, for then you would be among the losers. **96**Indeed, those for whom the word of your Lord has effect will not believe, **97**Even though every sign comes to them, until they see the painful doom. **98**If only there had been a community that believed and profited by its belief, as did the people of Jonah. When they believed, we removed the torment of disgrace from them in the life of this world and gave them comfort for a while. **99**And if your Lord willed, all who are on the earth would have believed together. Would you force men until they are believers? **100**It is not for any soul to believe except by the permission of Allah. He has set uncleanness upon those who have no sense. **101**Say, Look at what is in the heavens and the earth. But signs and warnings do not help people who will not believe. **102**What do they expect other than something like the days of those who passed away before them? Say, Expect, then. I am with you among those who expect. **103**Then we will save our messengers and the believers, in the same way. It is obligatory upon us to save believers. **104**Say, O mankind, if you are in doubt of my religion, then I do not worship those whom you worship instead of Allah, but I worship Allah, who causes you to die, and I have been commanded to be among the believers. **105**And set your face toward the religion as a *hanif*, and do not be among those who ascribe partners. **106**And do not call out to what cannot benefit you or hurt you, besides Allah, for if you did so, then you would be among the wrongdoers. **107**If Allah afflicts you with some injury, no one can remove it except him, and if he desires good for you, no one can repel his bounty. He strikes with it whom he wills among his slaves. He is the forgiving, the merciful. **108**Say, O mankind, now the truth from your Lord has come to you. So whoever is guided is guided only for his soul, and whoever goes astray, goes astray only against it. And I am not a guardian over you. **109**And follow what is inspired within you, and wait patiently until Allah gives judgment. And he is the best of judges.

---

96. Instead of "the word of your Lord," the Warsh Qur'an has "the words of your Lord."[20]

99. See 7:179 and 32:13.

104. See sura 109.

105. On *hanif*, see 2:135.

SURA 11

Hud

Hud

Introduction

This sura, like sura 10, is dated in Islamic tradition from late in the Meccan period, the first part of Muhammad's prophetic career. Its name comes from verses 50-60, which tell the story of the prophet Hud, who was according to Islamic tradition sent to the Ad people of Arabia around 2400 BC.

Sura 11 repeats in stronger terms the warnings of sura 10 concerning Allah's judgment. That, according to a hadith, caused Muhammad anxiety to the extent that once one of his leading followers, Abu Bakr, said to him, "O Messenger of Allah, truly your hair has turned gray."[1] Muhammad replied that this sura, along with suras 56, 77, 78, and 81, all of which deal with judgment day, "have turned my hair gray."[2]

In another tradition, however, he allows the dyeing of hair, but with a striking caveat: "Change gray hair, but do not imitate the Jews."[3] A third has him saying: "Some of the best things with which you can change gray hair are Henna and Katam."[4] It is not unusual to see devout Muslims with their beards dyed henna, in accord with this recommendation, to this day.

In his early eighth-century writings about Islam, John of Damascus refers to "the text of the Camel of God, about which he [that is, Muhammad] says that there was a camel from God."[5] The story of the "camel of Allah" appears

---

1 Ibn Kathir, V, 17.
2 Ibid.
3 Sunan an-Nasa'i, vol. 6, book 48, no. 5076.
4 Ibid., no. 5082.
5 John of Damascus, 487.

in this sura (11:64–65) and at three other places in the Qur'an (7:77; 26:154; 91:11–14), although each time it told elliptically, as if it is intended more as a reminder than as an exposition of the entire story. In any case, John's reference may indicate the existence at the time he wrote of a longer account of this tale. The traces that now exist of it in this sura and the other two could have initially been allusions to this fuller account, and that account could have been used as the source for the Qur'an's information about this incident.

Hud

In the name of Allah, the compassionate, the merciful.

1Alif. Lam. Ra. A book in which the signs are perfected and then explained, from one who is wise, informed. **2**Serve no one but Allah. Indeed, I am a warner and a bringer of good news from him to you. **3**Ask pardon of your Lord and turn to him repentant. He will cause you to enjoy a good situation until an appointed time. He gives his bounty to every bountiful one. But if you turn away, indeed, I fear for you the retribution of an awful day. **4**To Allah is your return, and he is able to do all things. **5**Indeed, now they fold up their hearts so that they might hide from him. At the very moment when they cover themselves with their clothing, Allah knows what they keep hidden and what they proclaim. Indeed, he is aware of what is in their hearts. **6**And there is not an animal on earth that does not depend for its sustenance upon Allah. He knows its dwelling place and its resting place. Everything is in a clear record. **7**And it is he who created the heavens and the earth in six days, and his throne was upon the water, so that he might test you, to see which of you is best in conduct. Yet if you say, Indeed, you will be raised again after death, those who disbelieve will surely say, This is nothing but mere sorcery. **8**And if we delay the doom for them until a reckoned time, they will surely say, What holds it back? Indeed on the day when it comes to them, it cannot be averted from them, and what they derided will surround them. **9**And if we cause man to taste some mercy from us and afterward withdraw it from him, indeed, he is despairing, ungrateful. **10**And if we cause him to taste favor after some misfortune that had come upon him, he says, The ills have left me. Indeed, he rejoices, boastful, **11**Except for those who persevere and do good works. Theirs will be forgiveness and a great reward. **12**A likely thing, that you would give up anything of that what has been revealed to you, and that your heart would be closed to it, because they say, Why hasn't a treasure been sent down for him, or an angel come with him? You are just a warner, and Allah is in charge of all things. **13**Or they say, He has fabricated it. Say, Then bring ten fabricated suras like it, and call on everyone you can besides Allah, if you are truthful. **14**And if

---

1. On the "mysterious letters," see 2:1.

The sura begins with a recapitulation of many themes touched on in sura 10, including the wisdom of the Qur'an itself (11:1); the necessity to worship only Allah (11:2) and the dependence of all creatures upon him (11:6); the worthlessness of idols (11:14); the deceptive glamour of this life (11:15); the dreadful punishment (11:16, 22) that awaits those who "invent a lie against Allah" (11:18); and the delightful gardens that await the blessed (11:23).

Ibn Kathir notes that several Islamic authorities consider this verse to be affirming that the Qur'an is "perfect in its wording, detailed in its meaning. Thus, it is complete in its form and its meaning."[1] For "this Qur'an descended, perfect and detailed, with the purpose of Allah's worship alone, without any partners."[2] The increasing discovery of variants in the Qur'anic text, however minor they may be, poses a challenge to these common affirmations of perfection in form as well as meaning.

5. Apparently some people wore clothes to conceal themselves from Allah, particularly during intimate moments. A hadith depicts Ibn Abbas explaining that "there were people who used to be shy to remove their clothes while answering the call of nature in an open space and thus be naked exposed to the sky. They were also ashamed of having sexual relations with their women due to fear of being exposed towards the sky. Thus, this was revealed concerning them."[3]

7. For the creation of the universe in six days, see 7:54.

Bell notes that between, "And it is he who created the heavens and the earth in six days, and his throne was upon the water" and the immediately subsequent, "so that he might test you, to see which of you is best in conduct," there is "a break in the sense, and possibly the concluding phrase is a separate scrap."[4]

13. The challenge to produce a sura comparable to those of the Qur'an is repeated; it appears also at 2:23 and 10:38. Here, however,

they do not answer your prayer, then know that it is revealed only in the knowledge of Allah, and that there is no God except him. Will you then become Muslims? **15**Whoever desires the life of this world and its splendor, we will repay them for their deeds in it, and in it they will not be wronged. **16**Those people are the ones for whom there is nothing in the hereafter except the fire. What they contrive here is useless and what they are inclined to do is fruitless. **17**Is he who relies on a clear proof from his Lord, and a witness from him recites it, and before it was the book of Moses, an example and a mercy? Such people believe in it, and whoever disbelieves in it among the tribes, the fire is his appointed place. So do not be in doubt about it. Indeed, it is the truth from your Lord, but most of mankind does not believe. **18**Who does a greater wrong than he who fabricates a lie about Allah? Such people will be brought before their Lord, and the witnesses will say, These people are the ones who lied about their Lord. Now the curse of Allah is upon wrong-doers, **19**Who bar people from the way of Allah and would make it crooked, and who are

unbelievers in the hereafter. **20**Such people will not escape in the earth, nor do they have any protecting friends besides Allah. For them the torment will be double. They could not bear to hear, and they did not see. **21**Such people are those who have lost their souls, and what they used to fabricate has failed them. **22**Surely they will be the greatest losers in the hereafter. **23**Indeed, those who believe and do good works and humble themselves before their Lord, such people are rightful companions of the garden, they will remain in it. **24**The two groups are like the blind and the deaf and the seer and the hearer. Are they equal in likeness? Will you not then be warned? **25**And we sent Noah to his people, Indeed, I am a plain warner to you. **26**So that you serve no one except Allah. Indeed, I fear the retribution of a painful day for you. **27**The chieftains of his people, who disbelieved, said, We see that you are just a mortal like us, and we do not see anyone follow you except the most abject among us, without reflection. We see in you no merit above us, no, we consider you to be liars. **28**He said, O my people, Do you think that if I rely on a clear proof

the difficulty is increased significantly, as skeptics are challenged to produce not just one but ten suras like it.

15. In connection with this verse and 11:16, the *Tafsir Anwarul Bayan* quotes a hadith in which Muhammad says: "No need of a believer (*Mu'min*) will be reduced in reward. Allah will grant him the reward for it in this world as well as in the Hereafter. However, whatever deeds the disbeliever (*kafir*) does for Allah's pleasure, will be rewarded only in this world. In the Hereafter he will have no deeds left to be rewarded."[5] There is a resonance here of Jesus's words: "Take heed then how you hear; for to him who has will more be given, and from him who has not, even what he thinks that he has will be taken away" (Luke 8:18).

25. Another telling of the story of Noah (see also 7:59, 10:71, 21:76, 23:23, 25:37, 26:105, 29:14, 37:75, 50:12, 51:46, 53:52, 54:9, 57:26, 69:11, and 71:1). There is a significant difference from the Biblical story: In Genesis 6-9, Noah has nothing to do with the unbelievers at all. God tells him, "I have determined to make an end of all flesh; for the earth is filled with violence through them; behold, I will destroy them with the earth" (Genesis 6:13) and tells

him to build the ark, but he doesn't tell him to go warn the people about the flood. But in the Qur'an, Noah comes to his people as a "plain warner" (11:25) that they should "serve no one except Allah" (11:26). So the corruption and violence of which the people are guilty in the Biblical account in the Qur'an become simply idolatry, or more precisely, *shirk*, the association of partners with Allah.

The messenger also comes to his people with a clear warning (14:52) that they should serve none but Allah (3:64). Thus in this account, as in other Qur'anic accounts of earlier prophets, Noah is kind of a prototype, preaching a message identical to that of the Qur'an (see 2:4, 3:67).

27. This denigration of Noah's followers is also echoed in the Muhammad legend. Heraclius, the seventh-century Byzantine emperor, is depicted as asking the Muslim commander Abu Sufyan about Muhammad: "Do the noblemen or the weak among people follow him?"[6] Abu Sufyan replies, "Rather the weak among them," to which Heraclius responds: "Such is the case with followers of the Messengers."[7] Despite this, however, the story does not record that Heraclius accepted Islam and of course has no historical basis.

from my Lord and there has come to me a mercy from his presence, and it has been made unclear to you, can we force you to accept it when you are averse to it? [29]And O my people, I ask no payment from you for it. My reward is the concern only of Allah, and I am not going to thrust away those who believe, indeed, they have to meet their Lord, but I find you to be people who are ignorant. [30]And, O my people, who would save me from Allah if I thrust them away? Will you not then think? [31]I don't say to you, I have the treasures of Allah, or I have knowledge of the unseen. Nor do I say, Indeed, I am an angel. Nor do I say to those whom your eyes scorn that Allah will not give them good, Allah knows best what is in their hearts. Indeed, then indeed I would be of the wrongdoers. [32]They said, O Noah, you have disputed with us and multiplied disagreements with us, now bring upon us what you threaten us with, if you are among the truthful. [33]He said, Only Allah will bring it upon you if he wills, and you can by no means escape. [34]My advice will not benefit you if I wanted to advise you, if it is Allah's will to keep you astray. He is your Lord and to him you will be brought back. [35]Or do they say, He has fabricated it? Say, If I have fabricated it, let

my crimes be upon me, but I am innocent of what you commit. [36]And it was inspired in Noah, No one of your people will believe except him who has already believed. Do not be distressed because of what they do. [37]Build the ship under our eyes and by our inspiration, and do not speak to me on behalf of those who do wrong. Indeed, they will be drowned. [38]And he was building the ship, and every time that chieftains of his people passed him, they mocked him. He said, Although you mock us, we mock at you even as you mock, [39]And you will know to whom a punishment comes that will confound him, and upon whom a lasting doom will fall. [40]Until, when our commandment came to pass and the oven gushed forth water, we said, Load in it two of every kind, a pair, and your family, except him against whom the word has already gone forth, and those who believe. And there were only a few who believed with him. [41]And he said, Embark in it, in the name of Allah will it sail and cast anchor. Indeed, my Lord is forgiving, merciful. [42]And it sailed with them amid waves like mountains, and Noah called out to his son, and he was standing aloof, O my son, come ride with us, and do not be with the unbelievers. [43]He said, I will go to some mountain

---

29. Instead of, "I find you," a Qur'anic manuscript examined by Mingana has, "I will show you."[8]

32. Instead of, "You have disputed with us," a Qur'anic manuscript examined by Mingana has, "You have disputed."[9]

34. Noah affirms that preaching to the unbelievers is pointless if Allah has determined to prevent them from believing. See 7:179, 10:99, and 32:13.

35. Traditionally, this verse is understood as illustrating that, like the messenger (11:13), Noah is accused of fabricating the revelations he receives from Allah. All this almost exactly replicates the experience of the messenger: Allah tells him to tell the unbelievers that he is just a man (18:110); they charge him with lying (42:24); and of course the messenger also teaches that if Allah wills to lead someone astray, no one can guide him (7:186). Indirectly emphasized is the identity of the messages of all the prophets and the obstinacy of the unbelievers before the manifest truth of Allah.

However, Barth points out that while 11:34 and 11:36 are about Noah, 11:35 is clearly referring to the Qur'an, as in 11:13, and "has no linkage to what precedes or what follows."[10] Noah, after all, is not given a book that he could have been accused of fabricating, so this is likely an interpolation from elsewhere.

42. Here begins the story of Noah's son, who declines to enter the ark and instead opts to take refuge on a mountain. He dies in the flood, and at 11:45, Noah reminds Allah of his promise to save his family (which came at 11:40). But Allah tells him, significantly, that he was not a member of his family, because he was an unbeliever (11:46). Belief and unbelief in Islam are more important than even family ties. Ibn Kathir adds that the drowning was punishment for his refusal to believe: "Thus, for his son, it had already been decreed that he would be drowned due to his disbelief and his opposition to his father."[11]

that will save me from the water. He said, Today there are none who will be saved from the commandment of Allah except him on whom he has had mercy. And the wave came in between them, so he was among the drowned. **44**And it was said, O earth, swallow your water and, O sky, be cleared of clouds. And the water was made to subside. And the commandment was fulfilled. And it came to rest upon al-Judi and it was said, A far removal for wrongdoing people. **45**And Noah called out to his Lord and said, My Lord, indeed, my son is of my family. Surely your promise is the truth and you are the most just of judges. **46**He said, O Noah, indeed, he is not of your family, indeed, he is of evil conduct, so do not ask me about what you have no knowledge of. I warn you so that you will not be among the ignorant. **47**He said, My Lord, indeed, in you do I seek refuge that I would ask you about something I have no knowledge of. Unless you forgive me and have mercy on me, I will be among the lost. **48**It was said, O Noah, go down with peace from us and blessings upon you and some nations from those with you. Nations to whom we will give enjoyment for a long while, and then a painful doom from us will overtake them. **49**This is among the news of the unseen which we inspire within you. You yourself did not know it, nor did your people before this. Then have patience. Indeed, the ending is for those who fear Allah. **50**And to Aad, their brother, Hud. He said, O my people, serve Allah. You have no other God except him. Indeed,

you just fabricate. **51**O my people, I ask no reward from you for it. Indeed, my reward is the concern only of him who made me. Do you then have no sense? **52**And, O my people, ask forgiveness of your Lord, then turn to him in repentance. He will cause the sky to rain abundance on you and will add to you strength to your strength. Do not turn away guilty. **53**They said, O Hud, you have brought us no clear proof, and we are not going to forsake our gods on your word, and we are not believers in you. **54**We say nothing except that one of our gods has possessed you in an evil way. He said, I call Allah to witness, and you bear witness, that I am innocent of the fact what you ascribe as partners, **55**Besides him. So circumvent me, all of you, give me no respite. **56**Indeed, I have put my trust in Allah, my Lord and your Lord. There is not an animal that he doesn't grasp by the forelock. Indeed, my Lord is on a straight path. **57**And if you turn away, still I have conveyed to you what I was sent to you with, and my Lord will set in your place a people other than you. You cannot injure him at all. Indeed, my Lord is guardian over all things. **58**And when our commandment came to pass, we saved Hud and those who believed with him by a mercy from us, we saved them from a harsh doom. **59**And such were Aad. They denied the signs of their Lord and disobeyed his messengers and followed the command of every defiant potentate. **60**And a curse was made to follow them in this world and on the day of resurrection. Indeed, Aad disbelieved in their

50. The story of the extrabiblical prophet Hud follows a roughly similar pattern to that of the story of Noah in 11:25-49. He tells the people of Ad to repent (11:52), but they complain that he has brought them no clear sign (11:53) and are destroyed, although like Noah and those with him in the ark, Hud and his people are saved (11:58). These are clearly more in the nature of sermons than of historical accounts.

Lord. A far removal for Aad, the people of Hud. **61**And to Thamud, their brother Salih. He said, O my people, serve Allah, you have no other God except him. He brought you forth from the earth and has made you tend it. So ask forgiveness of him and turn to him in repentance. Indeed, my Lord is near, responsive. **62**They said, O Salih, you have been among us before as the one in whom our hope was placed. Are you asking us not to worship what our fathers worshipped? Indeed, we truly are in grave doubt about what you're calling us to. **63**He said, O my people, consider, if I have clear proof from my Lord and there has come to me a mercy from him, who will save me from Allah if I disobey him? You would add nothing to me except perdition. **64**O my people, this is the camel of Allah, a sign to you, so allow her to feed on Allah's earth, and do not harm her, so that a swift punishment doesn't seize you. **65**But they hamstrung her, and then he said, Enjoy life in your dwelling-place for three days. This is a threat that will not be repudiated. **66**So when our commandment came to pass, we saved Salih and those who believed with him, by a mercy from us, from the disgrace of that day. Indeed, your Lord, he is the strong one, the mighty one. **67**And the cry overtook those who did wrong, so that morning found them prostrate in their dwellings, **68**As if they had not lived there. Indeed, Thamud disbelieved in their Lord. A far removal for Thamud. **69**And our messengers came to Abraham with

good news. They said, Peace. He answered, Peace, and did not delay in bringing a roasted calf. **70**And when he saw that their hands did not reach for it, he mistrusted them and conceived a fear of them. They said, Do not fear, indeed, we have been sent to the people of Lot. **71**And his wife, standing by, laughed when we gave her the good news of Isaac, and, after Isaac, of Jacob. **72**She said, Woe is me, will I bear a child when I am an old woman, and this my husband is an old man? Indeed, this is a strange thing. **73**They said, Are you amazed at the commandment of Allah? The mercy of Allah and his blessings be upon you, O people of the house! Indeed, he is the owner of praise, the owner of glory. **74**And when the awe departed from Abraham, and the glad news reached him, he pleaded with us on behalf of the people of Lot. **75**Indeed, Abraham was mild, imploring, penitent. **76**O Abraham, forsake this. Indeed, your Lord's commandment has gone forth, and indeed, there comes to them a doom that cannot be repelled. **77**And when our messengers came to Lot, he was distressed and did not know how to protect them. He said, This is a dreadful day.

78And his people came to him, running toward him, and before then they used to commit abominations. He said, O my people, here are my daughters. They are purer for you. Beware of Allah, and do not degrade me in my guests. Is there not any upright man among you? **79**They said, You well know that we have no right to your

---

61. Allah repeats the same pattern of the stories of Noah (11:25-49) and Hud (11:50-60) in telling the story of Salih, who was sent sometime after Noah's time to the Thamud people, who lived in northern Arabia. Allah gives them a sign of his power: the "camel of Allah, a sign to you" (11:64)—which according to some traditions emerged miraculously from a mountain. The Thamud are told not to harm it, but they do anyway (11:65) and are destroyed (11:67), except, once again, for Salih and the believers (11:66).

64. The camel of Allah is also mentioned at 7:77, 11:64, 26:155, and 91:11-14. See also the introduction to sura 11.

69. Here begins another Qur'anic retelling of the Biblical story of Abraham, Sarah, and Lot (Genesis 18-19), with a strong hint of an unnamed crime of sodomy (11:79), and culminating in the destruction of an unnamed Sodom and Gomorrah (11:82). See 7:80-4.

daughters, and you well know what we want. **80**He said, If only I had power over you or if I would go to a strong pillar. **81**They said, O Lot, indeed, we are messengers of your Lord, they will not reach you. So travel with your people in a part of the night, and do not let any of you turn round, except your wife. Indeed, what strikes them will strike her. Indeed, their meeting is in the morning. Isn't the morning near? **82**So when our commandment came to pass, we overthrew and rained upon it stones of clay, one after another, **83**Marked with fire in the providence of your Lord. And they are never far from the wrongdoers. **84**And to Midian, their brother Shu'aib. He said, O my people, serve Allah. You have no other God except him. And do not give short measure and short weight. Indeed, I see you who are wealthy, and indeed, I fear for you the torment of a day that is coming. **85**O my people, give full measure and full weight in justice, and do not wrong people regarding their goods. And do not do evil on the earth, causing corruption. **86**What Allah leaves with you is better for you if you are believers, and I am not a guardian over you. **87**They said, O Shu'aib, does your way of prayer command you that we should forsake what our fathers worshipped, or doing what we wish with our own property? Indeed, you are the mild one, the guide to right behavior. **88**He said, O my people, consider, if I am on a clear proof from my Lord and he sustains me with fair sustenance from him. I do not wish to

do behind your backs what I ask you not to do. I desire nothing except repentance, as far as I am able. My welfare is solely in Allah. In him do I trust and to Him do I turn. **89**And, O my people, do not the split with me cause you to sin, so that there comes upon you what came upon the people of Noah and the people of Hud, and the people of Salih, and the people of Lot are not far off from you. **90**Ask forgiveness of your Lord and then turn to him. Indeed, my Lord is merciful, loving. **91**They said, O Shu'aib, we do not understand much of what you are saying, and indeed, we see you weak among us. If it weren't for your family, we would have stoned you, for you are not strong against us. **92**He said, O my people, is my family more to be honored by you than Allah? And you put him behind you, neglected. Indeed, my Lord encompasses what you do. **93**And, O my people, act according to your power, indeed, I am acting. You will soon know on whom there comes a doom that will humiliate him, and who it is that lies. And watch. Indeed, I am a watcher with you. **94**And when our commandment came to pass, we saved Shu'aib and those who believed with him by a mercy from us, and the cry seized those who did injustice, and morning found them prostrate in their dwellings, **95**As if they had not lived there. A far removal for Midian, even as Thamud was removed far away. **96**And indeed we sent Moses with our signs and a clear justification **97**To Pharaoh and his chieftains, but they did follow the

---

80. Michael Schub sees this as an incomplete thought, noting that "some Quranic verses leave one up in the air."[12] This may be an indication of some textual dislocation.

84. The story of Shu'aib, prophet to the Midianites, is told in language very similar, and with an identical outcome, to the story of Hud (see also 7:85, 26:176).

87. Bell notes that "the grammar is a little uneven, and the phrase probably a Medinan insertion into an earlier verse."[13]

96. Once again, albeit quite briefly here, the Qur'an makes reference to Moses and Pharaoh. See also 2:49, 3:11, 7:103, 8:52, 10:75, 14:6, 17:101, 20:24, 23:46, 26:11, 27:12, 28:3, 29:39, 38:12, 40:24, 44:17, 50:13, 51:38, 54:41, 66:11, 69:9, 73:15, 79:15, 85:18, and 89:10.

command of Pharaoh, and the command of Pharaoh was not a right guide. ⁹⁸He will go before his people on the day of resurrection and will lead them to the fire for a watering place. Wretched is the watering place to which they are led. ⁹⁹A curse is made to follow them in this world and on the day of resurrection. Wretched is the gift given. ¹⁰⁰That is from the news of the towns. We relate it to you. Some of them are standing and some reaped. ¹⁰¹We did not wrong them, but they wronged themselves, and their gods on whom they call besides Allah did not help them in any way when your Lord's command came, they added to them nothing except ruin. ¹⁰²Even in this way is the grasp of your Lord when he grasps the towns while they are doing wrong. Indeed, his grasp is painful, very strong. ¹⁰³Indeed, truly in this there is a sign for those who fear the torment of the hereafter. That is a day to which mankind will be gathered, and that is a day that will be witnessed. ¹⁰⁴And we postpone it only to a term that has already been reckoned. ¹⁰⁵On the day when it comes, no soul will speak except by his permission. Some among them will be wretched, some glad. ¹⁰⁶As for those who will be wretched, they will be in the fire, sighing and wailing will be their share in it, ¹⁰⁷Remaining there as long as the heavens and the earth endure, except for what your Lord wills. Indeed, your Lord is the doer of what he wills. ¹⁰⁸And as for those who will be glad, they will be in the garden, remaining there as long as the heavens and the earth endure, except for what your Lord wills, an unfailing gift. ¹⁰⁹So do not be in doubt about what these people worship. They worship only as their fathers worshipped previously. Indeed, we will pay them what they deserve, undiminished. ¹¹⁰And we indeed gave to Moses the book, and there was strife over it, and if it had not been for a word that had already gone forth from your Lord, the case would have been judged between them, and indeed, they are in grave doubt about it. ¹¹¹And indeed, to each person your Lord will indeed repay his works in full. Indeed, he is informed of what they do. ¹¹²So walk the straight path as you are commanded, and those who turn with you, and do not transgress. Indeed, he is the seer of what you do. ¹¹³And do not get close to those who do wrong, so that the fire does not touch you, and you have no protecting friends against Allah, and afterward you would not be helped. ¹¹⁴Establish prayer at the two ends of the day and in some watches of the night. Indeed, good deeds annul evil deeds. This is a reminder for the mindful. ¹¹⁵And have patience, for indeed, Allah does not lose the wages of the good. ¹¹⁶If only there had been among the generations before you men possessing a remnant to warn people away from corruption in the earth, as a few of those whom we saved from them did. The wrongdoers pursued their own luxury, and were guilty. ¹¹⁷In truth, your Lord did not destroy the towns unjustly while their people were doing

---

103. Both those who reject Allah and those who accept him will face a fearsome judgment, leading to hellfire for the unbelievers and Paradise for the believers.

110. Allah gave Moses the Torah, but there are disputes about it, which Allah would have already settled were it not for this word (*kalimah*) that went forth from him. Tabari explains, "If it were not

that the punishment had already been delayed until an appointed time, then Allah would have decided the matter between you now. The word Kalimah carries the meaning that Allah will not punish anyone until the proof has been established against him and a Messenger has been sent to him."¹⁴

right. [118]And if your Lord had willed, he would indeed have made mankind one nation, yet they do not stop disagreeing, [119]Except him on whom your Lord has mercy, and for that he created them. And the word of your Lord has been fulfilled, Indeed I will fill Gehenna with the jinn and mankind together. [120]And all that we relate to you of the story of the messengers is so that that by it we may make your heart firm. And in this the truth has come to you, and an exhortation and a reminder for believers. [121]And say to those who do not believe, Act according to your power. Indeed, we are acting. [122]And wait. Indeed, we are waiting. [123]And the invisible thing of the heavens and the earth belong to Allah, and to him the whole matter will be returned. So worship him and put your trust in him. Indeed, your Lord is not unaware of what you do.

---

118. Allah does not make all of mankind into one nation because, says the *Tafsir Anwarul Bayan*, "Allah will not force all to become Muslims."[15] But whether he forces some to be unbelievers is an open question; see 7:179 and 32:13.

119. See 7:179. On Gehenna, see 2:206.

SURA 12

Joseph

Yusuf

Introduction

Here is another Biblical story recast and retold in the Qur'an, and like the overwhelming majority of Biblical stories in the Qur'an, is employed to make the same point: the messenger is a true prophet, he is being mistreated like all other prophets, and those who are ridiculing and rejecting him will be severely punished.

This sura tells the story of the Biblical patriarch Joseph, who is presented as another prototype of the messenger. This was done in sura 11 with the stories of other prophets. The Qur'anic tale of Joseph is an abbreviated version of the story in Genesis 37–50, with some notable differences from the Biblical account.

Islamic tradition classifies this as another late Meccan sura. It was revealed, says Maududi, when "the Quraysh were considering ways of how to get over the threat posed by the Prophet (peace be upon him): whether to kill, or banish, or imprison him."[1]

---

1 Mawdudi, IV, 143.

Joseph

In the name of Allah, the compassionate, the merciful.

1Alif. Lam. Ra. These are verse of the book that makes things clear. **2**Indeed, we have revealed it, a Qur'an in Arabic, so that you may understand. **3**We narrate to you the best of narratives in that we have inspired this Qur'an in you, although previously you were among the heedless. **4**When Joseph said to his father, O my father, indeed, I saw in a dream eleven planets and the sun and the moon, I saw them prostrating themselves to me. **5**He said, O my dear son, do not tell your brothers about your vision, so that they do not plot against you. Indeed, Satan is for man an open enemy.

---

1. On the "mysterious letters," see 2:1.

2. The Qur'an repeatedly proclaims its Arabic character; see also 13:37, 16:103, 20:113, 26:195, 39:28, 41:3, 42:7, 43:3, 46:12. The ninth-century jurist Abu Ubayda articulated the general Islamic view when he wrote: "Whoever suggests there is anything other than the Arabic language in the Qur'an has made a serious charge against God."[1]

The Qur'an's numerous non-Arabic words, however, cause difficulties for this dogma, and their presence in the book may account for the defensiveness and insistence of this verse, as they hindered efforts to situate Islam in Arabia. Indeed, the fact that it was seen necessary to have the Qur'an repeatedly insist that it was in Arabic suggests that there was widespread awareness that it was not, at least not entirely. There is considerable evidence of non-Arabic influence in the Qur'an; see 2:23, 2:120, 2:135, 3:4, 5:114, 24:31, 74:26, and elsewhere.

Contemporary linguist Robert Kerr explains: "The fact that both the script and language of the Qur'an point to the Classical *Arabia Petraea* of Syro-Palestine, and not *Arabia Deserta*, is further supported by the fact that the Qur'an's vocabulary is largely borrowed from Aramaic, especially Syriac, the liturgical language of the local churches."[2] According to linguist Jan Retsö, "Many of the most important and frequent words in the Qur'an are clear Aramaic borrowings, which can be shown by a comparison with Syriac."[3] These include such key words in Islam as "Lord," "merciful," "prostrate," "repent," "offering," "salvation," "alms," "Christ," and even "ayat," "sura," and "Qur'an" itself.[4] This coincides with research showing that the earliest mosques faced not Mecca but Petra in modern-day southern Jordan, where Syriac was spoken. See 3:96.

What's more, from the standpoint of classical Arabic, Qur'anic Arabic features numerous grammatical errors, which is curious in a book proclaimed to be pure and clear Arabic.[5] Both the foreign words and grammatical errors indicate that the language itself was in a process of intense development. The Qur'an is the first example of written Arabic literature, and it was not created in a vacuum. Arabic antecedents, however, were difficult, if not impossible, to find. The contemporary linguist Pierre Larcher observes that the traditional view, "that the Arabic of the Qur'an is itself the very language of Muhammad, that is to say, a hypothetical 'dialect of Quraysh,'" is "hypothetical in the sense that it is not documented in an independent manner."[6] That is, there is no evidence aside from the Qur'an itself of the Arabic of the Quraysh, so the assumption that the Qur'an is written in the Qurayshi dialect remains just that, an assumption, unsupported by any evidence. Larcher further notes that pre-Islamic Arabic poetry is likewise "a hypothetical construct"; none existed in written form until after the Qur'an appeared.[7]

The foreign derivation of many key Qur'anic words and concepts has not gone unnoticed over the centuries. The thirteenth-century Islamic scholar Ibn al-Naqib attempted to explain it as part of the Qur'an's universal mission and applicability: "Other books were revealed only in the language of the nation to whom they were addressed, while the Qur'an contains words from all Arabic dialects, and from Greek, Persian, and Ethiopic besides."[8]

Meanwhile, Ibn Kathir expresses the mainstream Islamic view when he notes that the Qur'an is not only in Arabic but is perfect: "The Arabic language is the most eloquent, plain, deep and expressive of the meanings that might arise in one's mind. Therefore, the most honorable Book, was revealed in the most honorable language, to the most honorable Prophet and Messenger, delivered by the most honorable angel, in the most honorable land on earth, and its revelation started during the most honorable month of the year, Ramadan. Therefore, the Qur'an is perfect in every respect."[9]

This perspective, which is mainstream in Islamic theology, is severely challenged by the existence of variants in the Qur'anic text.

4. The story of Joseph that takes up the bulk of the sura begins here. According to Maududi, one of the principal purposes of this account was yet again to warn people not to reject Muhammad. Its aim, he said, was to apply the story of Joseph being rejected by his brothers to Muhammad's tribe that rejected him, the Quraysh, to serve as "a reminder to the Quraysh that their attitude towards the Prophet (peace be upon him) was similar to that of Joseph's brothers. Now, Joseph's brothers failed to defeat God's plan. Instead, they lay humbled at the feet of their brother, a brother whom once they had callously cast into a pit. The implication being that the Quraysh will meet a similar end: their machinations against God's plan will be reduced to naught."[10]

Dreams are to be taken seriously: Ibn Kathir attributes to Ibn Abbas the claim that "the dreams of Prophets are revelations from Allah."[11] In a hadith, Muhammad explains this as not applying just to the prophets but as a general principle: "A good dream is from Allah, and a bad dream is from Satan. So whoever has seen (in a dream) something he dislikes, then he should spit without saliva, thrice on his left and seek refuge with Allah from Satan, for it will not harm him, and Satan cannot appear in my shape."[12]

⁶In this way your Lord will prefer you and will teach you the interpretation of events, and will perfect his grace upon you and upon the family of Jacob, as he perfected it upon your forefathers, Abraham and Isaac. Indeed, your Lord is the knower, the wise one. ⁷Indeed in Joseph and his brothers are signs for the inquiring. ⁸When they said, Indeed Joseph and his brother are dearer to our father than we are, although we are many. Indeed, our father is clearly mistaken. ⁹Kill Joseph or cast him into some land, so that your father's favor may be all for you, and you may afterward be righteous people. ¹⁰One among them said, Do not kill Joseph, but if you must do so, throw him into the depth of the pit, some caravan will find him. ¹¹ They said, O our father, why won't you trust us with Joseph, when indeed, we are good friends to him? ¹²Send him with us tomorrow so that he may enjoy himself and play. And indeed, we will take good care of him. ¹³He said, Indeed, in truth it saddens me that you should take him with you, and I fear that the wolf might devour him while you are not paying attention to him. ¹⁴They said, If the wolf devours him when we are a group, then surely we should have already perished. ¹⁵Then, when they led him off, and were in agreement that they should place him in the depth of the pit, we inspired in him, You will tell them of this deed of theirs when they do not know. ¹⁶And they came weeping to their father in the evening. ¹⁷Saying, O our father, we went racing one with another, and left Joseph by our things, and the wolf devoured him, and you do not believe what we are saying even when we speak the truth. ¹⁸And they came with false blood on his shirt. He said, No, but your minds have seduced you into something. Patience is appropriate. And Allah it is whose help is to be sought in what you describe. ¹⁹And there came a caravan, and they sent their water-drawer. He let down his pail. He said, What a stroke of good fortune! Here is a young man. And they hid him as a treasure, and Allah was aware of what they did. ²⁰And they sold him for a low price, a number of silver coins, and they attached no value to him. ²¹And the Egyptian man who bought him said to his wife, Receive him honorably. Perhaps he may be useful to us or we may adopt him as a son. In this way we established Joseph in the land, so that we might teach him the interpretation of events. And Allah was predominant in his career, but most of mankind do not know. ²²And when he reached his prime, we gave him wisdom and knowledge. In this way we reward the good. ²³And she, in whose house he was, asked him to do an evil act. She bolted the doors and said, Come! He said, I seek refuge in Allah. Indeed, he is my lord, who has treated me honorably. Indeed, wrongdoers never prosper. ²⁴She indeed desired him, and he would have desired her if it had not been that he saw the argument of his Lord. It was this way so that we might ward off evil from him, and lewdness. Indeed, he

---

6. Jacob's prediction of Joseph's preeminence differs from the Biblical account in which Jacob rebukes Joseph after learning of his dream (Genesis 37:10). Maududi states that "the Qur'anic account is in greater harmony with Jacob's character as a Prophet than the Biblical one."[13]

7. Maududi asserts that this verse encapsulates the purpose of the entire sura.[14]

18. In another departure from the Biblical account, Jacob doesn't believe the brothers' claim that Joseph is dead. This was because, according to the *Tafsir Anwarul Bayan*, "they failed to rip up the shirt to indicate that the wolf devoured" Joseph.[15]

24. Another detail not contained in the Biblical account is that Joseph would have desired the Egyptian's wife except that Allah prevented him from doing evil. This action to prevent Joseph from

was of our chosen slaves. **25**And they raced with one another to the door, and she tore his shirt from behind, and they met her lord and master at the door. She said, What will be his reward, who wishes evil upon your people, except prison or a painful doom? **26**He said, It was she who asked me to do an evil act. And a witness of her own people testified, If his shirt is torn from the front, then she speaks truth and he is among the liars. **27**And if his shirt is torn from behind, then she has lied and he is among the truthful. **28**So when he saw his shirt torn from behind, he said, Indeed, this is from the guile of you women. Indeed, your guile is very great. **29**O Joseph, turn away from this, and you, ask forgiveness for your sin. Indeed, you are among the sinful. **30**And women in the city said, The ruler's wife is asking an evil deed of her slave boy. Indeed, he has smitten her to the heart with love. We see that she is clearly mistaken.

31And when she heard about their sly talk, she sent to them and prepared a cushioned couch for them and gave every one of them a knife and said, Come out to them. And when they saw him, they praised him and cut their hands, exclaiming, Allah is blameless! This is not a human being. This is nothing other than some gracious angel. **32**She said, This is he because of whom you blamed me. I asked an evil act of him, but he abstained, but if he does not do my bidding he indeed will be imprisoned, and indeed will be among those who are brought low. **33**He said, O my Lord, prison is preferable to what they are urging upon me, and if you do not fend off their wiles from me, I will get close to them and become one of the foolish. **34**So his Lord heard his prayer and fended off their wiles from him. Indeed, He is the hearer, the knower. **35**And it seemed good to them, after they had seen the signs, to imprison him for a time. **36**And two young men went to prison with him. One of them said, I dreamed that I was pressing wine. The other said, I dreamed that I was carrying upon my head bread of which the birds were eating. Explain to us the interpretation, for we see you are among those who are good. **37**He said, The food that you are given will not come to you without my telling you the interpretation before it comes to you. This is what my Lord has taught me. Indeed, I have forsaken the religion of people who do not believe in Allah and are unbelievers in the hereafter. **38**And I have followed the religion of my fathers, Abraham and Isaac and Jacob. It never was for us to attribute anything as partner to Allah. This is of the bounty of Allah to us

sinning is the obverse of Allah's creating souls for hell (7:179, 32:13) and leading people astray (4:88, 6:39, 7:186, 76:29-30). Joseph apparently has this privilege only because he is "chosen," not in view of his own actions or character.

25. The Egyptian's wife accuses Joseph of impropriety, but Joseph's innocence is established when it is found that his cloak is torn in the back, not in the front. He was, in other words, fleeing from her (11:27-8). This detail is not in the Biblical account, which simply says, "She caught him by his garment, saying, 'Lie with me.' But he left his garment in her hand, and fled and got out of the house" (Genesis 39:12).

Maududi finds it improbable both that Joseph would be wearing a garment that could be so easily pulled off and that he would run away naked; accordingly, he writes that these and other differences prove "beyond any shadow of doubt the absurdity of the Orientalists' allegation that the Prophet (peace be upon him) had taken over the stories of the Prophets from the Israelites. On the contrary, the fact is that it is the Qur'an which purged the Israelite stories of their demeaning errors."[16] However, the Qur'anic detail regarding the tearing of the cloak in the back, not the front is also taken from the Jewish tradition.[17]

31. Ibn Kathir explains: "They thought highly of him and were astonished at what they saw. They started cutting their hands in amazement at his beauty, while thinking that they were cutting the citron with their knives."[18] The ruler's wife felt exonerated: "When they felt the pain, they started screaming and she said to them, 'You did all this from one look at him, so how can I be blamed?'"[19]

37. When two fellow prisoners ask him to interpret their dreams, he first tells them that he is a good Muslim (cf. 2:4, 3:67).

and to mankind, but most men do not give thanks. **39**O my fellow prisoners, are various lords better, or Allah, the one, almighty? **40**Those whom you worship besides him are just names that you have named, you and your fathers. Allah has revealed no justification for them. The decision rests with Allah alone, who has commanded you to worship no one save Him. This is the right religion, but most men do not know. **41**O my two fellow prisoners, as for one of you, he will pour out wine for his lord to drink, and as for the other, he will be crucified so that the birds will eat from his head. In this way is the case about which you inquired judged. **42**And he said to the one of the two who he knew would be released, Mention me in the presence of your lord. But Satan caused him to forget to mention it to his lord, so he stayed in prison for some years. **43**And the king said, Indeed, I saw in a dream seven fat cows which seven lean cows were eating, and seven green ears of corn and others dry. O notables, explain my vision for me, if you can interpret dreams. **44**They answered, Confused dreams. And we are not knowledgeable in the interpretation of dreams. **45**And he of the two who was released, and finally remembered, said, I am going to announce to you the interpretation, therefore send me forth. **46**Joseph! O you truthful one, explain for us the seven fat cows which seven lean

cows were eating and the seven green ears of corn and others dry, so that I may return to the people, so that they may know. **47**He said, You will sow for seven years as usual, but what you reap, leave it in its ear, all except a little that you eat. **48**Then after that seven hard years will come which will devour all that you have prepared for them, except a little of what you have stored. **49**Then after that will come a year when the people will have plenteous crops and when they will press. **50**And the king said, Bring him to me. And when the messenger came to him, he said, Return to your lord and ask him what was the case of the women who cut their hands. Indeed, my Lord knows their guile. **51**He said, What happened when you asked Joseph to do an evil act? They answered, Allah is blameless! We know nothing evil about him. The wife of the ruler said, Now the truth is out. I asked him to do an evil act, and he is surely of the truthful. **52**From this, he may know that I did not betray him in secret, and that surely Allah does not guide the trap of the betrayers. **53**I do not acquit myself. Indeed, the soul commands one to do evil, except when my Lord has mercy. Indeed, my Lord is forgiving, merciful. **54**And the king said, Bring him to me so that I may have him work for me. And when he had talked with him, he said, Indeed, you are today established in our presence and trusted. **55**He said, Set me over the

---

42. Maududi notes that this passage has been "interpreted by some Qur'an-commentators to mean that Satan caused Joseph to become negligent in remembering God, his Lord, and asked a creature of God to secure his release by bringing his case to the attention of his master (that is, the Egyptian king). It was for this reason that God punished Joseph and why he languished in prison for several years."[20] However, Maududi himself rejects that interpretation, preferring instead the one offered by Ibn Kathir and others, that "what the verse means is that Satan caused this person [that is, the prisoner who was spared] to forget mentioning the case of Joseph to his lord."[21]

50. In the Biblical account, there is this: "Then Pharaoh sent and called Joseph, and they brought him hastily out of the dungeon; and when he had shaved himself and changed his clothes, he came in before Pharaoh" (Genesis 41:14). Maududi finds this distasteful and states that a Talmudic account in which Joseph is dazzled by the splendor of the Egyptian court is "even more degrading," as it would require Joseph to bow before the king.[22] "If Joseph was truly as degraded a character as the Talmud would have us believe," Maududi asserts, "it does not make sense that the Egyptian king would have entrusted to him control over his whole dominion.... Thus, the Qur'anic account seems considerably more plausible and

storehouses of the land. Indeed, I am a skilled caretaker. [56]In that way we gave power in the land to Joseph. He was the owner of it where he pleased. We reach those whom we will with our mercy. We do not lose the reward of the good. [57]And the reward of the hereafter is better, for those who believe and fear Allah. [58]And Joseph's brethren came and presented themselves before him, and he knew them, but they did not know him. [59]And when he provided them with their provision, he said, Bring a brother of yours from your father to me. Do you not see that I fill up the food supply and I am the best of hosts? [60]And if you do not bring him to me, then there will be no food for you with me, nor will you draw near. [61]They said, We will try to win him from his father, that we will surely do. [62]He said to his young men, Place their goods in their saddlebags, so that they may know it when they go back to their people, and so will come again. [63]So when they went back to their father, they said, O our father, the supplies have been denied us, so send our brother with us so that we may obtain the food, surely we will guard him well. [64]He said, Can I entrust him to you except in the way that I entrusted his brother to you previously? Allah is the best guardian, and he is the most merciful of those who show mercy. [65]And when they opened their belongings, they discovered that their goods had been returned to them. They said, O our

father, what can we ask? Here are our goods returned to us. We will get provision for our people and guard our brother, and we will have the extra provision of a camel-load. This is a light measure. [66]He said, I will not send him with you until you give me an oath in the name of Allah that you will bring him back to me, unless you are surrounded. And when they gave him their oath, he said, Allah is watchful over what we say. [67]And he said, O my sons, do not go in by one gate, go in by different gates. I cannot help you in any way against Allah. Indeed, the decision rests with Allah alone. In him do I put my trust, and in him let all the trusting put their trust. [68]And when they entered in the manner which their father had commanded, it would not have helped them in any way against Allah, but it was a need of Jacob's soul which he satisfied in this way, and indeed, he was a lord of knowledge because we had taught him, but most of mankind do not know. [69]And when they went in before Joseph, he took his brother to him, saying, Indeed, I, even I, am your brother, therefore do not sorrow for what they did. [70]And when he provided them with their provision, he put the drinking-cup in his brother's saddlebag, and then a voice cried, O camel-riders! Indeed, you are surely thieves! [71]They called out, coming toward them, What is it you have lost? [72]They said, We have lost the king's cup, and he who brings it will have a camel-load,

consistent with reason and common sense than the Biblical and Talmudic ones."[23]

55. Maududi states that Joseph's life "offers the lesson that even a single righteous believer suffices to bring about an Islamic revolution by dint of his character and wisdom."[24] He rejects that interpretations of "scholars during a period of Muslim decline," who used Joseph's story offering one's services to an "un-Islamic government," and "brought down a very noble Prophet–Joseph–to the degrading level of serving an un-Islamic form of government."[25] See also 9:29.

64. Instead of "guardian," the Warsh Qur'an has "preservation."[26]

67. Ibn Kathir invokes several earlier authorities in support of the view that Jacob told his sons to enter by different gates because "he feared the evil eye for them, because they were handsome and looked beautiful and graceful. He feared that people might direct the evil eye at them, because the evil eye truly harms, by Allah's decree, and brings down the mighty warrior-rider from his horse."[27]

and I am answerable for it. ⁷³They said, By Allah, you know well that we did not come to do evil in the land, and are no thieves. ⁷⁴They said, And what will be the penalty for it, if you are liars? ⁷⁵They said, The penalty for it, he in whose bag it is found, he is the penalty for it. In this way we repay wrongdoers. ⁷⁶Then he began the search with their bags before his brother's bag, then he produced it from his brother's bag. This is what we contrived for Joseph. He could not have taken his brother according to the king's law unless Allah willed. We raise by grades those whom we will, and over every lord of knowledge there is one who is more knowing. ⁷⁷They said, If he steals, a brother of his stole before. But Joseph kept it secret in his soul and did not reveal it to them. He said, You are in a worse situation, and Allah knows best what you claim. ⁷⁸They said, O ruler of the land, indeed, he has a very aged father, so take one of us instead of him. Indeed, we see that you are among those who do kindness. ⁷⁹He said, Allah forbid that we should seize anyone except him with whom we found our property, then indeed we would be wrongdoers. ⁸⁰So when they despaired of him, they conferred together apart. The eldest of them said, Do you not know how your father took an oath from you in Allah's name and how you failed in the case of Joseph previously? Therefore I will not leave from the land until my father gives permission or Allah judges for me. He is the best of judges. ⁸¹Return to

your father and say, O our father, indeed, your son has stolen. We testify only to what we know, we are not guardians of the unseen. ⁸²Ask the town where we were, and the caravan with which we travelled here. Indeed, we speak the truth. ⁸³He said, No, but your minds have seduced you into something. Patience is appropriate. It may be that Allah will bring them all to me. Indeed, he, and he alone, is the knower, the wise one. ⁸⁴And he turned away from them and said, Alas, my grief for Joseph! And his eyes were whitened with the sorrow that he was suppressing. ⁸⁵They said, By Allah, you will never stop remembering Joseph until your health is ruined or you are among those who perish. ⁸⁶He said, I expose my distress and anguish only to Allah, and I know from Allah what you do not know. ⁸⁷Go, O my sons, and seek news about Joseph and his brother, and do not despair of the spirit of Allah. Indeed, no one despairs of the spirit of Allah except disbelieving people. ⁸⁸And when they came before him, they said, O ruler, misfortune has touched us and our people, and we bring only poor goods, so fill up the food supply for us and be charitable to us. Indeed, Allah will repay the charitable, ⁸⁹He said, Do you know what you did to Joseph and his brother in your ignorance? ⁹⁰They said, Is it indeed you who are Joseph? He said, I am Joseph, and this is my brother. Allah has shown us favor. Indeed, he who fears Allah and endures, indeed, Allah does not lose the wages of the kindly. ⁹¹They

---

76. This verse encapsulates the point of the Qur'anic story, that Allah orders all events, and none can thwart his will. Maududi observes that "He could not have taken his brother according to the king's law unless Allah willed" indicates that it was "unbecoming of Joseph, as a Prophet, to follow Egyptian law in a matter that related to him personally." To follow the king's law rather than Allah's law would have been "unbecoming of a Prophet who had taken authority into his own hands in order to replace man-made laws with those of God."[28]

83. Barth suggests that the repetition of, "No, but your minds have seduced you into something. Patience is appropriate" from 12:18, where it refers to Joseph, in this verse, where it refers to Benjamin, "makes one suspect that they are repeated here in place of a lost answer by Jacob."[29]

84. Jacob expresses sorrow not for the new loss of Benjamin but for the long-ago loss of Joseph (also in 12:18). Barth states: "At the very least, something about Benjamin must have stood here."[30]

said, By Allah, indeed Allah has preferred you above us, and we were indeed sinful. **92**He said, Have no fear this day. May Allah forgive you, and he is the most merciful of those who show mercy. **93**Go with this shirt of mine and lay it on my father's face, he will become a seer, and come to me with all your people. **94**When the caravan departed, their father had said, Indeed I am conscious of the breath of Joseph, though you call me senile. **95**They said, By Allah, indeed, you are in your old delusion. **96**Then, when the bearer of good news came, he laid it on his face and he became a seer once more. He said, Did I not say to you that I know from Allah what you do not know? **97**They said, O our father, ask forgiveness of our sins for us, for indeed, we were sinful. **98**He said, I will ask forgiveness for you from my Lord. Indeed, he is the forgiving, the merciful. **99**And when they came in before Joseph, he took his parents to him, and said, Come into Egypt safe, if Allah wills. **100**And he placed his parents on the throne and they fell down before him prostrate, and he said, O my father, this is the interpretation of my dream of old. My Lord has made it true, and he has shown me kindness, since he took me out of prison and has brought you from the desert after Satan had made strife between me and my brothers. Indeed, my Lord is kind to those whom he wills. He is the knower, the wise. **101**O my Lord, you have given me of the dominion and have taught me the interpretation of events, creator of the heavens and the earth. You are my protecting guardian in this world and the hereafter. Make me die a Muslim, and join me to the righteous. **102**This is among the news of the unseen which we inspire within you. You were not present with them when they fixed their plan and they were scheming. **103**And though you try a great deal, most men will not believe. **104**You ask them no fee for it. It is nothing other than a reminder to the peoples. **105**How many a sign is there in the heavens and the earth which they pass by with their faces averted. **106**And most of them do not believe in Allah except that they attribute partners. **107**Do they consider themselves secure from the overwhelming punishment of Allah coming upon them, or the sudden coming of the hour while they are unaware? **108**Say, This is my way, I call on Allah with certain knowledge, I and whoever follows me. Glory be to Allah, and I am not among the idolaters. **109**We did not send any before you except men to whom we revealed from among the people of the towns. Haven't they traveled in the land and seen the nature of the consequences for those who were before them? And indeed the dwelling place of the hereafter, for those who fear Allah, is best. Do you then have no sense? **110**Until, when the messengers despaired and thought that they were denied, then our help came to them, and those whom we willed were saved. And our wrath cannot be warded off from the guilty. **111**In their history indeed there is a lesson for men of understanding. It is no invented story, but a confirmation of the existing and a detailed explanation of everything, and a guidance and a mercy for people who believe.

99. While an Egyptian buys Joseph as a slave, and he is established in the unnamed "land" in 12:21, this is the first explicit mention of Joseph actually going to Egypt. For Barth, this is one of "several things in this Joseph sura" that "are so disjointed that one must suspect that something has been lost."[31]

109. Instead of "to whom we revealed," the Warsh Qur'an has "to whom he revealed."[32]
111. The Qur'an again repeats that this is not an invented tale but a confirmation of existing scripture (which did not actually confirm this message). See 5:44, 5:47.

The Thunder

Ar-Ra'd

Introduction

Islamic tradition holds that this sura, like suras 6, 7, 10, 11, and 12, dates from late in the Meccan period. According to Bell, the sura "seems to consist largely of scraps, which have been revised and added to at some time in Medina."[1] He bases this assessment primarily on the sura's shifting and inconsistent rhyme scheme.

Its main theme is summed up by 13:1, in which Allah tells the messenger: "These are verses of the book. What is revealed to you from your Lord is the truth, but most of mankind do not believe." This is, of course, a theme sounded in many other places in the Qur'an as well.

The sura's name comes from a phrase in 13:13, "The thunder sings his praise."

---

1 Bell, I, 228.

The Thunder

IN THE NAME OF ALLAH, THE COMPASSIONATE, THE MERCIFUL.

¹Alif. Lam. Mim. Ra. These are verses of the book. What is revealed to you from your Lord is the truth, but most people do not believe. ²It is Allah who raised up the heavens without visible supports, then mounted the throne, and compelled the sun and the moon to be of service, each running to an appointed term. He orders the course, he details the signs, so that perhaps you may be certain of the meeting with your Lord. ³And it is he who spread out the earth and placed firm hills and flowing streams in it, and of all fruits he placed in it, two spouses. He covers the night with the day. Indeed, in this are truly signs for people who think. ⁴And in the earth are neighboring tracts, vineyards and ploughed lands, and date-palms, like and unlike, which are watered with one water source. And we have made some of them to be superior to others in fruit. Indeed, in this truly are signs for people who have sense. ⁵And if you are amazed, then their saying is amazing, When we are dust, are we then in a new creation? Such people are those who disbelieve in their Lord, such people have shackles on their necks, such people are rightful companions of the fire, they will remain in it. ⁶And they call upon you to bring evil rather than good, when exemplary punishments have indeed occurred in front of them. But indeed, your Lord is rich in pardon for mankind despite their wrong, and indeed, your Lord is strong in punishment. ⁷Those who disbelieve say, If only some sign were sent down upon him from his Lord.

1. On the "mysterious letters," see 2:1. Like many other Islamic scholars, Ibn Kathir sees the four Arabic letters that begin this sura, and similar unexplained letters beginning many suras of the Qur'an, as confirmation of its miraculous character: "Every Surah that starts with separate letters affirms that the Qur'an is miraculous and is an evidence that it is a revelation from Allah, and that there is no doubt or denying in this fact."[1]

Despite the mystery of these letters, however, he goes on to assert that the Qur'an is "clear, plain and unequivocal," and that "most men will still not believe, due to their rebellion, stubbornness and hypocrisy."[2] The *Tafsir al-Jalalayn* asserts that the "most people" who will not believe are the people of Mecca at the time when they rejected Muhammad's prophetic claim.[3]

2. The section that begins here emphasizes Allah's power in all things. The idea that the heavens rest on invisible supports, presumably fixed on earth, manifests a prescientific understanding that belies contemporary Islamic apologists' claims that the Qur'an shows awareness of modern cosmology and other aspects of modern scientific understanding that weren't discovered until centuries after it was written. Ibn Kathir expands even more upon this when he writes: "The distance between the first heaven and the earth is five hundred years from every direction, and its thickness is also five hundred years. The second heaven surrounds the first heaven from every direction, encompassing everything that the latter carries, with a thickness also of five hundred years and a distance between them of five hundred years."[4]

These physical distances do not necessarily assume a physical Allah. "Vision does not comprehend him" (6:103), and he is nearer to man "than the jugular vein" (50:16), which suggests that he is not physical. Some argue that even though Allah is nearer than the jugular vein, he is not everywhere. Some modern Muslims argue that to affirm otherwise would be to fall into pantheism and *shirk*.[5] They argue this from the fact that Allah has "mounted the throne" (13:2, also 7:54). The imam Abul Hasan al-Ashari (874-936) argued against the claim of the rationalist-minded Mu'tazilite sect that this verse meant that Allah was everywhere. "If it were as they asserted," he asked, "then what difference would there be between the Throne and the earth?"[6] And the tenth-century scholar of hadith Ibn Khuzaymah declared: "Whoever does not affirm that Allah is above His heavens, upon His Throne and that He is distinct from His creation; must be forced to repent. If he does not repent, then he must be beheaded and then thrown into a garbage dump, so that the Muslims and the Ahl-Dhimma (the Christians and the Jew) will not suffer from his stinking smell."[7]

3. Here begins a passage in which Allah expatiates upon his power in creation. The natural world, like the Qur'an, is full of "signs" of Allah's presence and power.

6. The unbelievers, perverse as ever, ask Muhammad to "bring evil rather than good," that is, they ask him in derision to bring divine chastisements upon them. The *Tafsir al-Jalalayn* says that they "asked for the punishment to be hastened out of mockery."[8]

7. The unbelievers demand signs when signs are all around them in nature (13:3) and in every verse of the Qur'an.

You are only a warner, and for every people a guide. **⁸**Allah knows what every female bears and what the wombs absorb and what they grow. And everything with Him is measured. **⁹**He is the knower of the invisible and the visible, the great, the highly exalted. **¹⁰**It is the same whether any of you conceals what he says and he who declares it openly, he who lurks in the night and he who goes about freely in the daytime. **¹¹**For him are angels ranged in front of him and behind him, who guard him by Allah's command. Indeed, Allah does not change the condition of a people until they change what is in their hearts, and if Allah wills misfortune for a people, there is no one who can repel it, nor do they have a defender besides him. **¹²**It is he who shows you the lightning, a fear and a hope, and raises the heavy clouds. **¹³**The thunder sings his praise, and the angels, for awe of him. He launches the thunderbolts and strikes with them those whom he will while they dispute about Allah, and he is mighty in wrath. **¹⁴**To him is the real prayer. Those to whom they pray besides Allah do not respond to them at all, except like someone who stretches forth his hands toward water so that it may come to his mouth, and it will never reach it. The prayer of unbelievers goes astray. **¹⁵**And to Allah falls prostrate whoever is in the heavens and the earth, willingly or unwillingly, as do their shadows in the morning and the evening hours. **¹⁶**Say, Who is Lord of the heavens and the earth? Say, Allah. Say, Do you then take others besides him for protectors, which, even for themselves, have neither benefit nor harm? Say, Is the blind man equal to the seer, or is darkness equal to light? Or do they assign to Allah partners who created the likeness of his creation, so that their creation looks the same to them? Say, Allah is the creator of all things, and he is the one, the almighty. **¹⁷**He sends down water from the sky, so that valleys flow according to their measure, and the flood bears swelling foam, which they heat in the fire in order to make ornaments and tools rises a foam like it. In this way Allah compares the true and the false. Then, as for the foam, it passes away as scum upon the banks, while, as for what is of use to mankind, it remains in the earth. In this way Allah makes comparisons. **¹⁸**For those who answered Allah's call is bliss, and for those who did not answer his call, if they had all that is in the earth, and with it more like it, they would offer it as ransom. Such people will have a woeful

---

11. Each believer, meanwhile, is guarded by angels. Ibn Kathir notes that there are four: two guards, one in back and one in front, and two who record the Muslim's good and bad deeds.⁹ The believer greets the recording angels during prayer, turning to his right and left shoulder and saying each time, "Peace be upon you."

"Allah does not change the condition of a people until they change what is in their hearts" suggests that human beings do have free will. The *Tafsir al-Jalalayn* explains that Allah never "removes blessings" from people until they "exchange their good state for disobedience."¹⁰ This is difficult to reconcile with 13:31 and 13:33, as well as other passages that state that one's belief or unbelief is up to Allah (see 7:179, 10:99-100, 32:13). The twelfth-century Hanbali jurist Ibn Abi Ya'la describes the Qadari sect, which affirmed free will, as the worst of heretics for making such a claim: "They are those who claim that they possess in full the capacity to act

(al-istitâ'a), free will (al-mashî'a), and effective power (al-qudra). They consider that they hold in their grasp the ability to do good and evil, avoid harm and obtain benefit, obey and disobey, and be guided or misguided. They claim that human beings retain full initiative, without any prior status within the will of Allah for their acts, nor even in His knowledge of them. Their doctrine is similar to that of Zoroastrians and Christians. It is the very root of heresy."¹¹

14. A return to familiar themes: the idols are useless (13:14-16); the righteous will enter Paradise (13:20-24, 35); those who break Allah's covenant are accursed (13:25); the unbelievers demand a sign (13:27) and will be punished in this world and the next (13:34); the unbelievers ascribe partners to Allah (13:33) and reject part of the Qur'an (13:36).

17. Instead of "they heat," the Warsh Qur'an has "you heat."¹²

18. On Gehenna, see 2:206.

reckoning, and their dwelling place will be Gehenna, an evil bed. **19**Is he who knows what is revealed to you from your Lord is the truth like him who is blind? But only men of understanding pay attention, **20**Such people as those who keep the pact of Allah, and do not break the covenant, **21**Such people as those who unite what Allah has commanded should be joined, and fear their Lord, and dread a woeful reckoning, **22**Such people as those who persevere in seeking their Lord's face and are regular in prayer and spend out of what we bestow upon them secretly and openly, and overcome evil with good. Theirs will be the ending of the home, **23**Gardens of Eden which they enter, along with all who do right among their fathers and their wives and their descendants. The angels enter to them from every gate, **24**Peace be upon you, because you persevered. So how excellent will be the ending of the home. **25**And those who break the covenant of Allah after ratifying it, and sever what Allah has commanded should be joined, and spread corruption on the earth, theirs is the curse and theirs the evil dwelling place. **26**Allah enlarges the provision for those whom he wills, and limits it, and they rejoice in the life of this world, whereas the life of this world is only brief comfort as compared with the hereafter. **27**Those who disbelieve say, If only a sign were sent down upon him from his Lord! Say, Indeed, Allah leads astray those whom he wills, and guides to himself all who turn, **28**Who have believed and whose hearts have rest in the remembrance of Allah. Truly in the remembrance of Allah do hearts find rest. **29**Those who believe and do right, joy is for them, and bliss at journey's end. **30**In this way do we send you to a nation, before which other nations have passed away, so that you may recite to them what we have inspired within you, while they are unbelievers in Ar-Rahman. Say, He is my Lord, there is no God except him. In him do I put my trust, and to him is my recourse. **31**If it had been possible for a Qur'an to cause the mountains to move, or the earth to be torn apart, or the dead to speak, no, but the whole command is Allah's. Don't those who believe know that, if Allah had willed, he could have guided all mankind? As for those who disbelieve, disaster does not stop striking them because of what they do, or it dwells near their home until the threat of Allah comes to pass. Indeed, Allah does not fail to keep the appointment. **32**And indeed messengers were mocked before you, but I bore with those who disbelieved for a long time. Finally I seized them, and how was my punishment? **33**Is he who is aware of what every soul deserves? Yet they ascribe partners to Allah. Say, Name them. Is it that you would inform him of something on the earth that he doesn't know? Or is it just a way of speaking? No, but their fabrication is made to seem good for those who disbelieve, and they are kept from the right road. He whom Allah leads astray, for him there is no guide. **34**For them is torment in the life of this world, and indeed the torment of the hereafter is more painful, and they have no defender from Allah. **35**A description of the

---

26. Instead of "Allah," a Qur'anic manuscript examined by Mingana has "and Allah."[13]

30. On Ar-Rahman, see 17:110 and 38:5.

31. The unbelievers' demand for a miracle is dismissed; the Qur'an is better than a miracle. The *Tafsir al-Jalalayn* explains that "this *ayat* was revealed when they said to him, 'If you are a Prophet, then make these mountains of Makka move away before us and make rivers and springs flow in it so that we can plant and cultivate, and resurrect for us our dead fathers to tell us that you are a prophet.'"[14] But even if those things happened, they still wouldn't believe.

garden which is promised to those who keep their duty, under it rivers flow, its food is everlasting, and its shade, this is the reward of those who keep their duty, while the reward of unbelievers is the fire. **36**Those to whom we gave the book rejoice in what is revealed to you. And of the tribes there are those who deny some of it. Say, I am commanded only to serve Allah and I ascribe to him no partner. To him I call, and to him is my return. **37**In this way we have revealed it, a decisive utterance in Arabic, and if you would follow their desires after what has come to you of knowledge, then indeed you would have no protecting friend or defender from Allah. **38**And indeed we sent messengers before you, and we appointed for them wives and offspring, and it was not for any messenger to bring a sign except by Allah's permission. For everything there is a prescribed time. **39**Allah deletes or confirms what he wills, and with him is the mother of the book. **40**Whether we let you see something of what we have promised them, or make you die, yours is just the proclamation. Ours is the reckoning. **41**Don't they see how we target the land, stripping it of its outlying parts? When Allah dooms, there is no one who can postpone his doom, and he is swift at reckoning. **42**Those who were before them plotted, but all plotting is Allah's. He knows what each soul earns. The unbelievers will come to know for whom will be the ending of the home. **43**Those who disbelieve say, You are no messenger. Say, Allah, and whoever has knowledge of the book, is sufficient witness between me and you.

---

37. See 12:2.

39. The *Tafsir al-Jalalayn* says that the phrase "Allah deletes or confirms what he wills, and with him is the mother of the book" refers to the Qur'an: "Allah erases whatever ruling or anything else He wills, or endorses it.... The Master Copy of the Book (*Umm al-Kitab*) is in His Hands. *Umm al-Kitab* is the source of Revelation in which nothing is changed and it was what was written before time."[15] This remains the orthodox view of the Qur'an: that it is a perfect, unchanging copy of the Mother of the Book that has existed forever with Allah. See 43:4.

42. Instead of "the unbelievers," the Warsh Qur'an has "the unbeliever."[16]

SURA 14

Abraham

Ibrahim

Introduction

This is, Islamic tradition tells us, yet another late Meccan sura. Its name comes from 14:35, where Abraham appears and prays, but following the convention of the naming of Qur'an suras, this name has little to do with the content of this sura; more is said about Abraham elsewhere in the Qur'an (see especially sura 60).

Bell states: "This surah, like the preceding, seems to consist largely of fragments, and shows also the same variation of rhyme."[1]

---

1 Bell, I, 235.

Abraham

In the name of Allah, the compassionate, the merciful.

¹Alif. Lam. Ra. A book which we have revealed to you, so that by it you may bring forth mankind from darkness to light, by the permission of their Lord, to the path of the mighty, the owner of praise, ²Allah, to whom belongs whatever is in the heavens and whatever is in the earth, and woe to the unbelievers from an awful doom, ³Those who love the life of this world more than the hereafter, and bar people from the way of Allah and would make it crooked, such people are far astray. ⁴And we never sent a messenger except with the language of his people, so that he might make it clear for them. Then Allah leads astray those whom he wills, and guides those whom he wills. He is the mighty, the wise. ⁵We indeed sent Moses with our signs, saying, Bring your people forth from darkness to light. And remind them of the days of Allah. Indeed, in them are signs for each steadfast, thankful one. ⁶And how Moses said to his people, Remember Allah's favor to you when he delivered you from Pharaoh's people who were afflicting you with dreadful torment, and were killing your sons and leaving your women alive, that was a tremendous trial from your Lord. ⁷And when your Lord proclaimed, If you give thanks, I will give you more, but if you are ungrateful, indeed, my punishment is severe. ⁸And Moses said, Although you and all who are on earth prove ungrateful, indeed, Allah indeed is absolute, the owner of praise. ⁹Hasn't the history of those before you reached you, the people of Noah, and Aad and Thamud, and those after them? No one knows them except Allah. Their messengers came to them with clear proofs, but they thrust their hands into their mouths, and said, Indeed, we disbelieve in what you have been sent with, and indeed, we are in grave doubt about what you call us to. ¹⁰Their messengers said, Can there be doubt concerning Allah, the creator of the heavens and the earth? He calls you so that he may forgive you your sins and give you a reprieve until an appointed term. They said,

---

1. On the "mysterious letters," see 2:1. The book is, of course, the Qur'an. In the words of Ibn Kathir, it is "the most honored Book, that Allah sent down from heaven to the most honored Messenger of Allah sent to all the people of the earth, Arabs and non-Arabs alike."¹

2. In another indication of the centrality of Muhammad in Islam, Ibn Kathir makes the last part of this verse, which does not mention the messenger, refer to Muhammad: "Woe to them on the Day of Judgment because they defied you, O Muhammad, and rejected you."²

3. They are, in the words of the *Tafsir Anwarul Bayan*, "ever vigilant to expose any defect that they hope to find in the religion (*D'in*) of Islam."³ This avidity to oppose Islam is generally taken to be a sign of the perversity of the infidels and their rejection of Allah; Islamic scholars never link it to passages such as 9:5, 9:29, 47:4, 48:29, and 98:6, among others.

4. Allah has sent messengers to people speaking in their own language so they can understand the message clearly. On Allah leading people astray, see 7:179, 10:99, and 32:13.

6. On Pharaoh, see also 2:49, 3:11, 7:103, 8:52, 10:75, 17:101, 20:24, 23:46, 26:11, 27:12, 28:3, 29:39, 38:12, 40:24, 44:17, 50:13, 51:38, 54:41, 66:11, 69:9, 73:15, 79:15, 85:18, and 89:10.

9. "It is said," explains Ibn Kathir, "that they pointed to the Messengers' mouths asking them to stop calling them to Allah, the Exalted and Most Honored. It is also said that it means, they placed their hands on their mouths in denial of the Messengers. It was also said that it means that they did not answer the call of the Messengers, or they were biting their hands in rage."⁴

10. The dialogue between the unbelievers and the messengers that begins here appears to be meant to apply to all the experiences of all the prophets Allah has sent to the world, but which once again, as in other suras that are traditionally considered to have come from the late Meccan period, closely traces and universalizes the messenger's dealings with his own people.

You are only mortals like us, who want to turn us away from what our fathers used to worship. Then bring some clear justification. **11**Their messengers said to them, We are only mortals like you, but Allah gives favor to those of his slaves whom he wills. It is not for us to bring you justification unless by the permission of Allah. In Allah let believers put their trust. **12**How should we not put our trust in Allah when he has shown us our ways? We surely will endure the harm you do to us. In Allah let the trusting put their trust. **13**And those who disbelieved said to their messengers, Indeed we will drive you out from our land, unless you return to our religion. Then their Lord inspired them, Indeed we will destroy the wrongdoers, **14**And indeed we will make you dwell in the land after them. This is for him who fears my majesty and fears my threats. **15**And they sought help and every defiant potentate was bought to nothing, **16**Gehenna is before him, and he is made to drink fetid water, **17**Which he sips but can hardly swallow, and death comes to him from every side while he still cannot die, and before him is a harsh doom. **18**A comparison of those who disbelieve in their Lord, Their works are like ashes which the wind blows hard upon a stormy day. They have no control of anything that they have earned. That is the extreme failure. **19**Haven't you seen that Allah has created the heavens and the earth with truth? If he wills, he can remove you and bring some new creation, **20**And that is no great matter for Allah. **21**They all come forth to their Lord. Then those who were despised say to those who were scornful, We merely followed you, can you then avert from us any part of Allah's doom? They say, If Allah had guided us, we would have guided you. Whether we rage or patiently endure is all the same for us, we have no place of refuge. **22**And Satan says, when the matter has been decided, Indeed, Allah promised you a promise of truth, and I promised you, then failed you. And I had no power over you except that I called to you and you obeyed me. So don't blame me, blame yourselves. I cannot help you, nor can you help me. Indeed, I disbelieved in what you ascribed to me before. Indeed, for wrongdoers is a painful doom. **23**And those who believed and did good works are made to enter gardens under which rivers flow, remaining in them by permission of their Lord, their greeting in them, Peace! **24**Don't you see how Allah makes a comparison, a good saying is like a good tree, its root set firm, its branches reaching into heaven, **25**Giving its fruit at every season by permission of its Lord? Allah

---

13. This verse "clearly indicates," Maududi says, "that the *surah* was revealed at a time when the persecution of the Muslims in Makkah had reached its apex. In the manner of the earlier unbelievers, the Makkans were bent on banishing the believers from their land."[5] The persecution of the Muslims is portrayed in 2:191 and 2:217 as worse than contravening laws in order to slaughter the unbelievers who are responsible for the persecution, and being driven out of one's land triggers the divine command to recover that land, as also per 2:191.

"Truly we will destroy the wrongdoers, and truly we will make you dwell in the land after them" refutes the often-repeated claim that the Qur'an promises the land of Israel to the Jews. This claim is based on 5:21, which warns the children of Israel not to "turn back as losers." But the Jews did turn back, earning the curse of Allah: see 2:89, 3:112, 9:30. This verse shows that the Muslims inherit the land they were promised.

16. On Gehenna, see 2:206, as also at 14:29.

18. Instead of "the wind," the Warsh Qur'an has "the winds."[6]

22. According to Ibn Kathir, quoting an earlier authority, Satan will tell the unbelievers at that point, when it's too late: "I deny being a partner with Allah, the Exalted and Most Honored."[7] Ibn Kathir adds: "Iblis, may Allah curse him, will stand and address" those whom he led astray, "in order to add depression to their depression, sorrow to their sorrow and grief to their grief."[8]

makes comparisons for mankind so that they may reflect. **26**And the comparison of a bad saying is as a bad tree, uprooted from upon the earth, possessing no stability. **27**Allah confirms those who believe by a firm saying in the life of this world and in the hereafter, and Allah leads wrongdoers astray. And Allah does what he wills. **28**Haven't you seen those who exchanged the favor of Allah for ingratitude and led their people down to the dwelling place of loss, **29**Gehenna? They are exposed to it. A wretched end. **30**And they set up rivals to Allah so that they might mislead people from his way. Say, Enjoy life, for indeed, your journey's end will be the fire. **31**Tell my slaves who believe to establish prayer and spend out of what we have given them, secretly and publicly, before a day comes when there will be neither trade nor friendship. **32**Allah is he who created the heavens and the earth, and causes water to descend from the sky, thereby producing fruits as food for you, and makes the ships to be of service to you, that they may run upon the sea

at his command, and has made the rivers of service to you, **33**And makes the sun and the moon, constant in their courses, to be of service to you, and has made the night and the day of service to you. **34**And he gives you of all you ask of him, and if you would count the bounty of Allah, you would not be able to number it. Indeed, man is truly a wrongdoer, an ingrate. **35**And when Abraham said, My Lord, make this territory safe, and preserve me and my sons from serving idols. **36**My Lord, indeed, they have led astray many of mankind. But who follows me, he indeed is of me. And whoever disobeys me, still you are forgiving, merciful. **37**Our Lord, I have settled some of my descendants in an uncultivated valley near your sacred house, our Lord, so that they might establish prayer. So make the people incline their hearts toward them and provide for them from the fruits, so that they might be grateful. **38**Our Lord, indeed, you know what we conceal and what we proclaim. Nothing on the earth or in the heaven is hidden from Allah.

---

26. The "bad tree" is faintly reminiscent of Jesus's statement, "Every sound tree bears good fruit, but the bad tree bears evil fruit" (Matthew 7:17). A hadith depicts Muhammad telling his companions, "There is a tree among the trees which is as blessed as a Muslim," and explained, "It is the date-palm tree."9 This may have been because of the spiritual powers of dates. Muhammad is also depicted as saying: "He who eats seven Ajwa dates every morning, will not be affected by poison or magic on the day he eats them."10

27. A hadith has Muhammad explaining this "firm saying in the life of this world and in the hereafter": "When a Muslim is questioned in his grave, he will testify that none has the right to be worshipped but Allah and that Muhammad is Allah's Apostle, and that is what is meant by Allah's statement."11

28. In a hadith, Muhammad identifies these people as "the disbelieving pagans of Mecca," which is likely the source of Maududi's assessment of this sura as a warning to the Quraysh when tensions between them and the Muslims were high (see 14:13).12

35. Islamic tradition identifies "this territory" with Mecca, but the Qur'an makes no specific identification.

36. Ibn Kathir states that according to one of Muhammad's companions, Abdullah bin Amr, Muhammad recited part of

Abraham's prayer after reciting this verse and wept, crying out three times: "O Allah, Save my Ummah [community]!"13 In another indication of the importance that Islamic tradition places upon Muhammad, Allah is said to have sent Gabriel with these instructions: "Go to Muhammad and tell him this; We will make you pleased with your Ummah, O Muhammad, and will not treat them in a way you dislike."14

37. Islamic tradition identifies the "sacred house" as the Ka'ba in Mecca, but here again, the Qur'an does not make this identification. See 2:142.

The only men whose hearts are to be drawn near are Muslims. Ibn Kathir explains: "Had Ibrahim said, 'The hearts of mankind', Persians, Romans, the Jews, the Christians and all other people would have gathered around" the Ka'ba.15 But Abraham, they explain, said "some among men," thus "making it exclusive to Muslims only."16

Instead of, "So make the people incline their hearts toward them and provide for them from the fruits, so that they might be grateful," some early manuscripts have: "So you incline their hearts toward them and provide for them from the fruits, so that they might be grateful."17 Still other early manuscripts speak of

³⁹Praise be to Allah who has given me, in my old age, Ishmael and Isaac. Indeed, my Lord is indeed the hearer of prayer. ⁴⁰My Lord, make me establish proper prayer, and some of my posterity, our Lord, and accept my prayer. ⁴¹Our Lord, forgive me and my parents and the believers on the day when the account is established. ⁴²Do not think that Allah is unaware of what the wicked do. He only gives them a respite until a day when eyes will stare, ⁴³As they come hurrying on in fear, their heads upraised, their gaze not returning to them, and their hearts as air. ⁴⁴And warn mankind of a day when the doom will come upon them, and those who did wrong will say, Our Lord, give us a reprieve for a little while. We will obey your call and will follow the messengers. Didn't you swear before that there would be no end for you? ⁴⁵And you lived in the dwellings of those who wronged themselves and it became plain to you how we dealt with them and made examples for you. ⁴⁶Indeed they have plotted their plot, and their plot is with Allah, even if their plot were one by which the mountains would be moved. ⁴⁷So do not think that Allah will fail to keep his promise to his messengers. Indeed, Allah is mighty, able to repay. ⁴⁸On the day when the earth will be changed to something other than the earth, and the heavens, and they will come forth to Allah, the one, the almighty, ⁴⁹You will see the guilty on that day linked together in chains, ⁵⁰Their clothing black, and the fire covering their faces, ⁵¹So that Allah may repay each soul what it has earned. Indeed, Allah is swift at reckoning. ⁵²This is a clear message for mankind so that they may be warned by it, and that they may know that he is only one God, and that men of understanding may be reminded.

---

making the people "incline their group toward them," rather than their "hearts."¹⁸

41. Instead of, "Our Lord, forgive me and my parents and the believers on the day when the account is established," seventeen early Qur'an manuscripts omit a single letter (*alif*), which could make the passage read, "Our Lord, forgive me and my children and the believers on the day when the account is established."¹⁹

42. Allah then repeats still another time that the sinners who remain heedless of his truth will nonetheless face his dreadful judgment.

The Rock

Al-Hijr

Introduction

The title of sura 15, al-Hijr, is translated variously as "The Valley of Stone," "Stoneland," "Rock City," "Rocky Tract," and the like. Many translations do not render it in English at all, since it is a place name, referred to in 15:80: Al-Hijr was yet another place that rejected the messengers of Allah and was destroyed.

Islamic tradition holds that this is another late Meccan sura, revealed, like sura 14, at a time of great tension between the Muslims and the pagan Quraysh of Mecca, and at a time when Muhammad himself was apparently feeling a bit discouraged, so that Allah makes some effort to improve his spirits.

The Rock

In the name of Allah, the compassionate, the merciful.

1Alif. Lam. Ra. These are signs of the book and a clear Qur'an. **2**It may be that those who disbelieve ardently wish that they were Muslims. **3**Let them eat and enjoy life, and let hope fool them. They will come to know. **4** And we destroyed no township but there was a known decree for it. **5**No nation can surpass its term, nor can they lag behind. **6**And they say, O you to whom the reminder is revealed, indeed, you are indeed a madman. **7**Why don't you bring angels to us, if you are among the truthful? **8**We do not send down the angels except with the truth, and in that case they would not be tolerated. **9**Indeed, we, even we, reveal the reminder, and indeed, we indeed are its guardian. **10**We indeed sent before you among the factions of the men of old. **11**And there never came a messenger to them except that they did mock him. **12**In this way we make it enter the hearts of the guilty, **13**They do not believe in it, though the example of the men of old has gone before. **14**And even if we opened a gate of heaven to them and they kept ascending to it, **15**They would say, Our eyes are dazzled, no, but we are bewitched people. **16**And indeed in the heaven we have set mansions of the stars, and we have beautified it for those who see it. **17**And we have guarded it from every outcast satan, **18**Except him who eavesdrops, and a clear flame pursues them. **19**And the earth we have spread out, and placed firm hills in it, and caused everything to grow there in balance. **20**And we have given you livelihoods in it, and to those for whom you do not provide. **21**And there is not a thing that the storehouses of it are not with us. And we do not send it down except in appointed measure. **22**And we send the fertilizing winds, and cause water to descend from the sky, and give it you to drink. It is not you who are the holders of its storehouse. **23**Indeed, it is we, surely we, who bring to life and give death, and we are the inheritor. **24**And indeed we know the eager among you and indeed we know those who lag behind. **25**Indeed, your Lord will gather them together. Indeed, he is wise, aware. **26**Indeed we created man out of clay

---

1. On the "mysterious letters," see 2:1. On the clarity of the Qur'an, see 3:7.

2. Ibn Kathir invokes several early authorities for the view that this verse responds to the taunts of the unbelievers to the sinful Muslims in hell. When the idolaters tell the Muslims that "what you used to worship on earth has not helped you," Allah will be angry and will remove the sinful Muslims from hell—and then the unbelievers, left in hell, will wish they had accepted Islam.[1]

4. No one can escape the doom decreed by Allah. This sura seems to envision that doom as coming on the day of judgment, but see 9:14.

8. Instead of, "We do not send down [nunazzelu] the angels," the Warsh Qur'an has, "The angels do not descend [tanazzalu]."[2]

9. Allah will protect the Qur'an, asserts the Tafsir al-Jalalayn, "from alteration, distortion, additions, or deletions."[3] This is why many see textual variants as a threat; they would seem to negate Allah's promise in this verse.

11. Once again Allah comforts the messenger (see 2:144). Ibn Kathir explains: "Consoling His Messenger for the rejection of the disbelieving Quraysh, Allah says that He has sent Messengers before him to the nations of the past, and no Messenger came to a nation but they rejected him and mocked him. Then He tells him that He lets disbelief enter the hearts of those sinners who are too stubborn and too arrogant to follow His guidance."[4] Here again, disbelief is a matter of the will of Allah, which cannot be rejected or overridden (see 7:179, 10:99, 32:13).

18. On this eavesdropping, see 37:7-10.

23. "The Inheritor," that is, the one who survives when all else perishes.

of altered black mud, **27**And the jinn we created previously of essential fire. **28**And when your Lord said to the angels, Indeed, I am creating a mortal out of clay of altered black mud, **29**So when I have made him and have breathed into him of my spirit, fall down, prostrating yourselves to him. **30**So the angels fell prostrate, all of them together, **31**Except Iblis. He refused to be among the prostrate. **32**He said, O Iblis, what ails you that you are not among the prostrate? **33**He said, I am not one to prostrate myself to a mortal whom you have created out of clay of altered black mud. **34**He said, Then go forth from here, for indeed, you are outcast. **35**And indeed, the curse will be upon you until the day of judgment. **36**He said, My Lord, give me a reprieve until the day when they are raised. **37**He said, Then indeed, you are among those reprieved, **38**Until the day of the appointed time. **39**He said, My Lord, because you have sent me astray, I will indeed adorn the path of error for them on the earth, and will mislead every one of them, **40**Except those among them who are your perfectly devoted slaves. **41**He said, This is a right course obligatory upon me, **42**Indeed, as for my slaves, you have no power over any of them except those who follow you who are defiant, **43**And indeed, for all such people, Gehenna will be the promised place. **44**It has seven gates, and each gate has an appointed share. **45**Indeed, those who fear Allah are among gardens and water springs. **46**Enter them in peace, safely. **47**And we remove whatever anger may be in their hearts. As brothers, face to face, on couches raised. **48**Labor doesn't come to them there, nor will they be expelled from there. **49**Announce to my slaves that indeed I am the forgiving, the merciful, **50**And that my doom is the painful doom. **51**And tell them about Abraham's guests, **52**When they came in to him, and said, Peace, he said, Indeed, we are afraid of you. **53**They said, Be not afraid. Indeed, we bring you good news of a boy possessing wisdom. **54**He said, You bring me good news when old age has overtaken me? What then can you bring good news about? **55**They said, We bring you good news in truth. So do not be among the despairing. **56**He said, And who despairs of the mercy of his Lord except those who are astray? **57**He said, And afterward what is your business, O you messengers? **58**They said, We have been sent to a guilty people, **59**Except the family of Lot. We will deliver every one of them, **60**Except his wife, about whom we had decreed that she should be among those who stay behind. **61**And when the messengers came to the family of Lot, **62**He said, Indeed, you are people unknown. **63**They said, No, but we come to you with what they keep doubting, **64**And bring you the truth, and indeed, we are truth-tellers. **65**So travel with your family in a portion of the night, and follow their backs. Let none of you turn round, but go where you

---

28. This account of the creation of Adam parallels 2:30-39 and 7:11-25.

42. The *Tafsir al-Jalalayn* explains that the two groups in this verse are simply believers and unbelievers.[5]

43. On Gehenna, see 2:206.

44. According to the *Ruhul Ma'ani,* "One door will be reserved for the entry of the sinful Muslims," and "another door will be for the Jews, another for the Christians, another for the Sabians, another for the fire worshippers, another for the Polytheists and the last will be for the hypocrites."[6]

51. Here begins another retelling of the story of Abraham, Lot, and the unnamed Sodom and Gomorrah, paralleling the account found in Genesis 17-19 and repeated at 7:80 and 11:69. Like other Qur'anic retellings of Biblical stories, the Qur'anic account is streamlined and shorn of subplots, so as to focus sharply on one sole theme: the rejection of truth and subsequent punishment of the unbelievers.

56. Barth suggests that "he said" is "to be deleted," as "the verse continues the address of the angels," and Abraham doesn't actually speak until the following verse.[7]

are commanded. ⁶⁶And we made plain the decision to him, that their root was to be cut in the early morning. ⁶⁷And the people of the city came, rejoicing at the news. ⁶⁸He said, Indeed, they are my guests. Do not embarrass me. ⁶⁹And keep your duty to Allah, and do not shame me. ⁷⁰They said, Haven't we forbidden you from people? ⁷¹He said, Here are my daughters, if you must be doing this. ⁷²By your life, they moved blindly in the frenzy of approaching death. ⁷³Then the cry overtook them at sunrise. ⁷⁴And we turned the land upside down, and we rained down on them stones of heated clay. ⁷⁵Indeed, in this there are indeed signs for those who read the signs. ⁷⁶And indeed, it is upon a road still existing. ⁷⁷Indeed, in this is indeed a sign for believers. ⁷⁸And the dwellers in the wood indeed were evildoers. ⁷⁹So we took vengeance on them, and indeed, they are both on a high road, plain to see. ⁸⁰And the dwellers in the rock denied messengers. ⁸¹And we gave them our signs, but they were turned away from them. ⁸²And they used to carve out dwellings from the hills, secure. ⁸³But the cry overtook them at the morning hour, ⁸⁴And what

they tended to consider as gain did not help them. ⁸⁵We did not create the heavens and the earth and all that is between them except with truth, and indeed, the hour is surely coming. So forgive, with a gracious forgiveness. ⁸⁶Indeed, your Lord. He is the all-wise creator. ⁸⁷We have given you seven oft-repeated and the great Qur'an. ⁸⁸Do not strain your eyes toward what we have given to groups of them to enjoy, and do not be grieved because of them, and lower your wing for the believers. ⁸⁹And say, Indeed, I, surely I, am a plain warner, ⁹⁰Such as we send down for those who make division, ⁹¹Those who break the Qur'an into parts. ⁹²By your Lord, we will question them, every one of them, ⁹³About what they used to do. ⁹⁴So proclaim what you are commanded, and withdraw from the idolaters. ⁹⁵Indeed, we defend you from the scoffers, ⁹⁶Who set up some other god along with Allah. But they will come to know. ⁹⁷We know well that your heart is oppressed by what they say, ⁹⁸But sing the praise of your Lord, and be among those who make prostration. ⁹⁹And serve your Lord until the inevitable comes to you.

---

72. Barth points out that this verse "does not fit this context," but that it fits perfectly after 15:66: "And we made plain the decision to him, that their root was to be cut in the early morning. By your life, they moved blindly in the frenzy of approaching death."[8]

78. The "dwellers in the wood," says Ibn Kathir, were the people of Shu'aib (see 7:85, 11:84, 26:176). "Their evildoing," he explained, "included associating partners with Allah (Shirk), banditry and cheating in weights and measures."[9]

80. Ibn Kathir states that the "dwellers in the rock" were "the people of Thamud who rejected their Prophet, Salih."[10] This prophet "brought them signs to prove that what he was telling them was true, such as the she-camel which Allah created for them out of a solid rock in response to the supplication of Salih. This she-camel was grazing on their lands, and the people and the camel took water on alternate days that were well-known," but then "rebelled and killed it."[11] On the camel of Allah, see 11:64, 26:155, and 91:11-14, as well as the introduction to sura 11.

85. Another section in which Allah consoles the messenger for the rejection and ridicule he has encountered from the unbelievers.

87. The "seven oft-repeated" are the seven verses of sura 1, the Fatihah, the most often-repeated prayer in Islam.

88. Muslims should, in the words of Ibn Kathir, "be content with the Grand Qur'an that Allah has given to you, and do not long for the luxuries and transient delights that they have," that is, the unbelievers.[12]

91. These people are, according to a statement attributed to Ibn Abbas, "the People of the Book, who divided the Book into parts, believing in some of it, and rejecting some of it."[13] Others in Islamic tradition, however, say that it refers to the Quraysh, who, by charging that Muhammad was insane or possessed, were making the Qur'an into parts. Ibn Kathir depicts Muhammad's foremost early biographer, Ibn Ishaq, as saying that the Quraysh held a meeting on who they thought Muhammad really was, considering the possibility that he might be a soothsayer, or crazy, or a poet, or a sorcerer, before finally deciding on the latter and triggering the revelation of 15:94.[14]

The Bee

An-Nahl

Introduction

Sura 16, "The Bee," is traditionally considered to be another in the string of late Meccan suras that began with sura 10. Its title comes from 16:68, which tells us that Allah taught the bee to perform its distinctive functions.

The Bee

In the name of Allah, the compassionate, the merciful.

¹The commandment of Allah will come to pass, so do not try to hasten it. Glorified and exalted is he above all that they associate. ²He sends down the angels with the spirit of his command to those whom he will among his slaves, Warn mankind that there is no God except me, so keep your duty to me. ³He has created the heavens and the earth with truth. May he be highly exalted above all that they associate. ⁴He has created man from a drop of fluid, yet look, he is an open adversary. ⁵And he has created the cattle, from which you have warm clothing and uses, and of which you eat, ⁶And in which there is beauty for you, when you bring them home, and when you take them out to pasture. ⁷And they bear your loads for you to a land you could not reach except with great trouble to yourselves. Indeed, your Lord is full of kindness, merciful. ⁸And horses and mules and asses so that you may ride them, and for ornament. And he creates what you do not know. ⁹And the direction of the way belongs to Allah, and some do not go straight. And if he had willed, he would have led you all rightly. ¹⁰It is he who sends down water from the sky, from which you have drink, and from which are trees on which you send your animals to pasture. ¹¹In them he causes crops to grow for you, and the olive and the date-palm and grapes and all kinds of fruit. Indeed, in this is indeed a sign for people who reflect. ¹²And he has subjected the night and the day and the sun and the moon to be of service to you, and the stars are made submissive by his command. Indeed, in this indeed are signs for people who have sense. ¹³And whatever he has created for you on the earth of various colors, indeed, in this is indeed a sign for people who take notice. ¹⁴And it is he who has subjected the sea to be of service, so that you eat fresh meat from there, and bring forth from it ornaments which you wear. And you see the ships ploughing it so that you may seek of his bounty and that perhaps you may give thanks. ¹⁵And he has cast onto the earth firm hills so that it does not quake with you, and streams and roads so that you may find a way. ¹⁶And landmarks, and by the star they find a way. ¹⁷Is he then who creates like him who does not create? Will you not then remember? ¹⁸And if you would count the favors of Allah, you cannot number it. Indeed, Allah is truly forgiving, merciful. ¹⁹And Allah knows what you keep hidden and what you proclaim. ²⁰Those whom they invoke besides Allah created nothing, but are themselves created. ²¹Dead, not living. And they do not know when they will be raised. ²²Your God is one God. But as for those who do not believe in the hereafter, their hearts refuse to know, for they are proud. ²³Surely Allah knows what they keep hidden and what they proclaim.

Allah begins by emphasizing that he has created all things, and provides for all of humanity's needs, and that all created beings bear witness to him (vv. 1-19).

9. Ibn Kathir says that the "ways that turn aside" from the straight path of Islam are "various opinions and whims, such as Judaism, Christianity and Zoroastrianism."¹ The *Tafsir Ibn Abbas* concurs, saying: "It is Allah Who guides to monotheism, and some of the religions are crooked and unjust such as Judaism, Christianity and Zoroastrianism. And if Allah had willed, He would have guided you all to His religion."² So once again, belief or unbelief is up to Allah, not to the individual. See 7:179, 10:99, and 32:13.

20. Instead of "they invoke," the Warsh Qur'an has "you invoke."³

Indeed, he does not love the proud. ²⁴And when it is said to them, What has your Lord revealed?, they say, Fables of the men of old, ²⁵So that they may bear their burdens undiminished on the day of resurrection, with some of the burdens of those whom they mislead without knowledge. What they bear is evil. ²⁶Those before them plotted, so Allah struck at the foundations of their building, and then the roof fell down upon them from above them, and doom came on them from what they did not know, ²⁷Then on the day of resurrection, he will disgrace them and say, Where are my partners, for whose sake you opposed? Those who have been given knowledge will say, Disgrace this day and evil are upon the unbelievers, ²⁸Whom the angels cause to die while they are wronging themselves. Then they will make full submission, We used to do no wrong. No, surely Allah is the knower of what you used to do. ²⁹So enter the gates of Gehenna, to dwell in it forever. Woeful indeed will be the lodging of the arrogant. ³⁰And it is said to those who fear Allah, What has your Lord revealed? They say, Good. For those who do good in this world there is good, and the home of the hereafter will be better. Pleasant indeed will be the home of those who fear Allah, ³¹Gardens of Eden which they enter,

under which rivers flow, in which they have what they wish. In this way Allah repays those who fear Allah, ³²Those whom the angels cause to die pure. They say, Peace be upon you, enter the garden because of what you used to do. ³³Are they waiting for the angels to come to them or that your Lord's command would come to pass? That is what those who were before them did. Allah did not wrong them, but they wronged themselves, ³⁴So that the evils of what they did struck them, and what they used to mock surrounded them. ³⁵And the idolaters say, If Allah had willed, we would not have worshipped anything besides Him, we and our fathers, nor would we have forbidden anything without him. That is what those who were before them did. Are the messengers given the responsibility for anything except plain conveyance? ³⁶And indeed we have raised in every nation a messenger, Serve Allah and avoid *taghut*. Then there were some whom Allah guided, and some upon whom error had a justified hold. Just travel in the land and see the nature of the consequences for the deniers. ³⁷Even if you want them to be rightly guided, still Allah surely will not guide him who misleads. Such people have no helpers. ³⁸And they swear by Allah their most binding oaths that Allah will not raise up

---

24. "They say," according to the *Tafsir al-Jalalayn*, that the Qur'anic revelations are "fables of the men of old" that are meant to "misguide people."[4] See 3:37.

Instead of "when," a Qur'anic manuscript examined by Mingana has "where."[5]

29. On Gehenna, see 2:206.

35. The unbelievers make a reasonable complaint in light of the Qur'an's repeated statements about Allah leading people astray and having the ability to make everyone believers if he had desired (see 7:179, 10:99, and 32:13). But here this excuse is rejected, since Allah has sent messengers to every people, telling them to worship Allah alone (16:36).

Ibn Kathir tries to mitigate the harshness of the idea that if Allah had willed, all mankind would believe, by explaining that

Allah doesn't actually want anyone to disbelieve, and sends them messengers so that they won't do so, but simply allows them to if they so choose: "The legislative will of Allah is clear and cannot be taken as an excuse by them, because He had forbidden them to do that upon the tongue of His Messengers, but by His universal will (i.e., by which He allows things to occur even though they do not please Him) He allowed them to do that as it was decreed for them. So there is no argument in that for them. Allah created Hell and its people both the Shayatin (devils) and disbelievers, but He does not like His servants to disbelieve."[6]

36. On *taghut*, see 2:256.

37. Ibn Kathir asks, "the one whom He has caused to go astray, so who can guide him apart from Allah? No one."[7] See 7:179, 10:99, and 32:13.

him who dies. No, but it is a promise upon him in truth, but most of mankind do not know, **39**So that he may explain to them what they disagree about, and so that those who disbelieved may know that they were liars. **40**And our word to a thing, when we intend it, is only that we say to it, Be, and it is. **41**And those who have emigrated for the sake of Allah after they had been oppressed, we indeed will give them good lodging in the world, and surely the reward of the hereafter is greater, if they only knew, **42**Those who are steadfast and put their trust in Allah. **43**And we did not send before you anyone other than men whom we inspired. Ask the people of the message if you do not know. **44**With clear proofs and writings, and we have revealed to you the message so that you might explain to mankind what has been revealed for them, and that perhaps they may reflect. **45**Are those who plan evil deeds then secure that Allah will not cause the earth to swallow them, or that doom will not come upon them from what they do not know? **46**Or that he will not seize them in their moving around, so that there is no escape for them? **47**Or that he will not seize them with a gradual wasting? Indeed, your Lord is indeed full of kindness, merciful. **48**Have they not observed all things that Allah has created, how their shadows incline to the right and to the left, making prostration to Allah, and they are humble? **49**And to Allah whatever is in the heavens and whatever is in the earth of living creatures makes prostration, and the angels, and they are not proud. **50**They fear their Lord above them, and do what they are told. **51**Allah has said, Do not choose two gods. There is only one God. So be in awe of me, only me. **52**To Him belongs whatever is in the heavens and the earth, and religion is his forever. Will you then fear anyone other than Allah? **53**And whatever you enjoy of comfort, it is from Allah. Then when misfortune reaches you, to Him you cry for help. **54**And afterward, when he has rid you of the misfortune, look, a group among you attributes partners to their Lord, **55**So as to deny what we have given them. Then enjoy life, for you will come to know. **56**And they assign a portion of what we have given them to what they do not know. By Allah, but you will indeed be asked about what you used to fabricate. **57**And they assign daughters to Allah. May he be glorified. And to themselves, what they desire, **58**When if one of them receives news of the birth of a female, his face remains darkened, and he is inwardly angry. **59**He hides himself from the people because of the evil of what he has received news about. Will he keep her in contempt, or bury her beneath the earth? Indeed evil is their judgment. **60**For those who do not believe in the hereafter is an evil comparison, and the sublime comparison belongs to Allah. He is the mighty, the wise. **61**If Allah were to seize mankind for

40. Allah accomplishes everything he intends to do, and "nothing," says Ibn Kathir, "can stop Him or oppose Him."[8] But if that is so, the conundrum Ibn Kathir intended to solve remains: Allah condemns some people to eternal torture in hell because of their unbelief, but they don't believe because it is Allah's will that they don't.

41. Those who emigrate for the sake of Allah, that is, those who leave their homelands to bring Islam to a new land, will be rewarded in both this world and the next (see 4:100). Islamic tradition generally regards the first of these as the Muslims who fled

Mecca with Muhammad and settled in Medina; Ibn Kathir, however, identifies them as the Muslims who earlier fled to Abyssinia to escape the persecution of the pagan Quraysh.

57. The polytheists even dare to say that Allah has daughters, while they themselves have sons. The *Tafsir al-Jalalayn* states that "they allot Him daughters, which they dislike, when He is far exalted above having any children; and they allot themselves the sons, which they prefer, so that they have what is more glorious than what they attribute to Him."[9]

their wrongdoing, he would not leave on it a living creature, but he gives them a reprieve until an appointed term, and when their term comes, they cannot put it off an hour nor advance it. ⁶²And they assign to Allah what they dislike, and their tongues expound the lie so that the better portion will be theirs. Surely theirs will be the fire, and they will be abandoned. ⁶³By Allah, we indeed sent messengers to the nations before you, but Satan made their deeds seem good to them. So he is their patron this day, and theirs will be a painful doom. ⁶⁴And we have revealed the book to you alone so that you might explain to them what they disagree about, and a guidance and a mercy for a people who believe. ⁶⁵Allah sends down water from the sky and with it revives the earth after her death. Indeed, in this is indeed a sign for a people who hear. ⁶⁶And indeed, in cattle there is a lesson for you. We give you to drink of what is in their bellies, from between the refuse and the blood, pure milk palatable to the drinkers. ⁶⁷And of the fruits of the date-palm, and grapes, from which you derive strong drink and good nourishment. Indeed, in this is indeed a sign for people who have sense. ⁶⁸And your Lord inspired the bee, saying, Choose dwelling places in the hills and in the trees and in what they build, ⁶⁹Then eat of all fruits, and follow the ways of your Lord, made easy. There comes forth from their bellies a drink of various colors, in which is healing for mankind. Indeed, in this is indeed a sign for people who reflect. ⁷⁰And Allah creates you, then causes you to die, and among you is he who is brought back to the most humble stage of life, so that he knows nothing after knowledge. Indeed, Allah is the knower, powerful. ⁷¹And Allah has favored some of you above others in provision.

Now those who are more favored will by no means hand over their provision to those whom their right hands possess, so that they may be equal with them in that respect. Is it then the favor of Allah that they deny? ⁷²And Allah has given you wives of your own kind, and has given you, from your wives, sons and grandsons, and has made provision of good things for you. Is it then in vanity that they believe and in the favor of Allah that they disbelieve? ⁷³And they worship besides Allah what possess no provision whatsoever for them from the heavens or the earth, nor do they have any power. ⁷⁴So do not make comparisons for Allah. Indeed, Allah knows, you do not know. ⁷⁵Allah makes a comparison, a slave, who has control of nothing, and one on whom we have bestowed a fair provision from us, and he spends from it secretly and openly. Are they equal? Praise be to Allah. But most of them do not know. ⁷⁶And Allah makes a comparison, Two men, one of them dumb, having control of nothing, and he is a burden on his owner, wherever he directs him to go, he brings no good. Is he equal with one who enjoins justice and follows a straight path? ⁷⁷And to Allah belongs the unseen of the heavens and the earth, and the matter of the hour is but as a twinkling of the eye, or it is nearer still. Indeed, Allah is able to do all things. ⁷⁸And Allah brought you forth from the wombs of your mothers knowing nothing, and gave you hearing and sight and hearts so that perhaps you might give thanks. ⁷⁹Have they not seen the birds obedient in midair? No one holds them except Allah. Indeed, in this, truly, are signs for a people who believe. ⁸⁰And Allah has given you in your houses a dwelling place, and has given you, from the hides of cattle, houses which you find light on the day of migration and on the day of pitching camp, and of their wool and their fur and their hair, furnishings and comfort for a while. [81]And Allah has given you, of what he has created, shelter from the sun, and has given you places of refuge in the mountains, and has given you coats to ward off the heat from you, and coats to save you from your own foolhardiness. In this way, he perfects his favor to you, so that you may submit.

[82]Then, if they turn away, your duty is just clear proclamation.

[83]They know the favor of Allah and then deny it. Most of them are ingrates. [84]And the day when we raise up a witness from every nation, then there is no permission for unbelievers, nor are they allowed to make amends. [85]And when those who did wrong see the doom, it will not be made light for them, nor will they be reprieved. [86]And when those who ascribed partners to Allah see those partners of theirs, they will say, Our Lord, these are our partners to whom we used to call upon instead of to you. But they will throw back to them the saying, Indeed, you truly are liars. [87]And they offer submission to Allah on that day, and all that they used to fabricate has failed them. [88]For those who disbelieve and bar people from the way of Allah, we add doom to doom, because they spread corruption, [89]And the day when we raise in every nation a witness against them from their own people, and we bring you as a witness against these. And we reveal the book to you as an explanation of all things, and

a guidance and a mercy and good news for the Muslims. [90]Indeed, Allah commands justice and kindness, and giving to relatives, and forbids lewdness and abomination and wickedness. He exhorts you so that you may be mindful. [91]Fulfil the covenant of Allah when you have made a covenant, and do not break your oaths after you have taken them, and after you have made Allah a witness over you. Indeed, Allah knows what you do. [92]And do not be like her who unravels the thread after she has made it strong, to thin filaments, making your oaths a deceit between you because of a nation being more numerous than a nation. Allah only tests you in this, and he indeed will explain to you on the day of resurrection what you disagreed about.

[93]If Allah had willed, he could have made you one nation, but he leads astray those whom he wills and guides those whom he wills, and you will indeed be asked about what you used to do. [94]Do not make your oaths a deceit between you, so that a foot doesn't slip after being firmly planted and you taste evil for barring people from the way of Allah, and yours would be an awful doom. [95]And do not buy a small gain at the price of Allah's covenant. Indeed, what Allah has is better for you, if you only knew. [96]What you have wastes away, and what Allah has remains. And indeed we reward those who are steadfast in proportion to the best of what they used to do. [97]Whoever does right, whether male or female, and is a believer, indeed we will give him new life,

---

93. The *Tafsir al-Jalalayn* glosses this verse as: "If Allah had willed, He would have made you one community having a single *din* [religion], but He misguides anyone He wills and guides anyone He wills."[10] Without noting any discrepancy, he continues: "You will be questioned on the Day of Rising about what you did and then you will be repaid for it."[11]

Instead of, "He leads astray," a Qur'anic manuscript examined by Mingana has, "Allah leads astray."[12]

96. Instead of "we reward," the Warsh Qur'an has "he rewards."[13]

and we will reward them in proportion to the best of what they used to do. **98**And when you recite the Qur'an, seek refuge in Allah from Satan the outcast. **99**Indeed, he has no power over those who believe and put trust in their Lord. **100**His power is only over those who make a friend of him, and those who ascribe partners to him. **101**And when we put a sign in place of a sign, and Allah knows best what he reveals, they say, indeed, you are just fabricating. Most of them do not know. **102**Say, The holy spirit has delivered it from your Lord with truth, so that it may confirm those who believe, and as guidance and good news for the Muslims. **103**And we know well that they say, Only a man teaches him. The speech of him about whom they falsely hint is foreign, and this is clear Arabic. **104**Indeed, those who disbelieve the signs of Allah, Allah does not guide them and theirs will be a painful doom. **105**They only invent falsehood who do not believe Allah's signs, and they are the liars. **106**Whoever disbelieves in Allah after his belief, except he who is forced to do so and whose heart is still content with the faith, but whoever finds ease in disbelief, on them is wrath from Allah. Theirs will be an awful doom. **107**That

is because they have chosen the life of the world rather than the hereafter, and because Allah does not guide the disbelieving people. **108**Such people are those whose hearts and ears and eyes Allah has sealed. And such are the heedless. **109**Surely in the hereafter they are the losers. **110**Then indeed, your Lord, for those who became fugitives after they had been persecuted, and then fought and were steadfast, indeed, your Lord afterward is indeed forgiving, merciful. **111**On the day when every soul will come pleading for itself, and every soul will be repaid for what it did, and they will not be wronged. **112**Allah makes a comparison, a town that dwelled secure and content, its provision coming to it in abundance from every side, but it disbelieved in Allah's favors, so Allah made it experience the clothing of dearth and fear because of what they used to do. **113**And indeed there had come to them a messenger from among them, but they denied him, and so the torment seized them while they were wrongdoers. **114**So eat of the lawful and good food which Allah has provided for you, and thank the bounty of your Lord if it is him you serve. **115**He has forbidden for you only carrion and blood and the flesh of

---

101. On abrogation, see 2:106.

103. The unbelievers claim that the messenger is learning the contents of the Qur'an from a man and then passing them off as divine revelation, but the one they have in mind is a foreigner, while the Qur'an is in pure Arabic. Ibn Kathir grants that "maybe the Messenger of Allah used to sit with him sometimes and talk to him a little, but he was a foreigner who did not know much Arabic, only enough simple phrases to answer questions when he had to."14

In Islamic tradition several people have been identified as the person to whom this verse is referring. Some suggest Muhammad's wife's uncle Waraqa, who first identified him as a prophet, and who used to, according to Islamic tradition, "write from the Gospel in Hebrew as much as Allah wished him to write."15

Another possibility is that the man of foreign tongue was one of Muhammad's companions, Salman the Persian: the Arabic word translated here as "foreign" is *ajami*, which also means Persian.

Since all these traditions date from the ninth century, and there is no trace of them earlier, their historical value for illuminating events of the seventh century cannot be assumed to be high. It may be that this verse is designed to counter the fact that Persian traditions were used in the compilation of the Qur'an and that this was known to critics of the new religion. For Persian influence in the Qur'an, see 17:1 and 55:72. For the Qur'an's repeatedly proclaimed Arabic character, see 12:2.

106. In a notable departure from the Christian concept of martyrdom, Allah allows Muslims to deny their faith when forced to do so. Ibn Kathir explains: "This is an exception in the case of one who utters statements of disbelief and verbally agrees with the *Mushrikin* [unbelievers] because he is forced to do so by the beatings and abuse to which he is subjected, but his heart refuses to accept what he is saying, and he is, in reality, at peace with his faith in Allah and His Messenger."16 This is another foundation for the idea of religious deception in Islam. See also 3:28.

pigs and what has been sacrificed in the name of anyone other than Allah, but he who is forced to this, neither craving nor transgressing, indeed, then Allah is forgiving, merciful. **116**And do not speak about what your own tongues describe, the falsehood, This is lawful, and this is forbidden, so that you invent a lie against Allah. Indeed, those who invent a lie against Allah will not succeed. **117**A brief enjoyment, and theirs a painful doom. **118**And to those who are Jews, we have forbidden what we have already told you. And we did not wrong them, but they were inclined to wrong themselves. **119**Then indeed, your Lord, for those who do evil in ignorance and afterward repent and change, indeed, your Lord is afterward indeed forgiving, merciful. **120**Indeed, Abraham was a nation obedient to Allah, a *hanif*, and he was not among the idolaters, **121**Thankful for his bounties, he chose him and he guided him to a straight path. **122**And we gave him good in the world, and

in the hereafter he is among the righteous. **123**And afterward we inspired you, Follow the religion of Abraham, *hanif*. He was not among the idolaters. **124**The sabbath was established only for those who disagreed about it, and indeed, your Lord will judge between them on the day of resurrection over what they used to disagree about.

125 Call them to the way of your Lord with wisdom and beautiful preaching, and reason with them in the better way. Indeed, your Lord is best aware of the one who departs from his path, and he is best aware of those who are guided. **126**If you punish, then punish with the equivalent of what you were afflicted with. But if you endure patiently, indeed it is better for the patient. **127**Endure patiently. Your endurance is only by Allah. Do not grieve for them, and do not be in distress because of what they devise. **128**Indeed, Allah is with those who keep their duty to him and those who are doers of good.

---

120. On *hanif*, see 2:135, as also at 16:123.

125. "Wisdom and beautiful preaching" is an appealing phrase; however, in a hadith, Muhammad has been depicted as telling Muslims to follow up the "invitation," if refused, with a second invitation asking non-Muslims to enter the Islamic social order as dhimmis, with institutionalized second-class status; or if they refuse both, to go to war with them: "Fight against those who disbelieve in Allah. Make a holy war...When you meet your enemies who are polytheists, invite them to three courses of action. If they respond to any one of these you also accept it and withhold yourself from doing them any harm. Invite them to (accept) Islam; if they respond to

you, accept it from them and desist from fighting against them.... If they refuse to accept Islam, demand from them the Jizya. If they agree to pay, accept it from them and hold off your hands. If they refuse to pay the tax, seek Allah's help and fight them."17 See 9:29.

126. One should respond to attacks by striking the attacker in the same way (cf. 2:194, 5:45), but patient endurance is better, although it does not remove the obligations of 8:39, 9:29, and the like. As those passages from sura 8 and 9 are generally considered in Islamic tradition to have been revealed after this verse, they take precedence over it (see 2:106).

The Night Journey

Al-Isra

Introduction

A hadith has one of Muhammad's companions, Abdullah ibn Masud, who is said to have made his own version of the Qur'an, say of this sura, along with suras 18 and 19: "They are among the earliest and most beautiful Surahs and they are my treasure."[1]

In another hadith, Aisha says: "The Prophet would not sleep until he recited Surat Bani Isra'il and Az-Zumar." Surat Bani Isra'il, the sura of the tribe of Israel, is an alternate name for this sura. Az-Zumar, The Troops, is sura 39.

---

1 Ibn Kathir, V, 550.

The Night Journey

In the name of Allah, the compassionate, the merciful.

1May he be glorified who carried his servant by night from the sacred mosque to the farthest mosque, around which we have blessed, so that we might show him some of our signs. Indeed, he, only he, is the hearer, the seer. **2**We gave Moses the book, and we established it as a guidance for the children of Israel, saying, Choose no guardian besides me. **3**The descendants of those whom we carried along with Noah. Indeed, he was a grateful slave. **4**And we decreed for the children of Israel in the book, You indeed will spread corruption on the earth twice, and you will become great tyrants. **5**So when the time for the first of the two came, we raised up against you slaves of ours of great might who ravaged the country, and it was a threat performed. **6**Then we gave you once again your turn against them, and we aided you with wealth and children and made you better soldiers. **7**If you do good, you do good for your own souls, and if you do evil, it is for them. So when the time for the second, they came to ravage you, and to enter the Temple even as they entered it the first time, and to lay waste to all that they conquered with an utter wasting. **8**It may be that your Lord will have mercy on you, but if you repeat, we will repeat, and we have established Gehenna as a dungeon for the unbelievers. **9**Indeed, this Qur'an guides people to what is straightest, and gives the news to the believers who do good works that theirs will be a great reward. **10**And that those who do not believe in the hereafter, for them we have prepared a painful doom. **11**Man

1. The Islamic claim to Jerusalem is based upon Muhammad's Night Journey to the city, which is mentioned only in the hadith and sira literature. According to ninth-century traditions, Muhammad was miraculously transported from Mecca to the Temple Mount, and from there to paradise itself. There he is greeted by a succession of earlier prophets, including Adam, John the Baptist, Jesus, Joseph, Moses, and others, and is given the command for the Muslims to pray five times a day.

The Qur'an's only reference to this journey is in this verse, which says that Allah took the messenger "from the sacred mosque to the farthest [al-aqsa] mosque." There was no mosque in Jerusalem at this time that Muhammad is supposed to have lived, so the "farthest" mosque could not have been the Al-Aqsa Mosque that was built on the Temple Mount toward the end of the seventh century, unless the Qur'an passage itself was written after that mosque was built. Given the absence of evidence for the existence of the Qur'an before the time around which the Al-Aqsa Mosque was built, this is entirely possible.

William St. Clair Tisdall notes that this tradition is incorporated from the Zoroastrian tradition, and so may be an example of the Persian influence on the Qur'an that is heatedly denied at 16:103. Tisdall states that "a Pahlavi book called *Arta Viraf Namak*, written in the days of Ardashir, some four hundred years before the Hegira," contains an account of the Magi of Persia "sending a Zoroastrian of the above name [that is, Arta Viraf] up to heaven, with the view of bringing down tidings of what was going on there. This messenger ascended from one heaven to another, and having seen it all, was commanded by Ormazd [the Zoroastrian deity] to return to the earth, and tell it to his people."[1] Tisdall concludes: "There is no doubt a singular resemblance between the ascent of this Magian messenger, and that also told of Mohammed, to the heaven above."[2]

Instead of "around which we have blessed," a Qur'anic manuscript examined by Mingana has "around which we have knelt down."[3]

4. Regarding "corruption on the earth," see 5:33. Ibn Kathir elaborates: "Allah tells us that He made a declaration to the Children of Israel in the Scripture, meaning that He had already told them in the Book which He revealed to them, that they would cause mischief on the earth twice, and would become tyrants and extremely arrogant, meaning they would become shameless oppressors of people."[4]

5. The identity of the "slaves of ours of great might" whom Allah raised up against the Jews is unclear. Ibn Kathir doesn't trust accounts from Jewish sources, apparently including Jewish Scriptures: "Some of them are fabricated, concocted by their heretics, and others may be true, but we have no need of them, praise be to Allah. What Allah has told us in His Book (the Qur'an) is sufficient and we have no need of what is in the other books that came before. Neither Allah nor His Messenger required us to refer to them."[5] For the Jews' disobedience to Allah, "Their humiliation and subjugation was a befitting punishment."[6]

8. On Gehenna, see 2:206, as also at 17:18, 17:39, 17:63, and 17:97.

prays for evil as he prays for good, for man was always hasty. **12**And we establish the night and the day two signs. Then we make dark the sign of the night, and we make the sign of the day brightness, so that you may seek bounty from your Lord, and so that you may know the computation of the years, and the reckoning, and we have explained everything with a clear explanation. **13**And every man's fate we have fastened to his own neck, and we will bring forth for him on the day of resurrection a book that he will find wide open. **14**Read your Book. Your soul is sufficient as reckoner against you this day. **15**Whoever goes right, it is only for his own soul that he goes right, and whoever goes astray, goes astray only to its hurt. No burdened soul can bear another's load, we never punish until we have sent a messenger. **16**And when we wish to destroy a town, we command its people who live at ease, and afterward they commit abominations in it, and so the word has effect for it, and we destroy it with complete annihilation. **17**How many generations we have destroyed since Noah. And Allah is sufficient as the knower and watcher of the sins of his slaves. **18**Whoever desires what hastens away, we hasten for him what we will, for those whom we please. And afterward we have appointed Gehenna for him, he will endure the heat of it, condemned, rejected. **19**And whoever desires the hereafter and works for it with the necessary effort, being a believer, for such people, their effort finds favor.

20We supply each, both these and those, from the bounty of your Lord. And the bounty of your Lord can never be walled up. **21**See how we prefer one of them above another, and indeed the hereafter will be greater in degrees and greater in preferment. **22**Do not set up any other god with Allah, so that you do not sit down reproved, forsaken. **23**Your Lord has decreed that you worship no one except him, and kindness to parents. If one of them or both of them attain old age with you, do not say a word of contempt to them or repulse them, but speak a gracious word to them. **24**And lower the wing of submission to them through mercy, and say, My Lord, have mercy on them both, as they cared for me when I was little. **25**Your Lord is best aware of what is in your minds. If you are righteous, then indeed, he was always forgiving to those who turn.

26Give the relative his due, and the needy, and the wayfarer, and do not waste in wantonness. **27**Indeed, the wasteful have always been brothers of the satans, and Satan has always been ungrateful to his Lord. **28**But if you turn away from them, seeking mercy from your Lord, for which you hope, then speak to them a reasonable word. **29**And do not let your hand be chained to your neck, and do not open it with a complete opening, so that you do not sit down rebuked, destitute. **30**Indeed, your Lord enlarges the provision for those whom he wills, and reduces. Indeed, he has always been the knower, the seer of his slaves. **31**Do not kill

---

15. No one can bear another's burdens, but 29:13 says that unbelievers "will truly bear their own burdens and other burdens beside their own."

22. Here begins the elucidation of a specific moral code, the closest the Qur'an gets to anything like the Ten Commandments. Muslims should worship Allah alone (17:22); be kind to their parents (17:23, but see 9:23 and 60:4); provide for their relatives, the needy, and travelers, and not be wasteful (17:26); not kill their

children for fear of poverty (17:31); not commit adultery (17:32); "not take life, which Allah has made sacred," with a notable caveat: "except for a just cause," and to make restitution for wrongful death (17:33, see 2:178); not seize the wealth of orphans (17:34); "give full measure when you measure, and weigh with a right balance" (17:35); "not follow what you have no knowledge about" (17:36); "not walk on the earth insolently" (17:37). Theft is not listed here but is at 5:38.

your children, fearing a fall into poverty. We will provide for them and for you. Indeed, the killing of them is great sin. **32**And do not come near to adultery. Indeed, it is an abomination and an evil way. **33**And do not take life, which Allah has made sacred, except for a just cause. Whoever is wrongfully killed, we have given power to his heir, but do not let him commit excess in killing. Indeed, he will be helped. **34**Do not come near the wealth of the orphan except with what is better until he comes to strength, and keep the covenant. Indeed, the covenant will be asked about. **35**Give full measure when you measure, and weigh with a right balance, that is fitting, and better in the end. **36**Do not follow what you have no knowledge about. Indeed, the hearing and the sight and the heart, each of these will be asked about. **37**And do not walk on the earth insolently. Indeed, you cannot tear the earth apart, nor can you stretch to the height of the hills. **38**The evil of all of that is hateful in the sight of your Lord. **39**This is some of that wisdom with which your Lord has inspired you. And do not set up with Allah any other god, so that you will not be thrown into Gehenna, reproved, abandoned. **40**Has your Lord then distinguished you by giving you sons, and has chosen for himself females from among the angels? Indeed, truly you speak an awful word. **41**We indeed have displayed in this Qur'an so that they may take note, but it increases nothing in them except aversion. **42**Say, If there were other gods along with him, as they say, then they would have searched for a way against the Lord of the throne. **43**May he be glorified and highly exalted above what they say. **44**The seven heavens and the earth and all that is in them praise him, and there is not a thing that does not sing his praise, but you do not understand their praise. Indeed, he is always merciful, forgiving. **45**And when you recite the Qur'an, we place a hidden veil between you and those who do not believe in the hereafter, **46**And we place veils upon their hearts so that they do not understand it, and in their ears a deafness, and when you make mention of your Lord alone in the Qur'an, they turn their backs in aversion. **47**We are best aware of what they wish to hear when they give ear to you and when they have secret consultations, when the evildoers say, You're just following a bewitched man. **48**See what comparisons they make for you, and in this way all are astray, and cannot find a path. **49**And they say, When we are bones and fragments, will we really be raised up as a new creation? **50**Say, Even if you were stones or iron, **51**Or some created thing that is even greater in your thoughts. Then they will say, Who will bring us back? Say, He who created you at first. Then will they shake their heads at you, and say, When will it be? Say, It will perhaps be soon, **52**A day when he will call you and you will answer with his praise, and you will think that you have lingered only a little while. **53**Tell my slaves to speak what is kindlier. Indeed, Satan sows discord among them. Indeed, Satan is an open enemy for man. **54**Your Lord is best aware of you. If he wills, he will have mercy on you, or if he wills, he will punish you. We have not sent you as a guardian over them. **55**And your Lord is best aware of all who are in the heavens and the earth. And we preferred some of the prophets above others, and to David we gave the

---

40. See 16:57.
42. Instead of "as they say," the Warsh Qur'an has "as you say."7

46. See 7:179, 10:99, and 32:13.
55. See 3:184.

Psalms. **56**Say, Call upon those whom you assume besides him, yet they have no power to rid you of misfortune nor to change. **57**Those to whom they call seek the way of approach to their Lord, which among them will be the nearest, they hope for his mercy and they fear his doom. Indeed, the torment of your Lord is to be shunned. **58**There is not a town that we will not destroy before the day of resurrection, or punish it with severe punishment. That is set forth in the book.

59Nothing hinders us from sending signs except that the people of old denied them. And we gave Thamud the camel, a clear sign in order to warn. **60**And when we told you, Indeed, your Lord encompasses mankind, and we appointed the sight which we showed you as an ordeal for mankind, and the cursed tree in the Qur'an. We warn them, but it increases them in nothing except gross impiety. **61**And when we said to the angels, Fall down prostrate before Adam and they fell prostrate, all except Iblis, he said, Will I fall prostrate before what you have created out of clay? **62**He said, Do you see this whom you have honored above me, if you give me favor until the day of resurrection I will indeed seize his descendants, except for a few. **63**He said, Go, and whoever among them follows you, indeed, Gehenna will be your payment, ample payment. **64**And startle with your voice any of them whom you can, and urge your horse and foot against them, and be a partner in their wealth and children, and

promise them. Satan promises them only in order to deceive. **65**Indeed, my slaves, over them you hast no power, and your Lord is sufficient as guardian. **66**Your Lord is he who steers the ship on the sea for you so that you may seek his bounty. Indeed, he has always been merciful toward you. **67**And when harm touches you upon the sea, all those whom you call upon fail except him, but when he brings you safely to land, you turn away, for man has always been ungrateful. **68**Do you then feel secure that he will not cause a slope of the land to engulf you, or send a sandstorm upon you, and then you will find that you have no protector? **69**Or do you feel secure that he will not return you to that a second time, and send against you a hurricane of wind and drown you for your ingratitude, and then you will not find in it that you have any avenger against us? **70**Indeed we have honored the children of Adam. We carry them on the land and the sea, and have made provision of good things for them, and have preferred them above many of those whom we created with a definite preference. **71**On the day when we will summon all men with their record, whoever is given his book in his right hand, such people will read their book and they will not be wronged even a bit. **72**Whoever is blind here will be blind in the hereafter, and even farther from the road. **73**And they indeed tried hard to seduce you away from what we have inspired you with, so that you would invent against us something other than

59. See 11:64.

61. See 7:11.

64. Luxenberg points out that to say that Satan should "startle" people with his voice contradicts 114:5, where "the evil whisperer," who is presumably Satan, "whispers in the hearts of mankind." Examining the Syro-Aramaic substratum of the Qur'anic passage, he posits that the passage actually reads: "And turn away with your voice any of them whom you can, outwit them with your snare and

your lies and deception, tempt them with wealth and children, and promise them. Satan promises them only in order to deceive."[8]

68. See 3:137.

73. The *Ruhul Ma'ani* says that the Quraysh "asked the Holy Prophet to replace the verses containing punishment to verses containing mercy and vice versa," which would make the verses of mercy much more plentiful.[9] But Allah kept Muhammad from being thus beguiled. For another explanation, see 53:19.

it, and then they would have accepted you as a friend. [74]And if we had not made you wholly firm, you might almost have inclined to them a little. [75]Then we would have made you taste double of living and double of dying, then you would have found no helper against us. [76]And they indeed wanted to scare you away from the land so that they might drive you out from there, and then they would have stayed only a little while after you. [77]Our method in the case of those whom we sent before you, and you will not find in our method anything that has changed. [78]Establish prayer at the setting of the sun until the dark of night, and the Qur'an at dawn. Indeed, the Qur'an at dawn is always witnessed. [79]And some part of the night awaken for it, an additional prayer for you. It may be that your Lord will raise you to a praised status. [80]And say, My Lord, cause me to come in with a firm entrance and to go out with a firm exit. And give me a sustaining power from your presence. [81]And say, Truth has come and falsehood has vanished away. Indeed, falsehood is always bound to vanish. [82]And we reveal of the Qur'an what is a healing and a mercy for believers, though it increases the evildoers in nothing except ruin. [83]And when we make life pleasant to man, he turns away and is averse, and when evil touches him, he is in despair. [84]Say, Each one acts according to his rule of conduct, and your Lord is best aware of him whose way is right. [85]They are asking you about the spirit. Say, The spirit is by command of my Lord, and of knowledge you have been given only a little. [86]And if we willed, we could withdraw what we have revealed to you, then you would find no guardian for you against us in regard to it, [87]Except mercy from your Lord. Indeed, his kindness to you has always been great. [88]Say, Indeed, even if mankind and the jinn assembled to produce something like this Qur'an, they could not produce anything like it, even though they were helpers one of another. [89]And indeed we have displayed for mankind in this Qur'an all kind of comparisons, but most of mankind refuse anything except disbelief. [90]And they say, We will not put faith in you until you cause a spring to gush forth from the earth for us, [91]Or you have a garden of date-palms and grapes, and cause rivers to gush forth in it abundantly, [92]Or you cause the heaven to fall upon us in pieces, as you have pretended, or bring Allah and the angels as a justification, [93]Or you have a house of gold, or you ascend up into heaven, and even then we will put no faith in your ascension until you bring down for us a book that we can read. Say, May my Lord be glorified! Am I anything except a mortal messenger? [94]And nothing prevented mankind from believing when the guidance came to them except the fact that they said, Has Allah sent a mortal as messenger? [95]Say, If there were angels walking secure on the earth, we would have sent down from heaven for them an angel as messenger. [96]Say, Allah is sufficient as a witness between

---

Instead of, "And they indeed tried hard to seduce you away from what we have inspired you with," the Shi'ite Bankipur Qur'an manuscript has, "And they indeed tried hard to seduce you away from what we have inspired you with in Ali."[10] See 2:59 and the Appendix: Two Apocryphal Shi'ite Suras.

82. See 9:14. Instead of, "though it increases the evildoers in nothing except ruin," the Shi'ite Bankipur Qur'an manuscript has, "though it increases those who wrong the family of Muhammad in nothing except ruin."[11] See 2:59 and the Appendix: Two Apocryphal Shi'ite Suras.

88. See 2:23 and 10:38.

me and you. Indeed, he is the knower, the seer of his slaves. **97**And he whom Allah guides, he is led rightly, while as for him whom he leads astray, for them you will find no protecting friends beside him, and we will assemble them on the day of resurrection on their faces, blind, dumb and deaf, their dwelling place will be Gehenna, whenever it abates, we increase the flame for them. **98**That is their reward because they disbelieved our signs and said, When we are bones and fragments, will we really be raised up as a new creation? **99**Haven't they seen that Allah who created the heavens and the earth is able to create something like them, and has established for them an end of which there is no doubt? But the wrongdoers refuse anything except disbelief. **100**Say, If you possessed the treasures of the mercy of my Lord, you would surely hold them back for fear of spending, for man has always been grudging. **101**And indeed we gave nine signs to Moses, clear proofs. Ask the children of Israel how he came to them, then Pharaoh said to him, Indeed, I consider you to be bewitched, O Moses. **102**He said, In truth you know that no one sent these down as proofs except the Lord of the heavens and the earth, and indeed, I consider you lost, O Pharaoh. **103**And he wished to frighten them out of the land, but we drowned him and those with him, all together. **104**And we said to the children of Israel after him, Dwell in the land, but when the promise of the hereafter comes to pass, we will bring you as a crowd gathered out of various nations. **105**With truth have we sent it down, and with truth it has descended. And we have sent you as nothing else except a bearer of good news and a warner. **106**And a Qur'an that we have divided, so that you might recite it to mankind at intervals, and we have revealed it by sign. **107**Say, Believe in it or do not believe, indeed, those who were given knowledge before it, when it is read to them, fall down prostrate on their faces, adoring, **108**Saying, Glory to our Lord! Indeed the promise of our Lord must be fulfilled. **109**They fall down on their faces, weeping, and it increases humility in them. **110**Say, Call upon Allah, or cry to Ar-Rahman, to whichever one you call upon. His are the most beautiful names. And you, don't be loud in your prayer or silent in it, but follow a way between. **111**And say, Praise be to Allah, who has not taken to himself a son, and who has no partner in the dominion, nor has he any protecting friend through dependence. And magnify him with all magnificence.

---

97. See 7:179, 10:99, and 32:13. "Flame" is *sa'ir*; see 4:10.

101. Another telling of the story of Moses and Pharaoh (see also 2:49, 3:11, 7:103, 8:52, 10:75, 11:96, 14:6, 17:101, 20:24, 23:46, 26:11, 27:12, 28:3, 29:39, 38:12, 40:24, 44:17, 50:13, 51:38, 54:41, 66:11, 69:9, 73:15, 79:15, 85:18, and 89:10). Pharaoh remains obstinate and denies Moses's claims in language similar to the unbelievers' dismissal of the messenger in 17:47. On the paradigmatic character of the prophetic stories, see 7:59.

104. The *Tafsir Ibn Abbas* identifies "the land" as "Jordan and Palestine."[12] But see 5:21 and 14:13.

110. "The compassionate" is Ar-Rahman, the middle term of the Islamic invocation *Bismillah Ar-Rahman Al-Rahim*, "In the name of Allah, the compassionate, the merciful." This verse appears to be addressing some who believed Ar-Rahman was a deity distinct from Al-Lah, and the messenger is instructed to tell them that they are but two different names for the same being. According to Ibn Kathir, "One of the idolaters heard the Prophet saying when he was prostrating: 'O Most Gracious, O Most Merciful.' The idolator said, he claims to pray to One, but he is praying to two! Then Allah revealed this Ayah [verse, or sign]."[13]

Ar-Rahman was the name of a pagan god in pre-Islamic Arabia. Thus the Qur'an's use of the name may have been an attempt to bring together two gods into one, in order to unify the camps of those who worshipped each. There is even a hint of this in the Qur'an: see 38:5.

The use of Ar-Rahman in this verse and elsewhere may also be an indication of traditions, and likely even written material, connected to the worship of this god being incorporated into Islam.

SURA 18

The Cave

Al-Kahf

Introduction

This sura is traditionally classified as another Meccan sura; it occupies a unique place in Muslim piety. A tradition depicts Muhammad saying that one who memorized the first ten verses of this sura (or, in some versions, the last ten) would "be protected from the trial of the dajjal," the Islamic version of the anti-Christ.[1] Another hadith has him saying that if a Muslim recites sura 18 on a Friday, "it will illuminate him with light from one Friday to the next."[2]

Sura 18 contains some key material for Islamic folklore and Sufi mysticism. According to Ibn Hisham, this sura was revealed after the pagan Quraysh sent an emissary to the Jewish rabbis of Medina, asking them about Muhammad's prophetic claims. The rabbis responded: "Ask him about three things of which we will instruct you; if he gives you the right answer then he is an authentic prophet, but if he does not, then the man is a rogue, so form your own opinion about him. Ask him what happened to the young men who disappeared in ancient days, for they have a marvelous story."[3] That story is told in this sura (18:9–26); the young men disappeared into a cave, from which the title of this sura comes.

The rabbis continued: "Ask him about the mighty traveler who reached the confines of both East and West."[4] That story is at 18:83–98 "Ask him

---

1 Mishkat al-Masabih, 2146https://sunnah.com/mishkat/8/37; *Sunan Abu Dawud* 4323.
2 Mishkat al-Masabih, 2175https://sunnah.com/mishkat/8/65.
3 Ibn Ishaq, 136.
4 Ibid.

what the spirit is. If he can give you the answer, then follow him, for he is a prophet. If he cannot, then he is a forger and treat him as you will."[5] So this sura is offered, at least in this view, as a validation of Muhammad's claim to be a prophet. Whether the sura came first or these questions regarding what became its contents, however, is unclear.

Sura 18's importance in Muslim piety is affirmed in numerous hadiths. In one, a man was reciting the sura when "a cloud came down and spread over that man, and it kept on coming closer and closer to him till his horse started jumping (as if afraid of something). When it was morning, the man came to the Prophet, and told him of that experience. The Prophet said, 'That was As-Sakina (tranquility) which descended because of (the recitation of) the Qur'an.'"[6] As-Sakina is an adaptation of the Hebrew Shekinah, which refers in Jewish tradition to God's presence in the world, and the cloud clearly recalls the cloud that accompanies God's presence in Biblical passages such as Exodus 40:35. Like other Biblical concepts imported into Islam—notably, Jesus as the "Word of God"—it doesn't have this strong a connotation in Islamic thought. It occurs in the Qur'an at 2:248, 9:26, 9:40, 48:4, 48:18, and 48:26, and is generally translated simply as "tranquility."

Another hadith has Muhammad describe the anti-Christ figure of Islamic eschatology, the dajjal, as "a young man with very curly hair with one eye protruding (with which he cannot see)." When he appears, "he who amongst you survives to see him, should recite over him the opening Ayat of Surat Al-Kahf (i.e., Surat 18: Verses 1–8). He will appear on the way between Syria and Iraq and will spread mischief right and left."[7]

5 Ibid.
6 Bukhari, vol. 6, book 66, no. 5011.
7 Riyad-us-Saliheen, 1808.

The Cave

IN THE NAME OF ALLAH, THE COMPASSIONATE, THE MERCIFUL.

1Praise be to Allah, who has revealed the book to his slave, and has not placed any crookedness in it, **2**Straight, to give warning of stern punishment from him, and to bring to the believers who do good works the news that a fair reward will be theirs, **3**In which they will remain forever, **4**And to warn those who say, Allah has chosen a son, **5**They have no knowledge of this, nor their fathers, Dreadful is the word that comes out of their mouths. They speak nothing but a lie. **6**Yet it may be, if they do not believe in this statement, that you will torment your soul with grief over their footsteps. **7**Indeed, we have placed all that is on the earth as an ornament of it so that we might test them, which of them is best in conduct. **8**And indeed, we will make all that is on it a barren mound. **9**Or do you think that the companions of the cave and the inscription are a wonder among our signs? **10**When the young men fled for refuge to the cave and said, Our Lord, give us mercy from your presence, and show us right conduct in our ordeal. **11**Then we sealed up their hearing in the cave for a number of years. **12**And afterward we raised them up so that we might know which of the two groups would best calculate the time that they had remained. **13**We narrate their story to you with truth. Indeed, they were young men who believed in their Lord, and we increased them in guidance. **14**And we made their hearts firm when they stood forth and said, Our Lord is the Lord of the heavens and the earth. We call upon no God besides him, for then we would utter an untruth. **15**These, our people, have chosen gods besides him, although they bring no clear justification to them. And who does greater wrong than he who fabricates a lie about Allah? **16**And when you withdraw from them and what they worship besides Allah, then seek refuge in the cave, your Lord will spread out his mercy for you and will prepare a pillow for you in your ordeal. **17**And you might have seen the sun when it rose move away from their cave to the right, and when it set go past them on the left, and they were in the cleft of it. That was among the signs of Allah. He whom Allah guides, he indeed is led rightly, and he whom he leads astray, for him you

---

1. The *Tafsir Anwarul Bayan* explains that the Qur'an's lack of "crookedness" means that "there are neither iniquities nor muddling of words in the Qur'an. There is also no shortage of eloquence in it, nor any discrepancies."[1] This is why textual variants cause such controversy among believing Muslims.

4. See 2:116, 9:30, and 19:35.

6. See 2:144.

9. Here begins the story of the "companions of the cave [al-kahf] and the inscription [al-raqim]." The young men slept in the cave for 309 years (18:25), miraculously protected by Allah. There is no agreement on the meaning of al-raqim; some Islamic authorities say it refers to a nearby valley or mountain, while others contend it was the name of a nearby town.[2] Another view is that it was "a tablet of stone on which they wrote the story of the people of the Cave, then they placed it at the entrance to the Cave"—hence, "the Inscription."[3]

This is an adaptation of the Christian story of the Seven Sleepers of Ephesus, who are revered as saints in Byzantine Christianity. These are young men who sought refuge in a cave from the pagans in the pre-Christian Roman Empire, were miraculously protected, and who woke up after the Empire had been Christianized. (Ibn Kathir, however, thinks the story is pre-Christian, since the Jewish rabbis know of it and ask Muhammad about it as one of their tests of his prophethood.[4])

13. The "companions of the cave" were, according to Ibn Kathir, "boys or young men" who were "more accepting of the truth and more guided than the elders who had become stubbornly set in their ways and clung to the religion of falsehood."[5] They acknowledge the oneness of Allah and reject the idols of their people; Allah protects them from the idolaters by sheltering them in the cave.

will not find a guiding friend. **¹⁸**And you would have thought them awake although they were asleep, and we caused them to turn over to the right and the left, and their dog stretching out his paws on the threshold. If you had observed them closely, you would surely have turned away from them and fled, and would have been filled with awe of them. **¹⁹**And in the same way we awakened them so that they might question one another. A speaker from among them said, How long have you remained? They said, We have remained a day or some part of a day. They said, Your Lord knows best how long you have remained. Now send one of you with this silver coin of yours to the city, and let him see what food is purest there and bring you a supply of it. Let him be courteous and let no man know about you. **²⁰**For they, if they come to know about you, will stone you or turn you back to their religion, then you will never prosper. **²¹**And in the same way we revealed them, so that they might know that the promise of Allah is true, and that, as for the hour, there is no doubt about it. When they disagreed about their case among themselves, they said, Build over them a building, their Lord knows best about them. Those who won their point said, We indeed will build a mosque over them. **²²**They will

say, There were three of them, their dog the fourth, and they say, Five, their dog the sixth, guessing at random, and they say, Seven, and their dog the eighth. Say, My Lord is best aware of their number. No one knows them except a few. So do not argue about them except on a clear matter, and do not ask anyone among them to speak about them. **²³**And do not say about anything, Indeed, I will do that tomorrow, **²⁴**Except if Allah wills. And remember your Lord when you forget, and say, It may be that my Lord will guide me to a nearer way of truth than this. **²⁵**And they remained in their cave three hundred years, and nine additional. **²⁶**Say, Allah is best aware of how long they remained. His is the invisible one of the heavens and the earth. How clear of sight he is, and keen of hearing! They have no protecting friend besides him, and he allows no one to share in his government. **²⁷**And recite what has been revealed to you of the book of your Lord. There is no one who can change his words, and you will find no refuge besides him. **²⁸**Restrain yourself along with those who call upon their Lord in the morning and evening, seeking his face, and do not let your eyes overlook them, desiring the splendor of the life of this world, and do not obey him whose heart we have made heedless of our

---

18. Allah "caused them to turn over to the right and the left" presumably to preserve their bodies from decay while they slept, for, in a statement attributed to Ibn Abbas, "If they did not turn over, the earth would have consumed them."⁶ Their dog, meanwhile, was "stretching out his paws on the threshold," indicating that he wasn't precisely inside the cave, so that he wouldn't keep angels from entering it. "He was sitting outside the door," explains Ibn Kathir, "because the angels do not enter a house in which there is a dog, as was reported in As-Sahih, nor do they enter a house in which there is an image, a person in a state of ritual impurity or a disbeliever, as was narrated in the Hasan Hadith."⁷ *Sahih* means "reliable," that is, a hadith that is considered to be authentic; *hasan* is "good," a hadith that cannot be authenticated to the degree to which a sahih hadith can be, but one that is nevertheless trustworthy.

Bukhari records that tradition, in which Muhammad is depicted as saying: "Angels do not enter a house wherein there is a dog or a picture of a living creature."⁸ Nevertheless, continues Ibn Kathir: "The blessing they enjoyed extended to their dog, so the sleep that overtook them overtook him too. This is the benefit of accompanying good people, and so this dog attained fame and stature."⁹

22. The uncertainty as to the number of sleepers is difficult to reconcile with the Qur'an's self-definition as the dictation of the omniscient deity.

27. The message in the passage that begins here is the same as that of Luke 12:15-21: "Fool! This night your soul is required of you; and the things you have prepared, whose will they be?"

remembrance, who follows his own lust and whose case has been abandoned. **29**Say, The truth from your Lord. Then whoever wills, let him believe, and whoever wills, let him disbelieve. Indeed, we have prepared fire for unbelievers. Its tent encloses them. If they ask for showers, they will be showered with water like molten lead that burns their faces. Calamitous the drink and evil the resting-place. **30**Indeed, as for those who believe and do good works, indeed, we do not allow the reward of one whose work is good to be lost. **31**As for such people, theirs will be gardens of Eden, in which rivers flow beneath them, in which they will be given armlets of gold and will wear green robes of finest silk and gold embroidery, reclining upon thrones in them. Blessed the reward, and fair the resting-place. **32**Make a comparison for them. Two men, to one of whom we assigned two gardens of grapes, and We surrounded both with date-palms and had put fields between them. **33**Each of the gardens gave its fruit and withheld none of it. And we caused a river to gush forth in them. **34**And he had fruit. And he said to his comrade, when he spoke with him, I have more than you in wealth, and am stronger in respect of men. **35**And he went into his garden, while he did wrong to himself. He said, I do not think that all this will ever perish. **36**I do not think that the hour will ever come, and if indeed I am brought back to my Lord, I surely will find better than this as a resort. **37**His comrade, when he spoke with him, exclaimed, Do you disbelieve in him who created you out of dust, and then of a drop, and then fashioned you a man? **38**But He is Allah, my Lord, and I ascribe no partner to my Lord. **39**If only, when you entered your garden, you had said, What Allah wills. There is no strength except in Allah. Although you see me as less than you in wealth and children, **40**Yet it may be that my Lord will give me better than your garden, and will send on it a bolt from heaven, and some morning it will be a smooth hillside, **41**Or some morning its water will be lost in the earth so that you cannot find it. **42**And his fruit was ruined. Then he began to lament over all that he had spent upon it, when it was all ruined on its trellises, and to say, If only I had not ascribed any partner to my Lord! **43**And he had no troop of men to help him against Allah, nor could he save himself. **44**In this case there is protection only from Allah, the true, he is the best for reward, and best for consequences. **45**And make the comparison of the life of this world as water that we send down from the sky, and the vegetation of the earth mingles with it and then becomes dry twigs that the winds scatter. Allah is able to do all things. **46**Wealth and children are an ornament of the life of this world. But the good deeds that endure are better in your Lord's sight for reward, and better in respect of hope. **47**And the day when we remove the hills and you see the earth emerging, and we gather them together so as not to leave one of them behind. **48**And they are set before your Lord in ranks, Now indeed you have come to us as we created you at the beginning. But you thought that we had set no appointment

---

29. Instead of, "Indeed, we have prepared fire for unbelievers," the Shi'ite Bankipur Qur'an manuscript has, "Indeed, we have prepared fire for those who deprive the family of Muhammad of its due."[10] See 2:59 and the Appendix: Two Apocryphal Shi'ite Suras.

36. Instead of "better than this" (*minha*) the Warsh Qur'an has "better than both of them" (*minhumaa*).[11]

for you. [49]And the book is placed, and you see the guilty fearful of what is in it, and they say, What kind of a book is this that doesn't leave a small thing or a great thing, but has counted it. And they find all that they did confronting them, and your Lord wrongs no one. [50]And when we said to the angels, Fall prostrate before Adam, and they fell prostrate, all except Iblis. He was one of the jinn, so he rebelled against his Lord's command. Will you choose him and his descendants for your protecting friends instead of me, when they are an enemy to you? What a terrible exchange for evildoers. [51]I did not make them to witness the creation of the heavens and the earth, or their own creation, nor did I choose misleaders for helpers. [52]And the day when he will say, Call those whom you pretended were my partners. Then they will call upon them, but they will not hear their prayer, and we will set a gulf of doom between them. [53]And the guilty see the fire and know that they are about to fall in it, and they find no way of escape from it. [54]And indeed we have displayed for mankind in this Qur'an all manner of comparisons, but man is contentious more than anything. [55]And nothing hinders mankind from believing when the guidance comes to them, and from asking forgiveness of their Lord

unless that the judgment of the men of old should come upon them or they should be confronted with the doom. [56]We do not send the messengers except as bearers of good news and warners. Those who disbelieve contend with falsehood in order to refute the truth by it. And they take our signs and that with which they are threatened as a joke. [57]And who does greater wrong than he who has been reminded of the signs of his Lord, yet turns away from them and forgets what his hands send forward? Indeed, on their hearts we have placed coverings so that they do not understand, and in their ears a deafness. And though you call them to the guidance, in that case they can never be led rightly. [58]Your Lord is the forgiver, full of mercy. If he rebuked them for what they earn, he would hasten on the doom for them, but theirs is an appointed term from which they will find no escape. [59]And those towns, we destroyed them when they did wrong, and we appointed a fixed time for their destruction. [60]And when Moses said to his servant, I will not give up until I reach the point where the two rivers meet, though I march on for ages. [61]And when they reached the point where the two met, they forgot their fish, and it went its way into the waters, being free. [62]And when they had gone farther, he said to his

---

50. Satan's refusal to bow down to Adam is recalled again (see 2:34, 7:11). Here Satan is identified as one of the jinns, as opposed to his identification as an angel at elsewhere (2:34, 7:11, 15:28-31, 20:116, 38:71-74).

60. Here begins one of the strangest, most arresting stories in the entire Qur'an: that of the journey of Moses and the unnamed man who is known in Islamic tradition as Khidr, "the Green Man." Some identify him as one of the prophets, others as a *wali*, a Muslim saint. Whoever he was, he leads Moses through a series of incidents that are all designed to illustrate the point that one should trust in Allah in all circumstances.

The twentieth-century Qur'an translator Abdullah Yusuf Ali offers four lessons from the story, including the idea that "even as the whole stock of the knowledge of the present day, the sciences

and the arts, and in literature, (if it could be supposed to be gathered in one individual), does not include all knowledge. Divine knowledge, as far as man is concerned, is unlimited," and, "There are paradoxes in life: apparent loss may be real gain; apparent cruelty may be real mercy; returning good for evil may really be justice and not generosity (18:79-82). Allah's wisdom transcends all human calculation."[12]

Khidr looms large in Islamic mystical tradition. The eighth-century Sufi mystic Ibrahim Bin Adham (Abou Ben Adhem) once claimed, "In that wilderness I lived for four years. God gave me my eating without any toil of mine. Khidr the Green Ancient was my companion during that time—he taught me the Great Name of God."[13] Some Qur'anic scholars, such as the famed medieval-era commentator Ibn Taymiyya, even consider Khidr to be immortal.[14]

servant, Bring us our breakfast. Indeed we have found fatigue on this journey. **⁶³**He said, Did you see, when we took refuge on the rock, and I forgot the fish, and no one but Satan caused me to forget to mention it, it went its way into the waters in a marvelous way. **⁶⁴**He said, This is what we have been seeking. So they retraced their steps again. **⁶⁵**Then they found one of our slaves, to whom we had given our mercy, and had taught him knowledge from our presence. **⁶⁶**Moses said to him, May I follow you, so that you might teach me right conduct from what you have been taught? **⁶⁷**He said, Indeed, you cannot be patient with me. **⁶⁸**How can you be patient about something you cannot comprehend? **⁶⁹**He said, Allah willing, you will find me patient and I will not in any way disobey you. **⁷⁰**He said, Then if you go with me, do not ask me about anything until I myself mention it to you. **⁷¹**So the two set out until, when they were in the ship, he made a hole in it. He said, Have you made a hole in it to drown the people in it? You have indeed done a dreadful thing. **⁷²**He said, Didn't I tell you that you could not be patient with me? **⁷³**He said, Do not be angry with me that I forgot, and do not be hard upon me for my fault. **⁷⁴**So the two journeyed on until, when they met a boy, he killed him. He said, What? Have you killed an innocent soul who has not killed any man? Indeed you have

done a horrid thing. **⁷⁵**He said, Didn't I tell you that you could not be patient with me? **⁷⁶**He said, If I ask you about anything after this, do not stay with me. You have received an excuse from me. **⁷⁷**So the two journeyed on until, when they came to the people of a certain town, they asked its people for food, but they refused to make them guests. And they found in it a wall on the point of falling into ruin, and he repaired it. He said, If you had wished, you could have taken payment for it. **⁷⁸**He said, This is the parting between you and me. I will explain to you the interpretation of what you could not bear with patience. **⁷⁹**As for the ship, it belonged to poor people working on the river, and I wished to sink it for there was a king behind them who is taking every ship by force. **⁸⁰**And as for the boy, his parents were believers and we were afraid that he would oppress them by rebellion and disbelief. **⁸¹**And we intended that their Lord would exchange him for them for one better in purity and nearer to mercy. **⁸²**And as for the wall, it belonged to two orphan boys in the city, and there was beneath it a treasure belonging to them, and their father had been righteous, and your Lord intended that they should come to their full strength and should bring forth their treasure as a mercy from their Lord, and I did not do it upon my own initiative Such is the interpretation of what you could not

---

80. A hadith asserts that Muhammad "used not to kill the children, so thou shouldst not kill them unless you could know what Khadir had known about the child he killed, or you could distinguish between a child who would grow up to be a believer (and a child who would grow up to be a non-believer), so that you killed the (prospective) non-believer and left the (prospective) believer aside."¹⁵ This may help to explain the persistent phenomenon of

honor killing in Islamic countries and even among Muslims in the West.

Besides Jewish and Christian traditions, Islam also contains some traces of pagan traditions. In fact, the Ka'aba, the Meccan shrine to which every Muslim, if able, is obligated to make at least one pilgrimage, was a pagan Arab shrine and a center of pilgrimage long before Muhammad began preaching Islam.

be patient about. **83**They will ask you about Dhul-Qarnayn. Say, I will recite to you a remembrance of him. **84**Indeed, we made him strong in the land and gave him the means to achieve everything. **85**And he followed a road, **86**Until, when he reached the setting-place of the sun, he found it setting in a spring of muddy water, and found a people nearby. We said, O Dhul-Qarnayn, either punish them or show them kindness. **87**He said, As for him who does wrong, we will punish him, and then he will be brought back to his Lord, who will punish him with awful punishment. **88**But as for him who believes and does right,

good will be his reward, and we will speak a mild command to him. **89**Then he followed a road, **90**Until, when he reached the rising-place of the sun, he found it rising on a people for whom we had appointed no shelter from it. **91**So it was, and we knew everything about him. **92**Then he followed a road, **93**Until, when he came between the two mountains, he found on one side a people that could barely understand word. **94**They said, O Dhul-Qarnayn, indeed, Gog and Magog are spoiling the land. So may we pay you tribute on the condition that you set a barrier between us and them? **95**He said, That in which my Lord has

---

83. According to Islamic tradition, at one point a group of skeptical rabbis devised a test for Muhammad's claim to be a prophet: "Ask him about a man who travelled a great deal and reached the east and the west of the earth. What was his story?"[16] Responding to this challenge, the Qur'an here begins the story of that traveler. Ibn Kathir explains that Dhul-Qarnayn had "dominion over the east and the west, all countries and their kings submitted to him, and all the nations, Arab and non-Arab, served him."[17] Dhul-Qarnayn means "the one with two horns"; Ibn Kathir explains that he got his name "because he reached the two 'Horns' of the sun, east and west, where it rises and where it sets."[18]

The *Tafsir al-Jalalayn* says that "he was not a prophet" and that his name was Alexander, that is, Alexander the Great, who was depicted on coins with two ram's horns on his head.[19] Maududi notes that "early commentators on the Qur'an were generally inclined to believe" that Dhul-Qarnayn was Alexander.[20] The twentieth-century Egyptian scholar Muhammad Al-Ghazali says that Alexander the Great is "high on the list of possibilities."[21] See 18:87 for more on this.

86. This verse has caused Muslims some embarrassment, as it appears to assume a flat earth over which the sun rises and sets. That was standard cosmology at the time the Qur'an was compiled, so this is the most likely understanding of this passage, but even in Ibn Kathir's day it was seen as needing to be explained. According to Ibn Kathir, Dhul-Qarnayn "followed a route until he reached the furthest point that could be reached in the direction of the sun's setting, which is the west of the earth."[22] He didn't actually see the sun setting, he was just watching it from the shore: "He saw the sun as if it were setting in the ocean. This is something which everyone who goes to the coast can see: it looks as if the sun is setting into the sea but in fact it never leaves its path in which it is fixed."[23] So where do people get crazy ideas such as that he actually "reached the setting-place of the sun" in a literal sense? Ibn Kathir blames the Jews and Christians: "Most of these stories come from the myths of the People of the Book and the fabrications and lies of their heretics."[24]

Instead of "spring of muddy water" (*hami'atin*), the Ibn Amir Qur'an has "spring of extremely hot water" (*haameiyatin*).[25]

87. Unlike Alexander the Great, Dhul-Qarnayn was a pious Muslim. Modern-day Islamic scholars show some embarrassment over the fact that earlier commentators insisted that the manifestly pagan Alexander the Great was identified as a Muslim in the Qur'an.[26] Still, the Islamic holy book appropriates numerous non-Muslim figures as Muslims, including Abraham, Moses, all the other Biblical prophets, and Jesus. Thus the appropriation of Alexander the Great is not inconsistent or singular.

Some have suggested instead that Dhul-Qarnayn was Cyrus the Great of Persia or some other great ancient king. But as Muhammad Asad observes, all these pre-Islamic figures were pagans, whereas the Qur'an here depicts Dhul-Qarnayn as a strict Muslim. The consensus today, therefore, is that his exact identification is unknown. Asad concludes that the Qur'anic account "has nothing to do with history or even legend, and that its sole purport is a parabolic discourse on faith and ethics, with specific reference to the problem of worldly power."[27]

As Asad notes, however, because so many commentators have identified Dhul-Qarnayn with Alexander, it is not uncommon to find Muslims asserting this. It also coincides neatly with the Islamic idea, based on a hadith, that Islam was mankind's original religion, and all other religions are simply later corruptions of it. Thus there were in every pre-Islamic age pure monotheists such as Dhul-Qarnayn who were essentially proto-Muslims.

94. Gog and Magog are, according to Ibn Kathir, "among the progeny of Adam."[28] They will "emerge into the land of the Turks and spread mischief there, destroying crops and people."[29] They are important in Islamic eschatology. In a hadith, Muhammad explains that in the end times, "Allah will send Ya'juj and Ma'juj (Gog and Magog people) and they will sworn down from every slope. The first of them will pass the Lake Tabariyah (near the Dead Sea in Palestine) and drink all its water. And when the last of them will pass, he will say: 'There was once water there.'"[30] Jesus will pray to Allah, who will "send insects which will attack their (Ya'juj and Ma'juj people) neck until they all will perish like a single person."[31] Jesus and his disciples "will then come down" (see 4:159), and "they will

established me is better. Just help me with strength, I will set a barrier between you and them. **96**Give me pieces of iron, until, when he had levelled up between the cliffs, he said, Blow, until, when he had made it a fire, he said, Bring me molten copper to pour on it. **97**And they were not able to surmount it, nor could they pierce it. **98**He said, This is a mercy from my Lord, but when the promise of my Lord comes to pass, He will lay it low, for the promise of my Lord is true. **99**And on that day we will let some of them surge against others, and the trumpet will be blown. Then we will gather them together in one gathering. **100**On that day, we will present Gehenna to the unbelievers, clear to view, **101**Those whose eyes were fooled from my reminder, and who could not bear to hear. **102**Do the unbelievers think that they can choose my slaves as protecting friends besides me? Indeed, we have prepared Gehenna as a welcome for the unbelievers. **103**Say, Should we inform you who will be the greatest losers by their works? **104**Those whose effort goes astray in the life of this world, and yet think that they do good work. **105**Those are the ones who disbelieve in the signs of their Lord and in the meeting with him. Therefore their works are vain, and on the day of resurrection, we assign no weight to them. **106**That is their reward, Gehenna, because they disbelieved, and made a joke of our signs and our messengers. **107**Indeed, those who believe and do good works, theirs are the gardens of paradise for welcome, **108**In which they will remain, with no desire to be removed from there. **109**Say, Even if the sea became ink for the words of my Lord, indeed the sea would be used up before the words of my Lord were exhausted, even if we brought something like it to help. **110**Say, I am only a mortal like you. My Lord inspires in me that your God is only one God. And whoever hopes for the meeting with his Lord, let him do righteous work, and make no one share in the worship due to his Lord.

---

not find in the earth as much space as a single span which would not be filled with their corpses and their stench."[32]

No one knows when this will be, but it will be a fearsome day. A hadith depicts one of Muhammad's wives, Zainab bint Jahsh (see 33:37), recounting that one day Muhammad "awoke from sleep with a flushed red face," and said: "Woe to the Arabs from the evil drawn near. Today a gap has been made in the wall of Ya'juj and Ma'juj like this," and he drew a shape in the air with his finger.[33] Zainab asked, "O Messenger of Allah! Shall we be destroyed while there are righteous among us?"[34] He answered: "Yes, when the evil abounds."[35] Another hadith has Muhammad warning that only one out a thousand people would be saved: "one-thousand will be from Gog and Magog, and the one (to be saved will be) from you [Muslims]."[36]

96. Dhul-Qarnayn walls Gog and Magog in between two mountains. This is another reason why he is identified with Alexander the Great, who according to pre-Islamic legend built the Gates, or Wall, of Alexander in the Caucasus in order to protect his empire from the barbarians of the northern regions, who were associated with Gog and Magog of Ezekiel 38-39.

100. On Gehenna, see 2:206, as also at 18:102 and 18:106.

105. A hadith has Muhammad say: "On the Day of Resurrection, a huge fat man will come who will not weigh, the weight of the wing of a mosquito in Allah's Sight."[37] Then he recited this verse.

SURA 19

Mary

Maryam

Introduction

This is, according to Islamic tradition, another Meccan sura. It is said that in the first part of Muhammad's career, a group of Muslims migrated from Arabia to Abyssinia. The legend has it that when the enemies of the Muslims demanded that the Negus, the Christian ruler of Abyssinia, turn the Muslims over to them, one of the Muslims recited part of this sura to the ruler. According to Ibn Hisham, "The Negus wept until his beard was wet and the bishops wept until their scrolls were wet, when they heard what he read to them. Then the Negus said, 'Of a truth, this and what Jesus brought have come from the same niche. You two may go, for by God, I will never give them up to them and they shall not be betrayed.'"[1]

The Muslims' enemies then scheme to get the Negus to change his mind by explaining to him that the Muslims reject the Christian understanding of Jesus as the Son of God. But after hearing the Muslims' defense of their position, the Negus is portrayed as saying: "By God, Jesus, son of Mary, does not exceed what you have said by the length of this stick."[2] He was thus one of the believers among the People of the Book, not one of the "vile" ones who remain unbelievers by not becoming Muslim (see 98:6).

---

1 Ibn Ishaq, 151.
2 Ibid.

Mary

IN THE NAME OF ALLAH, THE COMPASSIONATE, THE MERCIFUL.

[1]Kaf. Ha. Ya. A'in. Sad. [2]A mention of the mercy of your Lord to his slave Zechariah. [3]When he cried out to his Lord a cry in secret, [4]Saying, My Lord, indeed, my bones are getting feeble and my head is shining with grey hair, and I have never been unblessed in prayer to you, my Lord. [5]Indeed, I fear for my relatives after me, since my wife is barren. Give me a heir from your presence, [6]Who will inherit from me and inherit from the house of Jacob. And make him, my Lord, acceptable. [7]O Zechariah, indeed, we bring you news of a son whose name is John, we have given the same name to no one before. [8]He said, My Lord, how can I have a son when my wife is barren and I have reached infirm old age? [9]He said, So it will be. Your Lord says, It is easy for me, even as I created you before, when you were nothing. [10]He said, My Lord, appoint some sign for me. He said, Your sign is that you, with no bodily defect, will not speak to mankind for three nights. [11]Then he came forth to his people from the sanctuary, and signified to them, Glorify your Lord at the break of day and the at nightfall. [12]O John, hold fast to the book. And we gave him wisdom when he was a child, [13]And compassion from our presence, and purity, and he was devout, [14]And dutiful toward his parents. And he was not arrogant, rebellious. [15]Peace on him on the day he was born, and the day he dies, and the day he will be raised alive. [16]And make mention of Mary in the book, when she had withdrawn from her people to a chamber looking East, [17]And had chosen seclusion from them. Then we sent our spirit to her and it assumed for her the likeness of a perfect man. [18]She said, Indeed, I seek refuge in Ar-Rahman from you, if you fear Allah. [19]He said, I am only a messenger of your Lord, so that I may bestow on you a holy son. [20]She said, How can I have a son when no mortal has touched me, nor have I been unchaste? [21]He said, So it will be. Your Lord says,

---

1. On the "mysterious letters," see 2:1.

2. The account of the births of John the Baptist and Jesus generally follows the sequence of the account in Luke 1:5-80, with some differences highlighting the divergences between Christian and Islamic theology. The Qur'anic account begins, as does Luke's account, with the story of Zechariah, the father of John the Baptist, encountering an angel (Luke 1:11). The angel tells him he will become a father despite his old age and his wife's barrenness (19:8). In the Qur'an, unlike in the Gospel, this comes as an answer to his prayer for a son (19:4-6).

10. In both the Gospel (Luke 1:20) and this verse, Zechariah is unable to speak after this vision, although the Qur'an, unlike the Gospel, does not present this as punishment for his unbelief but only as a sign of Allah's power.

There is nothing in the Qur'an paralleling the Gospel's connection of Zechariah's son, John, with Elijah (Luke 1:17), the prophet who was to return before the Lord's coming (Malachi 4:5-6). John is not the messenger sent to prepare the way of the Lord; he is simply pious ("meaning that he was pure and had no inclination to do sins," says Ibn Kathir, in an echo of some Christian traditions that John committed no sins), devout, and kind to his parents (19:13-14).[1]

15. Here begins the story of the birth of Jesus; like the account of the birth of John, it differs significantly from the Gospel account (see 19:19, 19:24).

17. The messenger (19:19) to Mary is not identified in the Qur'an, as in Luke 1:19, as Gabriel. Nor is Mary addressed by a group of angels, as she is at 3:42. Instead, here she is spoken to by "our spirit," in the "likeness of a perfect man." This personage is identified as Gabriel in Islamic tradition.[2] This verse and 26:193 have given rise to the common idea that Gabriel is the Holy Spirit; in Islamic theology, however, this appellation has none of the significance it has in Christianity.[3]

18. On Ar-Rahman, see 17:110 and 38:5.

19. The spirit messenger tells Mary that she will be the mother of a "holy son"; there is nothing about his being "Son of the Most High" (Luke 1:32), a concept rejected again at 19:35.

20. Jesus is virginally conceived, as in Christianity. Ibn Kathir says that many scholars believe she conceived by the breath of the angel Gabriel: "Many scholars of the predecessors (Salaf) have mentioned that at this point the angel (who was Jibril [Gabriel]) blew into the opening of the garment that she was wearing. Then the breath descended until it entered into her vagina and she conceived the child by the leave of Allah."[4]

It is easy for me. And so that we may make him a sign for mankind and a mercy from us, and it is a thing that is ordained. **22**And she conceived him, and she withdrew with him to a far place. **23**And the pangs of childbirth drove her to the trunk of the palm-tree. She said, Oh, if only I had died before this and had become nothing, forgotten. **24**Then he called out to her from beneath her, saying, Do not grieve. Your Lord has placed a stream beneath you, **25**And shake the trunk of the palm-tree toward you, you wilt cause ripe dates to fall upon you. **26**So eat and drink and be consoled. And if you meet any mortal, say, Indeed, I have vowed a fast to Ar-Rahman, and may not speak this day to any mortal. **27**Then she brought him to her own people, carrying him. They said, O Mary, You have come with an amazing thing. **28**O sister of Aaron, your father was not a wicked man, nor was your mother unchaste. **29**Then she pointed to him. They said, How can we talk to one who is in the cradle, a young boy? **30**He spoke, Indeed, I am the slave of Allah. He has given me the book and has appointed me a prophet, **31**And has made me blessed wherever I may be, and has commanded for me prayer and almsgiving as long as I remain alive, **32**And dutiful toward her who bore me, and has not made me arrogant, unblessed. **33**Peace be upon me on the day I was born, and the day I die, and the day I will be raised alive. **34**Such was Jesus, the son of Mary, a statement of the truth about which they doubt. **35**It is not fitting for Allah that he should take to himself a son. Glory be to him, when he decrees a thing, he says to it only, Be, and it is. **36**And indeed, Allah is my Lord and your Lord. So serve him. That is the right path. **37**The sects among them disagree, but woe to the unbelievers from the meeting of an awful day. **38**See and hear them on the day they come to us. Yet the evildoers are today in obvious error. **39**And warn them of the day of anguish when the case has been decided. Now they are in a state of carelessness, and they do not believe. **40**Indeed, we, and we alone, inherit the earth and all who are on it, and to us they are returned. **41**And mention Abraham in the book. Indeed, he was a saint, a prophet. **42**When he said to his father, O my father, why do you worship what does not or see, nor can help you in any way? **43**O my father, indeed, there has come to me knowledge that did not come to you. So follow me, and I will lead you on a right path. **44**O my father, do not worship Satan. Indeed, Satan is a rebel to Ar-Rahman. **45**O my father, Indeed, I fear that a punishment from Ar-Rahman might overtake you so that you become a

---

23. Mary still suffers the pains of childbirth, while in some Christian traditions she does not, since those are the result of the sin (Genesis 3:16) that Jesus is taking upon himself and expiating (I Corinthians 15:22).

24. Mary gives birth to Jesus under a palm tree, not in a manger as in Luke 2:7. It is unclear from the text who is speaking (the newborn Jesus or someone else?) and what the nature of the stream that Allah places beneath Mary is. Luxenberg, however, finds that this passage has nothing to do with streams. Rather, it refers to Mary's delivering a virgin birth. In Luxenberg's philological reconstruction based on the Syro-Aramaic understanding of the key words here, the infant Jesus is telling the virgin: "Do not be sad, your Lord has made your delivery legitimate."[5]

Numerous Islamic authorities identify the voice that spoke from beneath Mary as Gabriel, while others agree it was the baby Jesus,

who speaks soon enough anyway (19:30).[6] One later tradition notes that when Jesus (or Gabriel) tells Mary in this verse not to grieve, she responds, "How can I not grieve when you are with me and I have no husband nor am I an owned slave woman?"[7] On slave women, see 4:3.

26. On Ar-Rahman, see 17:110 and 38:5.

28. On "sister of Aaron," see 3:35.

30. On Jesus speaking in the cradle, see 3:46.

35. Jesus is not the Son of God but the "slave of Allah," for to have a son is not befitting Allah's majesty (see 4:171).

41. Here the Qur'an returns to the story of Abraham, recounting his breach with his father when his father refused to give up his idol worship (as also in 9:114).

44. On Ar-Rahman, see 17:110.

companion of Satan. **⁴⁶**He said, Do you reject my gods, O Abraham? If you do not stop, I will surely stone you. Leave me for a long while. **⁴⁷**He said, Peace be upon you. I will ask forgiveness for you from my Lord. Indeed, he has always been favorable to me. **⁴⁸**I will withdraw from you and what you pray to besides Allah, and I will pray to my Lord. It may be that, in prayer to my Lord, I will not be unblessed. **⁴⁹**So when he had withdrawn from them and what they were worshipping besides Allah, we gave him Isaac and Jacob. Each of them we made a prophet. **⁵⁰**And we gave them some of our mercy, and assigned to them a high and true renown. **⁵¹**And make mention of Moses in the book. Indeed, he was chosen, and he was a messenger, a prophet. **⁵²**We called him from the right slope of the mountain, and brought him near in communion. **⁵³**And we bestowed upon his brother Aaron, a prophet, some of our mercy.

⁵⁴And mention Ishmael in the book. Indeed, he was a keeper of his promise, and he was a messenger, a prophet. **⁵⁵**He commanded prayer and almsgiving from his people, and was acceptable in the sight of his Lord. **⁵⁶**And mention Idris in the book. Indeed, he was a saint, a prophet, **⁵⁷**And we raised him to high a station. **⁵⁸**These are the ones to whom Allah showed favor from among the prophets, from the descendants of Adam and of those whom we carried with Noah, and of the descendants of Abraham and Israel, and from among those whom we guided and chose. When the signs of Ar-Rahman were recited to them, they fell down, adoring and weeping. **⁵⁹**Now there has succeeded them a later generation who have ruined worship and have followed lusts. But they will meet deception. **⁶⁰**Except him who will repent and believe and do right. Such people will enter the garden, and they will not be wronged in anything, **⁶¹**Gardens of Eden, which Ar-Rahman has promised to his slaves in the unseen. Indeed, his promise is always sure of fulfillment. **⁶²**They hear in them no idle talk, but only peace, and in them they have food for morning and evening. **⁶³**Such is the garden which we cause the devout among our slaves to inherit. **⁶⁴**We do not come down except by commandment of your Lord. To him belongs all that is in front of us and all that is behind us and all that is between those two, and your Lord was never forgetful, **⁶⁵**Lord of the heavens and the earth and of all that is between them. Therefore, worship him and be steadfast in his service. Do you know someone who can be named along with him? **⁶⁶**And man says, When I am dead, will I really be brought forth alive? **⁶⁷**Doesn't man remember that we created him before, when he was nothing? **⁶⁸**And by your Lord, indeed we will assemble them and the satans, then we will bring them, crouching, around Gehenna. **⁶⁹**Then we will pluck out from every sect whoever among them was the most stubborn in rebellion to Ar-Rahman. **⁷⁰**And surely we are best aware of those most worthy to be burned in it. **⁷¹**There is not one of you who will not approach it. That is a fixed command of your Lord. **⁷²**Then

---

47. Abraham prays that Allah will forgive his father, but in 60:4, in asking for this forgiveness, Abraham is not an example for the Muslims.

58. On Ar-Rahman, see 17:110 and 38:5, as also for 19:61, 19:69, 19:75, 19:78, 19:85, 19:88, 19:91, 19:92, 19:93, and 19:96.

68. On the oath "by your Lord," see 34:3. On Gehenna, see 2:206, as also at 19:86.

71. The Muslims, like the unbelievers, will experience hellfire, but according to Islamic tradition, only at a distance, and temporarily. Ibn Kathir quotes a tradition explaining: "The passing of the Muslims (over the Hellfire) means their passing over a bridge that is over it. But the passing of the idolators over the Hellfire refers to their admission to the Fire."[8]

we will rescue those who avoided evil, and leave the evildoers crouching there. ⁷³And when our clear signs are recited to them, those who disbelieve say to those who believe, Which of the two parties is in a better position, and more imposing as an army? ⁷⁴How many a generation have we destroyed before them, who were more imposing in respect of gear and appearance. ⁷⁵Say, As for him who is in error, Ar-Rahman will indeed prolong his span of life until, when they see what they were promised, whether it be punishment or the hour, they will know who is in a worse position and who is weaker as an army. ⁷⁶Allah increases in right guidance those who walk rightly, and the good deeds that endure are better in your Lord's sight for reward, and better to resort to. ⁷⁷Have you seen him who disbelieves in our signs and says, Surely I will be given wealth and a child? ⁷⁸Has he examined the unseen, or has he made a pact with Ar-Rahman? ⁷⁹No, but we will record what he says and prolong for him a span of torment. ⁸⁰And we will inherit from him what he spoke about, and he will come to us, alone. ⁸¹And they have chosen gods besides Allah so that they may be power for them. ⁸²No, but they will deny their worship of them, and become their enemies. ⁸³Don't you see that we have set the satans on the unbelievers to push them to do evil? ⁸⁴So make no haste against them. We just number a sum to them,

⁸⁵On the day when we will gather the righteous to Ar-Rahman, an honored company. ⁸⁶And drive the guilty to Gehenna, a weary herd, ⁸⁷They will have no power of intercession, except for him who has made a covenant with his Lord. ⁸⁸And they say, Ar-Rahman has taken to himself a son. ⁸⁹Surely you say a monstrous thing, ⁹⁰By which the heavens are almost torn, and the earth is split apart and the mountains fall in ruins, ⁹¹That you ascribe to Ar-Rahman a son, ⁹²When it is not fitting for Ar-Rahman that he should have a son. ⁹³There is no one in the heavens and the earth who does not come to Ar-Rahman as a slave. ⁹⁴Indeed he knows them and numbers them with numbering. ⁹⁵And each one of them will come to him on the day of resurrection, alone. ⁹⁶Indeed, those who believe and do good works, Ar-Rahman will appoint love for them. ⁹⁷And we have made it easy on your tongue, only so that you may bear good news with it to those who are righteous, and warn the defiant people with it. ⁹⁸And how many a generation before them have we destroyed. Can you see a single man of them, or hear from them the slightest sound?

---

73. The unbelievers are ready to determine which religion to follow based on the level of earthly prosperity of its adherents. "In this," according to Ibn Kathir, "they were saying, 'How can we be upon falsehood while we are in this manner of successful living?'"⁹ However, Allah has destroyed countless generations before them (19:74).

77. Instead of "a child" (*waladan*), the version of Khalaf, one of the transmitters of Hamza's reading, has "children" (*wuldan*).¹⁰

89. The idea that Allah has begotten a son is "a monstrous thing," as it implies Allah's insufficiency and need for a helper (see 2:116).

97. Regarding *yassara*, rendered here as "made it easy," Luxenberg notes that in Arabic, the word "does in fact mean '*to facilitate, to make easy*.'"¹¹ However, he points out that the Syro-Aramaic word from which it is derived, *passeq*, means "to translate" as well as "to make easy."¹² He posits that a more precise rendering of the verse may be: "And we have translated it into your language…."¹³ This reading also fits at 44:58, 54:17, 54:22, 54:32, and 54:40. For the foreign origin of the Qur'an, see 16:103 and 41:44.

Ta Ha

Ta Ha

Introduction

This sura is traditionally considered to date from the early Meccan period. It "has no rival," says the twentieth-century Islamic scholar Muhammad al-Ghazali, "in its uncompromising affirmation of the Absolute Unity of Allah."[1]

It takes its name from the two Arabic letters that begin it, *ta* and *ha*. Ibn Abbas and other early commentators have suggested that *ta ha* is actually a phrase from an ancient Arabic dialect, meaning "O man," in which case it may be that here Allah is addressing the messenger.

---

1 Muhammad al-Ghazali, *Journey Through the Qur'an: The Content and Context of the Suras*, Aisha Bewley, trans. (London: Dar al-Taqwa, 1998), 216.

Ta Ha

IN THE NAME OF ALLAH, THE COMPASSIONATE, THE MERCIFUL.

¹Ta. Ha. ²We have not revealed this Qur'an to you so that you would be distressed, ³But as a reminder to him who fears, ⁴A revelation from him who created the earth and the high heavens, ⁵Ar-Rahman, who is established on the throne. ⁶To him belongs whatever is in the heavens and whatever is on the earth, and whatever is between them, and whatever is beneath the ground. ⁷And if you speak out loud, then indeed, he knows the secret and more hidden. ⁸Allah. There is no God except him. His are the most beautiful names. ⁹Has there come to you the story of Moses? ¹⁰When he saw a fire and said to his people, Indeed, wait, I see a fire far off. Perhaps I may bring you a brand from it or may find guidance at the fire. ¹¹And when he reached it, he was called by name, O Moses, ¹²Indeed, it is I, your Lord, so take off your shoes, for indeed, you are in the holy valley of Tuwa. ¹³And I have chosen you, so listen to what is inspired. ¹⁴Indeed, I, and I alone, am Allah. There is no God except me. So serve me and establish prayer for my remembrance.

¹⁵Indeed, the hour is surely coming. But I will to keep it hidden, so that every soul may be rewarded for what it strives for. ¹⁶Therefore, do not let him who does not believe in it turn you aside from it and follows his own desire, so that you do not perish. ¹⁷And what is that in your right hand, O Moses? ¹⁸He said, This is my staff on which I lean, and with which I bring down branches for my sheep, and with which I find other uses. ¹⁹He said, Throw it down, O Moses. ²⁰So he threw it down, and indeed, it was a serpent, gliding. ²¹He said, Grasp it and do not be afraid. We will return it to its former state. ²²And thrust your hand under your armpit, it will come forth white without harm. Another sign. ²³So that we may show you some of our greater signs, ²⁴Go to Pharaoh. Indeed, he has transgressed. ²⁵He said, My Lord, relieve my mind, ²⁶And ease my task for me, ²⁷And loosen a knot from my tongue, ²⁸So that they may understand what I say. ²⁹Appoint for me a helper from my people, ³⁰Aaron, my brother. ³¹Confirm my strength with him, ³²And let him share my task, ³³So that we may glorify you a great deal, ³⁴And remember you a great deal.

1. On the "mysterious letters," see 2:1.

2. See 2:144.

5. On Ar-Rahman, see 17:110 and 38:5.

9. Here begins another retelling of the story of Moses and the Exodus, also told beginning at 2:49, 7:103, 10:75, 17:101, and 26:10. But, as Al-Ghazali observes, "Every time the story appears different aspects of it emerge. Each version has details which are not included in any other version."¹ The repeated aspects have their usefulness as well. Al-Ghazali also points out that this sura is very concerned with reminding and bidding the faithful to remember truths that they have already learned, which is clear from the fact that so many of its themes have been sounded before.

10. Sufis say that when Moses approached the Burning Bush and heard the voice of Allah, he attained the states of *fana*, or absorption of the self into the deity, and *baqaa*, life in union with Allah. His shoes, they say, represented his separation from Allah, which is why Allah tells him to take them off (20:12). According to the

eleventh-century Qur'anic scholar and jurist Ibn Masud Baghavi in *Ma'alimut-tanzil*, what Moses saw wasn't actually fire at all but the heavenly light (*Nur*) of Allah.²

12. The meaning of "Tuwa" is unknown and has been the subject of speculation. Ibn Kathir offers several possibilities: "Ibn Abbas said, 'It is the name of the valley.' Others have said the same. This is merely mentioned as something to give more explanation [i.e., background] to the story. It has also been said that it is a figure of speech, which comes from the command to place his feet down. It has also been said that it means 'doubly sacred' and that Tuwa is something that has repetitious blessings. However, the first opinion is most correct."³

Bell suggests that "Tuwa" is "perhaps based on a misreading of the Syriac *tura* = Mount."⁴

24. On Pharaoh, see also 2:49, 3:11, 7:103, 8:52, 10:75, 14:6, 17:101, 23:46, 26:11, 27:12, 28:3, 29:39, 38:12, 40:24, 44:17, 50:13, 51:38, 54:41, 66:11, 69:9, 73:15, 79:15, 85:18, and 89:10.

[35]Indeed, you are always seeing us. [36]He said, You are granted your request, O Moses. [37]And indeed, another time, already we have shown you favor, [38]When we inspired in your mother what is inspired, [39]Saying, Throw him into the ark, and throw it into the river, then the river will throw it on to the bank, and there an enemy to me and an enemy to him will take him. And I filled you with love from me so that you might be trained according to my will, [40]When your sister went and said, Shall I show you one who will nurse him? And we restored you to your mother so that her eyes might be refreshed and might not sorrow. And you killed a man and we delivered you from great distress, and tested you with a heavy trial. And you remained years among the people of Midian. Then you came here by providence, O Moses, [41]And I have attached you to myself. [42]Go, you and your brother, with my signs, and do not be faint in remembrance of me. [43]Go, both of you, to Pharaoh. Indeed, he has transgressed. [44]And speak to him a gentle word, that perhaps he may heed or fear. [45]They said, Our Lord, indeed, we are afraid that he may be quick to harm us or that he may play the tyrant. [46]He said, Do not fear. Indeed, I am with you two, hearing and seeing. [47]So go to him and say, Indeed, we are two messengers of your Lord. So let the children of Israel go with us, and do not torment them. We bring you a sign from your Lord. And peace will be for him who follows right guidance. [48]Indeed, it has been revealed to us that the doom will be for him who denies and turns away. [49]He said, Who then is the Lord of you two, O Moses? [50]He said, Our Lord is he who gave everything its nature, then guided it rightly. [51]He said, What then is the status of the generations of old? [52]He said, The knowledge of that is with my Lord in a book. My Lord neither errs nor forgets, [53]He has established the earth as a bed and has threaded roads for you in it and has sent down water from the sky and by it we have brought forth various kinds of vegetation, [54]Eat and feed your cattle. Indeed, in this truly are signs for men of thought. [55]We created you from it, and we return you to it, and from it we bring you forth a second time. [56]And we truly showed him all our signs, but he denied them and refused. [57]He said, Have you come to drive us out from our land by your sorcery, O Moses? [58]But we surely can produce for you sorcery like this, so make an appointment between us and you, which neither we nor you will fail to keep, at a convenient place. [59]He said, Your appointment will be the day of the feast, and let the people assemble when the sun has risen high. [60]Then Pharaoh went and gathered his strength, then came. [61]Moses said to them, Woe to you! Do not fabricate a lie against Allah, so that he does not destroy you by some punishment. He who lies fails miserably. [62]Then they debated with one another about what they must do, and conversed in secret. [63]They said, Indeed, these are two wizards who would drive you out from your country by their sorcery, and destroy your best traditions, [64]So arrange your plan, and come in battle line. Whoever is uppermost on this day will be indeed successful. [65]They said, O Moses, either throw first, or let us be the first to throw. [66]He said, No, you throw. Then indeed, their cords and their staves, by their sorcery, appeared to him as if they ran. [67]And Moses began to be afraid. [68]We said, Do not fear. Indeed, you will prevail. [69]Throw what is in your right hand. It will eat up what they have made. Indeed, what they have made is just

a wizard's artifice, and a wizard will not be successful to whatever point he may attain. **⁷⁰**Then the wizards were flung down prostrate, calling out, We believe in the Lord of Aaron and Moses. **⁷¹**He said, You are putting faith in him before I give you permission. Indeed, he is your chief who taught you sorcery. Now surely I will cut off your hands and your feet on opposite sides, and I will crucify you on the trunks of palm trees, and you will know for certain which of us has sterner and more lasting punishment. **⁷²**They said, We do not choose you above the clear proofs that have come to us, and above him who created us. So decree what you will decree. You will end for us only the life of this world. **⁷³**Indeed, we believe in our Lord, so that he may forgive us our sins and the sorcery to which you forced us. Allah is better and more lasting. **⁷⁴**Indeed, whoever comes guilty to his Lord, indeed for him is Gehenna. There he will neither die nor live. **⁷⁵**But whoever comes to him a believer, having done good works, for such people are the high positions, **⁷⁶**Gardens of Eden under which rivers flow, in which they will remain forever. That is the reward of him who grows. **⁷⁷**And indeed we inspired Moses, saying, Take away my slaves by night and strike a dry path in the sea for them, not fearing to be overtaken, nor being afraid.

⁷⁸Then Pharaoh followed them with his armies and there covered them what did cover them of the sea. **⁷⁹**And Pharaoh led his people astray, he did not guide them. **⁸⁰**O children of Israel, we delivered you from your enemy, and we made a covenant with you on the holy mountain's side, and sent down on you the manna and the quails, **⁸¹**Eat of the good things with which we have provided you, and do not transgress over them so that my wrath does not come upon you, and he on whom my wrath comes, he is lost indeed. **⁸²**And indeed, truly I am forgiving toward him who repents and believes and does good, and afterward walks rightly. **⁸³**And what has made you hasten from your people, O Moses? **⁸⁴**He said, They are close upon my track. I hastened to you, my Lord, so that you might be pleased. **⁸⁵**He said, Indeed, we have tested your people in your absence, and As-Samiri has misled them. **⁸⁶**Then Moses went back to his people, angry and sad. He said, O my people, hasn't your Lord promised you a fair promise? Did the time appointed then appear too long for you, or did you wish that wrath from your Lord would come upon you, so that you broke your promise with me? **⁸⁷**They said, We did not break our promise with you of our own will, but we were laden with the burdens of the ornaments of the people, then threw them, for that was what As-Samiri proposed. **⁸⁸**Then he produced for them a calf, of saffron color, which gave forth a lowing sound. And they called out, This is your god and the god of Moses, but he has forgotten. **⁸⁹**Did they not see, then, that it returned no saying to them and possessed for

---

71. "I will cut off your hands and your feet on opposite sides, and I will crucify you on the trunks of palm trees": this is the punishment for those who spread "corruption on the earth," as prescribed in 5:33.

74. On Gehenna, see 2:206.

83. Moses ascends the mountain to meet Allah, but significantly, he doesn't receive the Ten Commandments. Instead, Allah asks him why he hurried up the mountain in advance of his people.

85. Allah tells Moses that he is testing Moses's people by allowing Samiri to lead them astray. Samiri, who fashions the idol of the calf, is not mentioned by name in other Qur'anic versions of this story. Ibn Kathir attributes to Ibn Abbas the statement: "As-Samiri was a man from the people of Bajarma, a people who worshipped cows. He still had the love of cow worshipping in his soul. However, he acted as though he had accepted Islam with the Children of Israel. His name was Musa bin Zafar."⁵

them neither hurt nor use? **90**And Aaron indeed had told them beforehand, O my people! You are just being seduced with it, for indeed, your Lord is Ar-Rahman, so follow me and obey my order. **91**They said, We will by no means stop being devoted to it until Moses returns to us. **92**He said, O Aaron, what held you back when you saw that they had gone astray, **93**That you did not follow me? Have you then disobeyed my order? **94**He said, O son of my mother, do not clutch my beard or my head. I was afraid that you would say, You have caused division among the children of Israel, and have not waited for my word. **95**He said, And what do you have to say, O Samiri? **96**He said, I perceived what they did not perceive, so I seized a handful from the footsteps of the messenger, and then threw it in. In this way my soul prompted me. **97**He said, Then go. And indeed, in this life it is for you to say, Do not touch me. And indeed, there is for you an appointment that you cannot break. Now look upon your god to which you have remained devoted. Indeed we will burn it and will scatter its dust over the sea. **98**Your God is only Allah, other than whom there is no God. He encompasses all things in his knowledge. **99**In this way do we relate to you some news of what happened of old, and we have given you a reminder from our presence. **100**Whoever turns away from

it, he indeed will bear a burden on the day of resurrection, **101**Remaining under it, an evil burden for them on the day of resurrection, **102**The day when the trumpet is blown. On that day we assemble the guilty white-eyed, **103**Murmuring among themselves, You have remained just ten. **104**We are best aware of what they say when the best among them in conduct say, You have remained just a day. **105**They will ask you about the mountains. Say, My Lord will break them into scattered dust. **106**And leave it as an empty plain, **107**In which you see neither a curve nor an uneven place. **108**On that day they follow the caller who does not deceive, and voices are hushed for Ar-Rahman, and you hear just a faint murmur. **109**On that day no intercession helps except that of him to whom Ar-Rahman has given permission and whose word he accepts. **110**He knows what is in front of them and what is behind them, while they cannot encompass it in knowledge. **111**And faces humble themselves before the living one, the eternal one. And he who carries wrongdoing is indeed a failure.

112 And he who has done some good works, being a believer, he does not fear injustice or deprivation.

113 In this way we have revealed it as a Qur'an in Arabic, and have displayed certain threats in it,

---

90. On Ar-Rahman, see 17:110 and 38:5.

96. The *Tafsir al-Jalalayn* states that the "handful" was earth "from the tracks left by the hooves of Jibril's horse," that is, Gabriel's.[6]

97. Ibn Kathir explains: "This means, 'Just as you took and touched what was not your right to take and touch of the messenger's footprint, such is your punishment in this life, that you will say, "Do not touch (me)." This means, 'You will not touch the people and they will not touch you.'"[7] This may be a hint that Samiri is a Samaritan, as his name suggests: a people who generally did not (and do not) intermingle with outsiders.

99. The story of Moses has been retold as a "reminder from our presence." This is intended to explain the repetition of the story,

which may stem from the combination of material from various traditions, all containing a version of this story, into the Qur'an.

108. On Ar-Rahman, see 17:110 and 38:5.

109. Intercession with Allah's permission is accepted (cf. 10:3, 21:28, 34:23, and 53:26). However, elsewhere the Qur'an says that everyone will stand alone before Allah; no intercession from others will be accepted (2:48, 2:123, 6:94, 23:101, 39:43, 42:46).

113. This is one of the verses that establishes the proposition that it is an essential part of the nature of the Qur'an that it is in Arabic, and hence it cannot be translated; only its meaning can be rendered. See 10:38 and 12:2.

so that perhaps they may keep from evil or that it may cause them to take notice. **114**Then exalted be Allah, the true king. And do not hasten with the Qur'an before its revelation has been perfected to you, and say, My Lord, increase me in knowledge. **115**And indeed we made a covenant of old with Adam, but he forgot, and we found no constancy in him. **116**And when we said to the angels, Fall prostrate before Adam, they fell prostrate, except Iblis, he refused. **117**Therefore we said, O Adam, this is an enemy to you and to your wife, so do not let him drive you both out of the garden so that you fall into misery. **118**It is given to you that you do not hunger in it, nor are naked, **119**And that you do not thirst in it, nor are exposed to the sun's heat. **120**But Satan whispered to him, saying, O Adam, Shall I show you the tree of immortality and power that does not waste away? **121**Then the two ate of it, so that their shame became clear to them, and they began to hide by heaping on themselves some of the leaves of the garden. And Adam disobeyed his Lord, and so went astray. **122**Then his Lord chose him, and relented toward him, and guided him. **123**He said, Go down from here, both of you, one of you an enemy to the other. But when guidance from me comes to you, then whoever follows my guidance, he will not go astray or come to grief. **124**But he who turns away from remembrance of me, his life will be narrow, and I will bring him blind to the assembly on the day of resurrection. **125**He will say, My Lord, Why have you gathered me blind, when I was able to see? **126**He will say, So it must be. Our signs came to you, but you forgot them. In a similar way, you are forgotten on this day. **127**In this way do we reward him who is wasteful and does not believe the signs of his Lord, and indeed the torment of the hereafter will be sterner and more lasting. **128**Isn't it a guidance for them, how many a generation we destroyed before them, amid whose dwellings they walk? Indeed, in this are truly signs for men of thought. **129**And if not for a decree that had already gone forth from your Lord, and a term already fixed, the judgment would have been inevitable. **130**Therefore, bear with what they say, and celebrate the praise of your Lord before the rising of the sun and before its setting. And glorify him some hours of the night and at the two ends of the day, so that you may find acceptance. **131**And do not strain your eyes toward what we cause some groups among them to enjoy, the flower of the life of this world, so that we may test them by it. The provision of your Lord is better and more lasting. **132**And command prayer upon your people, and be constant in it. We do not ask a provision from you, we provided for you. And the ending is for righteousness. **133**And they say, If only he would bring us a miracle from his Lord. Hasn't there come to them the proof of what is in the former scriptures? **134**And if we had destroyed them with some punishment before this, they would surely have said, Our Lord, if only you had sent to us a messenger, so that we might have followed your signs before we were humbled and disgraced. **135**Say, Each person is waiting, so wait. You will come to know who are the companions of the path of justice, and who is right.

---

114. This is because, as Ibn Kathir relates, crediting Ibn Abbas, Muhammad would recite revelations rapidly as they were being revealed, trying to remember them. He should trust in Allah's power to make him remember.[8] This could also be intended to account at least in part for the changing contents of the Qur'an at the time when this passage was first published.

120. Satan tempts Adam to eat from the Tree of Eternity, not the tree of the knowledge of good and evil, as in Genesis 2:17.

SURA 21

The Prophets

Al-Anbiyya

Introduction

After several suras have recounted the message and reception of various prophets in strikingly similar terms, this sura discusses the phenomenon of prophecy and the way it is received in general (usually with scoffing). It also touches on several prophets specifically, including Abraham, David, Solomon, Job, and Zechariah.

This is traditionally regarded as a late Meccan sura, revealed against the backdrop of the ongoing strife between Muhammad and the leaders of the pagan Quraysh tribe of Mecca—a tribe of which Muhammad was a member, but which had rejected his prophetic claim. This sura is full of both direct and implied references to their skepticism as well as replies to their objections.

The Prophets

IN THE NAME OF ALLAH, THE COMPASSIONATE, THE MERCIFUL.

¹The judgment draws near for mankind, while they turn away heedless. ²There never comes to them a new reminder from their Lord except that they listen to it while they play, ³With hearts preoccupied. And they confer in secret. The wrongdoers say, Is this man other than a mortal like you? Will you then succumb to sorcery when you see? ⁴He said, My Lord knows what is spoken in the heaven and the earth. He is the hearer, the knower. ⁵No, they say, muddled dreams, no, he has just invented it, no, he is but a poet. Let him bring us a sign even as those of old were sent. ⁶Not a town believed of those which we destroyed before them, would they then believe? ⁷And we did not send before you other than men whom we inspired. Ask the people of the reminder if you do not know. ⁸We did not give them bodies that would not eat food, nor were they immortals. ⁹Then we fulfilled the promise to them. So we delivered them and those whom we willed, and we destroyed the wasteful.

¹⁰Now we have revealed a book to you in which is your reminder. Have you then no sense? ¹¹How many a community that dealt unjustly have we destroyed, and raised up after them another people? ¹²And when they felt our might, look at them fleeing from it. ¹³Do not flee, but return to your luxuries and your dwellings, so that you may be questioned. ¹⁴They called out, Alas for us, we were wrongdoers. ¹⁵And their crying did not stop until we made them as reaped corn, extinct. ¹⁶We did not create the heaven and the earth and all that is between them while playing. ¹⁷If we had wished to find a pastime, we could have found it in our presence, if we ever did. ¹⁸No, but we throw the true against the false, and it breaks its head and indeed, it vanishes. And yours will be woe for what you ascribe. ¹⁹To him belongs whoever is in the heavens and the earth. And those who dwell in his presence are not too proud to worship him, nor do they grow weary, ²⁰They glorify night and day, they do not slacken. ²¹Or have they chosen gods from the earth who raise the dead? ²²If there were gods in it besides Allah,

1. In a passage extending to 21:47, Allah speaks generally of how the unbelievers always scorn the signs of his creative power and the messages of the prophets.

3. Instead of, "The wrongdoers say," the Shi'ite Bankipur Qur'an manuscript has, "Those who have deprived the family of Muhammad of its due say."[1] See 2:59 and the Appendix: Two Apocryphal Shi'ite Suras.

4. Instead of "he said," the Warsh Qur'an has "say."[2]

5. "Here," according to Ibn Kathir, "Allah tells us of the stubbornness and heresy of the disbelievers, and the various things they said about the Qur'an, and how they were confused and misguided about it. Sometimes they described it as magic, and sometimes they described it as poetry, or mixed up false dreams, or a fabrication."[3] The unbelievers, meanwhile, demand a sign when every verse of the Qur'an is a sign (see 6:35).

7. The "people of the reminder," states Ibn Kathir, are "the people of knowledge among the nations such as the Jews and Christians and other groups."[4] See 10:94.

9. See 7:179, 10:99, and 32:13.

17. According to the *Tafsir al-Jalalayn*, "If We had desired to have some amusement – in the form of a wife or child – We would have derived it from Our Presence – from the houris or angels."[5] The "houris" are the virgins of paradise (see 44:54).

18. The *Tafsir al-Jalalayn* states that "the word used here means to strike a fatal blow which exposes the brain and removes it."[6]

22. The unbelievers can't be correct that their objects of worship are really gods besides Allah, because this multiplicity would create confusion not only in heaven but also on earth. The assumption is apparently that a multiplicity of gods would give conflicting commands, while Allah remains consistent (although see 5:64). This in

then indeed both were disordered. May Allah be glorified, the Lord of the throne, from all that they ascribe. ²³He cannot be questioned about what he does, but they will be questioned. ²⁴Or have they chosen other gods besides Allah? Say, Bring your proof. This is the reminder of those with me and those before me, but most of them do not know the Truth and so they are averse. ²⁵And we sent no messenger before you unless we inspired him, There is no God except me, so worship me. ²⁶And they say, Ar-Rahman has taken to himself a son. May he be glorified. No, but they are honored slaves, ²⁷They do not speak until he has spoken, and they act by his command. ²⁸He knows what is in front of them and what is behind them, and they cannot intercede except for him whom he accepts, and they quake for awe of him. ²⁹And one of them who would say, Indeed, I am a god besides him, that one we would repay with Gehenna. In this way we repay wrongdoers. ³⁰Have not those who disbelieve known that the heavens and the earth were of one piece, then we parted them, and we made every living thing out of water? Will they not then believe? ³¹And we have placed in the earth firm hills so that it does not quake with them, and we have placed streams in it as roads so that perhaps they may find their way. ³²And we have made the sky a preserved roof. Yet they turn away from its signs. ³³And it is

he who created the night and the day, and the sun and the moon. They float, each in an orbit. ³⁴We appointed immortality for no mortal before you. What? If you die, can they be immortal? ³⁵Every soul must taste of death, and we test you with evil and with good, as an ordeal. And to us you will be returned. ³⁶And when the unbelievers see you, they mock you, Is this he who makes mention of your gods? And they would deny all mention of Ar-Rahman. ³⁷Man is made of haste. I will show you my signs, but do not ask me to hasten. ³⁸And they say, When will this promise be fulfilled, if you are truthful? ³⁹If those who disbelieved only knew the time when they will not be able to drive off the fire from their faces and from their backs, and they will not be helped! ⁴⁰No, but it will come upon them unawares so that it will baffle them, and they will be unable to repel it, nor will they be reprieved. ⁴¹Messengers before you, indeed, were mocked, but those who mocked were overwhelmed by what they mocked. ⁴²Say, Who guards you in the night or in the day from Ar-Rahman? No, but they turn away from mention of their Lord. ⁴³Or do they have gods who can shield them from us? They cannot help themselves, nor can they be defended from us. ⁴⁴No, but we gave these men and their fathers ease until life grew long for them. Do they not see how we advance to their land, reducing it of its outlying

---

turn assumes that divine law has a political aspect that is implemented on earth.

23. Says Ibn Kathir: "He is the Ruler Whose rule cannot be overturned and none can object to it, because of His might, majesty, pride, knowledge, wisdom, justice and subtlety."⁷ See 7:179, 10:99, and 32:13.

26. Those who say, "Ar-Rahman has taken to himself a son" are not just the Christians but the pagan Arabs who worshiped the daughters of Allah (see 16:57 and 53:19).

On Ar-Rahman, see 17:110 and 38:5, as also at 21:36 and 21:42.

28. Intercession with Allah's permission is accepted (cf. 10:3, 34:23, and 53:26). However, elsewhere the Qur'an says that everyone will stand alone before Allah; no intercession from others will be accepted (2:48, 2:123, 6:94, 23:101, 39:43, 42:46).

29. On Gehenna, see 2:206.

41. Barth suggests that there has been some dislocation here, as this verse would make more sense after the first part of 21:36: "And when the disbelievers see you, they mock you. Messengers before you, indeed, were mocked, but those who mocked were overwhelmed by what they mocked."⁸

parts? Can they then be the victors? ⁴⁵Say, I warn you only by the inspiration. But the deaf do not hear the call when they are warned. ⁴⁶And if a breath of your Lord's punishment were to touch them, they surely would say, Alas for us, indeed, we were wrongdoers. ⁴⁷And we set a just balance for the day of resurrection so that no soul is wronged in anything. Even if it is the weight of a grain of mustard seed, we bring it. And we are sufficient as reckoners. ⁴⁸And we indeed gave Moses and Aaron the *furqan* and a light and a reminder for those who keep from evil, ⁴⁹Those who fear their Lord in secret and who dread the hour. ⁵⁰This is a blessed reminder that we have revealed, will you then reject it? ⁵¹And we indeed gave Abraham of old his proper course, and we were aware of him, ⁵²When he said to his father and his people, What are these images to which you are devoted? ⁵³They said, We found our fathers worshippers of them. ⁵⁴He said, Indeed you and your fathers were in plain error. ⁵⁵They said, Do you bring us the truth, or are you some joker? ⁵⁶He said, No, but your Lord is the Lord of the heavens and the earth, who created them, and I am among those who testify to that. ⁵⁷And by Allah, I will circumvent your idols after you have gone away and turned your backs. ⁵⁸Then he reduced them to fragments, all except the chief of them, so that perhaps they might have recourse

to it. ⁵⁹They said, Who has done this to our gods? Surely it must be some evildoer. ⁶⁰They said, We heard a youth mention them, who is called Abraham. ⁶¹They said, Then bring him before the people's eyes so that they may testify. ⁶²They said, Is it you who have done this to our gods, O Abraham? ⁶³He said, But this, their chief has done it. So question them, if they can speak. ⁶⁴Then they gathered together in a different place and said, Indeed, you yourselves are the wrongdoers. ⁶⁵And they reversed themselves, and they said, You know well that these do not speak. ⁶⁶He said, Do you then worship instead of Allah what cannot benefit you at all, nor harm you? ⁶⁷Shame on you and all that you worship instead of Allah. Have you then no sense? ⁶⁸They called out, Burn him and stand by your gods, if you are going to act. ⁶⁹We said, O fire, be coolness and peace for Abraham, ⁷⁰And they wished to set a trap for him, but we made them the greater losers. ⁷¹And we rescued him and Lot to the land that we have blessed for peoples. ⁷²And we bestowed upon him Isaac, and Jacob as a grandson. Each of them we made righteous. ⁷³And we made them chiefs who guide by our command, and we inspired in them the doing of good deeds and the right establishment of prayer and the giving of alms, and they were worshippers of us. ⁷⁴And to Lot we gave judgment and knowledge, and we delivered him from

---

47. Everyone's smallest good deed, even the size of a mustard seed, will not go unnoticed. There is, however, no quantification in Islamic tradition about how much various good deeds or bad deeds weigh. However, one may tip the scales decisively in one's favor by waging jihad. A hadith has Muhammad being asked, "Instruct me as to such a deed as equals Jihad (in reward)," and answering, "I do not find such a deed."[9]

48. On *furqan*, see 3:4.

51. Another telling of the story of Abraham confronting his idolatrous people. See 9:17, 9:114.

74. Here begins a quick succession of brief references to Lot (21:74-75); Noah (21:76-77); David and Solomon (21:78-82); Job (21:83-84); Ishmael, Idris (Enoch), and Dhul-Kifl (Ezekiel) (21:85); Dhu'n-Nun (Jonah) (21:87-88); Zechariah (21:89-90); and Mary and Jesus (21:91), all of whom, we are reminded here, remained faithful to Allah through various kinds of difficulty and distress (and, often, scorn from unbelievers). These are all assumed to be Muslims (see 3:67).

the community that did abominations. Indeed, they were people of evil, lewd. [75]And we brought him in to our mercy. Indeed, he was among the righteous. [76]And Noah, when he called out of old, we heard his prayer and saved him and his family from the great affliction. [77]And delivered him from the people who denied our signs. Indeed, they were people of evil, therefore we drowned them all. [78]And David and Solomon, when they gave judgment concerning the field, when people's sheep had strayed and browsed in it by night, and we were witnesses to their judgment. [79]And we made Solomon to understand, and to each of them we gave judgment and knowledge. And we subdued the hills and the birds to sing praise along with David. It was we who did this. [80]And we taught him the art of making garments to protect you in your fighting. Are you then grateful? [81]And to Solomon the wind in its raging. It set by his command toward the land that we had blessed. And of everything we are aware. [82]And of the evil ones, some who dived for him and did other work, and we were guardians to them. [83]And Job, when he called out to his Lord, Indeed, adversity afflicts me, and you are the most merciful of all who show mercy. [84]Then we heard his prayer and removed that adversity from which he suffered, and we gave him his family and more like them, a mercy from our storehouse, and a remembrance for the worshippers, [85]And Ishmael, and Idris, and Dhul-Kifl. All were among the steadfast. [86]And we brought them in to our mercy. Indeed, they are among the righteous. [87]And Dhu'n-Nun, when he went off in anger and considered that we had no power over him, but he cried out in the darkness, saying, There is no God except you. May you be glorified. Indeed, I have been a wrongdoer. [88]Then we heard his prayer and saved him from the anguish. In this way do we save believers. [89]And Zechariah, when he called out to his Lord, My Lord, do not leave me not childless, although you are the best of inheritors. [90]Then we heard his prayer, and bestowed upon him John, and made his wife fertile for him. Indeed, they used to compete with one another in good deeds, and they called out to us in longing and in fear, and were submissive to us. [91]And she who was chaste, therefore we breathed into her some of our spirit and made her and her son a sign for peoples. [92]Indeed, this, your religion, is one religion, and I am your Lord, so worship me. [93]And they have broken their religion among them, all are returning to us. [94]Then whoever does some good works and is a believer, there will be no rejection of his effort. Indeed, we record for him. [95]And there is a ban upon any community which we have destroyed, so that they shall not return. [96]Until, when Gog and Magog are let loose, and they hasten out of every mound, [97]And the true promise draws near, then look at them, staring wide, the eyes of those who disbelieve. Alas for us, we are in forgetfulness of

---

76. See also 7:59, 10:71, 11:25, 23:23, 25:37, 26:105, 29:14, 37:75, 50:12, 51:46, 53:52, 54:9, 57:26, 69:11, and 71:1.

87. Dhu'n-Nun is "companion of the fish," a fitting name for Jonah.

92. All these prophets and Mary shared a single religion, Islam, although those who followed after these prophets "have broken their religion among them" (21:93). The original religion of all

the prophets was Islam, and when someone claims to follow one of those prophets (Abraham, Moses, Jesus, and so on) but rejects Islam, he is rejecting the true message of those prophets in favor of a later corrupted version that was devised not by the prophets themselves but by evildoers among their followers.

97. See 18:94.

this, but we were wrongdoers. ⁹⁸Indeed, you and what you worship besides Allah are the fuel of Gehenna. You will come to it. ⁹⁹If these had been gods they would not have come there, but all will live in it. ¹⁰⁰Wailing is their portion in it, and in it they do not hear. ¹⁰¹Indeed, those to whom kindness has gone forth from us before, they will be far removed from there. ¹⁰²They will not hear the slightest sound from it, while they remain in what their souls desire. ¹⁰³The supreme horror will not grieve them, and the angels will welcome them, This is your day which you were promised, ¹⁰⁴The day when we will roll up the heavens like the rolling up of a *sijill*. As we began the first creation, we will repeat it. A promise upon us. Indeed, we will perform it. ¹⁰⁵And indeed we have written in the Psalms, after the reminder, that my righteous slaves will inherit the earth, ¹⁰⁶Indeed, there is a plain statement for people who are devout. ¹⁰⁷We did not send you except as a mercy for the peoples. ¹⁰⁸Say, It is only inspired in me that your God is one God. Will you then become Muslims? ¹⁰⁹But if they are averse, then say, I have warned you all equally, although I do not know whether what you are promised is near or far. ¹¹⁰Indeed, he knows what is said openly, and what you conceal. ¹¹¹And I do not know if this is a trial for you, and enjoyment for a while. ¹¹²He said, My Lord, you judge with truth. Our Lord is Ar-Rahman, whose help is to be implored against what you ascribe.

---

98. On Gehenna, see 2:206.

104. Arthur Jeffery, author of *The Foreign Vocabulary of the Qur'an*, notes that the meaning of *sijill* was "unknown to the early interpreters of the Qur'an."[10] He adds, "Some took it to be the name of an Angel, or of the Prophet's amanuensis."[11] Ibn Kathir reflects the confusion in his commentary: "What is meant by *Sijill* is book."[12] He quotes an early Islamic authority explaining: "*As-Sijill* is an angel who is entrusted with the records; when a person dies, his Book (of deeds) is taken up to *As-Sijill*, and he rolls it up and puts it away until the Day of Resurrection."[13] Then he adds that "the correct view is that *sijill* "refers to the record (of deeds). This was also reported from him by Ali bin Abi Talhah and Al-Awfi. This was also stated by Mujahid, Qatadah and others. This was the view favored by Ibn Jarir, because this usage is well-known in the (Arabic) language."[14]

The parenthetical "Arabic" was added by the English translator. In reality, according to Jeffery, *sijill* is not an Arabic word at all but is derived from the Greek *sigillon*, meaning an "imperial edict." Jeffery notes that the first Arabic use appears to be in this very passage of the Qur'an; at least no earlier Arabic usage has been found.[15]

105. In one of the closest linguistic parallels between the Bible and the Qur'an, Psalm 37:29 says: "The righteous shall inherit the land, and dwell upon it forever." See also 3:184.

112. On Ar-Rahman, see 17:110 and 38:5.

Instead of "he said," the Warsh Qur'an has "say."[16]

The Pilgrimage

Al-Hajj

Introduction

Islamic scholars are divided over whether this sura dates from the Meccan or Medinan period of Muhammad's prophetic career. Ibn Kathir is among the notable authorities who say it is Meccan, while the *Tafsir Anwarul Bayan* and others maintain that it is Medinan.

Maududi splits the difference by noting a stylistic change between verses 1–24 and verses 25–78, and postulating that the first part comes from Mecca and the second from Medina. That stylistic change may also be evidence of the combination of two or more separate documents.

The Pilgrimage

IN THE NAME OF ALLAH, THE COMPASSIONATE, THE MERCIFUL.

¹O mankind, fear your Lord. Indeed, the earthquake of the hour is a dreadful thing. ²On the day when you see it, every nursing mother will forget her nursing child and every pregnant one will be delivered of her burden, and you will see mankind as drunk, yet they will not be drunk, but the torment of Allah will be strong. ³Among mankind is he who disagrees about Allah without knowledge, and follows each defiant satan, ⁴For him it is decreed that whoever takes him for friend, he indeed will mislead him and will guide him to the punishment of the flame. ⁵O mankind, if you are in doubt concerning the resurrection, then indeed, we have created you from dust, then from a drop of seed, then from a clot, then from a little lump of flesh shapely and shapeless, that we may make clear for you. And we cause what we will to remain in the wombs for an appointed time, and afterward we bring you forth as infants, then you attain your full strength. And among you there is he who dies, and among you there is he who is brought back to the most humble time of life, so that, after knowledge, he knows nothing. And you see the earth barren, but when we send down water on it, it stirs and swells and puts forth every lovely kind. ⁶That is because Allah, he is the truth and because he gives life to the dead, and because he is able to do all things, ⁷And because the hour will come, there is no doubt about it, and because Allah will raise those who are in the graves. ⁸And among mankind is he who disagrees about Allah without knowledge or guidance or a book giving light, ⁹Turning away in pride to seduce from the way of Allah. For him there is disgrace in this world, and on the day of resurrection we make him taste the torment of burning. ¹⁰This is for what your two hands have sent before, and because Allah is no oppressor of his slaves. ¹¹And among mankind is he who worships Allah on the borderline, so that if good comes upon him he is content with it, but if a trial comes upon him, he completely falls away utterly. He loses both this world and the hereafter. That is the complete loss. ¹²He calls upon, besides Allah, those who do not hurt him or benefit him. That is straying very far away. ¹³He calls out to him whose harm is closer than his benefit, indeed an evil patron and indeed an evil friend. ¹⁴Indeed, Allah causes those who believe and do good works to enter gardens under which rivers flow. Indeed, Allah does what he intends. ¹⁵Whoever thinks that Allah will not give him victory in this world and the hereafter, let him stretch a rope up to the roof, and let him hang himself. Then let him see whether his strategy can remove what he rages against.

---

4. "Flame" is *sa'ir*; see 4:10.

5. Maududi explains the prescientific character of this account of human gestation by saying: "The stages of gestation known today with the help of powerful microscopes, and through them alone, are not mentioned in the Qur'an. Instead, only those major changes are mentioned with which even the illiterate bedouin of the time were familiar."[1]

15. Those who doubt that Allah will help the messenger in this world and the next should hang themselves. "This," says Ibn Kathir, "was also the view of Mujahid, Ikrimah, Ata, Abu Al-Jawza, Qatadah and others. The meaning is: whoever thinks that Allah will not support Muhammad and His Book and His Religion, let him go and kill himself if it annoys him so much."[2]

¹⁶In this way do we reveal it as plain signs, and indeed Allah guides those whom he wills. ¹⁷Indeed, those who believe, and those who are Jews, and the Sabaeans and the Christians and the Zoroastrians and the idolaters, indeed, Allah will decide between them on the day of resurrection. Indeed, Allah is witness over all things. ¹⁸Haven't you seen that to Allah prostrates whoever is in the heavens and whoever is in the earth, and the sun, and the moon, and the stars, and the hills, and the trees, and the animals, and many of mankind, while there are many for whom the doom is justly deserved? He whom Allah humiliates, there is no one to give him honor. Indeed, Allah does what he will. ¹⁹These two are two groups that disagree about their Lord. But as for those who disbelieve, garments of fire will be cut out for them, boiling fluid will be poured down on their heads, ²⁰By which what is in their bellies, and their skins too, will be melted, ²¹And for them are hooked rods of iron. ²²Whenever, in their anguish, they would leave there, they are driven back to it, and, taste the torment of burning. ²³Indeed, Allah will cause those who believe and do good works to enter gardens under which rivers flow, in which they will be allowed armlets of gold, and pearls, and their clothing there will be silk. ²⁴They are guided to gentle speech, they are guided to the path of the glorious one. ²⁵Indeed, those who disbelieve and bar people from the way of Allah and from the sacred mosque, which we have appointed for mankind together, the dweller in it and the nomad, whoever seeks wrongful partiality in it, him we will cause to taste a painful doom. ²⁶And when we prepared the place of the house for Abraham, saying, Do not ascribe anything as a partner to me, and purify my house for those who walk around it, and those who stand and those who bow and make prostration. ²⁷And proclaim to

---

17. This is not as tolerant a statement as it may immediately appear to be. "Although the disbelievers are divided into many different religions," says the *Tafsir Anwarul Bayan*, "and creeds, they all share the common factor of disbeliefs. For this reason, they are collectively antagonistic towards Islam....Allah will decide on the Day of Judgement between them and disclose to them that only the Muslims were guided aright."³ See 2:62.

18. Even the sun, moon, stars, and all created beings worship Allah. A hadith depicts Muhammad describing the sunset in pre-scientific terms that appear to assume a flat earth: "It goes (i.e. travels) till it prostrates itself underneath the Throne and takes the permission to rise again, and it is permitted."⁴

19. A hadith has Muhammad say that 999 out of every thousand people will be sent to hell. On that day, Adam will ask Allah: "O Allah! How many are the people of the Fire?"⁵ Allah will answer: "From every one thousand, take out nine-hundred-and-ninety-nine."⁶ Muhammad goes on to explain in the same hadith that one person saved would be a Muslim, telling his companions: "Rejoice with glad tidings; one person will be from you and one-thousand will be from Gog and Magog."⁷ On Gog and Magog, see 18:94.

Maudidi is unusual among Muslim commentators on the Qur'an in noting a textual problem. He states that "some commentators" believe that this verse "belongs to the Madinan period," and explains that this view is based on the idea that the "two groups" mentioned in the verse are the Muslims and the Quraysh, and that this verse was written after the Battle of Badr, which took place after the Muslims emigrated from Mecca to Medina. "However," Maudidi concludes, "had there been any connection between this verse and the Battle of Badr it would have been located in *Surah al-Anfal* [sura 8] rather than in the present *surah* or in this particular context. If one accepts such a line of argument, it implies that the verses revealed subsequently were placed quite arbitrarily according to the whims of people and without any regard for textual coherence. On the contrary, we find a highly cohesive order in the Qur'an, something which is in itself, emphatic refutation of such an argument."⁸

25. Maudidi suggests that verses 25-78 were revealed not long after the Muslims migrated from Mecca to Medina, and around the time of the Hajj, the pilgrimage to Mecca, were feeling particularly homesick. According to Islamic tradition, the pagan Quraysh controlled Mecca at that time. Maudidi explains: "Blatant polytheism was rampant both in and around the Holy Mosque, whereas the followers of the One True God were barred from entering it. Thereafter, the Muslims were granted permission to fight against those oppressors, to dismantle their power, and to establish that righteous order of life under which goodness flourishes and evils are suppressed."⁹

26. On the sacred mosque, see 6:92.

mankind the pilgrimage. They will come to you on foot and on every lean camel, they will come from every deep ravine, **28**So that they may witness things that are of benefit to them, and mention the name of Allah on appointed days over the cattle that he has bestowed upon them. Then eat of them and feed the poor and unfortunate with them. **29**Then let them end their untidiness and pay their vows and walk around the ancient house. **30**That, and whoever magnifies the sacred things of Allah, it will be well for him in the sight of his Lord. The cattle are lawful to you except what has been told you. So shun the filth of idols, and shun lying speech, **31**Hanifs to Allah, not ascribing partners to him, for whoever ascribes partners to Allah, it is as if he had fallen from the sky and the birds had snatched him or the wind had blown him to a far-off place. **32**That, and whoever magnifies the offerings consecrated to Allah, it surely is from devotion of their hearts, **33**In them are benefits for you for an appointed term, and afterward they are brought for sacrifice to the ancient house. **34**And for every nation we have appointed a ritual, so that they may mention the name of Allah over the cattle that he has given them for food, and your God is one God, therefore submit to Him. And give good news to the humble, **35**Whose hearts fear when Allah is mentioned, and are patient amid whatever may come upon them, and those who establish worship and who spend out of that we have bestowed on them. **36**And the camels, we have established them among the ceremonies of Allah. In them you have much good. So mention the name of Allah over them when they are drawn up in lines. Then when their flanks fall, eat of them and feed the beggar and the suppliant. In this way we have made them subject to you, so that perhaps you may give thanks. **37**Their flesh and their food do not reach Allah, but devotion from you reaches him. In this way we have made them subject to you so that you may magnify Allah, that he has guided you. And give good news to the good. **38**Indeed, Allah defends those who are true. Indeed, Allah does not love each treacherous ingrate. **39**Permission is given to those who fight because they have been wronged, and Allah is indeed able to give them victory, **40**Those who have been driven from their homes unjustly only because they said, Our Lord is Allah, for if it had not been for Allah's repelling some men by means of others, monasteries and churches and oratories and mosques, in which the name of Allah is frequently mentioned, would surely have been destroyed. Indeed Allah helps someone who helps him. Indeed, Allah is strong, almighty. **41**Those who, if we give them power in the land, establish prayer and give alms and command

---

31. On *hanif*, see 2:135.

39. According to numerous Islamic authorities, "this was the first Ayah which was revealed about Jihad."[10] Maududi makes clear what kind of jihad is envisioned when he says that it is "the first verse that grants the Muslims permission to wage war."[11] Osama bin Laden began his October 6, 2002, letter to the American people with two Qur'an quotations, this verse and 4:76.[12]

40. Without jihad warfare, "monasteries and churches and oratories and mosques, in which the name of Allah is frequently mentioned, would surely have been destroyed." This would seem to be a blanket prohibition against the destruction of churches and other Christian edifices.

However, its specification that houses of worship in which "the name of Allah is frequently mentioned" must not be destroyed may assume the distinction between Christians who accept Islam and those who do not (see 2:62, 98:6).

41. The "prayer" that is to be established by the ruler is salat, Islamic prayer, and the alms to be given are *zakat*, Islamic almsgiving. Muhsin Khan and Hilali explain that the right that the ruler should command is "Islamic Monotheism and all that Islam orders

what is right and forbid what is wrong. And the outcome of events belongs to Allah. **42**If they deny you, in the same way the people of Noah, and Aad and Thamud, before you, denied, **43**And the people of Abraham and the people of Lot, **44**The dwellers in Midian. And Moses was denied, but I indulged the unbelievers for a long while, then I seized them, and how I condemned them! **45**How many a town have we destroyed while it was sinful, so that it lies in ruins, and a deserted well and lofty tower. **46**Haven't they travelled in the land, and do they have hearts with which to feel and ears with which to hear? For indeed, it is not the eyes that grow blind, but it is the hearts, which are within the bosoms, that grow blind. **47**And they will ask you to hasten on the doom, and Allah does not fail to keep his promise, but indeed, a day with Allah is as a thousand years of what you reckon. **48**And how many a town did I have patience with for a long time although it was sinful. Then I grasped it. To me is the return. **49**Say, O mankind, I am only a plain warner to you. **50**Those who believe and do good works, for them is pardon and a rich provision, **51**While those who try to thwart our signs, such people are rightful companions of the fire. **52**We never sent a messenger or a prophet before you who, except that when he recited, Satan would throw into it. But Allah abrogates what Satan proposes. Then Allah establishes his signs. Allah is the knower, the wise one, **53**So that he may make what Satan proposes a temptation for those in whose hearts is a disease, and those whose hearts are hardened. Indeed, the evildoers are in open antagonism, **54**And so that those who have been given knowledge may know that it is the truth from your Lord, so that they may believe in it and their hearts may submit humbly to him. Indeed, Allah truly is guiding those who believe to a right path. **55**And those who disbelieve will not stop being in doubt about it until the hour comes upon them unawares, or there come to them the torment of a disastrous day. **56**The dominion on that day will belong to Allah, he will judge between them. Then those who believed and did good works will be in gardens of delight, **57**While those who disbelieved and denied our signs, for them will be a shameful doom. **58**Those who emigrated for the cause of Allah and then were killed or died, Allah indeed will provide for them a good provision. Indeed, Allah, he truly is the best of all those who make provision. **59**Surely he will cause them to enter by an entry that they will love. Indeed, Allah truly is the knower, the indulgent. **60**That, and whoever retaliates with equivalent of what he was made to suffer and then has been wronged, Allah will help

---

one to do," while the wrong that he forbids is "disbelief, polytheism and all that Islam has forbidden."[13] See 3:110.

47. For Allah, a day is as a thousand years (cf. 2 Peter 3:8), but in 70:4 a day for Allah is as fifty thousand years.

52. Satan has interfered with the messages of all previous prophets, but Allah abrogates whatever falsehood he throws in (see 81:25 and 6:115, where it is asserted that no one can tamper with the revelations of Allah). Ibn Kathir says at this point many commentators of the Qur'an discuss the Satanic Verses incident; for that, see 53:19.

58. Ibn Kathir highlights both the importance of emigration for the sake of Allah (see 4:100) and of jihad warfare: "Allah tells us that those who migrate for the sake of Allah, seeking to earn His pleasure and that which is with Him, leaving behind their homelands, families and friends, leaving their countries for the sake of Allah and His Messenger to support His religion, then they are killed, i.e., in Jihad, or they die, i.e., they pass away without being involved in fighting, they will have earned an immense reward."[14]

59. Ibn Kathir states, invoking earlier authorities, that "this was revealed about a skirmish in which the Companions encountered some of the idolaters. The Muslims urged them not to fight during the Sacred Months, but the idolaters insisted on fighting and initiated the aggression. So the Muslims fought them and Allah granted them victory."[15] See 2:191 and 2:217.

him. Indeed, Allah truly is mild, forgiving. **61**That is because Allah makes the night pass into the day and makes the day pass into the night, and because Allah is the hearer, the seer. **62**That is because Allah, he is the true one, and what they invoke instead of him, it is false, and because Allah, he is the high one, the great one. **63**Don't you see how Allah sends down water from the sky and then the earth becomes green on the next day? Indeed, Allah is subtle, aware. **64**To him belongs all that is in the heavens and all that is on the earth. Indeed, Allah, he truly is the absolute, the owner of praise. **65**Haven't you seen how Allah has made all that is in the earth submissive to you? And the ship runs upon the sea by his command, and he holds back the heaven from falling on the earth unless it is by his permission. Indeed, Allah is, for mankind, full of kindness, merciful. **66**And it is he who gave you life, then he will cause you to die, and then will give you life. Indeed, man is truly an ingrate. **67**To each nation we have given sacred rites which they are to perform, so do not let them argue with you about this matter, but call them to your Lord. Indeed, you truly follow right guidance. **68**And if they argue with you, say, Allah is best aware of what you do. **69**Allah will judge between you on the day of resurrection regarding what you used to disagree about. **70**Haven't you known that Allah knows all that is in the heaven and the earth? Indeed, it is in a record. Indeed, that is easy for Allah. **71**And they worship instead of Allah what he has sent down

no justification for, and about which they have no knowledge. For evildoers there is no helper. **72**And when our signs are recited to them, you know the denial in the faces of those who disbelieve, they all just attack those who recite our signs to them. Say, Shall I proclaim to you something even worse than that? The fire. Allah has promised it[17] for those who disbelieve. A wretched journey's end. **73**O mankind, a comparison is made, so pay attention to it. Indeed, those you call upon besides Allah will never create a fly, even if they combined together for the purpose. And if the fly took something from them, they could not rescue it from it. The seeker and the sought are so weak! **74**They do not accord to Allah his rightful measure. Indeed, Allah is strong, almighty. **75**Allah chooses messengers from the angels, and from mankind. Indeed, Allah is the hearer, the seer. **76**He knows all that is in front of them and all that is behind them, and to Allah all things are returned. **77**O you who believe, bow down and prostrate yourselves, and worship your Lord, and do good, so that perhaps you may prosper. **78**And wage jihad for Allah with the jihad that is his right. He has chosen you and has not laid upon you any hardship in religion, the faith of your father Abraham. He has named you Muslims of old time and in this, so that the messenger may be a witness against you, and so that you may be witnesses against mankind. So establish prayer, give alms, and hold fast to Allah. He is your protecting friend. A blessed patron and a blessed helper.

---

62. Instead of "they invoke," the Warsh Qur'an has "you invoke."[16]

65. The sky would fall upon the earth were it not for the fact that Allah holds it up. Ibn Kathir explains: "If He willed, He could give the sky permission to fall on the earth, and whoever is in it would

be killed, but by His kindness, mercy and power, He withholds the heaven from falling on the earth, except by His leave."[17] The Qur'an assumes a prescientific cosmology, as at 18:86 and 36:38-40.

78. "Wage jihad": see 2:218.

SURA 23

The Believers

Al-Mu'minun

Introduction

Sura 23 is regarded in Islamic tradition as coming from the middle of Muhammad's Meccan period, during the time of a famine in Mecca, which is referred to obliquely in 23:75–6.

Umar, the second caliph of the Muslims, is depicted in a hadith as saying that Muhammad promised paradise to those who adhered to the opening ten verses of this sura: "When the Revelation came down to the Messenger of Allah, a sound could be heard near his face like the buzzing of bees. We waited a while, then he turned to face the qiblah and raised his hands, then he said: 'O Allah, give us more (blessing) and do not give us less; honour us and do not humiliate us, give to us and do not deprive us, give precedence to us and do not give others precedence over us; be pleased with us and make us pleased.' Then he said: 'Ten verses have been revealed to me; whoever adheres to them will enter Paradise.' Then he recited to us: 'Successful indeed are the believers' [al-Mu'minoon 23:1] until he completed the ten verses."[1]

---

1 Musnad Ahmad 223, https://sunnah.com/ahmad/2/140.

The Believers

IN THE NAME OF ALLAH, THE COMPASSIONATE, THE MERCIFUL.

¹The believers are successful indeed, ²Who are humble in their prayers, ³And who shun vain conversation, ⁴And who give alms, ⁵And who guard their private parts, ⁶Except from their wives or those that their right hands possess, for then they are not blameworthy, ⁷But whoever craves beyond that, such people are transgressors, ⁸And who are shepherds of their pledge and their covenant, ⁹And who pay attention to their prayers. ¹⁰These are the heirs ¹¹Who will inherit paradise. There they will remain. ¹²Indeed we created man from a product of wet earth, ¹³Then placed him as a drop in a safe lodging, ¹⁴Then we fashioned from the drop a clot, then we fashioned from the clot a little lump, then we fashioned the little lump bones, then clothed the bones with flesh, and then produced it as another creation. So blessed be Allah,

the best of creators. ¹⁵Then indeed, after that you surely die. ¹⁶Then indeed, on the day of resurrection you are raised. ¹⁷And we have created seven paths above you, and we are never unmindful of creation. ¹⁸And we send down from the sky water in measure, and we give it lodging in the earth, and indeed, we are able to withdraw it. ¹⁹Then with it, we produce for you gardens of date-palms and grapes, in which is much fruit for you and of which you eat, ²⁰And a tree that springs forth from Mount Sinai, that grows oil and seasoning for the eaters. ²¹And indeed, in the cattle there is truly a lesson for you. We give you to drink of what is in their bellies, and you have many uses in them, and of them you eat, ²²And on them and on the ship you are carried. ²³And we indeed sent Noah to his people, and he said, O my people, serve Allah. You have no other God except him. Will you not fear Allah? ²⁴But the chieftains of

---

1. The observation that the believers are successful recalls the muezzin's call to prayer from the minaret, which says in part: "Come to prayer, come to success," and the Qur'anic promise that the believers will prosper in this world as well as in the next (3:139, 3:148).

6. The exemption from the obligation of chastity with one's slave girls makes clear for what purpose they are intended (see 4:3). The *Tafsir al-Jalalayn* explains that one must guard one's chastity: "except from their wives or those they own as slaves, in which case they are not blameworthy in approaching them."¹ Writing in the twentieth century, Maududi says that "it is made clear that one need not guard one's private parts from two kinds of women – one's wives and slave-girls."²

The rape of captive women is also sanctioned in a hadith that depicts Muslim warriors asking Muhammad if they must practice *coitus interruptus* when having sexual intercourse with "some excellent Arab women" whom they have captured.³ Muhammad is made to respond only by addressing the question at hand, "It does not matter if you do not do it, for every soul that is to be born up to the Day of Resurrection will be born."⁴ He and those who are asking both take for granted that the captive women may permissibly be used in this way.

17. On the "seven paths above you," Ibn Kathir explains that "Allah knows what goes into the earth and what comes out of it, what comes down from heaven and what goes up into it. He is with you wherever you are, and Allah sees what you do. No heaven is

hidden from Him by another and no earth is hidden from Him by another. There is no mountain but He knows its features, and no sea but He knows what is in its depths. He knows the numbers of what is in the mountains, in the hills, the sands, the seas, the landscapes and the trees."⁵

A hadith recorded in the *Mishkat al-Masabih* depicts Muhammad offering a determinist view of why some people are good and others evil: "Allah took a handful of sand from all over the earth and mixed it with water so that it became mud. Allah then cast the mould of Sayyidina [Master] Adam from this mud. Allah then blew the soul into it. The progeny of Sayyidina Adam will therefore be like the portion of sand they were created from. Among them are reddish people, white people, black people and others between these complexions. Some of them are soft, others hard, some good, others bad (according to the type of sand)."⁶

23. Here begins another return to the stories of various prophets: Noah from here to 23:30, an unnamed prophet in the generation after Noah (23:31-41), other unnamed prophets sent to other people (23:42-44), Moses and Aaron (23:45-49), and Jesus (23:50). These again serve as parables for the reception accorded to the messenger and the need to accept him. On Noah, see also 7:59, 10:71, 11:25, 21:76, 25:37, 26:105, 29:14, 37:75, 50:12, 51:46, 53:52, 54:9, 57:26, 69:11, and 71:1.

24. The opponents of the Muslims are depicted as saying the same things that the enemies of the prophets of old said. Noah's

his people, who disbelieved, said, This is only a man like you, who would make himself superior to you. If Allah had willed, he surely could have sent down angels. We have not heard of this in the case of our fathers of old. **25**He is only a man in whom is a madness, so watch him for a while. **26**He said, My Lord, help me because they deny me. **27**Then we inspired him, saying, Build the ship under our eyes and our inspiration. Then, when our command comes and the oven boils over, introduce into it two spouses of every kind, and your family except him against whom the word has already gone forth. And do not plead with me on behalf of those who have done wrong. Indeed, they will be drowned. **28**And when you are on board the ship, you and whoever is with you, then say, Praise be to Allah who has saved us from the wrongdoing people. **29**And say, My Lord, cause me to disembark at a blessed place, for you are best of all who enable to disembark. **30**Indeed, in this truly are signs, for indeed, we are always putting to the test. **31**Then, after them, we brought forth another generation, **32**And we sent among them a messenger of their own, saying, Serve Allah, You have no other God except him. Will you not fear Allah? **33**And the chieftains of his people, who disbelieved and denied the meeting of the hereafter, and whom we had made soft in the life of this world, said, This is only a mortal like you, who eats what you eat and drinks what you drink. **34**If you were to obey a mortal like yourselves, then, indeed, you would surely be losers. **35**Does he promise you that you, when you are dead and have become dust and bones, will be raised up? **36**Impossible, impossible is what you are promised. **37**There is nothing but our life of this world, we die and we live, and we shall not be raised.

38He is only a man who has invented a lie about Allah. We are not going to put faith in him. **39**He said, My Lord, Help me because they deny me. **40**He said, In a little while they will surely become repentant. **41**So the cry rightfully overtook them, and we made them like wreckage. A far removal for wrongdoing people. **42**Then after them we brought forth other generations. **43**No nation can go beyond its term, or postpone it. **44**Then we sent our messengers one after another. Whenever its messenger came to a nation, they denied him, so we caused them to follow one another and we made them into reports. A far removal for people who do not believe. **45**Then we sent Moses and his brother Aaron with our signs and a clear justification, **46**To Pharaoh and his chiefs, but they scorned and were despotic people. **47**And they said, Shall we put faith in two mortals like ourselves, and whose people serve us? **48**So they denied them and became among those who were destroyed. **49**And we indeed gave Moses the book, so that perhaps they might go right. **50**And we made the son of Mary and his mother a sign, and we gave them refuge on a height, a place of flocks and water springs. **51**O you messengers, eat of the good things, and do right. Indeed, I am aware of

---

enemies scoff that he is just "a man like you"; the critics of an unnamed prophet say the same thing (23:33); the messenger is also just an ordinary man (18:110).

25. They say Noah is possessed, just as they say about the messenger (44:14).

37. The unbelievers deny that the dead will be raised, just as they did to the messenger (19:66).

46. On Pharaoh, see also 2:49, 3:11, 7:103, 8:52, 10:75, 14:6, 17:101, 20:24, 26:11, 27:12, 28:3, 29:39, 38:12, 40:24, 44:17, 50:13, 51:38, 54:41, 66:11, 69:9, 73:15, 79:15, 85:18, and 89:10.

what you do. ⁵²And indeed, this your religion is one religion and I am your Lord, so keep your duty to me. ⁵³But they have divided their religion among them into sects, each group rejoicing in its tenets. ⁵⁴So leave them in their error until the time comes. ⁵⁵They think that in the wealth and sons with which we provide them ⁵⁶We hasten to them with good things. No, but they do not perceive. ⁵⁷Indeed, those who go in awe for fear of their Lord, ⁵⁸And those who believe in the signs of their Lord, ⁵⁹And those who do not ascribe partners to their Lord, ⁶⁰And those who give what they give with their hearts full of fear because they are about to return to their Lord, ⁶¹These people race for the good things, and they will win them in the race. ⁶²And we do not burden any soul beyond its ability, and with us is a book that speaks the truth, and they will not be wronged. ⁶³No, but their hearts are in ignorance of this, and they have other deeds as well that they are doing, ⁶⁴Until when we seize their luxurious ones with the punishment, look, they call out for help. ⁶⁵Do not call for help today. Surely you will not be helped by us. ⁶⁶My signs were recited to you, but you used to turn back on your heels, ⁶⁷In scorn of it. Every night you spoke nonsense together. ⁶⁸Have they not pondered over the word, or has something come to them which did not come to their fathers of old? ⁶⁹Or do they not know their messenger, and so reject him? ⁷⁰Or do they say, There is a madness in him? No, but he brings them the truth, and most of them are haters of the truth. ⁷¹And if the truth had followed their

desires, indeed the heavens and the earth and whoever is in them would have been corrupted. No, we have brought them their reminder, but they now turn away from their reminder. ⁷²Or do you ask for any payment from them? But the bounty of your Lord is better, for he is best of all who make provision. ⁷³And indeed, you truly call them to a straight path. ⁷⁴And indeed, those who do not believe in the hereafter are indeed astray from the path. ⁷⁵Though we had mercy on them and relieved them of the harm afflicting them, they still would wander blindly on in their insolence. ⁷⁶Already we have seized them with punishment, but they do not humble themselves to their Lord, and they do not pray, ⁷⁷Until, when we open the gate of extreme punishment for them, look, they are appalled at it. ⁷⁸It is he who has created ears and eyes and hearts for you. You give small thanks. ⁷⁹And it is he who has dispersed you all over the earth, and to him you will be gathered. ⁸⁰And it is he who gives life and causes death, and the difference of night and day is his. Do you then have no sense? ⁸¹No, but they say the kind of thing that the men of old said, ⁸²They say, When we are dead and have become dust and bones, shall we then really be raised again? ⁸³We were already promised this, we and our forefathers. Indeed, this is nothing but fables of the men of old. ⁸⁴Say, To whom do the earth and whoever is on it belong, if you have knowledge? ⁸⁵They will say, To Allah. Say, Will you not then remember? ⁸⁶Say, Who is Lord of the seven heavens, and Lord of the great throne? ⁸⁷They will

---

52. Again it is emphasized that the messenger is bringing the same message as that of the earlier prophets (see 3:3, 3:50).

86. Instead of "Lord of the seven heavens," an eighth-century manuscript now in the National Library of France has "Lord of the

heavens," although the missing word has been added by a different hand at a later date, bringing the text in line with the version published in Cairo in 1924.[7]

say, To Allah. Say, Will you not then keep duty? ⁸⁸Say, In whose hand is the dominion over all things and he protects, while against him there is no protection, if you have knowledge? ⁸⁹They will say, To Allah. Say, How then are you bewitched? ⁹⁰No, but we have brought them the truth, and indeed, they are liars. ⁹¹Allah has not chosen any son, nor is there any god along with him, or else each god would surely have championed what he created, and some of them would surely have overcome others. May Allah be glorified above everything that they claim. ⁹²Knower of the invisible and the visible, and may he be exalted over all that they ascribe as partners. ⁹³Say, My Lord, if you would show me what they are promised, ⁹⁴My Lord, then do not place me among the wrongdoing people. ⁹⁵And indeed we are able to show you what we have promised them. ⁹⁶Repel evil with what is better. We are best aware of what they claim. ⁹⁷And say, My Lord, I seek refuge in you from suggestions of the satans, ⁹⁸And I seek refuge in you, my Lord, so that they do not be present with me, ⁹⁹Until, when death comes to one of them, he says, My Lord, send me back, ¹⁰⁰So that I may do right in what I have left behind. But no, it is just a word that he speaks, and behind them is a barrier until the day when they are raised. ¹⁰¹And when the trumpet is blown, there will be no kinship among them that day, nor will they ask about one another. ¹⁰²Then those whose scales are heavy, they are the successful. ¹⁰³And

those whose scales are light are those who lose their souls, remaining in Gehenna. ¹⁰⁴The fire burns their faces, and they grimace within it. ¹⁰⁵Weren't my signs recited to you, and then you used to deny them? ¹⁰⁶They will say, Our Lord, our evil fortune conquered us, and we were misguided people. ¹⁰⁷Our Lord, bring us out of here. If we return, then indeed we will be wrongdoers. ¹⁰⁸He says, Away with you in it, and do not speak to me. ¹⁰⁹Indeed, there was a group of my slaves who said, Our Lord, we believe, therefore forgive us and have mercy on us, for you are best of all who show mercy, ¹¹⁰But you made them a laughingstock until they caused you to forget the remembrance of me, while you laughed at them. ¹¹¹Indeed, I have rewarded them today for being steadfast in that they, even they are the triumphant. ¹¹²He will say, How long did you remain on the earth, counting by years? ¹¹³They will say, We remained a day or part of a day. Ask those who keep count. ¹¹⁴He will say, You remained only a little, if you only knew. ¹¹⁵Did you think then that we had created you for nothing, and that you would not be returned to us? ¹¹⁶Now may Allah, the true king, be exalted. There is no God except him, the Lord of the throne of favor. ¹¹⁷He who calls upon any other god along with Allah has no proof of it. His reckoning is only with his Lord. Indeed, unbelievers will not be successful. ¹¹⁸And say, My Lord, forgive and have mercy, for you are the best of all who show mercy.

---

91. Ibn Kathir explains: "If it were decreed that there should be a plurality of deities, each of them would have exclusive control over whatever he had created, so there would never be any order in the universe. But what we see is that the universe is ordered and cohesive, with the upper and lower realms connected to one another in the most perfect fashion."[8]

101. On Judgment Day, the scoffers will have no one to help them. Everyone will stand alone before Allah; no intercession from

others will be accepted (2:48, 2:123, 6:94, 39:43, 42:46). However, the Qur'an elsewhere accepts intercession with Allah's permission (10:3, 21:28, 34:23, and 53:26).

102. See 7:8, 21:47.

103. On Gehenna, see 2:206.

104. The *Tafsir al-Jalalayn* says: "The Fire will sear their faces, making them grimace horribly in it, their lips drawn back from their teeth."[9]

SURA 24

The Light

An-Nur

Introduction

According to Islamic tradition, this is a Medinan sura that was revealed after the Muslims' defeat of a pagan Arab tribe, the Banu al-Mustaliq. Much of it is preoccupied with one of the most notorious events in early Islamic history as recorded in the foundational Islamic texts: the rumors that Muhammad's favorite wife, Aisha, had committed adultery—an incident that has repercussions for Muslim women down to this day.

The Light

In the name of Allah, the compassionate, the merciful.

1A sura which we have revealed and commanded, and in which we have revealed clear signs, that perhaps you may be mindful. **2**The adulterer and the adulteress, lash each one of them a hundred times. And do not let pity for the two prevent you from obedience to Allah, if you believe in Allah and the last day. And let a group of believers witness their punishment. **3**The adulterer will not marry anyone except an adulteress or an idolatress, and no one will marry the adulteress except an adulterer or an idolater. All that is forbidden to believers. **4**And those who accuse honorable women but do not bring four witnesses, lash them eighty times and never accept their testimony, they indeed are evildoers, **5**Except those who afterward repent and make amends. Indeed, Allah is forgiving, merciful. **6**As for those who accuse their wives but have no witnesses except themselves, let the testimony of one of them be four testimonies by Allah, that he is among those who speak the truth, **7**And yet a fifth, invoking the curse of Allah on him if he is among those who lie. **8**And it will avert the punishment from her if she bears witness before Allah four times that the thing he says is indeed false, **9**And a fifth that the wrath of Allah be upon her if he speaks the truth. **10**And if it had it not been for the favor of Allah and his mercy to you, and that Allah is merciful, wise, **11**Indeed, those who spread the slander are a gang among you. Do not think it is a bad thing for you, no, it is good for you. To every man among them, what he has earned of the sin, and as for him among them who had the greater share in it, his will be an awful doom. **12**Why didn't the believers, men and women, when you heard it, think good of their own people, and say, It is an obvious untruth? **13**Why didn't they produce four witnesses? Since they do not produce witnesses, they indeed are liars in the sight of Allah. **14**If it had not been for

2. On the penalties of lashing (which is prescribed here) and stoning to death for adultery, see 4:15.

4. On the need for four witnesses, see 24:13.

11. Beginning here, the Qur'an furiously castigates a group that has "spread the slander" against a chaste woman and the believers for believing them (24:12). This is a "most serious" matter (24:15), but the Qur'an gives little context regarding what exactly is being discussed.

13. The details of the incident that is the subject of this passage are filled in by several hadiths. It states that Allah had recently ordered the veiling of women (a command that is transmitted at 24:31), so Muhammad's child bride Aisha, when she accompanied him to a battle, was carried in a curtained howdah on the back of a camel. The caravan stopped, and Aisha got out to answer "the call of nature."[1] While returning, she lost her necklace and stopped to search for it. Meanwhile, her attendants, who were forbidden to look at or speak to a wife of Muhammad, loaded the howdah back onto the camel without realizing that she wasn't in it. "At that time," Aisha explains, "I was still a young lady," and what's more, "women were light in weight for they did not get fat."[2]

Thus the caravan left without her, and Aisha was stranded. Presently a Muslim warrior who was traveling behind the army came along and was considerably startled to find Aisha alone. "I veiled my face with my head cover at once," Aisha insisted, "and by Allah, we did not speak a single word, and I did not hear him saying any word besides his Istirja"—a prayer spoken in times of distress.[3] The warrior carried Aisha on his camel to the Muslims' camp—and almost immediately rumors started. Aisha explains: "After we returned to Medina, I became ill for a month. The people were propagating the forged statements of the slanderers while I was unaware of anything of all that, but I felt that in my present ailment, I was not receiving the usual kindness from Allah's Messenger which I used to receive when I got sick."[4]

Ali bin Abi Talib, who later became the founding figure for the Shi'ite Muslims, ungallantly reminds Muhammad that there were "plenty of women" available to him; Aisha never forgot or forgave this, and according to Islamic tradition, it became a basis for the Sunni-Shi'ite split, as Aisha later actually led an army against Ali's forces.[5]

The traditions record that Muhammad was distressed by all this, as he loved Aisha. In due time he received a revelation as Aisha watched: "So there overtook him the same hard condition which used to overtake him (when he was Divinely Inspired) so that the drops of his sweat were running down, like pearls, though it was

the favor of Allah and his mercy to you in the world and the hereafter, an awful doom would had overtaken you for what you whispered about. **15**When you welcomed it with your tongues, and spoke with your mouths what you had no knowledge about, you considered it a small matter. In the sight of Allah, it is very serious. **16**Why, when you heard it, didn't you say, It is not for us to speak of this? Glory be to you. This is awful slander. **17**Allah warns you not ever to repeat anything like it, if you are believers. **18**And he explains the signs to you. Allah is the knower, the wise one. **19**Indeed, those who love the idea that slander would be spread about those who believe, theirs will be a painful punishment in this world and the hereafter. Allah knows. You do not know. **20**If it had not been for the favor of Allah and his mercy to you, and that Allah is compassionate, merciful. **21**O you who believe, do not follow the footsteps of Satan. To whomever follows the footsteps of Satan, indeed, he commands filthiness and wrong. If it had not been for the favor of Allah and his mercy to you, not one of you would ever have grown pure. But Allah causes those whom he wills to grow. And Allah is the hearer, the knower. **22**And do not let those who possess dignity and ease among you swear not to give to near relatives and to the needy, and to migrants for the sake of Allah. Let them forgive and show

indulgence. Don't you long for Allah to forgive you? Allah is forgiving, merciful. **23**Indeed, as for those who falsely accuse virtuous, believing, unwary women are cursed in this world and the hereafter. Theirs will be an awful doom **24**On the day when their tongues and their hands and their feet testify against them about what they used to do, **25**On that day, Allah will pay them their just reward, and they will know that Allah, he is the clear truth. **26**Vile women are for vile men, and vile men for vile women. Good women are for good men, and good men for good women, such people are innocent of what people say, for them is pardon and a bountiful provision. **27**O you who believe, do not enter houses other than your own without first announcing your presence and invoking peace upon the people in them. That is better for you, so that you may be mindful. **28**And if you find no one in them, still do not enter until permission has been given. And if it be said to you, Go away again, then go away, for it is purer for you. Allah knows what you do. **29**No sin for you to enter uninhabited houses in which is comfort for you. Allah knows what you proclaim and what you hide. **30**Tell the believing men to lower their gaze and be modest. That is purer for them. Indeed, Allah is aware of what they do. **31**And tell the believing women to lower their gaze and be modest, and to display of their adornment only

---

a (cold) winter day, and that was because of the heaviness of the Statement which was revealed to him. When that state of Allah's Apostle was over, and he was smiling when he was relieved, the first word he said was, 'Aisha, Allah has declared your innocence.'"6 The revelation from Allah also required that adultery and other sexual crimes could only be established on the testimony of four witnesses.

This ninth-century folk tale is thus the basis for the fact that it remains part of Islamic law to this day that four male Muslim witnesses must be produced in order to establish a crime of adultery or related indiscretions.

22. See 4:100.

26. Ibn Kathir, quoting an earlier authority, says that this is about the slander against Aisha: "Allah would not have made Aishah the wife of His Messenger unless she had been good, because he is the best of the best of mankind. If she had been evil, she would not have been a suitable partner either according to His Laws or His decree."7

30. Says Ibn Kathir: Men "should look only at what is permissible for them to look at, and lower their gaze from forbidden things. If it so happens that a person's gaze unintentionally falls upon something forbidden, he should quickly look away."8

what is apparent, and to draw their veils over their bosoms, and not to reveal their adornment except to their own husbands or fathers or husbands' fathers, or their sons or their husbands' sons, or their brothers or their brothers' sons or sisters' sons, or their women, or their slaves, or male attendants who lack desire, or children who know nothing of women's nakedness. And do not let them stamp their feet so as to reveal what they hide of their adornment. And turn to Allah together, O believers, so that you may succeed. [32]And marry off those among you who are single and the pious among your slaves and maidservants. If they are poor, Allah will enrich them from his bounty. Allah is of ample means, aware. [33]And let those who cannot find a match keep chaste until Allah gives them independence by his favor. And those among your slaves as seek a writing, write it for them if you are aware of anything good in them, and bestow upon them from the wealth of Allah which he has bestowed upon you. Do not force your slave-girls to become whores so that you may seek enjoyment of the life of this world, if they wish to preserve their chastity. And if one forces them, then after they are forced, indeed, Allah will be forgiving, merciful. [34]And indeed we have sent down for you signs that make clear, and the example of those who passed away before you. A warning to those who fear Allah. [35]Allah is the light of the heavens and the earth. The comparison of his light is as a niche in which is a lamp. The lamp is in a glass. The glass is like a shining star, kindled from a blessed tree, an olive neither of the east nor of the west, whose oil would almost glow forth though no fire touched it. Light upon light. Allah guides those

---

31. This is not a matter of choice, as is often claimed today, but a divine commandment. Ibn Kathir explains: "This is a command from Allah to the believing women, and jealousy on His part over the wives of His believing servants. It is also to distinguish the believing women from the women of the Jahiliyyah [the society of unbelievers] and the deeds of the pagan women."[9]

The *Tafsir al-Jalalayn* states that this verse means that when in public women should cover "everything other than their face and hands."[10] In a hadith, Aisha is made to recount that Muhammad said that "when a woman reaches the age of menstruation, it does not suit her that she displays her parts of body except this and this, and he pointed to her face and hands."[11] In another hadith, a woman with a veil over her face came to see Muhammad; she was looking for her son, who had been killed in battle. Muhammad asked her: "You have come here asking for your son while veiling your face?"[12] She responded: "If I am afflicted with the loss of my son, I shall not suffer the loss of my modesty."[13] Pleased, Muhammad told her: "You will get the reward of two martyrs for your son," because "the people of the Book have killed him."[14]

Regarding women stamping their feet, Ibn Kathir states: "During Jahiliyyah, when women walked in the street wearing anklets and no one could hear them, they would stamp their feet so that men could hear their anklets ringing. Allah forbade the believing women to do this."[15] And: "Women are also prohibited from wearing scent and perfume when they are going outside the home, lest men should smell their perfume."[16]

However, Christoph Luxenberg notes that the traditional understanding of this verse is a "conjectural and unsuccessful interpretation" demonstrating that "the Arabic commentators did not know what to do with this, to their ears, foreign-sounding expression."[17] Noting that the earliest manuscripts of the Qur'an do not contain the diacritical marks that allow many Arabic letters to be distinguished from one another (see 2:2), Luxenberg reads the passage as if it had been written in Syro-Aramaic and finds it to be a paraphrase of Isaiah 3:16: "Because the daughters of Zion are haughty and walk with outstretched necks, glancing wantonly with their eyes, mincing along as they go, tinkling with their feet." The Syro-Aramaic word here rendered as "mincing," however, he says is closer to "hopping." Accordingly, he offers a variant reading of this section of this verse: instead of, "Do not let them stamp their feet so as to reveal what they hide of their adornment," he reads it as, "They should not (walk around) with their feet hopping…so that their concealed charms stand out."[18]

33. Muslims should free their slaves upon their request, "provided," says Ibn Kathir, "that the servant has some skill and means of earning so that he can pay his master the money that is stipulated in the contract."[19] Muslims should not force their slave girls to become prostitutes and live off the profits, if the slave girls want to remain chaste. This, however, does not abrogate the slave-owner's right to use them, as specified in 4:3, 4:24, 23:6, 33:50, and 70:30.

Instead of, "And let those who cannot find a match keep chaste until Allah gives them independence by his favor," the Shi'ite Bankipur Qur'an manuscript has, "And let those who cannot find a match keep chaste through temporary marriage until Allah gives them independence by his favor."[20] See 4:24 on temporary marriage, as well as 2:59 and the Appendix: Two Apocryphal Shi'ite Suras regarding the Bankipur manuscript.

35. Allah is the light of the heavens and the earth; this is the verse that gives this sura its name.

whom he wills to his light. And Allah speaks to mankind in allegories, for Allah is knower of all things. **36**In houses which Allah has allowed to be exalted and that his name will be remembered within. In them, offer praise to him in the morning and evening. **37**Men who are seduced from remembrance of Allah and constancy in prayer and paying alms to the poor by neither buying nor selling, who fear a day when hearts and eyes will be overturned, **38**So that Allah may reward them with the best of what they did, and increase reward for them from his bounty. Allah gives blessings without limit to those whom he wills. **39**As for those who disbelieve, their deeds are like a mirage in a desert. The thirsty one thinks it is water until he comes to it and finds it to be nothing, and finds in its place Allah who pays him his due, and Allah is swift at reckoning. **40**Or as darkness on a vast, abysmal sea. There covers him a wave, above which is a wave, above which is a cloud. Layer upon layer of darkness. When he holds out his hand, he can barely see it. And he for whom Allah has not appointed light, for him there is no light. **41**Haven't you seen that Allah, it is he whom all who are in the heavens and the earth praise, and the birds in their flight? Of each he knows indeed the prayer and the praise, and Allah is aware of what they do. **42**And to Allah belongs the dominion of the heavens and the earth, and to Allah is the journeying. **43**Haven't you seen how Allah makes the clouds move gently, then gathers them, then makes them layers, and you see the rain come forth from between them, he sends down from the heaven mountains

in which are hail, and strikes with it those whom he wills, and turns it away from those whom he wills. The flashing of his lightning almost snatches away the sight. **44**Allah causes the revolution of the day and the night. Indeed, in this is indeed a lesson for those who see. **45**Allah has created every animal of water. Among them is one that goes upon its belly and one that goes upon two legs and one that goes upon four. Allah creates what he wills. Indeed, Allah is able to do all things. **46**Indeed we have sent down signs and explained them. Allah guides those whom he wills to a straight path. **47**And they say, we believe in Allah and the messenger, and we obey, then after that a faction of them turn away. Such people are not believers. **48**And when they appeal to Allah and his messenger to judge between them, indeed, a faction of them turn away, **49**But if right had been with them, they would have come to him willingly. **50**Is there a disease in their hearts, or so they have doubts, or are they afraid that Allah and his messenger will wrong them in judgment? No, but such people are evildoers. **51**The saying of believers when they appeal to Allah and his messenger to judge between them is only that they say, We hear and we obey. And such people are those who are successful. **52**He who obeys Allah and his messenger, and fears Allah, and keeps duty, such people indeed are victorious. **53**They solemnly swear by Allah that, if you order them, they will go forth. Say, Do not swear, known obedience. Indeed, Allah is informed of what you do. **54**Say, Obey Allah and obey the messenger. But if you turn away, then for

---

52. Those who obey Allah and Muhammad will be victorious in the end, a conviction that has sustained many a jihadist throughout Islamic history through setbacks and defeats.

53. "Go forth," says the *Tafsir al-Jalalayn*, "to do jihad."[21] See 2:218, 9:29. Ibn Kathir explains: "Allah says about the hypocrites who had promised the Messenger and sworn that if he were to

him only what he has been charged with, and for you only what you have been charged with. If you obey him, you will be guided. But the messenger has no other responsibility than to convey plainly. ⁵⁵Allah has promised those of you who believe and do good works that he will surely make them succeed on the earth even as he caused those who were before them to succeed, and that he will surely establish for them their religion which he has approved for them, and will give them in exchange safety after their fear. They serve me. They ascribe no thing as partner to me. Those who disbelieve from now on, they are the wrong-doers. ⁵⁶Establish prayer and give alms and obey the messenger, so that perhaps you may find mercy. ⁵⁷Do not think that the unbelievers can escape in the land. Fire will be their home, a wretched journey's end. ⁵⁸O you who believe, let your slaves, and those of you who have not come to puberty, ask permission of you at three times, before the dawn prayer, and when you lay aside your clothing for the heat of noon, and after the night prayer. Three times of privacy for you. It is no sin for them or for you at other times, when some of you move about, attendant upon others. In this way Allah makes the signs clear for you. Allah is the knower, the wise one. ⁵⁹And when the children among you come to puberty then let them ask permission in the same way as those

before them used to ask it. In this way Allah makes his signs clear for you. Allah is the knower, the wise one. ⁶⁰As for women who are past child-bearing age, who have no hope of marriage, it is no sin for them if they adjust their clothing in such a way as not to show adornment. But to refrain is better for them. Allah is the hearer, the knower. ⁶¹No blame is there upon the blind nor any blame upon the lame nor any blame upon the sick nor on yourselves if you eat from your houses, or the houses of your fathers, or the houses of your mothers, or the houses of your brothers, or the houses of your sisters, or the houses of your fathers' brothers, or the houses of your fathers' sisters, or the houses of your moth-ers' brothers, or the houses of your mothers' sisters, or from where you hold the keys, or of a friend. It will be no sin for you whether you eat together or apart. But when you enter houses, greet one another with a greeting from Allah, blessed and sweet. In this way Allah makes his signs clear for you, so that perhaps you may understand. ⁶²They only are the true believers who believe in Allah and his messenger and, when they are with him on some common errand, do not go away until they have asked permission from him. Indeed, those who ask permission from you, those are the ones who believe in Allah and his messenger. So if they ask your permission

---

command them to go out for battle, they would go."²² However, of the hypocrites "it is known that your obedience is merely verbal and is not accompanied by action. Every time you swear an oath you lie."²³

55. A momentous promise. "This is a promise," says Ibn Kathir, "from Allah to His Messenger that He would cause his Ummah [community] to become successors on earth, i.e., they would become the leaders and rulers of mankind, through whom He would reform the world and to whom people would submit, so that they would have in exchange a safe security after their fear."²⁴ Ibn

Kathir then says, "This is what Allah did indeed do," and recounts some of the early Islamic conquests.²⁵

58. Slaves and children must ask permission before coming into the presence of the messenger. This passage and others like it have been adduced to make the case that Muhammad was using the Qur'an to dictate his personal preferences, and thus indirectly estab-lishing his historicity, as it is difficult to see why such instructions would be invented for a legendary figure. However, it is possible that these instructions were originally given by someone whose tradi-tions were later incorporated into the Muhammad legend.

for some matter of theirs, give permission to those whom you will of them, and ask forgiveness of Allah for them. Indeed, Allah is forgiving, merciful. ⁶³Do not make the call of the messenger among you like your calling of one another. Allah knows those of you who steal away, hiding themselves. And let those who conspire to evade orders beware, so that grief or painful punishment do not come upon them. ⁶⁴Indeed, truly to Allah belongs whatever is in the heavens and the earth. He knows your situation. And the day when they are returned to him so that he may inform them of what they did. Allah is knower of all things.

SURA 25

The Furqan

Al-Furqan

Introduction

On the meaning of *furqan*, usually translated as "criterion," see 3:4. In the first verse of this sura, it is identified as the Qur'an. The *Tafsir al-Jalalayn* says that the Qur'an is "so called because it discriminates between the true and the false."[1]

Allah sent it to the messenger, the *Tafsir al-Jalalayn* continues, "so that he can be a warner—about the punishment of Allah—to all beings—human beings and jinn, but not angels."[2] Why not to the angels? Perhaps because the angels "do not resist Allah in what he commands them" (66:6), and thus have no need of Muhammad's warning. But he has been sent to everyone on earth, as he himself explains in a hadith: "Every Prophet used to be sent to his nation only but I have been sent to all mankind."[3]

This is traditionally regarded as a late Meccan sura. However, the *Tafsir al-Jalalayn* asserts that verses 68, 69, and 70 are Medinan, which may be an indication of some textual dislocation.[4]

---

1 *Tafsir al-Jalalayn*, 770.
2 Ibid.
3 Bukhari, vol. 1, book 7, no. 335.
4 *Tafsir al-Jalalayn*, 770.

The Furqan

IN THE NAME OF ALLAH, THE COMPASSIONATE, THE MERCIFUL.

1Blessed is he who has revealed the *furqan* to his slave, so that he may be a warner for the worlds. **2**He to whom the dominion of the heavens and the earth belong, he has chosen no son nor has he any partner in the dominion. He has created everything and has determined a measure for it. **3**Yet they choose besides him other gods who create nothing but are themselves created, and possess neither harm nor profit for themselves, and possess neither death nor life, nor power to raise the dead. **4**Those who disbelieve say, This is nothing but a lie that he has invented, and other people have helped him with it, so that they have produced a slander and a lie. **5**And they say, Fables of the men of old which he has had written down so that they are dictated to him in the morning and evening. **6**Say, he who knows the secret of the heavens and the earth has revealed it. Indeed, he is always forgiving, merciful. **7**And they say, What is wrong with this messenger that he eats food and walks in the markets? Why isn't an angel sent down to him, to be a warner with him? **8**Or treasure thrown down to him, or why doesn't he have a paradise from which to eat? And the evildoers say, You are just following a bewitched man. **9**See how they make comparisons for you, so that they are all astray and cannot find a road. **10**Blessed is he who, if he wills, will assign you better than that. Gardens under which rivers flow, and will assign you mansions. **11**No, but they deny the hour, and for those who deny the hour we have prepared a flame. **12**When it sees them from afar, they hear its crackling and roar. **13**And when they are flung into a narrow place of it, chained together, they pray for destruction there. **14**Do not pray that day for one destruction, but pray for many destructions. **15**Say, Is that better, or the garden of immortality which is promised to those who fear Allah? It will be their reward and journey's end. **16**Remaining in

---

1. As noted at 3:4, *furqan*, here and generally in Islamic tradition rendered as "criterion," is a Syriac word meaning "redemption, salvation."[1] This would make this verse read that Allah "has revealed salvation," and would make it one example of the Qur'an's Aramaic Christian substratum. This possibility becomes more likely in light of 25:1. Heger also notes that the word translated as "warner" is *nadhir*, which in Syriac is "votive gift" or "sacrifice." In this light, the verse reads: "Blessed is he who has revealed salvation to his servant, so that he may be a sacrifice for the worlds"—a Christian confession.

This verse is also one of the apparent (and unacknowledged by Islamic commentators) exceptions to the rule that Allah is the lone speaker in the Qur'an—unless he is blessing himself for delivering the Qur'an to the messenger.

2. Regarding Allah's not having a son, see 2:116, 19:35.

3. This could be a reference to the Christian Trinity, or to the pagan Arabs who worshiped Allah along with many other gods, or both.

5. See 3:37 and 16:103. Then there is an unnamed figure who, according to a hadith, "was a Christian who embraced Islam and read Surat-al-Baqara [sura 2] and Al-Imran [sura 3], and he used

to write (the revelations) for the Prophet."[2] That is, he used to transcribe Muhammad's Qur'anic recitations. Evidently this experience disabused him of the notion that they were divinely inspired, for "later on he returned to Christianity again and he used to say: 'Muhammad knows nothing but what I have written for him.'"[3]

The Qur'an reacts with fury to one person who made these charges: Allah points out that the man was "illegitimate" and promises to brand him on the nose (68:10-16). See also 2:79 and 3:78. These and other passages suggest that some people around the messenger mocked his prophetic pretensions by representing their own writings, or folkloric or apocryphal material, as divine revelation and selling them to him. This could be based on an event in the life of one of the people whose legends are incorporated into Muhammad's story, or could reflect the reactions of people to alterations in the Qur'an as the text was being finalized and responses to those reactions.

7. Here begins another section about the perversity of the unbelievers, the rewards awaiting the just, and the pangs of regret that the damned will feel on the day of judgment.

11. "Flame" is *sa'ir*, on which see 4:10.

it, they have all that they desire. For your Lord, it is a promise that must be fulfilled. **17**And on the day when he will gather them and what they worship instead of Allah and will say, Was it you who misled these my slaves, or did they wander from the way? **18**They will say, May you be glorified, it was not for us to choose any protecting friends beside you, but you gave them and their fathers ease until they forgot the warning and became lost people. **19**In this way they will give you the lie regarding what you say, then you can neither turn away nor obtain help. And whoever among you does wrong, we will make him taste great torment. **20**We never sent before you any messengers but indeed, they indeed ate food and walked in the markets. And we have appointed some of you as a test for others. Will you be steadfast? And your Lord is ever the seer. **21**And those who do not look for a meeting with us say, Why aren't angels sent down to us and we do not see our Lord? Surely they think too highly of themselves and are scornful with great pride. **22**On the day when they see the angels, on that day there will be no good news for the guilty, and they will cry, A forbidding ban. **23**And we will turn to the work they did and make it scattered dust. **24**Those who have earned the garden on that day will be better in their home and happier in their place of noonday rest, **25**A day when the heaven with the clouds will

be torn asunder and the angels will be sent down, a grand descent. **26**The dominion on that day will be the true, belonging to Ar-Rahman, and it will be a hard day for unbelievers. **27**On the day, when the wrongdoer gnaws his hands, he will say, If only I had chosen a way together with the messenger. **28**Alas for me! If only I had never taken such a person for a friend. **29**He indeed led me astray from the reminder after it had reached me. Satan has always been man's deserter in the hour of need. **30**And the messenger says, O my Lord, indeed, my own people consider this Qur'an of no importance. **31**Even so have we appointed to every prophet an adversary from among the guilty, but Allah is sufficient for a guide and helper. **32**And those who disbelieve say, Why isn't the Qur'an revealed to him all at once? It is this way so that we may strengthen your heart with it, and we have arranged it in right order. **33**And they bring you no comparison except that we bring you the truth, and a better one as argument. **34**Those who will be gathered on their faces to Gehenna, such people are worse in plight and further from the right road. **35**We indeed gave Moses the book and placed his brother Aaron with him as helper. **36**Then we said, Go together to the people who have denied our signs. Then we destroyed them, a complete destruction. **37**And Noah's people, when they denied the messengers, we drowned them

---

17. Instead of "he will gather them," the Warsh Qur'an has "we will gather them."[4]

19. Instead of "you can," the Warsh Qur'an has "they can."[5]

26. On Ar-Rahman, see 17:110 and 38:5.

28. The seventeenth-century Shi'ite hadith collection *Bihar al-Anwar* quotes the Sixth Imam, Jafar as-Sadiq, that in Ali's copy of the Qur'an, instead of, "If only I had never taken such a person for a friend," the passage reads, "If only I had never taken the second for a friend."[6] Jafar added: "And this will appear one day."[7] "The second" refers to Abu Bakr, who in Islamic tradition was the caliph

after Muhammad's death; Shi'ites reject his caliphate as a usurpation of what rightly belonged to Ali.

34. On Gehenna, see 2:206, as also at 25:65.

35. In the section beginning here, the Qur'an once again recalls Moses and Noah, and notes that the people to whom they and other prophets were sent received them with scorn also, and were utterly destroyed. Yet they continue to mock the messenger's claim to be a prophet and will soon receive their penalty. See 7:59.

37. See also 7:59, 10:71, 11:25, 21:76, 23:23, 26:105, 29:14, 37:75, 50:12, 51:46, 53:52, 54:9, 57:26, 69:11, and 71:1.

and made them a sign for mankind. We have prepared a painful doom for evildoers. **38**And Aad and Thamud, and the dwellers in Ar-Rass, and many generations in between. **39**Each we warned by examples, and each we brought to utter ruin. **40**And indeed they have passed by the town on which was rained the fatal rain. Can it be that they have not seen it? No, but they hope for no resurrection. **41**And when they see you, they treat you only as a joke, Is this he whom Allah sends as a messenger? **42**He would have led us far away from our gods if we had not been devoted to them. They will know, when they see the doom, who is more astray from the road. **43**Have you seen him who chooses his own lust for his god? Would you then be guardian over him? **44**Or do you think that most of them hear or understand? They are like cattle, no, but they are farther astray. **45**Haven't you seen how your Lord has spread the shade, and if he willed, he could have made it still, then we have made the sun its pilot, **46**Then we withdraw it to us, a gradual withdrawal? **47**And it is he who makes night a covering for you, and sleep rest, and makes day a resurrection. **48**And it is he who sends the winds, good news heralding his mercy, and we send down purifying water from the sky, **49**So that we may give life by it to a dead land, and we give it to many animals and men that we have created to drink of it. **50**And indeed we have repeated it among them so that they might remember, but most of mankind persist in their ingratitude. **51**If we willed, we could raise up a warner in every village. **52**So do not obey the unbelievers, but wage jihad against them with a great jihad. **53**And it is he who has given independence to the two seas, one palatable, sweet, and the other salty, bitter, and has set a bar and a forbidding ban between them. **54**And it is he who has created man from water, and has appointed for him relatives by blood and by marriage, for your Lord is always powerful. **55**Yet they worship instead of Allah what can neither benefit them nor harm them. The disbeliever has always been a partisan against his Lord. **56**And we have sent you only as a bearer of good news and a warner. **57**Say, I ask of you no reward for this, except that whoever wills may choose a way to his Lord. **58**And trust in the living one who does not die, and sing his praise. He is sufficient as the knower of the sins of his slaves,

59Who created the heavens and the earth and all that is between them in six days, then he

---

38. According to Ibn Kathir, the "dwellers at Ar-Rass" were "the people of one of the villages of Thamud."[8] He also notes a tradition stating "Ar-Rass was a well where they buried (Rassu) their Prophet."[9]

The people of Thamud also appear at 11:61, 14:9, 17:59, 22:42, 26:141, 27:45, 29:38, 38:13, and 40:31, always in the context of their having rejected the messenger sent to them, who is identified as Salih at 7:73 and elsewhere. The people of Aad also appear at 7:65, 9:70, 11:50, 14:9, 22:42, 25:38, 26:123, 29:38, 38:12, 46:7, and elsewhere, likewise always in the context of their having rejected the messenger sent to them, who is identified as Hud at 11:50 and elsewhere.

44. See 8:55, 98:6.

48. Instead of "good news," the Warsh Qur'an has "proclamation."[10]

51. This is not necessary in light of 25:1.

52. See 2:218. According to the *Tafsir Ibn Abbas*, this should be done "by means of the Qur'an" and "by the sword."[11]

56. This means, says Ibn Kathir, that the messenger is "a bringer of good news to the believers, a warner to the disbelievers; bringing good news of Paradise to those who obey Allah, and bringing warnings of a dreadful punishment for those who go against the commandments of Allah."[12]

59. Allah here creates the universe in six days, as he does at 10:3, 11:7, 25:59, 32:4, and 50:38. However, at 41:9-12, he does it in eight days.

On Ar-Rahman, see 17:110 and 38:5, as also for 25:60 and 25:63. Ibn Kathir asserts that this usage of Ar-Rahman comes from the time of the Treaty of Hudaybiyyah between Muhammad and the pagan Arabs of Mecca. When Muhammad ordered that the treaty

mounted the throne. Ar-Rahman. Ask anyone informed about him. ⁶⁰And when it is said to them, Adore Ar-Rahman, they say, And what is Ar-Rahman? Are we to adore whatever you tell us to? And it increases aversion in them. ⁶¹Blessed be he who has placed in the heaven mansions of the stars, and has placed in them a great lamp and a moon giving light. ⁶²And it is he who has appointed night and day in succession, for him who desires to remember, or desires thankfulness. ⁶³The slaves of Ar-Rahman are those who walk upon the earth modestly, and when the foolish ones address them, answer, Peace, ⁶⁴And who spend the night before their Lord, prostrate and standing, ⁶⁵And who say, Our Lord, turn the torment of Gehenna away from us, indeed, the torment of it is anguish, ⁶⁶Indeed, it is wretched as a dwelling place and resting place, ⁶⁷And those who, when they spend, are neither wasteful nor grudging, and there is always a firm station between the two, ⁶⁸And those who do not call upon any other god along with Allah, and do not take the life which Allah has forbidden except in justice, and do not commit adultery, and whoever does this will pay the penalty, ⁶⁹The doom will be doubled for him on the day of resurrection, and he will remain in it disdained forever, ⁷⁰Except him who repents and believes and does righteous work, as for such people, Allah will change their evil deeds to good deeds. Allah is ever forgiving, merciful. ⁷¹And whoever repents and does good, he indeed repents toward Allah with true repentance, ⁷²And those who will not witness vanity, but when they pass near senseless play, pass by with dignity. ⁷³And those who, when they are reminded of the signs of their Lord, do not fall deaf and blind over them. ⁷⁴And who say, Our Lord, allow us the comfort of our wives and of our offspring, and make us models for those who fear Allah. ⁷⁵They will be awarded the high place because they were steadfast, and they will meet in it with welcome and the ward of peace, ⁷⁶Remaining there forever. It is happy as a dwelling place and resting place. ⁷⁷Say, My Lord would not concern himself with you except for your prayer. But now you have denied, therefore there will be judgment.

---

begin with, "In the Name of Allah, Ar-Rahman (the Most Gracious), Ar-Rahim (the Most Merciful)," they responded: "We do not know Ar-Rahman or Ar-Rahim. Write what you used to write: 'Bismika Allahumma (in Your Name, O Allah).'"[13] This, along with 25:3, is another indication that Allah was one of the gods worshiped by the pagans before the advent of Islam.

60. This is one of several Qur'anic verses that are designated in Islamic tradition as verses of prostration: the believer is to make a prostration whenever the verse is recited.

68. Note the caveat on the prohibition of killing here, as at 17:22.

The Poets

Ash-Shu'ara

Introduction

This is traditionally thought to be a Meccan sura. Its name comes from 26:224, where Allah says that only those who are going astray follow the poets. The import of this is that the messenger is not a poet, and the Qur'an not merely a poetical work but a divine revelation, although the pagans of Mecca persistently refuse to accept this.

The Poets

In the name of Allah, the compassionate, the merciful.

[1]Ta. Sin. Mim. [2]These are signs of the book that makes clear. [3]It may be that you torment yourself because they do not believe. [4]If we will, we can send down on them from the sky a sign so that their necks would remain bowed before it. [5]There never comes to them a fresh reminder from Ar-Rahman, except that they turn away from it. [6]Now they have denied, but there will come to them news of what they used to scoff at. [7]Have they not seen the earth, how much of every fruitful kind we make to grow in it? [8]Indeed, in this is indeed a sign, yet most of them are not believers. [9]And indeed, your Lord, he is indeed the mighty, the merciful. [10]And when your Lord called Moses, saying, Go to the wrongdoing people, [11]The people of Pharaoh. Will they not fear Allah? [12]He said, My Lord, indeed, I fear that they will deny me, [13]And I will be embarrassed, and my tongue will not speak plainly, therefore send for Aaron. [14]And they have a criminal charge against me, so I fear that they will kill me. [15]He said, No, indeed. So go, you two, with our signs. Indeed, we will be with you, hearing. [16]And come together to Pharaoh and say, Indeed, we bear a message from the Lord of the worlds, [17]Let the children of Israel go with us. [18]He said, Did we not raise you among us as a child? And you lived many years of your life among us, [19]And you committed your deed that you did, and you were one of the ingrates. [20]He said, I did it then, when I was of those who are astray. [21]Then I fled from you when I feared you, and my Lord granted me a command and established me among those sent. [22]And this is the past favor with which you reproach me, that you have enslaved the children of Israel. [23]Pharaoh said, And what is the Lord of the worlds? [24]He said, The Lord of the heavens and the earth and all that is between them, if only you had sure belief. [25]He said to those around him, Do you not hear? [26]He said, Your Lord and the Lord of your fathers. [27]He said, Indeed, your messenger who has been sent to you is indeed a madman. [28]He said, Lord of the east and the west and all that is between them, if only you understood. [29]He said, If you choose a god other than me, I surely will place you among the prisoners. [30]He said, Even though I show you something clear? [31]He said, Produce it, then, if you are among the truthful! [32]Then he flung down his staff and it became a clear serpent, [33]And he drew forth his hand and indeed, it was white to those who saw it. [34]He said to the chiefs around him, Indeed, this is truly a knowledgeable wizard, [35]Who would drive you out of your land by his

---

1. On the "mysterious letters," see 2:1.
2. See 2:144.
4. See 7:179, 10:99, and 32:13.
10. Here is yet another telling of the story of Moses, also told beginning at 2:49, 7:103, 10:75, 17:101, and 20:9, as well as more briefly elsewhere. The comparisons to the messenger's story are frequent and unmistakable. When Allah tells him to go to preach to "the people of Pharaoh" (26:11), Moses says to Allah: "I do fear that they will charge me with falsehood" (26:12), just as they

charged the messenger (25:4). Moses is afraid the unbelievers will kill him (26:14), just as they plotted to kill the messenger (8:30). After Moses preaches to him, Pharaoh says Moses is a "veritable madman" (26:27), just as the pagan Arabs have said about the messenger (15:6).
11. On Pharaoh, see also 2:49, 3:11, 7:103, 8:52, 10:75, 14:6, 17:101, 20:24, 23:46, 27:12, 28:3, 29:39, 38:12, 40:24, 44:17, 50:13, 51:38, 54:41, 66:11, 69:9, 73:15, 79:15, 85:18, and 89:10.

sorcery. Now what do you advise? **36**They said, Put him off, and his brother, and send summoners into the cities **37**Who will bring to you every knowledgeable wizard. **38**So the wizards were gathered together at a set time on an appointed day. **39**And it was said to the people, Are you gathering? **40**Yes, so that we may follow the wizards if they are the winners. **41**And when the wizards came, they said to Pharaoh, Will there surely be a reward for us if we are the winners? **42**He said, Yes, and you will then surely be among those brought near. **43**Moses said to them, Throw what you are going to throw. **44**Then they threw down their cords and their staves and said, By Pharaoh's might, indeed, we truly are the winners. **45**Then Moses threw his staff, and indeed, it swallowed what they falsely showed. **46**And the wizards were flung prostrate, **47**Calling out, We believe in the Lord of the worlds, **48**The Lord of Moses and Aaron. **49**He said, You put your faith in him before I give you permission. Indeed, he is no doubt your chief who taught you sorcery. But indeed you will come to know. Indeed I will cut off your hands and your feet on opposite sides, and indeed I will crucify every one of you. **50**They said, It is no hurt, for indeed, to our Lord we will return. **51**Indeed, we ardently hope that our Lord will forgive us our sins, because we are the first of the believers. **52**And we inspired Moses, saying, Take away my slaves by night, for you will be pursued. **53**Then Pharaoh sent summoners into the cities, **54**Indeed, these truly are just a little troop, **55**And indeed, they are offenders against us. **56**And indeed, we are a ready army. **57**In this way we took them away from gardens and water springs, **58**And treasures and excellent dwellings, **59**In this way, and we caused the children of Israel to inherit them. **60**And they overtook them at sunrise. **61**And when the two hosts saw each other, those with Moses said, Indeed, we are truly caught. **62**He said, No, truly, for indeed, my Lord is with me. He will guide me. **63**Then we inspired Moses, saying, Strike the sea with your staff. And it parted, and each part was like a high mountain. **64**Then we brought the others near that place. **65**And we saved Moses and those with him, every one, **66**And we drowned the others. **67**Indeed, in this is indeed a sign, yet most of them are not believers. **68**And indeed, your Lord, he is truly the mighty, the merciful. **69**Recite to them the story of Abraham, **70**When he said to his father and his people, What do you worship? **71**They said, We worship idols, and are always devoted to them. **72**He said, Do they hear you when you call out? **73**Or do they benefit or harm you? **74**They said, No, but we found our fathers acting in this way.

---

49. This is the same punishment that Allah commands for those who spread "corruption on the earth."

69. A retelling of the story of Abraham, also told at 7:80, 9:17, 9:114, 11:69, 15:51, 19:41, 21:51, and 29:16, again showing him confronting his people in their worship of idols.

74. "They knew that their idols could not do anything," says Ibn Kathir, "but they had seen their fathers doing this, so they made haste to follow in their footsteps."[1] This recalls Ibn Hisham's ninth-century account of a delegation of Christians who came from the Yemeni city of Najran to see Muhammad (see the introduction to sura 3). One of the leaders of this delegation was a bishop, Abu Haritha ibn Alqama, who received money, servants, and other favors from "the Christian kings of Byzantium."[2] Abu Haritha, says Ibn Ishaq, knew that Muhammad was a prophet, and told the other members of the delegation that he was, but refused to accept him for fear of losing the loot that the Byzantines were lavishing upon him.

This shows that whether out of cultural inertia or love of money, the unbelievers are in bad faith: there is no consideration of the possibility that people might reject Islam simply because they don't think it is true. Everyone knows it is true, but some find it inconvenient, for various reasons, to admit that. Maududi offers a glimpse into the mindset of the disbeliever: "Yes, we know that these are idols made of wood and stone, but our religious faith demands that we keep worshipping them with total devotion."[3]

75He said, See now what you worship, 76You and your forefathers. 77Indeed, they are an enemy to me, except the Lord of the worlds, 78Who created me, and he guides me, 79And who feeds me and gives me water. 80And when I sicken, then he heals me, 81And who causes me to die, then gives me life, 82And who, I ardently hope, will forgive me my sin on the day of judgment. 83My Lord, grant me wisdom and unite me to the righteous. 84And give me a good report in later generations. 85And place me among the inheritors of the garden of delight, 86And forgive my father. Indeed, he is among those who go astray. 87And do not humiliate me on the day when they are raised, 88The day when wealth and sons do not help 89Except him who brings a sound heart to Allah. 90And the garden will be brought near for those who fear Allah. 91And fire will appear in full view to those who are astray. 92And it will be said to them, Where is what you used to worship 93Instead of Allah? Can they help you or help themselves? 94Then will they be thrown in it, they and the seducers 95And the armies of Iblis, together. 96And they will say, when they are arguing in it, 97By Allah, in truth we were in clear error 98When we made you equal with the Lord of the worlds. 99It was only the guilty who misled us. 100Now we have no intercessors 101Nor any loving friend. 102If only we had another chance, so that we might be among the believers. 103Indeed, in this is indeed a sign, yet most of them are not believers. 104And indeed, your Lord, he is indeed the mighty, the merciful. 105Noah's people denied the messengers, 106When their brother Noah said

to them, Will you not fear Allah? 107Indeed, I am a faithful messenger to you, 108So keep your duty to Allah, and obey me. 109And I ask of you no wage for this, my wage is the concern only of the Lord of the worlds. 110So keep your duty to Allah, and obey me. 111They said, Shall we put faith in you, when the lowest follow you? 112He said, And what knowledge do I have of what they may have been doing? 113Indeed, their reckoning is the concern of my Lord, if only you knew, 114And I am not to drive believers away. 115I am only a plain warner. 116They said, If you don't stop, O Noah, you will surely be among those who are stoned. 117He said, My Lord! Indeed, my own people deny me. 118Therefore judge between us a judgment, and save me and those believers who are with me. 119And we saved him and those with him in the laden ship. 120Then afterward we drowned the others. 121Indeed, in this is indeed a sign, yet most of them are not believers. 122And indeed, your Lord, he is truly the mighty, the merciful. 123Aad denied the messengers. 124When their brother Hud said to them, Will you not fear Allah? 125Indeed, I am a faithful messenger to you, 126So keep your duty to Allah and obey me. 127And I ask of you no wage for this, my wage is the concern only of the Lord of the worlds. 128Do you build you on every high place a monument for vain delight? 129And do you seek you out strongholds, so that perhaps you may last forever? 130And if you seize by force, do you seize as tyrants? 131Rather keep your duty to Allah, and obey me. 132Keep your duty toward him who has aided you with what you know, 133Has aided you

---

105. Another telling of the story of Noah (see also 7:59, 10:71, 11:25, 21:76, 23:23, 25:37, 29:14, 37:75, 50:12, 51:46, 53:52, 54:9, 57:26, 69:11, and 71:1).

115. Noah tells the unbelievers that he is only a "plain warner," like the messenger (7:184).

123. Another account of the prophet Hud (see 7:65, 11:50).

with cattle and sons. **134**And gardens and water springs. **135**Indeed, I fear for you the retribution of an awful day. **136**They said, It is all the same to us whether you preach or are not among those who preach, **137**This is just a fable of the men of old, **138**And we will not be doomed. **139**And they denied him, therefore we destroyed them. Indeed, in this is indeed a sign, yet most of them are not believers. **140**And indeed, your Lord, he is truly the mighty, the merciful. **141**Thamud denied the messengers **142**When their brother Salih said to them, Will you not fear Allah? **143**Indeed, I am a faithful messenger to you, **144**So keep your duty to Allah and obey me. **145**And I ask of you no wage for this, my wage is the concern only of the Lord of the worlds. **146**Will you be left secure in what is here before us, **147**In gardens and water springs. **148**And tilled fields and heavy-sheathed palm-trees, **149**Though you carve out dwellings in the mountain, being skillful? **150**Therefore keep your duty to Allah and obey me, **151**And do not obey the command of the wasteful, **152**Who spread corruption on the earth, and do not act righteously. **153**They said, You are just one of the bewitched, **154**You are just a mortal like us. So bring some sign if you are among the truthful. **155**He said, This camel. She has the right to drink, and you have the right to drink, on an appointed day.

156 And do not touch her with evil so that there does not come upon you the retribution of an awful day. **157**But they hamstrung her, and then were penitent. **158**So the retribution came on them. Indeed, in this is truly a sign, yet most of them are not believers. **159**And indeed, your Lord, he is truly the mighty, the merciful. **160**The people of Lot denied the messengers, **161**When their brother Lot said to them, Will you not fear Allah? **162**Indeed, I am a faithful messenger to you, **163**So keep your duty to Allah and obey me. **164**And I ask of you no wage for this, my wage is the concern only of the Lord of the worlds. **165**What? Of all creatures you come to the males, **166**And leave the wives your Lord created for you? No, you are defiant people. **167**They said, If you do not stop, O Lot, you will soon be among the outcast. **168**He said, I am in truth among those who hate your conduct. **169**My Lord, save me and my family from what they do. **170**So we saved him and his family, every one, **171**Except an old woman among those who stayed behind. **172**Then afterward we destroyed the others. **173**And we rained on them a rain. And dreadful is the rain of those who have been warned. **174**Indeed, in this is indeed a sign, yet most of them are not believers. **175**And indeed, your Lord, he is truly the mighty, the merciful. **176**The dwellers in the wood denied the messengers,

---

141. The prophet Salih appears previously at 7:73, 11:61, and is also at 27:45.

154. Here is told again the story of the "camel of Allah," a miraculous beast Salih brings forth in answer to the people's demand for a sign (see 7:77, 11:64, and 91:11-14, as well as the introduction to sura 11). Says Ibn Kathir: "A crowd of them gathered and demanded that he immediately bring forth from the rock a she-camel that was ten months pregnant, and they pointed to a certain rock in their midst. Allah's Prophet Salih made them promise that if he responded to their request, they would believe in him and follow him. So they agreed to that. The Prophet of Allah Salih, peace be upon him, stood and prayed, then he prayed to Allah to grant

them their request. Then the rock to which they had pointed split open, revealing a she-camel that was ten months pregnant, exactly as they had requested. So some of them believed, but most of them disbelieved."4

160. The story of Lot is also told at 7:80, 11:69, 15:51, 21:74, and 27:54.

165. Lot castigates the unbelievers for their homosexuality. A hadith depicts Muhammad saying: "Whomever you find doing the actions of the people of Lut then kill the one doing it, and the one it is done to."5

176. The prophet Shu'aib also appears at 7:85, 11:84, and 29:36; see also 15:78.

¹⁷⁷When Shu'aib said to them, Will you not fear Allah? ¹⁷⁸Indeed, I am a faithful messenger to you, ¹⁷⁹So keep your duty to Allah and obey me. ¹⁸⁰And I ask of you no wage for this, my wage is the concern only of the Lord of the worlds. ¹⁸¹Give full measure, and do not be among those who give less. ¹⁸²And weigh with the true balance. ¹⁸³Do not wrong mankind in their goods, and do not evil, spreading corruption in the earth. ¹⁸⁴And keep your duty to him who created you and the generations of the men of old. ¹⁸⁵They said, You are just one of the bewitched, ¹⁸⁶You are just a mortal like us, and indeed, we consider you to be one of the liars. ¹⁸⁷Then make fragments of the heaven fall upon us, if you are among the truthful. ¹⁸⁸He said, My Lord is best aware of what you do. ¹⁸⁹But they denied him, so there came on them the retribution of the day of gloom. Indeed, it was the retribution of an awful day. ¹⁹⁰Indeed, in this is indeed a sign, yet most of them are not believers. ¹⁹¹And indeed, your Lord, he is indeed the mighty, the merciful. ¹⁹²And indeed, it is a sign of the Lord of the worlds, ¹⁹³Which the true spirit has brought down ¹⁹⁴Upon your heart, so that you may be among the warners, ¹⁹⁵In plain Arabic speech. ¹⁹⁶And indeed, it is in the scriptures of the men of old. ¹⁹⁷Is it not a sign for them that the scholars among the children of Israel know it? ¹⁹⁸And if we had revealed it to one among any nation other than the Arabs, ¹⁹⁹And he had read it

to them, they would not have believed in it. ²⁰⁰In this way we make it enter the hearts of the guilty. ²⁰¹They will not believe in it until they see the painful doom, ²⁰²So that it will come upon them suddenly, when they are not aware. ²⁰³Then they will say, Are we to be given a reprieve? ²⁰⁴Would they hasten on our doom? ²⁰⁵Haven't you then seen, if we make them content for years, ²⁰⁶And then what they were promised comes, ²⁰⁷That what they were contented with doesn't help them at all? ²⁰⁸And we destroyed no town except if it had its warners ²⁰⁹As a reminder, for we never were oppressors. ²¹⁰The satans did not bring it down. ²¹¹It is not fitting for them, nor is it in their power, ²¹²Indeed, truly they are banished from the hearing. ²¹³Therefore do not invoke another god with Allah, so that you do not be one of the doomed. ²¹⁴And warn your tribe of near relatives, ²¹⁵And lower your wing to those believers who follow you. ²¹⁶And if they disobey you, say, Indeed, I am innocent of what they do. ²¹⁷And put your trust in the mighty, the merciful. ²¹⁸Who sees you when you stand up ²¹⁹And your abasement among those who fall prostrate. ²²⁰Indeed, he, only he, is the hearer, the knower. ²²¹Shall I tell you upon whom the satans descend? ²²²They descend on every sinful, false one. ²²³They listen eagerly, but most of them are liars. ²²⁴As for poets, those who go astray follow them. ²²⁵Haven't you seen how they stray in every valley, ²²⁶And how

185. The unbelievers charge that Shu'aib is bewitched, just as they say about the messenger (17:47).
186. The unbelievers charge Shu'aib with being just a mortal man like them, and a liar, again, just like the messenger (17:93, 25:4).
195. See 12:2, as well as 2:23, 2:120, 2:135, 3:4, 5:114, and 24:31.
197. Ibn Kathir asks, "Is it not sufficient witness to the truth for them that the scholars of the Children of Israel found this Qur'an mentioned in the Scriptures which they study?"⁶ He asserts that "the fair-minded among them admitted that the attributes of Muhammad and his mission and his Ummah were mentioned in

their Books, as was stated by those among them who believed, such as Abdullah bin Salam, Salman Al-Farisi and others who met the Prophet."⁷
214. Instead of, "And warn your tribe of near relatives," the Shi'ite Bankipur Qur'an manuscript has a preface in Persian stating that according to the Eighth Shi'ite Imam, the Qur'an of Ubayy ibn Ka'b read: "And warn your tribe of near relatives and your purified family."⁸ See 2:59 and the Appendix: Two Apocryphal Shi'ite Suras.
224. Poets were generally considered to be under demonic influence and deranged as a result.

they say what they do not do? [227]Except those who believe and do good works, and remember Allah a great deal, and vindicate themselves after they have been wronged. Those who do wrong will come to know by what a reverse they will be overturned.

227. Instead of, "Those who do wrong," the Shi'ite Bankipur Qur'an manuscript invokes the Sixth Shi'ite Imam, Jafar as-Sadiq, to affirm this reading: "Those who have wronged the family of Muhammad."[9] See 2:59 and the Appendix: Two Apocryphal Shi'ite Suras.

The Ant

An-Naml

Introduction

Islamic tradition designates this as another Meccan sura. In another indication of the fluidity of the Qur'anic text, a hadith credits several of Muhammad's companions, Al-sha'bl, Abu Malik, Qatadah, and Thabit b. 'Umarah, with the assertion that "the prophet (may peace be upon him) did not write 'In the name of Allah, the compassionate, the merciful' until Surah al-naml was revealed."[1] Its title comes from 27:18.

As this is a ninth-century tradition, it may be an indication that the heading "in the name of Allah, the compassionate, the merciful" only started to be added to the sura headings at some time after the Qur'an, or parts of it, began circulating, and that the omission of it was still recent enough to be remembered by those to whom this hadith was directed as an explanation. This heading now appears at the beginning of 113 of the 114 suras; only sura 9 does not include it.

---

1 *Sunan Abu Dawud,* 787.

The Ant

In the name of Allah, the compassionate, the merciful.

¹Ta. Sin. These are the verses of the Qur'an, the clear book, ²A guidance and good news for believers ³Who establish prayer and give alms and are sure of the hereafter. ⁴Indeed, as for those who do not believe in the hereafter, we have made their works seem good to them, so that they are all astray. ⁵Those are the ones for whom is the worst of punishments, and in the hereafter they will be the greatest losers. ⁶Indeed, as for you, you truly receive the Qur'an from the presence of one who is wise, aware. ⁷When Moses said to his family, Indeed, I spy a fire far off, I will bring you news from there, or bring to you a borrowed fire so that you may warm yourselves. ⁸But when he reached it, he was called, saying, Blessed is whoever is in the fire and whoever is around about it. And may Allah, the Lord of the worlds, be glorified. ⁹O Moses, indeed, it is I, Allah, the mighty, the wise. ¹⁰And throw down your staff. But when he saw it writhing as if it were a jinn, he turned to flee headlong. O Moses, do not fear, the emissaries do not fear in my presence, ¹¹Except him who has done wrong and afterward has changed evil for good. And indeed, I am forgiving, merciful. ¹²And put your hand into the bosom of your robe, it will come forth white but unhurt, among nine signs for Pharaoh and his people, indeed, they have always been rebellious people. ¹³But when our signs came to them, plain to see, they said, This is mere sorcery, ¹⁴And they denied them, although their souls acknowledged them, for spite and arrogance. Then see the nature of the consequences for the wrongdoers. ¹⁵And we indeed gave knowledge to David and Solomon, and they said, Praise be to Allah, who has preferred us above many of his believing slaves. ¹⁶And Solomon was David's heir. And he said, O mankind, indeed, we have been taught the language of birds, and have been given of all things. This surely is obvious favor. ¹⁷And there were gathered together to Solomon his armies of the jinn and mankind, and of the birds, and they

---

1. On the "mysterious letters," see 2:1.

2. On the clarity of the Qur'an, see 2:7.

4. The *Tafsir al-Jalalayn* explains: "As for those who do not believe in the Next World, We have made their ugly actions—instigated by their lower appetites—appear good to them, and they wander about blindly—confused about them, because they consider them good whereas Allah does not."¹

7. The story of Moses, which is also told beginning at 2:49, 7:103, 10:75, 17:101, 20:9, and 26:10, as well as more briefly elsewhere, is again retold. This account of Moses encountering the burning bush is derived from Exodus 3:2ff, but there is no revelation of the Name of God (Exodus 3:14). Instead, the Qur'anic account fast-forwards to Exodus 4:2-6, and once again the stories are told of Moses's rod becoming a serpent (27:10), his hand turning white (27:12), and Pharaoh and his court rejecting these signs (27:14), all of which appear in other tellings of the story.

12. On Pharaoh, see also 2:49, 3:11, 7:103, 8:52, 10:75, 14:6, 17:101, 20:24, 23:46, 26:11, 28:3, 29:39, 38:12, 40:24, 44:17, 50:13, 51:38, 54:41, 66:11, 69:9, 73:15, 79:15, 85:18, and 89:10.

15. The story of Solomon focuses primarily on his meeting with the Queen of Sheba (1 Kings 10:1-13).

17. This conference of the birds, the subject of a celebrated poem by the twelfth-century Persian poet Farid ud-Din Attar, is derived from the Targum Sheni, or Second Targum of the Book of Esther, which scholars date from anywhere between the fourth and eleventh centuries, or from sources common to both the Targum and the Qur'an. "At another time," the Targum states, "when the heart of Solomon was gladdened with wine, he gave orders for the beasts of the land, the birds of the air, the creeping things of the earth, the demons from above and the Genii, to be brought, that they might dance around him, in order that all the kings waiting upon him might behold his grandeur."² The ultimate jumping-off point for this folk tale may be, in Bell's view, I Kings 4:33, which says this of Solomon: "He spoke of trees, from the cedar that is in Lebanon to the hyssop that grows out of the wall; he spoke also of beasts, and of birds, and of reptiles, and of fish."³

were set in battle order, **18**Until, when they reached the valley of the ants, an ant exclaimed, O ants, enter your dwellings so that Solomon and his armies do not crush you without realizing. **19**And he smiled, laughing at her speech, and said, My Lord, make me thankful for your favor with which you have favored me and my parents, and to do good that will be pleasing to you, and include me among your righteous slaves. **20**And he searched among the birds and said, How is it that I do not see the hoopoe, or is he among the absent? **21**I indeed will punish him with hard punishment or I indeed will kill him, or he indeed will bring me a clear excuse. **22**But he was not long in coming, and he said, I have found out what you do not understand, and I come to you from Sheba with sure news. **23**Indeed, I found a woman ruling over them, and she has been given of all things, and hers is a mighty throne. **24**I found her and her people worshipping the sun instead of Allah, and Satan makes their works seem good to them, and bars them from the way, so that they are not guided, **25**So that they do not worship Allah, who brings forth the hidden in the heavens and the earth, and knows what you conceal and what you proclaim, **26**Allah, there is no God except him, the Lord of the mighty throne. **27**He said, We will see whether you speak truth or whether you are among the liars. **28**Go with this my letter and throw it down to them, then turn away and see what they return, **29**She said, O chieftains, indeed, there has been thrown to me a noble letter. **30**Indeed, it is from Solomon, and indeed, it is in the name of Allah, the compassionate, the merciful, **31**Do not exalt yourselves against me, but come to me as Muslims. **32**She said, O chieftains, pronounce for me in my case. I decide no case until you are present with me. **33**They said, We are lords of might and lords of great prowess, but it is for you to command, so consider what you will command. **34**She said, Indeed, kings, when they enter a township, ruin it and make the honor of its people shame. They will do this. **35**But indeed, I am going to send a present to them, and to see

---

18. Bell posits regarding the talking ants story that "this also is found in Jewish literature but of doubtful date; it is no doubt ultimately based on Prov. vi. 6," which says: "Go to the ant, O sluggard; consider her ways, and be wise," but says nothing about talking ants.[4]

20. This also is similar to the Targum Sheni, which has: "Just then the redcock, enjoying itself, could not be found; and King Solomon said that they should seize and bring it by force, and indeed he sought to kill it."[5]

22. The Targum Sheni depicts the redcock saying: "Then I found the fortified city *Qitor* in the Eastern lands, and around it are stones of gold and silver in the streets plentiful as rubbish, and trees planted from the beginning of the world, and rivers to water it, flowing out of the garden of Eden. Many men are there wearing garlands from the garden close by. They shoot arrows, but cannot use the bow. They are ruled by a woman, called queen of Sheba."[6]

25. Instead of "what you conceal and what you proclaim," the Warsh Qur'an has "what they conceal and what they proclaim."[7]

26. The hoopoe is himself a pious Muslim.

28. The Targum Sheni also has its bird deliver a letter from Solomon to the queen.

30. The letter begins with the standard Islamic invocation *Bismillah ar-Rahman ar-Rahim*—In the name of Allah, the compassionate, the merciful—and calls upon the queen and her people to embrace Islam (27:31). On Solomon being a Muslim, see 3:67 on Abraham.

35. Ibn Kathir explains this passage as "meaning, 'I will send him a gift befitting for one of his status, and will wait and see what his response will be. Perhaps he will accept that and leave us alone, or he will impose a tax which we can pay him every year, so that he will not fight us and wage war against us.'"[8] This idea seems modeled on the jizya, the tax prescribed for the dhimmis (9:29): the Queen of Sheba seems prepared to pay a tax as a symbol of her submission to Solomon's authority. Ibn Kathir quotes a statement attributed to Qatadah, one of Muhammad's companions: "May Allah have mercy on her and be pleased with her—how wise she was as a Muslim and (before that) as an idolater! She understood how gift-giving has a good effect on people."[9]

with what the messengers return. ³⁶So when he came to Solomon, he said, What? Would you help me with wealth? But what Allah has given me is better than what he has given you. No, it is you who rejoice in your gift. ³⁷Return to them. We indeed will come to them with armies that they cannot resist, and we will drive them out from there with shame, and they will be humiliated. ³⁸He said, O chiefs, which of you will bring me her throne before they come to me as Muslims? ³⁹An ifrit among the jinn said, I will bring it you before you can rise from your place. Indeed, I truly am strong and trusty for such work. ⁴⁰One with whom was knowledge of the book said, I will bring it you before your gaze returns to you. And when he saw it set in his presence, he said, This is of the bounty of my Lord, that he may test me whether I give thanks or am ungrateful. Whoever gives thanks only gives thanks for his own soul, and whoever is ungrateful, indeed, my Lord is absolute in independence, bountiful. ⁴¹He said, Disguise her throne for her so that we may see whether she will be guided or be among those who are not rightly guided. ⁴²So when she came, it was said, Is your throne like this? She said, As if it were the very one. And, We were given the knowledge before her and we became Muslims. ⁴³And what she was inclined to worship instead

of Allah hindered her, for she came among disbelieving people. ⁴⁴It was said to her, Enter the hall. And when she saw it, she thought it was a pool and bared her legs. He said, Indeed, it is a hall, made smooth, of glass. She said, My Lord, indeed, I have wronged myself, and I submit with Solomon to Allah, the Lord of the worlds. ⁴⁵And we indeed sent to Thamud their brother Salih, saying, Worship Allah. And indeed, they then became two groups arguing. ⁴⁶He said, O my people, why will you hasten the evil rather than the good? Why won't you ask pardon of Allah, so that you may receive mercy? ⁴⁷They said, we consider you and those with you a bad omen. He said, Your omen is with Allah. No, but you are people that are being tested. ⁴⁸And there were in the city nine persons who spread corruption in the land and did not act righteously. ⁴⁹They said, Swear to one another by Allah that we indeed will attack him and his family by night, and afterward we will surely say to his friend, We did not witness the destruction of his family. And indeed, we are truth-tellers. ⁵⁰So they plotted a plot, and we plotted a plot, while they did not realize. ⁵¹Then see the nature of the consequences of their plotting, for indeed, we destroyed them and their people, every one. ⁵²See, over there are their empty dwellings, in ruins because they did wrong. Indeed, in

---

36. Solomon rejects the gifts, intent instead on converting the queen to Islam. Ibn Kathir paraphrases his response to the gifts: "Are you trying to flatter me with wealth so that I will leave you alone with your Shirk [worshipping others besides Allah] and your kingdom?"¹⁰

39. *Ifrit*, says Bell, "is probably Persian, Afrid = creature."¹¹

42. The queen recognizes her throne even though it is disguised; according to Ibn Kathir, this shows "the ultimate in intelligence and strong resolve."¹²

44. In the Targum Sheni, "sat down in the palace of glass. When the queen of Sheba saw it, she thought that the glass floor was water, and so in crossing over lifted up her garments. When Solomon

seeing the hair about her legs, cried out to her: 'Thy beauty is the beauty of women, but thy hair is as the hair of men; hair is good in man, but in woman it is not becoming.' On this she said: 'My Lord, I have three enigmas to put to thee. If thou canst answer them, I shall know that thou art a wise man: but if not thou art like all around thee.' When he had answered all three, she replied, astonished: 'Blessed be the Lord thy God, who hath placed thee on the throne that thou mightest rule with right and justice.' And she gave to Solomon much gold and silver; and he to her whatsoever she desired."¹³ See also 3:93.

Solomon devised the further test, according to the *Tafsir al-Jalalayn*, to get a look at the queen's legs: "She was told: 'Enter the

this is truly a sign for a people who have knowledge. ⁵³And we saved those who believed and used to fear Allah. ⁵⁴And Lot, when he said to his people, Will you knowingly commit abominations? ⁵⁵Must you lust after men instead of women? No, but you are people who act senselessly. ⁵⁶But the answer of his people was nothing except that they said, Expel the family of Lot from your town, for they are people who would keep clean. ⁵⁷Then we saved him and his family except his wife. We destined her to be among those who stayed behind. ⁵⁸And we rained a rain upon them. Dreadful is the rain of those who have been warned. ⁵⁹Say, Praise be to Allah, and peace be upon his slaves whom he has chosen. Is Allah best, or what you ascribe as partners? ⁶⁰Is not he who created the heavens and the earth, and sends down for you water from the sky with which we cause to spring forth joyous orchards, whose trees it has never been yours to cause to grow? Is there any God besides Allah? No, but they are people who ascribe equals. ⁶¹Is not he who made the earth a fixed dwelling, and placed rivers in its folds, and placed firm hills on it, and has set a barrier between the two seas? Is there any God besides Allah? No, but most of them do not know. ⁶²Is not he who answers the wronged one when he calls out to him and removes the evil, and has made you caliphs of the earth? Is there any God besides Allah? Little do they reflect. ⁶³Is not he who guides you in the darkness of the land and the sea, he who sends the winds as heralds of his mercy? Is there any God besides Allah? May Allah be highly exalted from all that they ascribe as a partner. ⁶⁴Is not he who produces creation, then reproduces it, and who provides for you from the heaven and the earth? Is there any God besides Allah? Say, Bring your proof, if you are truthful. ⁶⁵Say, No one in the heavens and the earth knows the unseen except Allah, and they do not know when they will be raised. ⁶⁶No, but does their knowledge reach to the hereafter? No, for they are in doubt concerning it. No, for they cannot see it. ⁶⁷Yet those who disbelieve say, When we have become dust like our fathers, will we indeed be brought forth? ⁶⁸We were promised this, we and our fathers. This is nothing but fables of the men of old. ⁶⁹Say, Travel in the land and see the nature of the ending for the guilty. ⁷⁰And do not grieve for them, nor be in distress because of what they plot. ⁷¹And they say, When this promise, if you are truthful? ⁷²Say, It may be that a part of what you would hasten on is close behind you. ⁷³Indeed, your Lord is full of bounty for mankind, but most of them do not give thanks. ⁷⁴Indeed, your Lord knows surely all that

---

courtyard, which was paved with transparent crystal under which were flowing fresh water and fish; Suleyman had it constructed when he had been told that her legs and feet were those of a donkey—but when she saw it she supposed it to be a pool and bared her legs ready to enter it; Suleyman was on his throne in the center of the courtyard and he saw that her legs and feet were beautiful. He said to her: 'It is a courtyard paved with glass,' and invited her to Islam."[14] Solomon "wanted to marry her but disliked the hair on her legs and so the *shaytans* prepared a depilatory and she removed the hair with it. He married her and loved her and confirmed her as the ruler over her kingdom."[15] Why they accept this aid from demons is left unexplained.

45. The prophet Salih appears previously at 7:73, 11:61, and 26:141.
54. The story of Lot is also told at 7:80, 11:69, 15:51, 21:74, 26:160, and 29:28.
55. See 26:165.
59. Instead of "you ascribe," the Warsh Qur'an has "they ascribe."[16]
62. On "caliphs of the earth," see 2:30.
69. See 3:137.

their bosoms hide, and all that they proclaim. **75**And there is nothing hidden in the heaven or the earth except that it is in a clear book. **76**Indeed, this Qur'an narrates to the children of Israel most of the things about which they disagree. **77**And indeed, it is a guidance and a mercy for believers. **78**Indeed, your Lord will judge between them from his wisdom, and he is the mighty, the wise. **79**Therefore put your trust in Allah, for you are on the clear truth. **80**Indeed, you cannot make the dead hear, nor can you make the deaf hear the call when they have turned to flee, **81**Nor can you lead the blind out of their error. You can make no one hear, except those who believe our signs and who have become Muslims. **82**And when the word is fulfilled concerning them, we will bring forth an animal of the earth to speak to them, because mankind did not have faith in our signs. **83**And the day when we will gather out of every nation a host of those who denied our signs, and they will be set in ranks, **84**Until, when they come, he will say, Did you deny my signs when you could not understand them in knowledge, or what was it that you did? **85**And the word will be fulfilled regarding them because they have done wrong,

and they will not speak. **86**Haven't they seen how we have appointed the night that they may rest in it, and the day giving sight? Indeed, in this truly are signs for a people who believe. **87**And the day when the trumpet will be blown, and all who are in the heavens and the earth will be afraid, except him whom Allah wills. And all come to him, humbled. **88**And you see the hills you consider to be solid flying with the flight of clouds, the doing of Allah, who perfects all things. Indeed, he is informed of what you do. **89**Whoever brings a good deed will have better than its worth, and such people are safe from fear on that day. **90**And whoever brings an evil deed, such people will be flung down on their faces in the fire. Are you rewarded for anything except what you did? **91**I am commanded only to serve the Lord of this land which he has hallowed, and to whom all things belong. And I am commanded to be among those who surrender, **92**And to recite the Qur'an. And whoever goes right, goes right only for his own soul, and as for him who goes astray, say, Indeed, I am only a warner. **93**And say, Praise be to Allah, who will show you his signs so that you will know them. And your Lord is not unaware of what you do.

---

76. See 4:157.

The Narration

Al-Qasas

Introduction

Ibn Kathir relates a story told by the ninth-century Islamic jurist Ahmad ibn Hanbal, about an early Muslim being asked to recite this sura: "We came to Abdullah and asked him to recite to us *Ta Sin Mim*, the two hundred."[1] "Ta Sin Mim" is this sura, called in this story by the three Arabic letters in 28:1. "The two hundred" means that the sura has two hundred verses; sura 28 in its present form, however, has only eighty-eight verses. Islamic scholars generally consider this to be an erroneous reference to sura 26, which has 227 verses; it may, however, simply indicate that part of this sura has been lost or moved elsewhere.

Sura 28 is considered in Islamic tradition to be a Meccan sura. However, Bell notes that "the Medinan date of, at least, the final form is confirmed by vv. 43–46, similar assurances of the truth of stories being Medinan, cf. III, 39, XI, 51, XII, 103."[2] If the sura was put into its final form long after the traditional dating of the Meccan and Medinan periods, this could be evidence that several manuscripts or at least narratives were combined into this sura.

---

1 Ibn Kathir, VII, 375.
2 Bell, II, 373.

The Narration

In the name of Allah, the compassionate, the merciful.

¹Ta. Sin. Mim. ²These are the signs of the clear book. ³We narrate to you some of the story of Moses and Pharaoh with truth, for people who believe. ⁴Indeed, Pharaoh exalted himself on the earth and divided its people into sects. He oppressed a tribe among them, killing their sons and leaving their women alive. Indeed, he was of those who work corruption. ⁵And we desired to show favor to those who were oppressed in the earth, and to make them examples and to make them the inheritors, ⁶And to establish them in the earth, and to show Pharaoh and Haman and their hosts what they feared from them. ⁷And we inspired the mother of Moses, saying, Nurse him and, when you fear for him, then throw him into the river and do not fear or grieve. Indeed, we will bring him back to you and will make him among our messengers. ⁸And the family of Pharaoh took him up, so that he might become for them an enemy and a sorrow, indeed, Pharaoh and Haman and their armies were always sinning. ⁹And the wife of Pharaoh said, A consolation for me and for you. Do not kill him. Perhaps he may be of use to us, or we may choose him for a son. And they did not realize. ¹⁰And the heart of the mother of Moses became empty, and she would have betrayed him if we had not fortified her heart, so that she might be among the believers. ¹¹And she said to his sister, Follow him. So she observed him from afar, and they did not realize. ¹²And we had previously forbidden foster-mothers for him, so she said, Shall I show you a family that will raise him for you and take care of him? ¹³So we restored him to his mother, so that she might be comforted and not grieve, and so that she might know that the promise of Allah is true. But most of them do not know. ¹⁴And when he reached his full strength and had matured, we gave him wisdom and knowledge. In this way do we reward the good. ¹⁵And he entered the city at a time of carelessness among its people, and he found in it two men fighting, one of his own group, and the other of his enemies, and he who was from his group asked him for help against him who was of his enemies. So Moses struck him with his fist and killed him. He said, This is Satan's doing. Indeed, he is an enemy, a mere misleader. ¹⁶He said, My Lord, indeed, I have wronged my soul, so forgive me. Then he forgave him. Indeed, he is the forgiving, the merciful. ¹⁷He said, My Lord,

---

1. On the "mysterious letters," see 2:1.

2. On the clarity of the Qur'an, see 2:7.

3. Here begins still another retelling of the story of Moses (see also 2:49, 7:103, 10:75, 17:101, 20:9, 26:10, and 27:7). There is a great deal of repetition and overlap, but there are also unique features of most every retelling. Each one has its own homiletic point: details of Moses's life are used to warn unbelievers or exhort believers to greater piety. Maududi notes that it is told in suras 26, 27, and this one, and asserts that "these surahs taken together complete Moses's story."[1]

Many elements of the Biblical account are echoed, but the recurring preoccupation with Moses reinforces his status as a prophet of Islam, as well as the perversity of the Jews in not recognizing the congruence of the messenger's message with that of Moses and then becoming Muslims. Maududi emphasizes that the point of these retellings of Moses's story is not to make a point about Moses but about Muhammad: this sura, he says, "both dispels the doubts and refutes the objections made about the Prophethood of Muhammad (peace be on him). It also exposes the hollowness of the excuses put forward by people for not believing in him."[2]

3. On Pharaoh, see also 2:49, 3:11, 7:103, 8:52, 10:75, 14:6, 17:101, 20:24, 23:46, 26:11, 27:12, 29:39, 38:12, 40:24, 44:17, 50:13, 51:38, 54:41, 66:11, 69:9, 73:15, 79:15, 85:18, and 89:10.

8. Haman is imported from the Book of Esther to become Pharaoh's assistant.

Because you have favored me, I will never be a supporter of the guilty. **18**And morning found him in the city, fearing, vigilant, when look, he who had appealed to him the day before called out to him for help. Moses said to him, Indeed, you are indeed a mere troublemaker. **19**And when he would have fallen upon the man who was an enemy to them both, he said, O Moses, wouldst you kill me as you killed a person yesterday? You would be nothing but a tyrant in the land, you would not be among the righteous. **20**And a man came from the uttermost part of the city, running. He said, O Moses, indeed, the chiefs are conspiring against you to kill you, therefore escape. Indeed, I am among those who give you good advice. **21**So he escaped from there, fearing, vigilant. He said, My Lord, deliver me from the wrongdoing people. **22**And when he turned his face toward Midian, he said, Perhaps my Lord will guide me on the right road. **23**And when he came to the water of Midian, he found there a whole tribe of men, watering. And he found apart from them two women keeping back. He said, What ails you? The two said, we cannot give them to drink until the shepherds return from the water, and our father is a very old man. **24**So he watered for them. Then he turned aside into the shade, and said, My Lord, I need whatever good you send down for me. **25**Then there came to him one of the two women, walking shyly. She said, Indeed, my father calls for you, so that he may reward you with a payment for watering for us. Then, when he came to him and told him the story, he said, Do not be afraid. You have escaped from the wrongdoing people. **26**One of the two women said, O my father, hire him, for the best

that you can hire is the strong, the trustworthy. **27**He said, Indeed, I would like to marry you to one of these two daughters of mine, on the condition that you hire yourself to me for eight pilgrimages. Then if you complete ten, it will be of your own accord, for I would not make it hard for you. Allah willing, you will find me among the righteous. **28**He said, That is between you and me. Whichever of the two terms I fulfill, there will be no injustice to me, and Allah is witness over what we say. **29**Then, when Moses had fulfilled the term, and was traveling with his family, he saw in the distance a fire and said to his family, Wait. Indeed, I see in the distance a fire, perhaps I will bring you news from there, or a brand from the fire so that you may warm yourselves. **30**And when he reached it, he was called from the right side of the valley in the blessed field, from the tree, O Moses, indeed, I, and I alone, am Allah, the Lord of the worlds, **31**Throw down your staff. And when he saw it writhing as it had been a jinn, he turned to flee headlong, O Moses, draw near and do not fear. Indeed, you are among those who are secure. **32**Thrust your hand into the bosom of your robe, it will come forth white without hurt. And guard your heart from fear. Then these will be two proofs from your Lord to Pharaoh and his chiefs. Indeed, they are rebellious people. **33**He said, My Lord, indeed, I killed a man among them and I fear that they will kill me. **34**My brother Aaron is more eloquent than I am in speech. Therefore send him with me as a helper to confirm me. Indeed, I fear that they will lie to me. **35**He said, We will strengthen your arm with your brother, and we will give to you both power so that they cannot reach you for our signs.

You two, and those who follow you, will be the winners. **36**But when Moses came to them with our clear signs, they said, This is nothing but invented sorcery. We never heard of this among our fathers of old. **37**And Moses said, My Lord is best aware of him who brings guidance from his presence, and the final home will be his. Indeed, wrongdoers will not be successful. **38**And Pharaoh said, O chiefs, I do not know that you have a god other than me, so kindle for me, O Haman, to bake the mud, and set up for me a lofty tower so that I may inspect the God of Moses, and indeed, I consider him among the liars. **39**And he and his hosts were haughty in the land without justification, and thought that they would never be brought back to us. **40**Therefore we seized him and his armies, and abandoned them to the sea. See the nature of the consequences for evildoers. **41**And we made them leaders that invite people to the fire, and on the day of resurrection they will not be helped. **42**And we made a curse to follow them in this world, and on the day of resurrection they will be among the hateful. **43**And we indeed gave the book to Moses after we had destroyed the generations of old, clear testimonies for mankind, and a guidance and a mercy, so that perhaps they might reflect. **44**And you were not on the western side when we explained the commandment to Moses, and you were not among those present, **45**But we brought forth generations, and their lives dragged on for them. And you were not a dweller in Midian, reciting our signs to them, but we kept sending. **46**And you were not beside the mountain when we called, but a mercy from your Lord that you may warn a people to whom no warner came before you, so that perhaps they may be mindful. **47**Otherwise, if disaster should afflict them because of what their own hands have sent before, they might say, Our Lord, why did you send no messenger to us, so that we might have followed your signs and been among the believers? **48**But when there came to them the truth from our presence, they said, Why is he not given something like what was given to Moses? Did they not disbelieve in what was given to Moses of old? They say, Two works of sorcery that support each other, and they say, Indeed, in both we are unbelievers. **49**Say, Then bring a book from the presence of Allah that gives clearer guidance than these two. I may follow it, if you are truthful. **50**And if they do not answer, then know that what they follow is their lusts. And who goes farther astray than he who follows his lust without guidance from Allah? Indeed, Allah does not guide wrongdoing people. **51**And now indeed we have caused the word to reach them, so that perhaps they may be mindful. **52**Those to whom we gave the book before it, they believe in it, **53**And when it is recited to them, they say, We believe in it. Indeed, it is the truth from our Lord. Indeed, even before it we were among the Muslims. **54**These will be given their reward twice over,

---

36. Pharaoh dismisses Moses's preaching as "sorcery" just as the unbelievers will say about the messenger (11:7, 15:15).

44. The fact that the messenger knows these details of Moses's life, when he wasn't there to witness them, is proof that he is a prophet. Ibn Kathir explains: "Allah points out the proof of the prophethood of Muhammad, whereby he told others about matters of the past, and spoke about them as if he were hearing and seeing them for himself. But he was an illiterate man who could not read books, and he grew up among a people who knew nothing of such things."[3]

48. Instead of "two works of sorcery," the Warsh Qur'an has "two sorcerers."[4]

52. "This was revealed," says the *Tafsir al-Jalalayn*, "about a group of the Jews who became Muslims…and Christians who came from Abyssinia and from Syria."[5] Those Christians also became Muslims. For those who did not, see 98:6.

because they are steadfast and repel evil with good, and spend from what we have provided them with, **55**And when they hear vanity they withdraw from it and say, To us our works and to you your works. Peace be upon you, we do not seek out the ignorant. **56**Indeed, you do not guide those whom you love, but Allah guides those whom he wills. And he is best aware of those who walk rightly. **57**And they say, If we were to follow the guidance with you, we would be torn out of our land. Have we not established for them a sure sanctuary, to which the produce of all things is brought, a provision from our presence? But most of them do not know. **58**And how many a community have we destroyed that was ungrateful for its means of livelihood. And over there are their dwellings, which have not been inhabited after them except a little. And we, even we, were the inheritors. **59**And never did your Lord destroy the towns until he had raised up in their mother a messenger reciting our signs to them. And never did we destroy the towns unless the people of them were evildoers. **60**And whatever you have been given is a comfort of the life of this world and an ornament of it, and what Allah has is better and more lasting. Have you then no sense? **61**Is he to whom we have promised a good promise like him whom we allow to enjoy for awhile the comfort of the life of this world, then on the day of resurrection he will be among those arraigned? **62**On the day when he will call to them and say, Where are my partners whom you imagined? **63**Those concerning whom the word will have

come true will say, Our Lord, these are the ones whom we led astray. We led them astray even as we ourselves were astray. We declare our innocence before you, they never worshipped us. **64**And it will be said, Call upon your partners. And they will call out to them, and they will give no answer to them, and they will see the doom. If only they had been guided. **65**And on the day when he will call to them and say, What answer did you give to the messengers? **66**On that day news will be dimmed for them, nor will they ask about one another, **67**But as for him who will repent and believe and do right, he perhaps may be one of the successful. **68**Your Lord makes happen what He wills and chooses. They never have any choice. May Allah be glorified and exalted above all that they associate. **69**And your Lord knows what their hearts conceal, and what they make known. **70**And he is Allah, there is no God except him. His is all praise in the former and the latter, and his is the command, and to him you will be brought back. **71**Say, Have you thought, if Allah made night everlasting for you until the day of resurrection, who is a god besides Allah who could bring you light? Will you then not hear? **72**Say, Have you thought, if Allah made day everlasting for you until the day of resurrection, who is a god besides Allah who could bring you the night in which you rest? Will you then not see? **73**Out of his mercy he has appointed the night and the day for you, so that in it you may rest, and that you may seek his bounty, and that perhaps you may be grateful. **74**And on the day when he will

---

56. See 7:179, 10:99, and 32:13. This verse "was revealed," Ibn Kathir explains, "concerning Abu Talib, the paternal uncle of the Messenger of Allah"—and the father of Ali, the hero of the Shi'ites. Abu Talib "used to protect the Prophet, support him and stand by him. He loved the Prophet dearly, but this love was a natural love,

i.e., born of kinship, not a love that was born of the fact that he was the Messenger of Allah. When he was on his deathbed, the Messenger of Allah called him to Faith and to enter Islam, but the decree overtook him and he remained a follower of disbelief, and Allah's is the complete wisdom."[6]

call to them and say, Where are my partners whom you pretended? ⁷⁵And we will take out from every nation a witness and we will say, Bring your proof. Then they will know that Allah has the truth, and all that they invented will have failed them. ⁷⁶Now Korah was among Moses' people, but he oppressed them, and we gave him so much treasure that the stores of it would indeed have been a burden for a troop of mighty men. When his own people said to him, Do not boast, indeed, Allah does not love those who boast, ⁷⁷But seek the dwelling place of the hereafter in what Allah has given you and do not neglect your portion of the world, and be kind even as Allah has been kind to you, and do not seek corruption on the earth, indeed, Allah does not love corrupters, ⁷⁸He said, I have been given it only because of knowledge I possess. Didn't he know that Allah had already destroyed the generations before him of men who were mightier than him in strength and built up greater wealth? The guilty are not asked about their sins. ⁷⁹Then he went forth before his people in his pomp. Those who desired the life of this world said, If only we had something like what has been given to Korah! Indeed, he is lord of rare good fortune. ⁸⁰But those who had been given knowledge said, Woe to you, the reward of Allah for him who believes and does right is better, and only the steadfast will obtain it. ⁸¹So we caused the earth

to swallow him and his dwelling-place. Then he had no army to help him against Allah, nor was he among those who can save themselves. ⁸²And morning found those who had longed for his place just the day before calling out, Alas, Allah enlarges the provision for those whom he wills among his slaves and reduces it. If Allah had not been favorable to us, he would have caused it to swallow us. Alas, the unbelievers never prosper. ⁸³As for that dwelling place of the hereafter, we assign it to those who do not seek oppression in the earth, or corruption. The ending is for those who fear Allah. ⁸⁴Whoever brings a good deed, he will have better than it, while as for him who brings an evil deed, those who do evil deeds will be repaid only for what they did. ⁸⁵Indeed, he who has given you the Qur'an for a law will surely bring you home again. Say, My Lord is best aware of him who brings guidance and him who is in clear error. ⁸⁶You had no hope that the book would be inspired in you, but it is a mercy from your Lord, so never be a helper to the unbelievers. ⁸⁷And do not let them divert you from the signs of Allah after they have been sent down to you, but call to your Lord, and do not be among those who ascribe partners. ⁸⁸And do not call upon any other god along with Allah. There is no God except him. Everything will perish except his face. His is the command, and to him you will be brought back.

---

76. Korah, who rebels against Moses, is based on the account at Numbers 16:1-40.

86. The messenger should "never be a helper to the disbelievers," but "rather," says Ibn Kathir, "separate from them, express your hostility towards them and oppose them."[7]

88. The *Tafsir Ibn Abbas* explains that "all works that are for other than Allah's Countenance will not be accepted except that which is meant for the sake of His Countenance; it is also said that this means: every countenance changes except Allah's and every kingdom will vanish except His."[8]

The Spider

Al-Ankabut

Introduction

This sura's name comes from 29:41, which compares those who trust in anyone or anything besides Allah to spiders, who labor to build webs that are "the flimsiest of houses."

Maududi says that sura 29 was revealed during a time when the Muslims were suffering severe persecution in Mecca. He considers and then dismisses the possibility that the first section, since it rails against the hypocrites who, according to Islamic tradition, so plagued Muhammad in Medina, was revealed later, during the Medinan period. This may once again be evidence of textual dislocation.

The Spider

IN THE NAME OF ALLAH, THE COMPASSIONATE, THE MERCIFUL.

1Alif. Lam. Mim. **2**Do men imagine that they will be left because they say, We believe, and will not be tested with affliction? **3**Indeed, we tested those who were before you. In this way Allah knows those who are sincere, and knows those who are liars. **4**Or do those who do evil deeds imagine that they can escape us? What they decide is evil.

5Whoever looks forward to the meeting with Allah, Allah's reckoning is surely near, and he is the hearer, the knower. **6**And whoever wages jihad, wages jihad only for himself, for indeed Allah is altogether independent of creatures. **7**And as for those who believe and do good works, we will remit from them their evil deeds and will repay them the best that they did. **8**We have commanded kindness to parents upon man, but if they struggle to make you join with me that about which you have no knowledge, then do not obey them. To me is your return and I will tell you what you did. **9**And as for those who believe and do good works, we indeed will make them enter in among the righteous. **10**Among mankind is he who says, We believe in Allah, but if he be made to suffer for the sake of Allah, he mistakes the persecution of mankind for Allah's punishment, and then, if victory comes from thy Lord, he will say, Indeed we were with you. Is not Allah best aware of what is in the bosoms of creatures? **11**Indeed Allah knows those who believe, and indeed he knows the hypocrites. **12**Those who disbelieve say to those who believe, Follow our way and we will indeed bear your sins. They cannot bear anything of their sins. Indeed, they truly are liars. **13**But they will indeed bear their own burdens and other burdens beside their own, and they indeed will be asked on the day of resurrection about what they invented. **14**And indeed we sent Noah to his people, and he continued with them for a thousand years except for fifty years, and the flood engulfed them, for they were wrongdoers. **15**And we rescued him and those who were with him in the ship, and made it a sign for the peoples. **16**And Abraham, when he said to his people, Serve Allah and keep your duty to him, that is better for you, if only you knew. **17**You serve instead of Allah only idols, and you only fabricate a lie. Indeed, those whom you serve instead of Allah have no provision for you. So seek your provision from Allah, and serve him, and give thanks to him, to him you will be brought back. **18**But if you deny, then nations have denied before you. The messenger is only to convey clearly. **19**Do they not see how Allah produces creation, then reproduces it? Indeed, for Allah that is easy. **20**Say, Travel in the land and see how

---

1. On the "mysterious letters," see 2:1.

8. Unbelievers can wage *jihad* as well as believers. The word alone generally means "struggle," which is its import here. "Jihad for the sake of Allah," however, refers specifically to jihad warfare. See 2:218.

Even if a believer's own parents urge one to worship anything or anyone besides Allah, he shouldn't obey them. Ibn Kathir elucidates this: "If they are idolaters, and they try to make you follow them in their religion, then beware of them, and do not obey them in that."[1] See also 9:23, 9:84, 9:113, 31:15, and 60:4.

14. Another telling of the story of Noah (see also 7:59, 10:71, 11:25, 21:76, 23:23, 25:37, 26:105, 37:75, 50:12, 51:46, 53:52, 54:9, 57:26, 69:11, and 71:1).

16. A retelling of the story of Abraham, also told at 7:80, 9:17, 9:114, 11:69, 15:51, 19:41, 21:51, and 26:69.

he originated creation, then Allah brings forth the later growth. Indeed, Allah is able to do all things. ²¹He punishes those whom he wills and shows mercy to those whom he wills, and to him you will be turned. ²²You cannot escape in the earth or in the sky, and besides Allah there is no friend or helper for you. ²³Those who disbelieve in the signs of Allah and in meeting with him, such people have no hope of my mercy. For such people there is a painful doom. ²⁴But the answer of his people was only that they said, Kill him or Burn him. Then Allah saved him from the fire. Indeed, in this truly are signs for people who believe. ²⁵He said, You have chosen only idols instead of Allah. The love between you is only in the life of this world. Then on the day of resurrection, you will deny each other and curse each other, and your dwelling will be the Fire, and you will have no helpers. ²⁶And Lot believed him, and said, Indeed I am a fugitive to my Lord. Indeed he, only he, is the mighty, the wise. ²⁷And we bestowed Isaac and Jacob on him, and we established the prophethood and the book among his descendants, and we gave him his reward in this world, and indeed in the hereafter he indeed is among the righteous. ²⁸And Lot, when he said to his people, Indeed, you commit lewdness such as no creature did before you. ²⁹For do not come in to males, and do not block the path, and do not commit abominations in your meetings. But the answer of his people was only that they said,

Bring Allah's doom upon us if you are a truth-teller. ³⁰He said, My Lord, give me victory over people who work corruption. ³¹And when our messengers brought Abraham the good news, they said, Indeed, we are about to destroy the people of that town, for its people are wrongdoers. ³²He said, Indeed, Lot is there. They said, We are best aware of who is there. We are to deliver him and his family, all except his wife, who is among those who stay behind. ³³And when our messengers came to Lot, he was troubled because of them, for he could not protect them, but they said, Do not fear or grieve. Indeed, we are to deliver you and your family, except your wife, who is among those who stay behind. ³⁴Indeed, we are about to bring down upon the people of this town a fury from the sky because they are transgressors. ³⁵And indeed in that we have left a clear sign for people who have sense. ³⁶And to Midian we sent Shu'aib, their brother. He said, O my people, serve Allah, and look forward to the last day, and do not do evil, spreading corruption on the earth. ³⁷But they denied him, and the dreadful earthquake took them, and morning found them prostrate in their dwelling place. ³⁸And Aad and Thamud, it is clear to you from their dwellings. Satan made their deeds seem good to them and so barred them from the way, although they were keen observers. ³⁹And Korah, Pharaoh and Haman, Moses came to them with clear proofs, but they were boastful in the land.

---

21. See 7:179, 10:99, and 32:13. Says Ibn Kathir, "He is the Ruler Who is in control, Who does as He wishes and judges as He wants, and there is none who can put back His judgement. None can question Him about what He does; rather it is they who will be questioned, for His is the power to create and to command, and whatever He decides is fair and just, for He is the sovereign who cannot be unjust in the slightest."²

28. The story of Lot is also told at 7:80, 11:69, 15:51, 21:74, 26:160, and 27:54.

36. The prophet Shu'aib also appears at 7:85, 11:84, and 26:176; see also 15:78.

39. Says Maududi: "The stories mentioned in this Surah also impress the same point mostly, as if to say, 'Look at the Prophets of the past: they were made to suffer great hardships and were

And they were not winners. ⁴⁰So we took each one in his sin, among them was he on whom we sent a hurricane, and among them was he who was overtaken by the cry, and among them was he whom we caused the earth to swallow, and among them was he whom we drowned. It was not for Allah to wrong them, but they wronged themselves. ⁴¹The comparison of those who choose patrons other than Allah is the comparison of the spider when she takes a house for herself, and indeed the flimsiest of all houses is the spider's house, if only they knew. ⁴²Indeed Allah knows what thing they invoke instead of him. He is the mighty, the wise. ⁴³As for these comparisons, we make them for mankind, but no one will grasp their meaning except the wise. ⁴⁴Allah created the heavens and the earth with truth. Indeed, in this is indeed a sign for believers. ⁴⁵Recite what has been inspired within you of the book, and establish prayer. Indeed, prayer preserves from lewdness and iniquity, but indeed remembrance of Allah is more important. And Allah knows what you do. ⁴⁶And do not argue with the people of the book unless it be in what is better, except with those among them who do wrong, and say, We believe in what has been revealed to us and revealed to you, our Allah and your Allah is one, and to him we are Muslims. ⁴⁷In like manner we have revealed the book to you, and those to whom we gave the book previously will believe in it, and among these, there are some who believe in it. And no one denies our signs except the unbelievers. ⁴⁸And you were not a reader of any book before it, nor did you write it with your right hand, for then those who follow falsehood might have doubted. ⁴⁹But it is clear signs in the hearts of those who have been given knowledge, and no one denies our signs except

---

treated cruelly for long periods. Then, at last they were helped by Allah. Therefore, take heart: Allah's succour will certainly come. But a period of trial and tribulation has to be undergone.' Besides teaching this lesson to the Muslims, the unbelievers also have been warned, as if to say, 'If you are not being immediately seized by Allah, you should not form the wrong impression that you will never be seized. The signs of the doomed nations of the past are before you. Just see how they met their doom and how Allah succoured the Prophets.'³ The warning to those who have heard and rejected the messenger is clear.

On Pharaoh, see also 2:49, 3:11, 7:103, 8:52, 10:75, 14:6, 17:101, 20:24, 23:46, 26:11, 27:12, 28:3, 38:12, 40:24, 44:17, 50:13, 51:38, 54:41, 66:11, 69:9, 73:15, 79:15, 85:18, and 89:10.

42. Instead of "they invoke," the Warsh Qur'an has "you invoke."⁴

43. Ibn Kathir asserts that one early Muslim remarked: "I never came across an Ayah of the Book of Allah that I did not know, but it grieved me," because his lack of understanding indicated that he didn't have the requisite knowledge.⁵ This verse may be why it is so common today for Muslims to charge that non-Muslims who speak about Islam do not understand Islamic texts and teachings; if they did understand them, they would become Muslims.

46. Muslims, Jews, and Christians all worship the same deity. Although there are significant differences in each religion's conception of God, this Qur'anic assertion has come to be taken for granted among massive numbers of non-Muslims. The *Tafsir al-Jalalayn* says that Muslims should not argue with Jews and Christians except by "calling people to Allah by His Signs and calling attention to His proofs—except in the case of those of them who do wrong by

fighting you and refusing to pay the *jizya*, in which case argue with them by means of the sword until they become Muslim or pay the *jizya*."⁶ On the jizya, see 9:29.

A hadith attributes to Ibn Abbas the idea that it was unnecessary to ask the Jews and Christians religious questions when the Muslims had the Qur'an: "Why do you ask the people of the scripture about anything while your Book (Quran) which has been revealed to Allah's Apostle is newer and the latest? You read it pure, undistorted and unchanged, and Allah has told you that the people of the scripture (Jews and Christians) changed their scripture and distorted it, and wrote the scripture with their own hands and said, 'It is from Allah,' to sell it for a little gain. Does not the knowledge which has come to you prevent you from asking them about anything?"⁷ For an opposing view, see 10:94.

47. Regarding those who deny Allah's signs, the *Tafsir al-Jalalayn* states: "This refers to the Jews who denied when it was clear to them that the Qur'an was the truth and the one who brought it was speaking the truth. They still denied it."⁸

48. The messenger is reminded that he never read or recited any scripture before the Qur'an. Allah was telling him, says Ibn Kathir, that "you lived among your people for a long time before you brought this Qur'an. During this time you never read any book or wrote anything. Your people, as well as others all know that you are an unlettered man who does not read or write."⁹ This, of course, is the substance of the miracle claimed of the Qur'an itself, that this sublime poetry came to an illiterate man. On the messenger being illiterate, see 7:157.

wrongdoers. **50**And they say, Why aren't signs sent down upon him from his Lord? Say, Signs are with Allah alone, and I am just a plain warner. **51**Is it not enough for them that we have sent down to you the book which is read to them? Indeed, in this truly is mercy, and a reminder for people who believe. **52**Say, Allah is sufficient for witness between me and you. He knows whatever is in the heavens and the earth. And those who believe in vanity and disbelieve in Allah, it is they who are the losers. **53**They ask you to hasten on the doom. And if a term had not been appointed, the doom would surely have come to them. And indeed it will come upon them suddenly, when they do not realize. **54**They ask you to hasten on the doom, when indeed Gehenna will indeed encompass the unbelievers. **55**On the day when the doom will overwhelm them from above them and from under their feet, and he will say, Taste what you used to do. **56**O my slaves who believe, indeed, my earth is spacious. Therefore serve me only. **57**Every soul will taste of death. Then to us you will be returned. **58**Those who believe and do good works, them indeed we will house in lofty dwellings of the garden under which rivers flow. There they will dwell secure. How sweet the reward of the laborers, **59**Who persevere, and put their trust in their Lord. **60**And how many an animal there is that does not bear its own provision. Allah provides for it and for you. He is the hearer, the knower. **61**And if you were to ask them, Who created the heavens and the earth, and constrained the sun and the moon, they would say, Allah. How then are they turned away? **62**Allah makes the provision wide for those whom he wills among his slaves, and reduces it for those whom he wills. Indeed, Allah is aware of all things. **63**And if you were to ask them, Who causes water to come down from the sky, and with it revives the earth after its death, they would indeed say, Allah. Say, Praise be to Allah. But most of them have no sense. **64**The life of this world is but a pastime and a game. Indeed, the home of the hereafter, that is life, if only they knew. **65**And when they embark upon ships they pray to Allah, making their faith pure for him only, but when he brings them safely to land, look, they ascribe partners, **66**So that they may disbelieve in what we have given them, and so that they may take their ease. But they will come to know. **67**Have they not seen that we have appointed a sanctuary that is immune while mankind is ravaged all around them? Do they then believe in falsehood and disbelieve in the bounty of Allah? **68**Who does greater wrong than he who invents a lie about Allah, or denies the truth when it comes to him? Is there not a home in Gehenna for unbelievers? **69**As for those who wage jihad in our way, we surely guide them to our paths, and indeed Allah is with the good.

---

49. The *Tafsir al-Jalalayn* explains that the Qur'an is clear for "those who believe in it and memorise it."[10] It reiterates that the wrongdoers who deny Allah's signs are the Jews, who "deny them after they have become clear to them."[11]

54. On Gehenna, see 2:206, as also at 29:68.
69. On jihad in the way of Allah, see 2:218.

The Romans

Ar-Rum

Introduction

According to Maududi, "The period of the revelation of this Surah is determined absolutely by the historical event that has been mentioned at the outset. It says: 'The Romans have been vanquished in the neighboring land.' In those days the Byzantine occupied territories adjacent to Arabia were Jordan, Syria and Palestine, and in these territories the Romans were completely overpowered by the Iranians in 615 A. D. Therefore, it can be said with absolute certainty that this Surah was sent down in the same year."[1]

This would place sura 30 in Mecca, seven years before the emigration to Medina. However, Bell observes that "the phraseology of the passage points rather to a later period, in particular, the phrase 'the affair belongs to Allah' [30:4] is not used in its early eschatological sense, but has reference to mundane affairs," as in 3:154, "and is probably Medinan."[2]

Maududi adds: "The prediction made in the initial verses of this Surah is one of the most outstanding evidences of the Quran's being the Word of Allah and the Holy Prophet Muhammad's being a true Messenger of Allah."[3] This is because, he explains, it correctly predicts that the Romans (i.e., the Byzantines) will be victorious in their wars against the Persians in the 620s, after an initial setback, and that is exactly what happened.

---

1 Maududi, EnglishTafsir.com, https://www.englishtafsir.com/Quran/30/index.html.
2 Bell, II, 392.
3 Maududi, EnglishTafsir.com, https://www.englishtafsir.com/Quran/30/index.html.

The idea that this is a fulfilled prophecy, however, depends entirely on this sura having been written, or at least memorized, and known to exist before the events to which it alludes took place. There is no manuscript evidence, or indeed, evidence of any kind, to establish this claim.

The Romans

In the name of Allah, the compassionate, the merciful.

1Alif. Lam. Mim. **2**The Romans have been defeated **3**In the nearer land, and after their defeat they will be victorious **4**In a few years. The affair belongs to Allah before and after. And in that day, believers will rejoice **5**In Allah's help to victory. He helps to victory those whom he wills. He is the mighty, the merciful. **6**It is a promise of Allah. Allah does not fail in his promise, but most of mankind do not know. **7**They know only some appearance of the life of this world, and are heedless of the hereafter. **8**Haven't they thought about themselves? Allah did not create the heavens and the earth, and what is between them, except with truth and for a destined end. But indeed many of mankind are unbelievers in the meeting with their Lord. **9**Haven't they traveled in the land and seen the fate of those who were before them? They were stronger than them in power, and they dug the earth and built upon it more than these have built. Messengers of their own came to them with clear proofs. Surely Allah did not wrong them, but they wronged themselves. **10**Then evil were the consequences for those who dealt in evil, because they rejected the signs of Allah and

1. On the "mysterious letters," see 2:1.

2. After many passages in which the unbelievers ask the messenger for a sign that he is a genuine prophet but are rebuffed (including 6:37, 10:20, 13:7, 13:27), here he delivers what appears to be an actual prophesy. It regards the fate of the Byzantine, or Eastern Roman Empire. The Byzantines have been defeated but will be victorious within a few years (30:4).

The Persians defeated the Byzantines in 615 AD, taking Jerusalem. According to the *Tafsir al-Jalalayn*, the pagan Arabs used this news to taunt the Muslims: "The unbelievers of Makka were delighted by that event," that is, the defeat of the Byzantines. "They said to the Muslims, 'We will defeat you as Persia defeated the Romans.'"1 However, in 622, the Byzantines defeated the Persians and soon drove them out of Asia Minor. In 630, they retook Jerusalem.

4. The word translated "a few years" (*bidaai sineena*) means literally "a period of three to nine years." Why Allah would not be more specific when he knows everything (6:59) is not explained. A hadith states that "on the day that these Ayat were revealed, the Persians had defeated the Romans, and the Muslims had wanted the Romans to be victorious over them, because they were the people of the Book."2 However, "the Quraish wanted the Persians to be victorious since they were not people of the Book, nor did they believe in the Resurrection."3 The story holds that this prophecy excited one of Muhammad's foremost companions, Abu Bakr, who became the first caliph of the Muslims after Muhammad died. The Quraysh, according to the story, offered to make a bet with Abu Bakr that the Byzantines would not actually defeat the Persians within a few years; "this was before betting has been forbidden," for which see 5:90.4 Abu Bakr agreed to the bet (which in another version of the story was made in particular with one of the Quraysh, Ubai ibn Khalaf). Since the key word meant "something between three and nine years," they split the difference: the Romans would have to defeat the Persians within six years for Abu Bakr to win the bet.5

"Then six years passed without the Romans being victorious. The idolaters took what they won in the bet from Abu Bakr. When the seventh year came and the Romans were finally victorious over the Persians, the Muslims rebuked Abu Bakr for agreeing to six years. He said: 'Because Allah said: In Bid years,'" that is, between three and nine years.6 The hadith concludes: "At that time, many people became Muslims," presumably because they saw this prophecy fulfilled.7

However, the nineteenth-century Islamic scholar C. G. Pfander notes a simple change in the diacritical marks on several key words makes for a variant reading of 30:2-4 that reverses the sense of the passage as it is generally understood: "The Byzantine have conquered in the nearest part of the land, and they shall be defeated in a small number of years."8 Pfander adds: "If this be the correct reading, the whole story about Abu Bakr's bet with Ubai must be a fable, since Ubai was dead long before the Muslims began to defeat the Byzantines, and even long before the victories which Heraclius won over the Persians. This shows how unreliable such Traditions are."9 Indeed.

The value of this passage as a prophecy, however, would depend upon its having been written before these events took place; there is no independent evidence for that.

9. Between "the fate" (*aqibatu*) and "of those" (*alladhina*), there is a substantial erasure of at least one word in a Qur'anic fragment now found in the National Library of Russia. The word that was removed cannot be determined, but its removal brings the text in line with the standard version.10

10. Ibn Kathir explains that this refers to unbelievers, for whom "evil was their inevitable end, because they rejected the signs of Allah and made fun of them."11 On September 17, 2001, US President George W. Bush appeared at the Islamic Center of Washington, DC, in the company of several prominent Muslim leaders and quoted this verse as evidence that the September 11 attacks were "acts of violence against innocents" that "violate the

mocked them. **11**Allah produces creation, then he reproduces it, then to him you will be returned. **12**And on the day when the hour arises the unrighteous will despair. **13**There will be no one to intercede for them among those whom they made equal with Allah. And they will reject their partners. **14**In the day when the hour comes, on that day they will be split into groups. **15**As for those who believed and did good works, they will be made happy in a garden. **16**But as for those who disbelieved and denied our revelations, and denied the meeting of the hereafter, such people will be brought to doom. **17**So glory be to Allah when you enter the night and when you enter the morning. **18**To him be praise in the heavens and the earth. And at the sun's decline and in the noonday. **19**He brings forth the living from the dead, and he brings forth the dead from the living, and he revives the earth after her death. And even so you will be brought forth. **20**And among his signs is this, he created you from dust, and look at you human beings, scattered about. **21**And among his signs is this, he created for you wives from yourselves so that you might find rest in them, and he ordained between you love and mercy. Indeed, in this indeed are signs for people who reflect. **22**And among his signs is the creation of the heavens and the earth, and the difference of your languages and colors. Indeed, in this indeed are signs for men of knowledge. **23**And among his signs is your slumber by night and by day, and your seeking of his bounty. Indeed, in it indeed are signs for people who are mindful. **24**And of his signs is this, he shows you the lightning for a fear and for a hope, and sends down water from the sky, and thereby brings the earth to life after her death. Indeed, in this indeed are signs for people who understand. **25**And among his signs is this, the heavens and the earth stand fast by his command, and afterward, when he calls you, indeed, from the earth you will emerge. **26**To him belongs whoever is in the heavens and the earth. All are obedient to him. **27**It is he who produces creation, then reproduces it, and it is easier for him. The sublime comparison in the heavens and the earth is his. He is the mighty, the wise. **28**He makes for you a comparison of yourselves. Have you, from among those whom your right hands possess, partners in the wealth we have bestowed upon you, equal with you in respect of it, so that you fear them as you fear each other? In this way we display the revelations for people who have sense. **29**No, but those who do wrong follow their own lusts without knowledge. Who is able to guide him whom Allah has sent astray? For such people there are no helpers. **30**So set your face for religion as *hanifs*, the nature of Allah, in which he has created man. There is no altering Allah's creation.

---

fundamental tenets of the Islamic faith."[12] However, the verse is referring to those who rejected Allah's signs, not those who believed in them. Hence it provides more of a justification for than a condemnation of those attacks.

21. Ibn Kathir explains: "If Allah had made all of Adam's progeny male, and created the females from another kind, such as from Jinn or animals, there would never have been harmony between them and their spouses. There would have been revulsion if the spouses had been from a different kind. Out of Allah's perfect mercy He made their wives from their own kind, and created love and kindness between them."[13]

29. See 7:179, 10:99, and 32:13.

30. A hadith has Muhammad say: "Every child is born with a true faith (i.e. to worship none but Allah Alone) but his parents convert him to Judaism or to Christianity or to Magainism, as an animal delivers a perfect baby animal. Do you find it mutilated?"[14] Upon hearing this, according to the story, one of Muhammad's companions, Abu Huraira, recited this verse, making clear that Islam is indeed the religion in which Allah created human beings.

On *hanif*, see 2:135.

That is the right religion, but most men do not know. **31**Turning to him, and be careful of your duty to him and establish prayer, and do not be among those who ascribe partners, **32**Among those who split up their religion and became sectarians, each sect rejoicing in its tenets. **33**And when harm touches men, they cry to their Lord, turning to him in repentance, then, when they have tasted of his mercy, look, some of them attribute partners to their Lord, **34**So as to disbelieve in what we have given them. Enjoy yourselves awhile, but you will come to know. **35**Or have we revealed to them any justification which speaks of what they associate with him? **36**And when we cause mankind to taste of mercy, they rejoice in it, but if an evil thing comes upon them as the consequence of their own deeds, indeed, they are in despair. **37**Do they not see that Allah enlarges the provision for those whom he will, and reduces. Indeed, in this indeed are signs for people who believe. **38**So give to the relative his due, and to the needy, and to the traveler. That is best for those who seek Allah's face. And such people are those who are successful. **39**What you give in usury so that it may increase on people's property has no increase with Allah, but what you give in charity, seeking Allah's face, has a great increase. **40**Allah is the one who created you and then sustained you, then causes you to die, then gives life to you again. Do any of your partners do any of that? Praised and exalted be he above what they associate. **41**Corruption appears on land and sea because of what men's hands have done, so that he may make them taste a part of what they have done, so that they may return. **42**Say, Travel in the land, and see the nature of the consequences for those who were before you. Most of them were idolaters. **43**So set your purpose resolutely for the right religion, before the inevitable day comes from Allah. On that day mankind will be split apart, **44**Whoever disbelieves must bear the consequences of his disbelief, while those who do right make provision for themselves. **45**So that he may reward out of his bounty those who believe and do good works. Indeed, he does not love the unbelievers. **46**And among his signs is this, he sends winds bearing good news to make you taste his mercy, and so that the ships may sail at his command, and so that you may seek his favor, and that perhaps you may be grateful. **47**Indeed we sent before you messengers to their own people. Then we took revenge upon those who were guilty. To help believers is always obligatory upon us. **48**Allah is he who sends the winds so that they raise clouds, and spreads them along the sky as he pleases, and causes them to break and you see the rain pouring down from within them. And when he makes it fall upon those whom he wills among his slaves. Indeed, they rejoice, **49**Though before that, even before it was sent down upon them, they were in despair. **50**Look, therefore, at the signs of Allah's mercy, how he brings the earth to life after her

---

32. Ibn Kathir says that this refers to "the Jews, Christians, Zoroastrians, idol worshippers and all the followers of false religions, besides the followers of Islam."[15] This divisiveness will affect the Muslims as well, according to a hadith; see 10:93. Ibn Kathir continues: "The followers of the religions before us had differences of opinions and split into false sects, each group claiming to be following the truth. This Ummah too has split into sects, all of which are misguided apart from one, which is Ahlus-Sunnah Wal-Jama'ah [the People of the Prophet's Way and Community], those who adhere to the Book of Allah and the Sunnah of the Messenger of Allah and what was followed by the first generations, the Companions, their followers, and the Imams of the Muslims of earlier and later times."[16]

death. Indeed, he truly is the one who gives life to the dead, and he is able to do all things. [51]And if we sent a wind and they saw it as yellow, they indeed would still continue in their disbelief. [52]For indeed you cannot make the dead hear, nor can you make the deaf hear the call when they have turned to flee. [53]Nor can you guide the blind out of their error. You can make no one hear except those who believe in our signs so that they are Muslims. [54]Allah is he who formed you out of weakness, then appointed after weakness strength, then, after strength, appointed weakness and grey hair. He creates what he wills. He is the knower, the mighty. [55]And on the day when the hour arises, the guilty will vow that they delayed only an hour. In this way they were always deceived. [56]But those to whom knowledge and faith are given will say, The truth is that you have delayed, by Allah's decree, until the day of resurrection. This is the day of resurrection, but you did not know. [57]On that day their excuses will not profit those who did injustice, nor will they be allowed to make amends. [58]Indeed we have made all kinds of comparisons for mankind in this Qur'an, and indeed if you came to them with a miracle, those who disbelieve would indeed exclaim, You are just tricksters. [59]In this way does Allah seal the hearts of those who do not know. [60]So have patience. Allah's promise is the very truth, and do not let those who have no certainty make you impatient.

59. See 30:29.

SURA 31

Luqman

Luqman

Introduction

Maududi dates this sura to the Meccan period, at a time when the Muslims had just begun to be persecuted for their faith, and adduces 31:15 about abjuring even loyalty to one's parents if they are not faithful Muslims as evidence of this. However, Bell sees this sura as "a number of loosely connected pieces," some dating from later periods.[1]

The sura is named for Luqman the Wise (31:12), the subject of many legends. A hadith has this: "A black man came to Sa'id bin Al-Musayyib to ask him a question, and Sa'id bin Al-Musayyib said to him: 'Do not be upset because you are black, for among the best of people were three who were black," including "Luqman the Wise, who was a black Nubian with thick lips."[2]

---

1 Bell, II, 400.
2 Ibn Kathir, VII, 576.

Luqman

In the name of Allah, the compassionate, the merciful.

¹Alif. Lam. Mim. ²These are signs of the wise book, ³A guidance and a mercy for the good, ⁴Those who establish prayer and give alms, and have sure faith in the hereafter. ⁵Such people have guidance from their Lord. Such people are the successful. ⁶And among mankind is he who buys amusing discourse, so that he may mislead people from Allah's way without knowledge, and makes it the butt of mockery. For such people there is a shameful doom. ⁷And when our revelations are recited to him, he turns away in pride as if he did not hear them, as if there were a deafness in his ears. So give him news of a painful doom. ⁸Indeed, those who believe and do good works, for them are the gardens of delight, ⁹In which they will remain. It is a promise of Allah in truth. He is the mighty, the wise. ¹⁰He has created the heavens without supports that you can see, and has cast into the earth firm hills, so that it does not quake with you, and he has dispersed in it all kinds of animals. And we send down water from the sky and we cause every noble kind to grow in it. ¹¹This is the creation of Allah. Now show me what those besides him have created. No, but the wrongdoers are in clear error. ¹²And indeed we gave Luqman wisdom, saying, Give thanks to Allah, and whoever gives thanks, he gives thanks for his soul. And whoever refuses, indeed, Allah is absolute, the owner of praise. ¹³And when Luqman said to his son, when he was exhorting him, O my dear son, ascribe no partners to Allah. Indeed, to ascribe partners is an immense wrong, ¹⁴And we have commanded man regarding his parents, his mother bears him in weakness upon weakness, and his weaning is in two years. Give thanks to me and to your parents. To me is the journeying. ¹⁵But if they struggle with you to make you ascribe to me as a partner what you have no knowledge about, then do not obey them. Spend time with them in the world in kindness, and

---

1. On the "mysterious letters," see 2:1.

6. Ibn Kathir notes the contrast here between those people who "have guidance from their Lord" (31:5) and "the doomed, those who turn away from the Qur'an and do not benefit from hearing the Words of Allah. Instead, they turn to listening to flutes and singing accompanied by musical instruments."[1]

According to Maududi, this verse refers to someone who "wants to make fun of the Divine Revelations by alluring and absorbing the people in legends and tales and music. He intends that the invitation of the Qur'an should be derided and ridiculed and laughed away. He plans to fight the Religion of God with the strategy that as soon as Muhammad (upon whom be Allah's peace) should come out to recite Revelations of God to the people, there should be a charming, sweet-voiced damsel giving her performance in a musical concert on the one hand, and a glib-tongued storyteller telling tales and legends of Iran, on the other, and the people should become so absorbed in these cultural activities that they may not be in a mood to hear anything about God and the morals and the Hereafter."[2]

13. "Allah," Ibn Kathir states, "tells us how Luqman advised his son. His full name was Luqman bin Anqa bin Sadun, and his son's name was Tharan, according to a saying quoted by As-Suhayli.

Allah describes him in the best terms, and states that he granted him wisdom. Luqman advised his son, the closest and most beloved of all people to him, who deserved to be given the best of his knowledge."[3]

Bell suggests that Luqman "should be identified with Solomon, the address to his son being suggested by the beginning of the Book of Proverbs; if we suppose the initial *sin* to have been blurred, it is a possible misreading of the name."[4]

Luqman tells his son not to join partners with Allah, for it is "an immense wrong"; Ibn Kathir adds, "meaning, it is the greatest wrong."[5] See 6:21.

14. This verse and the next one interrupts Luqman's advice to his son, although it has the loose connection of the parent/child theme. It is likely an interpolation. These two verses would fit better after 31:21, expanding upon the unbelievers' excuse that they follow what they found with their fathers to explain that if one's parents enjoin worship of anything other than Allah, they should not be obeyed.

15. One's kindness toward one's parents stops if they are trying to turn the believer away from Islam. See also 9:23, 9:84, 9:113, 29:8, and 60:4. Ibn Kathir recounts a legend attributed to one

follow the path of him who repents to me. Then to me will be your return, and I will tell you what you used to do. ¹⁶O my dear son, indeed, though it be only the weight of a grain of mustard-seed, and though it be in a rock, or in the heavens, or on the earth, Allah will bring it forth. Indeed, Allah is subtle, aware. ¹⁷O my dear son, establish prayer and command kindness and forbid iniquity, and persevere whatever may come upon you. Indeed, that is a resolve to which to aspire. ¹⁸Do not turn away from people, and do not walk with arrogance in the land. Indeed, Allah does not love any arrogant braggart. ¹⁹Be modest in your walk and lower your voice. Indeed, the harshest of all voices is the voice of the donkey. ²⁰Do you not see how Allah has made for your service whatever is in the skies and whatever is in the earth and has loaded you with his favors both visible and hidden? Yet among mankind is he who argues about Allah, without knowledge or guidance or a book giving light. ²¹And if it is said to them, Follow what Allah has revealed, they say, No, but we follow what we found with our fathers. What? Even if Satan were inviting them to the torment of flame? ²²Whoever submits his purpose to Allah while doing good, he has indeed grasped the firm handhold. To Allah belongs the ending of all things. ²³And whoever disbelieves, do not let his disbelief afflict you. To us is their return, and we will tell them what they did. Indeed, Allah

is aware of what is in the hearts. ²⁴We give them comfort for a while, and then we drive them to a heavy doom. ²⁵If you asked them, Who created the heavens and the earth, they would answer, Allah. Say, Praise be to Allah. But most of them do not know. ²⁶To Allah belongs whatever is in the heavens and the earth. Indeed, Allah, he is the absolute, the owner of praise. ²⁷And if all the trees on earth were pens, and the sea, with seven more seas to help it, the words of Allah could not be exhausted. Indeed, Allah is mighty, wise. ²⁸Your creation and your raising are only as a single soul. Indeed, Allah is the hearer, the knower. ²⁹Haven't you seen how Allah causes the night to pass into the day and causes the day to pass into the night, and has subjected the sun and the moon, each running to an appointed term, and that Allah is informed of what you do? ³⁰That is because Allah, he is the true, and what they invoke besides him is the false, and because Allah, he is the sublime, the great. ³¹Haven't you seen how the ships glide on the sea by Allah's favor, so that he may show you some of his wonders? Indeed, in this indeed are signs for every steadfast, grateful one. ³²And if a wave overwhelms them like a canopy, they call out to Allah, making their faith pure for him only. But when he brings them safely to land, some of them compromise. No one denies our signs except every ungrateful traitor. ³³O mankind, keep your duty to your Lord and fear a day

---

of Muhammad's companions, Sa'd ibn Malik: "I was a man who honored his mother, but when I became Muslim, she said: 'O Sa'd! What is this new thing I see you doing? Leave this religion of yours, or I will not eat or drink until I die, and people will say: "Shame on you," for what you have done to me, and they will say that you have killed your mother.' I said, 'Do not do that, O mother, for I will not give up this religion of mine for anything.' She stayed without eating for one day and one night, and she became exhausted; then she

stayed for another day and night without eating, and she became utterly exhausted. When I saw that, I said: 'O my mother, by Allah, even if you had one hundred souls and they were to depart one by one, I would not give up this religion of mine for anything, so if you want to, eat, and if you want to, do not eat.' So she ate."⁶

21. "Flame" is *sa'ir*, on which see 4:10.

30. Instead of "they invoke," the Warsh Qur'an has "you invoke."⁷

when the parent will not be able to help the child in anything, nor the child to help the parent. Indeed, Allah's promise is the very truth. Do not let the life of this world seduce you, and do not let the deceiver seduce you, in regard to Allah.

34Indeed, Allah, with him is knowledge of the hour. He sends down the rain, and knows what is in the wombs. No soul knows what it will earn tomorrow, and no soul knows in what land it will die. Indeed, Allah is the knower, the aware.

---

34. Only Allah has "knowledge of the hour," that is, of the end times and the coming of the day of judgment, but several hadiths depict Muhammad giving some information regarding this. In one that is repeated frequently with minor variations in the hadith literature, he is depicted as saying: "The last hour would not come unless the Muslims will fight against the Jews and the Muslims would kill them until the Jews would hide themselves behind a stone or a tree and a stone or a tree would say: Muslim, or the servant of Allah, there is a Jew behind me; come and kill him; but the tree Gharqad would not say, for it is the tree of the Jews."[8]

Another hadith has the Muslims asking Muhammad, "O Messenger of Allah, when will the Hour be?"[9] He answers: "The one who is asked about it does not know more than the one who is asking. But I will tell you of its portents. When the slave woman gives birth to her mistress, that is one of its portents. When the barefoot and naked become leaders of the people, that is one of its portents. When shepherds compete in constructing buildings, that is one of its portents. (The Hour) is one of five (things) which no one knows except Allah."[10] Then, according to the story, Muhammad recited this verse.

SURA 32

The Prostration

As-Sajda

Introduction

Sura 32, "The Prostration," is traditionally dated from the middle of the Meccan period, although Bell sees it as containing primarily later material. It repeats many preoccupations of other chapters of the Qur'an. Maududi says that "the main theme of the Surah is to remove the doubts of the people concerning Tauhid [the absolute oneness of Allah], the Hereafter and the Prophethood, and to invite them to all these three realities."[1]

The importance of this sura in Islamic tradition is illustrated by the hadith that asserts that Muhammad "used to recite in the morning prayer on Friday" this sura and sura 71.[2] The sura's title comes from the reference to prostration at 32:15.

---

1 Maududi, EnglishTafsir.com, http://www.englishtafsir.com/Quran/32/index.html.
2 *Sunan Abu Dawud*, 1069.

The Prostration

In the name of Allah, the compassionate, the merciful.

1Alif. Lam. Mim. **2**The revelation of the book of which there is no doubt is from the Lord of the worlds. **3**Or they say, he has fabricated it. No, but it is the truth from your Lord, so that you might warn a people to whom no warner came before you, so that perhaps they may walk rightly. **4**It is Allah who created the heavens and the earth, and what is between them, in six days. Then he mounted the throne. You do not have, besides him, any protecting friend or mediator. Will you not then remember? **5**He directs affairs from the heaven to the earth, then it ascends to him in a day, of which the measure is a thousand years of that you reckon. **6**That is the knower of the invisible and the visible, the mighty, the merciful, **7**Who made all things good which he created, and he began the creation of man from clay, **8**Then he made his seed from a drop of contemptible fluid, **9**Then he fashioned him and breathed into him some of his spirit, and appointed for you hearing and sight and hearts. You give small thanks. **10**And they say, When we are lost in the earth, how can we then be recreated? No, but they are unbelievers in the meeting with their Lord. **11**Say, The angel of death, who has charge over you, will gather you, and afterward to your Lord you will be returned. **12**If only you could see when the guilty hang their heads before their Lord, Our Lord, we have now seen and heard, so send us back, we will do right, now we are sure. **13**And if we had so willed, we could have given every soul its guidance, but the word from me concerning evildoers took effect, that I will fill Gehenna with the jinn and mankind together. **14**So taste, you forgot the meeting of this your day, indeed, we forget you. Taste the torment of immortality, because of what you used to do. **15**Only those believe in our signs who, when they are reminded

---

1. On the "mysterious letters," see 2:1.

3. See 3:37, 16:103.

4. Allah here creates the universe in six days, as he does at 7:54, 10:3, 11:7, 25:59, and 50:38. However, at 41:9-12, he does it in eight days.

7. The statement that everything Allah created is good appears to contradict the idea that Allah created many jinns and men for hell (see 7:179, 10:99, and 32:13).

8. See 22:5.

13. Here is another indication that Allah does not, unlike the God of the Bible, will "that all men be saved and come to the knowledge of the truth" (I Timothy 2:3).

Maududi offers a paraphrase that attempts to soften the jarring import of this Qur'anic verse: "That is, 'Had it been Our will to give guidance to the people after having made them observe and experience the reality, We would not have brought you here after making you undergo this hard test in the world. We could have given you such guidance even before. But We had a different scheme for you from the very beginning. We wanted to test you by keeping the reality hidden from your eyes and senses in order to see whether you could recognize it by your intellect after perceiving its signs in the universe and in your own selves or not, whether you could take advantage of the help that We provided to you through Our Prophets and Our Books to recognize the reality or not, and whether after knowing the reality you could attain such control over yourself or not that you should free yourselves from the service of your desires and lusts and believe in the reality and mend your ways and attitudes accordingly. You have failed in this test. Now setting the same test once again will be useless. If the second test is set in a condition when you remember everything that you have seen and heard here, it will be no test at all. And if, like before, you are given re-birth in the world, while you do not remember anything and the reality is kept hidden from you, and you are set the test once again as before the result will not be, any different.'"[1] However, this explanation ignores the arbitrariness of the verse, positing that the damned person has "failed in this test" when no such failure, or test, is mentioned in the Qur'an. See also 7:179 and 10:99. On Gehenna, see 2:206.

15. This is one of several Qur'anic verses that are designated in Islamic tradition as verses of prostration: the believer is to make a prostration whenever the verse is recited.

of them, fall down prostrate and sing the praise of their Lord, and they are not scornful, **16**Who forsake their beds to call upon their Lord in fear and hope, and spend out of what we have bestowed on them. **17**No soul knows what is kept hidden for them of joy as a reward for what they used to do. **18**Is he who is a believer like him who is a transgressor? They are not alike. **19**But as for those who believe and do good works, for them are the gardens of retreat, a welcome for what they used to do. **20**And as for those who do evil, their retreat is the fire. Whenever they desire to leave there, they are brought back to it. To them it is said, Taste the torment of the fire which you used to deny. **21**And indeed we make them taste the lesser punishment before the greater, so that perhaps they may return. **22**And who does greater wrong than he who is reminded of the signs of his Lord, then turns from them. Indeed, we will repay the guilty. **23**We indeed gave Moses the book, so do not be in doubt of his receiving it, and we established it a guidance for the children of Israel. **24**And when they became steadfast and believed firmly in our signs, we appointed leaders from among them who guided by our command. **25**Indeed, your Lord will judge between them on the day of resurrection over what they used to disagree about. **26**Is it not a guidance for them, how many generations we destroyed before them, amid whose dwelling places they walk? Indeed, in this truly are signs. Will they not then pay attention? **27**Haven't they seen how we lead the water to the barren land and bring forth crops with it, from which their cattle eat, and they themselves? Will they not then see? **28**And they say, When will this victory come, if you are truthful? **29**Say, On the day of the victory, the faith of those who disbelieve will not help them, nor will they get a reprieve. **30**So withdraw from them and wait. Indeed, they are waiting.

---

16. In a hadith, one of the early Muslims asks Muhammad: "O Messenger of Allah, tell me of an action that will gain me admittance to Paradise and keep me far away from Hell."² Muhammad answers: "You have asked for something great, but it is easy for the one for whom Allah makes it easy. Worship Allah and do not associate anything in worship with Him, establish prayer, pay charity, fast Ramadan, and perform Hajj to the House." Then he adds: "Shall I not tell you of the means of goodness? Fasting is a shield, and charity extinguishes sin as water extinguishes fire, and a man's prayer in the middle of the night," and recited this verse and the one following. After that, he said: "Shall I not tell you of the head of the matter, and its pillar and pinnacle? (It is) Jihad."³ See 9:41.

18. The unbelievers are not equal to the believers, for the believers are the "best of people" (3:110) while the unbelievers are "the most vile of created beings" (98:6).

21. Ibn Kathir attributes to Ibn Abbas the idea that the "lesser punishment" refers to "diseases and problems in this world, and the things that happen to its people as a test from Allah to His servants so that they will repent to Him."⁴ Verses 9:14-5 and 9:29 suggest that these tests are in part to be instituted by the Islamic state, imposing second-class status and institutionalized discrimination upon the dhimmis in order to move them to repentance and conversion.

23. Maududi emphasizes that the point here in mentioning Moses is to convey once again the importance of Muhammad: "Then it is said: 'This is not the first and novel event of its kind that a Book has been sent down upon a man from God. Before this the Book had been sent upon Moses also, which you all know. There is nothing strange in this at which you should marvel. Be assured that this Book has come down from God, and note it well that the same will happen now as has already happened in the time of Moses. Leadership now will be bestowed only on those who will accept this Divine Book. Those who reject it shall be doomed to failure.'"⁵

26. See 3:137.

SURA 33

The Allies

Al-Ahzab

Introduction

Sura 33 is traditionally regarded as being from Medina. In Islamic tradition, it provides a principal foundation for the central role of Muhammad, and hence of the hadith (traditions of his words and deeds), in the formulation of Islamic law. It also contains a dramatic example of Allah's solicitude for his prophet, further solidifying his pivotal role.

According to a hadith, this sura was originally 127 verses longer than it is in the canonical text. Muhammad's wife Aisha is made to say: "Surat al-Ahzab used to be recited in the time of the Prophet with two hundred verses, but when Uthman wrote out the codices he was unable to procure more of it than what there is today."[1] The circulation of such traditions in the ninth century suggests that some were raising a question that others felt necessary to answer: the length of this sura had changed within living memory, and that change had to be accounted for or at least noted.

---

1 Arthur Jeffery, "Abu 'Ubaid on the Verses Missing from the Koran," in Ibn Warraq, *The Origins of the Koran*, 153.

The Allies

IN THE NAME OF ALLAH, THE COMPASSIONATE, THE MERCIFUL.

¹O prophet, keep your duty to Allah and do not obey the unbelievers and the hypocrites. Indeed, Allah is the knower, the wise one. ²And follow what is inspired in you from your Lord. Indeed, Allah is aware of what you do. ³And put your trust in Allah, for Allah is sufficient as trustee. ⁴Allah has not assigned to any man two hearts within his body, nor has he made your wives whom you declare your mothers, nor has he made those whom you claim your sons. This is just a saying of your mouths. But Allah tells the truth and he shows the way. ⁵Proclaim their real parentage. That will be more just in the sight of Allah. And if you do not know their fathers, then your brothers in the faith, and your clients. And there is no sin for you in the mistakes that you make unintentionally, but what your hearts do intentionally. Allah is always forgiving, merciful. ⁶The prophet is closer to the believers than their selves, and his wives are their mothers. And blood relatives are closer one to another in the decree of Allah than believers and the fugitives, except that you should do kindness to your friends. This is written in the book. ⁷And when we made a covenant with the prophets, and from you and from Noah and Abraham and Moses and Jesus son of Mary. We took a solemn covenant from them, ⁸So that he may ask the loyal about their loyalty. And he has prepared a painful doom for the unfaithful. ⁹O you who believe, remember Allah's favor to you when armies came against you, and we sent against them a great wind and

4. In those days, men would divorce their wives by telling them, "You are to me like the back of my mother." The Qur'an is saying that this doesn't affect any real change or make them actually into their mothers, but the point here is not about divorce. Rather, the passage is apparently intended to end the practice of adoption. Ibn Kathir explains: "This was revealed concerning Zayd bin Harithah, may Allah be pleased with him, the freed servant of the Prophet. The Prophet had adopted him before prophethood, and he was known as Zayd bin Muhammad. Allah wanted to put an end to this naming and attribution."[1]

5. An adopted son should be known by the name of his natural father: he can never truly enter into his adoptive household. See 33:37.

6. A hadith depicts Muhammad as saying: "There is no believer but I, of all the people, I am the closest to him both in this world and in the Hereafter."[2] Islamic tradition holds that Muhammad was in every respect a mortal man like every other, but this Qur'an verse and the accompanying hadith provide some insight into how he has come to hold such an exalted status in Islamic popular piety.

9. Here begins what Islamic tradition regards as a discussion of the Battle of the Trench, extending to 33:27. This was a battle against the Muslims by the confederates, the combined forces of the pagan Quraysh who were besieging the city (and held back by the trench Muhammad had ordered dug), and the Jewish Qurayzah, who had betrayed the Muslims and were working against them inside the city (cf. 5:82). According to Ibn Hisham, a new convert to Islam, Nu'aym bin Mas'ud, came to Muhammad offering to trick the enemy. Muhammad responded, according to Ibn Ishaq: "You are only one man among us, so go and awake distrust among the enemy to draw them off us if you can, for war is deceit."[3] Nu'aym's deception turned the confederates against each other and against their Jewish allies; soon afterward, they ended the siege. Nu'aym's deception had saved Islam.

A hadith has Aisha recount, "When Allah's Apostle returned on the day (of the battle) of Al-Khandaq (i.e. Trench), he put down his arms and took a bath. Then Gabriel whose head was covered with dust, came to him saying, 'You have put down your arms! By Allah, I have not put down my arms yet.' Allah's Apostle said, 'Where (to go now)?' Gabriel said, 'This way,' pointing towards the tribe of Bani Quraiza. So Allah's Apostle went out towards them."[4]

Ibn Hisham recounts that Muhammad addressed the Qurayzah Jews contemptuously: "You brothers of monkeys, has God disgraced you and brought His vengeance upon you?"[5] (See 2:62-65, 5:59-60, and 7:166.) The Muslims laid siege to the Qurayzah strongholds until, said Ibn Hisham, the Jews "were sore pressed" and Allah "cast terror into their hearts."[6] After they surrendered, according to Ibn Hisham, "The apostle went out to the market of Medina (which is still its market today) and dug trenches in it. Then he sent for [the men of the Qurayzah] and struck off their heads in those trenches as they were brought out to him in batches."[7] Ibn Hisham puts the number of those massacred at "600 or 700 in all, though some put the figure as high as 800 or 900."[8] Another ninth-century biographer of Muhammad, Ibn Sa'd, says "they were between six hundred and seven hundred in number."[9]

armies you could not see. And Allah is always the seer of what you do. **10**When they came upon you from above you and from below you, and when eyes grew wild and hearts reached to the throats, and you were imagining vain thoughts about Allah. **11**There the believers were severely tested, and shaken with a mighty shock. **12**And when the hypocrites, and those in whose hearts is a disease, were saying, Allah and his messenger promised us nothing but delusion. **13**And when a group of them said, O people of Yathrib, there is no stand for you, therefore turn back. And certain of them asked permission of the prophet, saying, Our homes lie open. And they did not lay open. They just wanted to flee. **14**If the enemy had entered from all sides and they had been exhorted to treachery, they would have committed it, and would have hesitated about it only briefly. **15**And indeed they had already sworn to Allah that they would not turn their backs. An oath to Allah must be answered for. **16**Say, Flight will not help you if you flee from death or killing, and then you dwell in comfort for only a little while. **17**Say, Who is he who can preserve you from Allah if he intends harm for you, or intends mercy for you? They will not find that they have any friend or helper other than Allah. **18**Allah already knows those of you who hinder, and those who say to their brothers, Come here to us. And they do not come to the stress of battle except for a little while, **19**Being sparing of their help to you. But when the fear comes, then you see them looking at you with rolling eyes like one who faints away

to death. Then, when the fear departs, they excoriate you with sharp tongues in their greed for wealth. Such people have not believed. Therefore Allah makes their deeds fruitless. And that is easy for Allah. **20**They claim that the tribes have not retired, and if the tribes would advance, they would want to be in the desert with the nomadic Arabs, asking for the news of you, and if they were among you, they would not participate in battle, except a little. **21**Indeed in the messenger of Allah you have an excellent example for him who looks to Allah and the last day, and remembers Allah a great deal. **22**And when the true believers saw the tribes, they said, This is what Allah and his messenger promised us. Allah and his messenger are true. It only confirmed them in their faith and submission. **23**Among the believers are men who are true to the covenant they made with Allah. Some of them have paid their vow by death, and some of them still are waiting, and they have not changed in the least, **24**So that Allah may reward the true men for their truth, and punish the hypocrites if he wills, or relent toward them. Indeed, Allah is forgiving, merciful. **25**And Allah repulsed the unbelievers in their wrath, they gained nothing good. Allah turned their attack away from the believers. Allah is always strong, mighty. **26**And he brought those among the people of the book who supported them down from their strongholds, and cast terror into their hearts. Some you killed, and some you made captive. **27**And he caused you to inherit their land and their houses and their wealth, and land you

---

21. The messenger being an "excellent example" is understood in an absolutist sense in Islamic tradition: if Muhammad did it, it is good, and if he didn't, it is not. See 2:144.

26. This has generally been taken as an oblique reference to the massacre of the Jews (see 33:9).

have not trodden. Allah is always able to do all things. **²⁸**O prophet, say to your wives, If you desire the life of this world and its adornment, come. I will make you content and will release you with a good release. **²⁹**But if you desire Allah and his messenger and the dwelling place of the hereafter, then indeed, Allah has prepared an immense reward for the good among you. **³⁰**O you wives of the prophet, whoever among you commits obvious lewdness, the punishment for her will be doubled, and that is easy for Allah. **³¹**And whoever among you is submissive to Allah and his messenger and does what is right, we will give her reward to her twice over, and we have prepared for her a rich provision. **³²**O you wives of the prophet, you are not like any other women. If you keep your duty, then do not speak too softly, so that he in whose heart is a disease does not lust, but speak in a normal tone. **³³**And stay in your houses. Do not display yourselves with the display of the time of ignorance. Be regular in prayer, and give alms, and obey Allah and his messenger. Allah's wish is only to remove uncleanness far from you, O people of the house, and cleanse you with a thorough cleansing. **³⁴**And bear in mind what is recited in your houses of the signs of Allah and wisdom. Indeed, Allah is subtle, aware. **³⁵**Indeed, men who surrender to Allah, and women who surrender, and men who believe and women who believe, and men who obey and women who obey, and men who speak the truth and women who speak the truth, and men who persevere and women who persevere, and men who are humble and women who are humble, and men who give alms and women who give alms, and men who fast and women who fast, and men who guard their modesty and women who guard, and men who remember Allah a great deal and women who remember, Allah has prepared for them forgiveness and a vast reward. **³⁶**And it is not fitting for a believing man or a believing woman, when Allah and his messenger have settled a matter, that they should claim any say in the matter, and whoever is rebellious to Allah and his messenger, he indeed goes astray in obvious error. **³⁷**And when you said to him on whom

---

28. Modesty and piety are enjoined upon the wives of the messenger. See 24:13.

36. Ibn Kathir declares: "This Ayah is general in meaning and applies to all matters, i.e., if Allah and His Messenger decreed a matter, no one has the right to go against that, and no one has any choice or room for personal opinion in this case."¹⁰ Islamic tradition fills in the details of this verse and the oblique one that follows it. Zaynab bint Jahsh had been married to Muhammad's adopted son Zayd bin Haritha (see 33:4). According to the *Tafsir al-Jalalayn*, Muhammad asked for Zaynab's hand on behalf of Zayd; Zaynab and her brother "disliked that," for "they had thought that the Prophet, may Allah bless him and grant him peace, himself would ask to marry her."¹¹ But they ultimately agreed because of the admonition here to obey the messenger.

37. The *Tafsir al-Jalalayn* says that Muhammad "looked at" Zaynab and "felt love for her," while Zayd "disliked her" and told Muhammad, "I want to divorce her."¹² But Muhammad told him: "Keep your wife to yourself, and fear Allah." A hadith has Aisha remark: "If Allah's Apostle were to conceal anything (of the Quran) he would have concealed this Verse," because it shows him unwilling to accept Allah's will, which was that he marry Zaynab.¹³

But then, according to the tenth-century historian Tabari, Muhammad went to Zayd's house and found Zaynab wearing only a chemise. Muhammad hastened away, murmuring, "Glory be to God the Almighty! Glory be to God, who causes hearts to turn!"¹⁴ Soon afterward, according to Tabari, Muhammad was talking with Aisha when "a fainting overcame him."¹⁵ Then he smiled and asked, "Who will go to Zaynab to tell her the good news, saying that God has married her to me?"¹⁶ He then recited this verse, in which Allah scolds him for being concerned about what people might think and thus refusing to marry Zaynab. The *Tafsir al-Jalalayn* explains what Allah is telling Muhammad here: Muhammad was "concealing something in yourself which Allah wished to bring to light—meaning his love for her and that if Zayd were to divorce her, he would marry her—you were fearing people—and that they would say, 'He has married his son's wife,' when Allah has more right to your fear in every matter, so that you should not fear what people say."¹⁷

According to Tabari, Aisha was not caught up in the enthusiasm of the moment: "I became very uneasy because of what we heard about her beauty and another thing, the greatest and loftiest of matters—what God had done for her by giving her in marriage. I said that she would boast of it over us."¹⁸ A hadith depicts Zaynab doing

Allah has conferred favor and you have conferred favor, Keep your wife to yourself and fear Allah. And you hid in your mind what Allah was going to bring to light, and you feared mankind, whereas Allah has a better right that you should fear him. So when Zayd had performed that necessary formality from her, we gave her to you in marriage, so that there may be no sin for believers in regard to the wives of their adopted sons, when the latter have performed the necessary formality from them. The commandment of Allah must be fulfilled. [38]There is no reproach for the prophet in what Allah has prescribed for him. That was Allah's way with those who passed away of old, and the commandment of Allah is certain destiny, [39]Who delivered the messages of Allah and feared him, and feared no one except Allah. Allah keeps good account. [40]Muhammad is not the father of any of your men, but he is the messenger of Allah and the seal of the prophets, and Allah is always aware of all things. [41]O you who believe, remember Allah with much remembrance. [42]And glorify him early and late. [43]It is he who prays for you, and his angels, so that he may bring you forth from darkness to light, and he is always merciful to the believers. [44]Their greeting on the day when they meet him will be, Peace. And he has prepared for them a noble reward. [45]O prophet, indeed, we have sent you as a witness and a bringer of good news and a warner. [46]And as a summoner to Allah by his permission, and as a lamp that gives light. [47]And announce to the believers the good news that they will have great bounty from Allah. [48]And do not get close to the unbelievers and the hypocrites. Disregard their noxious talk, and put your trust in Allah. Allah is sufficient as trustee. [49]O you who believe, if you marry believing women and divorce them before you have touched them, then there is no period that you should reckon. But provide for them and release them honorably. [50]O prophet, indeed, we have made lawful to you your wives to whom you

exactly that, saying to Muhammad's other wives: "You were given in marriage by your families, while I was married (to the Prophet) by Allah from over seven Heavens."[19]

This episode has generally been understood as the reason for the abolition of adoption (33:4), so as to remove the appearance of impropriety from Muhammad that was created by his marriage to a woman who had been his daughter-in-law.

40. Muhammad (mentioned by name here, as also at 3:144, 47:2, and 48:29, and nowhere else in the Qur'an) is the seal of the prophets, as he himself is made to explain in a hadith: "Messengership and Prophethood have come to an end, and there will be no more Messengers or Prophets."[20] In the Qur'an, most or all of the prophets are related to one another (6:84), and thus likely received their prophetic spirit as something of an inheritance. If, therefore, Muhammad had a son who survived into adulthood (Islamic tradition holds that he had as many as five sons, all of whom died before reaching puberty), the son would almost certainly have been a prophet as well, and Muhammad would not have been the last prophet, the "seal of the prophets."[21] Aisha is made to say in a hadith: "Had Zayd outlived Muhammad, he would have appointed him as his successor."[22] The *Tafsir al-Jalalayn* says that the claim that "Muhammad is not the father of any of your men" refers to Zayd, but adds: "He was not the father of any man and no one after him would be a Prophet."[23]

The idea that Muhammad's son, natural or adopted, would himself be a prophet is reflected in Shi'ite theology, which holds that the leader of the Islamic community must be a member of Muhammad's household and that such a man will have something of Muhammad's prophetic spirit.

In order, therefore, to ensure the centrality of Muhammad in Islamic tradition, and to establish a religious orthodoxy that could withstand challenge from outside, the narrative had to be devised emphasizing that Muhammad had neither natural nor adopted sons. A delegitimization of adoption had the added benefit of striking at Islam's chief spiritual rival, Christianity, with its doctrine of Gentiles as adopted sons of God. Thus the story of Zayd and Zaynab and Muhammad's scandalous marriage may have been invented to seal Muhammad's status within the Muslim community.

43. On Allah praying for the believers, see 2:157 and 33:56.

49. More regulations concerning marriage, as in 4:24.

50. While the messenger may marry women who offer themselves to him, believers do not share this privilege. Ibn Kathir has an early Muslim explain: "This means, it is not permissible for anyone else to marry a woman who offers herself to him; if a woman offers herself to a man, it is not permissible for him (to marry her) unless he gives her something."[24]

"Those whom your right hand possesses" are specified here as "spoils of war"; see 4:3, 4:24, 23:6, and 70:30.

have paid their dowries, and those whom your right hand possesses of those whom Allah has given you as spoils of war, and the daughters of your uncle on the father's side and the daughters of your aunts on the father's side, and the daughters of your uncle on the mother's side and the daughters of your aunts on the mother's side who emigrated with you, and a believing woman if she gives herself to the prophet and the prophet desires to take her in marriage, a privilege for you alone, not for the believers. We are aware of what we commanded them regarding their wives and those whom their right hands possess, so that you may be free from blame, for Allah is always forgiving, merciful. **51**You can delay those whom you will among them and receive to you those whom you will, and whomever you desire among those whom you have set aside, it is no sin for you, that is better, that they may be comforted and not grieve, and may all be pleased with what you give them. Allah knows what is in your hearts, and Allah is always forgiving, merciful. **52**It is not allowed for you to take women from now on, nor that you should exchange them for other wives, even though their beauty pleased you, except those whom your right hand possesses. And

Allah is always the watcher over all things. **53**O you who believe, do not enter the dwellings of the prophet for a meal without waiting for the proper time, unless permission is granted to you. But if you are invited, enter, and, when your meal is ended, then depart. Do not linger for conversation. Indeed, that would cause annoyance to the prophet, and he would be shy of you, but Allah is not shy of the truth. And when you ask anything of them, ask it of them from behind a curtain. That is purer for your hearts and for their hearts. And it is not for you to cause annoyance to the messenger of Allah, nor that you should ever marry his wives after him. Indeed, that would be an offense in Allah's sight.

54Whether you divulge a thing or keep it hidden, indeed, Allah is always the knower of all things. **55**It is no sin for them to converse with their fathers, or their sons, or their brothers, or their brothers' sons, or the sons of their sisters or of their own women, or their slaves. O women, keep your duty to Allah. Indeed, Allah is always the witness over all things. **56**Indeed, Allah and his angels pray for the prophet. O you who believe, ask blessings on him and greet him with a worthy greeting. **57**Indeed, those who malign

---

51. In a hadith, Aisha is depicted as saying to Muhammad when this verse was revealed: "I feel that your Lord hastens in fulfilling your wishes and desires."[25]

53. Allah tells believers to be circumspect about barging into the messenger's house or staying there too long after dinner, for such behavior "annoys the Prophet"; they should also only speak to his wives from behind screens. This reinforces the exalted status of Muhammad in Islamic tradition as being the object of Allah's unique concern (see 2:144). This could be evidence of the personal convenience of the revelations Muhammad received or of the convenience of another figure whose traditions were incorporated into the Muhammad legend.

56. Allah also prays for the believers at 2:157 and 33:43. This idea creates obvious theological problems, resulting in the claim

that the verb in question, *yusalloona*, means "blesses" rather than "prays." However, there are traces in Islamic tradition of the idea that Allah does indeed pray. In a hadith, Muhammad is depicted as saying: "Indeed Allah, His Angels, the inhabitants of the heavens and the earths—even the ant in his hole, even the fish—say Salat [prayers] upon the one who teaches the people to do good."[26]

Ibn Kathir relates another hadith that reinforces this. An early Muslim explains: "Allah's Salah [prayer] is His praising him before the angels, and the Salah of the angels is their supplication."[27] So evidently Allah praises himself before the angels, but this would not constitute praying for the believers or the messenger. It is unclear whether these Qur'anic passages are evidence of a polytheistic source text, careless editing, or simply scribal error.

Allah and his messenger, Allah has cursed them in this world and the hereafter, and has prepared for them a humiliating punishment. **58**And those who malign believing men and believing women undeservedly, they bear the guilt of slander and obvious sin. **59**O prophet, tell your wives and your daughters and the women of the believers to draw their veils close around them. That will be better, so that they may be recognized and not molested. Allah is always forgiving, merciful. **60**If the hypocrites and those in whose hearts is a disease and the alarmists in the city do not stop, we will indeed urge you on against them, then they will be your neighbors in it only for a little while. **61**Cursed, they will be seized wherever they are found and killed with a slaughter. **62**That was the way of Allah in the case of those who passed away of old, you will not find anything changed in the way of Allah. **63**Men ask you about the hour. Say, The knowledge of it is with Allah alone. What can convey it to you? It may be that the hour is near. **64**Indeed, Allah has cursed the unbelievers, and has prepared for them a flaming fire, **65**In which they will remain forever. They will find no

protecting friend nor helper. **66**On the day when their faces are turned over in the fire, they say, If only we had obeyed Allah and had obeyed his messenger. **67**And they say, Our Lord, indeed, we obeyed our princes and great men, and they misled us from the way. **68**Our Lord, give them double torment and curse them with a great curse. **69**O you who believe, do not be like those who slandered Moses, but Allah proved his innocence regarding what they claimed, and he was well esteemed in Allah's sight. **70**O you who believe, guard your duty to Allah, and speak words straight to the point, **71**He will adjust your works for you and will forgive you your sins. Whoever obeys Allah and his messenger, he indeed has gained a splendid victory. **72**Indeed, we offered the trust to the heavens and the earth and the hills, but they shrank from bearing it and were afraid of it. And man assumed it. Indeed, he has proved a tyrant and a fool. **73**So Allah punishes hypocritical men and hypocritical women, and idolatrous men and idolatrous women. But Allah pardons believing men and believing women, and Allah is always forgiving, merciful.

59. The idea that women must cover themselves so that they may not be molested unfortunately implies that if they are not covered, they may lawfully be importuned. See 4:3.

68. Instead of "a great curse," the Warsh Qur'an has "many curses."[28]

69. Ibn Kathir explains that Moses "was a shy and modest man who would never show anything of his skin because of his shyness," which led some Jews to claim: "He only keeps himself covered because of some defect in his skin, either leprosy or scrotal hernia or some other defect."[29] So Allah, wanting to clear Moses, did so one day when Moses "was alone, so he took off his garment and put

it on a rock, then he took a bath. When he had finished, he turned back to pick up his garment, but the rock moved away, taking his garment with it."[30] Moses chased the rock "until he reached a group of the Children of Israel, who saw him naked and found that he was the best of those whom Allah had created. Thus he was cleared of what they had said about him."[31]

72. Allah offered the *al-amanah*, the obedience of created things, to the heavens and the earth and the mountains, but they refused it. Man took it, but performed badly, so now Allah must punish the hypocrites and unbelievers.

SURA 34

Sheba

Saba

Introduction

Sura 34 is traditionally dated from the Meccan period, during a time when, according to Maududi, "the Islamic movement was being suppressed…by resort to derision and ridicule, rumor mongering, false allegations and casting of evil suggestions in the people's minds."[1] It is noteworthy how large such incidents loom in Islamic sacred history; they help illuminate the furious reaction some modern-day Muslims have had to mild ridicule in the form of cartoons.

Bell sees abundant evidence of the sura having undergone considerable editing: "It probably contains a good deal of Meccan material, but there are Medinan revisions and additions."[2]

The title comes from 34:15.

---

1 Maududi, EnglishTafsir.com, http://www.englishtafsir.com/Quran/34/index.html.
2 Bell, II, 420.

Sheba

IN THE NAME OF ALLAH, THE COMPASSIONATE, THE MERCIFUL.

1Praise be to Allah, to whom belongs whatever is in the heavens and whatever is in the earth. His is the praise in the hereafter, and he is the wise, the aware. **2**He knows what goes into the earth and what comes forth from it, and what descends from the heaven and what ascends into it. He is the merciful, the forgiving. **3**The unbelievers say, The hour will never come to us. Say, No, by my Lord, but it is surely coming to you. The knower of the unseen. Not an atom's weight, or less than that or greater, escapes him in the heavens or on the earth, but it is in a clear book, **4**So that he may reward those who believe and do good works. For them is forgiveness and a rich provision. **5**But those who strive against our signs, challenging, theirs will be a painful torment of wrath. **6**Those who have been given knowledge see that what is revealed to you from your Lord is the truth and leads to the path of the mighty one, the owner of praise. **7**The unbelievers say, Will we show you a man who will tell you when you have become dispersed in dust with the most complete dispersal, yet even then you will be created anew? **8**Has he invented a lie about Allah, or is there a madness in him? No, but those who disbelieve in the hereafter are in torment and are far astray. **9**Haven't they observed what is in front of them and what is behind them of the sky and the earth? If we will, we can make the earth swallow them, or cause obliteration from the sky to fall on them. Indeed, in this is surely a sign for every slave who turns repentant. **10**And surely we gave David favor from us, O you hills and birds, sing his praises with him. And we made iron pliable to him, **11**Saying, Make long coats of mail and measure the links. And do what is right. Indeed, I am the seer of what you do. **12**And to Solomon the wind, of which the morning course was a month's journey and the evening course a month's journey, and we caused the fountain of copper to gush forth for him, and some of the jinn who worked before him by permission of his Lord. And those among them who deviated from our command, we caused them to taste the punishment of flaming fire. **13**They made what he willed for him, synagogues and statues, basins like wells and boilers built into the ground. Give thanks, O house of David. Few of my slaves are thankful. **14**And when we decreed death for him, nothing showed his death to them except a creeping

---

1. This is another verse that is difficult to reconcile with the Islamic claim that Allah is the sole speaker throughout the Qur'an (see 1:2). Ibn Kathir is typical of the classical exegetes in ignoring the difficulty and glossing the verse as meaning that "Allah tells us that all praise belongs to Him alone in this world and in the Hereafter."[1]

3. Here and at 34:7, 34:9, 34:31, and 34:43, objections to the messenger's message are repeated, each introduced by the phrase "the unbelievers say," and Allah at each point answers them.

The oath "by my Lord" also appears at 4:65, 10:53, and 64:7. At 19:68 there is "by your Lord"; "by the Lord of the heavens and the earth" at 51:23; and "I swear by the Lord of the rising-places and the setting-places of the planets" at 70:40. These oaths are also (see

34:1) difficult to reconcile with the claim that only Allah speaks throughout the Qur'an. These texts appear to presuppose that the messenger, not Allah, is speaking, unless Allah is referring to himself in the third person or even invoking another deity (see 33:56).

8. See 16:103.

10. Ibn Kathir says that Allah had blessed David "with a mighty voice. Such that when he glorified Allah, the firm, solid, high mountains joined him in glorifying Allah, and the free-roaming birds, who go out in the morning and come back in the evening, stopped for him, and he was able to speak all languages."[2]

12. Solomon is discussed more fully in the passage starting at 27:15.

creature of the earth which gnawed away his staff. And when he fell, the jinn saw clearly how, if they had known the unseen, they would not have continued in despised labor. **15**There was indeed a sign for Sheba in their dwelling place, Two gardens on the right hand and the left, Eat of the provision of your Lord and give thanks to him. A good land and an indulgent Lord. **16**But they were defiant, so we sent on them the flood of the dam, and in exchange for their two gardens gave them two gardens bearing bitter fruit, the tamarisk and here and there a lote-tree. **17**This we awarded them because of their ingratitude. Do we ever punish anyone except the ingrates? **18**And we set, between them and the towns which we had blessed, towns easy to be seen, and we made the distance between them easy, Travel in them safely both by night and day. **19**But they said, Our Lord, make the distance between our journeys longer. And they wronged themselves, therefore we made them notorious and scattered them abroad, a total scattering. Indeed, in this truly are signs for each steadfast, grateful one. **20**And Satan indeed found his calculation true concerning them, for they follow him, all except a group of true believers. **21**And he had no justification at all against them, except that we would know him

who believes in the hereafter from him who is in doubt about it, and your Lord takes note of all things. **22**Say, Call upon those whom you set up besides Allah. They do not possess even an atom's weight either in the heavens or on the earth, nor have they any share in either, nor does he have a helper among them. **23**No intercession helps with him except for him whom he permits. Yet when fear is banished from their hearts, they say, What was it that your Lord said? They say, The truth. And he is the sublime, the great. **24**Say, Who gives you provision from the sky and the earth? Say, Allah, indeed, we or you are surely rightly guided or obviously astray. **25**Say, You will not be asked about what we did, nor will we be asked about what you do. **26**Say, Our Lord will bring us all together, then he will judge between us with truth. He is the all-knowing judge. **27**Say, Show me those whom you have joined to him as partners. No, for he is Allah, the mighty, the wise· **28**And we have not sent you except as a bringer of good news and a warner to all mankind, but most of mankind do not know. **29**And they said, When is this promise, if you are truthful? **30**Say, Yours is the promise of a day which you cannot postpone nor hasten by an hour. **31**The unbelievers say, we do not believe in this Qur'an nor in what was

---

16. Here the people of Sheba reject Allah, but at 27:44, the Queen of Sheba professes her Islamic faith.

Bell says that "the flood of the dam" refers to "the dam of Ma'rib, the bursting of which (c. A.D. 450) is associated with the migration of many tribes from South Arabia."[3]

17. This verse strongly supports the commonly held idea that piety in Islam will equal earthly success, and rejecting Allah will bring disaster in this world as well as in the next. Ibn Kathir attributes these words to an early Muslim: "He does not punish anyone except the disbelievers."[4]

23. Intercession with Allah's permission is accepted (cf. 10:3, 20:109, 21:28). However, elsewhere the Qur'an says that everyone will stand alone before Allah; no intercession from others will be accepted (cf. 2:48, 2:123, 6:94, 23:101, 39:43, 42:46).

25. The messenger must disown the unbelievers because, according to Ibn Kathir, "you do not belong to us and we do not belong to you, because we call people to Allah, to believe that He is the Only God and to worship Him alone. If you respond, then you will belong to us and we to you, but if you reject our call, then we have nothing to do with you and you have nothing to do with us."[5]

27. In a hadith, Muhammad is made to say, "By Him in Whose hand is the life of Muhammad, he who amongst the community of Jews or Christians hears about me, but does not affirm his belief in that with which I have been sent and dies in this state (of disbelief), he shall be but one of the denizens of Hell-Fire."[6] See 3:19, 3:85.

before it, but if you could see when the wrongdo-ers are brought up before their Lord, how they cast the blame upon one another, how those who were despised say to those who were proud, If it hadn't been for you, we would have been believ-ers. **32**Those who were proud say to those who were despised, Did we drive you away from the guidance after it had come to you? No, but you were guilty. **33**Those who were despised say to those who were proud, No, but scheming night and day, when you commanded us to disbelieve in Allah and set up rivals to him. And they are filled with remorse when they behold the doom, and we place shackles on the necks of those who disbelieved. Are they repaid for anything except what they used to do? **34**And we did not send a warner to any town except that its wealthy ones declared, Indeed, we are unbelievers in what you have been sent with. **35**And they said, we are more in wealth and children. We are not the punished ones. **36**Say, Indeed, my Lord enlarges the provi-sion for those whom he wills and reduces it. But most of mankind do not know. **37**And it is not your wealth or your children that will bring you near to us, but he who believes and does good. As for such people, theirs will be twofold reward for what they did, and they will dwell secure in lofty halls. **38**And as for those who strive against our signs, challenging, they will be brought to the doom. **39**Say, Indeed, my Lord enlarges the provi-sion for those whom he wills among his slaves, and reduces it. And whatever you spend, he reim-burses it. And he is the best of providers. **40**And on the day when he will gather them all together,

he will say to the angels, Did these people wor-ship you? **41**They will say, May you be glorified. You are our guardian, not them. No, but they worshipped the jinn, most of them were believers in them. **42**On that day you will possess no benefit or harm for one another. And we will say to those who did wrong, Taste the torment of the fire that you used to deny. **43**And if our signs are recited to them in plain terms, they say, This is nothing but a man who would turn you away from what your fathers used to worship, and they say, This is nothing but an invented lie. The unbelievers say of the truth when it reaches them, This is nothing but mere sorcery. **44**And we have given them no books that they study, nor did we send them any warner before you. **45**Those before them denied, and these have not received a tenth of what we bestowed on them, yet they denied my messen-gers. How severe then was my condemnation. **46**Say, I exhort you to only one thing, that you wake up, for Allah's sake, by twos and individu-ally, and then think, There is no madness in your comrade. He is nothing but a warner to you in the face of a terrible doom. **47**Say, Whatever reward I might have asked from you is yours. My reward is the concern of Allah alone. He is the witness over all things. **48**Say, Indeed, my Lord throws the truth. The knower of hidden things. **49**Say, The truth has come, and falsehood does not show its face and will not return. **50**Say, If I am astray, I am astray only to my own loss, and if I am rightly guided, it is because of what my Lord has revealed to me. Indeed, he is the hearer, close by. **51**If only you could see when they are terrified with no

---

35. Instead of "they said," a Qur'anic manuscript dating from the eighth or ninth century has "he said," although the text was erased and later corrected to bring it into line with the standard version.[7]

40. Instead of "he will gather them," the Warsh Qur'an has "we will gather them."[8] Instead of "he will say," the Warsh Qur'an has "we will say."[9]

escape, and are seized from close by, [52]And say, we believe in it. But how can they reach from afar off, [53]When they disbelieved in it before? They aim at the unseen from afar off. [54]And a gulf is set between them and what they desire, as was done for people of their kind previously. Indeed, they were in hopeless doubt.

The Angels

Al-Malaika

Introduction

This sura is also known as *Fatir*, "The Creator"; both titles come from 35:1. Traditionally it is regarded as Meccan, although Bell sees several passages in it as Medinan; they may be additions that came later in the editing process.

Sura 35 repeats many familiar themes. Says Maududi: "The discourse is meant to warn and reprove the people of Makkah [Mecca] and their chiefs for their antagonistic attitude that they had then adopted towards the Holy Prophet's message of Tauhid [the unity of Allah]."[1]

---

1 Maududi, EnglishTafsir.com, http://www.englishtafsir.com/Quran/35/index.html.

The Angels

IN THE NAME OF ALLAH, THE COMPASSIONATE, THE MERCIFUL.

¹Praise be to Allah, the creator of the heavens and the earth, who appoints the angels as messengers having wings, two, three and four. He multiplies in creation what he wills. Indeed, Allah is able to do all things. ²What Allah opens to mankind of mercy, no one can withhold it, and what he withholds, no one can release after that. He is the mighty, the wise. ³O mankind, remember Allah's favor toward you. Is there any creator other than Allah who provides for you from the sky and the earth? There is no God except him. To where, then, are you turned? ⁴And if they deny you, messengers were denied before you. To Allah all things are brought back. ⁵O mankind, indeed, the promise of Allah is true. So do not let the life of the world seduce you, and do not let the seducer seduce you with regard to Allah. ⁶Indeed, Satan is an enemy for you, so treat him as an enemy. He only summons his group to be companions of the flaming fire. ⁷Those who disbelieve, theirs will be an awful doom, and those who believe and do good works, theirs will be forgiveness and a great reward. ⁸Is he whose evil deeds are made to seem good to him so that he considers them good? Allah indeed leads astray those whom he wills, and guides those whom he wills, so do not let your soul expire in grieving for them. Indeed, Allah is aware of what they do. ⁹And it is Allah who sends the winds and they raise a cloud, then we lead it to a dead land and revive the earth with it after its death. Such is the resurrection. ¹⁰Whoever desires power, all power belongs to Allah. To him good words ascend, and he exalts the pious deed, but those who plot iniquities, theirs will be an awful doom, and the plotting of such people will come to nothing. ¹¹Allah created you from dust, then from a little fluid, then he made you pairs. No female bears or brings forth except with his knowledge. And no one grows old who grows old, nor is anything lessened of his life, without it being recorded in a book, Indeed, that is easy for Allah. ¹²And the two seas are not alike, this, fresh, sweet, good to drink, this bitter, salty. And from them both you eat fresh meat and derive the ornament that you wear. And you see the ship cleaving them with its prow so that you may seek his bounty, and that perhaps you may give thanks. ¹³He makes the night pass into the day and he makes the day pass into the night. He has subjected the sun and moon to service. Each runs to an appointed term. Such is Allah, your Lord, his is the dominion, and those to whom you pray instead of him do not own even as much as the white spot on a date-stone. ¹⁴If you pray to them, they do not hear your prayer, and if they heard, they could not grant it to you. On the day of resurrection, they will disown association with you. No one can inform you like him who is aware.

---

1. See 34:1.

8. Maududi explains that this means "that Allah deprives, of the grace of guidance, those who become so perverted mentally, and leaves them to wander aimlessly in the ways in which they themselves wish to remain lost. After making the Holy Prophet realize this fact Allah exhorts him to the effect: 'It is not within your power to bring such people to the right path; therefore, have patience in their regard. Just as Allah is indifferent about them, so should you also avoid being unduly anxious about their reformation.'"¹ This does not, however, explain Allah's declaration that he could have guided all people to the truth but chose not to do so. See 7:179, 10:99, and 32:13.

¹⁵O mankind, you are the poor in your relation to Allah. And Allah, he is the absolute, the owner of praise. ¹⁶If he wills, he can be rid of you and bring some new creation. ¹⁷That is not a hard thing for Allah. ¹⁸And no burdened soul can bear another's burden, and if one who is heavily burdened calls out over his burden, nothing of it will be lifted even though he be a relative. You warn only those who fear their Lord in secret, and have established prayer. He who grows, grows only for himself. To Allah is the journeying. ¹⁹The blind man is not equal to the seer, ²⁰Nor is darkness light, ²¹Nor is the shadow equal to the sun's full heat, ²²Nor are the living equal with the dead. Indeed, Allah makes those whom he wills able to hear. You cannot reach those who are in the graves. ²³You are just a warner. ²⁴Indeed, we have sent you with the truth, a bearer of glad news and a warner, and there is not a nation except that a warner has passed among them. ²⁵And if they deny you, those before them also denied. Their messengers came to them with clear proofs, and with the Psalms and the enlightening book. ²⁶Then I seized those who disbelieved, and how intense was my condemnation. ²⁷Haven't you seen that Allah causes water to fall from the sky, and we produce with it fruit of various colors, and among the hills are white and red streaks, of various colors, and black, ²⁸And among men and animals and cattle, in the same way, various colors? The learned among his slaves fear Allah

alone. Indeed, Allah is mighty, forgiving. ²⁹Indeed, those who read the book of Allah, and establish prayer, and spend out of what we have bestowed on them secretly and openly, they look forward to imperishable gain, ³⁰So that he will pay them their wages and increase his favor upon them. Indeed, he is forgiving, responsive. ³¹As for what we inspire within you of the book, it is the truth confirming what was before it. Indeed, Allah is indeed the observer, the seer of his slaves. ³²Then we gave the book as inheritance to those whom we chose among our slaves. But among them are some who wrong themselves and among them are some who are lukewarm, and among them are some who surpass through good deeds, by Allah's permission. That is the great favor. ³³Gardens of Eden. They enter them wearing armlets of gold and pearls and their clothing in them is silk. ³⁴And they say, Praise be to Allah who has put grief away from us. Indeed, Our Lord is forgiving, bountiful, ³⁵Who, out of his favor, has installed us in the mansion of eternity, where labor does not touch us, nor can weariness affect us. ³⁶But as for those who disbelieve, for them is fire of Gehenna, it does not take complete effect upon them so that they can die, nor is its torment lightened for them. In this way do we punish every ingrate. ³⁷And they cry for help there, Our Lord, release us, we will do right, not what we used to do. Didn't we grant you a life long enough for him who was thoughtful to think in it? And the

18. See 10:3, 20:109, 21:28, and 34:23, where the door appears to have been opened to the possibility that others might intercede for the person being judged. However, Maududi states that "in the sight of Allah everyone is responsible for his own actions and for no one else's. There is no possibility that Allah will place the burden of one man's responsibility upon the other, nor is there the possibility that a person will take the burden of another's responsibility upon himself and get himself seized for the crime committed by

the other. This thing has been said here because the polytheist kinsmen and relatives of the people who were embracing Islam in Makkah, used to urge them, saying, Give up Islam and return to your ancestral faith. We take the responsibility of any punishment etc. on ourselves."² This also could be an anti-Christian reference, denying the salvific nature of the death of Christ.

25. See 3:184.

36. On Gehenna, see 2:206.

warner came to you. Now taste, for evildoers have no helper. ³⁸Indeed, Allah is the knower of the unseen of the heavens and the earth. Indeed, he is aware of the secret of hearts. ³⁹It is he who has made you caliphs on earth, so he who disbelieves, his disbelief is on his own head. Their disbelief increases for the unbelievers, in their Lord's sight, nothing but condemnation. For the unbelievers, their disbelief increases nothing but loss. ⁴⁰Say, Have you seen your partner gods to whom you pray besides Allah? Show me what they created of the earth. Or do they have any portion in the heavens? Or have we given them a book so that they act on clear proof from it? No, the evildoers promise one another only to deceive. ⁴¹Indeed, Allah holds the heavens and the earth so that they do not deviate, and if they were to deviate, there is not one who could hold them after him. Indeed, he is always merciful, forgiving. ⁴²And they swore by Allah their most binding oath, that if a warner came to them, they would be more guided than any of the nations, yet when a warner came to them, it aroused in them nothing but repugnance, ⁴³Behaving arrogantly in the land and plotting evil, and the evil plot only closes in on the men who make it. Then can they expect anything but the treatment of the people of old? You will not find any substitute for Allah's way of treatment, nor will you find any power to change Allah's way of treatment. ⁴⁴Haven't they traveled in the land and seen the nature of the consequences for those who were before them, and they were mightier than these in power? Allah is not such that anything in the heavens or in the earth escapes him. Indeed, he is the wise one, the mighty one. ⁴⁵If Allah took mankind to task by what they deserve, he would not leave a living creature on the surface of the earth, but he gives them a reprieve to an appointed term, and when their term comes, then indeed Allah is always the seer of his slaves.

---

39. On "caliphs on earth," see 2:30.

42. Maududi explains: "Before the advent of the Holy Prophet, the same thing used to be said by the Arabs, in general, and by the Quraish, in particular, when they witnessed the moral degeneration of the Jews and the Christians."³

44. See 3:137.

Ya Sin

Ya Sin

Introduction

This is traditionally regarded as a Meccan sura. According to Bell, it "shows puzzling breaks in connection which render it difficult to give a satisfactory account of its composition. It may be suggested that it consisted of two strands which have been intertwined."[1]

It takes its name from the two Arabic letters that begin it (36:1), and as with all the chapters that begin with such letters, in the words of the *Tafsir al-Jalalayn*, "Allah knows best what is meant by that."[2] A hadith depicts Muhammad promising: "Whoever recites Ya Sin in the night, seeking the Face of Allah, will be forgiven," and in another, he is made to say that "the Qur'an's heart is Ya Sin."[3] Maududi explains that this is because it "presents the message of the Qur'an in a most forceful manner, which breaks the inertness and stirs the spirit of man to action."[4]

Another hadith has Muhammad say, "Recite Surah Ya-Sin over your dying men."[5] This should be done, says Maududi, "not only to revive and refresh the whole Islamic creed in the mind of the dying person but also bring before him, in particular, a complete picture of the Hereafter so that he may know what stages he would have to pass through after crossing the stage of this worldly life."[6] This sura does indeed "revive and refresh the whole Islamic creed," as it sounds a goodly number of the same themes that are also set out in many other suras.

---

1 Bell, II, 434.
2 *Tafsir al-Jalalayn*, 941.
3 Ibn Kathir, VIII, 167; *Jami at-Tirmidhi*, vol. 5, book 42, no. 2887.
4 Maududi, EnglishTafsir.com, http://www.englishtafsir.com/Quran/36/index.html.
5 *Sunan Abu Dawud*, 3115.
6 Maududi, EnglishTafsir.com, http://www.englishtafsir.com/Quran/36/index.html.

Ya Sin

IN THE NAME OF ALLAH, THE COMPASSIONATE, THE MERCIFUL.

[1]Ya Sin. [2]By the wise Qur'an, [3]Indeed, you are among those sent [4]On a straight path, [5]A revelation of the mighty, the merciful, [6]So that you may warn a people whose fathers were not warned, so they are heedless. [7]Already the judgment has proved true of most of them, for they do not believe. [8]Indeed, we have put shackles on their necks reaching to their chins, so that they are made stiff-necked. [9]And we have set a bar in front of them and a bar behind them, and have covered them so that they do not see. [10]Whether you warn them or you do not warn them, it is all the same for them, for they do not believe. [11]You warn only him who follows the reminder and fears Ar-Rahman in secret. To him bring news of forgiveness and a rich reward. [12]Indeed, it is we who bring the dead to life. We record what they send before, and their footprints. And all things we have kept in a clear record. [13]Make a comparison for them, The people of the city when those who had been sent came to them, [14]When we sent two to them, and they denied them both, so we reinforced them with a third, and they said, Indeed, we have been sent to you. [15]They said, You are just men like us. Ar-Rahman has revealed nothing. You just lie. [16]They answered, Our Lord knows that we are indeed sent to you, [17]And our duty is just clear conveyance. [18]They said, we see an evil omen in you. If you do not stop, we will surely stone you, and grievous torture will come upon you at our hands. [19]They said, Your evil omen be with you. Is it because you are reminded? No, but you are defiant people. [20]And there came a man running from the uttermost part of the city. He called out, O my people, follow those who have been sent. [21]Follow those who ask no fee of you, and who are rightly guided. [22]For what cause should I not serve him who has created me, and to whom you will be brought back? [23]Shall I take gods in place of him when, if Ar-Rahman should wish me any harm, their intercession will not help me in any way, nor can they save? [24]Then indeed I would be in clear error. [25]Indeed, I have believed in your Lord, so hear me. [26]It was said, Enter paradise.

---

1. On the "mysterious letters," see 2:1.

2. Allah's swearing by the Qur'an is odd, as generally one swears by something greater than oneself. See also 34:3.

6. The people who had not been warned before are, says Ibn Kathir, "the Arabs, for no warner had come to them before him."[1] However, he adds, "the fact that they alone are mentioned does not mean that others are excluded," and "the mission of the Prophet is universal."[2]

9. The *Tafsir al-Jalalayn* says, "This is another metaphor for how the path of faith is barred to them."[3] The *Tafsir Ibn Abbas* agrees, stating that this verse means that Allah has "covered the insight of their hearts (so that they see not) the Truth and guidance."[4] Ibn Kathir depicts an early Muslim saying that "Allah placed this barrier between them and Islam and Iman [faith], so that they will never reach it."[5] Ibn Kathir also paraphrases this passage as, "We [i.e., Allah] have blinded their eyes to the truth."[6] See 7:179, 10:99, and 32:13.

10. Ibn Kathir explains: "Allah has decreed that they will be misguided, so warning them will not help them and will not have any effect on them."[7]

11. Only believers will benefit from the messenger's warning. On Ar-Rahman, see 17:10, as also at 36:15 and 36:23.

13. He begins a recapitulation in the form of a parable of a story that is told many times in the Qur'an in connection with specific prophets: messengers come to a city (identified as Antioch by many Muslim commentators), but the people reject them, saying they're only "men like us" (36:15), just as those who rejected Noah said about him (11:27, 23:24), and as the messenger is also just an ordinary man (18:110).

17. The messengers respond by saying that their "duty is just clear conveyance," as is the messenger (5:92, 5:99).

He said, If only my people knew **27**With what my Lord has pardoned me and made me among the honored ones. **28**We did not send down against his people after him a host from heaven, nor do we ever send. **29**It was just one shout, and indeed, they were extinct. **30**Alas for the slaves! A messenger never came to them except that they mocked him. **31**Haven't they seen how many generations we destroyed before them, which indeed did not return to them, **32**But all, without exception, will be brought before us. **33**A sign to them is the dead earth. We revive it, and we bring forth grain from it so that they eat of it, **34**And we have placed in it gardens of the date-palm and grapes, and we have caused springs of water to gush forth in it, **35**So that they may eat of the fruit of it, and their hands did not make it. Will they not, then, give thanks? **36**Glory be to him who created all the pairs, of what the earth grows, and of themselves, and of what they do not know. **37**A sign to them is night. We strip it of the day, and indeed, they are in darkness. **38**And the sun runs on to a resting place for him. That is the measuring of the mighty, the wise one. **39**And for the moon we have appointed mansions until she returns like an old shriveled palm-leaf. **40**It is not for the sun to overtake the moon, nor does the night surpass the day. They each float in an orbit. **41**And a sign to them is that we bear their offspring in the laden ship, **42**And have created for them something like them, on which they ride. **43**And if we will, we drown them,

and there is no help for them, nor can they be saved, **44**Unless by mercy from us and as comfort for awhile. **45**When it is said to them, Beware of what is in front of you and what is behind you, so that perhaps you may find mercy. **46**There never came a sign from the signs of their Lord to them, except that they turned away from it. **47**And when it is said to them, Spend out of what Allah has provided you with, those who disbelieve say to those who believe, Will we feed those whom Allah, if he willed, would feed? You are in nothing but clear error. **48**And they say, When will this promise be fulfilled, if you are truthful? **49**They await just one shout, which will surprise them while they are arguing. **50**Then they cannot make bequest, nor can they return to their own people. **51**And the trumpet is blown and indeed, from the graves they go to their Lord, **52**Calling out, Woe to us, who has raised us from our place of sleep? This is what Ar-Rahman promised, and the messengers spoke truth. **53**It is just one shout, and look at them brought together before us. **54**This day no soul is wronged in anything, nor are you repaid for anything except what you used to do. **55**Indeed, those who deserve paradise this day are busy in joyful things, **56**They and their wives, in pleasant shade, reclining on thrones, **57**Theirs the fruit and theirs what they ask for, **58**The word from a merciful Lord is peace. **59**But go apart, O you guilty, today. **60**Didn't I order you, O you sons of Adam, not to follow Satan? Indeed, he is your

---

31. See 3:137.

38. See 22:18. Once again, the Qur'an assumes a flat earth with the sun orbiting around it.

52. On Ar-Rahman, see 17:110 and 38:5.

55. Ibn Kathir attributes to two companions of Muhammad a disagreement over the "joyful things" with which the blessed would be busy. He states that Ibn Abbas thought "busy in joyful things" meant "listening to stringed instruments." Abu Haatim, on the other hand, contended that Ibn Abbas "misheard the phrase *iftidaad al-abkaar* (deflowering virgins) and thought it was *samaa' al-awtaar* (listening to stringed instruments)." Ibn Kathir concludes: "In fact the correct phrase is *iftidaad al-abkaar* (deflowering virgins)."[8] On the virgins, see 44:54 and 55:56.

open enemy, **61**But to worship me? That was the right path. **62**Yet he has led astray a great multitude among you. Did you then have no sense? **63**This is Gehenna which you were promised. **64**Burn in it today for disbelieving. **65**This day we seal up their mouths, and their hands speak out to us, and their feet bear witness about what they used to earn. **66**And if we had willed, we indeed could have blotted out their eyesight so that they would struggle for the way. Then how could they have seen? **67**And if we had willed, we indeed could have fixed them in their place, making them powerless to go forward or turn back. **68**He whom we bring to old age, we reverse him in creation. So won't they understand? **69**And we have not taught him poetry, nor is it fitting for him. This is nothing but a reminder and a clear Qur'an, **70**To warn whoever lives, and so that the word may be fulfilled against the unbelievers. **71**Haven't they seen how we have created the cattle for them of our handiwork, so that they are their owners,

72And have subjected them to them, so that some of them they have for riding, some for food? **73**They have benefits and drinks from them. Will they not then give thanks? **74**And they have taken gods besides Allah, so that they may be helped. **75**It is not in their power to help them, but they are an army in arms to them. **76**So do not let their speech grieve you. Indeed, we know what they conceal and what they proclaim. **77**Has not man seen that we have created him from a drop of seed? Yet indeed, he is an open enemy. **78**And he has made a comparison for us, and has forgotten the fact of his creation, saying, Who will revive these bones when they have rotted away? **79**Say, He will revive them who produced them at the first, for he is the knower of every creation, **80**Who has established for you fire from the green tree, and look, you kindle from it. **81**Is not he who created the heavens and the earth able to create things like them? Yes, he is. For he is the all-wise creator, **82**But his command, when he intends something, is only that he says to it, Be! And it is. **83**Therefore glory be to him in whose hand is the dominion over all things. To him you will be brought back.

---

63. On Gehenna, see 2:206.

66. The *Tafsir Ibn Abbas* paraphrases this as, "If We willed, We could have misguided them all away from true guidance, so how could they be guided."9 See 7:179, 10:99-100, 16:37, 32:13, and 36:9.

68. Instead of "they understand," the Warsh Qur'an has "you understand."10

76. See 2:144.

SURA 37

Those Ranged in Ranks

As-Saffat

Introduction

A hadith has one of Muhammad's companions say, "The Messenger of Allah used to enjoin upon us to make the prayer short, but he would lead us in prayer and recite As-Saffat."[1] Maududi says this is a Meccan sura; Bell notes that it also "contains passages from different dates."[2] The title comes from 37:1 and 37:165.

---

1 Sunan an-Nasa'i, vol. 1, book 10, no. 827.
2 Bell, II, 440.

Those Ranged in Ranks

IN THE NAME OF ALLAH, THE COMPASSIONATE, THE MERCIFUL.

¹By those who ranged the ranks in battle order ²And those who drive away with reproof ³And those who read for a reminder, ⁴Indeed, your Lord is surely one, ⁵Lord of the heavens and of the earth and all that is between them, and Lord of the sun's risings. ⁶Indeed, we have adorned the lowest heaven with an ornament, the planets, ⁷With security from every defiant satan. ⁸They cannot listen to the highest chiefs, for they are pelted from every side, ⁹Outcast, and theirs is a perpetual torment, ¹⁰Except him who snatches a fragment, and a piercing flame pursues him. ¹¹Then ask them, Are they stronger as a creation, or those whom we have created? Indeed, we created them from sticky clay. ¹²No, but you are amazed when they mock ¹³And do not pay attention when they are reminded, ¹⁴And seek to scoff when they see a sign. ¹⁵And they say, Indeed, this is mere sorcery, ¹⁶When we are dead and have become dust and bones, will we then really be raised? ¹⁷And our forefathers? ¹⁸Say, You, in truth, you will be brought low. ¹⁹There is just one shout, and indeed, they see, ²⁰And say, Alas for us, this is the day of judgment. ²¹This is the day of separation, which you used to deny. ²²Assemble those who did wrong, together with their wives and what they used to worship ²³Instead of Allah, and lead them to the path to the blaze, ²⁴And stop them, for they must be questioned. ²⁵What ails you that you do not help one another? ²⁶No, but this day they make full submission. ²⁷And some of them draw near to others, questioning each other. ²⁸They say, Indeed, you used to come to us, imposing, ²⁹They answer, No, but you were not believers. ³⁰We had no power over you, but you were transgressing people. ³¹Now the word of our Lord has been fulfilled concerning us. Indeed, we are about to taste. ³²Thus we misled you. Indeed, we were astray. ³³Then indeed, this day they are sharers in the doom. ³⁴Indeed, in this way we deal with the guilty. ³⁵For when it was said to them, There is no God except Allah, they were scornful ³⁶And said, Shall we forsake our gods for a mad poet? ³⁷No, but he brought the truth, and he confirmed those sent. ³⁸Indeed, truly you taste the painful doom ³⁹You are repaid for nothing except what you did ⁴⁰Except single-minded slaves of Allah, ⁴¹For them there is a known provision, ⁴²Fruits. And they will be honored ⁴³In the gardens of delight, ⁴⁴On couches facing one another,

---

1. "Those who set the ranks in battle order" are the angels.¹

7. The angels are apparently ranged in ranks in order to keep the rebellious demons from listening in to the exalted assembly. Says Ibn Kathir: "They cannot reach the higher group—which refers to the heavens and the angels in them—when they speak of what has been revealed by Allah of His Laws and decrees."²

8. Apparently the angels pelt the satans with the planets to prevent them from hearing the heavenly assembly. See 67:5.

10. Some devils, however, do manage to hear and snatch away a bit of Allah's revelation. Ibn Kathir attributes to Ibn Abbas the statement that "when they heard the revelation, they would come down to earth and to every word they would add nine of their own."³ This

may be the cosmic derivation of the Scriptural corruptions that the Jews (5:13) and the Christians (5:14) engaged in.

23. "The blaze" is *al-jahim*, about which see 5:10, as also for 37:55, 37:64, 37:68, and 37:163.

29. Barth points out that this passage makes much more sense if 37:32 is placed before 37:30: "29. They answer, No, but you were not believers. 32. Thus we misled you. Indeed, we were astray. 30. We had no power over you, but you were transgressing people."⁴

37. What the messenger says is true and confirms the messages of the earlier prophets (see 3:67, 21:74, 21:92).

40. Here begins a more detailed description of what the blessed will enjoy in paradise than the Qur'an has presented previously.

⁴⁵A cup from a gushing spring is brought around for them, ⁴⁶White, delicious to the drinkers, ⁴⁷In it there is no harm, nor are they made intoxicated by it. ⁴⁸And with them are those of modest gaze, with lovely eyes, ⁴⁹As if they were closely guarded pearls. ⁵⁰And some of them draw near to others, questioning each other. ⁵¹A speaker among them says, Indeed, I had a comrade ⁵²Who used to say, Are you in truth among those who put faith? ⁵³Can we, when we are dead and have become mere dust and bones, can we indeed receive reward or punishment? ⁵⁴He says, Will you look? ⁵⁵Then he looks and sees him in the depth of the blaze. ⁵⁶He says, By Allah, you indeed all but caused my ruin, ⁵⁷And if it had not been for the favor of my Lord, I, too, would have been among those called forth. ⁵⁸Are we then not to die ⁵⁹Except for our former death, and are we not to be punished? ⁶⁰Indeed, this is the supreme victory. ⁶¹For the like of this, then, let laborers labor. ⁶²Is this better as a welcome, or the tree of zaqqum? ⁶³Indeed, we have appointed it a torment for wrongdoers. ⁶⁴Indeed, it is a tree that springs up in the heart of the blaze. ⁶⁵Its fruit is like the heads of satans ⁶⁶And indeed, they indeed must eat of it, and fill bellies with it. ⁶⁷And afterward, indeed, on top of that they have a drink of boiling water ⁶⁸And afterward, indeed, their return is surely to the blaze. ⁶⁹They indeed found their fathers astray, ⁷⁰But they make haste in their footsteps. ⁷¹And indeed most of the men of old went astray before them, ⁷²And indeed we sent warners among them. ⁷³Then see the nature of the consequences for those who were warned, ⁷⁴Except single-minded slaves of Allah. ⁷⁵And Noah indeed prayed to us, and the hearer of his prayer was favorable ⁷⁶And we saved him and his family from the great distress, ⁷⁷And made his descendants the survivors, ⁷⁸And left for him among the later people, ⁷⁹Peace be upon Noah among the peoples. ⁸⁰Indeed, in this way do we reward the good. ⁸¹Indeed, he is one of our

---

45. The "gushing spring" will, says the *Tafsir al-Jalalayn*, be filled with "wine which flows on the surface of the earth like rivers of water in this world, as white as driven snow—whiter than milk, delicious to those who drink—unlike the wine of this world which is unpleasant."⁵ Ibn Kathir adds that "Zayd bin Aslam said, 'White flowing wine,' meaning, with a bright, shining color, unlike the wine of this earth with its ugly, repulsive colors of red, black, yellow and turbid shades, and other features which are repugnant to anyone of a sound nature."⁶

48. These maidens will, says the *Tafsir al-Jalalayn*, "confine their eyes to their husbands" and "not look at anyone other than them."⁷ These are the virgins of paradise, in search of whom Muslims have fought against unbelievers and sought death throughout history, knowing that paradise is guaranteed to those who "kill and are killed" for Allah (9:111).

49. "This refers," according to the *Tafsir al-Jalalayn*, "to their colour; they are like the white of ostriches, covered with their feathers so that dust does not reach them. This whitish yellow is the best complexion for women."⁸ However, the *Tafsir Anwarul Bayan* differs: "Some commentators say that since extremely white women (resembling the colour of eggs) are disliked by many, the women of Heaven will vary according to the taste of people. Some will have the reddish shade of rubies, while others will have different complexions."⁹

62. At the heart of hell the damned will find the zaqqum tree, with its fruit like devils' heads. It is identified with the "cursed tree" of 17:60; see also 44:43 and 56:52. Ibn Kathir ascribes to an early Muslim the statement that "the tree of Zaqqum is mentioned as a test for those who are misguided."¹⁰ Ibn Kathir adds that the zaqqum tree "is nourished by the fire, for it was created from fire."¹¹ He ascribes to Abu Jahl ("may Allah curse him"), a notorious enemy of Muhammad in the ninth-century Islamic literature, the statement: "Zaqqum means dates and butter which I eat [*Atazaqqamuhu*]."¹² According to Bell, "*Zaqqum* is said to have been the name of a tree with bitter fruit growing in the Hijaz. The word occurs in Syriac, meaning 'hog-bean,' which would suit the context here."¹³

75. On Noah, see also 7:59, 10:71, 11:25, 21:76, 23:23, 25:37, 26:105, 29:14, 50:12, 51:46, 53:52, 54:9, 57:26, 69:11, and 71:1.

78. This is repeated at 37:108, 37:119, and 37:129. The *Tafsir al-Jalalayn* explains it as meaning that the "later people" would remain "in praise until the Day of Rising" of those righteous ones who went before.¹⁴ However, Barth notes that this usage of *taraka alayhi*, "we left for him," is unusual in the extreme and may be evidence of textual corruption, for this phrase "without an object in the accusative is against all Arabic usage, even against that of the Koran."¹⁵

believing slaves. **82**Then we drowned the others. **83**And indeed, of his persuasion indeed was Abraham **84**When he came to his Lord with a whole heart, **85**When he said to his father and his people, What is it that you worship? **86**Is it a falsehood, gods besides Allah, that you desire? **87**What then is your opinion of the Lord of the worlds? **88**And he glanced a glance at the stars **89**Then said, Indeed, I feel sick. **90**And they turned their backs and went away from him. **91**Then he turned to their gods and said, Will you not eat? **92**What ails you that you do not speak? **93**Then he attacked them, striking with his right hand. **94**And they came toward him, hastening. **95**He said, Do you worship what you yourselves carve **96**When Allah has created you and what you make? **97**They said, Build for him a building and fling him in the red hot fire. **98**And they designed a trap for him, but we made them inferior. **99**And he said, Indeed, I am going to my Lord who will guide me. **100**My Lord, grant me one from among the righteous. **101**So we gave him news of a gentle son. **102**And when he was old enough to walk with him, he said, O my dear son, I have seen in a dream that I must sacrifice you. So look, what do you think?

He said, O my father, do what you are commanded. Allah willing, you will find me among the steadfast. **103**Then, when they had both submitted, and he had flung him down upon his face, **104**we called to him, O Abraham, **105**You have already fulfilled the vision. Indeed, in this way do we reward the good. **106**Indeed, that was truly a clear test. **107**Then we ransomed him with a mighty victim. **108**And we left for him among the later people, **109**Peace be upon Abraham. **110**In this way do we reward the good. **111**Indeed, he is one of our believing slaves. **112**And we gave him news of the birth of Isaac, a prophet of the righteous. **113**And we blessed him and Isaac. And of their descendants are some who do good, and some who plainly wrong themselves. **114**And we indeed gave favor to Moses and Aaron, **115**And saved them and their people from the great distress, **116**And helped them so that they became the victors. **117**And we gave them the clear book **118**And showed them the right path. **119**And we left for them among the later people, **120**Peace be upon Moses and Aaron. **121**Indeed, in this way do we reward the good. **122**Indeed, they are two of our believing slaves. **123**And indeed, Elias was among

---

83. On Abraham, see also 7:80, 9:17, 9:114, 11:69, 15:51, 19:41, 21:51, 26:69, 29:16, 60:4, and elsewhere.

101. Abraham sees in a dream that he must sacrifice his son, but Allah stops him just before he is about to do it; it was all a test. The son is not named in the Qur'anic text, but Isaac's birth follows (37:112), which strongly implies that the son who was almost sacrificed was Ishmael, as Isaac had not yet been born at the time of this incident. Ibn Kathir explains the view of virtually all Islamic scholars: the sacrificial son was Ishmael, and the Jews and Christians corrupted the text of their Scriptures to make the claim that he was Isaac. "This child was Ismail," writes Ibn Kathir. "The Muslims and the People of the Book agree, and indeed it is stated in their Book, that Ismail, peace be upon him, was born when Ibrahim, peace be upon him, was eighty-six years old, and Ishaq [Isaac] was born when Ibrahim was ninety-nine years old."¹⁶

This makes the identification certain and demonstrates that the Jews and Christians have corrupted their scriptures: "According

to their Book, Allah commanded Ibrahim to sacrifice his only son, and in another text it says his firstborn son. But here they falsely inserted the name of Ishaq. This is not right because it goes against what their own Scripture says. They inserted the name of Ishaq because he is their ancestor, while Isma'il is the ancestor of the Arabs. They were jealous of them, so they added this idea and changed the meaning of the phrase 'only son' to mean 'the only son who is with you,' because Isma'il had been taken with his mother to Makkah [Mecca]. But this is a case of falsification and distortion, because the words 'only son' cannot be said except in the case of one who has no other son. Furthermore, the firstborn son has a special status that is not shared by subsequent children, so the command to sacrifice him is a more exquisite test."¹⁷

114. On Moses, see also 2:49, 7:103, 10:75, 17:101, 20:9, 26:10, 27:7, 28:3, and elsewhere.

123. See 6:85.

those sent, **124**When he said to his people, Will you not fear Allah? **125**Will you cry to Baal and forsake the best of creators, **126**Allah, your Lord and Lord of your forefathers? **127**But they denied him, so they surely will be called forth **128**Except single-minded slaves of Allah. **129**And we left for him among the later people, **130**Peace be upon Eliases. **131**Indeed, in this way do we reward the good. **132**Indeed, he is one of our believing slaves. **133**And indeed, Lot truly was of those sent. **134**When we saved him and his family, every one, **135**Except an old woman among those who stayed behind, **136**Then we destroyed the others. **137**And indeed, you truly pass by them in the morning **138**And at night, do you then have no sense? **139**And indeed, Jonah truly was among those sent **140**When he fled to the laden ship, **141**And then drew lots and was of those rejected, **142**And the fish swallowed him while he was blameworthy, **143**And if he had not been one of those who glorify, **144**He would have remained in its belly until the day when they are raised, **145**Then we threw him on a desert shore while he was sick, **146**And we caused a tree of gourd to grow above him, **147**And we sent him to a hundred thousand or more **148**And they believed, therefore we gave them comfort for a while. **149**Now ask them, Does your Lord have daughters while they have sons? **150**Or did we create the angels females while they were present? **151**Indeed, it is part of their falsehood that they say, **152**Allah has children. Allah. Truly they tell a lie. **153**He has preferred daughters to sons. **154**What ails you? How do you judge? **155**Will you not then reflect? **156**Or do you have a clear justification? **157**Then bring your book, if you are truthful. **158**And they imagine kinship between him and the jinn, whereas the jinn know well that they will be brought before. **159**May Allah be glorified from what they attribute, **160**Except single-minded slaves of Allah. **161**Indeed, truly, you and what you worship, **162**You cannot seduce anyone against him **163**Except him who is to burn in the blaze. **164**There is not one of us who does not have his known position. **165**Indeed, we, even we are those who ranged the ranks, **166**Indeed, we, even we are those who sing his praise **167**And indeed, they used to say, **168**If only we had a reminder from the men of old, **169**We would be single-minded slaves of Allah. **170**Yet they disbelieve in it, but they will come to know. **171**And indeed our word went forth of old to our slaves who

---

130. Instead of "peace be upon Eliases" (*Il Yaaseen*), the Warsh Qur'an has "peace be upon the family of Eliases" (*Aali Yaasseen*).[18] The Warsh reading may be an attempt to resolve a difficulty. Ibn Warraq explains: "Many of the verses in this sura end with the rhyme -in. For the sake of this rhyme, the second instance of Elias (verse 130) is rendered *Ilyasin*, as though it were a plural."[19] Making the passage be about Elias's family and saying "the Eliases," a la "the Smiths" or "the Joneses," excuses the plural.

139. Jonah also appears at 21:87 and 68:48 as Dhu'n-Nun, the "companion of the fish," which may indicate source material differing from what is used here.

148. In the Bible, they repent (Jonah 3:5), but here, they believe, which is the all-important act in the Qur'an, that of accepting the message.

149. Here begins a polemic against the pagan Arabs who worshiped "daughters of Allah" (see 16:57 and 53:19).

152. See 2:116.

157. It is assumed that the earlier revelations will confirm what the Qur'an says (see 2:4, 5:44).

were sent [172]So that they would indeed be helped, [173]And that our army, they indeed would be the victors. [174]So withdraw from them awhile, [175]And watch, for they will see. [176]Would they hasten on our doom? [177]But when it comes home to them, then it will be a wretched morning for those who have been warned. [178]Withdraw from them awhile [179]And watch, for they will see. [180]May your Lord be glorified, the Lord of majesty, from what they attribute [181]And peace be upon the messengers. [182]And praise be to Allah, Lord of the worlds.

173. Allah's forces will be victorious, as the *Tafsir al-Jalalayn* explains: "It is Our army (the believers) which will be victorious over the unbelievers by the proof and victory over them in this world. If some of them are not victorious in this world, they will be in the Next World."[20] See 9:14, 9:111.

SURA 38

Sad

Sad

Introduction

This sura takes its name from the Arabic letter *sad*, with which it begins. As always, the letters that begin many suras are left unexplained, and the commentators say that Allah alone knows what he means by these letters.

Sura 38 is traditionally regarded as Meccan, but Bell asserts that "the end of the surah, vv. 67–88, which may not in itself be a unity, is in a different rhyme and does not properly belong to it. Its presence may be due to vv. 49–66 having been written on the back of it. In any case it seems earlier than that passage."[1]

1 Bell, II, 450.

Sad

In the name of Allah, the compassionate, the merciful.

1Sad. By the renowned Qur'an, **2**No, but those who disbelieve are in false pride and opposition. **3**How many a generation did we destroy before them, and they cried out when it was no longer the time for escape. **4**And they are amazed that a warner from among themselves has come to them, and the unbelievers say, This is a wizard, a charlatan. **5**Does he make the gods into one Allah? Indeed, that is an astounding thing. **6**The chiefs among them go around, exhorting, Go and be faithful to your gods! Indeed, this is something to be desired. **7**We have not heard of this in the last religion. This is nothing but an invention. **8**Has the reminder been to him among us? No, but they are in doubt about my reminder, no, but they have not yet tasted my doom. **9**Or are theirs the treasures of the mercy of your Lord, the mighty, the bestower? **10**Or is the kingdom of the heavens and the earth and all that is between them theirs? Then let them ascend by ropes. **11**A defeated army are the groups that are there. **12**The people of Noah before them denied, and Aad, and Pharaoh firmly planted, **13**And Thamud, and the people of Lot, and the dwellers in the wood, these were the groups. **14**Each denied the messengers, therefore my doom was justified, **15**These wait for just one shout, there will be no second after it. **16**They say, Our Lord, hasten on our fate for us before the day of reckoning. **17**Bear with what they say, and remember our slave David, lord of might, indeed, he was always turning in repentance. **18**Indeed, we subjected the hills to sing the praises with him at nightfall and sunrise, **19**And the birds assembled, all were turning to him. **20**We made his kingdom strong and gave him wisdom and decisive speech. **21**And has the story of the litigants come to you? How they climbed the wall into the royal chamber, **22**How they burst in upon David, and he was afraid of them. They said, Be not afraid. Two litigants, one of whom has wronged the other, therefore judge rightly between us, do not be unjust, and show us the good way. **23**Indeed, this my brother has ninety and nine ewes while I had one ewe, and he said, Entrust it to me, and he conquered me in speech. **24**He said, He has wronged you in demanding

---

1. On the "mysterious letters," see 2:1.

5. The question reflects puzzlement among the audience of the Qur'an over its assertion that pre-Islamic gods such as Ar-Rahman ("The Merciful") were in reality simply attributes of the one Allah; see 17:110. The Qur'anic passages mentioning Ar-Rahman may have originally been the writings of people worshiping a different god, until Ar-Rahman was conflated with Allah, and these passages were incorporated into the Islamic holy book, with verses such as this one remaining as markers of a time when the two gods were distinct from one another, and the conflation had to be explained.

7. Ibn Kathir attributes to Ibn Abbas the paraphrase: "We have not heard of this from the religion of these later days (meaning Christianity); if this Qur'an were true, the Christians would have told us about it."[1]

11. In sum, as Maududi puts it, "Allah says that the actual reason with those people for their denial is not any defect in the message of Islam but their own arrogance, jealousy and insistence on following the blind."[2] See 2:18.

12. On Pharaoh, see also 2:49, 3:11, 7:103, 8:52, 10:75, 14:6, 17:101, 20:24, 23:46, 26:11, 27:12, 28:3, 29:39, 40:24, 44:17, 50:13, 51:38, 54:41, 66:11, 69:9, 73:15, 79:15, 85:18, and 89:10.

17. Here begins a Qur'anic retelling of the parable that the prophet Nathan tells King David in 2 Samuel 12:1-9. In the Bible, the point of the story of the rich man with many ewes who takes the single ewe of the poor man is to bring home to David the enormity of his having had Uriah the Hittite killed so that he could take Uriah's wife Bathsheba. In the Qur'an is none of this, however, except the story of the rich man who took the poor man's ewe, followed by David's realization that Allah had tried him (38:24).

24. Ibn Kathir says, "In discussing this passage, the scholars of Tafsir [Qur'an commentary] mention a story which is mostly based upon Isra'iliyat [Israelite] narrations. Nothing has been reported about this from the Infallible Prophet that we could accept as

your ewe in addition to his ewes, and indeed, many partners oppress one another, except those who believe and do good works, and they are few. And David guessed that we had tested him, and he sought forgiveness of his Lord, and he bowed himself and fell down prostrate and repented. ²⁵So we forgave him that, and indeed, he had access to our presence and a happy journey's end. ²⁶O David, indeed, we have set you as a caliph on the earth, therefore judge rightly between mankind, and do not follow desire, so that it does not seduce you from the way of Allah. Indeed, those who stray from the way of Allah have an awful doom, for they forgot the day of reckoning. ²⁷And we did not create the heaven and the earth and all that is between them in vain. That is the opinion of those who disbelieve. And woe to those who disbelieve, from the fire. ²⁸Shall we treat those who believe and do good works like those who spread corruption on the earth, or shall we treat the pious like the wicked? ²⁹A book that we have revealed to you, full of blessing, so that they may ponder its signs, and that men of understanding may reflect. ³⁰And we bestowed Solomon upon David. How excellent a slave! Indeed, he was

always turning in repentance. ³¹When there were shown to him in the evening well-trained horses ³²And he said, indeed, I have preferred the good things to the remembrance of my Lord, until they were taken out of sight behind the veil. ³³Bring them back to me, and he fell to stroking their legs and necks. ³⁴And indeed we tested Solomon, and set upon his throne a lifeless body. Then he repented. ³⁵He said, My Lord, forgive me and bestow dominion on me such as shall not belong to any after me. Indeed, you are the bestower. ³⁶So we made the wind subservient to him, to flow gently by his command wherever he intended. ³⁷And the unruly, every builder and diver, ³⁸And others linked together in chains, ³⁹This is our gift, so bestow it, or withhold, without reckoning. ⁴⁰And indeed, he has favor with us, and a happy journey's end. ⁴¹And mention our slave Job, when he called out to his Lord, Indeed, Satan afflicts me with distress and torment. ⁴²Strike the ground with your foot. This is a cool bath and a refreshing drink. ⁴³And we bestowed on him his family and with it more like it, a mercy from us, and a memorial for men of understanding. ⁴⁴And, Take in your hand a branch and strike with it, and

---

true."³ Yet the *Tafsir al-Jalalayn* reveals the dependence in saying that David "realised with certainty that We had put him to the test—meaning that he had fallen into affliction because of his love for that woman. He begged forgiveness from his Lord and fell down prone, prostrating, and repented."⁴

26. On "caliph on the earth," see 2:30.

31. Regarding Solomon's horses, Ibn Kathir tells a story in which Muhammad happens upon one of the toys of his child bride, Aisha: a horse with cloth wings. He asks her, "Did you not hear that Sulayman, peace be upon him, had a horse that had wings?"⁵ Then, says Aisha, "The Messenger of Allah smiled so broadly that I could see his molars."⁶ Legends of this kind support the idea, frequently denied today, that Aisha was indeed a child, still playing with toys, when the prophet of Islam married her, a marriage with important implications (see 33:21).

34. The *Tafsir al-Jalalayn* explains: "That came about because he married a woman he was passionately in love with and she used to worship an idol in his house without his knowledge. The power

over his kingdom resided in his signet ring. He removed it once when he went to the lavatory and left it with his wife, Umayna, as was his custom. A jinn came in the form of Suleyman and took it from her. The name of the jinn was Sakhr, or possibly something else. He sat on the throne of Suleyman and the birds and other creatures devoted themselves to him. Suleyman came out looking different from his normal appearance and saw him on his throne. He said to the people, 'I am Suleyman,' but they did not recognise him. Then he repented. Then after some days Suleyman was restored to his kingdom because he regained his ring and put it on and sat on his throne."⁷

41. Here begins another survey of prophets: Job (38:41-44); Abraham, Isaac, and Jacob (38:45-47); and Ishmael, Elisha, and Dhul-Kifl (Ezekiel) (38:48).

44. Ibn Kathir explains that Job "got angry with his wife and was upset about something she had done, so he swore an oath that if Allah healed him, he would strike her with one hundred blows. When Allah healed him, how could her service, mercy, compassion

do not break your oath. Indeed, we found him steadfast, how excellent a slave! Indeed, he was ever turning in repentance. **45**And make mention of our slaves, Abraham, Isaac and Jacob, men of strength and vision. **46**Indeed, we purified them with a pure thought, remembrance of the home. **47**Indeed, in our sight they are truly among the elect, the excellent. **48**And mention Ishmael and Elisha and Dhu'l-Kifl. All are among the chosen. **49**This is a reminder. And indeed, for those who fear Allah is a happy journey's end, **50**Gardens of Eden, of which the gates are opened for them, **51**In which, reclining, they call for plenteous fruit and cool drink in it. **52**And with them are those of modest gaze, of equal age. **53**This it is what you are promised for the day of reckoning. **54**Indeed, this is in truth our provision, which will never waste away. **55**This, and indeed, for the transgressors there with be an evil journey's end, **56**Gehenna, where they will burn, an evil bed. **57**Then they will taste it, a boiling fluid, and a murky, intensely cold fluid, **58**And other of the kind in pairs. **59**Here is an army rushing blindly with you. No word of welcome for them. Indeed, they will roast at the fire. **60**They say, No, but you, for you there is no word of welcome. You prepared this for us. Now wretched is our plight. **61**They say, Our Lord, whoever prepared this for us, give him double

portion of the fire. **62**And they say, What ails us that we do not see men whom we were inclined to count among the wicked? **63**Did we take them for a laughing-stock, or have our eyes missed them? **64**Indeed, that is very truth, the argument of the dwellers in the fire. **65**Say, I am only a warner, and there is no God except Allah, the one, the absolute, **66**Lord of the heavens and the earth and all that is between them, the mighty, the forgiving. **67**Say, It is tremendous news **68**From which you turn away. **69**I had no knowledge of the highest chiefs when they argued, **70**It is revealed to me only so that I might be a plain warner. **71**When your Lord said to the angels, Indeed, I am about to create a mortal out of mire, **72**And when I have fashioned him and breathed into him of my spirit, then fall down before him prostrate, **73**The angels fell down prostrate, every one, **74**Except Iblis, he was scornful and became one of the unbelievers. **75**He said, O Iblis, what hinders you from falling prostrate before what I have created with both my hands? Are you too proud or are you among the highly exalted? **76**He said, I am better than him. You created me from fire, while you created him from clay. **77**He said, Go forth from here, for indeed, you are outcast, **78**And indeed, my curse is upon you until the day of judgment. **79**He said, My Lord, give me a reprieve until the

---

and kindness be repaid with a beating So Allah showed him a way out, which was to take a bundle of thin grass, with one hundred stems, and hit her with it once. Thus he fulfilled his oath and avoided breaking his vow."8 However, see 4:34.

45. Instead of, "And make mention of our slaves [*ibaadanaa*], Abraham, Isaac and Jacob, men of strength and vision," the version of al-Bazzi, one of the transmitters of Hamza's reading, has, "And make mention of our slave [*abdanaa*], Abraham, Isaac and Jacob, men of strength and vision."9

52. The women of "modest gaze" in paradise will be of "equal age," which the *Tafsir al-Jalalayn* explains as meaning that "they will have the same age: thirty-three years."10

56. On Gehenna, see 2:206.

69. The "highest chiefs" seems to be a reference to the exalted assembly of Allah and his angels (37:7-8).

71. The story of the creation of mankind and Iblis's refusal to bow down to Adam is also at 2:30-39, 7:11-25, and 15:28-42. The idea that the angels should bow down before a human being is a vestige of the Biblical idea that human beings are created in the image of God; however, this idea does not appear in the Qur'an.

day when they are raised. [80]He said, Indeed, you are among those reprieved [81]Until the day of the appointed time. [82]He said, Then, by your might, I surely will seduce every one of them, [83]Except your single-minded slaves among them. [84]He said, The truth is, and the truth I speak, [85]That I will fill Gehenna with you and with those among them who follow you, together. [86]Say, I ask no fee for this from you, and I am not pretending. [87]Indeed, it is nothing other than a reminder for all peoples [88]And you will come in time to know the truth of it.

---

85. See 7:179, 10:99, and 32:13. On Gehenna, see 2:206.

The Throngs

Az-Zumar

Introduction

This is traditionally regarded as a Meccan sura that was revealed fairly early in Muhammad's career. However, Bell observes that "from v. 28 onwards the surah seems to have been pieced together from earlier passages, some of which may possibly be Meccan, though some seem early Medinan."[1]

A hadith depicts Aisha saying: "The Messenger of Allah used to fast until we would say, 'He does not want to break fast,' and he would not fast until we would say, 'He does not want to fast.' And he used to recite Bani Isra'il [Al-Isra] and Az-Zumar every night"—that is, suras 17 and 39.[2] The connection between fasting and not fasting and reciting these suras is unexplained. Since the section about fasting appears elsewhere without reference to these suras, it is possible that these are divergent traditions that were combined in one version more or less at random, or for reasons that have been lost.[3] In any case, this is yet more evidence of the fluidity of Islamic tradition in the ninth century, when the hadith literature was being compiled.

The sura's title comes from 39:71 and 39:73.

---

1 Bell, II, 457.
2 Ibn Kathir, VIII, 355.
3 Sunan an-Nasa'i, vol. 3, book 22, no. 2349.

The Throngs

In the name of Allah, the compassionate, the merciful.

[1]The revelation of the book is from Allah, the mighty, the wise. [2]Indeed, we have revealed the book to you with truth, so worship Allah, making religion pure for him. [3]Surely pure religion is for Allah alone. And those who choose protecting friends besides him, We worship them only so that they may bring us near to Allah. Indeed, Allah will judge between them concerning what they disagree about. Indeed, Allah does not guide him who is a liar, an ingrate. [4]If Allah had willed to choose a son, he could have chosen what he wished from what he has created. May he be glorified, he is Allah, the one, the absolute. [5]He has created the heavens and the earth with truth. He makes night to succeed day, and he makes day to succeed night, and he subjects the sun and the moon to give service, each running on for an appointed term. Is not he the mighty one, the forgiver? [6]He created you from one being, then from that he made its mate, and he has provided for you eight kinds of cattle. He created you in the wombs of your mothers, creation after creation, in three layers of darkness. This is Allah, your Lord. The dominion is his. There is no God except him. How then are you turned away? [7]If you are ungrateful, yet Allah is independent of you, though he is not pleased with ingratitude from his slaves, and if you are thankful he is pleased with it for you. No burdened soul will bear another's burden. Then you will return to your Lord, and he will tell you what you used to do. Indeed, he knows what is in the hearts. [8]And when some harm touches man, he calls out to his Lord, turning to him. Then, when he grants him a favor from him, he forgets what he had called out to him for, and sets up rivals to Allah so that he may seduce from his path. Say, Take pleasure in your disbelief for awhile. Indeed, you are among the companions of the fire. [9]Is he who worships devoutly in the watches of the night, prostrate and standing, fearing the hereafter and hoping for the mercy of his Lord? Say, Are those who know equal with those who do not know? But only men of understanding will be mindful. [10]Say, O my slaves who believe, observe your duty to your Lord. For those who do good in this world there is good, and Allah's earth is spacious. Indeed the steadfast will be paid their wages without

---

3. "We worship them only so that they may bring us near to Allah" is the explanation of "those who choose protecting friends besides him," although "say" is absent here. This verse, in any case, dismisses the core assumption involved in the intercession of the saints, that they bring one closer to God, with greater precision and accuracy than he demonstrated in his dismissal of the idea of the Trinity (5:116).

4. See 2:116.

8. Barth notes that this verse and 39:49, both of which contain "the rare" *khawwalahu ni'amatan* ("he grants him a favor"; at 39:49, *khawwalnahu ni'amatan*, "we have granted him a favor"), "can be absent without detriment to the present context."[1]

9. The believer and the unbeliever are not equal. This notion has many implications; the emphasis here is on the fact that they will not receive equal treatment on the day of judgment. The statement also underscores the idea that the Muslims are the "best of people" (3:110), and the unbelievers are the "most vile of created beings" (98:6). There is no compatibility of this with the idea of the equality of dignity of all people as created by the same God. Instead, there is a sharp dichotomy between believer and unbeliever; see 48:29.

According to Barth, the questions here and at 39:19, 39:22, and 39:24 "belong by dint of their identical question form to a coherent construction that was not originally separated, as it is now, by a series of other verses."[2] However, he concludes that "whether the verses belong together in this way is uncertain, given the nature of the tradition."[3]

limit. **11**Say, Indeed, I am commanded to worship Allah, making religion pure for him. **12**And I am commanded to be the first of those who are Muslims. **13**Say, Indeed, if I should disobey my Lord, I fear the torment of a mighty day. **14**Say, I worship Allah, making my religion pure for him. **15**Then worship what you will besides him. Say, The losers will be those who lose themselves and their family on the day of resurrection. That will be the clear loss. **16**They have tents of fire above them and beneath them. With this does Allah frighten his slaves. O my slaves, therefore fear me.**17**And those who put away *taghut* so that they would not worship it and turn to Allah in repentance, for them there is glad news. Therefore give good news to my slaves **18**Who hear advice and follow the best of it. Such people are those whom Allah guides, and such are men of understanding. **19**Is he on whom the word of doom is fulfilled, and can you rescue him who is in the fire? **20**But those who keep their duty to their Lord, for them are lofty mansions with lofty mansions above them, built, beneath which rivers flow. A promise of Allah. Allah does not fail in his promise. **21**Haven't you seen how Allah has sent down water from the sky and has caused it to penetrate the earth as water springs, and afterward by it produces crops of various colors, and afterward they wither and you see them turn yellow, then he makes them chaff. Indeed, in this is indeed a reminder for men of understanding. **22**Is he whose bosom Allah has expanded for Islam, so that he follows a light from his Lord? Then woe to those whose hearts are hardened against remembrance of Allah. Such people are in clear error. **23**Allah has revealed the most beautiful statement, a book, its parts resembling one another, oft-repeated, at which the flesh creeps of those who fear their Lord, so that their flesh and their hearts soften to Allah's reminder. This is Allah's guidance, with which he guides those whom he wills. And for him whom Allah leads astray, for him there is no guide. **24**Is he, then, one who will strike his face against the awful doom upon the day of resurrection? And it will be said to the wrongdoers, Taste what you used to earn. **25**Those before them denied, and so the doom came upon them from where they did not know. **26**In this way Allah made them taste humiliation in the life of this world, and indeed the torment of the hereafter will be greater, if only they knew. **27**And indeed we have made in this Qur'an all kinds of comparisons for mankind, so that perhaps they may reflect, **28**An Arabic Qur'an, containing no crookedness, that perhaps they may fear Allah. **29**Allah makes a comparison, A man in relation to whom

---

12. This contradicts the claim that Abraham was a Muslim (3:67), as were the other prophets (6:84). However, Islamic exegetes smooth over the contradiction by saying that this refers to Muhammad's community specifically, not to the earlier communities of believers. "The Ummah [community] of the Holy Prophet," explains the *Tafsir Anwarul Bayan*, "is the last Ummah to appear on earth. The first believer of this Ummah was none other than the Holy Prophet himself."4

16. The "tents of fire" of the damned are contrasted with the "lofty mansions" of the blessed (39:20). Barth accordingly suggests that the two intervening verses were not originally placed there.5

17. On *taghut*, see 2:256.

19. See 39:9, as also at 39:22 and 39:24.

23. Ibn Kathir quotes an earlier authority saying: "This means that the entire Qur'an's parts resemble each other and are oft-repeated," and another: "One *Ayah* resembles another, and one letter resembles another."6 And a third: "It is oft-repeated so that people will understand what their Lord tells them."7 Ibn Kathir explains that when Muhammad's companions heard the Qur'an recited, "Their skins would shiver, and their hearts would soften to the remembrance of Allah."8

28. "No crookedness," according to the *Tafsir al-Jalalayn*, means "no confusion or disagreement."9 Regarding Arabic, see 12:2.

are several part-owners, arguing, and a man belonging wholly to one man. Are the two equal in comparison? Praise be to Allah, but most of them do not know. ³⁰Indeed, you will die, and indeed, they will die, ³¹Then indeed, on the day of resurrection, you will argue before your Lord. ³²And who does greater wrong than he who tells a lie against Allah, and denies the truth when it reaches him? Will not the home of unbelievers be in Gehenna? ³³And whoever brings the truth and believes in it, such people are the dutiful. ³⁴They will have what they wish from their Lord's bounty. That is the reward of the good, ³⁵That Allah will remit from them the worst of what they did, and will pay them as reward the best of what they used to do. ³⁶Will not Allah defend his slave? Yet they would frighten you with those besides him. He whom Allah leads astray, for him there is no guide. ³⁷And he whom Allah guides, for him there can be no misleader. Is not Allah mighty, able to repay? ³⁸And indeed, if you asked them, Who created the heavens and the earth?, they will say, Allah. Say, Do you think then about those whom you worship besides Allah, that if Allah willed some injury for me, could they remove his injury from me, or if he willed some mercy for me, could they restrain his mercy? Say, Allah is my everything. In him do the trusting put their trust. ³⁹Say, O my people, act in your manner. Indeed, I am acting. In this way you will come to know ⁴⁰Who it is to whom a doom comes that will humiliate him, and on whom there falls everlasting doom. ⁴¹Indeed, we have revealed to you the book for mankind with truth. Then whoever goes right, it is for his soul, and whoever strays, strays only to its harm. And you are not a guardian over them. ⁴²Allah receives souls at the time of their death, and what does not die in its sleep. He keeps that for which he has ordained death and dismisses the rest until an appointed term. Indeed, in this truly are signs for people who think. ⁴³Or do they choose intercessors other than Allah? Say, What? Even though they have power over nothing and have no intelligence? ⁴⁴Say, To Allah belongs all intercession. His is the dominion over the heavens and the earth. And afterward you will be brought back to him. ⁴⁵And when Allah alone is mentioned, the hearts of those who do not believe in the hereafter are repelled, and when those besides him are mentioned, look, they are glad. ⁴⁶Say, O Allah, creator of the heavens and the earth, knower of the invisible and the visible, you will judge between your slaves about what they used to disagree over. ⁴⁷And although those who do wrong possess all that is in the earth, and with it as much again, they indeed will seek to ransom themselves with it from the awful doom on the day of resurrection, and there will appear to them, from their Lord, something they had not expected. ⁴⁸And the evils that they earned will appear to them, and what they used to scoff at will surround

---

32. On Gehenna, see 2:206, as also at 39:60, 39:71, and 39:72.

36. See 7:179, 10:99, and 32:13.

42. The twentieth-century Qur'an translator Abdullah Yusuf Ali explains this by asserting that sleep is a little death: "Sleep being twin-brother to Death, our souls are for the time being released from the bondage of the flesh. Allah takes them for the time being. If, as some do, we are to die peacefully in sleep, our soul does not come back to the physical body, and the later decays and dies. If we still have some period of life to fulfill according to Allah's decree, our soul comes back to the body, and we resume our function in this life."¹⁰

43. Everyone will stand alone before Allah; no intercession from others will be accepted (2:123, 6:94, 23:101, 42:46). However, the Qur'an elsewhere accepts intercession with Allah's permission (10:3, 20:109, 21:28, 34:23, 53:26).

them. [49]Now when harm touches a man, he calls out to us, and afterward when we have granted him a favor from us, he says, I obtained it only by force of knowledge. No, but it is a test. But most of them do not know. [50]Those before them said it, yet what they had earned did not help them, [51]But the evils that they earned struck them, and those who do wrong, the evils that they earn will strike them, they cannot escape. [52]Don't they know that Allah enlarges provision for whom he will, and reduces it. Indeed, in this truly are signs for people who believe. [53]Say, O my slaves who have been wasteful to their own harm, do not despair of the mercy of Allah, who forgives all sins. Indeed, he is the forgiving, the merciful. [54]Turn to your Lord in repentance, and submit to him, before the doom comes to you, when you cannot be helped. [55]And follow the better of what is revealed to you from your Lord, before the doom comes on you suddenly, when you do not know, [56]So that no soul says, Alas, my grief is that I was unmindful of Allah, and I was indeed among the scoffers. [57]Or says, If only Allah had guided me, I would have been among the dutiful. [58]Or says, when it sees the doom, If only I had a second chance, so that I might be among the righteous. [59]No, for my revelations came to you, but you denied them and were scornful and were among the unbelievers. [60]And on the day of resurrection, you see those who lied about Allah with their faces blackened. Isn't Gehenna the home of the scorners? [61]And Allah delivers those who fear Allah because of what they deserve. Evil does not touch them, nor do they grieve. [62]Allah is creator of all things, and he is guardian over all things. [63]His are the keys of the heavens and the earth, and those who disbelieve the revelations of Allah, such people are are the losers. [64]Say, Do you ask me to serve other than Allah? O you fools. [65]And indeed it has been revealed to you as it was to those before you, if you ascribe a partner to Allah, your work will fail and you will indeed be among the losers. [66]No, but you must serve Allah, and be among the grateful. [67]And they do not esteem Allah as he has the right to be esteemed, when the whole earth will be in his hand on the day of resurrection, and the heavens are rolled in his right hand. He is glorified and highly exalted from all that they ascribe as partner. [68]And the trumpet is blown, and all who are in the heavens and all who are in the earth will fall dead, except him whom Allah wills. Then it is blown a second time, and look at them standing and waiting. [69]And the earth shines with the light of her Lord, and the book is set up, and the prophets and the witnesses are brought, and it is judged between them with truth, and they are not wronged. [70]And each soul is paid in full for what it did. And he is best aware of what they do. [71]And those who disbelieve are driven to Gehenna in throngs, until when they reach it and its gates are opened, and its guards say to them, Didn't messengers of your own come to you, reciting the revelations of your Lord to you and warning you of the meeting of this your day? They say, Yes, indeed. But the word of torment of unbelievers is fulfilled. [72]It is said, Enter the gates of Gehenna to dwell in it. In this way the journey's end of the scorners is wretched. [73]And those who keep their

---

49. This verse may be a later interpolation; see 39:8.

71. "The unbelievers are driven to hell in throngs," and will again be reminded of the messengers they did not heed, while the believers "are driven to the garden in throngs" (39:73), the final outcome of their inequality (39:9). On Gehenna, see 2:206.

duty to their Lord are driven to the garden in throngs, until when they reach it, and its gates are opened, and its guards say to them, Peace be upon you. You are good, so enter, to dwell here, **74**They say, Praise be to Allah, who has fulfilled his promise to us and has made us inherit the land, sojourning in the garden where we will. So the wage of laborers is bounteous. **75**And you see the angels thronging around the throne, singing the praises of their Lord. And they are judged rightly. And it is said, Praise be to Allah, the Lord of the worlds.

SURA 40

The Forgiver

Ghafir

Introduction

"Everything has an essence," said Ibn Abbas in a tradition related by Ibn Kathir, "and the essence of the Qur'an is the family of Ha Mim," that is, suras 40 through 46, all of which begin with the Arabic letters *ha* and *mim*.[1] Of the Ha Mim suras, a tradition has the companion of Muhammad and compiler of the Qur'an Ibn Mas'ud say: "When I reach the family of Ha Mim, it is like reaching a beautiful garden, so I take my time."[2] There is some indication that the "Ha Mim" was added to some of these in order to group them together; see the introduction to sura 42.

These are all, according to Islamic tradition, Meccan suras, and they share the general characteristics of the chapters of that period: furious denunciations of the unbelievers, but none of the exhortations to warfare against them that mark the Medinan suras, and fewer specific denunciations of the Jews and Christians than appear in the chronologically later chapters.

The first of these, sura 40, is often called "The Believers," from 40:28, but since this is the same title as that of sura 23, it is also known as "The Forgiver," from 40:3. Islamic authorities generally assert that it was revealed right after sura 39, and it shares many of the themes of that sura, recapitulated here at the sura's beginning: the Qur'an is from Allah (40:2); there is no other god (40:3); only unbelievers dispute his signs (40:4), such as the people of Noah, whom Allah punished (40:5)—they and other unbelievers are "companions of the fire" (40:6).

---

1 Ibn Kathir, VIII, 439.
2 Ibid.

The Forgiver

In the name of Allah, the compassionate, the merciful.

1Ha. Mim. **2**The revelation of the book is from Allah, the mighty, the knower, **3**The forgiver of sin, the accepter of repentance, the stern in punishment, the bountiful. There is no God except him. To him is the journeying. **4**No one argues about the signs of Allah except those who disbelieve, so do not let their turn of fortune in the land deceive you. **5**The people of Noah and the groups after them denied before these, and every nation plotted to seize their messenger and argued falsely to refute the truth. Then I seized them, and how was my punishment. **6**In this way the word of your Lord about those who disbelieve was fulfilled, that they are companions of the fire. **7**Those who carry the throne, and all who are around it, sing the praises of their Lord and believe in him and ask forgiveness for those who believe, Our Lord, you comprehend all things in mercy and knowledge, therefore forgive those who repent and follow Your way. Ward off from them the punishment of the blaze. **8**Our Lord, and make them enter the gardens of Eden which you have promised them, with those among their fathers and their wives and their descendants who do right. Indeed, you, only you, are the mighty, the wise. **9**And ward off evil deeds from them, and he from whom you ward off evil deeds on that day, him indeed you have taken into mercy. That is the supreme victory. **10**Indeed, those who disbelieve are informed by proclamation, Indeed Allah's condemnation is more terrible than your condemnation of one another, when you were called to the faith but refused. **11**They say, Our Lord, twice you have made us die, and twice you have made us live. Now we confess our sins. Is there any way to go out? **12**This is because, when Allah alone was invoked, you disbelieved, but when some partner was ascribed to him, you were believing. But the command belongs only to Allah, the sublime, the majestic. **13**It is he who shows you his signs, and sends down for you provision from the sky. No one is mindful except him who turns repentant. **14**Therefore pray to Allah, making religion pure for him, however much the unbelievers hate it, **15**The exalter of ranks, the Lord of the throne. He sends the spirit down under his command upon those whom he wills among his slaves, so that he may warn of the day of meeting, **16**The day when they come forth, nothing about them being hidden from Allah. Whose is the dominion on this day? It is Allah's, the one, the almighty. **17**On this day each soul is repaid for what it has earned, no wrong on this day. Indeed, Allah is swift at reckoning. **18**Warn them about the day of the approaching, when hearts will be choking throats,

---

1. On the "mysterious letters," see 2:1.

6. Instead of "the word of your Lord," the Warsh Qur'an has "the words of your Lord."[1]

7. "The blaze" is *al-jahim*, about which see 5:10.

10. Allah hates the unbelievers even more than they hate themselves. Ibn Kathir articulates this idea in a quotation ascribed to Qatadah, one of Muhammad's companions: "Allah's hatred for the people of misguidance—when Faith is presented to them in this world, and they turn away from it and refuse to accept it—is greater than their hatred for themselves when they see the punishment of Allah with their own eyes on the Day of Resurrection."[2]

11. The *Tafsir al-Jalalayn* explains the two deaths and two lives: "They were dead sperm and then were brought to life. Then they were made to die and then brought to life for the Resurrection."[3] To the question of whether or not there is any way to get out of hell, the same tafsir says flatly: "The answer is: 'No.'"[4]

there will be no friend for the wrongdoers, nor any intercessor who will be heard. **19**He knows the traitor of the eyes, and what the bosoms hide. **20**Allah judges with truth, while those whom they invoke instead of him do not judge at all. Indeed, Allah, he is the hearer, the seer. **21**Haven't they travelled in the land to see the nature of the consequences for those who disbelieved before them? They were mightier than these in power and traces in the earth. Yet Allah seized them for their sins, and they had no protector from Allah. **22**That was because their messengers kept bringing them clear proofs but they disbelieved, so Allah seized them. Indeed, he is strong, severe in punishment. **23**And indeed we sent Moses with our signs and a clear justification **24**To Pharaoh and Haman and Korah, but they said, A lying sorcerer. **25**And when he brought them the truth from our presence, they said, Kill the sons of those who believe with him, and leave their women alive. But the plot of unbelievers is in nothing but error. **26**And Pharaoh said, Allow me to kill Moses, and let him call out to his Lord. Indeed, I fear that he will change your religion or that he will spread corruption in the land. **27**Moses said, Indeed, I seek refuge in my Lord and your Lord from every scorner who does not believe in a day of reckoning. **28**And a believing man of Pharaoh's family, who hid his faith, said, Would you kill a man because he says, My Lord is Allah, and

has brought you clear proofs from your Lord? If he is lying, then his lie is upon him, and if he is truthful, then some of what he threatens you with will strike you. Indeed, Allah does not guide one who is wasteful, a liar. **29**O my people, yours is the kingdom today, you being uppermost in the land. But who would save us from the wrath of Allah if it reached us? Pharaoh said, I just show you what I think, and I just guide you to wise policy. **30**And he who believed said, O my people, indeed, I fear a fate for you like that of the groups, **31**A plight like that of Noah's people, and Aad and Thamud, and those after them, and Allah wills no injustice for slaves. **32**And, O my people, indeed, I fear a day of summoning for you, **33**A day when you will turn to flee, having no preserver from Allah, and he whom Allah leads astray, for him there is no guide. **34**And indeed Joseph brought you clear proofs before, yet you did not stop being in doubt about what he brought you until, when he died, you said, Allah will not send any messenger after him. In this way does Allah deceive him who is wasteful, a doubter. **35**Those who argue about the signs of Allah without any justification that has come to them, it is greatly hateful in the sight of Allah and in the sight of those who believe. In this way Allah seals up every arrogant, disdainful heart. **36**And Pharaoh said, O Haman, build a tower for me so that perhaps I may reach the roads, **37**The roads of the heavens, and may look

20. Instead of "they invoke," the Warsh Qur'an has "you invoke."[5]
21. See 3:137.
23. Here yet again begins the story of Moses and Pharaoh (see also 2:49, 3:11, 7:103, 8:52, 10:75, 14:6, 17:101, 20:24, 23:46, 26:11, 27:12, 28:3, 29:39, 38:12, 44:17, 50:13, 51:38, 54:41, 66:11, 69:9, 73:15, 79:15, 85:18, and 89:10). There is emphasis here on Pharaoh's intention to kill Moses (40:26).
28. A believer from among Pharaoh's people asks him: "Would you kill a man because he says, My Lord is Allah?" According to

Maududi, this sura came to Muhammad when the unbelievers were plotting to kill him, so the parallels are obvious: the Qur'an tells the story of an earlier prophet solely in order to make a point about the reception of the messenger by his contemporaries.
33. Only the one who sends the affliction has the remedy. Ibn Kathir explains that "whomever Allah sends astray will have no other guide except Him."[6] See 7:179, 10:99, and 32:13.

upon the God of Moses, although indeed I think him a liar. In this way, the evil that he did was made to seem good to Pharaoh, and he was barred from the way. The plot of Pharaoh ended only in ruin. **38**And he who believed said, O my people, follow me. I will show you the way of right conduct. **39**O my people, indeed, the life of this world is just a passing comfort, and indeed, the hereafter, that is the enduring home. **40**Whoever does an evil deed, he will be repaid with one like it, while whoever does right, whether male or female, and is a believer, such people will enter the garden, where they will be nourished without limit. **41**And, O my people, what ails me that I call you to deliverance when you call me to the fire? **42**You call me to disbelieve in Allah and ascribe to him as partners what I have no knowledge about, while I call you to the mighty, the forgiver. **43**Surely that to which you call me has no claim in this world or in the hereafter, and our return will be to Allah, and the wasteful will be companions of the fire. **44**And you will remember what I say to you. I confide my cause to Allah. Indeed, Allah is the seer of slaves. **45**So Allah warded off from him the evils which they plotted, while a dreadful doom encompassed Pharaoh's people, **46**The fire, they are exposed to it morning and evening, and on the day when the hour comes, cause Pharaoh's people to enter the most awful doom. **47**And

when they argue in the fire, the weak say to those who were proud, Indeed, we were following you, will you therefore rid us of a part of the fire? **48**Those who were proud say, Indeed, we are all in it. Indeed, Allah has judged between slaves. **49**And those in the fire say to the guards of Gehenna, Ask your Lord to relieve us of a day of the torment. **50**They say, Didn't your messengers come to you with clear proofs? They say, Yes, truly. They say, Then you pray, although the prayer of unbelievers is useless. **51**Indeed, we truly do help our messengers, and those who believe, in the life of this world and on the day when the witnesses arise, **52**The day when their excuse does not help the evildoers, and theirs is the curse, and theirs the evil dwelling. **53**And we indeed gave Moses the guidance, and we caused the children of Israel to inherit the book, **54**A guide and a reminder for men of understanding. **55**Then have patience. Indeed, the promise of Allah is true. And ask forgiveness of your sin, and sing the praise of your Lord at the nightfall and in the early hours. **56**Indeed, those who argue about the signs of Allah without a justification having come to them, there is nothing else in their hearts except pride which they will never attain. So take refuge in Allah. Indeed, he, only he, is the hearer, the seer. **57**Surely the creation of the heavens and the earth is greater than the creation of mankind, but

---

51. Allah promises to make his messengers victorious. Ibn Kathir attributes to the eighth-century preacher as-Suddi this explanation: "Allah never sends a Messenger to a people and they kill him or some of the believers who call them to the truth, then that generation passes away, but He then sends them someone who will support their call and will seek vengeance for their blood from those who did that to them in this world. So the Prophets and believers may be killed in this world, but their call will prevail in this world."7

And indeed, Ibn Kathir adds, "Allah granted victory to His Prophet Muhammad and his Companions over those who had opposed him, disbelieved in him and shown hostility towards him. He caused His Word and His religion to prevail over all other religions... This religion will continue to prevail until the Hour begins."8

55. See 2:144.

56. The unbelievers, who are motivated by nothing but pride, see 2:18.

most of mankind do not know. ⁵⁸And the blind man and the seer are not equal, nor are those who believe and do good works and the evildoer. Little do you remember. ⁵⁹Indeed, the hour is surely coming, there is no doubt about it, yet most of mankind do not believe. ⁶⁰And your Lord has said, Pray to me and I will hear your prayer. Indeed, those who scorn my service, they will enter Gehenna, disgraced. ⁶¹It is Allah who has appointed for you night that you may rest in it, and day for seeing. Indeed, Allah is a Lord of bounty for mankind, yet most of mankind do not give thanks. ⁶²This is Allah, your Lord, the creator of all things, There is no God except him. How then are you deluded? ⁶³In this way they are deluded who deny the signs of Allah. ⁶⁴It is Allah who appointed for you the earth as a dwelling place and the sky as a canopy, and fashioned you and perfected your shapes, and has provided you with good things. This is Allah, your Lord. Then blessed be Allah, the Lord of the worlds. ⁶⁵He is the living one. There is no God except him. So pray to him, making religion pure for him. Praise be to Allah, the Lord of the worlds. ⁶⁶Say, I am forbidden to worship those to whom you call besides Allah since there have come to me clear proofs from my Lord, and I am commanded to surrender to the Lord of the worlds. ⁶⁷It is he who created you from dust, then from a drop, then from a clot, then brings you forth as a child, then that you attain full strength and afterward that you become old men, though some among you die before then, and that you reach an appointed term, so that perhaps you may understand. ⁶⁸It is

he who brings to life and gives death. When he decrees a thing, He says to it only, Be! And it is. ⁶⁹Haven't you seen those who argue about the signs of Allah, how they are turned away? ⁷⁰Those who deny the book and that what we send with our messengers. But they will come to know, ⁷¹When shackles are around their necks and chains. They are dragged ⁷²Through boiling waters, then they are thrust into the fire. ⁷³Then it is said to them, Where are those you used to make partners ⁷⁴Besides Allah? They say, They have failed us, but we used not to pray to anything before. In this way does Allah leads the unbelievers astray. ⁷⁵This is because you rejoiced on the earth without right, and because you were petulant. ⁷⁶Enter the gates of Gehenna, to dwell in it. Evil is the dwelling place of the scornful. ⁷⁷Then have patience. Indeed, the promise of Allah is true. And whether we let you see a part of what we promise them, or we cause you to die, still to us they will be brought back. ⁷⁸Indeed we sent messengers before you, among them those of whom we have told you about, and some of whom we have not told you about, and it was not given to any messenger to bring a sign except by Allah's permission, but when Allah's commandment comes, it is judged rightly, and the followers of vanity will then be lost. ⁷⁹It is Allah who has appointed cattle for you, so that you may ride on some of them, and eat of some. ⁸⁰You have benefits from them, and so that you may satisfy by their means a need that is in your hearts, and may be carried upon them as upon the ship. ⁸¹And he shows you his signs. Which, then, of the signs of

---

58. See 39:9. Instead of "you remember," the Warsh Qur'an has "they remember."⁹

60. On Gehenna, see 2:206, as also at 40:76.

Allah do you deny? [82]Haven't they travelled in the land to see the nature of the consequences for those before them? They were more numerous than these, and mightier in power and traces in the earth. But all that they used to earn did not help them. [83]And when their messengers brought them clear proofs, they rejoiced in the knowledge they possessed. And what they had mocked came upon them. [84]Then, when they saw our doom, they said, We believe in Allah alone and reject what we used to associate. [85]But their faith could not help them when they saw our doom. This is Allah's law, which has always taken its course for his slaves. And then the unbelievers will be ruined.

82. See 3:137.

Explained in Detail

Fussilat

Introduction

Traditionally, this is another Meccan sura. According to Ibn Hisham, it was revealed to Muhammad after Utba bin Rabi'a, a chieftain of the Quraysh, offered Muhammad a series of proposals "which if he accepts in part, we will give him whatever he wants, and he will leave us in peace."[1]

Utba approached Muhammad and reminded him that he was of the Quraysh tribe, although they had rejected his prophetic claim. "If what you want is money, we will gather for you of our property so that you may be the richest of us; if you want honor, we will make you our chief so that no one can decide anything apart from you; if you want sovereignty, we will make you king, and if this ghost which comes to you, which you see, is such that you cannot get rid of him, we will find a physician for you, and exhaust our means in getting you cured, for often a familiar spirit gets possession of a man until he can be cured of it."[2]

Muhammad, according to this ninth-century story, replied by reciting verses 1–37 of this sura. Then, Ibn Hisham recounts, "when Utba returned to his companions they noticed that his expression had completely altered, and they asked him what had happened. He said that he had heard words such as he had never heard before, which were neither poetry, spells, nor witchcraft. 'Take my advice and do as I do, leave this man entirely alone for,

1 Ibn Ishaq, 132.
2 Ibid.

by God, the words which I have heard will be blazed abroad. If (other) Arabs kill him, others will have rid you of him; if he gets the better of the Arabs, his sovereignty will be your sovereignty, his power your power, and you will be prosperous through him.'"[3]

The other Quraysh chiefs were scornful, saying, "He has bewitched you with his tongue."[4] But Utba stood his ground, saying only: "You have my opinion, you must do what you think fit."[5]

The title comes from 41:3.

---

3 Ibn Ishaq, 133.
4 Ibid.
5 Ibid.

Explained in Detail

In the name of Allah, the compassionate, the merciful.

[1]Ha. Mim. [2]A revelation from the compassionate, the merciful, [3]A book of which the signs are explained in detail, a Qur'an in Arabic for people who have knowledge, [4]Good news and a warning. But most of them turn away so that they do not hear. [5]And they say, Our hearts are protected from what you call us to, and in our ears there is a deafness, and between us and you there is a veil. Act, then. Indeed, we also will be acting. [6]Say, I am only a mortal like you. It is inspired in me that your God is one God, therefore take the straight path to him and seek forgiveness of him. And woe to the idolaters, [7]Who do not give alms, and who are unbelievers in the hereafter. [8]Indeed, as for those who believe and do good works, for them is an enduring reward. [9]Say, Do you indeed disbelieve in him who created the earth in two days, and do you ascribe rivals to him? He is the Lord of the worlds. [10]He placed on it firm hills rising above it, and blessed it and measured in it its sustenance in four days, equal for those who ask, [11]Then he turned to the heaven when it was smoke, and said to it and to the earth, Come both of you, willingly or not. They said, We come, obedient. [12]Then he decreed seven heavens in two days and inspired in each heaven its mandate, and we decorated the nether heaven with lamps, and rendered it inviolable. That is the measuring of the mighty, the knower. [13]But if they turn away, then say, I warn you of a thunderbolt like the thunderbolt of Aad and Thamud, [14]When their messengers came to them from in front of them and behind them, saying, Do not worship anyone but Allah. They said, If our Lord had willed, he surely would have sent down angels, so indeed, we are unbelievers in what you have been sent with. [15]As for Aad, they were arrogant in the land without right, and they said, Who is mightier than us in power? Couldn't they see that Allah who created them was mightier than them in power? And they denied our revelations. [16]Therefore we let loose on them a raging wind in evil days, so that we might make them taste the torment of disgrace in the life of the world. And indeed the torment of the hereafter will be more shameful, and they will not be helped. [17]And as for Thamud, we gave them guidance, but they preferred blindness to the guidance, so the bolt of the torment of humiliation overtook them because of what they used to earn. [18]And we delivered those who believed and used to keep their duty to Allah. [19]And on the day when the enemies of Allah are gathered to the fire, they are driven on [20]Until, when they reach it, their ears

---

1. On the "mysterious letters," see 2:1. This is the second of the "Ha Mim" suras; see the introduction to sura 40.

3. The "signs" (*ayat*) are the verses of the Qur'an, as well as natural phenomena. As for their being "explained in detail," see 2:7. Regarding Arabic, see 12:2.

9. Allah here creates the universe in eight days, but at 7:54, 10:3, 11:7, 25:59, 32:4, and 50:38, he does it in six days.

15. The people of Aad also appear at 7:65, 9:70, 11:50, 14:9, 22:42, 25:38, 26:123, 29:38, 40:31, and 46:7, always in the context of their having rejected the messenger sent to them, who is identified as Hud at 11:50 and elsewhere.

17. The people of Thamud also appear at 11:61, 14:9, 17:59, 22:42, 25:38, 26:141, 27:45, 29:38, 38:13, and 40:31, always in the context of their having rejected the messenger sent to them, who is identified as Salih at 7:73 and elsewhere.

Like the accounts of Hud in Aad and those of other prophets, this is a highly stylized account intended essentially about the messenger and the reception he is accorded.

and their eyes and their skins testify against them about what they used to do. [21]And they say to their skins, Why are you testifying against us? They say, Allah who gives speech to all things has given us speech, and who created you at the beginning, and to whom you are returned. [22]You did not hide yourselves so that your ears and your eyes and your skins would not testify against you, but you thought that Allah did not know much of what you did. [23]That thought of yours, that you thought about your Lord, has ruined you, and you find yourselves among the lost. [24]And even if they have patience, yet the fire is still their home, and if they ask for favor, yet they are not among those to whom favor can be shown. [25]And we assigned them comrades, who made their present and their past seem good to them. And the word concerning the nations of the jinn and mankind who passed away before them has effect for them. Indeed, they were always losers. [26]Those who disbelieve say, Do not pay attention to this Qur'an, and drown out the hearing of it, perhaps you may conquer. [27]But indeed we will cause those who disbelieve to taste an awful doom, and indeed we will repay them with the worst of what they used to do. [28]That is the reward of Allah's enemies, the fire. In it is their immortal home, payment for denying our revelations. [29]And those who disbelieve will say, Our Lord, show us those who seduced us from among the jinn and mankind. We will place them under our feet so that they may be among the lowest. [30]Indeed, those who say, Our Lord is Allah, and afterward are steadfast, the angels descend upon them, saying, Do not fear or grieve, but hear good news of the paradise which you are promised. [31]We are your protecting friends in the life of this world and in the hereafter. There you will have what your souls desire, and there you will have what you pray for. [32]A gift of welcome from one who is forgiving, merciful. [33]And who is better in speech than he who prays to his Lord and does right, and says, Indeed, I am among those who are Muslims? [34]The good deed and the evil deed are not alike. Repel the evil deed with one that is better, then indeed, he with whom you had enmity as if he were a bosom friend. [35]But no one is granted it except those who are steadfast, and no one is granted it except the owner of great happiness. [36]And if a whisper from Satan reaches you, then seek refuge in Allah. Indeed, he is the hearer, the knower. [37]And among his signs are the night and the day and the sun and the moon. Do not adore the sun or the moon, but adore Allah who created them, if it is in truth him whom you worship. [38]But if they are too proud, still those who are with your Lord glorify him night and day, and do not get tired. [39]And among his signs is that you see the earth withered, but when we send down water on it, it stirs and grows. Indeed, he who brings life is truly the one who brings life to the dead. Indeed, he is able to do all things. [40]Indeed, those who distort our revelations are not hidden from us. Is he who is thrown into the fire better, or he who comes safely on the day of resurrection? Do what you will. Indeed, he sees what you do. [41]Indeed, those who disbelieve in the reminder when it comes to them, for indeed, it is an unassailable book. [42]Falsehood cannot come at it from in front of it or from behind it. A revelation from

25. See 3:137.
37. See 6:74.

43. See 3:3, 5:47.

the wise, the owner of praise. **⁴³**Nothing is said to you except what was said to the messengers before you. Indeed, your Lord is the owner of forgiveness, and the owner of dire punishment. **⁴⁴**And if we had sent it as a Qur'an in a foreign tongue, they surely would have said, If only its signs were explained. What? A foreign tongue and an Arab? Say to them, For those who believe, it is a guidance and a healing, and as for those who disbelieve, there is a deafness in their ears, and it is blindness for them. Such people are called to from afar. **⁴⁵**And we indeed gave Moses the book, but there has been disagreement over it, and if not for a word that had already gone forth from your Lord, it would before now have been judged between them, but indeed, they are in hopeless doubt about it. **⁴⁶**Whoever does right, it is for his soul, and whoever does wrong, it is against it. And your Lord is not at all a tyrant to his slaves. **⁴⁷**To him is referred knowledge of the hour. And no fruits burst forth from their sheaths, and no female carries or brings forth except with his knowledge. And on the day when he calls to them, Where now are my partners?, they will say,

We declare to you, not one of us is a witness. **⁴⁸**And those to whom they used to call upon of old have failed them, and they realize they have no place of refuge. **⁴⁹**Man does not get tired of praying for good, and if evil touches him, then he is disheartened, desperate. **⁵⁰**And indeed, if we cause him to taste mercy after some harm that has touched him, he will say, This is my own, and I do not think that the hour will ever rise, and if I am brought back to my Lord, I surely will be better off with him. But we indeed will tell those who disbelieve what they did, and we indeed will make them taste hard punishment. **⁵¹**When we show favor to man, he withdraws and turns aside, but when evil touches him, then he abounds in prayer. **⁵²**Think. If it is from Allah and you reject it, who is farther astray than one who is in an open feud? **⁵³**We will show them our signs on the horizons and within themselves until it will be obvious to them that it is the truth. Doesn't your Lord suffice, since he is witness over all things? **⁵⁴**How are they still in doubt about the meeting with their Lord? Indeed, isn't he surrounding all things?

---

44. The unbelievers will never be satisfied. "This," says Maududi, "is the kind of the stubbornness that the Holy Prophet was confronting. The disbelievers said, 'Muhammad (upon whom be Allah's peace) is an Arab. Arabic is his mother tongue. How can one believe that the Arabic Qur'an that he presents has not been forged by himself but has been revealed to him by God? The Qur'an could be believed to be the Revelation of God if he had started speaking fluently in a foreign language unknown to him, like Persian, Latin, or Greek.'"[1] Yet see 16:103. The Qur'an's repeated insistence that it is

in Arabic, and repudiation of the idea that it could be in any other language, suggests a determination to refute and silence critics who pointed out traces of its foreign origins. See 12:2, as well as 2:23, 2:120, 2:135, 5:114.

45. Ibn Kathir says that this means that if Allah had not decreed to "delay the Reckoning until the Day of Resurrection," then "the punishment would have been hastened for them. But they have an appointed time, beyond which they will find no escape."[2]

SURA 42

The Consultation

Ash-Shura

Introduction

Maududi sees this sura, which is traditionally regarded as Meccan, as a "supplement" to sura 41. It is the third in the sequence of "Ha Mim" suras that begins with sura 40; however, the fact that there are two separate sets of unexplained Arabic letters at its beginning (42:1 and 42:2) suggests the possibility that "Ha Mim" was added at a later date so as to fit this sura into the series. Its name comes from 42:38.

The Consultation

In the name of Allah, the compassionate, the merciful.

¹Ha. Mim. **²**Ain. Sin. Qaf. **³**In this way Allah the mighty, the knower inspires you like those before you. **⁴**To him belongs all that is in the heavens and all that is on the earth, and he is the sublime, the mighty. **⁵**The heavens above might almost be torn asunder while the angels sing the praise of their Lord and ask forgiveness for those on the earth. Indeed, Allah, he is the forgiver, the merciful. **⁶**And as for those who choose protecting friends besides him, Allah is guardian over them, and you are in no way a guardian over them. **⁷**And in this way we have inspired in you an Arabic Qur'an, so that you may warn the mother of towns and those around it, and may warn of a day of assembling of which there is no doubt. A multitude will be in the garden, and a multitude of them in the flame. **⁸**If Allah had willed, he could have made them one community, but Allah brings those whom he wills into his mercy. And the wrongdoers have no friend nor helper. **⁹**Or have they chosen protecting friends besides him? But Allah, he is the protecting friend. he raises the dead, and he is able to do all things. **¹⁰**And in whatever you disagree, the verdict of it belongs to Allah. This is my Lord, in whom I put my trust, and to whom I turn. **¹¹**The creator of the heavens and the earth. He has made for you pairs of yourselves, and of the cattle also pairs, by which he multiplies you. Nothing is like him, and he is the hearer, the seer. **¹²**The keys of the heavens and the earth are his. He enlarges provision for whom he will and reduces. Indeed, he is knower of all things. **¹³**He has decreed for you that religion which he commended to Noah, and what we inspire in you, and what we commanded to Abraham and Moses and Jesus, saying, Establish the religion, and do not be divided over it. What you call the idolaters to is dreadful. Allah chooses for himself those whom he wills, and guides to himself him who turns. **¹⁴**And they were not divided until after the knowledge came to them, through rivalry among themselves, and if it had not been for a word that had already gone forth from your Lord for an appointed term, it surely had been judged between them. And those who were made to inherit the book after them are indeed in hopeless doubt concerning it. **¹⁵**To this, then, summon people. And be steadfast as you

---

1. On the "mysterious letters," see 2:1. This is the third of the "Ha Mim" suras; see the introduction to sura 40.

2. The unique second verse of mysterious letters suggests that "Ha Mim" may have been added to this sura later in order to fit it into the series.

7. The inspiration theme is continued from 42:3, suggesting that 42:4-6 could be an interpolation. "Flame" is *sa'ir*, on which see 4:10. On Arabic, see 12:2. On the mother of towns, see 6:92.

8. See 7:179, 10:99, and 32:13. Ibn Kathir sees this passage as more evidence of absolute determinism: Allah could have made human beings "either all following guidance or all following misguidance, but He made them all different, and He guides whomsoever He Wills to the truth and He sends astray whomsoever He Wills."¹ Verse 42:44 affirms this again.

10. The *Tafsir al-Jalalayn* explains: "The judgment concerning anything you differ about with the unbelievers regarding matters of the *din* [religion] and other things is Allah's concern on the Day of Rising. He will decide between you."²

The messenger here speaks in the first person, again causing difficulty for the contention that Allah is the sole speaker throughout the Qur'an. See 1:2, 34:1.

13. The religion of the messenger is the same as that of Noah, Abraham, Moses, and Jesus; see 3:3 and 5:47.

14. This verse is a foundation of the Islamic idea that the prophets of Judaism and Jesus must have taught Islam, and their message was corrupted by their followers.

are commanded, and do not follow their lusts, but say, I believe in whatever scripture Allah has sent down, and I am commanded to be just among you. Allah is our Lord and your Lord. To us our works and to you your works, no argument between us and you. Allah will bring us together, and to him is the journeying. **16**And those who argue about Allah after he has been acknowledged, their argument has no weight with their Lord, and wrath is upon them and theirs will be an awful doom. **17**It is Allah who has revealed the book with truth, and the balance. How can you know? It may be that the hour is near. **18**Those who do not believe in it seek to hasten it, while those who believe are afraid of it and know that it is the truth. Aren't those who dispute, in doubt regarding the hour, far astray? **19**Allah is favorable to his slaves. He provides for those whom he wills. And he is the strong, the mighty. **20**Whoever desires the harvest of the hereafter, we give him increase in its harvest. And whoever desires the harvest of this world, we give him of it, and he has no portion in the hereafter. **21**Or do they have partners who have made lawful for them in religion what Allah did not allow? And if not for a decisive word, it would have been judged between them. Indeed, for wrongdoers is a painful doom. **22**You see the wrongdoers afraid of what they have earned, and it will surely come upon them, while those who believe and do good works in flowering meadows of the gardens, having what they wish from their Lord. This is the great bounty. **23**It is this that Allah announces to his slaves who believe and do good works. Say, I ask no fee of you for this, except love among relatives. And whoever commits a good deed, we add to its good for him. Indeed, Allah is forgiving, responsive. **24**Or do they say, He has invented a lie about Allah? If Allah willed, he could have sealed your heart. And Allah will wipe out the lie and will vindicate the truth by his words. Indeed, he is aware of what is hidden in the hearts. **25**And it is he who accepts repentance from his slaves, and forgives the evil deeds, and knows what you do, **26**And accepts those who do good works, and gives increase to them from his bounty. And as for unbelievers, theirs will be an awful doom. **27**And if Allah were to enlarge the provision for his slaves, they would surely rebel on the earth, but he sends down by measure as he wills. Indeed, he is informed, a seer of his slaves. **28**And it is he who sends down the saving rain after they have despaired, and spreads out his mercy. He is the protecting friend, the praiseworthy one. **29**And of his signs is the creation of the heaven and the earth, and of whatever animals he has dispersed in it. And he is able to gather them when he wills. **30**Whatever strikes you of misfortune, it is for what your right hands have earned. And he forgives much. **31**You cannot escape on the earth, for besides Allah you have no protecting friend, nor any helper. **32**And of his signs are the ships, like banners on the sea, **33**If he wills, he calms the wind so that they keep still upon its surface.

---

16. This threat of punishment for those who argue about Allah can be a hindrance to asking questions about the faith. See 5:101.

21. Instead of "for them," the seventh-century Qur'an manuscript known as the Codex Parisino-Petropolitanus (which some claim to be a copy of Uthman's version) has "for him," although this has been erased and replaced with the standard wording.[3]

25. Instead of "what you do," the Warsh Qur'an has "what they do."[4]

30. Ibn Kathir explains that misfortune befalls one "because of sins that you have committed in the past."[5] This leads to the notion that the path to good fortune in this world is more fervent adherence to Allah's laws.

33. Instead of "the wind," the Warsh Qur'an has "the winds."[6]

Indeed, in this truly are signs for every steadfast grateful one. ³⁴Or he causes them to perish because of what they have earned, and he forgives much, ³⁵And that those who argue about our signs may know that they have no refuge. ³⁶Now whatever you have been given is just a passing comfort for the life of this world, and what Allah has is better and more lasting for those who believe and put their trust in their Lord, ³⁷And those who shun the worst of sins and indecencies and, when they are angry, forgive, ³⁸And those who answer the call of their Lord and establish prayer, and whose affairs are a matter of consultation, and who spend out of what we have bestowed on them, ³⁹And those who, when great wrong is done to them, defend themselves, ⁴⁰The reward of an evil deed is an evil like it. But whoever forgives and changes, his wage is the concern of Allah. Indeed, he loves not wrongdoers. ⁴¹And whoever defends himself after he has suffered wrong, for such, there is no way against them. ⁴²The way is only against those who oppress mankind, and wrongfully rebel on the earth. For such people there is a painful doom. ⁴³And indeed whoever is patient and forgives, indeed, that, truly, is the steadfast heart of things. ⁴⁴He whom Allah leads astray, for him there is no protecting friend after him. And you will see the evildoers when they see the doom, they say, Is there any way of return? ⁴⁵And you will see them exposed to it, made humble by disgrace, and looking with veiled eyes. And those who believe will say, Indeed, the losers are those who lose themselves and their family on the day of resurrection. Indeed, aren't the wrongdoers in perpetual torment? ⁴⁶And they will have no protecting friends to help them instead of Allah. He whom Allah leads astray, for him there is no road. ⁴⁷Answer the call of your Lord before there comes to you a day from Allah, which there is no averting. You have no refuge on that day, nor do you have any refusal. ⁴⁸But if they are averse, we have not sent you as a guardian over them. Yours is only to convey. And indeed, when we cause man to taste of mercy from us, he rejoices over it. And if some evil strikes them because of what their own hands have sent before, then indeed, man is an ingrate. ⁴⁹To Allah belongs the dominion of the heavens and the earth. He creates what he wills. He bestows females upon those whom he wills, and bestows males upon those whom he wills, ⁵⁰Or he mingles them, males and females, and he makes barren those whom he wills. Indeed, he is the knower, powerful. ⁵¹And it was not for any mortal that Allah should speak to him unless by revelation or from behind a veil, or he sends a messenger to reveal what he wills by his permission. Indeed, he is exalted, wise. ⁵²And in this way we have inspired in you a spirit of our command. You did not know what the book was, nor the faith. But we have made it a light by which we guide those of our slaves whom we will. And indeed, you indeed guide to a right path, ⁵³The path of Allah, to whom belongs whatever is in the heavens and whatever is in the earth. Do not all things reach Allah at last?

---

40. Forgiveness is good, but revenge is permitted (42:41).

46. Everyone will stand alone before Allah; no intercession from others will be accepted (2:48, 2:123, 6:94, 23:101, 39:43). However, the Qur'an elsewhere accepts intercession with Allah's permission (10:3, 20:109, 21:28, 34:23, 53:26).

49. See 16:57.

The Ornaments of Gold

Az-Zukhruf

Introduction

Maududi enunciates the traditional view when he says that sura 43 was revealed around the same time as suras 32, 40, and 42, when the Quraysh were plotting to kill him. He adds that Allah makes a reference to their secret plots in 43:79–80. Bell sees 43:9–13 and 43:67–78 as later interpolations, and indeed, these two sections can be omitted without harm to the sense of the surrounding passages. Its name is derived from 43:35 and 43:53.

The Ornaments of Gold

IN THE NAME OF ALLAH, THE COMPASSIONATE, THE MERCIFUL.

[1]Ha. Mim. [2]By the clear book, [3]Indeed, we have made it an Arabic Qur'an so that perhaps you may understand. [4]And indeed, in the mother of the book, which we possess, it is indeed sublime, decisive. [5]Shall we utterly ignore you because you are a transgressing people? [6]How many prophets did we send among the men of old? [7]And a prophet never came to them except they used to mock him. [8]Then we destroyed men mightier in prowess than these, and the example of the men of old has gone. [9]And if you ask them, who created the heavens and the earth, they will surely answer, The mighty, the knower created them, [10]Who made the earth a bed for you, and placed roads for you in it, so that perhaps you may find your way, [11]And who sends down water from the sky in measure, and we revive a dead land with it. Even so you will be brought forth, [12]He who created all the pairs, and established ships and cattle for you, on which you ride. [13]So that you may mount upon their backs, and may remember your Lord's favor when you mount on them, and may say, May he be glorified who has subjected these to us, and we were not capable, [14]And indeed, to our Lord we surely are returning. [15]And they give him a portion of his slaves. Indeed, man is truly a mere ingrate. [16]Or does he choose daughters out of all that he has created, and honors you with sons? [17]And if one of them has news of what he likens to Ar-Rahman, his countenance becomes black and he is full of inward rage. [18]Is then one bred amid outward show, and in dispute cannot make himself plain? [19]And they make the angels, who are the slaves of Ar-Rahman, females. Did they witness their creation? Their testimony will be recorded and they

1. On the "mysterious letters," see 2:1. This is the fourth of the "Ha Mim" suras; see the introduction to sura 40.

2. On the clarity of the Qur'an, see 3:7.

3. See 12:2.

4. The "mother of the book" (*umm al-kitab*) is, according to Islamic tradition, the copy of the Qur'an that has existed for all eternity with Allah. The Qur'an that is traditionally understood as having been delivered through Gabriel to Muhammad is supposed to be a perfect copy of this eternal book. Maududi describes the "mother of the book" as "the Book from which all the Books sent down to the Prophets have been derived."[1]

The *Tafsir al-Jalalayn* defines the "mother of the book" as "the source of all divinely revealed Books, the Preserved Tablet," which is mentioned at 85:21.[2] Maududi explains the preserved tablet as "the Tablet whose writing cannot be effaced, which is secure from every kind of interference."[3] This theology explains why variants in the Qur'anic text, and signs that it was edited and altered, pose such a thorny problem in Islamic theology.

Maududi ascribes the supposed unanimity of the messages of all the prophets, despite the fact that no trace exists of the Islamic messages of Abraham, Moses, Jesus, and the others, to their common source in the mother of the book: "By saying that the Qur'an is inscribed in Umm al-Kitab, attention has been drawn to an important truth. Different Books had been revealed by Allah in different ages to different Prophets for the guidance of different nations in different languages, but all these Books invited mankind to one and the same Faith: they regarded one and the same thing as the Truth; they presented one and the same criterion of good and evil; they propounded the same principles of morality and civilization; in short, they brought one and the same *Din* (Religion). The reason was that their source and origin was the same, only words were different; they had the same meaning and theme which is inscribed in a Source Book with Allah, and whenever there was a need, He raised a Prophet and sent down the same meaning and subject-matter clothed in a particular diction according to the environment and occasion."[4]

Ibn Kathir concludes: "This explains the high status of the Qur'an among the hosts on high (the angels), so that the people of earth will respect it, venerate it and obey it."[5]

8. Allah destroys the mockers; this may be by the hands of the believers, as per 9:14.

10. Instead of "a bed," the Warsh Qur'an has "beds."[6]

16. See 16:57 and 53:19. "Women," explains Ibn Kathir, "are regarded as lacking something, which they make up for with jewelry and adornments from the time of childhood onwards, and when there is a dispute, they cannot speak up and defend themselves clearly, so how can this be attributed to Allah?"[7]

19. Instead of "slaves [*ibaadu*] of Ar-Rahman," the version of Rawh, one of the transmitters of Yaqub's version, has "in the presence [*inda*] of Ar-Rahman."[8]

will be questioned. **20**And they say, If Ar-Rahman had willed, we would not have worshipped them. They have no knowledge whatsoever of that. They just guess. **21**Or have we given them any book before so that they are holding fast to it? **22**No, for they say only, Indeed, we found our fathers following a religion, and we are guided by their footprints. **23**And even so we did not send a warner before you into any town except that its luxurious ones said, Indeed, we found our fathers following a religion, and we are following their footprints. **24**He said, What? Even though I bring you better guidance than that you found your fathers following? They answered, Indeed, we are unbelievers in what you bring. **25**So we repaid them. Then see the nature of the consequences for the rejecters. **26**And when Abraham said to his father and his people, Indeed, I am innocent of what you worship, **27**Except he who created me, for he will surely guide me. **28**And he made it a word enduring among his descendants, so that perhaps they might return. **29**No, but I let these people and their fathers enjoy life until the truth would come to them and a messenger making plain. **30**And now that the truth has come to them, they say, This is mere sorcery, and indeed, we are unbelievers in it. **31**And they say, If only this Qur'an had been revealed to some great man of the two towns. **32**Is it they who apportion your Lord's mercy? We have apportioned among them their livelihood in the life of this world, and raised some of them above others in rank so that some of them may take labor from others, and the mercy of your Lord is better than what they amass. **33**And if it had not been that mankind would have become one community, we might well have appointed, for those who disbelieve in Ar-Rahman, roofs of silver for their houses and stairs by which to mount, **34**And for their houses, doors and couches of silver on which to recline, **35**And ornaments of gold. Yet all that would have been just a provision for the life of this world. And the hereafter with your Lord would have been for those who avoid evil. **36**And he whose sight is dim to the remembrance of Ar-Rahman, we assign to him a satan who becomes his comrade, **37**And indeed, they surely turn them from the way of Allah, and yet they think that they are rightly guided, **38**Until, when he comes to us, he says, If only there were the distance of the two horizons between me and you. An evil comrade. **39**And it does not profit you this day, because you did wrong, that you will be sharers in the doom. **40**Can you make the deaf hear, or can you guide the blind or him who is in clear error? **41**And if we take you away, we surely shall take revenge on them, **42**Or we show you we threaten them with, for indeed, we have complete command of them. **43**So hold fast to what is inspired in you. Indeed, you are on a right path. **44**And indeed, it is in truth a reminder for you and for your people, and you will be questioned. **45**And ask those among our messengers whom we sent before you, Did we ever establish gods to be worshipped besides

---

24. Instead of "he said," the Warsh Qur'an has "say."[9]

26. Abraham appears briefly; see also 7:80, 9:17, 9:114, 11:69, 15:51, 19:41, 21:51, 26:69, 29:16, 37:83, 60:4, and elsewhere.

39. Instead of, "And it does not profit you this day, because you did wrong," the Shi'ite Bankipur Qur'an manuscript has, "And it does not profit you this day, because you deprived the family of Muhammad of its due."[10] See 2:59 and the Appendix: Two Apocryphal Shi'ite Suras.

Ar-Rahman? ⁴⁶And indeed we sent Moses with our revelations to Pharaoh and his chiefs, and he said, I am a messenger of the Lord of the worlds. ⁴⁷But when he brought them our signs, look, they laughed at them. ⁴⁸And every sign that we showed them was greater than its sister, and we seized them with the torment, so that perhaps they might turn again. ⁴⁹And they said, O wizard, entreat your Lord for us by the agreement that he has made with you. Indeed, we truly will walk rightly. ⁵⁰But when we eased their torment, look, they broke their word. ⁵¹And Pharaoh caused a proclamation to be made among his people, saying, O my people, is not the dominion of Egypt and these rivers flowing under me mine? Can you not then discern? ⁵²I am surely better than this fellow, who is despicable and can hardly make himself clear. ⁵³Why, then, haven't ornaments of gold been set upon him, or angels sent along with him? ⁵⁴In this way he persuaded his people to make light, and they obeyed him. Indeed, they were a rebellious people. ⁵⁵So when they angered us, we punished them and drowned every one of them. ⁵⁶And we made them a people of the past, and an example for those after. ⁵⁷And when the son of Mary is quoted as an example, look, the people laugh out loud, ⁵⁸And say, Are our gods better, or is he? They do not raise the objection

except to argue. No, but they are a contentious people. ⁵⁹He is nothing but a slave on whom we bestowed favor, and we made him a model for the children of Israel. ⁶⁰And if we had willed, we could have set among you angels to be caliphs on the earth. ⁶¹And indeed, he truly is knowledge of the hour. So do not doubt about it, but follow me. This is the right path. ⁶²And do not let Satan turn you aside. Indeed, he is an open enemy for you. ⁶³When Jesus came with clear proofs, he said, I have come to you with wisdom, and to make clear some of what you disagree about. So keep your duty to Allah, and obey me. ⁶⁴Indeed, Allah, he is my Lord and your Lord. So worship him. This is a right path. ⁶⁵But the parties among them differed. Then woe to those who do wrong, from the torment of a painful day. ⁶⁶Are they waiting for anything except the hour, that it will come upon them suddenly, when they do not know? ⁶⁷Friends on that day will be enemies to one another, except those who kept their duty. ⁶⁸O my slaves, for you there is no fear this day, nor is it you who grieve, ⁶⁹Who believed our revelations and were Muslims, ⁷⁰Enter the garden, you and your wives, to be made glad. ⁷¹In it trays of gold and goblets are brought around, and in it is everything that souls desire and eyes find sweet. And you are immortal in it. ⁷²This is the garden

---

46. Moses reappears; see also 2:49, 7:103, 8:52, 10:75, 17:101, 20:43, 26:10, 27:12, 28:3, 40:23, and elsewhere. The parallels to the messenger are quite transparent here: the unbelievers ridicule his signs (43:47) and call him a sorcerer (43:49); ultimately Allah punished them (43:55).

59. See 5:17, 5:116, 9:30, 61:6.

60. On "caliphs on the earth," see 2:30.

61. The *Tafsir al-Jalalayn* explains that Jesus is "knowledge of the hour" because "he will descend then."[11] Ibn Kathir prescinds somewhat from the eschatological explanation, saying that "the miracles and signs that happened at his hands, such as raising the dead and healing the sick, are sufficient as signs of the approach of the

Hour."[12] The *Tafsir Anwarul Bayan* offers three possible interpretations: that this passage refers to Jesus's return to earth (see 4:159), or that it should be read as "it truly is knowledge of the hour" rather than "he truly is knowledge of the hour," and that "it" refers to the Qur'an, and, as Ibn Kathir suggests, the miracles of Jesus.[13]

65. Ibn Kathir explains that the followers of Jesus "differed and became parties and factions, some who stated that he (Isa) was the servant and Messenger of Allah—which is true—while others claimed that he was the son of Allah or that he himself was Allah—glorified be Allah far above what they say."[14] The fact that virtually all the sects of Christianity consider Jesus the divine son of God is not considered.

which you are made to inherit because of what you used to do. [73]In it there is plenty of fruit for you, from which to eat. [74]Indeed, the guilty live forever in Gehenna's torment. [75]It is not relaxed for them, and they despair in it. [76]We did not wrong them, but they it was who did the wrong. [77]And they call out, O master, let your Lord make an end of us. He says, Indeed, you must remain here. [78]We indeed brought the truth to you, but you were, most of you, averse to the truth. [79]Or do they determine anything? Indeed, we are determining. [80]Or do they think that we cannot hear their secret thoughts and private conversations? No, but our envoys, present with them, record them. [81]Say, If Ar-Rahman has a son, then I will be first among those who worship him. [82]May the Lord of the heavens and the earth, the Lord of the throne, be glorified from what they ascribe. [83]So let them flounder and play until they meet the day which they are promised. [84]And it is he who in the heaven is Allah, and in the earth Allah. He is the wise one, the knower. [85]And blessed be he to whom belongs the dominion over the heavens and the earth and all that is between them, and with whom is knowledge of the hour, and to whom you will be returned. [86]And those to whom they call out instead of him have no power of intercession, except him who knowingly bears witness to the truth. [87]And if you ask them who created them, they will surely say, Allah. How then are they turned away? [88]And he says, O my Lord, indeed, these are a people who do not believe. [89]Then bear with them and say, Peace. But they will come to know.

---

74. On Gehenna, see 2:206.
89. Instead of "they will come to know," the Warsh Qur'an has "you will come to know."[15]

The Smoke

Ad-Dukhan

Introduction

A hadith depicts Muhammad saying: "Whoever recites Ha Mim Ad-Dukhan during the night, in the morning seventy thousand angels seek forgiveness for him."[1] This is another of the Ha Mim suras, which are considered to be Meccan; Bell, however, sees signs of its beginning "having been altered to stand at the head of a chapter of the Book."[2] Its title is taken from 44:10.

---

1 *Jami at-Tirmidhi*, vol. 5, book 42, no. 2888.
2 Bell, II, 498.

The Smoke

IN THE NAME OF ALLAH, THE COMPASSIONATE, THE MERCIFUL.

[1]Ha. Mim. [2]By the clear book [3]Indeed, we revealed it on a blessed night, indeed, we are always warning, [4]On which every wise command is made clear [5]As a command from our presence, indeed, we are always sending, [6]A mercy from your Lord. Indeed, he, he alone is the hearer, the knower, [7]Lord of the heavens and the earth and all that is between them, if you would be sure. [8]There is no God except him. He brings to life and gives death, your Lord and the Lord of your forefathers. [9]No, but they play in doubt. [10]But watch for the day when the sky will produce visible smoke [11]That will envelop the people. This will be a painful torment. [12]Our Lord, relieve us of the torment. Indeed, we are believers. [13]How can there be remembrance for them, when a messenger making things clear had already come to them, [14]And they had turned away from him and said, One who was taught, a madman? [15]Indeed, we withdraw the torment a little. Indeed, you return. [16]On the day when we will seize them with the greater seizure, in truth we will punish. [17]And indeed before them we tested Pharaoh's people, when a noble messenger came to them, [18]Saying, Give up the slaves of Allah to me. Indeed, I am a faithful messenger to you. [19]And saying, Do not be proud against Allah. Indeed, I bring you a clear justification. [20]And indeed, I have sought refuge in my Lord and your Lord so that you do not stone me to death. [21]And if you put no faith in me, then let me go. [22]And he called out to his Lord, These are guilty people. [23]Then, Take away my slaves by night. Indeed, you will be followed, [24]And leave the sea behind at rest, for indeed, they are a drowned army. [25]How many were the gardens and the water springs that they left behind, [26]And the corn fields and the good land [27]And pleasant things in which they took delight. [28]Even so, and we made it an inheritance for other people, [29]And the heaven and the earth did not weep for them, nor were they reprieved. [30]And we delivered the children of Israel from the shameful doom, [31]From Pharaoh. Indeed, he was a tyrant among the transgressors. [32]And we chose them, intentionally, above the worlds. [33]And we gave them signs in which was a clear test. [34]Indeed, these people are saying, [35]There is nothing but our first death, and we will not be raised

---

1. On the "mysterious letters," see 2:1. This is the fifth of the "Ha Mim" suras; see the introduction to sura 40.

2. On the clarity of the Qur'an, see 3:7.

3. The "blessed night" is traditionally considered to be the "Night of Power" toward the end of Ramadan. See 2:185 and 97:1-5.

10. A hadith depicts Muhammad asking Allah to curse the Quraysh; another says that he asked him to give them seven years of famine, "so famine overtook them for one year and destroyed every kind of life to such an extent that the people started eating hides, carcasses and rotten dead animals. Whenever one of them looked towards the sky, he would (imagine himself to) see smoke because of hunger."[1] After the chief of the Quraysh appealed to Muhammad that his own kin were dying, Muhammad, the story goes, relented and prayed for them, and Allah revealed this passage.

17. Pharaoh reappears, challenged by a curiously unnamed Moses. See also 2:49, 3:11, 7:103, 8:52, 10:75, 14:6, 17:101, 20:24, 23:46, 26:11, 27:12, 28:3, 29:39, 38:12, 40:24, 50:13, 51:38, 54:41, 66:11, 69:9, 73:15, 79:15, 85:18, and 89:10.

32. Allah chose the children of Israel above other nations. Islamic commentators minimize the ongoing import of this. Ibn Kathir offers two explanations that he attributes to early Islamic authorities: "This means that they were chosen above those among whom they lived," and, "They were chosen above the other people of their own time, and it was said that in every period there are people who are chosen above others."[2] The *Tafsir Ibn Abbas* likewise says that the Israelites were chosen above others "of their time."[3] See also 5:13 and 7:129.

again. **36**Bring back our fathers, if you speak the truth. **37**Are they better, or the people of Tubba and those before them? We destroyed them, for surely they were guilty. **38**And we did not create the heavens and the earth, and all that is between them for amusement. **39**We did not create them except with truth, but most of them do not know. **40**Surely the day of sorting is the term for all of them, **41**A day when friend can help a friend in nothing, nor can they be helped, **42**Except him on whom Allah has mercy. Indeed, he is the mighty, the merciful. **43**Indeed, the tree of Zaqqum, **44**The food of the sinner. **45**Like molten brass, it boils in their bellies **46**Like the boiling of scalding water. **47**Take him and drag him into the midst of the blaze, **48**Then pour the torment of boiling water upon his head. **49**Taste. Indeed, truly you were mighty, noble. **50**Indeed, this is what you used to doubt. **51**Indeed, those who kept their duty will be in a secured place. **52**Amid gardens and water springs, **53**Clothed in silk and silk embroidery, facing one another. **54**Even so. And we will marry them to *houris* with wide, lovely eyes. **55**They call in it for every fruit in safety. **56**They do not taste death in it, except the first death. And he has saved them from the torment of the blaze, **57**A bounty from your Lord. That is the supreme victory. **58**And we have made it easy in your language only so that they may be mindful. **59**Wait, then. Indeed, they are waiting.

---

37. Bell states that the people of Tubba are the "Himyarites of South Arabia," but Gibson says that they "should not be confused with a king of Himyar by the same name."[4]

40. The "day of sorting" is the day of judgment. See 77:13-14, 77:38, 78:17.

43. On Zaqqum, see 37:62.

47. "The blaze" is *al-jahim*, about which see 5:10, as also for 44:56.

54. The Arabic word *hoor*, or *houris*, which is usually translated as "maidens" or "virgins," is central to the canonical understanding of these passages as referring to the virgins of paradise; see 37:48. But *hur* does not actually mean "virgins," as even Arabic philologists acknowledge. Rather, it is the plural form of an Arabic feminine adjective that means simply "white." Qur'an commentators and Arabic scholars often explain that it actually means "white-eyed," an expression that Qur'an translators have taken as an expression of the beauty of these virgins, translating it as "large-eyed," "wide-eyed," "with lustrous eyes," and similar expressions. A hadith also manifests the understanding of *houris* as "white" as it has Muhammad say that in paradise, "everyone will have two wives from the houris, (who will be so beautiful, pure and transparent that) the marrow of the bones of their legs will be seen through the bones and the flesh."[5] The beauty of women with skin so transparent that their bones are visible is taken for granted.

According to Islamic tradition, *hur* is the equivalent of *houri*, which does mean virgin, but Luxenberg argues that this is a clear misreading of the text. Examining the Qur'anic *rasm*, the original text without diacritical marks, the other contexts in which the word *hur* appears in the Qur'an, and the contemporary usage of the word *houris*, he concludes that the famous passages refer not to virgins but instead to white raisins, or grapes. White raisins were a prized delicacy in that region, and as such, make a more fitting symbol of the reward of paradise, which is frequently referred to in the Qur'an as a "garden," than sexual favors from virgins.[6] Luxenberg further demonstrates that metaphorical references to bunches of grapes are consonant with Christian homiletics expatiating on the refreshments that greeted the blessed in Heaven. He specifically cites the fourth-century hymns "on Paradise" of St. Ephraem the Syrian (306–373), which refer to "the grapevines of Paradise." Luxenberg explains that the fact that the Syriac word Ephraem used for "grapevine" was feminine "led the Arabic exegetes of the Koran to this fateful assumption" that the Qur'anic text referred to sexual playthings in paradise.[7]

The misreading of the word may have been understandable given other religious traditions that were circulating in the general region. According to Tisdall, "the books of the Zoroastrians and Hindus...bear the most extraordinary likeness to what we find in the Koran and Hadith. Thus in Paradise we are told of 'houris having fine black eyes,' and again of 'houris with large black eyes, resembling pearls hidden in their shells.'...The name *houry* too is derived from an Avesta or Pehlavi Source, as well as *jinn* for genii, and *bihisht* (Paradise), signifying in Avestic 'the better land.' We also have very similar tales in the old Hindu writings, of heavenly regions with their boys and girls resembling the houris and *ghilman* of the Koran."[8] On the boys, see 52:24.

58. See 19:97.

SURA 45

The Crouching

Al-Jathiya

Introduction

This is another "Ha Mim" sura, all of which are considered Meccan. Bell sees it as "rather confused," with some portions dating from the Medinan period.[1] Its title comes from 45:28.

---

1 Bell, II, 502.

The Crouching

IN THE NAME OF ALLAH, THE COMPASSIONATE, THE MERCIFUL.

1Ha. Mim. **2**The revelation of the book is from Allah, the mighty, the wise. **3**Indeed, in the heavens and the earth are signs for believers. **4**And in your creation, and all the animals that he scatters on the earth, are signs for a people whose faith is sure. **5**And the difference of night and day and the provision that Allah sends down from the sky and thereby brings the earth to life after her death, and the ordering of the winds, are signs for a people who have sense. **6**These are the signs of Allah which we recite to you with truth. Then in what fact, after Allah and his signs, will they believe? **7**Woe to each sinful liar, **8**Who hears the revelations of Allah recited to him, and then continues in pride as if he did not hear them. Give him news of a painful doom. **9**And when he knows anything about our signs, he makes it a joke. For such people there is a shameful doom. **10**Beyond them there is Gehenna, and what they have earned will not help them in any way, nor those whom they have chosen for protecting friends besides Allah. Theirs will be an awful doom. **11**This is guidance. And those who disbelieve the revelations of

their Lord, for them there is a painful torment of wrath. **12**It is Allah who has made the sea of service to you so that the ships may run on it by his command, and that you may seek of his bounty, and that perhaps you may be thankful, **13**And has made of service to you whatever is in the heavens and whatever is on the earth, it is all from him. Indeed, in this truly are signs for a people who reflect. **14**Tell those who believe to forgive those who do not hope for the days of Allah, so that he may repay people what they used to earn. **15**Whoever does right, it is for his soul, and whoever does wrong, it is against it. And afterward you will be brought back to your Lord. **16**And indeed we gave the children of Israel the book and the wisdom and the prophethood, and provided them with good things and favored them over the worlds, **17**And gave them clear commandments. And they did not disagree until after the knowledge came to them, through rivalry among themselves. Indeed, your Lord will judge between them on the day of resurrection over what they used to disagree about. **18**And now have we set you on a sharia of the matter, so follow it, and do not follow the whims of those who do not know.

---

1. On the "mysterious letters," see 2:1. This is the sixth of the "Ha Mim" suras; see the introduction to sura 40.

9. Allah destroys the mockers; this may be by the hands of the believers, as per 9:14.

10. On Gehenna, see 2:206.

14. The believers should forgive the unbelievers; however, Ibn Kathir explains that this was only a temporary provision: "Let the believers forgive the disbelievers and endure the harm that they direct against them. In the beginning of Islam, Muslims were ordered to observe patience in the face of the oppression of the idolaters and the People of the Scriptures so that their hearts may incline towards Islam. However, when the disbelievers persisted in stubbornness, Allah legislated for the believers to fight in Jihad."[1]

16. See 44:32, as well as 5:13 and 7:129.

18. *Sharia* is Islamic law, derived from the Qur'an and Sunnah, accepted practice, which is in turn derived from the reports (hadiths) of Muhammad's words and deeds that are considered authentic. This verse, however, does not carry all that weight, although it does open the way to further developments. Bell explains: "Sharia has the sense of 'watering-place,' 'an opening leading to water.' The later meaning 'law' is inappropriate here, when the sense is that Muhammad has been given independent access to revealed knowledge."[2]

Ibn Kathir warns that this passage "contains a warning to the Muslim Ummah as well. It warns them not to take the path [of] the Jews took nor adopt their ways."[3]

¹⁹Indeed, they cannot help you against Allah in anything. And indeed, as for the wrongdoers, some of them are friends of others, and Allah is the friend of those who fear Allah. ²⁰This is a clear indication for mankind, and a guidance and a mercy for a people whose faith is sure. ²¹Or do those who commit evil deeds think that we will make them like those who believe and do good works, the same in life and death? Their judgment is bad. ²²And Allah has created the heavens and the earth with truth, so that every soul might be repaid what it has earned. And they will not be wronged. ²³Have you seen him who makes his desire his god, and Allah sends him astray intentionally, and seals up his hearing and his heart, and sets a covering on his sight? Then who will lead him after Allah? Will you not then be mindful? ²⁴And they say, There is nothing but our life of the world, we die and we live, and nothing destroys us except time, when they have no knowledge whatsoever of that, they just guess. ²⁵And when our clear revelations are recited to them, their only argument is that they say, Bring our fathers. then, if you are truthful. ²⁶Say, Allah gives you life, then causes you to die, then gathers you to the day of resurrection of which there is no doubt. But most of mankind do not know. ²⁷And to Allah belongs the dominion of the heavens and the earth, and on the day when the hour arises, on that day those who follow falsehood will be lost. ²⁸And you will see each nation crouching, each nation summoned to its record. This day you are repaid for what you used to do. ²⁹This is our book and it pronounces against you with truth. Indeed, we have caused what you did to be recorded. ³⁰Then, as for those who believed and did good works, their Lord will bring them in to his mercy. That is the clear victory. ³¹And as for those who disbelieved, Were not our signs recited to you? But you were scornful and became a guilty people. ³²And when it was said, Indeed, Allah's promise is the truth, and there is no doubt of the coming of the hour, you said, We do not know what the hour is. We consider it nothing but speculation, and we are by no means convinced. ³³And the evils of what they did will appear to them, and what they used to deride will come upon them. ³⁴And it will be said, This day we forget you, even as you forgot the meeting of this your day, and your dwelling place is the fire, and there is no one to help you. ³⁵ This because you made the revelations of Allah a joke, and the life of this world seduced you. Therefore this day they do not come forth from there, nor can they make amends. ³⁶Then praise be to Allah, Lord of the heavens and Lord of the earth, the Lord of the worlds. ³⁷And to him belongs majesty in the heavens and the earth, and he is the mighty, the wise.

---

19. Instead of "in anything," a Qur'anic manuscript examined by Mingana has "in derision."4 Instead of "Allah," the same manuscript has "blow," as in a physical fight. He reconstructs the verse as, "In derision, they will not take the place of a blow, for you."5

29. Instead of, "This is our book and it pronounces against you with truth," the Shi'ite Bankipur Qur'an manuscript has, "This is our book and Muhammad and the people of his house pronounce against you with truth."6 See 2:59 and the Appendix: Two Apocryphal Shi'ite Suras.

SURA 46

The Dunes

Al-Ahkaf

Introduction

This is the seventh and last of the "Ha Mim" series (see sura 40) and hews closely to the themes of the others: the Qur'an is revealed by Allah (46:2); Allah created the heavens and the earth for a just purpose, but the unbelievers reject faith (46:3); those whom they pray to besides Allah are powerless (46:4–5); the unbelievers dismiss the Qur'an as "sorcery" (46:7), and the like. It is, like the other Ha Mim suras, traditionally regarded as Meccan. Bell, however, finds abundant evidence that this sura is "not all of a piece," and contains numerous interruptions and interpolations.[1] Its title comes from 46:21.

---

1 Bell, II, 507.

The Dunes

In the name of Allah, the compassionate, the merciful.

[1]Ha. Mim. [2]The revelation of the book is from Allah, the mighty, the wise. [3]We did not create the heavens and the earth and all that is between them except with truth, and for an appointed term. But those who disbelieve turn away from what they are warned about. [4]Say, Have you thought about all that you invoke besides Allah? Show me what they have created of the earth. Or do they have any portion in the heavens? Bring me a book before this, or some vestige of knowledge, if you are truthful. [5]And who is further astray than those who, instead of Allah, pray to those who do not hear their prayer until the day of resurrection, and are unconscious of their prayer, [6]And when mankind is gathered will become enemies for them, and will become deniers of having been worshipped. [7]And when our clear signs are recited to them, those who disbelieve say of the truth when it reaches them, This is mere sorcery. [8]Or say they, He has fabricated it. Say, If I have fabricated it, you still have no power to support me against Allah. He is best aware of what you say about it among yourselves. He is sufficient for a witness between me and you. And he is the forgiving, the merciful. [9]Say, I am no new thing among the messengers, nor do I know what will be done with me or with you. I do but follow what is inspired in me, and I am just a plain warner. [10]Think. If it is from Allah and you disbelieve in it, and a witness from the children of Israel has already testified to something like it and has believed, and you are too proud? Indeed, Allah does not guide wrongdoing people. [11]And those who disbelieve say of those who believe, If it had been good, they would not have been before us in attaining it. And since they will not be guided by it, they say, This is an ancient lie, [12]When before it there was the book of Moses, an example and a mercy, and this is a confirming book in the Arabic language, so that it may warn those who do wrong and bring good news for the righteous. [13]Indeed, those who say, Our Lord is Allah, and walk rightly thereafter, no fear will come upon them, nor will they grieve. [14]Such people are rightful owners of

---

1. On the "mysterious letters," see 2:1. This is the seventh and last of the "Ha Mim" suras; see the introduction to sura 40.

7. On the clarity of the Qur'an, see 3:7.

9. The messenger brings no new message; this is an implicit affirmation of the Islamic proposition that Islam was the original religion of all the earlier prophets, e.g., Abraham, Moses, Jesus, and so on, but their wicked followers corrupted their messages. See 2:4, 5:44.

10. Ibn Hisham and Bukhari identify this "witness from among the Children of Israel" who "testified" to the Qur'an's similarity to the Jewish scriptures as Abdullah bin Salam, a rabbi who was, according to ninth-century traditions, an early convert to Islam. He was, the story goes, convinced that Muhammad was a prophet when he correctly answered three questions "about three things which nobody knows unless he be a Prophet."[1] How Abdullah knew that Muhammad's answers were correct without being a prophet himself is not explained.

The idea that the Jews, like the Christians of Najran (see 26:74), knew that Muhammad was a prophet but rejected him for their own selfish reasons is emphasized in numerous Islamic traditions. In one, Ibn Sa'd recounts that Muhammad once went to a Jewish seminary, where he challenged the most learned rabbi: "Do you know that I am the Apostle of Allah?"[2] The rabbi answered, "By Allah! Yes, and the people know what I know. Verily your attributes and qualities are clearly mentioned in the Torah, but they are jealous of you."[3] It was only the sinful obstinacy of the Jews and Christians that prevented them from acknowledging this—indeed, that sin was so great that ultimately it led them, according to Islamic tradition, to alter their Scriptures in order to remove all references to Muhammad. The idea of Jews and Christians as sinful renegades from the truth of Islam would become a cornerstone of Islamic thought regarding non-Muslims.

12. On confirming the book of Moses, see 2:4, 5:44. On Arabic, see 12:2.

the garden, immortal in it, as a reward for what they used to do. **15**And we have enjoined on man doing good to his parents. His mother bears him with reluctance, and brings him forth with reluctance, and the bearing of him and the weaning of him is thirty months, until, when he attains full strength and reaches forty years, he says, My Lord, enable me to give thanks for the favor with which you have favored me and my parents, and that I may work righteousness that is acceptable to you. And be favorable to me in the matter of my descendants. Indeed, I have turned to you repentant, and indeed, I am one of the Muslims. **16**Those are the one from whom we accept the best of what they do, and we overlook their evil deeds, among the owners of the garden. This is the true promise which they were promised.

17And whoever says to his parents, Fie upon you both. Do you threaten me that I will be brought forth when generations before me have passed away? And those two call out to Allah for help, Woe to you! Believe. Indeed, the promise of Allah is true. But he says, This is nothing but fables of the men of old, **18**Such people are those on whom the word regarding nations of jinn and mankind which have passed away before them has effect. Indeed, they are the losers. **19**And for all there will be ranks from what they do, so that he may pay them for their deeds, and they will not be wronged. **20**And on the day when those who disbelieve are exposed to the fire, you squandered your good things in the life of this world and sought comfort therein. Now this day you are rewarded with the torment of disgrace because you were disdainful in the land without justification, and because you used to transgress. **21**And mention the brother of Aad, when he warned his people among the wind-curved dunes, and indeed warners came and went before and after him, saying, Serve no one but Allah. Indeed, I fear for you the torment of a mighty day. **22**They said, Have you come to turn us away from our gods? Then bring upon us what you threaten us with, if you are among the truthful. **23**He said, The knowledge is with Allah only. I convey to you what I have been sent with, but I see you are a people that does not know. **24**Then, when they saw it as a dense cloud coming toward their valleys, they said, Here is a cloud bringing us rain. No, but it is what you tried to hasten, a wind in which is painful torment, **25**Destroying all things by commandment of its Lord. And morning found them so that nothing could be seen except their dwellings. In this way do we reward the guilty people. **26**And indeed we had empowered them with that with which we have not empowered you, and had assigned them ears and eyes and hearts, but their ears and eyes and hearts did not help them in any way since they denied the revelations of Allah, and what they used to mock came upon them.

---

15. A good Muslim should honor his parents; however, see 9:23, 29:8, 31:15, and 60:4.

Bell points out that this section (46:15-18) is "of a different character from the rest."[4] Omitting it reveals a coherent passage that flows from 46:14 to 46:19, and therefore the section on kindness to parents appears to be a later interpolation.

Instead of "we have enjoined on man doing good [*ihsaanan*] to his parents," the version of Al Duri, one of the transmitters of Abu Amr's reading, has "we have enjoined on man beauty [*husnan*] to his parents."[5]

16. Instead of "we accept," the Warsh Qur'an has "is accepted."[6] Instead of "we overlook their evil deeds," the Warsh Qur'an has "their evil deeds are overlooked."[7]

19. Instead of "so that he may pay them," the Warsh Qur'an has "so that we may pay them."[8]

21. The prophet Hud and the people of Aad also appear at 7:65, 9:70, 11:50, 14:9, 22:42, 25:38, 26:123, 29:38, 38:12, and 40:31.

25. Instead of "nothing could be seen," the Warsh Qur'an has "you could see nothing."[9]

²⁷And indeed we have destroyed towns around you, and displayed our revelation, so that perhaps they might return. ²⁸Then why did those whom they had chosen for gods beside Allah as a way of approach not help them? No, but they failed them utterly. And that was their lie, and what they used to invent. ²⁹And when we came near you, some of the jinn, who wished to hear the Qur'an and, when they were in its presence, said, Give ear. And when it was finished, they turned back to their people, warning. ³⁰They said, O our people, indeed, we have heard a book that has been revealed after Moses, confirming what was before it, guiding to the truth and a right road. ³¹O our people, respond to Allah's summoner and believe in him. He will forgive you some of your sins and guard you from a painful doom. ³²And whoever does not respond to Allah's summoner cannot escape him anywhere on earth, and he has no protecting friends instead of him. Such people are in clear error. ³³Haven't they seen that Allah, who created the heavens and the earth and was not wearied by their creation, is able to give life to the dead? Yes, he is indeed able to do all things. ³⁴And on the day when those who disbelieve are exposed to the fire, Is not this real? They will say, Yes, by our Lord. He will say, Then taste the doom for what you disbelieved. ³⁵Then have patience, even as the steadfast among the messengers had patience, and do not try to hasten it for them. On the day when they see what they are promised, they will feel as if they had remained on earth for just an hour of daylight. A notification. Shall any people be destroyed except transgressors?

---

29. Ibn Kathir attributes to Ibn Abbas this explanation: "Allah's Messenger never recited Qur'an to the Jinns, nor did he see them."¹⁰ However, a group of jinns set out to discover why they can no longer engage in "eavesdropping on the news of the heavens," as they had done previously.¹¹ They happen upon Muhammad leading the Muslims in prayer, and "when the Jinns heard the recitation of the Qur'an, they stopped to listen to it, and then they said: 'By Allah! This is what has prevented you from eavesdropping on the news of the heavens.' Then they returned to their people and told them: 'Our people! We certainly have heard an amazing recitation (the Qur'an), it guides to the right path. So we have believed in it, and we will join none in worship with our Lord.'"¹²

35. Barth points out that "a notification" (balaghun) "stands quite unconnected, and cannot belong here. (The Arab exegesists [sic] have nothing decisive to say.)"¹³

Muhammad

Muhammad

Introduction

Maududi states that "the contents of this Surah testify that it was sent down after the hijrah at Madinah at the time when the fighting had been enjoined, though active fighting had not yet been undertaken."[1] Its title comes from 47:2, one of only four places where the name Muhammad appears in the Qur'an (the others are 3:144, 33:40, and 48:29).

---

1 Maududi, EnglishTafsir.com, http://www.englishtafsir.com/Quran/47/index.html.

Muhammad

IN THE NAME OF ALLAH, THE COMPASSIONATE, THE MERCIFUL.

1Those who disbelieve and turn from the way of Allah, he makes their actions useless. **2**And those who believe and do good works and believe in what is revealed to Muhammad, and it is the truth from their Lord, he rids them of their evil deeds and improves their condition. **3**That is because those who disbelieve follow falsehood and because those who believe follow the truth from their Lord. In this way Allah makes mankind's comparisons for them. **4**Now when you meet the unbelievers, strike the necks until, when you have subdued them, then make fast the bonds, and afterward either generosity or ransom until the war lays down its burdens. That, and if Allah willed, he could have punished them, but so that he may test some of you by means of others. And those who have been killed in the way of Allah, he does not make their actions useless. **5**He will guide them and improve their condition,

6And bring them into the garden which he has made known to them. **7**O you who believe, if you help Allah, he will help you and will make your foothold firm. **8**And those who disbelieve, perdition is for them, and he will make their actions useless. **9**That is because they hate what Allah has revealed, therefore he makes their actions fruitless. **10**Haven't they travelled in the land to see the nature of the consequences for those who were before them? Allah wiped them out. And for the unbelievers, there will be the same fate. **11**That is because Allah is the patron of those who believe, and because the unbelievers have no patron. **12**Indeed, Allah will cause those who believe and do good works to enter gardens under which rivers flow, while those who disbelieve take their comfort in this life and eat even as the cattle eat, and the fire is their dwelling place. **13**And how many a town stronger than your town, which has thrown you out, have we destroyed, and they had no helper. **14**Is he who relies on a clear proof

---

1. The refrain regarding those who oppose Islam that Allah will "make their actions useless" recurs at 47:8, 47:28, and 47:32. The *Tafsir Anwarul Bayan* explains: "Even though the disbelievers may carry out many good deeds and render great services to mankind, these deeds will not be recognized on the Day of Judgment on account of their disbelief."[1]

2. Contrasting with 47:1 is the promise that Allah will improve the condition of the believers, which is repeated in substance at 47:7 and 47:35.

This is one of only four places where the name Muhammad appears in the Qur'an (the others are 3:144, 33:40, and 48:29).

4. The literal understanding of this verse is paramount among Islamic commentators. Ibn Kathir says that it means that when Muslims "fight against" unbelievers, they should "cut them down totally with your swords" until "you have killed and utterly destroyed them."[2] The *Tafsir al-Jalalayn* concurs, explaining "strike the necks" as "meaning 'kill them.' Striking people's necks generally results in their death."[3] The twentieth-century Qur'an translator Abdullah Yusuf Ali, despite his general tendency to minimize aspects of the Qur'an that are jarring to Western non-Muslims,

likewise takes the injunction literally, justifying it by saying, "You cannot wage war with kid gloves."[4]

The same verse goes on to call for the taking of prisoners and allowing for "either generosity or ransom" of prisoners of war. This has been enshrined in Islamic law: a manual of Islamic jurisprudence certified by Al-Azhar University in Cairo, the most respected authority in Sunni Islam, as conforming "to the practice and faith of the orthodox Sunni community," lays out four options for prisoners, in line with this verse: "When an adult male is taken captive, the caliph considers the interests ... (of Islam and the Muslims) and decides between the prisoner's death, slavery, release without paying anything, or ransoming himself in exchange for money or for a Muslim captive held by the enemy."[5]

Instead of "those who have been killed" (*qutiluu*), the Warsh Qur'an has "those who fought" (*qaataluu*).[6]

10. See 3:137.

11. In a hadith, Muhammad is depicted as praying, "O Allah, I seek refuge with You from Kufr [unbelief] and poverty."[7] Someone asked him, "Are they equal?"[8] Muhammad answered, "Yes."[9]

from his Lord like those for whom the evil that they do is pleasing to them, while they follow their own lusts? **15**A comparison of the garden which those who keep their duty are promised, in it are rivers of fresh water, and rivers of milk of which the flavor does not change, and rivers of wine that is delicious to the drinkers, and rivers of pure honey. There is every kind of fruit in it for them, with forgiveness from their Lord. Is this like those who live forever in the fire and are given boiling water to drink so that it tears their bowels? **16**Among them are some who give ear to you until, when they go forth from your presence, they say to those who have been given knowledge, What was that he said just now? Those are the ones whose hearts Allah has sealed, and they follow their own lusts. **17**While as for those who walk rightly, he adds to their guidance, and gives them their protection. **18**Are they waiting for anything except the hour, that it should come upon them unawares? And the beginnings of it have already come. But how, when it has come upon them, can they take their warning? **19**So know that there is no God except Allah, and ask forgiveness for your sin and for believing men and believing women. Allah knows your place of turmoil and your place of rest. **20**And those who believe say, If only a surah were revealed! But when a decisive surah is revealed and war is mentioned in it, you see those in whose hearts is a disease looking at you with the look of men fainting to death. Therefore woe to them. **21**Obedience and a civil word. Then, when the matter is determined, if they are

loyal to Allah it will be well for them. **22**Would you then, if you were given the command, work corruption in the land and sever your ties of kinship? **23**Such are the people whom Allah curses so that he deafens them and makes their eyes blind. **24**Will they then not meditate on the Qur'an, or are there locks on the hearts? **25**Indeed, those who turn back after the guidance has been manifested to them, Satan has seduced them, and he gives them false hope. **26**That is because they say to those who hate what Allah has revealed, We will obey you in some matters, and Allah knows their secret conversation. **27**Then how, when the angels gather them, striking their faces and their backs? **28**That will be because they followed what angers Allah, and hated what pleases him. Therefore he has made their actions useless. **29**Or do those in whose hearts is a disease think that Allah will not bring their hates to light? **30**And if we wished, we could show them to you so that you would know them surely by their features. And you will know them by the tone of their conversation. And Allah knows your deeds. **31**And indeed we will test you until we know those of you who wage jihad and are steadfast, and until we test your record. **32**Indeed, those who disbelieve and turn from the way of Allah and oppose the messenger after the guidance has been manifested to them, they do not harm Allah at all, and he will make their actions useless. **33**O you who believe, obey Allah and obey the messenger, and do not make your actions useless. **34**Indeed, those who disbelieve and turn from the way of Allah and then die

---

20. Ibn Kathir explains that "Allah mentions that the believers were hoping that Jihad would be legislated. But when Allah ordained it, many of the people turned back."[10] He explains why they did so in a way that makes it clear that the jihad in question

involves hot war: they drew back, says Ibn Kathir, because of "their fear, terror, and cowardice concerning meeting the enemies."[11] See suras 8 and 9.

24. See 7:179, 10:99, 32:13.

unbelievers, Allah surely will not pardon them. [35]So do not falter and cry out for peace when you have the upper hand, and Allah is with you, and he will not deprive you of your actions. [36]The life of this world is just a game and a pastime. And if you believe and fear Allah, he will give you your wages, and will not ask you about your worldly wealth. [37]If he would ask you about it and press you, you would hoard it, and he would bring your hates to light. [38]Indeed, you are those who are called to spend in the way of Allah, yet among you there are some who hoard. And as for him who hoards, he hoards only from his soul. And Allah is the rich, and you are the poor. And if you turn away, he will exchange you for some other people, and they will not be like you.

---

35. Ibn Kathir states that one should not give way "in the condition of your superiority over your enemy. If, on the other hand, the disbelievers are considered more powerful and numerous than the Muslims, then the Imam (general commander) may decide to hold a treaty if he judges that it entails a benefit for the Muslims. This is like what Allah's Messenger did when the disbelievers obstructed him from entering Makkah and offered him treaty in which all fighting would stop between them for ten years."[12] That is a reference to the Treaty of Hudaybiyyah; see 9:7.

The Conquest

Al-Fath

Introduction

According to Maududi, Islamic tradition holds that this sura dates from the time of Muhammad's return to Mecca after concluding the Treaty of Hudaybiyyah with the Quraysh (see 9:7).[1] One hadith, however, holds that this sura, along with sura 5, were the last to be revealed.[2]

Its title is taken from 48:1 and actually encapsulates the general concerns of the sura.

In January 2018, as Turkish troops launched a military operation in Syria against the Syrian Kurdish People's Protection Units (YPG), ninety thousand mosques in Turkey prayed this sura. It was chosen for its preoccupation with conquest and victory over unbelievers.[3]

---

1 Maududi, EnglishTafsir.com, http://www.englishtafsir.com/Quran/48/index.html.
2 *Jami at-Tirmidhi*, vol. 5, book 44, no. 3063.
3 "'Conquest' prayers performed across Turkey's mosques for Afrin operation," *Hürriyet Daily News*, January 21, 2018.

The Conquest

In the name of Allah, the compassionate, the merciful.

¹Indeed, we have given you a clear conquest, ²So that Allah may forgive you of your sin what is past and what is to come, and may perfect his favor to you, and may guide you on a right path, ³And that Allah may help you with strong help, ⁴It is he who sent down *sakina* into the hearts of the believers so that they might add faith to their faith. The hosts of the heavens and the earth belong to Allah, and Allah is always the knower, the wise one, ⁵So that he may bring the believing men and the believing women into gardens under which rivers flow, in which they will remain, and may absolve them of their evil deeds. That, in the sight of Allah, is the supreme triumph, ⁶And may punish the hypocritical men and the hypocritical women, and the idolatrous men and the idolatrous women, who think an evil thought regarding Allah. For them is the evil turn of fortune, and Allah is angry with them and has cursed them, and has made ready for them Gehenna, an evil destination. ⁷The hosts of the heavens and the earth belong to Allah, and Allah is always mighty, wise. ⁸Indeed, we have sent you as a witness and a bearer of good news

and a warner, ⁹So that you may believe in Allah and his messenger, and may honor him, and may revere him, and may glorify him at early dawn and at the close of day. ¹⁰Indeed, those who swear loyalty to you, swear loyalty only to Allah. The hand of Allah is above their hands. So whoever breaks his oath, breaks it only to his soul's harm, while whoever keeps his covenant with Allah, he will bestow on him immense reward. ¹¹Those of the nomadic Arabs who were left behind will tell you, Our possessions and our familys occupied us, so ask forgiveness for us. They speak with their tongues what is not in their hearts. Say, Who can help you in any way against Allah, if he intends you harm, or intends you benefit? No, but Allah is always aware of what you do. ¹²No, but you thought that the messenger and the believers would never return to their own people, and that was made to seem good in your hearts, and you thought an evil thought, and you were worthless people. ¹³And so for him who does not believe in Allah and his messenger, indeed, we have prepared a flame for unbelievers. ¹⁴And Allah's is the dominion over the heavens and the earth. He forgives those whom he wills, and punishes those whom he wills. And Allah is always forgiving,

---

1. This conquest is generally, albeit not universally, regarded as referring to the Treaty of Hudaybiyyah, which Muhammad concluded on disadvantageous terms with the Quraysh tribe of Mecca before he conquered that city (see 9:7). A ninth-century hadith reflects some difficulty in reconciling a treaty concluded on unfavorable terms being called a victory. It depicts Umar ibn al-Khattab, who according to Islamic tradition was the second caliph of the Muslims after Muhammad's death, furiously asking Muhammad why he concluded the treaty on bad terms when the Muslims are right, and their dead are in paradise, while the Quraysh's dead are in hell. Muhammad answers, "O Ibn Al-Khattab! I am the Messenger of Allah and Allah will never degrade me."¹ At that point, the

story goes, this sura was revealed, and Muhammad "recited it to the end in front of Umar." Umar then asked him if the Treaty of Hudaybiyyah was, despite appearances, a victory, and Muhammad answered that it was. This would soon become clear (see 48:19).

4. On *sakina*, see 2:248.

6. On Gehenna, see 2:206.

10. See 2:144.

Instead of "he will bestow on him," the Warsh Qur'an has "we will bestow on him."²

11. See 9:90-91.

13. "Flame" is *sa'ir*, on which see 4:10.

merciful. **15**Those who were left behind will say, when you set forth to capture booty, Let us go with you. They would like to change the verdict of Allah. Say, You will not go with us. This Allah has said beforehand. Then they will say, You are envious of us. No, but they do not understand, except a little. **16**Say to those among the nomadic Arabs who were left behind, You will be called against a people of mighty prowess, to fight them until they submit, and if you obey, Allah will give you a good reward, but if you turn away as you did turn away before, he will punish you with a painful doom. **17**There is no blame for the blind, nor is there blame for the lame, nor is there blame for the sick. And whoever obeys Allah and his messenger, he will admit him to gardens under which rivers flow, and whoever turns back, he will punish him with a painful doom. **18**Allah was well pleased with the believers when they swore allegiance to you beneath the tree, and he knew what was in their hearts, and he sent down *sakina* on them, and has rewarded them with a near conquest, **19**And much booty that they will capture. Allah is always mighty, wise. **20**Allah promises that you will capture much booty, and has given you this in advance, and has kept men's hands

from you, so that it may be a sign for the believers, and so that he may guide you on a right path. **21**And other gains, which you have not been able to achieve, Allah will compass them, Allah is able to do all things. **22**And if those who disbelieve join battle with you, they will flee, and afterward they will find no protecting friend nor helper. **23**It is the law of Allah which has taken course beforehand. You will not find for the law of Allah anything that has changed. **24**And it is he who has kept men's hands from you, and has kept your hands from them, in the valley of Mecca, after he had made you conquerors over them. Allah is the seer of what you do. **25**It was these people who disbelieved and barred you from the sacred mosque, and barred the offering from reaching its goal. And if it had not been for believing men and believing women, whom you do not know, so that you do not trample them under foot and in this way incur guilt for them unknowingly, so that Allah might bring into his mercy those whom he wills, if they had been clearly separated, we indeed would have punished those among them who disbelieved with painful punishment. **26**When those who disbelieve had set up zealotry in their hearts, the zealotry of the age of ignorance, then

---

16. Islamic scholars differ as to which powerful people are meant, with most suggesting the Persians and/or Byzantines. This passage, however, may have been incorporated into the Qur'an from another source that originally referred to an entirely different powerful enemy.

17. The blind, lame, and ill need not fight in jihad warfare, but those who do will go to paradise. See 9:90-91.
Instead of "he will admit him," the Warsh Qur'an has "we will admit him."[3] Instead of "he will punish him," the Warsh Qur'an has "we will punish him."[4]

18. Ibn Kathir says there were 1,400 Muslims who pledged loyalty to Muhammad under a tree near Hudaybiyyah.[5] On *sakina*, see 2:248.

19. On the spoils of war, see sura 8. This conquest and promise of booty, according to Ibn Kathir, is "in reference to the goodness that Allah the Exalted and Most Honored caused to happen to the

Companions on account of the peace treaty between them and their disbelieving enemies. Ever after that, the Companions gained abundant, general and continuous benefits and accomplishments, leading to the conquest of Khaybar and Makkah and then the various surrounding provinces and areas. They earned tremendous glory, triumphs and an elevated and honorable status in this life and in the Hereafter."[6] At the oasis of Khaybar, according to Islamic tradition, Muhammad led a massacre of the Jews he had previously exiled from Medina. The spoils gained here and during the conquest of Mecca were the result of the disadvantageous treaty concluded at Hudaybiyyah (see 9:7 and 48:1), and thus vindicate the confident assertion put in Muhammad's mouth that the treaty was a victory. There is no independent historical record of these events dating earlier than the ninth century, thus it cannot be known exactly what is being discussed.

26. On *sakina*, see 2:248.

Allah sent down his *sakina* upon his messenger and upon the believers and imposed on them the word of self-restraint, for they were worthy of it and suited for it. And Allah is aware of all things. [27]Allah has fulfilled the vision for his messenger in very truth. You will indeed enter the sacred mosque, if Allah wills, secure, shaven and with hair cut, not fearing. But he knows what you do not know, and has given you a near conquest beforehand. [28]It is he who has sent his messenger with the guidance and the religion of truth, so that he may cause it to prevail over all religions. And Allah is sufficient as a witness. [29]Muhammad is the messenger of Allah. And those with him are ruthless against the unbelievers and merciful among themselves. You see them bowing and falling prostrate, seeking bounty from Allah and acceptance. The mark of them is on their foreheads from the traces of prostration. That is their comparison in the Torah and their comparison in the Gospel, like sown corn that sends forth its shoot and strengthens it and rises firm upon its stalk, delighting the sowers, so that he may enrage the unbelievers with them. Allah has promised, to those among them who believe and do good works, forgiveness and immense reward.

---

28. The idea that Islam is the religion of Allah and of truth is stated also at 3:19, 3:85, and 9:29, and that it will prevail over all other religions is additionally at 2:193, 8:39, 9:33, and 61:9. This victory over other religions evidently involves harshness toward those who believe in them, as per the following verse.

29. The *Tafsir al-Jalalayn* glosses this as saying that Muslims must "not show mercy" to unbelievers.[7] Ruthlessness or harshness toward unbelievers is a sign of one's devotion to Allah.

This presents a stark contrast to Jesus' injunction in the Sermon on the Mount to "love your enemies and pray for those who persecute you" (Matthew 5:44).

This verse is one of only four places where the name Muhammad appears in the Qur'an (the others are 3:144, 33:40, and 47:2). None of them contain or even hint at the existence of any of the voluminous biographical material found in the ninth-century hadith and sira literature.

SURA 49

The Private Apartments

Al-Hujurat

Introduction

According to Maududi, "this Surah is a collection of the commandments and instructions sent down on different occasions," and "the traditions also show that most of these commandments were sent down during the final stage of the Holy Prophet's life at Madinah."[1] Many of them have to do with how one is to behave in the presence of the unnamed messenger. The title of the sura comes from 49:4.

---

1 Maududi, EnglishTafsir.com, http://www.englishtafsir.com/Quran/49/index.html.

The Private Apartments

IN THE NAME OF ALLAH, THE COMPASSIONATE, THE MERCIFUL.

1O you who believe, do not go ahead in the presence of Allah and his messenger, and keep your duty to Allah. Indeed, Allah is hearer, knower. **2**O you who believe, do not raise your voices above the voice of the prophet, nor shout when speaking to him as you shout one to another, so that your works are not made useless while you do not realize. **3**Indeed, those who lower their voices in the presence of the messenger of Allah, those are the ones whose hearts Allah has proven to righteousness. Theirs will be forgiveness and immense reward. **4**Indeed, those who call you from behind the private apartments, most of them have no sense. **5**And if they had had patience until you came forth to them, it would have been better for them. And Allah is forgiving, merciful. **6**O you who believe, if a transgressor brings you news, verify it, so that you do not strike some people in ignorance and afterward repent of what you did. **7**And know that the messenger of Allah is among you. If he were to obey you in much of the government, you would surely be in trouble, but Allah has endeared the faith to you and has made it pleasing to your hearts, and has made disbelief and lewdness and rebellion hateful to you. Such people are the ones who are the rightly guided. **8**Bounty and favor from Allah, and Allah is the knower, the wise one. **9**And if two parties of believers begin fighting, then make peace between them. And if one party of them does wrong to the other, fight the group that does wrong until it returns to the decree of Allah, then, if it returns, make peace between them justly, and act equitably. Indeed, Allah loves the just. **10**The believers are nothing other than brothers. Therefore, make peace between your brothers and observe your duty to Allah, so that perhaps you may obtain mercy. **11**O you who believe, do not let a people deride a people who may be better than they, do not let women deride women who may be better than they are, nor defame one another, nor insult one another with nicknames. Evil is the name of lewdness after faith. And whoever does not turn in repentance, such people are evildoers. **12**O you who believe, shun much suspicion, for indeed, some suspicion is a

---

1. The sura begins with a series of instructions on how to behave in the presence of the messenger. One may wonder why a perfect and eternal book that contains religious and ethical instruction that is valid for all time would contain a section that applied only to people who lived in the first generation of Islam, but the answer to this is implied by the instruction to Muslims not to "go ahead" in the messenger's presence. This means, says Ibn Kathir, that they should "not rush in making decisions before him, rather, follow his lead in all matters."[1] The hadiths are designed to enable Muslims to do this by reporting Muhammad's words and deeds in an enormous variety of situations. The proliferation of forged hadiths (Bukhari is said to have collected six hundred thousand of them and certified only seven thousand of these as authentic) indicates that in the ninth century and probably before that as well, stories of Muhammad's words and deeds were fabricated in order to provide justification for a particular faction or point of view.

6. Here begins a series of more general instructions to the believers.

Instead of "verify it" (*fatabayyanuu*), the Khalaf Qur'an has "stand firm" (*fatathabbatuu*).[2]

7. On "the messenger of Allah is among you," see 33:6.

9. Believers should not fight against one another, but they should join together to fight against a rebellious group until it returns to Allah's truth. See 4:89 and 4:92.

10. Maududi explains that this brotherhood is absolute and transcends all other allegiances; "The national and racial distinctions that cause universal corruption in the world have been condemned."[3]

12. A hadith depicts Muhammad saying: "Avoid suspicion, for suspicion is the gravest lie in talk and do not be inquisitive about one another and do not spy upon one another and do not feel envy with the other, and nurse no malice, and nurse no aversion and

crime. And do not spy on one another, nor back-bite one another. Would one of you love to eat the flesh of his dead brother? You hate that. And keep your duty. Indeed, Allah is relenting, merciful. ¹³O mankind, indeed, we have created you male and female, and have made you nations and tribes so that you may know one another. Indeed, the noblest among you, in the sight of Allah, is the most righteous. Indeed, Allah is the knower, aware. ¹⁴The nomadic Arabs say, We believe. Say, You do not believe, but rather say, We submit, for the faith has not yet entered into your hearts. Yet if you obey Allah and his messenger, he will not withhold from you anything of your deeds. Indeed, Allah is forgiving, merciful. ¹⁵The

believers are only those who believe in Allah and his messenger and afterward do not doubt, but wage jihad with their wealth and their lives for the cause of Allah. Such people are the sincere ones. ¹⁶Say, Would you teach Allah your religion, when Allah knows all that is in the heavens and all that is on the earth, and Allah is aware of all things? ¹⁷They make it a favor to you that they have embraced Islam. Say, Do not consider your Islam a favor to me, but Allah confers a favor on you, for he has led you to the faith, if you are sincere. ¹⁸Indeed, Allah knows the unseen things of the heavens and the earth. And Allah is the seer of all that you do.

hostility against one another. And be fellow-brothers and servants of Allah."⁴ A Muslim does not spy on or gossip about another Muslim because one's allegiance to one's fellow Muslims transcends all other loyalties, as stated at 49:10. During a jihad financing investigation in April 1999, FBI agent Gamal Abdel-Hafiz refused to record a conversation with a fellow Muslim, explaining: "A Muslim does not record another Muslim. That is against my religion."⁵

13. Ibn Kathir explains: "Allah the Exalted declares to mankind that He has created them all from a single person, Adam, and from that person He created his mate, Hawwa [Eve]. From their offspring He made nations, comprised of tribe, which include subtribes of all

sizes. It was also said that nations refers to non-Arabs, while tribes refers to Arabs."⁶ This commonality of descent creates a certain equality of dignity among human beings that is, however, negated by unbelief in Islam: "Therefore, all people are the descendants of Adam and Hawwa and share this honor equally. The only difference between them is in the religion that revolves around their obedience to Allah the Exalted and their following of His Messenger."⁷ On the radical inequality of dignity and worth between Muslims and non-Muslims, see 2:178.

15. See 2:218.

Qaf

Qaf

Introduction

Islamic tradition holds that Muhammad used to recite this sura, which is generally regarded as Meccan, on the two great Islamic festivals, Eid al-Fitr and Eid al-Adha, the festivals at the end of Ramadan and the end of the pilgrimage to Mecca.[1]

---

1 Muwatta Malik, book 10, no. 438https://sunnah.com/urn/504380.

Qaf

IN THE NAME OF ALLAH, THE COMPASSIONATE, THE MERCIFUL.

[1]Qaf. By the glorious Qur'an, [2]No, but they are amazed that a warner of their own has come to them, and the unbelievers say, This is a strange thing, [3]When we are dead and have become dust? That would be a far return. [4]We know what the earth takes from them, and with us is a recording book. [5]No, but they have denied the truth when it came to them, therefore they are now in a confused state.

[6]Have they not then observed the sky above them, how we have constructed it and decorated it, and how there are no cracks in it? [7]And we have spread out the earth, and have flung firm hills upon it, and have caused some of every lovely kind to grow on it, [8]A vision and a reminder for every penitent slave. [9]And we send down blessed water from the sky, by which we give growth to gardens and the grain of crops, [10]And lofty date-palms with ranged clusters, [11]Provision for men, and with which we bring a dead land to life. The resurrection of the dead will be like this. [12]The people of Noah denied before them, and the dwellers at Ar-Rass and Thamud,

[13]And Aad, and Pharaoh, and the brothers of Lot, [14]And those who lived in the wood, and the people of Tubba, every one denied their messengers, therefore my threat took effect. [15]Were we then worn out by the first creation? Yet they are in doubt about a new creation. [16]We indeed created man and we know what his soul whispers to him, and we are nearer to him than his jugular vein. [17]When the two receivers receive, seated on the right hand and on the left, [18]He utters no word except that there is with him a ready observer. [19]And the agony of death comes in truth. This is what you were inclined to avoid. [20]And the trumpet is blown. This is the threatened day. [21]And every soul comes, and along with it a driver and a witness. [22]You were not mindful of this. Now we have removed your covering from you, and your sight today is piercing. [23]And his comrade says, This is what I have ready. [24]You two throw each stubborn disbeliever into Gehenna, [25]Hinderer of good, transgressor, doubter, [26]Who sets up another god along with Allah. You two throw him to the dreadful doom. [27]His comrade says, Our Lord, I did not cause him to rebel, but he was gone far astray. [28]He says, Do not argue in

---

1. On the "mysterious letters," see 2:1.

It is unclear who is swearing or what the oath is about. Abdullah Yusuf Ali suggests in a parenthetical note that it is an oath that Muhammad is a prophet: "By the Glorious Qur'an (you are Allah's Messenger)."[1] The *Tafsir al-Jalalayn*, in contrast, has it as an oath about the unbelievers: "The Qur'an is noble even though the unbelievers of Makka did not believe in Muhammad."[2]

Still, who is doing the swearing is unclear. According to Islamic doctrine, the only speaker in the Qur'an is Allah, but it is curious that he the all-powerful deity would need to swear on things lesser than himself to establish his veracity. See 34:3.

12. On Noah, see also 7:59, 10:71, 11:25, 21:76, 23:23, 25:37, 26:105, 29:14, 37:75, 51:46, 53:52, 54:9, 57:26, 69:11, and 71:1. On Ar-Rass and Thamud, see 25:38.

13. On Aad, see 25:38. On Pharaoh, see also 2:49, 3:11, 7:103, 8:52, 10:75, 14:6, 17:101, 20:24, 23:46, 26:11, 27:12, 28:3, 29:39, 38:12, 40:24, 44:17, 51:38, 54:41, 66:11, 69:9, 73:15, 79:15, 85:18, and 89:10. On Lot, see 7:80, 11:69.

14. See 44:37.

17. Each person is accompanied by two angels, one who records his good deeds and the other his bad deeds. During Islamic prayer, one turns to one's right and one's left to greet these two angels in turn.

24. On Gehenna, see 2:206.

my presence, when I had already offered to you the warning. ²⁹The sentence that comes from me cannot be changed, and I am in no way a tyrant to the slaves. ³⁰On the day when we will say to Gehenna, Are you filled? And it says, Can there be more to come? ³¹And the garden is brought near for those who avoided evil, no longer distant. ³²This is what you were promised, for every penitent and mindful one, ³³Who fears Ar-Rahman in secret and comes with a contrite heart. ³⁴Enter it in peace. This is the day of immortality. ³⁵There they have all that they desire, and there is more with us. ³⁶And how many a generation did we destroy before them, who were mightier than these in prowess, so that they overran the lands, if they had any place of refuge? ³⁷Indeed, in this is truly a reminder for him who has a heart, or gives ear with full intelligence. ³⁸And indeed we created the heavens and the earth, and all that is between them, in six days, and no weariness touched us. ³⁹Therefore bear with what they say, and sing the praise of your Lord before the rising and before the setting of the sun, ⁴⁰And sing his praise in the nighttime, and after the prostrations. ⁴¹And listen on the day when the voice calls from a place close by, ⁴²The day when they will hear the cry in truth. That is the day of coming forth.

⁴³Indeed, it is we who bring to life and give death, and to us is the journeying. ⁴⁴On the day when the earth splits asunder from them, hastening forth. That is a gathering that is easy for us. ⁴⁵We are best aware of what they say, and you are in no way a tyrant over them. But warn by the Qur'an him who fears my threat.

---

30. Instead of "we will say," the Warsh Qur'an has "he will say."³ On Gehenna, see 2:206.

39. On "bear with what they say," see 2:144.

The Winds

Adh-Dhariyat

Introduction

According to Maududi, "The subject matter and the style clearly show that it was sent down in the period when although the Holy Prophet's invitation was being resisted and opposed with denial and ridicule and false accusations stubbornly, persecution had not yet started. Therefore, this Surah also seems to have been revealed in the same period in which the Surah Qaf [sura 50] was revealed."[1]

The title comes from 51:1, in which the wind is what scatters dust.

---

1 Maududi, EnglishTafsir.com, http://www.englishtafsir.com/Quran/51/index.html.

The Winds

IN THE NAME OF ALLAH, THE COMPASSIONATE, THE MERCIFUL.

1By those that scatter dust **2**And those that bear the burden **3**And those that glide with ease **4**And those who distribute by command, **5**Indeed, what you are threatened with is indeed true, **6**And indeed, the judgment will indeed come upon you. **7**By the heaven full of paths, **8**Indeed, you certainly are of differing opinions. **9**The one who hates it is made to turn away from it. **10**Cursed be the liars **11**Who are careless in an abyss. **12**They ask, When is the day of judgment? **13**The day when they will be tormented at the fire, **14**Taste your torment. This is what you tried to hasten. **15**Indeed, those who keep from evil will dwell amid gardens and water springs, **16**Taking what their Lord gives them, for indeed, previously they were doers of good, **17**They used to sleep only a little at night, **18**And before the dawning of each day would ask forgiveness, **19**And in their wealth the beggar and the outcast had a due share. **20**And in the earth are signs for those whose faith is sure. **21**And in yourselves. Can you then not see? **22**And in the heaven is your provision and what you are promised, **23**And by the Lord of the heavens and the earth, it is the truth, even as is what you speak. **24**Has the story of Abraham's honored guests reached you? **25**When they came to him and said, Peace, he answered, Peace. People unknown. **26**Then he went apart to his family so that they brought a fatted calf, **27**And he set it before them, saying, Will you not eat? **28**Then he began to fear them. They said, Do not fear, and gave him news of a wise son. **29**Then his wife came forward, moaning and striking her face, and cried, A barren old woman! **30**They said, Even so your Lord says. Indeed, he is the wise one, the knower. **31**He said, And what is your errand, O you who have been sent? **32**They said, Indeed, we are sent to a guilty people, **33**So that we may send stones of clay upon them, **34**Marked by your Lord for the rebellious. **35**Then we brought forth those believers who were there. **36**But we found there only one house of Muslims. **37**And we left behind in it a sign for those who fear a painful doom. **38**And in Moses, when we sent him to Pharaoh with clear justification, **39**But he withdrew in his might, and said, A wizard or a madman. **40**So we seized him and his armies and threw them into the sea, for he was reprobate. **41**And in Aad, when we sent the fatal wind against them. **42**It spared nothing that it reached, but made it like dust. **43**And in Thamud, when it was told them, Take your ease for awhile. **44**But they rebelled against their Lord's decree, and so the thunderbolt overtook them even while they watched, **45**And they were unable to rise up, nor

---

1. On Allah's oaths, see 34:3 and 50:1.

23. On the oath, "by the Lord of the heavens and the earth," see 34:3.

24. This account of Abraham's "honored guests" is reminiscent of the visitation of the Lord and the "three men" to Abraham in Genesis 18.

29. As in Genesis, the visitors tell Abraham that his wife, unnamed in the Qur'an, will give birth to a son, and she expresses skepticism.

32. Also as in Genesis, the visitors go on to Sodom and Gomorrah, which are, like Sarah, not named here but are identified as a "guilty people" who will be destroyed after the righteous are evacuated.

38. On Moses and Pharaoh, see also 2:49, 3:11, 7:103, 8:52, 10:75, 14:6, 17:101, 20:24, 23:46, 26:11, 27:12, 28:3, 29:39, 38:12, 40:24, 44:17, 50:13, 54:41, 66:11, 69:9, 73:15, 79:15, 85:18, and 89:10.

41. On Aad, see 25:38.

43. On Thamud, see 25:38.

could they help themselves. [46]And the people of Noah previously. Indeed, they were licentious people. [47]We have built the heaven with might, and it is we who make its vast extent. [48]And we laid out the earth, how gracious is the spreader. [49]And we have created all things in pairs, so that perhaps you may reflect. [50]Therefore flee to Allah, indeed, I am a plain warner to you from him. [51]And do not set up any other god along with Allah, indeed, I am a plain warner to you from him. [52]Even so, there came no messenger to those before them except that they said, A wizard or a madman. [53]Have they handed it down as an heirloom to one another? No, but they are defiant people. [54]So withdraw from them, for you are in no way blameworthy, [55]And warn, for warning benefits believers. [56]I created the jinn and mankind only so that they might worship me. [57]I seek no livelihood from them, nor do I ask that they should feed me. [58]Indeed, Allah is the sustainer, the Lord of unbreakable power. [59]And indeed, for those who do wrong there is an evil day like the evil day of those like them, so do not let them ask me to hasten it on. [60]And woe to those who disbelieve, from their day that they are promised.

46. On Noah, see also 7:59, 10:71, 11:25, 21:76, 23:23, 25:37, 26:105, 29:14, 37:75, 50:12, 53:52, 54:9, 57:26, 69:11, and 71:1.

50. Here and in the following verse Allah is apparently telling the messenger various things he should say to the unbelievers. There is, however, no indication in this passage, as there is in so many other places in the Qur'an, that the speaker is really the deity, as the messenger speaks in the first person. See 1:2 and 34:3.

The Mountain

At-Tur

Introduction

Maududi states that "from the internal evidence of the subject matter it appears that this Surah too was revealed in the same stage of the Holy Prophet's life at Makkah in which the Surah Adh-Dhariyat [sura 51] was revealed. While going through it one can clearly feel that during the period of its revelation the Holy Prophet (peace and blessings of Allah be upon him) was being showered with objections and accusations but there is no evidence yet to show that severe persecution of the Muslims had started."[1] According to Bell, "this surah shows signs of various revisions."[2]

The sura's name comes from 52:1.

---

1 Maududi, EnglishTafsir.com, http://www.englishtafsir.com/Quran/52/index.html.
2 Bell, II, 535.

The Mountain

IN THE NAME OF ALLAH, THE COMPASSIONATE, THE MERCIFUL.

¹By the mountain of Tur, ²And the inscribed book ³Unrolled on fine parchment, ⁴And the house frequented, ⁵And the roof exalted, ⁶And the sea kept filled, ⁷Indeed, the torment of your Lord will surely come to pass, ⁸There is no one who can ward it off. ⁹On the day when the heaven will heave with heaving, ¹⁰And the mountains move away with movement, ¹¹Then woe that day to the deniers ¹²Who play in talk of serious matters, ¹³The day when they are thrust with a thrust into the fire of Gehenna ¹⁴This is the fire which you were wont to deny. ¹⁵Is this sorcery, or do you not see? ¹⁶Endure its heat, and whether you are patient about it or impatient about, it is all the same for you. You are only being paid for what you used to do. ¹⁷Indeed, those who kept their duty dwell in gardens and delight, ¹⁸Happy because of what their Lord has given them, and their Lord has warded off from them the torment of the blaze. ¹⁹Eat and drink in health for what you used to do, ²⁰Reclining on ranged couches. And we married them to *houris* with wide, lovely eyes. ²¹And they who believe and whose descendants follow them in faith, we cause their descendants to join them, and we deprive them of nothing of their work. Every man is a pledge for what he has earned. ²²And we provide them with fruit and meat as they desire. ²³There they pass from hand to hand a cup in which is neither vanity nor a cause of sin. ²⁴And there go around them, waiting on them, servant boys of their own, as if they were hidden pearls. ²⁵And some of them draw near to others, questioning, ²⁶Saying, Indeed, of old, when we were with our families, we were always anxious, ²⁷But Allah has been gracious to us and has preserved us from the torment of the breath of fire. ²⁸Indeed, we used to pray to him of old. Indeed, he is the benign, the merciful. ²⁹Therefore warn. By the favor of Allah, you are neither a soothsayer or a madman. ³⁰Or do they say, A poet, for whom we may expect some calamity of time? ³¹Say, Expect. Indeed, I am with you among the expectant. ³²Do their minds command them to do this, or are they an outrageous people? ³³Or do they say, He has fabricated it? No, but they will not believe. ³⁴Then let

---

13. On Gehenna, see 2:206.

18. "The blaze" is *al-jahim*, about which see 5:10.

20. On the women of paradise, see 7:11, 37:48.

21. The blessed will be joined by their families. Ibn Kathir and the *Tafsir al-Jalalayn* agree that this has to do with the levels of paradise: the believing children of pious people will be admitted to the levels their parents attained, even if they weren't as pious.[1]

24. The *Tafsir al-Jalalayn* elaborates: "Circulating among them there will be youths—as servants—like hidden pearls as regards their beauty and fineness. A pearl when it is protected in its shell is more beautiful there than it is elsewhere."[2] "Servant boys" is *ghilman*, a name that was applied to slave soldiers in various Islamic polities, beginning with the Abbasid caliphate and extending to the time of the nineteenth-century Qajar dynasty in Iran.[3]

This verse and 56:17 have often been invoked as the foundation for the widespread, albeit tacit, acceptance of homosexual activity in various areas of the Islamic world, notably Afghanistan. According to the Iranian Islamic scholar Janet Afary, "Two factors worked against homosexual intercourse on earth: the need for procreation and the use of the anus for defecation. Since there was no childbirth and no defecation in paradise, some sources have suggested that *lavat* [sodomy] might be permissible and the boys in descriptions of paradise could be construed as sexual companions."[4]

Luxenberg, however, contends on philological grounds that this passage, 56:17, and 76:19 actually have nothing to do with boys but with "white grapes," hence their repeated comparison to pearls, and that this is another example of Christian paradisal imagery of bountiful gardens that also gave rise to the virgins of paradise: see 44:54.

30. See 26:224.

34. See 2:23, 10:38.

them produce speech like it, if they are truthful. ³⁵Or were they created out of nothing? Or are they the creators? ³⁶Or did they create the heavens and the earth? No, but they are sure of nothing. ³⁷Or do they own the treasures of your Lord? Or have they been given charge? ³⁸Or do they have any stairway by means of which they overhear? Then let their listener produce some clear justification. ³⁹Or does he have daughters while you have sons? ⁴⁰Or do you ask a fee from them so that they are plunged in debt? ⁴¹Or do they possess the unseen so that they can write down? ⁴²Or do they seek to ensnare? But those who disbelieve, they are the ensnared. ⁴³Or do they have any god besides Allah? May Allah be glorified from all that they ascribe as partner.

⁴⁴And if they were to see a fragment of the heaven falling, they would say, A heap of clouds. ⁴⁵Then let them be, until they meet their day, in which they will be struck down, ⁴⁶A day in which their guile will not help them in any way, nor will they be helped. ⁴⁷And indeed, for those who do wrong, there is a punishment beyond that. But most of them do not know. ⁴⁸So wait patiently for your Lord's decree, for surely you are in our sight, and sing the praise of your Lord when you rise, ⁴⁹And at night also sing his praise, and at the setting of the stars.

39. See 16:57 and 53:19.
47. Instead of "for those who do wrong," the Shi'ite Bankipur Qur'an manuscript has "for those who deprive Muhammad's family of its due."⁵ See 2:59 and the Appendix: Two Apocryphal Shi'ite Suras.

The Star

An-Najm

Introduction

Maududi explains that according to traditions recorded by numerous Islamic authorities, this was the first sura containing a verse that required Muslims to perform a prostration upon hearing it. He adds that this was "the first Surah of the Qur'an, which the Holy Prophet (peace and blessings of Allah be upon him) had publicly recited before an assembly of the Quraish (and according to Ibn Marduyah, in the Ka'bah) in which both the believers and the disbelievers were present. At the end, when he recited the verse requiring the performance of a *sajdah* [prostration] and fell down in prostration, the whole assembly also fall down in prostration with him, and even those chiefs of the polytheists who were in the forefront of the opposition to the Holy Prophet (peace and blessings of Allah be upon him) could not resist falling down in prostration."[1]

Although Maududi gives no hint of it, this is a notorious incident in Islamic tradition (see 53:19).

Another hadith has Ibn Abbas say, "The Messenger of Allah prostrated for it—meaning (Surat) An-Najm—and so did the Muslims, the idolaters, the Jinns, and the people."[2]

---

1 Maududi, EnglishTafsir.com, http://www.englishtafsir.com/Quran/53/index.html.
2 *Jami at-Tirmidhi*, vol. 2, book 1, no. 575.

The Star

In the name of Allah, the compassionate, the merciful.

1By the star when it sets, **2**Your comrade is not astray, nor is he deceived, **3**Nor does he speak of desire. **4**It is nothing except an inspiration that is inspired, **5**Which one of mighty powers has taught him, **6**One vigorous, and he grew clear to view **7**When he was on the uppermost horizon. **8**Then he drew near and came down **9**Until he was two bows' length or even nearer, **10**And he revealed to his slave what he revealed. **11**The heart did not lie in what it saw. **12**Will you then dispute with him about what he sees? **13**And indeed he saw him still another time **14**By the lote-tree of the farthest boundary, **15**Nigh to which is the paradise of refuge. **16**When what shrouds enshrouded the lote-tree, **17**The eye did not turn aside, nor was it overbold. **18**Indeed he saw one of the greater revelations of his Lord. **19**Have you thought upon Al-Lat and Al-Uzza **20**And Manat, the third, the other? **21**Are yours the males and his the females? **22**That indeed is an unfair division. **23**They are just names that you have named, you and your fathers, for which Allah has revealed no justification. They follow only speculation and what they themselves desire. And now the guidance from their Lord has come to them. **24**Or shall man have what he covets? **25**But to Allah belongs the after and the former. **26**And how many angels are in the heavens whose intercession does not help in any way except after Allah gives permission to those whom he chooses and accepts.

19. Here begins the Qur'an's only mention of the notorious "Satanic verses" incident, which became in 1988 the inspiration for the novel *The Satanic Verses* by Salman Rushdie. For this novel, the Islamic Republic of Iran called for Rushdie's death and put a bounty on his head.

According to Ibn Hisham, in a passage preserved by Tabari, the incident took place because of Muhammad's worrying over the Quraysh rejecting his message: "The apostle was anxious for the welfare of his people, wishing to attract them as far as he could."[1] In fact, "He longed for a way to attract them."[2] At that point the leaders of the Quraysh came to him with an offer: "You will worship our gods, al-Lat and al-Uzza, for a year, and we shall worship your god for a year."[3] According to the story, Muhammad was so intent on reconciling his people that he wanted to do this, but Allah twice told him not to do so.

Then, however, according to the story, he received a revelation saying that it was legitimate for Muslims to pray to al-Lat, al-Uzza, and Manat, the three goddesses of Quraysh. This new message directly contradicted the substance of his preaching up to that point: he had scorned al-Lat, al-Uzza, and Manat as false gods and proclaimed Allah as the only God; now he seemed to be discarding this uncompromising monotheism.

At this point the meeting with the Quraysh took place that Islamic tradition still records; see Maududi's statement in the introduction to this sura. The Quraysh were elated at Muhammad's new revelation and prostrated themselves with Muhammad and the Muslims after Muhammad finished reciting it. Ibn Hisham says that the Quraysh were "delighted at what had been said about their gods, saying, 'Muhammad has spoken of our gods in splendid fashion. He alleged in what he read that they are the exalted Gharaniq

whose intercession is approved.'"[4] The Gharaniq, according to Islamic scholar Alfred Guillaume, were "'Numidian Cranes' which fly at a great height."[5] This meant that they were near Allah's throne and that it was legitimate for Muslims to pray to al-Lat, al-Uzza, and Manat, the three goddesses favored by the pagan Quraysh, as intercessors before Allah.

The story then continues with Gabriel scolding Muhammad, and the prophet of Islam repenting: "I have fabricated things against God and have imputed to Him words which He has not spoken."[6] Allah hadn't inspired these verses; Satan had. Allah gave Muhammad a stern warning (see 17:73) but was ultimately merciful; he "annulled what Satan had suggested and God established His verses i.e., you are just like the prophets and apostles."[7] Just like them, that is, in that Satan attempted to interfere with their messages also; see 22:52. This tale concludes with Allah sending down 53:19-23 to replace Satan's words about al-Lat, al-Uzza, and Manat (on abrogation, see 2:106).

Many modern Islamic scholars deny that this incident took place at all, as it causes acute embarrassment. If Satan could put words into Muhammad's mouth once and make him think they were revelations from Allah, who is to say that Satan did not use Muhammad as his mouthpiece on other occasions? However, it is recorded by Ibn Hisham and Tabari; Ibn Sa'd mentions it as well.[8] Thus it has the same claim to historical accuracy, or lack thereof, as the rest of Islamic tradition about Muhammad.

21. See 16:57.

26. Intercession with Allah's permission is accepted (10:3, 20:109, 21:28, 34:23). However, elsewhere the Qur'an states that everyone will stand alone before Allah and no intercession from others will be accepted (2:48, 2:123, 6:94, 23:101, 39:43, 42:46).

[27]Indeed, it is those who disbelieve in the hereafter who name the angels with the names of females. [28]And they have no knowledge of it. They follow only speculation, and indeed, a guess can never take the place of the truth. [29]Then withdraw from him who flees from our remembrance and desires only the life of this world. [30]That is their sum of knowledge. Indeed, your Lord is best aware of him who strays, and he is best aware of him who goes right. [31]And to Allah belongs whatever is in the heavens and whatever is in the earth, so that he may reward those who do evil with what they have done, and reward those who do good with goodness. [32]Those who avoid grave sin and abominations, except offenses they commit unwillingly, indeed, your Lord is of vast mercy. He is best aware of you when he created you from the earth, and when you were hidden in the bellies of your mothers. Therefore do not ascribe purity to yourselves. He is best aware of him who fears Allah. [33]Did you see him who turned away, [34]And gave a little, then was grudging? [35]Does he have knowledge of the unseen so that he sees? [36]Or has he not had news of what is in the books of Moses [37]And Abraham who paid his debt, [38]So that no burdened one would bear another's load, [39]And that man has only what he makes effort for, [40]And that his effort will be seen. [41]And afterward he will be repaid for it with fullest payment, [42]And that your Lord, he is the goal, [43]And that it is he who makes laugh, and makes weep, [44]And that it is he who gives death and gives life, [45]And that he creates the two spouses, the male and the female, [46]From a drop when it is poured forth, [47]And that he has decreed the second bringing forth, [48]And that it is he who enriches and makes content, [49]And that it is he who is the Lord of Sirius, [50]And that he destroyed the former Aad, [51]And he did not spare Thamud, [52]And the people of Noah previously, indeed, they were more unjust and more rebellious, [53]And he destroyed the ruined cities [54]So that there covered them what covered. [55]About which then, of the bounties of your Lord, can you dispute? [56]This is a warner of the warners of old. [57]The threatened hour is near. [58]No one besides Allah can disclose it. [59]Are you then amazed at this statement, [60]And laugh and do not weep, [61]While you amuse yourselves? [62]Instead, prostrate yourselves before Allah and serve him.

---

27. The reasoning behind female names for angels is likely the same as in the repeated claim that to say that Allah has daughters is ridiculous and insulting. See 16:57.

36. On Moses, see 2:49, 7:103, 10:75, 17:101, 26:10, and elsewhere.

37. On Abraham, see 7:80, 9:17, 9:114, 11:69, 15:51, 19:41, 21:51, 26:69, 29:16, 37:83, 60:4, and elsewhere.

49. Regarding Sirius, according to Ibn Kathir, "a group of Arabs used to worship" the "bright star."[9]

50. On Aad, see 25:38.

51. On Thamud, see 25:38.

52. On Noah, see also 7:59, 10:71, 11:25, 21:76, 23:23, 25:37, 26:105, 29:14, 37:75, 50:12, 51:46, 54:9, 57:26, 69:11, and 71:1.

53. Ibn Kathir states that "the ruined cities" are Sodom and Gomorrah.[10] See 3:137.

SURA 54

The Moon

Al-Qamar

Introduction

Ibn Kathir reports that Muhammad would recite sura 54, as well as sura 50, "during major gatherings and occasions because they contain Allah's promises and warnings, and information about the origin of creation, Resurrection, Tawhid [the oneness of Allah], the affirmation of prophethood, and so forth among the great objectives."[1]

The title comes from the first verse, which refers to the splitting of the moon—a miracle that, according to a hadith, took place during Muhammad's lifetime. As the Muslims looked agog at the moon split into two parts, Muhammad cried, "Witness, witness (this miracle)."[2] This hadith contradicts the Qur'an's statement that the messenger performs no miracles (see 6:37, 6:109, 10:20, and 13:7).

---

1 Ibn Kathir, IX, 344.
2 Bukhari, vol. 6, book 65, no. 4865.

The Moon

In the name of Allah, the compassionate, the merciful.

¹The hour drew near and the moon was split in two. ²And if they see a sign, they turn away and say, Prolonged illusion. ³They denied and followed their own lusts. Yet everything will come to a decision ⁴And surely there has come to them news of which should be a deterrent, ⁵Effective wisdom, but warnings do not help. ⁶So withdraw from them on the day when the summoner summons to a painful thing. ⁷With downcast eyes, they come forth from the graves as if they were locusts spread around, ⁸Hastening toward the summoner, the unbelievers say, This is a hard day. ⁹The people of Noah denied before them, yes, they denied our slave and said, A madman, and he was rejected. ¹⁰So he called out to his Lord, saying, I am vanquished, so help. ¹¹Then we opened the gates of heaven with pouring water ¹²And caused the earth to gush forth springs, so that the waters met for a predestined purpose. ¹³And we carried him upon a thing of planks and nails, ¹⁴That ran in our sight, as a reward for him who was rejected. ¹⁵And indeed we left it as a sign, but is there anyone who remembers? ¹⁶Then see how my punishment was after my warnings.

¹⁷And in truth we have made the Qur'an easy to remember, but is there anyone who remembers? ¹⁸Aad rejected warnings. Then how was my punishment after my warnings? ¹⁹Indeed, we let loose on them a raging wind on a day of constant calamity, ²⁰Sweeping men away as if they were uprooted trunks of palm-trees. ²¹Then see how my punishment was after my warnings. ²²And in truth we have made the Qur'an easy to remember, but is there anyone who remembers? ²³Thamud rejected warnings, ²⁴For they said, Is it a mortal man, alone among us, whom we are to follow? Then indeed we would fall into error and madness. ²⁵Has the remembrance been given to him alone among us? No, but he is a rash liar. ²⁶Tomorrow they will know who is the rash liar. ²⁷Indeed, we are sending the camel as a test for them, so watch them and have patience, ²⁸And inform them that the water is to be shared between them. Every drinking will be witnessed. ²⁹But they call their comrade and he took and hamstrung it. ³⁰Then see how my punishment was after my warnings. ³¹Indeed, we sent upon them one shout, and they became as the dry twigs, the builder of a cattle-fold. ³²And in truth we have made the Qur'an easy to remember, but

---

1. Some modern-day Muslims claim that this verse constituted a prophecy that was fulfilled during Neil Armstrong's moon landing in 1969, when the astronauts dug up a bit of the lunar soil and brought it back. In a classic example of *vaticinium ex eventu*, prophecy from the event, an Islamic apologetics website purports to explain "the extraordinary and simple mathematical miracle hidden behind 54:1 which relates to the Apollo 11 mission to the moon on 20 July 1969, followed by the fact that the same miracle 'splits' the Quran in a way that reveals in a stunning manner the Hijri Islamic lunar year of the event."¹ The numerological explanation that follows this is elaborate and inventive enough to illustrate the fact that virtually any proposition can be demonstrated as fact

once one departs from rational standards of the evaluation of evidence. The refutation of all such speculation lies in the simple fact that the astronauts did not actually split the moon in two; they just brought back a bit of moon dust from it.

9. On Noah, see 7:59, 7:71, 10:71, 11:25, 23:23, 29:14, and 37:75.

16. This is repeated as a refrain at 54:18, 54:21, and 54:30.

17. This is repeated as a refrain at 54:22, 54:32, and 54:40. See 19:97.

18. On Aad, see 25:38.

23. On Thamud, see 25:38.

27. On the camel, see 11:64, 26:155, and 91:11-14, as well as the introduction to sura 11.

is there anyone who remembers? ³³The people of Lot rejected warnings. ³⁴Indeed, we sent a storm of stones upon them, except the family of Lot, whom we rescued in the last watch of the night, ³⁵As grace from us. In this way do we reward him who gives thanks. ³⁶And he indeed had warned them of our blow, but they doubted the warnings. ³⁷They even asked his guests from him for an evil purpose. Then we blinded their eyes, Taste now my punishment after my warnings. ³⁸And in truth, the punishment decreed came upon them early in the morning. ³⁹Now taste my punishment after my warnings. ⁴⁰And in truth we have made the Qur'an easy to remember, but is there anyone who remembers? ⁴¹And warnings came in truth to the house of Pharaoh ⁴²Who denied our revelations, every one. Therefore we seized them with the grasp of the mighty, the powerful. ⁴³Are your unbelievers better than those, or do you have some immunity in the Psalms? ⁴⁴Or do they say, We are a victorious army? ⁴⁵The armies will all be routed and will turn and flee. ⁴⁶No, but the hour is their appointed meeting, and the hour will be more wretched and more bitter. ⁴⁷Indeed, the guilty are in error and madness. ⁴⁸On the day when they are dragged into the fire upon their faces, Feel the touch of *saqar*. ⁴⁹Indeed, we have created everything by measure. ⁵⁰And our commandment is just one, like the twinkling of an eye. ⁵¹And indeed we have destroyed your companions, but is there anyone who remembers? ⁵²And everything they did is in the Psalms, ⁵³And every small and great thing is recorded. ⁵⁴Indeed, the righteous will dwell among gardens and rivers, ⁵⁵Firmly established in the favor of a mighty king.

---

33. On Lot, see 7:80, 11:69.

41. On Pharaoh, see also 2:49, 3:11, 7:103, 8:52, 10:75, 14:6, 17:101, 20:24, 23:46, 26:11, 27:12, 28:3, 29:39, 38:12, 40:24, 44:17, 50:13, 51:38, 66:11, 69:9, 73:15, 79:15, 85:18, and 89:10.

43. See 3:184.

48. Zamakhshari says that *saqar* is one of the levels of hell: "The highest level is for the monotheists, the second for the Jews, the third for the Christians, the fourth for the Sabians, the fifth for the Magi, the sixth for the idolaters, and the seventh for the hypocrites."[2] *Saqar* is the level "for the Jews."[3]

However, this interpretation has been imposed upon the passage rather than being derived. The contemporary Islamic scholar Ibn Rawandi notes that "*saqar*, with the meaning: 'hellfire, heat of hell,' as assigned to it by Islamic tradition, has no certain origin in Arabic or any other Semitic language."[4] The understanding of the word in Islamic theology is derived solely from the context of the Qur'an passages where it appears (see also 74:26-7, 74:42). See 12:2, 16:103.

52. Although the word used (*zubur*) is the same, Ibn Kathir does not identify this as the Biblical Book of Psalms, but as "the Books of Record entrusted to the angels."[5] There is "nothing, whether large or small, but it is recorded and counted."[6] See also 3:184.

The Compassionate One

Ar-Rahman

Introduction

Maududi states that most authorities believe this to be a Meccan sura, but some think it is Medinan.[1] Its title comes from its first verse.

---

1 Maududi, EnglishTafsir.com, http://www.englishtafsir.com/Quran/55/index.html.

The Compassionate One

IN THE NAME OF ALLAH, THE COMPASSIONATE, THE MERCIFUL.

1Ar-Rahman **2**Has made known the Qur'an. **3**He has created man. **4**He has taught him speech. **5**The sun and the moon are made punctual. **6**The stars and the trees adore. **7**And the sky he has uplifted, and he has set the measure, **8**So that you do not exceed the measure, **9**But observe the measure strictly, and do not fall short of it. **10**And he has appointed the earth for creatures, **11**In which are fruit and sheathed palm-trees, **12**Husked grain and scented herb. **13**Which of your Lord's favors do you deny? **14**He created man from clay like the potter's, **15**And the jinn he created from smokeless fire. **16**Which of your Lord's favors do you deny? **17**Lord of the two easts, and Lord of the two wests. **18**Which of your Lord's favors do you deny? **19**He has loosed the two seas. They meet. **20**There is a barrier between them. They do not encroach. **21**Which of your Lord's favors do you deny? **22**There comes forth from both of them the pearl and coral-stone. **23**Which of your Lord's favors do you deny? **24**His are the ships displayed upon the sea, like banners. **25**Which of your Lord's favors do you deny? **26**Everyone who is on it will pass away, **27**There remains only the face of your Lord of might and glory. **28**Which of your Lord's favors do you deny? **29**All that are in the heavens and the earth entreat him. Every day he exercises power. **30**Which of your Lord's favors do you deny? **31**We will dispose of you, O you two dependents. **32**Which of your Lord's favors do you deny? **33**O company of jinn and men, if you have power to penetrate the regions of the heavens and the earth, then penetrate. You will never penetrate them except with permission. **34**Which of your Lord's favors do you deny? **35**There will be sent, against you both, heat of fire and flash of brass, and you will not escape. **36**Which of your Lord's favors do you deny? **37**And when the heaven splits asunder and becomes rosy like red hide, **38**Which of your Lord's favors do you deny? **39**On that day, neither man nor jinni will be asked about his sin. **40**Which of your Lord's favors do you deny? **41**The guilty will be known by their marks, and will be taken by the forelocks and the feet. **42**Which of your Lord's favors do you deny? **43**This is Gehenna, which the guilty deny. **44**They go circling around between it and fierce, boiling water. **45**Which of your Lord's favors do you deny? **46**But for him who fears the standing before his Lord, there are two gardens. **47**Which of your Lord's favors do you deny? **48**Of spreading branches. **49**Which of your Lord's favors do you deny? **50**In which are two flowing fountains. **51**Which of your Lord's favors do you deny?

---

1. On Ar-Rahman, see 17:110, 38:5.

13. This is repeated as a refrain at 55:16, 55:18, 55:21, 55:23, 55:25, 55:28, 55:30, 55:32, 55:34, 55:36, 55:38, 55:40, 55:42, 55:45, 55:53, 55:55, 55:59, 55:61, 55:65, 55:67, 55:69, and 55:77. The irregular length of the material between these repetitions suggests that there may have been interpolations.

17. The "two easts and two wests" refer, says Ibn Kathir, to "the sunrise of summer and winter and the sunset of summer and winter," a decidedly geocentric point of view.[1] See 18:86.

33. Says Maududi, "This is the only Surah of the Qur'an in which besides men the jinn also, who are the other creation of the earth endowed with freedom of will and action, have been directly addressed."[2]

43. On Gehenna, see 2:206.

⁵²In which is every kind of fruit in pairs. ⁵³Which of your Lord's favors do you deny? ⁵⁴Reclining upon couches lined with silk brocade, the fruit of both the gardens near to hand. ⁵⁵Which of your Lord's favors do you deny? ⁵⁶In them are those of modest gaze, whom neither man nor jinni will have touched before them. ⁵⁷Which of your Lord's favors do you deny? ⁵⁸Like the ruby and the coral-stone. ⁵⁹Which of your Lord's favors do you deny? ⁶⁰Is the reward of goodness anything except goodness? ⁶¹Which of your Lord's favors do you deny? ⁶²And beside them are two other gardens, ⁶³Which of your Lord's favors do you deny? ⁶⁴Dark green with foliage. ⁶⁵Which of your Lord's favors do you deny? ⁶⁶In which are two abundant springs. ⁶⁷Which of your Lord's favors do you deny? ⁶⁸In which is fruit, the date-palm and pomegranate. ⁶⁹Which of your Lord's favors do you deny? ⁷⁰In which are the good and beautiful ⁷¹Which of your Lord's favors do you deny? ⁷²Beautiful ones, close-guarded in pavilions ⁷³Which of your Lord's favors do you deny? ⁷⁴Whom neither man nor jinni will have touched before them ⁷⁵Which of your Lord's favors do you deny? ⁷⁶Reclining on green cushions and fair carpets. ⁷⁷Which of your Lord's favors do you deny? ⁷⁸Blessed be the name of your Lord, mighty and glorious.

---

56. These are, of course, the virgins of paradise. A hadith depicts Muhammad saying: "There is no one whom Allah will admit to Paradise but Allah will marry him to seventy-two wives, two from houris and seventy from his inheritance from the people of Hell, all of whom will have desirable front passages and he will have a male member that never becomes flaccid (i.e., soft and limp)."³

This is classified as a weak hadith, but the number seventy-two has nonetheless entered today into the popular understanding of Islamic paradise.

In another hadith, he is made to say, "The believer shall be given in paradise such and such strength in intercourse....He will be given the strength of a hundred" men.⁴ See 36:55 and 44:54.

The Inevitable Event

Al-Waqi'a

Introduction

A hadith has Abu Bakr say: "O Messenger of Allah! You have become gray."[1] He said: "I have gone gray from (Surat) Hud [11], Al-Waqi'ah [56], Al-Mursalat [77] and Amma Yatasa'alun [78] and Idhash-Shamsu Kuw-wirat [81]."[2]

This sura is traditionally considered to be Meccan; the title comes from 56:1.

---

1 *Jami at-Tirmidhi*, vol. 5, book 44, no. 3297.
2 Ibid.

The Inevitable Event

IN THE NAME OF ALLAH, THE COMPASSIONATE, THE MERCIFUL.

¹When the inevitable event takes place, ²There is no denying that it will come, ³Humiliating, exalting, ⁴When the earth is shaken with a shock ⁵And the hills are ground to powder ⁶So that they become a scattered dust, ⁷And you will be three kinds, ⁸Those on the right hand, what about those on the right hand? ⁹And those on the left hand, what about those on the left hand? ¹⁰And the foremost in the race, the foremost in the race, ¹¹Those are the ones who will be brought near ¹²In gardens of delight, ¹³A multitude of those of old ¹⁴And a few of those of later times. ¹⁵On lined couches, ¹⁶Reclining on them face to face. ¹⁷Immortal boys wait on them ¹⁸With bowls and ewers and a cup from a pure spring ¹⁹From which they get no aching of the head nor any intoxication, ²⁰And fruit that they prefer ²¹And flesh of fowls that they desire. ²²And beautiful ones with wide, lovely eyes, ²³Like hidden pearls, ²⁴Reward for what they used to do. ²⁵There hear they no vain speaking nor recrimination ²⁶Only the saying, Peace, peace. ²⁷And those on the right hand, what about those on the right hand? ²⁸Among thornless lote-trees ²⁹And clustered plantains, ³⁰And spreading shade, ³¹And water gushing, ³²And fruit in plenty ³³Neither out of reach nor forbidden, ³⁴And raised couches, ³⁵Indeed, we have created them a special creation ³⁶And made them virgins, ³⁷Lovers, friends, ³⁸For those on the right hand, ³⁹A multitude of those of old ⁴⁰And a multitude of those of later times. ⁴¹And those on the left hand, What about those on the left hand? ⁴²In scorching wind and scalding water ⁴³And shadow of black smoke, ⁴⁴Neither cool nor refreshing. ⁴⁵Indeed, before this they were soft with luxury ⁴⁶And used to persist in the awful sin. ⁴⁷And they used to say, When we are dead and have become dust and bones, shall we then really be raised again, ⁴⁸And also our forefathers? ⁴⁹Say, indeed, those of old and those of later times ⁵⁰Will all be brought together to the meeting of an appointed day. ⁵¹Then indeed, you, the ones who are astray, the deniers, ⁵²You indeed will eat from a tree called zaqqum ⁵³And will fill your bellies with it, ⁵⁴And on it you will drink boiling water, ⁵⁵Drinking even as the camel drinks. ⁵⁶This will be their welcome on the day of judgment. ⁵⁷We created you. Will you then admit the truth? ⁵⁸Have you seen what you emit? ⁵⁹Do you create it or are we the creator? ⁶⁰We decreed death among you, and we are not to be surpassed, ⁶¹So that we may transform you and make you what you do not know. ⁶²And indeed you know the first creation. Why, then, do you not reflect? ⁶³Have you seen what you cultivate? ⁶⁴Is it you who grow it, or are we the grower? ⁶⁵If we willed, we could indeed make it chaff, then would you not stop exclaiming, ⁶⁶Indeed, we are laden with debt. ⁶⁷No, but we are

---

17. See 52:24, 76:19.

35. See 36:55, 44:54, and 55:56.

36. See 36:55.

37. A hadith depicts Muhammad saying: "Whenever a woman harms her husband in this world (that is without any due right), his wife among the (Houris in Jannah [paradise]) says: 'You must not harm him. May Allah destroy you! He is only a passing guest with you and is about to leave you to come to us.'"[1]

52. See 37:62.

deprived. [68]Have you observed the water that you drink? [69]Is it you who brought it down from the raincloud, or did we bring it down? [70]If we willed, we could indeed make it bitter. Why then, don't you give thanks? [71]Have you observed the fire that you kindle, [72]Was it you who made the tree of it to grow, or were we the grower? [73]We, and we alone, appointed it a memorial and a comfort for the dwellers in the wilderness. [74]Therefore praise the name of your Lord, the mighty one. [75]No, I swear by the places of the stars [76]And indeed, that indeed is a mighty oath, if only you knew [77]That it is indeed a noble Qur'an [78]In a book kept hidden [79]Which no one touches except the purified, [80]A revelation from the Lord of the worlds. [81]Is it this statement that you scorn, [82]And make denial of it your livelihood? [83]Why, then, when it comes up to the throat [84]And you are at that moment looking [85]And we are nearer to him than you are, but you do not see [86]Why then, if you are not in bondage, [87]Do you not force it back, if you are truthful? [88]Thus if he is among those brought near, [89]Then breath of life, and plenty, and a garden of delight. [90]And if he is among those on the right hand, [91]Then peace for you, from those on the right hand. [92]But if he is among the rejecters, those who are astray, [93]Then the welcome will be boiling water [94]And roasting in blaze. [95]Indeed, this is certain truth. [96]Therefore praise the name of your Lord, the mighty one.

---

79. Non-Muslims, because they are unclean (see 9:28), are not to touch the Qur'an. This was why American guards at the prison camp at Guantanamo Bay in Cuba, where many jihad terrorists were held, would only touch the Qur'an while wearing gloves.

82. Islamic apologists today routinely insist that opponents of jihad violence and Sharia oppression of women and others are motivated solely by a desire for wealth; see 26:74.

94. "Blaze" is *jahim*, about which see 5:10.

SURA 57

The Iron

Al-Hadid

Introduction

Maududi notes that Islamic tradition is unanimous in regarding this as a Medinan sura; he says "it was probably sent down some time during the interval between the Battle of Uhud and the Truce of Hudaibiyah. This was the time when the tiny Islamic State of Madinah had been hemmed in by the disbelievers and the handful of the ill-equipped Muslims were entrenched against the combined power of entire Arabia. In this state Islam not only stood in need of the sacrifice of Life from its followers, but it also needed monetary help and assistance. In this Surah a forceful appeal has been made for the same."[1]

This is the first of Al-Musabbihat, that is, suras that begin by glorifying Allah. The others are 59, 61, 62, and 64. An Islamic tradition holds that Muhammad used to recite these before going to sleep at night.[2]

The title comes from 57:25, where iron is presented as a gift from Allah.

---

1 Maududi, EnglishTafsir.com, http://www.englishtafsir.com/Quran/57/index.html.
2 Ibn Kathir, IX. 460.

The Iron

In the name of Allah, the compassionate, the merciful.

¹All that is in the heavens and the earth glorifies Allah, and he is the mighty, the wise. ²His is the dominion over the heavens and the earth, he brings to life and he gives death, and he is able to do all things. ³He is the first and the last, and the outward and the inward, and he is the knower of all things. ⁴It is he who created the heavens and the earth in six days, then he mounted the throne. He knows all that enters the earth and all that emerges from it and all that comes down from the sky and all that ascends into it, and he is with you wherever you may be. And Allah is the seer of what you do. ⁵His is the dominion of the heavens and the earth, and to Allah things are brought back. ⁶He causes the night to pass into the day, and he causes the day to pass into the night, and he is the knower of all that is in the hearts. ⁷Believe in Allah and his messenger, and spend out of what he has entrusted you with, and for those of you who believe and spend, theirs will be a great reward. ⁸What ails you that you do not believe in Allah, when the messenger calls you to believe in your Lord, and he has already made a covenant with you, if you are believers? ⁹It is he who sends down clear revelations to his slave, so that he may bring you forth from darkness to light, and indeed, for you, Allah is full of kindness, merciful. ¹⁰And what ails you that you do not spend in the way of Allah when to Allah belongs the inheritance of the heavens and the earth? Those who spent and fought before the victory are not on the same level. They are greater in rank than those who spent and fought afterwards. To each Allah has promised good. And Allah is informed of what you do. ¹¹Who is he who will lend to Allah a good loan, so that he may double it for him and a rich reward may be his? ¹²On the day when you will see the believers, men and women, their light shining forth before them and on their right hands, Glad news for you this day, gardens under which rivers flow, in which you are immortal. That is the supreme victory. ¹³On the day when the hypocritical men and the hypocritical women will say to those who believe, Look at us so that we may borrow from your light, it will be said, Go back and seek for light. Then there will separate them a wall in which there is a gate, the inner side of which contains mercy, while the outer side of it is toward the doom. ¹⁴They will call out to them, Weren't we with you? They will say, Yes, indeed, but you tempted one another, and hesitated, and doubted, and vain desires seduced you until the decree of Allah came to pass, and the deceiver deceived you about Allah, ¹⁵So this day no ransom can be taken from you, nor from those who disbelieved. Your home is

---

8. Ibn Kathir paraphrases, "What prevents you from believing, while the Messenger is among you calling you to faith and bringing forward clear proofs and evidences that affirm the truth of what he brought you"?¹ Here again is the idea that one cannot be of sound mind and good intentions and reject Islam; see 26:74.

10. Maududi explains: "Those who sacrifice their lives and expend their wealth to further promote the cause of Islam when it is already strong cannot attain to the rank of those who struggled with their lives and their wealth to promote and uphold the cause of Islam when it was weak."²

12. See 4:124.

the fire, that is your patron, and a wretched journey's end. **16**Is not the time ripe for the hearts of those who believe to submit to Allah's reminder and to the truth which is revealed, so that they do not become like those who received the book of old? But the term was prolonged for them and so their hearts were hardened, and many of them are transgressors. **17**Know that Allah brings the earth to life after its death. We have made our signs clear for you, so that perhaps you may understand. **18**Indeed, those who give alms, both men and women, and lend to Allah a good loan, it will be doubled for them, and theirs will be a rich reward. **19**And those who believe in Allah and his messengers, they are the loyal ones, and the martyrs are with their Lord, they have their reward and their light, while as for those who disbelieve and deny our signs, they are owners of the blaze. **20**Know that the life of the world is only play, and idle talk, and pageantry, and boasting among you, and rivalry in respect of wealth and children, as the comparison of vegetation after rain, of which the growth is pleasing to the husbandman, but afterward it dries up and you see it turning yellow, then it becomes straw. And in the hereafter there is grievous punishment, and forgiveness from Allah and his good pleasure, while the life of this world is nothing but delusion. **21**Race one with another for forgiveness from

your Lord and a garden of which the breadth is as the breadth of the heavens and the earth, which is in store for those who believe in Allah and his messengers. That is the bounty of Allah, which he bestows upon those whom he wills, and Allah is of infinite bounty. **22**No disaster happens on earth or in yourselves except that it is in a book before we bring it into being, indeed, that is easy for Allah. **23**So that you do not grieve for the sake of what has escaped you, or rejoice because of what has been given. Allah does not love all prideful boasters, **24**Who hoard and who command greed upon the people. And whoever turns away, still Allah is the absolute, the owner of praise. **25**We indeed sent our messengers with clear proofs, and revealed with them the book and the balance, so that mankind may observe the right measure, and he sent down iron, in which is mighty power and uses for mankind, and so that Allah may know him who helps him and his messengers, although unseen. Indeed, Allah is strong, almighty. **26**And we indeed sent Noah and Abraham and placed the prophethood and the book among their descendants, and among them there is he who goes right, but many of them are transgressors. **27**Then we caused our messengers to follow in their footsteps, and we caused Jesus, son of Mary, to follow, and gave him the Gospel, and placed compassion and mercy in the hearts

---

16. Regarding not being like people of the book, a hadith depicts Aisha recalling that Muhammad, during his final illness, declared: "May Allah curse the Jews and Christians because they took the graves of their prophets as places of worship."[3] She added: "By that he warned his follower of imitating them, by doing that which they did."[4]

Another hadith has Muhammad saying: "The Jews and the Christians do not dye (their grey hair), so you shall do the opposite of what they do (i.e. dye your grey hair and beards)."[5]

19. "The blaze" is al-jahim, about which see 5:10.

22. The Tafsir al-Jalalayn explains: "Nothing occurs, either in the earth—such as drought—or in yourself—such as illness and

loss of children, without its being in a Book—the Preserved Tablet—before We create it and make it happen."[6] See 7:179, 10:99, and 32:13.

26. On Noah, see also 7:59, 10:71, 11:25, 21:76, 23:23, 25:37, 26:105, 29:14, 37:75, 50:12, 51:46, 53:52, 54:9, 69:11, and 71:1. On Abraham, see 7:80, 9:17, 9:114, 11:69, 15:51, 19:41, 21:51, 26:69, 29:16, 37:83, 60:4, and elsewhere.

27. Here is the distinction between the believers and unbelievers among the Christians; see 2:62 and 98:6. Ibn Kathir notes that this verse criticizes the Christians "in two ways: first, they invented things in their religion, things which Allah did not legislate for

of those who followed him. But they invented monasticism, we did not decree it for them, only seeking Allah's pleasure, and they did not observe with right observance. So we give those of them who believe their reward, but many of them are transgressors. **28**O you who believe, be mindful of your duty to Allah and put faith in his messenger. He will give you twofold of his mercy and will appoint for you a light in which you will walk, and will forgive you. Allah is forgiving, merciful, **29**So that the people of the book may know that they control nothing of the bounty of Allah, but that the bounty is in Allah's hand to give to those whom he wills. And Allah is of infinite bounty.

them. The second is that they did not fulfill the requirements of what they themselves invented and which they claimed was a means of drawing near to Allah, the Exalted and Most Honored."[7]

Ibn Kathir also quotes a tradition in which Ibn Abbas is made to say: "There were kings after Isa [Jesus] who changed the Tawrah [Torah] and the Injil [Gospel] when there were still believers who recited Tawrah and the Injil."[8] On the Jews and Christians corrupting their scriptures, see 2:4.

On the Christians inventing monasticism, which Allah had not decreed for them, Ibn Kathir quotes several traditions. In one, Muhammad is depicted as saying: "Every Prophet has Rahbaniyyah (monasticism); Jihad in the cause of Allah, the Exalted and Most Honored, is the Rahbaniyyah of this Ummah," that is, the worldwide Islamic community.[9] Ibn Kathir offers another version, in which Muhammad says: "Every Ummah has Rahbaniyyah; Jihad in the cause of Allah is the Rahbaniyyah of this Ummah."[10] Finally, he quotes a third tradition in which a companion of Muhammad says: "Fulfill the obligation of Jihad, because it is the Rahbaniyyah of Islam."[11]

29. The *Tafsir al-Jalalayn* says that this statement about the powerlessness of the Jews and Christians was contrary to their claims "that they were the ones whom Allah loved and those with whom He was pleased."[12] Ibn Kathir explains that this verse means that "they cannot prevent what Allah gives, or give what Allah prevents."[13]

The Pleading Woman

Al-Mujadila

Introduction

This is traditionally regarded as a Medinan sura. The title comes from 58:1.

The Pleading Woman

In the name of Allah, the compassionate, the merciful.

¹Allah has heard the saying of her who argues with you about her husband, and complains to Allah. And Allah hears your conversation. Indeed, Allah is the hearer, the knower. ²Those of you who put away your wives, they are not their mothers, no one are their mothers except those who gave them birth, they indeed speak an evil word and a lie. And indeed, Allah is forgiving, merciful. ³Those who put away their wives and afterward would go back on what they have said, in that case, the freeing of a slave before they touch one another. To this you are exhorted, and Allah is informed of what you do. ⁴And he who does not find, let him fast for two successive months before they touch one another, and for him who is unable to do so, the feeding of sixty needy ones. This, so that you may put trust in Allah and his messenger. Such are the limits, and for unbelievers is a painful doom. ⁵Indeed, those who oppose Allah and his messenger will be humiliated even as those before them were humiliated, and we have sent down clear signs, and for unbelievers is a shameful doom ⁶On the day when Allah will raise them all together and inform them of what they did. Allah has kept account of it while they forgot it. And Allah is witness over all things. ⁷Haven't you seen that Allah knows all that is in the heavens and all that is in the earth? There is no secret conference of three except that he is their fourth, nor of five except that he is their sixth, nor of less than that or more except that he is with them wherever they may be, and afterward, on the day of resurrection, he will inform them of what they did. Indeed, Allah is the knower of all things. ⁸Haven't you observed those who were forbidden conspiracy and afterward returned to what they had been forbidden, and conspire together for crime and wrongdoing and disobedience against the messenger? And when they come to you, they greet you with a greeting with which Allah does not greet you, and say within themselves, Why should Allah punish us for what we say? Gehenna will be sufficient for them, they will feel the heat of it, an evil destination. ⁹O you who believe, when you conspire together, do not conspire together for crime and wrongdoing and disobedience against the messenger, but conspire together for righteousness and piety,

---

1. In a hadith, Aisha is depicted as saying: "Praise is to Allah Whose hearing encompasses all voices. The woman who disputed concerning her husband (Al-Mujadilah) came to the Prophet when I was (sitting) in a corner of the house, and she complained about her husband, but I did not hear what she said. The Allah revealed: 'Indeed Allah has heard the statement of her that disputes with you concerning her husband.'"[1]

2. The dispute between the wife and her husband apparently involved his attempting to divorce her by telling her, "You are to me as my mother's back." A woman thus divorced could not remarry, and indeed had to remain in her ex-husband's household as, effectively, a domestic servant. Allah directs that such a divorce is not final but can be reversed if the husband frees a slave (58:3), fasts for two months, or feeds sixty poor people (58:4). See 33:4.

According to Islamic tradition, the woman mentioned here was named Khawlah bint Tha'labah, and her husband Aws bin as-Samit. Gabriel is said to have given this Qur'anic passage to Muhammad after Khawlah complained to the Islamic prophet about her plight. Here again, then, the reader of the Qur'an faces two choices: either the messenger was fabricating revelations that he said were from the supreme God in order to solve problems and settle issues he encountered in the course of his daily life, such that what claims to be an eternal book is actually filled with incidental minutiae from his life, or every detail of his life was mapped out for all eternity by the deity in order to teach some eternal truths, and he was therefore the most important person who ever existed. There is no other alternative. See 2:144.

8. On Gehenna, see 2:206.

and keep your duty toward Allah, to whom you will be gathered. **10**Indeed, conspiracy is only of Satan, so that he may trouble those who believe, but he cannot harm them at all unless by Allah's permission. In Allah let believers put their trust. **11**O you who believe, when it is said to you, Make room in assemblies, then make room. Allah will make way for you. And when it is said, Come up higher, go up higher, Allah will exalt those who believe among you, and those who have knowledge, to high ranks. Allah is informed of what you do. **12**O you who believe, when you hold a conversation with the messenger, offer alms before your conversation. That is better and purer for you. But if you cannot find, then indeed, Allah is forgiving, merciful. **13**Are you afraid to offer alms before your conversation? Then when you do not do it and Allah has forgiven you, establish prayer and give alms and obey Allah and his messenger. And Allah is aware of what you do. **14**Haven't you seen those who take for friends a people with whom Allah is angry? They are neither of you nor of them, and they knowingly swear a false oath. **15**Allah has prepared for them a dreadful doom. What they are inclined to do is indeed evil. **16**They make a shelter of their oaths and turn from the way of Allah, so theirs will be a shameful doom. **17**Their wealth and their children will not help them at all against Allah. Such people are rightful owners of the Fire, they will remain in it. **18**On the day when Allah will raise them all together, then will they swear to him as they swear to you, and they will imagine that they have some standing. Indeed, is it not they who are the liars? **19**Satan has taken hold of them and so has caused them to forget remembrance of Allah. They are Satan's party. Indeed, is it not Satan's party that will be the losers? **20**Indeed, those who oppose Allah and his messenger, they will be among the lowest. **21**Allah has decreed, Indeed, I truly will conquer, I and my messengers. Indeed, Allah is strong, almighty. **22**You will not find people who believe in Allah and the last day loving those who oppose Allah and his messenger, even though they be their fathers or their sons or their brothers or their tribe. As for such people, he has written faith upon their hearts and has strengthened them with a spirit from him, and he will bring them into gardens under which rivers flow, in which they will remain. Allah is well pleased with them, and they are well pleased with him. They are Allah's party. Indeed, is it not Allah's party that is successful?

---

11. Ibn Kathir attributes to one of Muhammad's companions the statement that this verse "was revealed about gatherings in places where Allah is being remembered. When someone would come to join in assemblies with the Messenger, they would hesitate to offer them space so that they would not lose their places. Allah the Exalted commanded them to spread out and make room for each other."[2]

12. One must pay for the privilege of an audience with the messenger. See 57:10.

19. Those who befriend those who are accursed by Allah are the party of Satan and will suffer in hell (58:17). Those accursed by Allah include Jews and Christians, as per 9:30.

SURA 59

The Exile

Al-Hashr

Introduction

This sura was revealed, according to Islamic tradition, after Muhammad had the Jewish an-Nadir tribe exiled from Medina. The title comes from 59:2.

This is the second of Al-Musabbihat, that is, suras that begin by glorifying Allah. The others are 57, 61, 62, and 64.[1]

---

1 Ibn Kathir, IX. 460.

The Exile

IN THE NAME OF ALLAH, THE COMPASSIONATE, THE MERCIFUL.

1All that is in the heavens and all that is on the earth glorifies Allah, and he is the mighty, the wise. **2**It is he who has caused those among the people of the book who disbelieved to go forth from their homes to the first exile. You did not think that they would go forth, while they thought that their strongholds would protect them from Allah. But Allah reached them from a place they did not expect, and cast terror in their hearts so that they ruined their houses with their own hands and the hands of the believers. So learn a lesson, O you who have eyes. **3**And if Allah had not decreed migration for them, he indeed would have punished them in the world, and in the hereafter theirs is the punishment of the fire. **4**That is because they were opposed to Allah and his messenger, and whoever is opposed to Allah, Allah is indeed stern in reprisal. **5**Any palm-trees you cut down or left standing on their roots, it was by Allah's permission, so that he might frustrate those who are evil. **6**And what Allah gave as spoils to his messenger from them, you did not urge on any horse or camel for the sake of it, but Allah gives his messenger lordship over those whom he wills. Allah is able to do all things. **7**What Allah gives as spoils to his messenger from the people of the towns, it is for Allah and his messenger and for the close relative and the orphans and the needy and the traveler, so that it does not become a commodity between the rich among you. And whatever the messenger gives you, take it. And whatever he forbids, abstain. And keep your duty to Allah. Indeed, Allah is stern in reprisal. **8**And for the poor fugitives who have been driven out of their homes and their belongings, who seek bounty from Allah and help Allah and his messenger. They are the loyal ones. **9**Those who entered the city and the faith before them love those who flee to them for refuge, and find in their hearts no need for what has been given them, but prefer above themselves, though poverty become their lot. And whoever is saved from his own greed,

---

2. Ibn Kathir explains: "When the Messenger of Allah migrated to Al-Madinah, he made a peace treaty with the Jews stipulating that he would not fight them and they would not fight him. They soon betrayed the treaty that they made with Allah's Messenger. Therefore, Allah sent His torment down on them; it can never be averted, and His appointed destiny touched them; it can never be resisted. The Prophet forced them to evacuate and abandon their fortified forts that Muslims did not think they would ever control. The Jews thought that their fortifications will save them from Allah's torment, but they did not help them against Allah in the least. Then, that which they did not expect came to them from Allah, and Allah's Messenger forced them to leave Al-Madinah."[1]
According to the historian Tabari, writing in the tenth century, the betrayal of the treaty was actually a conspiracy to kill Muhammad by some members of the Nadir, a Jewish tribe. Rather than appealing to the Nadir leaders to turn over the guilty men, Muhammad sent word to the Nadir: "Leave my country and do not live with me. You have intended treachery."[2] When the men of the Nadir protested and invoked that covenant, Muhammad's messenger replied: "Hearts have changed, and Islam has wiped out the old covenants."[3]

On "the people of the book who disbelieved," see 2:62, 98:6.
On terror, see 3:151, 8:12, and 8:60.
5. According to Islamic tradition, the Muslims besieged the Nadir's encampment and ordered that the date palms of the Banu Nadir be burned. The Jews, surprised, asked him: "O Muhammad! You used to forbid mischief in the earth and blame those who did it. Why is it that you had the date trees cut down and burned?" On mischief in the earth, see 5:33. This verse justifies the cutting of the trees as "by Allah's permission." It is a common contention of Islamic apologists today that Muhammad devised humane and just rules of warfare that included a prohibition on cutting down trees of the enemy. This verse states otherwise.
6. See 8:41.
8. A hadith has Umar say: "The properties abandoned by Banu Nadir were the ones which Allah bestowed upon His Apostle... These properties were particularly meant for the Holy Prophet...He would meet the annual expenditure of his family from the income thereof, and would spend what remained for purchasing horses and weapons as preparation for Jihad."[4]

such people are those who are successful. **¹⁰**And those who came after them say, Our Lord, forgive us and our brothers who were before us in the faith, and do not place in our hearts any anger toward those who believe. Our Lord, you are full of kindness, merciful. **¹¹**Haven't you observed those who are hypocrites, they tell their brothers who disbelieve among the people of the book, If you are driven out, we will surely go out with you, and we will never obey anyone against you, and if you are attacked, we will indeed help you. And Allah bears witness that they indeed are liars. **¹²**Indeed, if they are driven out, they do not go out with them, and indeed, if they are attacked, they do not help them, and indeed, if they had helped them, they would have turned and fled, and then they would not have been victorious. **¹³**Their fear of you is more intense in their hearts than their fear of Allah. That is because they are a people who do not understand. **¹⁴**They will not fight against you in a body except in fortified villages or from behind walls. Their adversity among themselves is very great. You think of them as a whole, whereas their hearts are varying. That is because they are a people who have no sense. **¹⁵**On the comparison of those a short time before them, they taste the ill-effects of their own conduct, and theirs is painful punishment. **¹⁶**On the comparison of Satan when he tells man

to disbelieve, then, when he disbelieves, says, Indeed, I am free of you, indeed, I fear Allah, the Lord of the worlds. **¹⁷**And the consequences for both will be that they are in the fire, remaining in it. This is the reward of evildoers. **¹⁸**O you who believe, observe your duty to Allah. And let every soul look to what it sends on before for the future. And observe your duty to Allah. Indeed, Allah is informed of what you do. **¹⁹**And do not be like those who forgot Allah, therefore he caused them to forget their souls. Such people are the evildoers. **²⁰**Not equal are the owners of the fire and the owners of the garden. The owners of the garden, they are the victorious. **²¹**If we had caused this Qur'an to descend upon a mountain, you indeed would have seen it humbled, torn apart by the fear of Allah. Such comparisons we make for mankind so that perhaps they may reflect. **²²**He is Allah, other than whom there is no God, the knower of the invisible and the visible. He is the compassionate, the merciful. **²³**He is Allah, other than whom there is no God, the sovereign Lord, the holy one, peace, the keeper of faith, the guardian, the majestic, the compeller, the superb. May Allah be glorified from all that they ascribe as partner. **²⁴**He is Allah, the creator, the shaper out of nothing, the fashioner. His are the most beautiful names. All that is in the heavens and the earth glorifies him, and he is the mighty, the wise.

---

11. The Islamic tradition that Tabari retells continues by saying that some of those whom the Qur'an designates as "hypocrites" urged the Banu Nadir not to go and promised to come to their aid if attacked. Relying on this, the Nadir told Muhammad: "We will not leave our settlements; so do as you see fit."⁵ Displacing

responsibility onto the enemy, Muhammad tells the Muslims, "The Jews have declared war."⁶

22. In this and the two succeeding verses are some of the legendary ninety-nine names of Allah found in Islamic tradition.

SURA 60

She Who Is
to Be Examined

Al-Mumtahana

Introduction

According to Islamic tradition, this sura was revealed after Muhammad
and the Muslims set out to conquer Mecca, and a Muslim named Hatib
bin Abi Balta'ah notified the Meccans of the impending attack because he
had relatives in Mecca. Hatib bin Abi Balta'ah was a veteran of the Battle of Badr, and so Muhammad declined Umar's request for permission
to behead him, saying, "He attended Badr. What can I tell you, perhaps
Allah looked at those who attended Badr and said, 'O the people of Badr,
do what you like, for I have forgiven you.'"[1] But then Muhammad received
this sura, which takes Hatib to task for taking as his friends the enemies
of Allah (60:1) and tells him that his relatives will not help him on the day
of judgment (60:3). He, and Muslims generally, should emulate Abraham's
hatred of his unbelieving relatives, and not his forgiveness of them (60:4).

The sura's name is taken from 60:10.

---

1 Ibn Kathir, IX, 584-5.

She Who Is to Be Examined

IN THE NAME OF ALLAH, THE COMPASSIONATE, THE MERCIFUL.

[1]O you who believe, do not choose my enemy and your enemy for allies. Do you give them friendship when they disbelieve in that truth which has come to you, driving out the messenger and you because you believe in Allah, your Lord? If you have come forth to wage jihad in my way and seeking my good pleasure, do you show friendship to them in secret, when I am best aware of what you hide and what you proclaim? And whoever does this among you, he indeed has strayed from the right path. [2]If they have the upper hand of you, they will be your foes, and will stretch out their hands and their tongues toward you with evil, and they long for you to disbelieve. [3]Your family ties and your children will not help you in any way on the day of resurrection. He will separate you. Allah is the seer of what you do. [4]There is an excellent example for you in Abraham and those with him, when they told their people, Indeed, we are guiltless of you and all that you worship besides Allah. We have done with you. And there has arisen between us and you hostility and hatred forever, until you believe in Allah alone, except what Abraham promised his father, I will ask forgiveness for you, although I own nothing for you from Allah. Our Lord, in you we put our trust, and to you we turn in repentance, and to you is the journeying. [5]Our Lord, do not make us a prey for those who disbelieve, and forgive us, our Lord. Indeed, you, only you, are the mighty, the wise one. [6]Indeed you have in them a good pattern for everyone who looks to Allah and the last day. And whoever may turn away, indeed, still Allah is the absolute, the owner of praise. [7]It may be that Allah will decree love between you and those of them with whom you are at enmity. Allah is mighty, and Allah is forgiving, merciful. [8]Allah does not forbid you to show kindness and deal justly with those who did not make war against you because of religion and did not drive you out of your homes. Indeed, Allah loves those who deal justly. [9]Allah only forbids to make friends of those who made war against you because of religion and have driven

---

1. Here are encapsulated several themes that are also stated elsewhere: the importance of not befriending unbelievers, and the idea that doing so is a sign that one has strayed from the straight path of Islam (cf. 3:28, 4:144, 5:51, 5:80); Islam is the religion of truth (cf. 9:13, 9:29, 9:30); one should wage jihad for the sake of Allah (cf. 4:74, 4:95, 9:41).

4. Abraham's willingness to sacrifice his son (who is again not named) is recounted beginning at 37:102. Allah designates Abraham as an "excellent example," a term applied to the messenger in 33:21, for telling his unbelieving family and people that "there has arisen between us and you hostility and hatred forever, until you believe in Allah alone." However, a specific exception is made: Abraham is *not* an excellent example when he tells his father, "I will ask forgiveness for you." Hatred is held up as exemplary; forgiveness is explicitly declared to be not exemplary, even for unbelieving relatives. See also 9:23, 9:84, 9:113, 29:8, and 31:15.

8. These are, says Ibn Kathir, "those who did not have a role in your expulsion," the expulsion of the Muslims from Mecca.[1]

Maududi explains: "Here a doubt may arise in the minds. It is all right to treat the disbelievers, who are not hostile, kindly, or should only they be treated unjustly? And should the disbelievers, who are hostile, be treated unjustly? The answer is that in this context, the word justice, in fact, has been used in a special sense. It means: 'Justice demands that you should not be hostile to those who are not hostile to you, for it is not justice to treat the enemy and the non-enemy alike. You have every right to adopt a stern attitude towards those who persecuted you for embracing Islam and compelled you to leave your homes and pursued you even after your expulsion. But as for those who were not partners in persecuting you, you should treat them well and should fulfill the right they have on you because of blood and other relationships.'"[2]

Some Islamic scholars today contend that this passage forbids anything but defensive warfare. This claim, however, is difficult to reconcile with 8:39 and 9:29.

you out from your homes and helped to drive you out. Whoever makes friends of them, such people are wrongdoers. **10**O you who believe, when believing women come to you as fugitives, examine them. Allah is best aware of their faith. Then, if you know them to be true believers, do not send them back to the unbelievers. They are not lawful for them, nor are they lawful for them. And give them what they have spent. And it is no sin for you to marry such women when you have given them their dowries. And do not hold to the ties of disbelieving women, and ask for what you have spent, and let them ask for what they have spent. That is the judgment of Allah. He judges between you. Allah is the knower, the wise one. **11**And if any of your wives have gone from you to the unbelievers and afterward you have your turn, then give to those whose wives have gone the equivalent of what they have spent, and keep your duty to Allah in whom you are believers. **12**O prophet, if believing women come to you, taking an oath of allegiance to you that they will ascribe no thing as partner to Allah, and will neither steal nor commit adultery nor kill their children, nor produce any lie that they have devised between their hands and feet, nor disobey you in what is right, then accept their allegiance and ask Allah to forgive them. Indeed, Allah is forgiving, merciful. **13**O you who believe, do not be friendly with a people with whom Allah is angry, who have despaired of the hereafter as the unbelievers despair of those who are in the graves.

---

10. In concluding the treaty of Hudaybiyyah, according to Islamic tradition, Muhammad shocked his men by agreeing to provisions that seemed highly disadvantageous to the Muslims: men fleeing the Quraysh and seeking refuge with the Muslims would be returned to the Quraysh, while men fleeing the Muslims and seeking refuge with the Quraysh would not be returned to the Muslims. But the fears of the companions were soon assuaged. A woman of the Quraysh, Umm Kulthum, joined the Muslims in Medina; her two brothers came to Muhammad, asking that they be returned "in accordance with the agreement between him and the Quraysh at Hudaybiya."³

But Muhammad refused: Allah forbade it. He gave Muhammad a new revelation consisting of this verse, basing the refusal to return Umm Kulthum on the fact that the Muslims had agreed to return any *man* who came to them, not any *woman*. Once the treaty was formally discarded, Islamic jurists enunciated the principle that truces in general could only be concluded on a temporary basis of up to ten years, and that they could only be entered into for the purpose of allowing weakened Muslim forces to gather strength to fight again more effectively. When they were no longer needed, they could be broken.

13. One people "with whom Allah is angry," according to many Islamic authorities, are the Jews (see 1:7).

The Battle Array

As-Saff

Introduction

About this sura, which is traditionally regarded as Medinan, Ibn Kathir ascribes this story to one of the companions of Muhammad: "We asked, 'Who among us should go to the Messenger and ask him about the dearest actions to Allah?' None among us volunteered. The Messenger sent a man to us and that man gathered us and recited this Surah, Surat As-Saff, in its entirety."[1] One of those actions that Allah loves is fighting for his cause in battle array (61:4), from which is derived the name of this sura.

Maududi notes that "it could not be known from any reliable tradition, but a study of its subject-matter shows that this Surah probably was sent down in the period closely following the Battle of Uhud, for by reading between the lines perceives a clear description of the conditions that prevailed in that period."[2] This is a manifestation of the uncertainty that surrounds the origins of much of the Qur'anic material.

This is the third of Al-Musabbihat, that is, suras that begin by glorifying Allah. The others are 57, 59, 62, and 64.[3]

---

1 Ibn Kathir, IX, 612.
2 Maududi, EnglishTafsir.com, http://www.englishtafsir.com/Quran/61/index.html.
3 Ibn Kathir, IX. 460.

The Battle Array

IN THE NAME OF ALLAH, THE COMPASSIONATE, THE MERCIFUL.

¹All that is in the heavens and all that is on the earth glorifies Allah, and he is the mighty, the wise. ²O you who believe, why do you say what you do not know? ³It is most hateful in the sight of Allah that you say what you do not know. ⁴Indeed, Allah loves them who battle for his cause in battle array, as if they were a solid structure. ⁵And when Moses said to his people, O my people, why do you persecute me, when you well know that I am Allah's messenger to you? So when they went astray, Allah led their hearts astray. And Allah does not guide the transgressing people. ⁶And when Jesus son of Mary said, O children of Israel, indeed, I am the messenger of Allah to you, confirming what was before me in the Torah, and bringing good news of a messenger who comes after me, whose name is Ahmad. Yet when he has come to them with clear proofs, they say, This is mere sorcery. ⁷And who does greater wrong than he who invents a lie against Allah when he is summoned to Islam? And Allah does not guide wrongdoing people. ⁸They want to extinguish the light of Allah with their mouths, but Allah will perfect his light, however much the unbelievers hate it. ⁹It is he who has sent his messenger with the guidance and the religion of truth, so that he may make it conqueror of all religion, however much idolaters may hate it. ¹⁰O you who believe, shall I show you a transaction that will save you from a painful doom? ¹¹You should believe in Allah and his messenger, and should wage jihad for the cause of Allah with your wealth and your lives. That is better for you, if only you knew. ¹²He will

---

2. Ibn Kathir says of this passage: "Some said that it was revealed about the gravity of fighting in battle, when one says that he fought and endured the battle, even though he did not do so."[1] He attributes to two companions of Muhammad the interpretation, "This Ayah was sent down to admonish some people who used to say that they killed, fought, stabbed, and did such and such during battle, even though they did not do any of it."[2]

4. Allah loves only the Muslims who fight in his cause; see 4:74, 4:95, 8:39, 8:61, 9:29, 47:4, 47:35. He does not love unbelievers; see 30:45.

5. See 7:179, 10:99, 32:13.

6. The dismissal of Jesus's miracles as "sorcery" recalls similar dismissals of Moses (28:36) and the messenger (28:48).

"Ahmad" means "the Most Praised One," and it is etymologically related to Muhammad, which means "Praised One." Mohammed Marmaduke Pickthall drives the connection home by translating "Ahmad" simply as "Praised One."

Muslims generally understand the verse as depicting Jesus predicting the coming of Muhammad. Many Muslim exegetes contend that this prophecy is the uncorrupted version of the words of Jesus that survive in corrupted form in John 14:16-17, where Jesus says: "And I will pray the Father, and he will give you another Counselor, to be with you forever, even the Spirit of truth, whom the world cannot receive, because it neither sees him nor knows him; you know him, for he dwells with you, and will be in you."

"Counselor" in John's Gospel is *paracletos*, or Paraclete. Some Islamic apologists have claimed that this is a corruption of *periclytos*, which means "famous" or "renowned," i.e., "Praised One." However, there is no textual evidence whatsoever for this. No manuscripts of the New Testament exist that use the word *periclytos* in this place. Nor is it likely that the two words might have been confused. That kind of confusion may be theoretically possible in Arabic, which does not write vowels and hence would present two words with identical consonant structures; the confusion is increased in regard to the Qur'an by the fact that the earliest manuscripts lack the diacritical marks that distinguish many consonants from one another (see 2:2). But Greek does write vowels, and so the words would never in Greek have appeared as even close to identical.

7. This liar is, says Ibn Kathir, "none is more unjust than he who lies about Allah and calls upon rivals and associates partners with Him, even while he is being invited to *Tawhid* [the divine unity] and sincerely worshipping Him."[3]

8. In the words of the *Tafsir al-Jalalayn*, the miscreants want to extinguish "the Law and proofs of Allah" by "saying it is magic, poetry and soothsaying."[4]

9. The idea that Islam will prevail over all other religions is additionally at 2:193, 8:39, and 9:33.

forgive you your sins and bring you into gardens under which rivers flow, and pleasant dwellings in gardens of Eden. That is the supreme victory. **13**And another which you love, help from Allah and present victory. Give good news to believers. **14**O you who believe, be Allah's helpers, even as Jesus son of Mary said to the disciples, Who are my helpers for Allah? They said, We are Allah's helpers. And a group among the children of Israel believed, while a group disbelieved. Then we strengthened those who believed against their enemies, and they gained the upper hand.

---

14. Ibn Kathir here outlines the Muslim view of both Jews and Christians. The Jews "rejected what Isa [Jesus] brought them, denied his prophethood and invented terrible lies about him and his mother. They are the Jews, may Allah curse them until the Day of Judgment."5 The Christians, meanwhile, "exaggerated over Isa, until they elevated him to more than the level of prophethood that Allah gave him. They divided into sects and factions, some saying that Isa was the son of Allah, while others said that he was one in a trinity, and this is why they invoke the father, the son and the holy ghost! Some of them said that Isa was Allah."6

SURA 62

The Friday Congregation

Al-Jumua

Introduction

A hadith has Muhammad's companion Abu Hurairah say: "We were with the Messenger of Allah when Surat Al-Jumuah was revealed, so he recited it until he reached: 'And other among them who have not yet joined them.' A man said to him: 'O Messenger of Allah! Who are these people who have not yet joined us?' But he did not say anything to him."[1] Abu Hurairah continues: "Salman [Al-Farsi] was among us. So the Messenger of Allah placed his hand upon Salman and said: 'By the One in whose Hand is my soul! If faith were on Pleiades then men among these people would reach it.'"[2] On Salman, see 16:103.

This is the fourth of Al-Musabbihat, that is, suras that begin by glorifying Allah. The others are 57, 59, 61, and 64.[3]

---

1 *Jami at-Tirmidhi*, vol. 5, book 44, no. 3310.
2 Ibid.
3 Ibn Kathir, IX. 460.

The Friday Congregation

IN THE NAME OF ALLAH, THE COMPASSIONATE, THE MERCIFUL.

¹All that is in the heavens and all that is on the earth glorifies Allah, the sovereign Lord, the holy one, the mighty one, the wise one. ²It is he who has sent among the unlettered ones a messenger of their own, to recite to them his signs and to make them grow, and to teach them the book and wisdom, though until now they were indeed in clear error, ³Along with others among them who have not yet joined them. He is the mighty, the wise one. ⁴That is the bounty of Allah; which he gives to those whom he wills. Allah is of infinite bounty. ⁵The comparison of those who are entrusted with the Torah, yet do not apply it, is as the comparison of the donkey carrying books. Wretched is the comparison of people who deny the signs of Allah. And Allah does not guide wrongdoing people. ⁶Say, O you who are Jews, if you claim that you are favored of Allah apart from mankind, then long for death if you are truthful. ⁷But they will never long for it because of all that their own hands have sent before, and Allah is aware of evildoers. ⁸Say, Indeed, the death from which you recoil will surely meet you, and afterward you will be returned to the knower of the invisible and the visible, and he will tell you what you used to do. ⁹O you who believe, when the call is heard for the prayer of the day of congregation, haste to the remembrance of Allah and leave your trading. That is better for you, if only you knew. ¹⁰And when the prayer is ended, then disperse in the land and seek Allah's bounty, and remember Allah a great deal, so that you may be successful. ¹¹But when they spot some merchandise or pastime they break away to it and leave you standing. Say, What Allah has is better than pastimes and merchandise, and Allah is the best of providers.

---

2. On the illiteracy of the messenger, see 7:157. The statement, "It is he who has sent among the unlettered ones a messenger of their own" is odd, as it suggests that the messenger was an illiterate who was sent to illiterates. The unlikelihood of this is reinforced by the fact that in classical Arabic, the word translated here as "unlettered ones," *omeyeen*, never referred to illiterates or to illiteracy. It referred, rather, to non-Jewish people, which would mean that this verse is saying that Allah has sent a gentile apostle to the gentiles. *Omeyeen* is an adjectival form of the Arabic noun for gentiles, and not all gentiles were illiterate during the time of Muhammad.

6. This chilling statement has become the springboard for a common theme in contemporary jihadism; see 2:94.

The Hypocrites

Al-Munafiqun

Introduction

This is traditionally regarded as a Medinan sura, based on 63:8; its title comes from 63:1.

The Hypocrites

In the name of Allah, the compassionate, the merciful.

1When the hypocrites come to you, they say, We bear witness that you are indeed Allah's messenger. And Allah knows that you are indeed his messenger, and Allah bears witness that the hypocrites indeed are speaking falsely. **2**They make their faith a pretext so that they may turn from the way of Allah. What they are inclined to do is indeed evil. **3**That is because they believed, then disbelieved, therefore their hearts are sealed so that they do not understand. **4**And when you see them, their outward appearance pleases you, and if they speak, you give ear to their speech, as if they were blocks of wood in striped cloaks. They consider every shout to be against them. They are the enemy, so beware of them. May Allah confound them. How deluded they are. **5**And when it is said to them, Come, the messenger of Allah will ask forgiveness for you, they turn away their faces and you see them turning away, disdainful. **6**Whether you ask forgiveness for them or do not ask forgiveness for them is all the same for them, Allah will not forgive them. Indeed, Allah does not guide the transgressing people. **7**It is they who say: Do not spend on behalf of those with Allah's messenger so that they might disperse, when Allah's are the treasures of the heavens and the earth, but the hypocrites do not understand. **8**They say, Surely, if we return to Medina, the honorable ones will soon drive out the dishonorable, when honor belongs to Allah and to his messenger and to the believers, but the hypocrites do not know. **9**O you who believe, do not let your wealth or your children distract you from the remembrance of Allah. Those who do so, they are the losers. **10**And spend out of what we have provided you with before death comes to one of you and he says, My Lord, if only you would give me a reprieve for a little while, then I would give alms and be among the righteous. **11**But Allah gives no soul a reprieve when its term comes, and Allah is informed of what you do.

---

1. According to Maududi, this revelation came to Muhammad in response to the machinations of one of the leaders of the hypocrites, Abdullah bin Ubayy. When the Jewish Qaynuqa tribe surrendered to the Muslims, some of the Qaynuqa who had made alliances among the Muslims came forward to plead their case before Muhammad. According to Tabari, Muhammad wanted to have all the men of the tribe put to death. However, Abdullah bin Ubayy implored Muhammad: "O Muhammad, deal kindly with my clients."[1] Muhammad ignored him, so Abdullah repeated the request, whereupon the Prophet of Islam turned his face away from Abdullah. Abdullah bin Ubayy then impetuously caught Muhammad by the collar of his robe, whereupon, according to Ibn Hisham, "the apostle was so angry that his face became almost black."[2] Muhammad said to Abdullah, "Confound you, let me go."[3] But Abdullah replied, "No, by God, I will not let you go until you deal kindly with my clients. Four hundred men without mail and three hundred mailed protected me from all mine enemies; would you cut them down in one morning? By God, I am a man who fears that circumstances may change."[4]

The story goes on to note that Muhammad then granted him his request, agreeing to spare the Qaynuqa as long as they turned over their property as booty to the Muslims and left Medina, which they did forthwith. Still, Muhammad was unhappy with the alliance Abdullah had made with the Jewish tribe. It was at this point, according to Islamic tradition, that he received a key revelation about the relationships that should prevail between Muslims and non-Muslims: 5:51.

8. Honor belongs to Allah, the messenger, and the believers, with unbelievers pointedly omitted. Maududi explains the verse this way: "All honor belongs to Allah in virtue of His essence, to the Prophet in virtue of his Prophethood, and to the Believers in virtue of their faith. As for the disbelievers and the wicked people and the hypocrites, they have no share whatever in the real, true honor."[5] This, along with 4:141, is the Qur'anic foundation for the Sharia provision that non-Muslims may not hold authority over Muslims, much less exercise political power, as that would bring them the honor that is due to the believers alone.

9. One's children, like one's parents, should not divert one from the service of Allah (see 9:23, 29:8, 31:15, and 60:4).

The Mutual Disillusion

At-Taghabun

Introduction

Islamic tradition is uncertain of the derivation of this sura. Maududi says: "Muqatil and Kalbi say that it was partly revealed at Makkah and partly at Madinah. Hadrat Abdullah bin Abbas and Ata bin Yasar say that vv. 1–13 were revealed at Makkah and vv. 14–18 at Madinah. But the majority of commentators regard the whole of the surah as a Madinan Revelation. Although there is no internal evidence to help determine its exact period of revelation, yet a study of its subject matter shows that it might probably have been sent down at an early stage at Madinah. That is why it partly resembles the Makkah surahs and partly the Madinan Surahs."[1] This uncertainty is a manifestation of the fact that there is no actual certain evidence regarding the origins of the Qur'an's various chapters.

This is the fifth and last of Al-Musabbihat, that is, suras that begin by glorifying Allah. The others are 57, 59, 61, and 62.[2]

---

1 Maududi, EnglishTafsir.com, http://www.englishtafsir.com/Quran/64/index.html.
2 Ibn Kathir, IX. 460.

The Mutual Disillusion

IN THE NAME OF ALLAH, THE COMPASSIONATE, THE MERCIFUL.

1All that is in the heavens and all that is on the earth glorifies Allah, to him belongs dominion and to him belongs praise, and he is able to do all things. **2**It is he who created you, but one of you is a disbeliever and one of you is a believer, and Allah is the seer of what you do. **3**He created the heavens and the earth with truth, and he shaped you and made your shapes good, and to him is the journeying. **4**He knows all that is in the heavens and the earth, and he knows what you conceal and what you proclaim. And Allah is aware of what is in the hearts. **5**Hasn't the story reached you of those who disbelieved of old and so tasted the evil consequences of their conduct, and theirs will be a painful doom? **6**That was because their messengers kept coming to them with clear proofs, but they said, Shall mere mortals guide us? So they disbelieved and turned away, and Allah was independent. Allah is absolute, the owner of praise. **7**Those who disbelieve claim that they will not be raised again. Say, Yes, indeed, by my Lord, you will be raised again and then you will be informed of what you did, and that is easy for Allah. **8**So believe in Allah and his messenger and the light which we have revealed. And Allah is informed of what you do. **9**The day when he will gather you to the day of gathering, that will be a day of loss and gain. And whoever believes in Allah and does right, he will absolve him of his evil deeds and he will admit him to gardens under which rivers flow, to remain in them forever. That is the supreme victory. **10**But those who disbelieve and deny our revelations, such people are owners of the fire, they will remain in it, a wretched journey's end. **11**No calamity comes except by Allah's permission. And whoever believes in Allah, he guides his heart. And Allah is the knower of all things. **12**Obey Allah and obey his messenger, but if you turn away, then the duty of our messenger is only to convey clearly. **13**Allah, there is no God except him. In Allah, therefore, let believers put their trust. **14**O you who believe, indeed, among your wives and your children there are enemies for you, therefore beware of them. And if you pardon and overlook and forgive, then indeed, Allah is forgiving, merciful. **15**Your wealth and your children are only a temptation, while with Allah

---

1. This sura repeats, yet again, oft-repeated themes: Allah has dominion over all things (64:1); he knows the secrets of every person's heart (64:2, 4); those who reject Allah's messengers will suffer a terrible punishment (64:5-6); they doubt that they will be raised from the grave and judged (64:7), but they will, and the righteous will enter Paradise (64:9) while the damned will go to hell (64:10).

7. On the oath "by my Lord," see 34:3.

9. Instead of "he will admit him," the Warsh Qur'an has "we will admit him."[1]

11. Ibn Kathir puts in the mouth of Ibn Abbas the statement that not only does nothing happen except by Allah's permission, but that nothing happens except "'By the command of Allah,' meaning from His decree and will."[2]

14. The warning that one's enemies may be his own wives and children echoes the warnings previously given about parents (9:23, 29:8, 31:15, 60:4) and children (63:9). Ibn Kathir attributes to Ibn Abbas this explanation: "There were men who embraced Islam in Makkah and wanted to migrate to Allah's Messenger. However, their wives and children refused to allow them. Later when they joined Allah's Messenger, they found that those who were with him (the Companions) have gained knowledge in the religion, so they were about to punish their wives and children"—whereupon Allah counseled them to forgive them.[3]

is an immense reward. [16]So keep your duty to Allah as best you can, and listen, and obey, and spend, that is better for your souls. And whoever is saved from his own greed, such people are the successful. [17]If you lend to Allah a good loan, he will double it for you and will forgive you, for Allah is responsive, merciful, [18]Knower of the invisible and the visible, the mighty, the wise.

The Divorce

At-Talaq

Introduction

Maududi opines that this sura "must have been sent down after those verses of surah Al-Baqarah in which commandments concerning divorce were given for the first time [2:227–241]. Although it is difficult to determine precisely what is its exact date of revelation, yet the traditions in any case indicate that when the people started making errors in understanding the commandments of Surah Al-Baqarah [sura 2], and practically also they began to commit mistakes, Allah sent down these instructions for their correction."[1]

---

1 Maududi, EnglishTafsir.com, http://www.englishtafsir.com/Quran/65/index.html.

The Divorce

IN THE NAME OF ALLAH, THE COMPASSIONATE, THE MERCIFUL.

¹O prophet, when you divorce women, divorce them for their waiting period and calculate the period, and keep your duty to Allah, your Lord. Do not expel them from their houses or let them go forth unless they commit open immorality. These are the limits of Allah, and whoever transgresses Allah's limits, he indeed wrongs his soul. You do not know, it may be that Allah will afterward bring some new thing to pass. **²**Then, when they have reached their term, take them back in kindness or part from them in kindness, and call to witness two just men among you, and keep your testimony upright for Allah. Whoever believes in Allah and the last day is exhorted to act in this way. And whoever keeps his duty to Allah, Allah will appoint a way out for him, **³**And will provide for him from where he does not expect. And whoever puts his trust in Allah, he will be sufficient for him. Indeed, Allah brings his command to pass. Allah has set a measure for all things. **⁴**And for those among your women who are past the age of menstruation, if you doubt, their period will be three months, along with those who do not yet menstruate. And for those who are with child, their period will be until they bring forth their burden. And whoever keeps his duty to Allah, he makes his course easy for him. **⁵**That is the commandment of Allah that he reveals to you. And whoever keeps his duty to Allah, he will absolve him of his evil deeds and magnify reward for him. **⁶**Let them live where you live, according to your wealth, and do not harass them so as to make life difficult for them. And if they are with child, then spend for them until they bring forth their burden. Then, if they are nursing for you, give them their due payment and consult together in kindness, but if you make difficulties for one another, then let some other woman nurse for him. **⁷**Let him who has abundance spend out of his abundance, and he whose provision is measured, let him spend out of what Allah has given him. Allah asks nothing of any soul except what he has given it. Allah will grant ease after hardship. **⁸**And how many a community revolted against the decree of its Lord and his messengers, and we called it to a stern account and punished it with severe punishment, **⁹**So that it tasted the evil consequences of its conduct, and the consequences of its conduct were loss. **¹⁰**Allah has prepared for them stern punishment, so keep your duty to Allah, O men of understanding, O you who believe, now Allah has sent down a reminder to you, **¹¹**A messenger reciting the revelations of Allah made plain to you, so that he may

---

1. In this verse, if a man wishes to divorce his wife, he has to wait through two menstrual cycles to make sure she isn't pregnant first; at 2:228, the waiting period is three menstrual cycles, and at 65:4, the waiting period of three months is specified for "women who are past the age of menstruation."

2. On taking wives back, see 2:228. In a hadith, Muhammad directs that in such a case, the divorced woman would have to consummate a marriage with another man and be divorced by him—only then could she return to her first husband if he wished her to do so: "Rifa'a Al-Qurazi married a lady and then divorced her whereupon she married another man. She came to the Prophet and said that her new husband did not approach her, and that he was completely impotent. The Prophet said (to her), 'No, (you cannot remarry your first husband) till you taste the second husband and he tastes you (i.e. till he consummates his marriage with you).'"[1]

4. The stipulation of the waiting period for "those who do not yet menstruate," assumes that the believers will be marrying, and divorcing, prepubescent girls.

11. Instead of "he will admit him," the Warsh Qur'an has "we will admit him."[2]

bring forth those who believe and do good works from darkness to light. And whoever believes in Allah and does right, he will admit him to gardens under which rivers flow, in which he will remain forever. Allah has made good provision for him.

[12]It is Allah who has created seven heavens, and of the earth the like of them. The commandment comes down among them slowly, so that you may know that Allah is able to do all things, and that Allah encompasses all things in knowledge.

---

12. Ibn Kathir states that this means, "He created seven earths."[3] He cites a hadith that also speaks of "seven earths" and adds: "Those who explained this Hadith to mean the seven continents have brought an implausible explanation that contradicts the letter of the Qur'an and the Hadith without having proof."[4] Maududi says that this verse "does not mean that He created as many earths as the heavens, but it means that He has also created several earths as He has created several heavens...the countless stars and planets seen in the sky are not all lying desolate, but like the earth there are many among them which are inhabited."[5]

SURA 66

The Prohibition

At-Tahrim

Introduction

This sura is traditionally regarded as Medinan. According to Maududi, "This is a very important Surah in which light has been thrown on some questions of grave significance with reference to some incidents concerning the wives of the Holy Prophet."[1] Bell, however, notes: "This surah is very disjointed, and seems to consist of a collection of discarded passages of various dates."[2] Its title comes from 66:1.

---

1 Maududi, EnglishTafsir.com, http://www.englishtafsir.com/Quran/66/index.html.
2 Bell, II, 589.

The Prohibition

In the name of Allah, the compassionate, the merciful.

¹O prophet, Why do you prohibit what Allah has made lawful for you, trying to please your wives? And Allah is forgiving, merciful. ²Allah has made lawful for you absolution from your oaths, and Allah is your protector. He is the knower, the wise one. ³When the prophet confided a fact to one of his wives and when she afterward revealed it and Allah told him about this, he made part of it known and passed over a part. And when he told it to her, she said, Who has told you? He said, The knower, the aware has told me. ⁴If you two turn in repentance to Allah for what your hearts desired, and if you help one another against him, then indeed, Allah, even he, is his protecting friend, and Gabriel and the righteous among the believers, and furthermore the angels are his helpers. ⁵It may happen that his Lord, if he divorces you, will give him in your place wives who are better than you, Muslim, believing, pious, penitent, devout, inclined to fasting, widows and maidens. ⁶O you who believe, ward off from yourselves and your families a fire of which the fuel is men and stones, over which are set angels strong, severe, who do not resist Allah in what he commands them, but do what they are commanded. ⁷O you who disbelieve, make no excuses for yourselves this day. You are only being paid for what you used to do. ⁸O you who believe, turn to Allah in sincere repentance. It may be that your Lord will absolve you of your evil deeds and bring you into gardens under which rivers flow, on the day when Allah will not humiliate the prophet and those who believe with him. Their light will run before them and on their right hands, they will say, Our Lord, perfect our light for us, and forgive us, indeed, you are able to do all things. ⁹O prophet, wage jihad against the unbelievers and the hypocrites, and be stern with them. Gehenna will be their home, an evil

---

4. A ninth-century hadith depicts Ibn Abbas asking Umar: "O Chief of the believers! Who were the two ladies from among the wives of the Prophet to whom Allah said: 'If you two return in repentance (66.4)'?"[1] Umar replied, "I am astonished at your question, O Ibn Abbas. They were Aisha and Hafsa." There is no certainty about this in Islamic tradition; Maududi identifies the two quarreling wives as Saffiyah and Maria the Copt.[2]

The hadith continues by stating that Hafsa, one of Muhammad's wives, had been angering the prophet by talking back to him. So when Umar learned that Muhammad had divorced all his wives, he was not surprised; in fact he was jubilant: "Hafsa is a ruined loser! I expected that would happen some day."[3] Umar explained that "the Prophet did not go to his wives because of the secret which Hafsa had disclosed to Aisha, and he said that he would not go to his wives for one month as he was angry with them when Allah admonished him (for his oath that he would not approach Maria). When twenty-nine days had passed, the Prophet went to Aisha first of all."[4]

The background of this, according to Islamic tradition, is that Hafsa had caught Muhammad in bed with Maria the Copt, on the day he was supposed to spend with Hafsa. Muhammad promised to stay away from Maria and asked Hafsa to keep the matter a secret, but Hafsa told Aisha. Then Allah stepped in with the revelation of the threat in this passage that Muhammad could simply divorce the complaining wives.

This story may have been formulated in order to emphasize Allah's solicitude for Muhammad and the futility of opposing him; see 2:144. However, for those who found this tale too salacious, another ninth-century tradition explains these Qur'an verses as concerning only his wives' jealousy (or perhaps Muhammad's bad breath) and his oath to stop drinking honey. In this case what the Prophet has held forbidden that Allah has made lawful for him would be honey. That is, Muhammad tried to please his consorts by promising to give up honey, and Allah is allowing him to break this oath and threatening the errant wives with divorce, which appears to be somewhat excessive as a punishment.[5]

The wide disparity between these two explanations of this passage, both found in canonical ninth-century hadiths, is another indication of the fact that many of the elements of Muhammad's biography as found in the hadith and sira literature were formulated in order to explain obscure passages of the Qur'an.

9. On "wage jihad," see 2:218. Ibn Kathir explains: "Allah the Exalted orders His Messenger to perform Jihad against the disbelievers and hypocrites, the former with weapons and armaments and the later by establishing Allah's legislated penal code."[6] On Gehenna, see 2:206.

destination. ¹⁰Allah cites an example for those who disbelieve, the wife of Noah and the wife of Lot, who were under two of our righteous slaves, yet betrayed them, so that they did not help them in any way against Allah and it was said, Enter the fire along with those who enter. ¹¹And Allah cites an example for those who believe, the wife of Pharaoh, when she said, My Lord, build for me a home with you in the garden, and deliver me from Pharaoh and his work, and deliver me from evildoing people, ¹²And Mary, the daughter of Imran, whose body was chaste, therefore we breathed into it something of our spirit. And she put faith in the words of her Lord and his books, and was among the obedient.

---

11. On Pharaoh, see also 2:49, 3:11, 7:103, 8:52, 10:75, 14:6, 17:101, 20:24, 23:46, 26:11, 27:12, 28:3, 29:39, 38:12, 40:24, 44:17, 50:13, 51:38, 54:41, 69:9, 73:15, 79:15, 85:18, and 89:10.

12. On "daughter of Imran," see 3:35, 19:28. On "we breathed into it something of our spirit," see 19:20.
Instead of "his books," the Warsh Qur'an has "his book."⁷

The Sovereignty

Al-Mulk

Introduction

According to Maududi, "It could not be known from any authentic tradition when this Surah was revealed, but the subject matter and the style indicate that it is one of the earliest Surahs to be revealed at Makkah."[1]

---

1 Maududi, EnglishTafsir.com, http://www.englishtafsir.com/Quran/67/index.html.

The Sovereignty

In the name of Allah, the compassionate, the merciful.

¹Blessed is he in whose hand is the dominion, and he is able to do all things. ²Who has created life and death so that he might test you to see which of you is best in conduct, and he is the mighty, the forgiving, ³Who has created seven heavens in harmony. You can see no fault in Ar-Rahman's creation, then look again, Can you see any cracks? ⁴Then look again and yet again, your sight will return to you weakened and made dim. ⁵And indeed we have decorated the world's heaven with lamps, and we have made them missiles for the satans, and for them we have prepared the torment of flame. ⁶And for those who disbelieve in their Lord, there is the torment of Gehenna, an evil destination. ⁷When they are flung into it, they hear its roaring as it boils up, ⁸As if it would burst with rage. Whenever a multitude is flung into it, its guards ask them, Didn't a warner come there to you? ⁹They say, Yes, indeed, a warner came to us, but we denied and said, Allah has revealed nothing, you are in nothing but a great error. ¹⁰And they say, If we had been inclined to listen or have sense, we would not have been among those who dwell in the flame. ¹¹So they acknowledge their sins, but those who dwell in the flame are far removed. ¹²Indeed, those who fear their Lord in secret, theirs will be forgiveness and a great reward. ¹³And keep your opinion secret or proclaim it, indeed, he is the knower of all that is in the hearts. ¹⁴Shouldn't he know what he created? And he is the subtle, the aware. ¹⁵It is he who has subjected the earth to you, so walk in its paths and eat of its provisions. And to him will be the resurrection. ¹⁶Have you taken security from him who is in the heaven, so that he will not cause the earth to swallow you when indeed it is convulsed? ¹⁷Or have you taken security from him who is in the heaven, so that he will not let loose a hurricane on you? But you will know the manner of my warning. ¹⁸And indeed those before them denied, then the manner of my wrath. ¹⁹Haven't they seen the birds above them spreading out their wings and closing them? Nothing holds them up except Ar-Rahman. Indeed, he is the seer of all things. ²⁰Or who is he who will be an army to you to help you instead of Ar-Rahman? The unbelievers are in nothing but delusion. ²¹Or who is he who will provide for you if he should withhold his provision? No, but they are set in pride and defiance. ²²Is he who goes groping on his face more rightly guided, or he who walks upright on a straight

---

3. On Ar-Rahman, see 17:110 and 38:5.

5. At this verse there is an abrupt change from the narrative that refers to Allah in the third person (67:1-4) to a first-person plural section; this may indicate some textual dislocation or the combination of two different sources.

Here begins a passage on Allah controls all things and designed his creation perfectly (vv. 1-5); the unbelievers will suffer the pains of hell and will at that point regret having rejected Allah's messengers (vv. 6-11); the righteous shall be rewarded (v. 12); Allah knows what is in everyone's heart (vv. 13-14); Allah sustains all things, and death can come without notice, so it is better to be mindful of Allah

and obey him than to ignore him (vv. 15-22). The sura concludes with Allah giving Muhammad six things to say to the unbelievers in response to their skepticism about whether and when the Day of Judgment will come (vv. 23-30).

The idea of the stars as missiles hurled at the satans manifests a decidedly prescientific world view (see 37:6-10; also 13:2, 22:5, 22:18).

"Flame" is sa'ir, on which see 4:10, as also for 67:10-11.

6. On Gehenna, see 2:206.

19. On Ar-Rahman, see 17:110 and 38:5, as also at 67:20 and 67:29.

road? **²³**Say, It is he who gave you being, and has assigned to you ears and eyes and hearts. You give small thanks. **²⁴**Say, It is he who multiplies you on the earth, and to whom you will be gathered. **²⁵**And they say, When will this promise be, if you are truthful? **²⁶**Say, The knowledge is with Allah alone, and I am just a plain warner, **²⁷**But when they see it near, the faces of those who disbelieve will be distressed, and it will be said, This is what you used to call for. **²⁸**Say, Have you considered, whether Allah causes me and those with me to perish or has mercy on us, still, who will protect the unbelievers from a painful doom? **²⁹**Say, he is Ar-Rahman. In him we believe and in him we put our trust. And you will soon know who it is that is in clear error. **³⁰**Say, Have you thought, If your water were to disappear into the earth, who then could bring you gushing water?

The Pen

Al-Qalam

Introduction

Maududi states: "This too is one of the earliest surahs to be revealed at Makkah, but its subject matter shows that it was sent down at the time when opposition to the Holy Prophet (upon whom be peace) had grown very harsh and tyrannical."[1] The possibility that this opposition stemmed from the nature of the message is not considered.

---

1 Maududi, EnglishTafsir.com, http://www.englishtafsir.com/Quran/68/index.html.

The Pen

IN THE NAME OF ALLAH, THE COMPASSIONATE, THE MERCIFUL.

¹Nun. By the pen and what they write, **²**You are not, for your Lord's favor to you, a madman. **³**And indeed, yours will indeed be an unfailing reward. **⁴**And indeed, you are of an exalted standard of character. **⁵**And you will see and they will see **⁶**Which one of you is the demented. **⁷**Indeed, your Lord is best aware of him who strays from his way, and he is best aware of those who walk rightly. **⁸**Therefore do not obey the rejecters **⁹**Who would have had you compromise, so that they may compromise. **¹⁰**Do not obey each feeble swearer either, **¹¹**Detractor, spreader abroad of slanders, **¹²**Hinderer of the good, transgressor, evildoer, **¹³**Cruel, and what's more, illegitimate. **¹⁴**It is because he has wealth and children **¹⁵**That when our revelations are recited to him, he says, Mere fables of the men of old. **¹⁶**We will brand him on the nose. **¹⁷**Indeed, we have tested them as we tested the owners of the garden when they vowed that they would pluck its fruit the next morning, **¹⁸**And made no exception, **¹⁹**Then a visitation from your Lord came upon it while they slept **²⁰**And in the morning it was as if it had already been plucked. **²¹**And they called out one to another in the morning, **²²**Saying, Run to your field if you would pluck it. **²³**So they went off, saying to one another in low tones, **²⁴**No needy man will enter it today against you. **²⁵**They went early, strong in purpose. **²⁶**But when they saw it, they said, Indeed, we are in error, **²⁷**No, but we are desolate, **²⁸**The best among them said, Didn't I say to you, Why do you not glorify? **²⁹**They said, May our Lord be glorified, Indeed, we have been wrongdoers. **³⁰**Then some of them drew near to others, reproaching themselves. **³¹**They said, Alas for us, in truth we were transgressors. **³²**It may be that our Lord will give us better than this in place of it. Indeed, we beseech our Lord. **³³**That was the punishment. And indeed the punishment of the hereafter is greater, if only they knew. **³⁴**Indeed, for those who keep from evil are gardens of bliss with their Lord. **³⁵**Shall we then treat those who have submitted in the same way that we treat the guilty? **³⁶**What ails you? How foolishly you judge, **³⁷**Or do you have a book in which you learn **³⁸**That you will indeed have everything that you choose? **³⁹**Or do you have a covenant on oath from us that reaches to the day of judgment, so that all that you decree will be yours? **⁴⁰**Ask them which of them will guarantee that, **⁴¹**Or do they have other gods? Then let them bring their other gods if they are truthful **⁴²**On the day when it comes upon them in earnest, and they are ordered to prostrate themselves but are not able, **⁴³**With downcast eyes, humiliation stupefying them. And they had been summoned

---

1. On the "mysterious letters," see 2:1.

2. On Allah consoling and reassuring the messenger, see 2:144.

4. See 33:21. According to a hadith, when asked about Muhammad's character, Aisha answered, "His character was the Qur'an."[1]

15. See 3:37.

16. See 25:5. The messenger's unnamed accuser is a violent, cruel slanderer; Islamic tradition identifies this unfortunate man as al-Walid bin al-Mughira, an opponent of Muhammad from the Quraysh. The *Tafsir al-Jalalayn* informs us that "his nose was cut by a sword during the Battle of Badr."[2]

33. Failure to heed the messenger's words will lead to ruin in both this life and the next (see 2:217, 3:173, 3:200, 9:14).

to prostrate themselves while they were still unhurt. **⁴⁴**Leave me with those who give the lie to this pronouncement. We will lead them on by steps from where they do not know. **⁴⁵**Yet I bear with them, for indeed, my scheme is firm. **⁴⁶**Or do you ask for a fee from them so that they are heavily taxed? **⁴⁷**Or is the unseen theirs so that they can write? **⁴⁸**But wait for your Lord's decree, and do not be like the companion of the fish, who cried out in despair. **⁴⁹**If it had not been that favor from his Lord had reached him, he would surely have been cast into the wilderness while he was reprobate. **⁵⁰**But his Lord chose him and placed him among the righteous. **⁵¹**And indeed, those who disbelieve want to disconcert you with their eyes when they hear the reminder, and they say, Indeed, he is truly mad, **⁵²**When it is nothing other than a reminder to creation.

---

48. The "companion of the fish" is Jonah; see 10:87.

51. They were, says the *Tafsir al-Jalalayn*, "looking at you harshly with a look which nearly fells you—when they hear the Reminder (the Qur'an) and say—out of envy that he is mad, because of the Qur'an which he brought—'He is quite mad.'"[3]

SURA 69

The Inevitable

Al-Haqqa

Introduction

"This too," says Maududi, "is one of the earliest surahs to be revealed at Makkah. Its subject matter shows that it was sent down at the time when opposition to the Holy Prophet (upon whom be peace) had started but had not yet become tyrannical."[1]

A hadith depicts Umar recounting that before he became a Muslim, he entered a mosque and stood behind Muhammad as he recited this sura. "I was amazed," Umar is made to recall, "by the way in which the Qur'an was composed. I said: By Allah, this man is a poet as Quraish said."[2] But at that moment, Muhammad recited the denial that the Qur'an is the work of a poet, at 69:40–41. Amazed, Umar decided Muhammad was a soothsayer and then heard the denial of this at 69:41. He concluded: "Then I felt an overwhelming attraction to Islam."[3] The title comes from 69:1–3.

1 Maududi, EnglishTafsir.com, http://www.englishtafsir.com/Quran/69/index.html.
2 Musnad Ahmad, 107, https://sunnah.com/ahmad:107.
3 Ibid.

The Inevitable

In the name of Allah, the compassionate, the merciful.

¹The inevitable. ²What is the inevitable? ³And what will convey unto you what the inevitable is? ⁴Thamud and Aad disbelieved in the judgment to come. ⁵As for Thamud, they were destroyed by lightning. ⁶And as for Aad, they were destroyed by a fierce roaring wind, ⁷Which he imposed on them for seven long nights and eight long days so that you would have seen men lying overthrown, as if they were hollow trunks of palm-trees. ⁸Can you see any remnant of them? ⁹And Pharaoh and those before him, and the communities that were destroyed, brought error, ¹⁰And they disobeyed the messenger of their Lord, therefore he seized them with a tightening grip. ¹¹Indeed, when the waters rose, we carried you upon the ship ¹²So that we might make it a memorial for you, and that remembering ears might remember. ¹³And when the trumpet will sound one blast ¹⁴And the earth with the mountains will be lifted up and crushed with one crash, ¹⁵Then, on that day the event will come. ¹⁶And the heaven will split asunder, for that day it will be frail. ¹⁷And the angels will be on its sides, and eight will hold up the throne of your Lord that day, above them. ¹⁸On that day you will be exposed, not a secret of yours will be hidden. ¹⁹Then, as for him who is given his record in his right hand, he will say, Take, read my book. ²⁰Surely I knew that I would have to meet my reckoning. ²¹Then he will be in blissful state ²²In a high garden ²³In which the clusters are in easy reach. ²⁴Eat and drink at ease for what you sent on before you in past days. ²⁵But as for him who is given his record in his left hand, he will say, If only I had not been given my book ²⁶And did not know what my reckoning was. ²⁷If only it had been death. ²⁸My wealth has not helped me, ²⁹My power has gone from me. ³⁰Take him and shackle him ³¹And then roast him in the blaze ³²And then insert him in a chain of which the length is seventy cubits. ³³Indeed, he used not to believe in Allah the mighty, ³⁴And did not encourage the feeding of the needy. ³⁵Therefore he has no friend here this day, ³⁶Nor any food except *ghislin*, ³⁷Which no one but sinners eat. ³⁸But no, I swear by all that you see ³⁹And all that you do not see ⁴⁰That it is indeed the speech of an illustrious messenger. ⁴¹It is not the speech of a poet. Little is it that you believe. ⁴²Nor soothsayer's speech. Little is it that you remember. ⁴³It is a revelation from the Lord of the worlds. ⁴⁴And if he had invented false sayings about us, ⁴⁵We surely would have taken

---

4. On Thamud and Aad, see 25:38.

9. On Pharaoh, see also 2:49, 3:11, 7:103, 8:52, 10:75, 14:6, 17:101, 20:24, 23:46, 26:11, 27:12, 28:3, 29:39, 38:12, 40:24, 44:17, 50:13, 51:38, 54:41, 66:11, 73:15, 79:15, 85:18, and 89:10.

11. On Noah, see also 7:59, 10:71, 11:25, 21:76, 23:23, 25:37, 26:105, 29:14, 37:75, 50:12, 51:46, 53:52, 54:9, 57:26, and 71:1.

31. "The blaze" is *al-jahim*, about which see 5:10.

36. Some scholars believe *ghislin* is a foreign word; in any case, its meaning is unclear even to the Islamic exegetes. The ninth-century historian Ibn al-Kalbi interprets *ghislin* as "what exudes from the bodies of the inmates of the Fire (i.e. Hell)."[1] Ibn Kathir records that while most authorities generally agree with Ibn al-Kalbi, saying, "It will be the worst food of the people of the Hellfire," or it "will be the blood and fluid that will flow from their flesh," or "the pus of the people of the Hellfire," there is also the conjecture that "it is a tree in Hell."[2]

him by the right hand ⁴⁶And then severed his aorta, ⁴⁷And not one of you could have held us off from him. ⁴⁸And indeed, it is a justification to those who fear Allah. ⁴⁹And indeed, we know that some among you will deny. ⁵⁰And indeed, it is indeed anguish for the unbelievers. ⁵¹And indeed, it is absolute truth. ⁵²So glorify the name of your mighty Lord.

---

46. The messenger did not invent this; if he had, Allah would sever his aorta. According to a hadith, Aisha says that Muhammad in his final illness exclaimed: "O Aisha! I still feel the pain caused by the food I ate at Khaibar, and at this time, I feel as if my aorta is being cut from that poison."[3] At the oasis of Khaibar, according to Islamic tradition, Muhammad massacred the Jews and was then poisoned by a Jewish woman he had enslaved and pressed into service as a cook.

The Ascending Stairways

Al-Ma'arij

Introduction

Maududi states: "The subject matter bears evidence that this Surah too was sent down in conditions closely resembling those under which Surah Al Haaqqah [sura 69] was sent down."[1] The title is taken from 70:3.

---

1 Maududi, EnglishTafsir.com, http://www.englishtafsir.com/Quran/70/index.html.

The Ascending Stairways

IN THE NAME OF ALLAH, THE COMPASSIONATE, THE MERCIFUL.

¹A questioner questioned concerning the doom about to fall ²Upon the unbelievers, which no one can repel, ³From Allah, Lord of the ascending stairways ⁴The angels and the spirit ascend to him in a day of which the span is fifty thousand years. ⁵But be patient with a patience good to see. ⁶Indeed, they see it far off ⁷While we see it near, ⁸The day when the sky will become as molten copper, ⁹And the hills become as flakes of wool, ¹⁰And no familiar friend will ask a question of his friend ¹¹Though they will be given sight of them. The guilty man will long to be able to ransom himself from the punishment of that day at the price of his children ¹²And his wife and his brother ¹³And his relatives that harbored him ¹⁴And all that are in the earth, if then it might deliver him. ¹⁵But no, for indeed, it is a flame ¹⁶Eager to roast, ¹⁷It calls him who turned and fled, ¹⁸And hoarded and withheld it. ¹⁹Indeed, man was created anxious, ²⁰Fretful when evil comes upon him ²¹And when good comes upon him, grudging, ²²Except worshippers. ²³Who are constant at their prayer ²⁴And in whose wealth there is an acknowledged right ²⁵Of the beggar and the destitute, ²⁶And those who believe in the day of judgment, ²⁷And those who are fearful of their Lord's doom— ²⁸Indeed, the torment of their Lord is before which no one can feel secure ²⁹And those who preserve their chastity ³⁰Except with their wives and those whom their right hands possess, for thus they are not blameworthy, ³¹But whoever seeks more than that, those are the ones who are transgressors, ³²And those who keep their trusts and their covenants, ³³And those who stand by their testimony ³⁴And those who are attentive at their prayer. ³⁵These people will dwell in gardens, honored. ³⁶What ails those who disbelieve, that they keep staring toward you, open-eyed, ³⁷On the right and on the left, in groups? ³⁸Does every man among them hope to enter the garden of delight? ³⁹No, truly, indeed, we created them from what they know. ⁴⁰But no, I swear by the Lord of the rising-places and the setting-places of the planets that we indeed are able ⁴¹To replace them by those who are better than them. And we are not to be surpassed. ⁴²So let them chat and play until they meet their day which they are promised, ⁴³The day when they come forth from the graves in haste, as if racing to a goal, ⁴⁴With eyes aghast, humiliation stupefying them, such is the day which they are promised.

---

3. The "ascending stairways," according to the *Tafsir al-Jalalayn*, are the means "by which the angels go up, meaning the heavens."[1]

4. Ibn Kathir explains, attributing the statement to a companion of Muhammad, that these are "creatures from the creation of Allah that resemble humans but they are not humans."[2] Jesus is a "spirit from Allah" in 4:171 and ascends to paradise at 3:55.

15. "Flame" is *laza*, which Zamakhshari, attributing the tradition to Ibn Abbas, identifies as the level of hell reserved for those who dedicated their lives to "serving the Fire," which presumably means dedicating their lives to activities that were sinful and turned people away from Allah.[3]

30. On "those whom their right hands possess," see 4:3, 4:24, 23:6, 33:50.

32. See 8:58, 9:1-5.

40. On the oath, "I swear by the Lord of the rising-places and the setting-places of the planets," see 34:3.

SURA 71

Noah

Nuh

Introduction

Maududi states: "This also is one of the earliest Surahs to be revealed at Makkah, but the internal evidence of its subject matter shows that it was sent down in the period when opposition to the Holy Prophet's message of Islam by the disbelievers of Makkah had grown very strong and active."[1] It is noteworthy that Maududi says that many other suras also were revealed at a time of furious opposition to the Islamic message. Bell notes that a "change of rhyme" at 71:5 shows that the sura "is not a unity in composition."[2] The title comes from 71:1.

---

1 Maududi, EnglishTafsir.com, http://www.englishtafsir.com/Quran/71/index.html.
2 Bell, II, 607.

Noah

IN THE NAME OF ALLAH, THE COMPASSIONATE, THE MERCIFUL.

1Indeed, we sent Noah to his people, Warn your people before the painful doom comes to them. **2**He said, O my people, indeed, I am a plain warner to you **3**Serve Allah and keep your duty to him and obey me, **4**So that he may forgive you some of your sins and give you a respite for an appointed term. Indeed, the term of Allah, when it comes, cannot be delayed, if only you knew. **5**He said, My Lord, indeed, I have called to my people night and day **6**But all my calling only makes them flee farther from me, **7**And indeed, whenever I call to them so that you might forgive them, they thrust their fingers in their ears and cover themselves with their clothes and persist and magnify themselves in pride. **8**And indeed, I have called to them aloud, **9**And indeed, I have made public proclamation to them, and I have appealed to them in private. **10**And I have said, Ask forgiveness from your Lord. Indeed, he has always been forgiving. **11**He will let loose the sky for you in abundant rain, **12**And will help you with wealth and sons, and will assign gardens to you and will assign rivers to you. **13**What ails you that you do not hope for dignity toward Allah

14When he created you by stages? **15**Don't you see how Allah has created seven heavens in harmony, **16**And has made the moon a light in it, and made the sun a lamp? **17**And Allah has caused you to grow as a growth from the earth, **18**And afterward he makes you return to it, and he will bring you forth again, a bringing forth. **19**And Allah has made the earth a wide expanse for you **20**That you may go around in it on broad roads. **21**Noah said, My Lord, indeed, they have disobeyed me and followed one whose wealth and children increase him in nothing except ruin, **22**And they have plotted a mighty plot, **23**And they have said, Do not forsake your gods. Do not forsake Wadd, or Suwa, or Yaghuth and Ya'uq and Nasr. **24**And they have led many astray, and you increase the wrongdoers in nothing except error. **25**Because of their sins they were drowned, then made to enter a fire. And they found they had no helpers in place of Allah. **26**And Noah said, My Lord, do not leave one of the unbelievers in the land. **27**If you leave them, they will mislead your slaves and will breed only lewd ingrates. **28**My Lord, forgive me and my parents and him who enters my house believing, and believing men and believing women, and do not increase the wrongdoers in anything except ruin.

---

1. On Noah, see also 7:59, 10:71, 11:25, 21:76, 23:23, 25:37, 26:105, 29:14, 37:75, 50:12, 51:46, 53:52, 54:9, 57:26, and 69:11.

2. Here again there are strong parallels between Noah's message and reception, and the message and reception of the messenger. As at 11:25 and 26:115, Noah is a "plain warner," as is the messenger: see 7:106, 15:89, 22:49, 29:50, 38:70, 46:9, 51:50-51, 67:26.

12. Allah will reward the believers in this world (see 3:139 and 3:200).

15. Like the messenger, Noah invokes the signs of Allah's power in creation.

23. A hadith attributes to Ibn Abbas the observation that "All the idols which were worshiped by the people of Noah were worshiped

by the Arabs later on.... The names (of the idols) formerly belonged to some pious men of the people of Noah, and when they died Satan inspired their people to prepare and place idols at the places where they used to sit, and to call those idols by their names. The people did so, but the idols were not worshiped till those people (who initiated them) had died and the origin of the idols had become obscure, whereupon people began worshiping them."[1]

26. The unbelievers do not deserve to live, for they will mislead the believers.

28. See 9:14

The Jinn

Al-Jinn

Introduction

According to a hadith, this sura was revealed when a group of jinns, puzzled that they could no longer hear what was happening in paradise, happened to hear Muhammad recite the Qur'an. "This is the thing," they said to each other, "which has intervened between you and the news of the Heavens."[1] Then they returned home and proclaimed 72:1–14. See also 46:29. The title comes from 72:1.

---

1 Bukhari, vol. 6, book 65, no. 4921.

The Jinn

In the name of Allah, the compassionate, the merciful.

[1]Say, It is revealed to me that a company of the jinn gave ear, and they said, Indeed, we have heard a marvelous Qur'an, [2]Which guides to righteousness, so we believe in it and we ascribe no partner to our Lord. [3]And that he, exalted be the glory of our Lord, has taken neither wife nor son, [4]And that the foolish one among us used to speak an atrocious lie about Allah. [5]And indeed, we had assumed that mankind and jinn would not speak a lie about Allah [6]And indeed, individual men used to invoke the protection of individual jinn, so that they increased them in transgression, [7]And indeed, they assumed, even as you assume, that Allah would not raise anyone [8]And we had sought the heaven but had found it filled with strong guards and meteors. [9]And we used to sit on places in it to listen. But he who listens now finds a flame in wait for him, [10]And we do not know whether harm is intended for all who are on the earth, or whether their Lord intends guidance for them. [11]And among us there are righteous people and among us there are those who are far from that. We are sects having different rules. [12]And we know that we cannot escape from Allah on the earth, nor can we escape by fleeing. [13]And when we heard the guidance, we believed in it, and whoever believes in his Lord, he fears neither loss nor oppression. [14]And there are some among us who have become Muslims, and there are some among us who are unjust. And whoever has become Muslim has taken knowingly taken the right path. [15]And as for those who are unjust, they are firewood for Gehenna. [16]If they tread the right path, we will give them water to drink in abundance [17]So that we may test them by it, and whoever turns away from the remembrance of his Lord, he will thrust him into ever-growing torment. [18]And the places of worship are only for Allah, so do not pray to anyone along with Allah. [19]And when the slave of Allah stood up in prayer to him, they crowded upon him, almost stifling. [20]Say, I pray to Allah only, and ascribe no partner to him. [21]Say, Indeed, I control neither harm nor benefit for you. [22]Say, Indeed, no one can protect me from Allah, nor can I find any refuge besides him [23]But conveyance from Allah and his messages, and whoever disobeys Allah and his messenger, indeed, his is fire of Gehenna, in which such people dwell forever. [24]Until they see what they are promised, but then they will know who is weaker in allies and less in multitude. [25]Say, I do not know whether what you are promised is near, or if my Lord has set a distant term for it. [26]The knower of the unseen, and he reveals

---

2. See 2:193, 4:31, 4:48, 6:21, 9:30.

3. See 6:100, 6:101, 9:30, 10:68, 17:40, 17:111, 18:4, 19:35, 19:88, 21:26, 25:2, 37:149, 39:4, 43:16, 43:81, 52:39, 53:21.

15. On Gehenna, see 2:206, as also at 72:23.

16. Once again that obedience to Allah brings earthly prosperity, specifically rain, as in 71:11.

18. Ibn Kathir ascribes this explanation to a companion of Muhammad: "Whenever the Jews and Christians used to enter their churches and synagogues, they would associate partners with Allah. Thus, Allah commanded His Prophet to tell them that they should single Him out alone for worship."[1]

20. Instead of "say," the Warsh Qur'an has "he said."[2]

his secret to no one, ²⁷Except to every messenger whom he has chosen, and then he makes a guard go before him and a guard behind him ²⁸So that he may know that they have indeed conveyed the messages of their Lord. He surrounds all their doings, and he keeps track of all things.

---

27. Instead of, "Except to every messenger whom he has chosen," the Shi'ite Bankipur Qur'an manuscript has a Persian preface stating that Abdullah ibn Masud's Qur'an read: "Except to every messenger or imam or deputy with whom he is satisfied."³ See 2:59 and the Appendix: Two Apocryphal Shi'ite Suras.

The Covered One

Al-Muzzammil

Introduction

Islamic tradition holds this to be a Meccan sura, although Maududi says of 73:20 that "although many of the commentators have expressed the opinion that this too was sent down at Makkah, yet some other commentators regard it as a Madani Revelation."[1] Also, Barth observes that "this sura cannot belong among the older of the Meccan ones, for the command to get up at night and recite the Koran (verse 4) already presupposes the existence in writing of a number of suras."[2]

The title comes from 73:1.

---

1 Maududi, EnglishTafsir.com, http://www.englishtafsir.com/Quran/73/index.html.

2 J. Barth, "Studies Contributing to Criticism and Exegesis of the Koran," in Ibn Warraq, ed., *What the Koran Really Says* (Amherst, New York: Prometheus, 2002), 405.

The Covered One

In the name of Allah, the compassionate, the merciful.

1O you wrapped up in your cloak, **2**Keep vigil all night long, except for a little, **3**Half of it, or a little less, **4**Or add to it, and recite the Qur'an at a measured pace, **5**For we will throw upon you a weighty word. **6**Indeed, the vigil of the night is when perception is keener and speech more certain. **7**Indeed, by day you have prolonged occupation. **8**So remember the name of your Lord and devote yourself with a complete devotion, **9**Lord of the East and the West, there is no God except him, so choose him alone for your defender, **10**And bear what they say with patience, and depart from them with courtesy. **11**Leave me to deal with the deniers, lords of ease and comfort, and give them respite for awhile. **12**Indeed, with us are heavy chains and a raging fire, **13**And food that chokes, and a painful doom **14**On the day when the earth and the hills rock, and the hills become a heap of running sand. **15**Indeed, we have sent a messenger to you as a witness against you, just as we sent a messenger to Pharaoh. **16**But Pharaoh rebelled against the messenger, whereupon we seized him with a severe seizure. **17**Then how, if you disbelieve, will you protect yourselves on the day that will turn children grey, **18**The very heaven being then torn asunder? His promise is to be fulfilled. **19**Indeed, this is a reminder. Let him who will, then, choose a way to his Lord. **20**Indeed, your Lord knows how you keep vigil sometimes nearly two-thirds of the night, or half, or a third of it, as do a group of those with you. Allah measures the night and the day. He knows that you do not count it, and turns to you in mercy. Recite, then, from the Qur'an what is easy for you. He knows that there are sick people among you, while others travel in the land in search of Allah's bounty, and others are fighting for the cause of Allah. So recite from it what is easy, and establish prayer and give alms, and lend Allah a good loan. Whatever good you send before you for your souls, you will find it with Allah, better and greater in the recompense. And seek forgiveness of Allah. Indeed, Allah is forgiving, merciful.

---

1. The *Tafsir al-Jalalayn* explains: "This is a reference to the Prophet, may Allah bless him and grant him peace, meaning the one wrapped up in his garment when Revelation came to him, out of fear of it and because of his great awe for it."[1]

15. According to Bell, the passage that begins here is "unconnected" to what comes before and after it, "being addressed to the people, not to the prophet, and probably come from some other place."[2]

On Pharaoh, see also 2:49, 3:11, 7:103, 8:52, 10:75, 14:6, 17:101, 20:24, 23:46, 26:11, 27:12, 28:3, 29:39, 38:12, 40:24, 44:17, 50:13, 51:38, 54:41, 66:11, 69:9, 79:15, 85:18, and 89:10.

20. The believers should read as much of the Qur'an as is easy for them, as Allah knows they're busy with jihad, or some may be ill or traveling. Ibn Kathir marvels that "this entire Surah was revealed in Makkah even though fighting was not legislated until after it was revealed. Thus, it is among the greatest of the signs of prophethood, because it informs about unseen matters of the future."[3]

The Cloaked One

Al-Muddaththir

Introduction

According to Maududi, citing numerous early authorities, the first seven verses of sura 74 "are the very earliest verses of the Qur'an to be revealed to the Holy Prophet."[1] However, he adds, that "the Muslim *Ummah* almost unanimously agreed" that the earliest revelation Muhammad received was 96:1–5.[2] Then, he says, Muhammad received no revelations for quite some time, until finally "he started going early to the tops of the mountains to throw himself down from them. But whenever he stood on the edge of a peak, the Angel Gabriel would appear and tell him that he was Allah's Prophet."[3] 74:8–56 was revealed, Maududi says, later in the Meccan period. Bell largely agrees, saying that "this surah contains a number of early passages of varying rhyme loosely fitted together."[4] The title comes from 74:1.

---

1 Maududi, EnglishTafsir.com, http://www.englishtafsir.com/Quran/74/index.html.
2 Ibid.
3 Ibid.
4 Bell, II, 616.

The Cloaked One

IN THE NAME OF ALLAH, THE COMPASSIONATE, THE MERCIFUL.

¹O you wrapped in your cloak, ²Arise and warn. ³Your Lord magnify, ⁴Your clothing purify, ⁵Shun pollution. ⁶And do not show favor, seeking worldly gain. ⁷For the sake of your Lord, be patient. ⁸For when the trumpet sounds, ⁹Surely that day will be a day of anguish, ¹⁰Not of ease, for unbelievers. ¹¹Leave me with him whom I created lonely, ¹²And then bestowed upon him ample means, ¹³And sons living in his presence ¹⁴And made it smooth for him. ¹⁵Yet he wants me to give more. ¹⁶No, for indeed, he has been stubborn to our revelations. ¹⁷On him I will impose a fearful doom. ¹⁸For indeed, he considered, then he planned. ¹⁹He is destroyed, how he planned. ²⁰Again, he is destroyed, how he planned. ²¹Then he looked, ²²Then he frowned and showed displeasure. ²³Then he turned away in pride ²⁴And said, This is nothing but sorcery from of old, ²⁵This is nothing but the speech of mortal man. ²⁶I will throw him to *saqar*. ²⁷What will convey to you what *saqar* is? ²⁸It leaves nothing, it spares nothing ²⁹It shrivels a man. ³⁰Above it are nineteen. ³¹We have appointed only angels to be wardens of the fire, and their number we have made to be a stumbling-block for those who disbelieve, so that those to whom the book has been given may have certainty, and that believers may increase in faith, and so that those to whom the book has been given and believers may not doubt, and so that those in whose hearts there is disease, and unbelievers, may say, What does Allah mean by this comparison? In this way Allah sends astray those whom he wills, and he guides those whom he wills. No one knows the multitudes

---

1. Ibn Kathir attributes this tradition to Ibn Abbas: "Verily, Al-Walid bin Al-Mughirah prepared some food for the Quraysh. So when they had eaten from it he said, 'What do you have to say about this man?' Some of them said, 'He is a magician.' Others said, 'He is not a magician.' Then some of them said, 'He is a soothsayer.' But others said, 'He is not a soothsayer.' Some of them said, 'He is a poet.' But others said, 'He is not a poet.' Some of them said, 'This is magic from that of old.' Thus, they eventually all agreed that it was magic from ancient times. Then, when this news reached the Prophet, he became grieved, covered his head and wrapped himself up. This is when Allah revealed" this verse.[1] On al-Walid bin al-Mughirah, see 68:16.

6. One is not to seek "worldly gain," but the spoils of war are not considered to be such. See 8:41.

26. On *saqar*, see 54:48.

30. This could be a fragment of what was originally a longer and clearer statement. Neither this verse nor any other states explicitly what there are "nineteen" of, or what these nineteen are exactly "over." Ibn Kathir enunciates the traditional Islamic view when he states that these are "the first of the guardians of Hell. They are magnificent in (their appearance) and harsh in their character."[2] While this interpretation is possible, this cryptic verse has become the foundation for numerous elaborate flights of Islamic numerology, attempting to show that this verse contains a hidden number-based key that demonstrates the Qur'an's miraculous character. The verse has also led to the development of a mysticism surrounding the number nineteen—such that some have opined, despite the many nominees for the role of "twentieth hijacker," that there is no such person, and the number of nineteen hijackers was chosen for the September 11, 2001, jihad missions because of the mystical significance of the number.

31. The twentieth-century Qur'an scholar Günter Lüling observes that 74:1-30 "is composed in a very homogeneous form, in that every verse has the same rhythmic style and approximate length of, on average, three to four words (indicating its having originally been a strophic text)."[3] This lengthy verse breaks the pattern of the line-length and rhythm, such that, Lüling notes, "Islamic Koran scholarship has...classified this over-length-verse 74.31 as a late insertion into an earlier text." According to those Islamic scholars, the editing took place during Muhammad's life, originating "in the Medinan period of the Prophet's activities as against his earlier Meccan period."[4] In any case, it is clear evidence that the original text has been altered.

This verse appears to have been inserted here because of its reference to the number of angels, so as to explain what is being numbered in the previous verse. The goal is to demonstrate the truth of the Qur'an, showing the people of the book that, as Ibn Kathir puts it, Muhammad "speaks according to the same thing that they have with them of heavenly revealed Scriptures that came to the Prophets before him."[5] But ultimately Allah is absolutely sovereign regarding who will accept Muhammad's message and who doesn't; see 7:179, 10:99, and 32:13.

of your Lord except him. This is nothing but a reminder to mortals. **32**No, by the moon **33**And the night when it withdraws **34**And the dawn when it shines forth, **35**Indeed, this is one of the greatest **36**As a warning to men, **37**To him among you who will advance or hang back. **38**Every soul is a pledge for its own deeds, **39**Except those who will stand on the right hand. **40**In gardens they will ask one another **41**About the guilty: **42**What has brought you to *saqar*? **43**They will answer, We were not among those who prayed **44**Nor did we feed the needy. **45**We used to wade with waders, **46**And we used to deny the day of judgment, **47**Until the inevitable came to us. **48**The mediation of no mediators will help them then. **49**Why now turn they away from the warning, **50**As if they were frightened donkeys **51**Fleeing from a lion? **52**No, but every one of them wants to be given open pages. **53**No, indeed. They do not fear the hereafter. **54**No, indeed. Indeed, this is a warning. **55**So whoever wills may be mindful. **56**And they will not be mindful unless Allah wills. He is the fountain of fear. He is the fountain of mercy.

42. See 74:26.
56. Instead of "they will not be mindful," the Warsh Qur'an has "you will not be mindful."6

The Resurrection

Al-Qiyama

Introduction

According to Maududi, "Although there is no tradition to indicate its period of revelation, yet there is in the subject matter of this Surah an internal evidence, which shows that it is one of the earliest Surahs to be sent down at Makkah."[1] The title comes from 75:1.

---

1 Maududi, EnglishTafsir.com, http://www.englishtafsir.com/Quran/75/index.html.

The Resurrection

In the name of Allah, the compassionate, the merciful.

1No, I swear by the day of resurrection, **2**No, I swear by the accusing soul. **3**Does man think that we will not assemble his bones? **4**Yes, indeed. We are able to restore his very fingers. **5**But man wants to deny what is before him. **6**He asks, When will this day of resurrection be? **7**But when sight is confounded **8**And the moon is eclipsed **9**And the sun and the moon are united, **10**On that day man will call out, Where to flee? **11**Alas, no refuge. **12**To your Lord is the recourse that day. **13**On that day, man is told the story of what he has sent before and left behind. **14**Rather, man will be a witness against himself, **15**Although he offers his excuses. **16**Do not try to hasten it with your tongue. **17**Indeed, upon us the putting together of it and the reading of it. **18**And when we read it, follow the reading, **19**Then indeed, upon us is its explanation. **20**No, but you love this fleeting world **21**And neglect the hereafter. **22**That day faces will be shining, **23**Looking toward their Lord, **24**And on that day other faces will be despondent, **25**You will know that some great disaster is about to fall upon them. **26**No, but when one's life comes up to the throat **27**And men say, Where is the wizard? **28**And he knows that it is the parting, **29**And agony is heaped on agony, **30**To your Lord that day will be the driving. **31**For he neither trusted, nor prayed. **32**But he denied and flouted. **33**Then went he to his people joyfully. **34**Nearer to you and nearer, **35**Again, nearer to you and nearer. **36**Do you think that man is to be left aimless? **37**Was he not a drop of fluid which gushed forth? **38**Then he became a clot, then he shaped and fashioned **39**And made of him a pair, the male and female. **40**Isn't he able to bring the dead to life?

---

1. On the oath here and in the next verse, see 34:3 and 50:1. These are, however, more precisely non-oaths. Ibn Kathir explains that "if the thing that is being sworn about is something that is being negated, then it is permissible to use the word 'La' (Nay) before the oath to emphasize the negation. Here, what is being sworn about is the affirmation of the final abode and the refutation against the claim of the ignorant that the resurrection of bodies will not occur. This is why Allah says, 'Nay! I swear by the Day of Resurrection. And nay! I swear by An-Nafs Al-Lawwamah.' Qatadah said, 'This means, I swear by both of these things.'"[1] How or why Allah would need to swear by something that of necessity must be incomparably lesser than himself is once again left unexplained.

16. The *Tafsir al-Jalalayn* says that Allah is warning the prophet not to "hasten the Qur'an before Jibril finishes conveying it, out of fear that you may lose some of it."[2] Allah will make sure he remembers it, as Ibn Kathir says: "Allah would make sure to collect it in his chest, and He would make it easy for him to recite it in the same way that it was revealed to him."[3] This passage doesn't discuss the possibility that Allah might cause some parts of the Qur'an to be forgotten, as mentioned in 2:106.

37. See 22:5.

SURA 76

The Man

Al-Insan

Introduction

Maududi notes a disagreement among Islamic exegetes regarding this sura: "Most of the commentators, including Allama Zamakhshari, Imam Razi, Qadi, Baidawi, Allama Nizam ad-Din Nisaburi, Hafiz Ibn Kathir and many others, regard it as a Makki Surah, and, according to Allama Alusi, the same is the opinion of the majority of scholars. However, some commentators hold the view that the Surah was revealed at Madinah, and some others say that it was revealed at Makkah but vv. 8–10 of it were sent down at Madinah."[1] This is another indication of how uncertainties and possible interpolations in the Qur'anic text have been noticed even by Islamic scholars. The title comes from 76:1.

---

1 Maududi, EnglishTafsir.com, http://www.englishtafsir.com/Quran/76/index.html.

The Man

IN THE NAME OF ALLAH, THE COMPASSIONATE, THE MERCIFUL.

1Has there come upon man any period of time in which he was an unremembered thing? **2**Indeed, we create man from a drop of thickened fluid to test him, so we make him hearing, knowing. **3**Indeed, we have shown him the way, whether he is grateful or disbelieving. **4**Indeed, we have prepared for unbelievers manacles and shackles and a raging fire. **5**Indeed, the righteous will drink of a cup of which the mixture is of camphor, **6**A spring of which the slaves of Allah drink, making it gush forth abundantly, **7**They perform the vow and fear a day of which the evil is widespread, **8**And feed the needy with food, the orphan and the prisoner, for love of him, **9**We feed you, for the sake of Allah alone. We wish for no reward nor thanks from you, **10**Indeed, we fear from our Lord a day of frowning and of fate. **11**Therefore Allah has warded off from them the evil of that day, and has made them find brightness and joy, **12**And has awarded them for all that they endured, a garden and silk clothing, **13**Reclining in it on couches, they will find there neither sun nor bitter cold. **14**Its shade is close upon them and its clustered fruits bow down. **15**Goblets of silver are brought around for them, and goblets of crystal **16**Crystal but silver, which they have measured to the measure. **17**There are they watered with a cup of which the mixture is of ginger, **18**A spring in it, named Salsabil. **19**There wait on them immortal youths, whom, when you see them, you would take them for scattered pearls. **20**When you look, you will see bliss and high estate there. **21**Their clothing will be fine green silk and gold brocade. They will wear bracelets of silver. Their Lord will quench their thirst with a pure drink. **22**Indeed, this is a reward for you. Your endeavor has found acceptance. **23**Indeed, we, and we alone, have revealed to you the Qur'an, a revelation, **24**So submit patiently to your Lord's command, and do not obey any guilty one or disbeliever among them. **25**Remember the name of your Lord in the morning and evening. **26**And worship him some of the night. And glorify him through the long night. **27**Indeed, these people love fleeting life, and put a grievous day behind them. **28**We, and we alone, created them, and strengthened their form. And when we will, we can replace them, bringing others like them instead of them. **29**Indeed, this is a warning, that whoever wills may choose a way to his Lord. **30**Yet you will not, unless Allah wills. Indeed, Allah is the knower, the wise one. **31**He makes those whom he wills to enter his mercy, and for evildoers has prepared a painful doom.

---

15. Bell states that this verse and the following one "are really unintelligible. Perhaps a gloss has become mixed with the text."[1]
18. "Salsabil" does not appear to be Arabic; Bell says that "the origin of this name is quite unknown."[2]

19. See 52:24, 56:17.
21. "Gold brocade" is *istabraq*, from the Syriac *istabarg*, "silk brocade."[3]

Those That Are Sent

Al-Mursalat

Introduction

A hadith asserts that this was the last sura Muhammad ever recited. A companion of Muhammad is depicted as saying: "I heard the Prophet reciting Surat-al-Mursalat Urfan (77) in the Maghrib [sunset] prayer, and after that prayer he did not lead us in any prayer till he died."[1] Another adds that as soon as he had finished reciting it, "suddenly a snake sprang at us and the Prophet said (ordered us): 'Kill it.' We ran to kill it but it escaped quickly. The Prophet said, 'It has escaped your evil and you too have escaped its evil.'"[2] The title comes from 77:1.

---

1 Bukhari, vol. 5, book 64, no. 4429.
2 Bukhari, vol. 3, book 28, no. 1830.

Those That Are Sent

IN THE NAME OF ALLAH, THE COMPASSIONATE, THE MERCIFUL.

[1]By those that are gently sent, [2]By the raging hurricanes, [3]By those that cause earth's vegetation to revive; [4]By those who winnow with a winnowing, [5]By those who bring down the reminder, [6]To excuse or to warn, [7]Surely what you are promised will come. [8]So when the stars are put out, [9]And when the sky is torn asunder, [10]And when the mountains are blown away, [11]And when the messengers are brought to their appointed time, [12]For what day is the appointed time? [13]For the day of sorting. [14]And what will convey to you what the day of sorting is? [15]Woe to the repudiators on that day. [16]Didn't we destroy the former people, [17]Then caused the later people to follow after? [18]In this way do we always deal with the guilty. [19]Woe to the repudiators on that day. [20]Didn't we create you from a base fluid [21]Which we laid up in a safe place [22]For a known term? [23]In this way we arranged. How excellent is our arranging. [24]Woe to the repudiators on that day. [25]Haven't we made the earth a lodging [26]Both for the living and the dead, [27]And placed on it high mountains and given you sweet water to drink in it? [28]Woe to the repudiators on that day. [29]Depart to what you used to deny, [30]Depart to the shadow falling threefold, [31]No relief nor shelter from the flame. [32]Indeed, it throws up sparks like the castles, [33]As if they were yellow camels. [34]Woe to the repudiators on that day. [35]This is a day on which they do not speak, [36]Nor are they permitted to put forth excuses. [37]Woe to the repudiators on that day. [38]This is the day of sorting, we have brought you and the men of old together. [39]If now you have any wit, outwit me. [40]Woe to the repudiators on that day. [41]Indeed, those who kept their duty are amid shade and fountains, [42]And such fruits as they desire. [43]Eat, drink and welcome, O you blessed, in return for what you did. [44]In this way we reward those who are good. [45]Woe to the repudiators on that day. [46]Eat and take your ease a little. Indeed, you are guilty. [47]Woe to the repudiators on that day. [48]When it is said to them: Bow down, they do not bow down. [49]Woe to the repudiators on that day. [50]In what statement, after this, will they believe?

---

1. Bell states that an alternative reading of this verse is, "By those that are sent one after the other." He explains: "The passage is usually interpreted as referring to angels in their various activities, but more probably it is the winds bringing up the storm clouds which give the picture of approaching doom."[1] Ibn Kathir records considerable disagreement among Islamic authorities over whether "the winds" or the "the angels" is meant, as well as attempts to harmonize the two interpretations.[2]

6. Referring to the two readings he offers for 77:1, Bell says that this verse "is not very intelligible on either interpretation, and is probably a later insertion."[3]

13. See 44:40. This is repeated at 77:14 and 77:38, as well as at 78:17.

15. This is the focus and refrain of this sura, repeated at 77:19, 77:24, 77:28, 77:34, 77:37, 77:40, 77:45, 77:47, and 77:49.

The News

An-Naba

Introduction

Maududi states of suras 75 through 79 that "all these seem to have been revealed in the earliest period at Makkah."[1] The title comes from 78:2.

---

1 Maududi, EnglishTafsir.com, http://www.englishtafsir.com/Quran/78/index.html.

The News

IN THE NAME OF ALLAH, THE COMPASSIONATE, THE MERCIFUL.

[1]What do they question one another about? [2]About the awful news, [3]Concerning which they are in disagreement. [4]No, but they will come to know. [5]No, again, but they will come to know. [6]Haven't we made the earth an expanse, [7]And the high hills bulwarks? [8]And we have created you in pairs, [9]And have appointed your sleep for repose, [10]And have appointed the night as a cloak, [11]And have appointed the day for livelihood. [12]And we have built above you seven strong, [13]And have appointed a dazzling lamp, [14]And have sent down from the rainy clouds abundant water, [15]By which to produce grain and plant, [16]And gardens of thick foliage. [17]Indeed, the day of sorting is a fixed time, [18]A day when the trumpet is blown and you come in multitudes, [19]And the heaven is opened and becomes as gates, [20]And the mountains will vanish, becoming like a mirage. [21]Indeed, Gehenna lurks in ambush, [22]A home for the rebellious. [23]They will remain in it for ages.

[24]In it they will taste neither coolness nor drink [25]Except boiling water and pus, [26]Proportionate reward. [27]For indeed, they did not look for a reckoning; [28]They called our revelations false with strong denial. [29]We have recorded everything in a book. [30]So taste. We do not give you any increase except of torment. [31]Indeed, for the righteous is achievement, [32]Enclosed gardens and vineyards, [33]And large-breasted women of equal age, [34]And a full cup. [35]There they will never hear useless talk, or lying [36]Repayment from your Lord, a gift in payment, [37]Lord of the heavens and the earth, and what is between them, Ar-Rahman; with whom no one can converse. [38]On the day when the angels and the spirit stand arrayed, they do not speak, except for him whom Ar-Rahman allows and who speaks rightly. [39]That is the true day. So whoever wills should seek recourse to his Lord. [40]Indeed, we warn you of a doom at hand, a day on which a man will look on what his own hands have sent before, and the disbeliever will call out, If only I were dust.

---

17. See 44:40, 77:13-14, 77:38.
21. On Gehenna, see 2:206.
33. Ibn Kathir attributes this interpretation to several early Muslims: "This means round breasts. They meant by this that the breasts of these girls will be fully rounded and not sagging, because they will be virgins, equal in age. This means that they will only have one age."[1] See 36:55, 44:54, and 55:56.
37. On Ar-Rahman, see 17:110 and 38:5.

Those Who Drag Forth

An-Naziat

Introduction

Islamic tradition regards this sura, like the others in this section, as an early Meccan sura. According to Bell, "the variation in the rhymes shows that this surah is not a unity."[1] The title comes from 79:1.

---

1 Bell, II, 532.

Those Who Drag Forth

In the name of Allah, the compassionate, the merciful.

1By those who drag forth to destruction, **2**By the meteors rushing, **3**By the lone stars floating, **4**By the angels hastening, **5**And those who govern the event, **6**On the day when the first trumpet sounds, **7**And the second follows it, **8**On that day hearts beat painfully **9**While eyes are downcast. **10**They are saying, Will we really be restored to our first state **11**Even after we are crumbled bones? **12**They say, Then that would be a useless proceeding. **13**Surely it will need just one shout, **14**And indeed, they will be awakened. **15**Has the history of Moses come to you? **16**How his Lord called him in the holy valley of Tuwa, **17**Go to Pharaoh, indeed, he has rebelled, **18**And say, Do you want to be purified? **19**Then I will guide you to your Lord and you shall fear. **20**And he showed him the mighty sign. **21**But he denied and disobeyed, **22**Then he turned away in haste, **23**Then he gathered and summoned **24**And proclaimed, I am your Lord the most high. **25**So Allah seized him as an example for the after and for the former. **26**Indeed, in this is truly a lesson for him who fears. **27**Are you harder to create, or is the heaven that he built? **28**He raised its height and put it in order, **29**And he made dark its night, and he brought forth its morning. **30**And after that he spread out the earth, **31**And produced from it its water and its pasture, **32**And he made fast the hills, **33**A provision for you and for your cattle. **34**But when the great disaster comes, **35**The day when man will call to mind his endeavor, **36**And the blaze will be visible to him who sees, **37**Then, as for him who rebelled **38**And chose the life of this world, **39**Indeed, the blaze will be his home. **40**But as for him who feared to stand before his Lord and restrained his soul from lust, **41**Indeed, the garden will be his home. **42**They ask you about the hour, When will it happen? **43**Why? What do you have to say about it? **44**To your Lord belongs its term. **45**You are just a warner to him who fears it. **46**On the day when they see it, it will be as if they had but remained only an evening or the morning of it.

---

1. On the oaths in this verse and the following ones, see 34:3 and 50:1. Why Allah needs to back up his own words with an oath on anything is again left unexplained.

15. On Moses and Pharaoh, see also 3:11, 7:103, 8:52, 10:75, 14:6, 17:101, 20:24, 23:46, 26:11, 27:12, 28:3, 29:39, 38:12, 40:24, 44:17, 50:13, 51:38, 54:41, 66:11, 69:9, 73:15, 85:18, and 89:10.

16. See 20:12.

36. "The blaze" is *al-jahim*, about which see 5:10, as also for 79:39.

SURA 80

He Frowned

Abasa

Introduction

Maududi explains: "The commentators and traditionists are unanimous about the occasion of the revelation of this Surah. According to them, once some big chiefs of Makkah were sitting in the Holy Prophet's assembly and he was earnestly engaged in trying to persuade them to accept Islam. At that very point, a blind man, named Ibn Umm Maktum, approached him to seek explanation of some point concerning Islam. The Holy Prophet (upon whom be peace) disliked his interruption and ignored him. Thereupon Allah sent down this Surah. From this historical incident the period of the revelation of this Surah can be precisely determined."[1] The title comes from 80:1.

---

1 Maududi, EnglishTafsir.com, http://www.englishtafsir.com/Quran/80/index.html.

He Frowned

IN THE NAME OF ALLAH, THE COMPASSIONATE, THE MERCIFUL.

[1]He frowned and turned away [2]Because the blind man came to him. [3]What could inform you that he might not grow [4]Or be mindful and so the reminder might help him? [5]As for him who thinks himself independent, [6]To him you pay regard. [7]Yet it is not your concern if he doesn't grow. [8]But as for him who comes to you with earnest purpose [9]And has fear, [10]From him you are distracted. [11]No, but indeed it is a warning, [12]So let whoever wills pay heed to it, [13]On honored leaves [14]Exalted, purified, [15]By scribes [16]Noble and righteous. [17]Man is destroyed, how ungrateful. [18]From what thing does he create him? [19]From a drop of seed he creates him and proportions him, [20]Then makes the way easy for him, [21]Then causes him to die, and buries him; [22]Then, when he wills, he brings him again to life. [23]No, but he hasn't done what he commanded him. [24]Let man consider his food, [25]How we pour water in showers [26]Then split the earth in clefts [27]And cause the grain to grow on it [28]And grapes and green herbs [29]And olive trees and palm trees [30]And gardens of thick foliage [31]And fruit and fodder, [32]Provision for you and your cattle. [33]But when as-sakhkhah comes [34]On the day when a man flees from his brother [35]And his mother and his father [36]And his wife and his children, [37]Every man that day will have concern enough to make him heedless. [38]On that day faces will be bright as dawn, [39]Laughing, rejoicing at good news, [40]And other faces, on that day, with dust upon them, [41]Veiled in darkness, [42]Those are the unbelievers, the wicked.

---

1. The one who frowned and turned away is generally understood in Islamic tradition to be the messenger. The Qur'an frequently tells Muslims to obey the messenger (3:32, 3:132, 4:13, 4:59, 4:69, 4:80, 5:92, 8:1, 8:20, 8:46, 9:71, 24:47, 24:51, 24:52, 24:54, 24:56, 33:33, 47:33, 49:14, 58:13, 64:12) and offers him as an "excellent example" for the conduct of individual Muslims (33:21), yet it also takes for granted that he is capable of sin, an element of his character that has dropped out of Muslim piety regarding Muhammad.

In yet another oddity involving the speaker and audience of the Qur'an, the sura begins by speaking of the messenger in the third person, although elsewhere in the Qur'an Allah usually addresses his prophet directly, with a few notable exceptions.

28. Qadb is a word of uncertain meaning; Ibn Warraq states that it denotes "probably 'green herbs' of some kind," and that is how it is rendered here.[1]

31. The word rendered "fodder" here is abb, another word of uncertain meaning. According to Jeffery, "The early authorities in Islam were puzzled by the word as is evident from the discussion by Tabari on the verse, and the uncertainty evidenced by Zamakhshari and Baydawi in their comments, an uncertainty which is shared by the Lexicons."[2]

33. There is uncertainty in Islamic tradition about what exactly as-sakhkhah is; it is not a clear Arabic word. Ibn Kathir offers several opinions, which he attributes to companions of Muhammad: "Ibn Abbas said, 'As-Sakhkhah is one of the names of the Day of Judgement that Allah has magnified and warned His servants of.' Ibn Jarir said, 'Perhaps it is a name for the blowing into Trumpet.' Al-Baghawi said, 'As-Sakhkhah means the thunderous shout of the Day of Judgement. It has been called this because it will deafen the ears. This means that it pierces the hearing to such an extent that it almost deafens the ears."[3]

The Folding Up

At-Takwir

Introduction

Maududi states that "the subject matter and the style clearly show that it is one of the earliest Surahs to be revealed at Makkah."[1] Bell notes that "the imagery is largely derived from Christian Apocalyptic, with adaptations to Arab ideas."[2]

A hadith depicts Muhammad saying: "Whoever wishes to look at the Day of Judgement as if he is seeing it with his own eyes, then let him read" this sura, along with suras 82 and 84.[3] The title comes from 81:1.

---

1 Maududi, EnglishTafsir.com, http://www.englishtafsir.com/Quran/81/index.html.
2 Bell, II, 638.
3 Ibn Kathir, X, 370.

The Folding Up

IN THE NAME OF ALLAH, THE COMPASSIONATE, THE MERCIFUL.

¹When the sun is folded up, ²And when the stars fall, ³And when the hills are moved, ⁴And when the camels big with young are abandoned, ⁵And when the wild beasts are herded together, ⁶And when the seas rise, ⁷And when souls are reunited, ⁸And when the girl child who was buried alive is asked ⁹For what sin she was killed, ¹⁰And when the pages are laid open, ¹¹And when the sky is torn away, ¹²And when the blaze is lit, ¹³And when the garden is brought near, ¹⁴Every soul will know what it has made ready. ¹⁵No, I swear by those that recede, ¹⁶That run and hide, ¹⁷By the night departing, ¹⁸And the morning breathing, ¹⁹That this is in truth the word of an honored messenger, ²⁰Mighty, established in the presence of the Lord of the throne, ²¹To be obeyed, and trustworthy, ²²And your comrade is not mad. ²³Surely he saw him on the clear horizon. ²⁴And he does not withhold knowledge of the unseen. ²⁵Nor is this the utterance of an outcast satan. ²⁶Where then are you going? ²⁷This is nothing other than a reminder to creation, ²⁸To those of you who determine to walk straight. ²⁹And you will not, unless Allah wills, the Lord of creation.

---

2. In a hadith, Ubayy bin Ka'b, a companion of Muhammad, is depicted as saying: "Six signs will take place before the Day of Judgement. The people will be in their marketplaces when the sun's light will go away. When they are in that situation, the stars will be scattered. When they are in that situation, the mountains will fall down upon the face of the earth, and the earth will move, quake and be in a state of mixed-up confusion. So the Jinns will then flee in fright to the humans and the humans will flee to the Jinns. The domestic beasts, birds and wild animals will mix together, and they will surge together in a wave (of chaos)."[1]

8. Ibn Kathir explains that this refers to "the female infant that the people of the pre-Islamic time of ignorance would bury in the dirt due to their hatred of girls. Therefore, on the Day of Judgment, the female infant will be asked what sin she committed that caused here [sic] to be murdered. This will be a means of frightening her murderer."[2] He attributes to a companion of Muhammad the statement: "She will ask, meaning she will demand restitution for her blood."[3] Ibn Kathir also relates a hadith in which Muhammad is asked about "interruption of sexual intercourse to prevent the male discharge from entering the womb of the woman," and he replies, "That is the minor infanticide and it is the female infant buried alive (Maw'udah) that will be questioned."[4]

12. "The blaze" is *al-jahim*, about which see 5:10.

15. The *Tafsir al-Jalalayn* explains that what is being referred to here and in the following verses are "the five planets: Saturn, Jupiter, Mars, Venus, and Mercury."[5] He says that "those that recede" and "run and hide" refers to the impression that the planets "appear to move backwards, in that sometimes you will see a planet at the end of a constellation and then it will go back to the beginning of it. They hide themselves when they go into occultation in various places, at which time they are no longer visible."[6]

29. See 7:179, 10:99, and 32:13.

The Cleaving

Al-Infitar

Introduction

Maududi notes: "This Surah and the Surah At-Takwir [81] closely resemble each other in their subject matter. This shows that both were sent down in about the same period."[1] The title comes from 82:1.

---

1 Maududi, EnglishTafsir.com, http://www.englishtafsir.com/Quran/82/index.html.

The Cleaving

IN THE NAME OF ALLAH, THE COMPASSIONATE, THE MERCIFUL.

[1]When the heaven is torn asunder, [2]When the planets are dispersed, [3]When the seas burst forth, [4]And the tombs are overturned, [5]A soul will know what it has sent before and what it has left behind. [6]O man, what has made you unconcerned about your Lord, the bountiful one, [7]Who created you, then fashioned, then proportioned you? [8]Into whatever form he wills, he casts you. [9]No, but you deny the judgment. [10]Indeed, there are guardians above you, [11]Generous and recording, [12]Who know what you do. [13]Indeed, the righteous will truly be in delight. [14]And indeed, the wicked will truly be in blaze. [15]They will burn in it on the day of judgment, [16]And will not be absent from it. [17]And what will convey to you what the day of judgment is? [18]Again, what will convey to you what the day of judgment is? [19]A day on which no soul has any power at all for any other soul. The command on that day belongs to Allah.

---

3. The meaning here, says Bell, is "uncertain."[1] That uncertainty is reflected in Islamic tradition. Ibn Kathir offers several interpretations, attributing each to a different companion of Muhammad: "Ali bin Abi Talhah reported from Ibn Abbas that he said, 'Allah will cause some of it to burst forth over other parts of it.' Al-Hasan said, 'Allah will cause some parts of it to burst forth over other parts of it, and its water will go away.' Qatadah said, 'Its fresh water will mix with its salt water.'"[2]

10. These are, according to the *Tafsir al-Jalalayn*, "angels who record actions."[3]

14. "Blaze" is *jahim*, about which see 5:10.

19. On that dreadful day, "no soul has any power at all for any other soul." Everyone will stand alone before Allah; no intercession from others will be accepted (2:123, 6:94, 23:101, 39:43, 42:46). However, the Qur'an elsewhere accepts intercession with Allah's permission (10:3, 20:109, 21:28, 34:23, 53:26).

The Defrauders

Al-Mutaffifin

Introduction

"The style of the Surah and its subject matter," says Maududi, "clearly show that it was revealed in the earliest stage at Makkah, when surah after surah was being revealed to impress the doctrine of the Hereafter on the people's minds."[1] The title comes from 83:1.

---

1 Maududi, EnglishTafsir.com, http://www.englishtafsir.com/Quran/83/index.html.

The Defrauders

IN THE NAME OF ALLAH, THE COMPASSIONATE, THE MERCIFUL.

¹Woe to the defrauders, ²Those who, when they take the measure from mankind, demand it in full, ³But if they measure or weigh for them, they cause them loss. ⁴Don't such men realize that they will be raised again ⁵To an awful day, ⁶The day when mankind stands before the Lord of the worlds? ⁷No, but the record of the vile is in *sijjin*, ⁸And what will convey to you what *sijjin* is? ⁹A written record. ¹⁰Woe to the repudiators on that day. ¹¹Those who deny the day of judgment ¹²Which no one denies except every criminal transgressor, ¹³Who, when you read our signs to him, says, Fables of the men of old. ¹⁴No, but what they have earned is rust upon their hearts. ¹⁵No, but surely on that day they will be screened off from their Lord. ¹⁶Then indeed, they will truly burn in the blaze, ¹⁷And it will be said, This is what you used to deny.

¹⁸No, but the record of the righteous is in *illiyyin*, ¹⁹And what will convey to you what *illiyyin* is? ²⁰A written record, ²¹Attested by those who are brought near. ²²Indeed, the righteous truly are in delight, ²³On couches, gazing, ²⁴You will know in their faces the radiance of delight. ²⁵They are given to drink of a pure wine, sealed, ²⁶The seal of which is musk, for this let those strive who strive for bliss, ²⁷And mixed with water of *tasnim*, ²⁸A spring from which those brought near drink. ²⁹Indeed, the guilty used to laugh at those who believed, ³⁰And wink at one another when they passed them, ³¹And when they returned to their own people, they returned joking, ³²And when they saw them, they said, Indeed, these people have gone astray. ³³Yet they were not sent as guardians over them. ³⁴This day it is those who believe who have the laugh of unbelievers, ³⁵On high couches, gazing. ³⁶Aren't the unbelievers paid for what they used to do?

---

7. *Sijjin* is not an Arabic word; nor is it a recognizable word from any other language. This passage is unclear, as *sijjin* is first identified as the place where the "record of the vile" is stored (it is "in *sijjin*") and then, almost immediately afterward, as that record itself (*sijjin* is "a written record" in 83:9).[1]

16. "The blaze" is *al-jahim*, about which see 5:10.

18. The meaning of *illiyyin* is unclear. Ibn Kathir asserts that it is "the opposite of Sijjin," and depicts a companion of Muhammad explaining that while *sijjin* is "the seventh earth and in it are the souls of the disbelievers," *illiyyin* is "the seventh heaven and it contains the souls of the believers."[2]

27. On *tasnim*, Bell states that "the meaning and derivation of this word are also unknown."[3]

The Splitting Asunder

Al-Inshiqaq

Introduction

Says Maududi, "This too is one of the earliest Surahs to be revealed at Makkah."[1] The title comes from 84:1.

---

1 Maududi, EnglishTafsir.com, http://www.englishtafsir.com/Quran/84/index.html.

The Splitting Asunder

IN THE NAME OF ALLAH, THE COMPASSIONATE, THE MERCIFUL.

¹When the heaven is split asunder ²And attentive to her Lord as it ought to be, ³And when the earth is spread out ⁴And has thrown out all that was in her, and is empty ⁵And attentive to her Lord in fear, ⁶You, indeed, O man, are working toward your Lord a work that you will meet. ⁷Then whoever is given his account in his right hand ⁸He indeed will receive an easy reckoning ⁹And will return to his people in joy. ¹⁰But whoever is given his account behind his back, ¹¹He surely will invoke destruction ¹²And be thrown to scorching fire. ¹³He indeed lived joyously with his people, ¹⁴He indeed thought that he would never return. ¹⁵No, but indeed, his Lord is always looking on him. ¹⁶So I swear by the afterglow of sunset, ¹⁷And by the night and all that it enshrouds, ¹⁸And by the moon when she is full, ¹⁹That you will journey on from layer to layer. ²⁰What ails them, then, that they do not believe ²¹And when the Qur'an is recited to them, do not fall prostrate? ²²No, but those who disbelieve will deny, ²³And Allah knows best what they are hiding. ²⁴So give them tidings of a painful doom, ²⁵Except those who believe and do good works, for theirs is an unfailing reward.

---

7. See 21:47.

19. Bell states that "the meaning is uncertain; the phrase is usually interpreted as, 'ye will experience one state after another.' Some read the verb in the singular, making it refer to the prophet.

It seems to me to refer to generations or communities rising, as it were, on the ruins of previous ones."[1]

20. Bell sees the passage beginning here as a later addition.[2]

The Constellations

Al-Buruj

Introduction

According to Maududi, "The subject matter itself indicates that this Surah was sent down at Makkah in the period when persecution of the Muslims was at its climax and the disbelievers of Makkah were trying their utmost by tyranny and coercion to turn away the new converts from Islam."[1] The title comes from 85:1.

---

1 Maududi, EnglishTafsir.com, http://www.englishtafsir.com/Quran/85/index.html.

The Constellations

In the name of Allah, the compassionate, the merciful.

1By the heaven, holding the constellations, **2**And by the promised day. **3**And by the witness and that to which he bears witness, **4**The owners of the ditch were destroyed **5**From the fuel-fed fire, **6**When they sat by it, **7**And were themselves the witnesses of what they did to the believers. **8**They had nothing against them except that they believed in Allah, the mighty, the owner of praise, **9**Him to whom belongs the dominion of the heavens and the earth, and Allah is the witness of all things. **10**Indeed, those who persecute believing men and believing women and do not repent, the torment of Gehenna will indeed be theirs, and theirs the torment of burning. **11**Indeed, those who believe and do good works, theirs will be gardens under which rivers flow. That is the great success. **12**Indeed, the punishment of your Lord is severe. **13**Indeed, it is he who produces, then reproduces, **14**And he is the forgiving, the loving, **15**Lord of the throne of glory, **16**The doer of what he wills. **17**Has there come to you the story of the armies **18**Of Pharaoh and Thamud? **19**No, but those who disbelieve live in denial **20**And Allah, all unseen, surrounds them. **21**No, but it is a glorious Qur'an. **22**On a preserved tablet.

---

4. Ibn Kathir explains: "This is information about a group of people who were among the disbelievers. They went after those among them who believed in Allah and they attempted to force them to give up their religion. However, the believers refused to recant, so they dug a ditch for them in the ground. Then they lit a fire in it and prepared some fuel for it in order to keep it ablaze. Then they tried to convince them (the believers) to [apostatize] from their religion (again), but they still refused them. So they threw them into the fire."[1]

10. On Gehenna, see 2:206.

18. On Pharaoh, see also 3:11, 7:103, 8:52, 10:75, 14:6, 17:101, 20:24, 23:46, 26:11, 27:12, 28:3, 29:39, 38:12, 40:24, 44:17, 50:13, 51:38, 54:41, 66:11, 69:9, 73:15, 79:15, and 89:10. On the people of Thamud, see also 11:61, 14:9, 17:59, 22:42, 26:141, 27:45, 29:38, 38:13, and 40:31.

22. Ibn Kathir explains "the preserved tablet" as "meaning, among the most high gathering, guarded from any increase, decrease, distortion, or change."[2] See also 13:39 and 43:4.

The Morning Star

At-Tariq

Introduction

Maududi asserts that "The style of its subject matter resembles that of the earliest Surahs revealed at Makkah," but once again, "this surah was sent down at a stage when the disbelievers of Makkah were employing all sorts of devices and plans to defeat and frustrate the message of the Qur'an and Muhammad."[1] The title is taken from 86:1–2.

---

1 Maududi, EnglishTafsir.com, http://www.englishtafsir.com/Quran/86/index.html.

The Morning Star

In the name of Allah, the compassionate, the merciful.

¹By the heaven and the morning star ²And what will tell you what the morning star is? ³The piercing star. ⁴No human soul lacks a guardian over it. ⁵So let man consider from what he is created. ⁶He is created from a gushing fluid ⁷Proceeding from between the backbone and the ribs. ⁸Indeed, he truly is able to return him ⁹On the day when hidden thoughts will be searched out. ¹⁰Then will he have no power nor any helper. ¹¹By the heaven that gives the returning rain, ¹²And the earth that splits

¹³Indeed, this is a conclusive word, ¹⁴It is not a joke. ¹⁵Indeed, they plot a plot ¹⁶And I plot a plot. ¹⁷So give a respite to the unbelievers. Deal gently with them for a while.

---

7. This passage, with its prescientific and unequivocally erroneous description of the location of semen production, has been a source of acute embarrassment for contemporary Islamic apologists. Many attempt to mitigate the difficulty by translating "backbone" (*sulb*) as "loins." However, Ibn Kathir understands the word as meaning "backbone" when he (again attributing the statement to Ibn Abbas) explains "proceeding from between the backbone and the ribs" as, "The backbone of the man and the ribs of the woman. It (the fluid) is yellow and fine in texture. The child will not be born except from both of them (i.e., their sexual fluids)."¹ This interpretation is unlikely as well, for the passage is clearly referring to a fluid that gushes forth from between the backbone and ribs of one individual.

Likewise in a hadith, Muhammad is depicted quoting Allah saying: "While you were in the backbone of Adam, I asked you much less than this, i.e. not to worship others besides Me, but you insisted on worshipping others besides me."² The hadith assumes that the wayward individual was fully present in the backbone, not needing the participation of anyone else to come into being.

In his twentieth-century translation of the Qur'an, Abdullah Yusuf Ali attempts to explain away the difficulty by stating that a man's "backbone is the source and symbol of his strength and personality," and thus is used metaphorically in this passage.³

17. "This means," says Ibn Kathir, "that you will see what befalls them of torment, punishment and destruction."⁴ That torment will not fail to materialize, and no man can hold it back.

The Most High

Al-Ala

Introduction

According to Maududi, "The subject matter shows that this too is one of the earliest Surahs to be revealed, and the words: 'We shall enable you to recite, then you shall never forget' of verse 6 also indicate that it was sent down in the period when the Holy Messenger (upon whom be Allah's peace) was not yet fully accustomed to receive Revelation and at the time Revelation came down he feared lest he should forget its words."[1] The title comes from 87:1.

---

1 Maududi, EnglishTafsir.com, http://www.englishtafsir.com/Quran/87/index.html.

The Most High

In the name of Allah, the compassionate, the merciful.

¹Praise the name of your Lord, the most high, ²Who creates, then proportions, ³Who measures, then guides, ⁴Who brings forth the pasturage, ⁵Then turns it to brown stubble. ⁶We shall enable you to recite, then you shall never forget ⁷Except what Allah wills. Indeed, he knows what is disclosed and what is still hidden, ⁸And we will ease your way to the state of ease.

⁹Therefore remind, for the reminder is useful. ¹⁰He who fears will be mindful, ¹¹But the most wretched will flout it, ¹²He who will be thrown into the great fire ¹³In which he will neither die nor live. ¹⁴He who grows is successful, ¹⁵And remembers the name of his Lord, and so prays, ¹⁶But you prefer the life of this world ¹⁷Although the hereafter is better and more lasting. ¹⁸Indeed, this is in the earlier scriptures. ¹⁹The books of Abraham and Moses.

---

1. See 1:2, 34:1.
7. See 2:106.
18. See 5:47.

19. In the Qur'an it is assumed that every prophet was given a book. In line with this, it is assumed that Abraham must have been given a book as well. See 5:46.

SURA 88

The Overwhelming Event

Al-Ghashiya

Introduction

Maududi says: "The whole subject matter of the Surah indicates that this too is one of the earliest Surahs to be revealed; but this was the period when the Holy Prophet (upon whom be peace) had started preaching his message publicly, and the people of Makkah were hearing it and ignoring it carelessly and thoughtlessly."[1]

Bell, however, asserts that "this surah shows much variation in rhyme and several interruptions in sense," indicating several interpolations.[2] The last word of each verse indicates the disruption in the rhyme scheme:

10. *aliya*	16. *mabthutha*
11. *laghiya*	17. *khuliqat*
12. *jariya*	18. *rufiat*
13. *marfua*	19. *nusibat*
14. *mawdua*	20. *sutihat*
15. *masfufa*	21. *mudhakkir*[3]

There is clearly a disruption at 88:17, clear also in the English text, which could indicate that two separate fragments have been combined.

The title comes from 88:1.

---

1 Maududi, EnglishTafsir.com, http://www.englishtafsir.com/Quran/88/index.html.
2 Bell, II, 652.
3 Ibn Warraq, "Introduction to Richard Bell," in Ibn Warraq, ed., *What the Koran Really Says* (Amherst, New York: Prometheus, 2002), 519-20.

The Overwhelming Event

In the name of Allah, the compassionate, the merciful.

[1]Has there come to you news of the overwhelming event? [2]On that day, faces will be downcast, [3]Laboring, weary, [4]Scorched by burning fire, [5]Drinking from a boiling spring, [6]No food for them except bitter thorn-fruit [7]Which does not nourish nor release from hunger. [8]On that day other faces will be calm, [9]Glad for their past effort, [10]In a lofty garden [11]Where they hear no idle talk, [12]In which is a running spring, [13]In which are couches raised [14]And goblets set at hand [15]And cushions ranged [16]And silken carpets spread. [17]Will they not consider the camels, how they are created? [18]And the heaven, how it is raised? [19]And the hills, how they are set up? [20]And the earth, how it is spread? [21]Remind them, for you are just one who reminds, [22]You are not at all an overseer over them. [23]But whoever is averse and disbelieves, [24]Allah will punish him with the most severe punishment. [25]Indeed, to us is their return [26]And ours is their reckoning.

---

6. Bell notes that the rhyme scheme is interrupted here, suggesting that this verse and 88:7 were added later, as the original rhyme scheme resumes at 88:8.

17. Here begins another interpolation with its own rhyme scheme, through 88:20.

21. The original rhyme scheme of 88:1-5 and 88:8-12 resumes here.

22. On "overseer," Bell states that "the meaning and derivation of the word is not quite certain."[1]

The Dawn

Al-Fajr

Introduction

Maududi says that sura 89, "The Dawn," "was revealed at the stage when persecution of the new converts to Islam had begun in Makkah."[1] The title comes from 89:1.

---

1 Maududi, EnglishTafsir.com, http://www.englishtafsir.com/Quran/89/index.html.

The Dawn

IN THE NAME OF ALLAH, THE COMPASSIONATE, THE MERCIFUL.

1By the dawn **2**And ten nights, **3**And the even and the odd, **4**And the night when it departs, **5**There surely is an oath for the thinking man. **6**Do you not consider how your Lord dealt with Aad? **7**With many-columned Iram, **8**The like of which was not created in the lands? **9**And with Thamud, who split the rocks in the valley, **10**And with Pharaoh, firm of might, **11**Who were rebellious in these lands, **12**And multiplied iniquity in them? **13**Therefore your Lord poured on them the disaster of his punishment. **14**Indeed, your Lord is always watchful. **15**As for man, whenever his Lord tests him by honoring him, and is favorable to him, he says, My Lord honors me. **16**But whenever he tests him by reducing his means of life, he says, My Lord despises me. **17**No, but you do not honor the orphan **18**And do not encourage the feeding of the poor. **19**And you devour inheritances with devouring greed. **20**And love wealth with abounding love. **21**No, but when the earth is ground to atoms, grinding, grinding, **22**And your Lord comes with angels, rank on rank, **23**And Gehenna is brought near on that day, on that day man will remember, but how will the remembrance be? **24**He will say, If only I had sent before me for my life. **25**No one punishes as he will punish on that day. **26**No one binds as he will then bind. **27**But you, soul at peace, **28**Return to your Lord, content in his good pleasure. **29**Enter among my slaves. **30**Enter my garden.

---

1. See 34:3 and 50:1.

2. According to Bell, "This is quite unintelligible even to the Moslem commentators."[1]

6. The people of Aad also appear at 7:65, 9:70, 11:50, 14:9, 22:42, 25:38, 26:123, 29:38, 38:12, and 40:31.

7. Jeffery notes numerous Islamic interpretations of "Iram," saying that this multiplicity "suggests of itself that [it] was a foreign one of which the exegetes could make nothing."[2]

Ibn Kathir explains: "These were the first people of Ad. They were the descendants of Ad bin Iram bin Aws bin Sam bin Nuh [Noah]. This was said by Ibn Ishaq. They are those to whom Allah sent His Messenger Hud. However, they rejected and opposed him. Therefore, Allah saved him and those who believed with him from among them, and He destroyed others with a furious, violent wind."[3]

The location of Aad is uncertain. In his *Atlas of the Qur'an*, Dr. Shauqi Abu Khalil records some uncertainty among Muslim exegetes: "The structures of this place are described in the Qur'an as being very tall like lofty pillars, the like of which were not created in the land. Some say that this place is Alexandria; others maintain that it is Damascus; and yet others, whose opinion is strongest by dint of stronger proofs, say that it is a city near Adan, between San'a and Hadramawt."[4] No trace of this people has ever been found. See 3:137.

9. On the people of Thamud, see also 11:61, 14:9, 17:59, 22:42, 26:141, 27:45, 29:38, 38:13, and 40:31.

10. On Pharaoh, see also 2:49, 3:11, 7:103, 8:52, 10:75, 14:6, 17:101, 20:24, 23:46, 26:11, 27:12, 28:3, 29:39, 38:12, 40:24, 44:17, 50:13, 51:38, 54:41, 66:11, 69:9, 73:15, 79:15, and 85:18.

13. "Disaster" may be, says Bell, "Ethiopic, meaning 'flood.'"[5]

23. On Gehenna, see 2:206.

27. For the passage beginning here and running through 89:30, the Shi'ite Bankipur Qur'an manuscript has, "But you, soul at peace in Muhammad and the family of Muhammad, return to your Lord, content in his guardianship, contenting with merit. Enter among my slaves, and enter my paradise."[6] See 2:59 and the Appendix: Two Apocryphal Shi'ite Suras.

The City

Al-Balad

Introduction

Once again Maududi states: "Its subject matter and style resemble those of the earliest Surahs revealed at Makkah, but it contains a pointer which indicates that it was sent down in the period when the disbelievers of Makkah had resolved to oppose the Holy Prophet (upon whom be Allah's peace), and made it lawful for themselves to commit tyranny and excess against him."[1]

Its title comes from 90:1. The city is identified in Islamic tradition as Mecca, but that is not stated here.

---

1 Maududi, EnglishTafsir.com, http://www.englishtafsir.com/Quran/90/index.html.

The City

IN THE NAME OF ALLAH, THE COMPASSIONATE, THE MERCIFUL.

¹No, I swear by this city ²And you are free in this city ³And the father and what was born of him, ⁴We indeed have created man in distress, ⁵Does he think that no one has power over him? ⁶And he says, I have squandered vast wealth, ⁷Does he think that no one see him? ⁸Didn't we assign to him two eyes ⁹And a tongue and two lips, ¹⁰And guide him to the parting of the mountain ways? ¹¹But he has not attempted the ascent, ¹²And what will convey to you what the ascent is? ¹³To free a slave, ¹⁴And to feed in the day of hunger. ¹⁵An orphan who is a close relative, ¹⁶Or some poor wretch in misery, ¹⁷And to be among those who believe and exhort one another to perseverance and exhort one another to mercy. ¹⁸Their place will be on the right hand. ¹⁹But those who disbelieve our revelations, their place will be on the left hand. ²⁰Fire will be a canopy over them.

---

1. See 34:3 and 50:1.
2. Ibn Kathir attributes to Ibn Abbas the assertion that this means: "O Muhammad! It is permissible for you to fight" in this city.[1]
3. Invoking many authorities, Ibn Kathir says that this means "by the begetter, Adam, and that which he begot is his children."[2]

He characterizes this view as "good and strong," explaining: "This is supported by the fact that Allah swears by the Mother of the Towns, which are dwellings. Then after it He swears by the dwellers therein, who is Adam, the father of mankind, and his children."[3] Why Allah would swear by something incomparably lesser than he is once again unexplained; see 34:3 and 50:1.

SURA 91

The Sun

Ash-Shams

Introduction

Here again, Maududi states: "The subject matter and the style show that this Surah too was revealed in the earliest period at Makkah at a stage when opposition to the Holy Prophet (upon whom be Allah's peace) had grown very strong and intense."[1] The title comes from 91:1.

1 Maududi, EnglishTafsir.com, http://www.englishtafsir.com/Quran/91/index.html.

The Sun

IN THE NAME OF ALLAH, THE COMPASSIONATE, THE MERCIFUL.

[1]By the sun and his brightness, [2]And the moon when she follows him, [3]And the day when it reveals him, [4]And the night when it enshrouds him, [5]And the heaven and him who built it, [6]And the earth and him who spread it out, [7]And a soul and him who perfected it [8]And inspired its wickedness and righteousness. [9]He is indeed successful who causes it to grow, [10]And he is indeed a failure who stunts it. [11]Thamud denied in their rebellious pride, [12]When the lowest of them broke forth [13]And the messenger of Allah said, It is the camel of Allah, so let her drink. [14]But they denied him, and they hamstrung her, so Allah doomed them for their sin and destroyed them. [15]And he does not fear the ending.

---

1. Allah swears by the sun in this verse, and then the moon (91:2), the day (91:3), the night (91:4), heaven (91:5), earth (91:6), and the soul (91:7). See 34:3 and 54:1.

8. Maududi explains of the soul that "the Creator has placed in it tendencies to both good and evil."[1] This is sharply different from the New Testament proposition that "God is light, and in Him there is no darkness at all" (I John 1:5), for to place evil in the soul, Allah must have it to give, which in the Christian conception would be utterly impossible and absurd, as evil is the absence of God. This also means that Allah is ultimately responsible not just for the soul's inclination toward good, but for its inclination toward evil as well. See 7:179, 10:99, and 32:13.

11. On Thamud and the camel of Allah, see 11:64, 26:155, and 91:11-14, as well as the introduction to sura 11.

15. Instead of, "And he does not fear," the Warsh Qur'an has, "Therefore he does not fear."[2]

SURA 92

The Night

Al-Layl

Introduction

According to Maududi, this sura's "subject matter so closely resembles that of Surah Ash-Shams [sura 91] that each Surah seems to be an explanation of the other. It is one and the same thing which has been explained in Surah Ash-Shams in one way and in this Surah in another. This indicates that both these Surahs were sent down in about the same period."[1] The title comes from 92:1.

---

1 Maududi, EnglishTafsir.com, http://www.englishtafsir.com/Quran/92/index.html.

The Night

IN THE NAME OF ALLAH, THE COMPASSIONATE, THE MERCIFUL.

¹By the night enshrouding ²And the day resplendent ³And him who has created male and female, ⁴Indeed, your effort is dispersed. ⁵As for him who gives and is dutiful ⁶And believes in goodness, ⁷Surely we will ease his way to the state of ease. ⁸But as for him who hoards and considers himself independent, ⁹And disbelieves in goodness, ¹⁰Surely we will ease his way to adversity.

¹¹His riches will not save him when he perishes. ¹²Indeed, ours is the guidance ¹³And indeed, to us belong the last and the first. ¹⁴Therefore I have warned you of the flame ¹⁵Which only the most wretched must endure, ¹⁶He who denies and turns away. ¹⁷Far removed from it will be the righteous ¹⁸Who gives his wealth so that he may grow. ¹⁹And no one has any favor for a reward with him, ²⁰Except for seeking the purpose of his Lord the most high. ²¹He indeed will be content.

---

1. See 34:3 and 50:1.

13. Ibn Kathir identifies "the last" with "the hereafter" and "the first" with "this world."[1]

14. Bell notes that 92:14-21 "cannot be strictly continuous with 5-13, because there Allah is the speaker, here Muhammad [that is, the messenger] speaks in his own person." He adds that verses 92:14-21 "appear to me to be later, perhaps Medinan, and to be either an addition to the surah or a substitute for 5-13."[2]

"Flame" is *laza*, for which see 72:15.

The Morning

Ad-Duha

Introduction

Maududi opines: "Its subject matter clearly indicates that it belongs to the earliest period at Makkah. Traditions also show that the revelations were suspended for a time, which caused the Holy Prophet (upon whom be Allah's peace) to be deeply distressed and grieved. On this account he felt very anxious that perhaps he had committed some error because of which his Lord had become angry with him and had forsaken him. Thereupon he was given the consolation that revelation had not been stopped because of some displeasure but this was necessitated by the same expediency as underlies the peace and stillness of the night after the bright day, as if to say: 'If you had continuously been exposed to the intensely bright light of Revelation (*Wahi*) your nerves could not have endured it. Therefore, an interval was given in order to afford you peace and tranquility.'"[1] The title comes from 93:1.

---

1 Maududi, EnglishTafsir.com, http://www.englishtafsir.com/Quran/93/index.html.

The Morning

IN THE NAME OF ALLAH, THE COMPASSIONATE, THE MERCIFUL.

[1]By the morning hours [2]And by the night when it is most still, [3]Your Lord has not forsaken you, nor does he hate you, [4]And indeed the latter portion will be better for you than the former, [5]And indeed your Lord will give to you so that you will be content. [6]Didn't he find you an orphan and protect? [7]Didn't he find you wandering and direct? [8]Didn't he find you destitute and enrich? [9]Therefore do not oppress the orphan, [10]Therefore do not drive away the beggar, [11]Therefore proclaim the bounty of your Lord.

---

1. See 34:3 and 50:1.

3. Islamic tradition holds that this passage was revealed in response to a woman who taunted Muhammad. According to a hadith, "The Prophet became ill, so he did not stand for prayer for a night or two. Then a woman came and said, 'O Muhammad! I think that your devil has finally left you.'"[1] Or, in another version that comes from Ibn Abbas, "When the Qur'an was revealed to the Messenger of Allah, Jibril [Gabriel] was delayed from coming to him for a number of days (on one occasion). Therefore, the Messenger of Allah was affected by this. Then the idolaters began to say, 'His Lord has abandoned him and hates him.'"[2] See 2:144.

6. According to Islamic tradition, Muhammad was an orphan, but in this passage as in many others, it is not clear which came first, the Qur'anic passage or the biographical material about Muhammad that purports to explain it and which only begins to appear in the ninth century.

9. Ibn Kathir explains: "This refers to the fact that his father died while his mother was still pregnant with him, and his mother, Aminah bint Wahb died when he was only six years old. After this he was under the guardianship of his grandfather, Abdul-Muttalib, until he died when Muhammad was eight years old. Then his uncle, Abu Talib, took responsibility for him and continued to protect him, assist him, elevate his status, honor him, and even restrain his people from harming him when he was forty years of age and Allah commissioned him with the prophethood."[3]

The Expansion

Al-Inshira

Introduction

Maududi says that this sura's "subject matter so closely resembles that of Surah Ad-Duha [sura 93] that both these Surah seem to have been revealed in about the same period under similar conditions."[1]

---

1 Maududi, EnglishTafsir.com, http://www.englishtafsir.com/Quran/94/index.html.

The Expansion

In the name of Allah, the compassionate, the merciful.

¹Haven't we expanded your heart for you? ²And eased you of the burden ³That weighed down your back, ⁴And exalted your fame? ⁵But indeed, with hardship goes ease, ⁶Indeed, with hardship goes ease, ⁷So when you are relieved, still labor ⁸And turn to your Lord with hope.

---

1. See 6:125. Ibn Kathir adds: "And just as Allah expanded his chest, He also made His Law vast, wide, accommodating and easy, containing no difficulty, hardship or burden."[1]
2. See 2:144.

3. See 48:2.
5. The *Tafsir al-Jalalayn* explains that the prophet "experienced harshness from the unbelievers but then had ease when he was given victory over them."[2]

SURA 95

The Fig

At-Tin

Introduction

Maududi notes a difference of opinion regarding whether this sura is Meccan or Medinan; such disagreements indicate that these judgments are generally based on interpretation of the sura's contents rather than upon any external evidence: "According to Qatadah, this Surah is Madani. Two different views have been reported from Ibn Abbas: first that it is a Makki Surah, and second that it is Madani. But the majority of scholars regard it as a Makki revelation, a manifest symbol of which is the use of the words *hadh-al-balad-il-amin* (this city of peace) [95:3] for Makkah. Obviously, if it had been revealed at Madinah, it would not be correct to use the words 'this city' for Makkah."[1] The title is taken from 95:1.

---

1 Maududi, EnglishTafsir.com, http://www.englishtafsir.com/Quran/95/index.html.

The Fig

IN THE NAME OF ALLAH, THE COMPASSIONATE, THE MERCIFUL.

¹By the fig and the olive, ²By Mount Sinai, ³And by this city of peace, ⁴Surely we created man of the best stature ⁵Then we reduced him to the lowest of the low, ⁶Except for those who believe and do good works, and theirs is an unfailing reward. ⁷So who from this point onward will lie to you about the judgment? ⁸Isn't Allah the most conclusive of all judges?

---

1. Regarding this oath, see 34:3 and 50:1.

According to Ibn Kathir, "the fig" refers to the mosque of Noah "that was built upon Mount Al-Judi" in southeastern Turkey, where Noah's ark is said to have come to rest.¹ "The olive," meanwhile, says Ibn Kathir, is the Al-Aqsa Mosque in Jerusalem.² See 17:1.

5. It is Allah who raised man high and then reduced him to the lowest of the low, except for the believers. See 7:179, 10:99, and 32:13.

SURA 96

The Clot

Al-Alaq

Introduction

Islamic tradition generally holds that 96:1–5 was the very first revelation that Muhammad received. However, this is not a unanimous view; see the introduction to sura 1. The title comes from 96:2.

The Clot

In the name of Allah, the compassionate, the merciful.

1Recite, in the name of your Lord who creates, **2**Creates man from a clot. **3**Recite, and your Lord is the most generous, **4**Who teaches by the pen, **5**Teaches man what he did not know.

6No indeed, but truly man is rebellious **7**That he thinks himself independent. **8**Indeed, to your Lord is the return. **9**Have you seen him who dissuades **10**A slave when he prays? **11**Have you seen if he relies on the guidance **12**Or commands piety? **13**Have you seen if he denies and

---

1. According to Islamic tradition, when Muhammad, a prosperous Arabian merchant from the Quraysh tribe of Mecca, was forty years old, he was praying in a cave in the mountains near Mecca. As he passed the entire night in devotion, an angel came to him and commanded him to read and recite what he read. According to a hadith in Bukhari's collection, Muhammad replied, "I do not know how to read."[1]

The angel, however, would brook no objections. He terrified Muhammad and even menaced him physically:

> (The Prophet added), "The angel caught me (forcefully) and pressed me so hard that I could not bear it anymore. He then released me and again asked me to read, and I replied, 'I do not know how to read.' Thereupon he caught me again and pressed me a second time till I could not bear it anymore. He then released me and asked me again to read, but again I replied, 'I do not know how to read (or, what shall I read?).' Thereupon he caught me for the third time and pressed me and then released me and said, 'Read! In the Name of your Lord, Who has created (all that exists). Has created man from a clot. Read! And Your Lord is Most Generous…[unto]…that which he knew not.'" (V. 96:5)[2]

In the standard Islamic version of this event as it has been retold through the ages, it was the angel Gabriel who appeared to Muhammad, but the Bukhari hadith does not give the angel's name. The ninth-century Islamic historian Ibn Sa'd recounts that the angel who originally visited Muhammad to begin giving him Qur'anic revelations was not Gabriel: "Verily the Apostle of Allah, may Allah bless him, was commissioned to prophethood when he was forty years old. Saraphel was with him for three years, then he was replaced by Gabriel who remained with him, at Makkah for ten years, and at the city of his migration, al-Madinah, for ten years."[3] However, no sooner does Ibn Sa'd mention this than he dismisses it: "Verily the learned and those versed in Sirah literature say: From the time the revelations commenced till he (Prophet), may Allah bless him, breathed his last none except Gabriel was with him."[4] Nevertheless, it is hard to see how anyone would have gotten the idea that another angel was involved with Muhammad if Islamic tradition had been absolutely certain from the first moment that it was Gabriel. The alternate tradition bears witness to the fact that these stories underwent considerable development; they were not historical records passed on faithfully throughout the ages.

Islamic tradition records that Muhammad returned to Khadija in tremendous distress. According to a tradition put into the mouth of Aisha: "Then Allah's Messenger returned with that (the Revelation), and his heart severely beating; (and the) muscles between his neck and shoulders were trembling till he came upon Khadija (his wife) and said, 'Cover me!' They covered him, till his fear was over, and after that he said, 'O Khadija! What is wrong with me? I was afraid that something bad might happen to me.' Then he told her all that had happened."[5] And he repeated to her his initial fears: "Woe is me poet or possessed."[6] He is, however, ultimately reassured that this terrifying vision was a heavenly visitation and begins his prophetic career. The atmosphere of all this could not be more different from that of angelic visions in the Bible, even Jacob's wrestling with the angel (Genesis 32:22-32), and particularly from the New Testament reassurances from Gabriel, "Be not afraid" (cf. Luke 1:13, 1:30).

5. The word *kalla*, "no indeed," occurs three times in sura 96: here and in verses 15 and 19. According to Ibn Rawandi, its appearance in this verse is "senseless, since it cannot be a negation of the preceding section no matter how those verses are interpreted."[7] Examining the Syriac substratum, Luxenberg contends that sura 96 was originally a Christian text: "The lexicological and syntactical analysis of this sura, examined under its Syriac connection, has revealed—contrary to the confusion which has reigned in its Arabic reading up to now—a clear and coherent composition in which the faithful is entreated to pray and participate in the liturgical service that the Koran designates as the Eucharist, corresponding to *iqtarib*, taken from the Syriac liturgical term *etqarrab*, which signifies 'take part in a liturgical service' as well as 'to receive the Eucharist.'"[8]

Specifically, he renders 96:19 not as "prostrate yourself, and draw near," but as a call to participate in the Eucharistic celebration: "Return to your religious practices and take part in the offering (= Eucharist)."[9] Luxenberg explains that the word *iqtarib*, normally translated as "draw near," is "in fact Arabic only in form and corresponds in reality to the liturgical Syriac term *el qarra / ethqarrab*, meaning 'to take part in the offering (Eucharistic)' as well as 'to receive the Eucharist.'"[10]

9. The sura shows signs of editing, as it appears to be in two parts: Verses 96:1–8 fit in with the traditional Muslim setting, in which Gabriel approached Muhammad on Mount Hira. But then the subject abruptly and unaccountably changes in this verse, denouncing some unnamed person who prevents a "slave" from praying. The culprit, according to Ibn Kathir, was a man of the Quraysh, "Abu Jahl, may Allah curse him. He threatened the Prophet for performing Salah [Islamic prayer] at the Ka'bah."[11]

is defiant? ¹⁴Is he then unaware that Allah sees? ¹⁵No indeed, but if he doesn't stop, we will seize him by the forelock, ¹⁶The lying, sinful forelock.

¹⁷Then let him call upon his comrades, ¹⁸We will call the *zabaniya*. ¹⁹No indeed, do not obey him. But prostrate yourself, and draw near.

---

15. Bell states of the passage that begins here that it seems "to have an individual in view" and is "perhaps a later insertion."[12]

18. Bell describes *zabaniya* as "a word the sense of which is not clear, it is usually taken as denoting the guards of hell, or the angels which carry off the soul at death."[13] Ibn Kathir identifies them as "the angels of torment."[14]

The Power

Al-Qadr

Introduction

Again demonstrating that the classification of the suras as Meccan or Medinan is not based on actual evidence of the circumstances of their composition, but on conjecture based on their contents, there is considerable disagreement in Islamic tradition about whether this brief sura is one or the other. Maududi states: "Whether it is a Makki or a Madani revelation is disputed. Abu Hayyan in *Al-Bahr al-Muhti* has made the claim that the majority of scholars regard it as a Madani Surah. Ali bin Ahmad al-Wahidi in his commentary says that this is the first Surah to be sent down in Madinah. Contrary to this, Al Mawardi says that according to the majority of scholars it is a Makki revelation, and the same view Imam Suyuti expressed in *Al-Itqan*. Ibn Mardayah has cited Ibn Abbas, lbn Az Zubair and Hadrat Aishah as saying that this Surah was revealed at Makkah. A study of the contents also shows that it should have been revealed at Makkah."[1] The title comes from 97:1.

---

1 Maududi, EnglishTafsir.com, http://www.englishtafsir.com/Quran/97/index.html.

The Power

IN THE NAME OF ALLAH, THE COMPASSIONATE, THE MERCIFUL.

¹Indeed, we revealed it on the night of power. ²And what will convey to you what the night of power is? ³The night of power is better than a thousand months. ⁴The angels and the spirit descend in it, by the permission of their Lord, with all decrees. ⁵Peace until the rising of the dawn.

---

1. This is, according to Islamic tradition, the night on which Muhammad received the first revelation of the Qur'an (that is, the one that is recorded at 96:1-5, according to most Islamic authorities). It is observed on the 27th night of Ramadan among Sunnis, and the 23rd night of Ramadan among Shi'ites, and is the occasion for particular commemorations, spiritual exercises, and other observances. See 2:185.

Ibn Kathir attributes this statement to Ibn Abbas and others: "Allah sent the Qur'an down all at one time from the Preserved Tablet (Al-Lawh Al-Mahfuz) to the House of Might (Baytul-Izzah), which is in the heaven of this world. Then it came down in parts to the Messenger of Allah based upon the incidents that occurred over a period of twenty-three years."¹ Ibn Kathir himself adds: "Then Allah magnified the status of the Night of Al-Qadr, which He chose for the revelation of the Mighty Qur'an."²

4. This is a night in which many Muslims engage in particular devotions, for, as Ibn Kathir explains, angels are visiting the earth: "The angels descend in abundance during the Night of Al-Qadr [the Night of Power] due to its abundant blessings. The angels descend with the descending of blessings and mercy, just as they descend when the Qur'an is recited, they surround the circles of *Dhikr* (remembrance of Allah) and they lower their wings with true respect for the student of knowledge. In reference to Ar-Ruh [the spirit], it is said that here it means the angel Jibril [Gabriel]."³

Instead of, "The angels and the spirit descend in it, by the permission of their Lord, with all decrees," the Shi'ite Bankipur Qur'an manuscript has, "The angels and the spirit descend in it, by the permission of their Lord, upon Muhammad and the family of Muhammad with all decrees."⁴ See 2:59 and the Appendix: Two Apocryphal Shi'ite Suras.

The Clear Proof

Al-Bayyina

Introduction

Islamic tradition holds that this sura is probably Medinan; it shares the bellicosity and contempt for the people of the book (primarily Jews and Christians) of the Medinan suras. Maududi says that its placement after suras 96 and 97 is "very meaningful. Surah Al-Alaq [96] contains the very first revelation, while Surah Al-Qadr [97] shows as to when it was revealed, and in this Surah it has been explained why it was necessary to send a Messenger along with this Holy Book."[1]

---

1 Maududi, EnglishTafsir.com, http://www.englishtafsir.com/Quran/98/index.html.

The Clear Proof

In the name of Allah, the compassionate, the merciful.

¹The unbelievers among the people of the book and the polytheists could not have cast off until the clear proof came to them, ²A messenger from Allah, reading purified pages ³Containing correct scriptures. ⁴Nor were the people of the book divided until after the clear proof came to them. ⁵And they are not ordered to do anything else but serve Allah, keeping religion pure for him, as *hanifs*, and to establish prayer and to give alms. That is true religion. ⁶Indeed, the unbelievers among the people of the book and the idolaters will remain in the fire of Gehenna. They are the most vile of created beings. ⁷Indeed, those who believe and do good works are the best of created beings. ⁸Their reward is with their Lord, gardens of Eden under which rivers flow, in which they dwell forever. Allah has pleasure in them and they have pleasure in him. This is for him who fears his Lord.

---

1. The Jews and Christians aren't going to forsake their falsehoods without clear proof. The unbelievers among the people of the book are the Jews and Christians who reject the messenger and do not become Muslims. See 2:62 and 57:27.

2. The clear proof is the messenger and the Qur'an. On "purified pages" and "correct scriptures" (98:3), see 2:4 and 10:94.

4. The *Tafsir al-Jalalayn* claims that before Muhammad came, the people of the book "used to agree that they would believe in him when he came. Those of them who rejected him envied him."[1] See 2:18, 2:174.

5. On *hanif*, see 2:135.

6. This verse is one of the most striking examples of the Qur'an's dehumanization of unbelievers. See 8:55. On Gehenna, see 2:206.

Instead of "created beings" (*al-bareiyyati*), the Warsh Qur'an has "innocent ones" (*al-bare'ati*).[2]

The Earthquake

Al-Zalzala

Introduction

Maududi notes once again, "Whether or not it was revealed at Makkah or Madinah is disputed."[1] There is no external information about its provenance and not enough to go on in its contents to have any idea of its derivation. The title comes from 99:1.

An Islamic tradition holds that this sura "is equivalent to one-fourth of the Qur'an."[2] The title comes from 99:1.

---

1 Maududi, EnglishTafsir.com, http://www.englishtafsir.com/Quran/99/index.html.
2 Ibn Kathir, X, 617.

The Earthquake

In the name of Allah, the compassionate, the merciful.

¹When Earth is shaken with her earthquake ²And Earth yields up her burdens, ³And man says, What ails her? ⁴That day she will relate her news, ⁵Because your Lord inspires her. ⁶On that day mankind will come forth in scattered groups to be shown their deeds. ⁷And whoever does an atom's weight of good will see it then, ⁸And whoever does an atom's weight of evil will see it then.

---

4. According to the *Tafsir al-Jalalayn*, "It will testify against every slave, male and female, to all that they did while on its surface," that is, the surface of the Earth.[1]

6. The *Tafsir al-Jalalayn* explains: "Some will go to the right to the Garden and some to the left to the Fire, so that they may see the repayment of their actions in the Garden or the Fire."[2]

7. See 21:47.

The Snorting Horses

Al-Adiyat

Introduction

Here yet again, Maududi notes: "Whether it is a Makki or a Madani Surah is disputed."[1]

---

1 Maududi, EnglishTafsir.com, http://www.englishtafsir.com/Quran/100/index.html.

The Snorting Horses

IN THE NAME OF ALLAH, THE COMPASSIONATE, THE MERCIFUL.

¹By the snorting horses, ²Striking sparks of fire ³And launching the raid at dawn, ⁴Then, with them, with their trail of dust, ⁵Cutting into the center, ⁶Indeed, man is an ingrate to his Lord ⁷And indeed, he is a witness to that, ⁸And indeed, in the love of wealth he is violent. ⁹Doesn't he know that when the contents of the graves are poured forth ¹⁰And the secrets of the hearts are made known, ¹¹On that day will their Lord be perfectly informed regarding them?

---

1. Ibn Kathir explains: "Allah swears by the horses when they are made to gallop into battle in His path (i.e., Jihad), and thus they run and pant, which is the sound that is heard from the horse when it runs."¹ On Allah swearing, see 34:3 and 50:1. On jihad, see 2:218, 8:39, 9:29.

3. "This is," says Ibn Kathir, "just as the Messenger of Allah used to perform raids in the early morning. He would wait to see if he heard the Adhan (call to prayer) from the people. If he heard it he would leave them alone, and if he didn't hear it he would attack."² The decision of whether or not to attack was based on whether the people in question were Muslim or not.

The Disaster

Al-Qaria

Introduction

According to Maududi, "There is no dispute about its being a Makki Surah. Its contents show that this too is one of the earliest Surahs to be revealed at Makkah."[1] Bell states that it is "a fragment, or a collection of fragments."[2] The title comes from 101:1–3.

---

1 Maududi, EnglishTafsir.com, http://www.englishtafsir.com/Quran/101/index.html.
2 Bell, II, 674.

The Disaster

IN THE NAME OF ALLAH, THE COMPASSIONATE, THE MERCIFUL.

¹The disaster. ²What is the disaster? ³And what will convey to you what the disaster is? ⁴A day on which mankind will be like thickly-scattered moths ⁵And the mountains will become as carded wool. ⁶Then, as for him whose scales are heavy, ⁷He will live a pleasant life. ⁸But as for him whose scales are light, ⁹His mother will be *hawiya*, ¹⁰And what will convey to you what it is? ¹¹Raging fire.

---

6. See 7:8, 21:47.

9. *Hawiya* is "childless." Bell describes this as "a phrase implying that the man will perish, or at least meet misfortune. The added explanation [in 101:10-11], takes *Hawiya* as a designation for Hell."¹ According to Zamakhshari, *hawiya* is one of the different levels of hell (see 2:206), the one for "the feigners of belief in the divinity," that is, hypocrites.²

10. Bell sees this and the following verse as "certainly in the nature of a gloss to the word *hawiya*."³

The Mutual Rivalry

At-Takathur

Introduction

Islamic tradition generally regards this as a Meccan sura, but a hadith has Ali say: "We were still in doubt concerning the torment of the grave, until 'the mutual rivalry diverts you' [sura 102] was revealed."[1] Maududi states that "this view has been regarded as an argument for Surah At-Takathur to be Madani on the ground that the torment of the grave was first mentioned at Madinah; no mention of it was ever made at Makkah. But this is wrong. In the Makki Surahs of the Quran, the torment of the grave has been mentioned at many places so clearly that there can be no room for any such doubt." He lists 6:93, 16:28, 23:99–100, and 40:45–46 in support of this, stating that these are all Meccan, and concludes that this illustrates that Ali's statement does not require this sura to be Medinan. The conjectural nature of the Meccan/Medinan classification is again illustrated.

Bell sees this sura as "also little more than a fragment. Whether it is a unity might be questioned, as the rhyme changes after v. 2."[2] The title comes from 102:1.

---

1 *Jami at-Tirmidhi*, vol. 5, book 44, no. 3355.
2 Bell, II, 675.

The Mutual Rivalry

IN THE NAME OF ALLAH, THE COMPASSIONATE, THE MERCIFUL.

1The mutual rivalry for worldly wealth diverts you **2**Until you come to the graves. **3**No, but you will come to know. **4**Again, no, but you will come to know. **5**No, if only you knew with a sure knowledge. **6**For you will see the blaze. **7**Yes, you will see it with sure vision. **8**Then, on that day, you will be asked about pleasure.

---

1. A hadith depicts one of the companions of Muhammad, Ubayy bin Ka'b, listening to a sermon in Mecca sometime after the death of the prophet of Islam. "O men!" the preacher says, "The Prophet used to say, 'If the son of Adam were given a valley full of gold, he would love to have a second one; and if he were given the second one, he would love to have a third, for nothing fills the belly of Adam's son except dust. And Allah forgives he who repents to Him.'" Ubai observes, "We considered this as a saying from the Qur'an till the Sura (beginning with) 'The mutual rivalry for piling up of worldly things diverts you...' (102.1) was revealed."[1] This ninth-century tale may be an attempt to explain edits in the Qur'anic text that took place within the living memory of the hearers.

Regarding worldly wealth, see also 8:67.

6. "The blaze" is *al-jahim*, about which see 5:10.

The Declining Day

Al-Asr

Introduction

Maududi notes disagreement about when this sura was revealed: "Although Mujahid, Qatadah and Muqatil regard it as a Madani Surah, yet a great majority of the commentators opine that it is Makki; its subject matter also testifies that it must have been sent down in the earliest stage at Makkah, when the message of Islam was being presented in brief but highly impressive sentences so that the listeners who heard them once could not forget them even if they wanted to, for they were automatically committed to memory."[1] The title comes from 103:1.

---

1 Maududi, EnglishTafsir.com, http://www.englishtafsir.com/Quran/103/index.html.

The Declining Day

IN THE NAME OF ALLAH, THE COMPASSIONATE, THE MERCIFUL.

1By the declining day, **2**Indeed, man is in a state of loss, **3**Except those who believe and do good works, and exhort one another to truth and exhort one another to steadfastness.

---

1. Ibn Kathir tells the story of a man who soon became a Muslim, Amr bin al-As, who went to visit an unbeliever, Musaylimah al-Kadhdhab, shortly after Muhammad began proclaiming that he was a prophet. Musaylimah asked Amr, "What has been revealed to your friend during this time?"[1] Amr then recited this brief sura, whereupon Musaylimah "thought for a while" and then replied, "Indeed, something similar has also been revealed to me," and recited: "O Wabr, O Wabr! You are only two ears and a chest, and the rest of you is digging and burrowing."[2] Amr responded by stating that Musaylimah was lying that this had been revealed to him.

The Wabr, says Ibn Kathir, "is a small animal that resembles a cat, and the largest thing on it is its ears and its torso, while the rest of it is ugly."[3] He explains: "Musaylimah intended by the composition of these nonsensical verses to produce something which would oppose the Qur'an. Yet it was not even convincing to the idol worshipper of that time."[4] Musaylimah may have intended to be responding to the Qur'an's challenge to produce a "sura like it" (see 2:23, 10:38).

Ibn Kathir also states that the jurist Ash-Shafi'i said, "If the people were to ponder on this Surah, it would be sufficient for them."[5]

3. Bell notes that "the form 'except...' is frequently the sign of an addition."[6] He also recounts that in Ibn Masud's Qur'an, the sura read: "1. By the afternoon. 2. Verily We have created men for loss. 3. And verily he is in it till the end of time. 4. Except those who have believed and counselled each other to piety and counselled each other to endurance."[7] Bell says that "there may be something original in his v. 3."[8]

SURA 104

The Slanderer

Al-Humaza

Introduction

According to Maududi, "All commentators are agreed that it is a Makki Surah; a study of its subject matter and style shows that this too is one of the earliest Surahs to be revealed at Makkah."[1] The title comes from 104:1.

---

1 Maududi, EnglishTafsir.com, http://www.englishtafsir.com/Quran/104/index.html.

The Slanderer

IN THE NAME OF ALLAH, THE COMPASSIONATE, THE MERCIFUL.

¹Woe to every slandering backbiter, ²Who has gathered wealth and arranged it. ³He thinks that his wealth will make him immortal. ⁴No, but indeed he will be thrown to *hutama*. ⁵And what will convey to you what *hutama* is? ⁶The fire of Allah, kindled, ⁷That leaps up over the hearts. ⁸Indeed, it is closed in on them ⁹In outstretched columns.

---

4. According to Bell, the word *al-hutama* "was apparently not well-understood; hence vv. 5-9 were later added in explanation of it."¹ Ibn Kathir states that it "is one of the descriptive names of the Hellfire. This is because it crushes whoever is in it."² The *Tafsir al-Jalalayn* agrees: "The word *hutama* is something which crushes everything that is thrown into it."³ Zamakhshari identifies it as the level of hell reserved for those who dedicated their lives to the "serving of idols."⁴

SURA 105

The Elephant

Al-Fil

Introduction

Maududi says: "This is unanimously a Makki Surah."[1]

---

1 Maududi, EnglishTafsir.com, http://www.englishtafsir.com/Quran/105/index.html.

The Elephant

IN THE NAME OF ALLAH, THE COMPASSIONATE, THE MERCIFUL.

1Haven't you seen how your Lord dealt with the owners of the elephant? **2**Didn't he bring their stratagem to nothing, **3**And send against them swarms of birds, **4**Which pelted them with stones of baked clay, **5**And made them like green crops devoured?

---

1. This is generally considered in Islamic tradition to refer to an event that was said to have taken place in 570 AD, the year Muhammad is traditionally regarded as having been born. The Yemeni Christian ruler Abrahah led a force into Arabia (a force that included elephants), intending to destroy the Ka'bah in Mecca. The guardians of the Ka'bah could offer no defense, but Allah sent flocks of birds who struck the invaders with stones (105:3-4). Here again is reinforced the idea that obedience to Allah will bring earthly success and prosperity, and disobedience to Allah will bring earthly ruin. See 2:217, 3:200.

3. "Swarms" is *ababil*; Ibn Warraq notes that "the sense of this term is not clear, and the word is rare."[1] It could be a proper name.

Quraysh

Quraysh

Introduction

Maududi here once again notes disagreement among Islamic authorities regarding when this sura was revealed, and even over whether it should stand alone as a separate sura at all: "its subject matter so closely relates to that of Surah Al-Fil [sura 105] that probably it was revealed immediately after it, without any other Surah intervening between them. On the basis of this very relevance, some of the earliest scholars regard the two Surahs as one entity. This view is strengthened by the traditions which say that in the Quran copy belonging to Hadrat Ubayy bin Ka'b these two were written as one Surah, i.e. without the insertion of the *Bismillah* between them. Furthermore, Hadrat Umar had once recited the two Surahs as one in the Prayer. But this view is not acceptable because in the Quran copy which Hadrat Uthman (may Allah bless him) had got written down officially by the cooperation of a large number of the Companions and sent to the centers of Islamic lands, the *Bismillah* was written between these two Surahs, and since then these two have been written as separate Surahs in all the copies of the Quran everywhere in the world. Moreover, the style of the two Surahs is so different that they manifestly appear as two separate Surahs."[1] This once again demonstrates that the text of the Qur'an in its early stages was considerably more fluid than is now taken for granted by both Muslim and non-Muslim scholars.

---

1 Maududi, EnglishTafsir.com, http://www.englishtafsir.com/Quran/106/index.html.

Quraysh

IN THE NAME OF ALLAH, THE COMPASSIONATE, THE MERCIFUL.

1For the security of Quraysh. **2**For their security, the caravans to set forth in winter and summer. **3**So let them worship the Lord of this house, **4**Who has fed them against hunger and has made them safe from fear.

---

1. According to Ibn Kathir, this security refers to the incident of the elephant alluded to in sura 105. He summarizes both suras 105 and 106 in this way: "We have prevented the Elephant from entering Makkah and We have destroyed its people in order to gather (Ilaf) the Quraysh, which means to unite them and bring them together safely in their city."[1]

3. This is traditionally understood to refer to the Ka'bah in Mecca. However, see 2:125.

Acts of Kindness

Al-Ma'un

Introduction

Here again, Maududi records disagreement among Islamic authorities over whether this sura is Meccan or Medinan.[1] The title comes from 107:7.

---

1 Maududi, EnglishTafsir.com, http://www.englishtafsir.com/Quran/107/index.html.

Acts of Kindness

IN THE NAME OF ALLAH, THE COMPASSIONATE, THE MERCIFUL.

¹Have you seen him who denies the judgment? ²That is he who pushes the orphan aside, ³And does not encourage the feeding of the needy. ⁴So woe to worshippers ⁵Who are inattentive of their prayer, ⁶Who would be seen ⁷Yet refuse small acts of kindness.

---

7. "Small acts of kindness" is *ma'un*, which Bell states is "a word of uncertain meaning, probably derived from the Hebrew ma'on, 'refuge,' but modified by the meaning of the Arabic root. It is usually interpreted as referring to the Zakkat [Islamic almsgiving], which, if the surah is Medinan, is possible."[1] Ibn Kathir records an Islamic tradition explaining *ma'un* as "what the people give to each other, like an axe, a pot, a bucket and similar items."[2]

The Abundance

Al-Kawthar

Introduction

Most Islamic authorities regard this sura as Meccan, although there is again an alternate tradition placing it as from Medina.[1] Bell opines that it is a fragment and that its rhyme scheme suggests that it would fit well after 74:39.[2]

Luxenberg declares that "this text is without a doubt pre-Koranic. As such it is a part of that *matrix out of which the Koran was originally constituted as a Christian liturgical book (Qeryana)*, and which as a whole has been designated in Western Koran studies as the *'first Meccan period.'* The address in the second person in this as in other Suras is moreover not necessarily directed at the Prophet himself. Rather, as is customary in liturgical books, each believer is addressed in the second person."[3]

On the Qur'an as originally a Christian liturgical text, see 2:185. Luxenberg adds: "Bell's suspicion that this is a fragment from Sura 74 cannot be ruled out, since this Sura as well as Sura 73 with their call to bedtime prayer, i.e. to the *vigils*, read in part like a *monastic rule*."[4]

Based on the Syro-Aramaic substratum of the text, Luxenberg offers this reading of this sura:

1. We have given you the (virtue of) *constancy*;
2. so pray to your Lord and *persevere* (in prayer);
3. your *adversary* (the devil) is (then) the *loser*.[5]

The title comes from 108:1.

---

1 Maududi, EnglishTafsir.com, http://www.englishtafsir.com/Quran/108/index.html.
2 Bell, II, 681.
3 Christoph Luxenberg, *The Syro-Aramaic Reading of the Koran* (Berlin: Verlag Hans Schiler, 2000), 301 Emphasis as in the original.
4 Ibid.
5 Luxenberg, *Syro-Aramaic*, 300. Emphasis as in the original.

The Abundance

IN THE NAME OF ALLAH, THE COMPASSIONATE, THE MERCIFUL.

¹Indeed, we have given you abundance, ²So pray to your Lord and sacrifice. ³Indeed, it is the one who insults you who has been cut off.

---

1. *Al-kawthar*, here translated as "abundance," is another mysterious word. Bell states that it is "from the root meaning 'many,'" and "is interpreted as meaning much wealth, or by others as referring to the number of his followers; others again take the word as the proper name of a river or pool in Paradise."¹ The *Tafsir al-Jalalayn* explains that "*Kawthar* is a river in the Garden from which the Basin of his Community is watered. *Kawthar* means immense good, in the form of Prophethood, Qur'an, intercession and other things."² However, Qurtubi offers seventeen different interpretations of *al-kawthar*; Qurtubi's thirteenth-century contemporary Ibn an-Naqib offers twenty-six.³

3. The *Tafsir al-Jalalayn* explains that this means "cut off from all good, or cut off from having descendants."⁴ He adds: "This was revealed about al-As ibn Wa'il, who called the Prophet abtar (cut off) when his son al-Qasim died."⁵ Islamic tradition holds that Muhammad never had a son who lived to adulthood; however, like all other elements of the Muhammad legend, this likely has a theological import. See 33:40 and, for punishment in kind as al-As receives here, 5:45.

The Unbelievers

Al-Kafirun

Introduction

Here again, Islamic authorities disagree about when this sura was revealed. Maududi notes the disagreement and concludes that "according to the majority of commentators, it is a Makki Surah, and the subject matter itself points to its being a Makki revelation."[1]

The subject matter points to its being Meccan because, according to Islamic tradition, the Muslims were a small, weak, embattled band, constantly threatened by the Quraysh, which would make this sura a plea for tolerance for the Muslims, not a magnanimous granting of tolerance to an opposition group.

Al-Wahidi, however, records a tradition that explains this sura as a rejection of an invitation from the Quraysh. They are depicted as saying to the Muslims: "Come follow our religion and we will follow yours. You worship our idols for a year and we worship your Allah the following year. In this way, if what you have brought us is better than what we have, we would partake of it and take our share of goodness from it; and if what we have is better than what you have brought, you would partake of it and take your share of goodness from it."[2] Muhammad rejected the offer: "Allah forbid that I associate anything with Him."[3]

---

1 Maududi, EnglishTafsir.com, http://www.englishtafsir.com/Quran/109/index.html.
2 Al-Wahidi, 280.
3 Ibid.

The Unbelievers

In the name of Allah, the compassionate, the merciful.

¹Say, O unbelievers, ²I do not worship what you worship, ³Nor do you worship what I worship. ⁴And I will not worship what you worship. ⁵Nor will you worship what I worship. ⁶To you your religion, and to me my religion.

---

6. This entire sura, with this culminating statement, is frequently invoked today as one of the Qur'an's statements of tolerance. However, the *Tafsir al-Jalalayn* says that this verse "was revealed before the command to fight came."[1] This would mean that this verse's tolerance is no longer applicable; see 2:106.

The twentieth-century Qur'anic scholar Muhammad al-Ghazali states: "Oppressing Islam and denying it the right to life cannot be tolerated. It must be explicitly stated that blood will continue to flow until this evil desire is removed and the power of Islam is restored and its Shari'a protected and its complete implementation guaranteed. Do the oppressors understand?"[2]

A hadith depicts Muhammad saying: "I have been commanded to fight against people, till they testify to the fact that there is no god but Allah, and believe in me (that) I am the messenger (from the Lord) and in all that I have brought. And when they do it, their blood and riches are guaranteed protection on my behalf except where it is justified by law, and their affairs rest with Allah."[3] Their blood and riches are not protected if they do not embrace Islam; that is, they can be lawfully robbed and killed. See 8:39, 9:29.

The Help

An-Nasr

Introduction

Maududi notes that several Islamic authorities agree that "this is the last Surah of the Quran to be revealed, i.e. no complete Surah was sent down to the Holy Prophet after it."[1] Ibn Kathir records a hadith to that effect.[2] However, another hadith asserts that suras 5 and 48 were the last to be revealed.[3]

An Islamic tradition holds that this sura "is equivalent to one-fourth of the Qur'an."[4] The title is taken from 110:1.

---

1 Maududi, EnglishTafsir.com, http://www.englishtafsir.com/Quran/110/index.html.
2 Ibn Kathir, X, 617.
3 *Jami at-Tirmidhi*, vol. 5, book 44, no. 3063.
4 Ibn Kathir, X, 617.

The Help

IN THE NAME OF ALLAH, THE COMPASSIONATE, THE MERCIFUL.

¹When Allah's help and the conquest comes ²And you see mankind entering the religion of Allah in crowds, ³Then sing the praises of your Lord, and seek his forgiveness. Indeed, he is always ready to show mercy.

---

1. Ibn Kathir states that "conquest" here refers to the conquest of Mecca, which in Islamic tradition led to the conquest of all Arabia. He quotes an early Muslim explaining that "when Makkah was conquered, all of the people rushed to the Messenger of Allah to profess their Islam. The various regions were delaying their acceptance of Islam until Makkah was conquered. The people used to say, 'Leave him and his people alone. If he is victorious over them he is a (true) Prophet.'"¹ Worldly success was unquestioningly equated with divine favor.

The Flame

Al-Lahab

Introduction

Islamic tradition is virtually unanimous in agreeing that this is a Meccan sura. Its title comes from 111:5.

The Flame

In the name of Allah, the compassionate, the merciful.

¹Perish the hands of Abu Lahab, and may he perish. ²His wealth and gains will not exempt him. ³He will be plunged into flaming fire, ⁴And his wife, the wood-carrier, ⁵Will have upon her neck a rope of palm-fiber.

---

1. In a hadith, Muhammad is depicted as climbing a mountain and calling the Quraysh. When they assembled, he told them: "I am a warner to you in face of a terrific punishment."[1] This annoyed Muhammad's uncle, who was known as Abu Lahab, "Father of Flame." According to the story, he shouted at Muhammad: "May your hands perish all this day. Is it for this purpose you have gathered us?"[2] Muhammad thereupon received this sura, cursing Abu Lahab and his wife to hellfire.

3. The "flaming fire" (*dhat lahab*) according to the *Tafsir al-Jalalayn*, "alludes to his nickname, Abu Lahab, lit. 'Father of Flame,' by which he was called due to the redness of his face."[3]

4. The *Tafsir al-Jalalayn* states that "she was named Umm Jamil. She carried wood and thorns and threw them in the path of the Prophet."[4] She will in hell receive punishment in kind; see 5:45.

The Sincerity

Al-Ikhlas

Introduction

According to Maududi, "Whether it is a Makki or a Madani Surah is disputed, and the difference of opinion has been caused by the traditions which have been related concerning the occasion of its revelation."[1] The divergence once again indicates that these traditions are more conjecture and factionalism than historical records.

---

1 Maududi, EnglishTafsir.com, http://www.englishtafsir.com/Quran/112/index.html.

The Sincerity

IN THE NAME OF ALLAH, THE COMPASSIONATE, THE MERCIFUL.

[1]Say, He is Allah, the one. [2]Allah, *as-samad.* [3]He has not fathered anyone, nor was he fathered. [4]And no one is comparable to him.

---

2. According to Bell, most modern scholars translate *as-samad* as "the eternal," but "no satisfactory derivation of the word in this sense has been suggested; Arab commentators take the word as meaning 'the one to whom recourse is had,' 'the chief.' The Semitic root, *smd*, seems to mean 'to bind together.' 'The Undivided' might give the sense."[1] Tabari offers a variety of meanings for the word, including "the one who is not hollow, who does not eat and drink," and "the one from whom nothing comes out," the latter being a familiar Qur'anic designation of Allah as the one who does not beget and is not begotten.[2] The philologist and historian Franz Rosenthal concludes that *as-samad* may be "an ancient Northwest

Semitic religious term, which may no longer have been properly understood by Muhammad himself."[3] Or by the person or persons who actually compiled the Qur'an.

3. This is a repudiation not only of Christianity but of the "daughters of Allah" worshiped by the Quraysh. See 2:116, 6:100, 9:30, 10:68, 17:40, 17:111, 18:4, 19:35, 19:88, 21:26, 25:2, 37:149, 39:4, 43:16, 43:81, 52:39, 53:21, 72:3. According to Islamic tradition, Muhammad briefly endorsed the idea of "daughters of Allah" during the Satanic Verses incident. See 53:19.

The Daybreak

Al-Falaq

Introduction

This sura and sura 114 are known collectively as *Al-Mu'awwidhatan*: the two suras of taking refuge in Allah from evil. They have a particular status in Islamic piety as incantations to ward off harm, as according to Islamic tradition, when Muhammad lay in bed with his final illness, he recited them over and over.

Here again, there is considerable disagreement among Islamic authorities as to whether these two suras date from the Meccan or the Medinan period.[1] The title comes from 113:1.

---

1 Maududi, EnglishTafsir.com, http://www.englishtafsir.com/Quran/113/index.html.

The Daybreak

IN THE NAME OF ALLAH, THE COMPASSIONATE, THE MERCIFUL.

[1]Say, I seek refuge in the Lord of the daybreak [2]From the evil of what he created, [3]From the evil of the darkness when it is intense, [4]And from the evil of malignant witchcraft, [5]And from the evil of the envious when he envies.

---

4. In a hadith, Aisha explains that "the Messenger of Allah was bewitched until he thought that he had relations with his wives, but he had not had relations with them."[1] It was worked by a man named Lubaid, or Labid, who was "an ally of the Jews" and a hypocrite.[2] This sura and sura 114 are presented in Islamic tradition as the remedy for such eventualities.

The Mankind

An-Nas

Introduction

Ibn Kathir records a tradition stating that one of those identified as an early compiler of the Qur'an, Ibn Mas'ud, "did not record the Mu'awwidhatayn [suras 113 and 114] in his Mushaf (copy of the Qur'an)."[1]

Maududi declares that "on the basis of these traditions the opponents of Islam had an opportunity to raise doubts about the Qur'an, saying that this Book, God forbid, is not free from corruption. For when, according to a Companion of the rank of Hadrat Abdullah bin Mas'ud, these two Surahs are an annexation to the Qur'an, many other additions and subtractions also might have been made in it."[2] Indeed.

However, Maududi attempts to resolve this difficulty by citing various authorities stating that Muhammad had included suras 113 and 114 in his Qur'an, and therefore Ibn Mas'ud was simply mistaken. As there is no independent evidence of any of this that goes back to the time Muhammad is supposed to have lived, all these differing traditions simply testify to the fluidity and variability of the Qur'anic text, as has been documented in this volume.

---

1 Ibn Kathir, X, 638.
2 Maududi, EnglishTafsir.com, http://www.englishtafsir.com/Quran/113/index.html.

The Mankind

IN THE NAME OF ALLAH, THE COMPASSIONATE, THE MERCIFUL.

1Say, I seek refuge in the Lord of mankind, **2**The king of mankind, **3**The God of mankind, **4**From the evil of the sneaking whisperer, **5**Who whispers in the hearts of mankind, **6**Of the jinn and mankind.

---

4. The whisperer is Satan, who "whispers and then when he is obeyed, he withdraws."[1]

6. Bell observes that this verse "may possibly be an afterthought," and thus a later interpolation.[2]

Two Apocryphal
Shi'ite Suras

Introduction

Around 1655, the Persian-language book *Dabestan-e Mazaheb* (School of Religions) was published in India, containing the texts of two chapters of the Qur'an, Sura al-Walaya ("The Guardian") and Sura al-Nurayn ("The Two Lights").

These two chapters are clearly meant to bolster the Shi'ite case. The guardian is Ali, and the two lights are obviously Muhammad and Ali. However, these two suras are almost certainly forgeries, and not only Sunnis, but Shi'ites also consider them inauthentic. This is in part because there is no mention of these suras in extant literature before the publication of *Dabestan-e Mazaheb*, although Arabic versions of both were discovered in Bankipur, India, in 1912 in a Qur'an manuscript that was at least two hundred or three hundred years old.[1]

Shi'ites also generally reject these two suras and other Qur'anic variants, even those that bolster their own case against the Sunnis, because they accept the mainstream Sunni Uthmanic Qur'anic text, although some say the order of the suras should be changed. However, the idea that Sunnis had altered the text of the Qur'an to remove passages that proved the rightness of the Shi'ite case persisted among some Shi'ites until at least the early eleventh century.[2]

---

1 William St. Clair Tisdall, "Shi'ah Additions To The Koran," *The Moslem World*, Vol. III, No. 3, July, 1913, 228.

2 Moojan Momen, *An Introduction to Shi'i Islam: The History and Doctrines of Twelver Shi'ism* (New Haven: Yale University Press, 1985), 172.

Although the Bankipur manuscript's pro-Shi'ite variations in the Qur'anic text may reflect or be derived from traditions predating that time, the historian and philologist William St. Clair Tisdall considers all of them to be forgeries with the "possible exception" of the sura of the Two Lights. He explains that "the style is imitated from that of the Koran, but not always very successfully. There are some grammatical errors, unless these are due to the transcriber." He also notes that some words are used with meanings they only acquired after the Qur'an was traditionally thought to have been compiled and states that the repetition of Qur'anic passages demonstrates "the writer's determination to prove what he wished to prove at all costs."[3]

However, there are so many grammatical errors and repetitions in the Qur'an as it stands that these cannot make the case for the inauthenticity of these two suras. The strongest case against them is based upon their relatively late appearance and clear apologetic intent, along with the fact that even though these passages are meant to establish the Shi'ite case, the Shi'ites reject them. Nevertheless, their very existence is noteworthy, as Islam's theology of the perfection and unchangeable character of the Qur'an did not deter their author from making edits in the holy text; they could be the product of a time when the Qur'anic text was still undergoing revision, and one was not risking one's life by making changes. If they originated later, that their author would have dared produce them is all the more striking in light of what were then and still are the prevailing beliefs and assumptions about the immutability of the Qur'anic text.

In any case, even if they originated close to the time of the publication of *Dabestan-e Mazaheb*, and the Arabic version is no older than the Persian, they attest to the fact that in some quarters, changes were indeed made in the Qur'anic text, and that text has never been static.

---

3 Tisdall, "Shi'ah Additions to the Koran," 229.

Al-Nurayn (The Two Lights)

IN THE NAME OF ALLAH, THE COMPASSIONATE, THE MERCIFUL.

1O you who have believed, believe in the two lights which we have sent down. They recite my signs to you, and they both warn you of the punishment of a great day.

2Two lights, one of them from the other, and indeed we are the hearer, the knower.

3Indeed those who faithfully perform their covenant with Allah and his messenger in his family, to them belong the gardens of delight.

4And those who have disbelieved after that they have believed, through their breaking their covenant and what the messenger agreed upon with them, shall be cast into the blaze,

5Indeed those who have wronged their own souls and have rebelled against the deputy of the messenger, those men shall be made drink of boiling water. Indeed it is Allah who has brightened the heavens and the earth with whatever he has willed, and has selected from the angels and from the messengers, and has made some of the believers guardians over mankind, Allah does whatever he wills. There is no God but he, the compassionate, the merciful.

6And indeed those who were before them practiced deceit with their messengers, therefore I punished them for their deceit: indeed my seizing is severe, painful.

7Indeed Allah destroyed Aad and Thamud because of what they had deserved, and he has made them a reminder to you. Will you not, therefore, fear Allah?

8And Pharaoh, because he was very obstinate towards Moses and Aaron, he drowned him and all who followed him,

9So that it might be a sign to you, and indeed most of you are sinful.

10Indeed Allah will gather them together in the day of gathering, and they will not be able to answer when they are questioned.

11Indeed, the blaze (*al-jahim*) will be their dwelling, and indeed Allah is all-knowing, all-wise.

12O messenger, announce my warning, accordingly they will know.

13They are, indeed, lost who have become renegades from my signs and my commandment.

14The comparison of those who faithfully perform their covenant with you is that I have rewarded them with the gardens of delight.

15Indeed Allah is certainly the Lord of pardon and of a great reward,

16And indeed Ali is among the pious,

17And indeed we will certainly pay him all of what he deserves on the day of judgment,

18Nor are we unaware of his being wronged.

---

1. The two lights are Muhammad and Ali, whom Shi'ites believe to be Muhammad's designated and rightful successor.
3. Here begins a collection of Qur'an quotations and paraphrases, assembled apparently at random with little regard for context. This also may be an attempt to imitate Qur'anic style and produce a "sura like it," answering the challenge of 2:23 and 10:38, but it is more likely that this pastiche of Qur'anic passages is meant to give the Shi'ite claims embedded within it an air of authenticity.

¹⁹And we have honored him above all your family,

²⁰For he and his seed are certainly patient.

²¹And indeed their opponent is the imam of sinners.

²²Say to those who have disbelieved after they believed, You have sought the adornment of the lower life, and were over-hasty about it, and you forgot what Allah and his messenger promised you, and you broke the covenants after confirming them. And we have indeed made the comparison for you beforehand, so that by chance you might be guided rightly.

²³O messenger, we have indeed sent down to you clear signs; in them whoever faithfully performs it is a believer, and whoever abandons it after you, they will be clear.

²⁴Therefore turn away from them, indeed they are renegades,

²⁵And indeed we summon them on a day when nothing will ease them, and they will not be granted mercy.

²⁶Indeed in the blaze they will have a place from which they will not depart.

²⁷Therefore praise the name of your Lord, and be among the worshippers.

²⁸And indeed, we certainly sent Moses, and Aaron when he wished to appoint a successor, consequently they rebelled against Aaron. Patience consequently was beautiful. We, therefore, made apes and pigs out of them, and we cursed them until a day when they will be raised up.

²⁹Be patient, therefore; then they will perceive clearly.

³⁰And indeed, we have surely brought you the command, as to those of the messengers who were before you,

³¹And we have made for you from among them a deputy, so that by chance they may return. ³²And whoever turns away from my decree, then indeed I am his place of return, consequently they will surely enjoy their unbelief only a little. Therefore you will not inquire about the covenant-breakers.

³³O messenger, we have indeed set for you a covenant on the necks of those who have believed. Accept it, therefore, and be among the grateful.

³⁴Indeed Ali is an adorer by night, a worshipper, he fears the next world and he hopes for the reward of his Lord. Say, Are they equal, those who have acted wrongfully? And they will know it in my punishment.

³⁵He will place iron collars about their necks, and they will be remorseful for what they did.

³⁶Indeed we give you good news of his seed, the upright ones.

³⁷And indeed they will not oppose our decree.

³⁸Therefore there will be blessing and mercy from me upon them, living and dead, on a day when they will be raised up.

³⁹And my wrath will be upon those who transgress against them after you, indeed they have become a people of evil, perishing.

⁴⁰And upon those who have walked their walk there will be mercy from me, and they will be in the upper rooms, safe.

⁴¹And praise be to Allah, the Lord of the worlds.

21. In Shi'ite Islam, the imam is a successor of Muhammad and a bearer of something of his prophetic spirit; the "imam of sinners" is the Sunni caliph.

Al-Walaya (The Guardian)

IN THE NAME OF ALLAH, THE COMPASSIONATE, THE MERCIFUL.

¹O you who have believed, believe in the prophet and in the guardian, both of whom we have raised up, they will guide you to the right path.

²A prophet and a guardian are two of them from one another, and I am the knower, the well-informed.

³Indeed those who faithfully perform Allah's covenant, to them belong the gardens of delight.

⁴And those who, when our signs are recited to them, have considered our signs to be lies,

⁵Indeed to them belongs a great place in the blaze, when it is proclaimed to them on the day of the resurrection, Where are the wrongdoers, those who consider the messengers liars?

⁶He did not create them, the messengers, except in the truth, and Allah was not going to reveal them until an appointed time near at hand.

⁷And praise your Lord and give thanks to him, and Ali is among the witnesses.

Acknowledgments

It is not surprising given the nature of this book and the political and cultural environment today that among the people to whom I owe gratitude for helping bring this critical edition of the Qur'an to fruition, there are more who must remain anonymous than those whom I can name.

Chief among the named, however, is the incomparable Ibn Warraq, the world's foremost scholar of the Qur'an and the origins of Islam, who carefully reviewed this manuscript and gave me invaluable suggestions for improvement and guidance for future inquiries. Likewise Hugh Fitzgerald and Loren Rosson, whose keen editorial eyes are responsible for any smoothness or ease of reading this book may feature.

Above all, there is that individual who carefully read the manuscript and gave me numerous useful suggestions for material I should include and topics I should discuss. I heeded virtually all of these suggestions, and this book is the better for it. You know who you are, and so do I, and you know how grateful I am.

Endnotes

SURA 1

1 Arthur Jeffery, "A Variant Text of the Fatiha," in Ibn Warraq, ed., *The Origins of the Koran* (Amherst, New York: Prometheus, 1998), 146.

2 Jeffery, 147.

3 "Quran—Comparing Hafs & Warsh for 51 textual variants," MuslimProphets.com, http://muslimprophets.com/article.php?aid=64.

4 Muhammad Ibn Ismail Al-Bukhari, *Sahih al-Bukhari: The Translation of the Meanings*, Muhammad M. Khan, trans. (Riyadh: Darussalam, 1997), vol. 1, book 10, no. 782. Jay Smith, *Qira'at Conundrum: Assessing the Many Qira'at Qur'ans*, n.d., 84.

5 Bukhari, vol. 5, book 63, no. 3827.

6 Ibn Kathir, *Tafsir Ibn Kathir* (abridged) (Riyadh: Darussalam, 2000), I, 87.

7 Jalalu'd-Din al-Mahalli and Jalalu'd-Din as-Suyuti, *Tafsir al-Jalalayn*, translated by Aisha Bewley (London: Dar Al Taqwa Ltd., 2007), 2.

8 Mahmoud M. Ayoub, *The Qur'an and Its Interpreters* (Albany, New York: State University of New York Press, 1984) I, 49.

SURA 2

1 *Tafsir al-Jalalayn*, 4.

2 Muhammad Muhsin Khan and Muhammad Taqi-ud-Din Al-Hilali, *Interpretation of the Meanings of the Noble Qur'an* (Riyadh: Darussalam, n.d.), II, 148.

3 Richard Bell, *The Qur'an: Translated, with a Critical Re-Arrangement of the Surahs* (Edinburgh: T. &. T. Clark, 1937), I, 3.

4 Christoph Luxenberg, *The Syro-Aramaic Reading of the Koran* (Berlin: Verlag Hans Schiler, 2000), 71.

5 Christoph Luxenberg, "Syriac Liturgy and the 'Mysterious Letters,'" in Ibn Warraq, ed., *Christmas in the Koran: Luxenberg, Syriac, and the Near Eastern and Judeo-Christian Background of Islam* (Amherst, New York: Prometheus Books, 2014), 527.

6 David Margoliouth, "Textual Variations of the Koran," in Ibn Warraq, *The Origins of the Koran*, 157.

7 Muhammad Asad, *The Message of the Qur'an* (Bristol, England, The Book Foundation, 2003), 11.

8 *Tafsir al-Jalalayn*, 524.

9 Ibn Kathir, I, 120.

10 Ignaz Goldziher, *Introduction to Islamic Theology and Law*, translated by Andras and Ruth Hamori (Princeton: Princeton University Press, 1981), 82.

11 G. F. Haddad, "The Qadariyya, Mu'tazila, and Shi'a," *Living Islam*, http://www.livingislam.org/n/qms_e.html.

12 Smith, 51.

13 J. Barth, "Studies Contributing to Criticism and Exegesis of the Koran," in Ibn Warraq, ed., *What the Koran Really Says* (Amherst, New York: Prometheus, 2002), 427.

14 Richard Bell, *The Qur'an: Translated, with a Critical Re-Arrangement of the Surahs* (Edinburgh: T. & T. Clark, 1937), I, 5.

15 Ibn Kathir, I, 176.

16 Ibn Warraq, "Introduction," in *What the Koran Really Says*, 48.

17 Arthur Jeffery, "The Qur'an Readings of Zaid b. Ali," in Ibn Warraq, ed., *Which Koran? Variants, Manuscripts, Linguistics* (Amherst, New York: Prometheus Books, 2011), 438.

18 R. H. Charles, *The Apocrypha and Pseudepigrapha of the Old Testament* (Oxford: Clarendon Press, 1913), 137.

19 Bell, I, 7.

20 Sayyid Abul A'la Mawdudi, *Towards Understanding the Qur'an (Tafhim al-Qur'an)*, Zafar Ishaq Ansari, trans. (Leicester, England: The Islamic Foundation, 1995), I, 70.

21 Jeffery, "Zaid," 438.

22 Ibn Kathir, I, 204.

23 Sayyid Qutb, *In the Shade of the Qur'an (Fi Zilal al-Qur'an)*, M. A. Salahi and A. A. Shamis, trans. (Leicester, England: The Islamic Foundation, 1999), I, 62.

24 Mawdudi, I, 73.

25 Ibn Kathir, I, 230.

26 "Quran - Comparing Hafs & Warsh."

27 W. St. Clair Tisdall, "Shi'ah Additions to the Koran," *The Moslem World*, Vol. III, No. 3, July, 1913, 234. Translation modernized for clarity.

28 Asad, 21.

29 Ibid.

30 Abu Abdullah al-Qurtubi, *Tafsir al-Qurtubi: Classic Commentary of the Holy Qur'an*, Aisha Bewley, trans. (London: Dar Al-Taqwa, 2003), I, 267.

31 Ibid.

32 Ibn Kathir, I, 250.

33 Ibid.

34 Judah Benzion Segal, "The Sabian Mysteries: The Planet Cult of Ancient Harran," in Edward Bacon, ed., *Vanished Civilizations of the Ancient World* (New York: McGraw Hill, 1963), 214.

35 Ibn Warraq, "Introduction," 43.

36 *Tafsir Ibn Abbas*, Mokrane Guezzou, trans. (Amman: Royal Aal al-Bayt Institute for Islamic Thought, 2020), https://www.altafsir.com/Tafsir.asp?tMadhNo=0&tTafsirNo=73&tSoraNo=2&tAyahNo=65&tDisplay=yes&UserProfile=0&LanguageId=2.

37 Qurtubi, I, 271.

38 Muhammad Aashiq Ilahi Bulandshahri, *Illuminating Discourses on the Noble Qur'an* (*Tafsir Anwarul Bayan*), Afzal Hussain Elias and Muhammad Arshad Fakhri, trans. (Karachi: Darul Ishaat, 2005), I, 79.

39 *Tafsir Anwarul Bayan*, I, 80.

40 *Tafsir al-Jalalayn*, 28.

41 Bukhari, vol. 4, book 58, no. 3169.

42 Ibid.

43 "Quran - Comparing Hafs & Warsh"; Smith, 91.

44 Ibn Kathir, I, 285.

45 David Brooks, "Among the Bourgeoisophobes: Why the Europeans and Arabs, each in their own way, hate America and Israel," *The Weekly Standard*, April 15, 2002.

46 Bell, I, 13.

47 Qurtubi, I, 312.

48 Ibid.

49 Qurtubi, I, 313.

50 Bell, I, 14.

51 Ibn Warraq, "Introduction," 48.

52 William St. Clair Tisdall, "The Sources of Islam," in Ibn Warraq, ed., *The Origins of the Koran: Classic Essays on Islam's Holy Book*, (Amherst, NY: Prometheus Books, 1998), 250.

53 Ibn Kathir, I, 323.

54 *Tafsir al-Jalalayn*, 38.

55 Qutb, I, 105.

56 "Quran—Comparing Hafs & Warsh"; Smith, 93.

57 Bell, I, 16.

58 Smith, 53.

59 Bell, I, 18.

60 Luxenberg, *Syro-Aramaic*, 56-7.

61 Smith, 54.

62 Asad, 39.

63 Jacob of Edessa, quoted in Crone and Cook, *Hagarism*, 173.

64 Barbara Finster, "Zu Der Neuauflage Von K.A.C. Creswells 'Early Muslim Architecture,' *Kunst Des Orients* 9, no. 1/2 (1973), 94. Author's translation.

65 Dan Gibson, *Early Islamic Qiblas: A Survey of Mosques Built between 1AH/622 C.E. and 263 AH/876 C.E.* (Vancouver: Independent Scholars Press, 2017), 7.

66 Gibson, *Early Islamic Qiblas*, 6.

67 For a detailed exposition of this, see Robert Spencer, *Did Muhammad Exist? An Inquiry into Islam's Obscure Editions, Revised and Expanded Edition* (New York: Bombardier Books, 2021).

68 Ibn Kathir, I, 429.

69 Muqtedar Khan, "The Legacy of Prophet Muhammad and the Issues of Pedophilia and Polygamy," *Ijtihad*, June 9, 2003.

70 Annemarie Schimmel, *And Muhammad Is His Messenger: The Veneration of the Prophet in Islamic Piety* (Chapel Hill: University of North Carolina Press, 1985), 21.

71 Schimmel, 35.

72 Ibid.

73 *Tafsir al-Jalalayn*, 60.

74 Bell, I, 24.

75 Ahmed ibn Naqib al-Misri, *Reliance of the Traveller: A Classic Manual of Islamic Sacred Law*, Nuh Ha Mim Keller, trans. (Beltsville, Maryland: Amana Publications, 1999), xx; o4.9.

76 Sultanhussein Tabandeh, *A Muslim Commentary on the Universal Declaration of Human Rights*, translated by F. J. Goulding, 1970.

77 Ibid.

78 Ibid.

79 Ibid.

80 Ibid.

81 Smith, 55.

82 *Mishkat al-Masabih*, 1965.

83 Roi Kais, "Qaedat al-Jihad claims responsibility for Burgas attack," *Ynet News*, July 21, 2012.

84 Yasmeen Serhan, "Is ISIS More Violent During Ramadan?," *The Atlantic*, June 26, 2017.

85 Luxenberg, *Syro-Aramaic*, 120-1.

86 Asad, 51.

87 *Tafsir al-Jalalayn*, 69.

88 Ibn Kathir, I, 527.

89 Ibid.

90 Ibn Hisham, *The Life of Muhammad: A Translation of Ibn Ishaq's Sirat Rasul Allah*, A. Guillaume, trans. (Karachi: Oxford University Press, 1955), 287.

91 Ibid.

92 Ibid.

93 Ibn Hisham, 288.

94 Qutb, I, 258.

95 Qutb, I, 259.

96 Qutb, I, 259-60.

97 Ibn Hisham, 314.

98 Ibn Kathir, I, 531.

99 *Tafsir Anwarul Bayan*, I, 235.

100 These include Ibn Abbas, Abu al-Aliyah, Mujahid, al-Hasan, Qatadah, ar-Rabi bin Anas, as-Suddi, Muqatil bin Hayyan, and Zayd bin Aslam.

101 *Tafsir al-Jalalayn*, 69.

102 *Tafsir al-Jalalayn*, 70.

103 August Fischer, "A Qur'anic Interpolation," Herbert Berg, trans., in Ibn Warraq, ed., *What the Koran Really Says*, 446.

104 Ibn Kathir, I, 589-90.

105 Ibn Kathir, I, 590.

106 Ibid.

107 *Tafsir Anwarul Bayan*, I, 266-67.

108 Karen Armstrong, "Balancing the Prophet," *Financial Times*, April 27, 2007.

109 Qurtubi, I, 549.

110 Smith, 56.

111 Ibn Kathir, I, 611-14.

112 Qutb, I, 273; Mawdudi, I, 173.
113 Muslim ibn al-Hajjaj, *Sahih Muslim*, translated by Abdul Hamid Siddiqi, (New Delhi: Kitab Bhavan), revised edition 2000, book 8, no. 3363.
114 Ibn Kathir, I, 675.
115 Bell, I, 36.
116 Smith, 57.
117 Ayoub, I, 247.
118 Ayoub, I, 248.
119 Ayoub, I, 247-8.
120 Bulugh al-Maram, book 2, no. 324, https://sunnah.com/bulugh/2/220.
121 Ayoub, I, 253.
122 Asad, 70.
123 *Sahih Muslim*, book 19, no. 4294.
124 Qutb, I, 330.
125 Ibid.
126 Qutb, I, 329.
127 Abu Dawud, *Sunan Abu Dawud, English Translation with Explanatory Notes,* Ahmad Hasan, trans. (New Delhi: Kitab Bhavan, 1990), book 37, no. 4310.
128 Bell, I, 37.
129 *Tafsir al-Jalalayn*, 97, 99.
130 "Taghut," in Thomas Patrick Hughes, ed., *A Dictionary of Islam* (Ottawa: Laurier Publications, 1996), 625.
131 Smith, 58.
132 Bukhari, vol. 1, book 6, no. 304.
133 Ibid.
134 Ibn Kathir, II, 105.
135 Ibid.

SURA 3

1 Ibn Kathir, II, 109.
2 Ibid.
3 Mahmoud M. Ayoub, *The Qur'an and Its Interpreters* (Albany, New York: State University of New York Press, 1992) II, 16.
4 Ayoub, II, 18.
5 C. Heger, "Koran XXV.1: Al-Furqan and the 'Warner,'" in *What the Koran Really Says*, 388.
6 Hughes, 132.
7 Shabbir Ahmed Usmani, *The Noble Qur'an (Tafseer-e-Usmani)*, Maulana Mohammad Ashfaq Ahmad, trans. (New Delhi: Idara Isha'at-e-Diniyat, 2006), I. 168.
8 Ibn Kathir, II, 110.
9 Ibn Kathir, II, 112.
10 *Tafsir al-Jalalayn*, 116.
11 Mawdudi, I, 229.
12 Al-Wahidi, 61.
13 Ibid.
14 Al-Wahidi, 60.
15 Maududi, I, 239.
16 Ibn Kathir, II, 122.
17 Ibn Kathir, II, 123.
18 Smith, 91.

19 Ibn Kathir, II, 132.
20 *Tafsir Anwarul Bayan*, I, 363.
21 Ibid.
22 Asad, 79.
23 Ibn Kathir, II, 141.
24 Etan Kohlberg, "Taqiyya in Shi'i Theology and Religion," in Hans Gerhard Kippenberg and Guy G. Stroumsa, eds., *Secrecy and Concealment: Studies in the History of Mediterranean and Near Eastern Religions* (Leiden: Brill, 1995), 351.
25 Kohlberg, 370.
26 Kohlberg, 355–56.
27 Kohlberg, 357–58.
28 Kohlberg, 373.
29 Kohlberg, 363.
30 Ibn Kathir, II, 142.
31 Raymond Ibrahim, "Islam, War, and Deceit: A Synthesis (Part I)," *Jihad Watch*, February 14, 2009.
32 Ibn Kathir, II, 146.
33 Tisdall, "Shi'ah Additions to the Koran," 234. Translation modernized for clarity.
34 Moojan Momen, *An Introduction to Shi'i Islam: The History and Doctrines of Twelver Shi'ism* (New Haven: Yale University Press, 1985), 172.
35 Ayoub, II, 90.
36 Ibn Kathir, III, 32.
37 *Sahih Muslim*, book 25, no. 5326.
38 *Sahih Muslim*, book 30, no. 5837.
39 *Tafsir Anwarul Bayan*, I, 375.
40 *Tafsir Anwarul Bayan*, I, 376.
41 Smith, 59.
42 Ibn Kathir, II, 158.
43 Ayoub, II, 131.
44 Abu Abdullah al-Qurtubi, *Tafsir al-Qurtubi: Classic Commentary of the Holy Qur'an*, Aisha Bewley, trans. (Bradford, England: Diwan Press, n.d.), III, 230.
45 Ayoub, II, 131.
46 "The Arabic Gospel of the Infancy of the Saviour," Alexander Walker, trans. *Ante-Nicene Fathers*, Vol. 8. Alexander Roberts, James Donaldson, and A. Cleveland Coxe, eds. (Buffalo, NY: Christian Literature Publishing Co., 1886.) Revised and edited for New Advent by Kevin Knight, http://www.newadvent.org/fathers/0806.htm.
47 Ayoub, II, 138.
48 *Tafsir Anwarul Bayan*, I, 384.
49 *Tafsir Anwarul Bayan*, I, 386.
50 "Infancy Gospel of Thomas," *The Apocryphal Gospels: Texts and Translations*, Bart Ehrman and Zlatko Plese, trans. (New York: Oxford University Press, 2011), 11.
51 *Tafsir Anwarul Bayan*, I, 386.
52 Ibid.
53 Smith, 84.
54 *Jami at-Tirmidhi*, vol. 6, book 45, no. 3551.
55 Ibn Kathir, II, 171.
56 Ibn Kathir, II, 172.

57 Ibid.
58 "Quran—Comparing Hafs & Warsh"; Smith, 90.
59 Ibn Hisham, 410.
60 "A Common Word between Us and You (Summary and Abridgement)," A Common Word, http://www.acommon word.com/index.php?lang=en&page=option1.
61 Sayyid Qutb, *Milestones* (Cedar Rapids, Iowa: Mother Mosque Foundation, n.d.), 263.
62 *Tafsir al-Jalalayn*, 134.
63 Ibn Kathir, II, 185.
64 Mawdudi, I, 264.
65 Ibn Kathir, II, 187.
66 Barth, 428.
67 Michael Schub, "Mauve Athena: The 'Translation' of the Qur'an into Modern Double-Standard Arabic," in *Which Koran?*, 202.
68 Ibn Kathir, II, 197.
69 Smith, 60.
70 "Quran—Comparing Hafs & Warsh"; Smith, 90.
71 Smith, 61.
72 Ayoub, II, 241.
73 Mawdudi, I. 271.
74 Ibid.
75 Ibid.
76 Ibn Kathir, II, 212.
77 Ibid.
78 Ibid.
79 Ibn Kathir, II, 212-3.
80 Ibn Kathir, II, 213.
81 Ibid.
82 Ibid.
83 Ibid.
84 Ibid.
85 *Tafsir al-Jalalayn*, 142.
86 Ibn Kathir, II, 216-7.
87 Ibn Warraq, "The Judeo-Christian Origins of Islam (Part 9)," *Jihad Watch*, July 21, 2011.
88 Dan Gibson, *Qur'anic Geography: A Survey and Evaluation of the Geographical References in the Qur'an with Suggested Solutions for Various Problems and Issues* (Saskatoon: Independent Scholars Press, 2011), 276-7.
89 Ibn Warraq and Markus Gross, "Makka, Bakka, and the Problem of Linguistic Evidence," in *Christmas in the Koran*, 795.
90 Ibn Kathir, II, 217.
91 Tisdall, "Shi'ah Additions to the Koran," 235. Translation modernized for clarity.
92 Ibn Kathir, II, 235.
93 Bukhari, vol. 6, book 65, no. 4557.
94 Momen, 173.
95 *Tafsir Anwarul Bayan*, I, 434.
96 *Tafsir Ibn Abbas*, 3:113, https://www.altafsir.com/Tafsir.asp?tMadhNo=0&tTafsirNo=73&tSoraNo=3&tAyahNo=113&tDisplay=yes&UserProfile=0&LanguageId=2.
97 Ibn Kathir, II, 249.
98 Ibn Kathir, II, 251.
99 Ibn Hisham, 300.
100 Ibid.
101 Ibid.
102 Ibid.
103 V. S. Naipaul, *Among the Believers: An Islamic Journey* (New York: Vintage Books, 1982), 141.
104 Ibn Kathir, II, 277.
105 Ibn Kathir, II, 284.
106 Smith, 62.
107 Abu Abd ar-Rahman al-Nasa'i, *Sunan an-Nasa'i*, Nasiruddin al-Khattab, trans. (Riyadh: Darussalam, 2007), vol. 1, book 4, no. 432.
108 Bukhari, vol. 4, book 56, no. 3039.
109 Barth, 428-9.
110 "Quran - Comparing Hafs & Warsh."
111 Ibn Warraq, *Virgins? What Virgins? And Other Essays* (Amherst, New York: Prometheus, 2010), 223.
112 Ibn Kathir, II, 307.
113 Ibn Kathir II, 328.

SURA 4

1 *Sahih Muslim* 3467.
2 Murtaza Motahhari, *Woman and Her Rights*, translated by M. A. Ansari, Al-Islam.org, http://www.al-islam.org/Womanrights/.
3 Al-Wahidi, 84.
4 Ibid.
5 Ibid.
6 Ibid.
7 Ibid.
8 *Mishkat al-Masabih*, 3236, https://sunnah.com/mishkat/13/154.
9 Ibn Kathir, II, 375.
10 Asad, 118.
11 *Tafsir Anwarul Bayan*, I, 501.
12 *Tafsir Anwarul Bayan*, I, 502.
13 *Mishkat al-Masabih*, 3095, https://sunnah.com/mishkat/13/16.
14 Ibn Kathir, II, 376.
15 Ibn Kathir, II, 377.
16 Smith, 84.
17 Fischer, 446.
18 Ibn Kathir, II, 389.
19 David S. Powers, *Studies in Qur'an and Hadith: The Formation of the Islamic Law of Inheritance* (Berkeley: University of California Press, 1986), ch. 1. Cf. *What the Koran Really Says*, 47–48.
20 Ibn Kathir, II, 395.
21 David S. Powers, *Muhammad Is Not the Father of Any of Your Men: The Making of the Last Prophet* (Philadelphia: University of Pennsylvania Press, 2009), 208.
22 Ibn Kathir, II, 395.
23 Ibid.
24 Powers, 209.

25 "Quran - Comparing Hafs & Warsh."

26 Ibn Kathir, II, 400.

27 Ibn Kathir, II, 401.

28 Bukhari, vol. 8, book 86, no. 6829, https://sunnah.com/bukhari/86/56.

29 Ibid.

30 Ibid.

31 *Tafsir al-Jalalayn*, 180.

32 Ibid.

33 Ibid.

34 Ibid.

35 *Tafsir al-Jalalayn*, 181.

36 *Sunan Ibn Majah*, vol. 3, book 9, no. 1977, https://sunnah.com/ibnmajah/9/133.

37 *Sahih Muslim* 3425.

38 Ibid.

39 Ibid.

40 "Malik's *Muwatta*," trans. 'A'isha 'Abdarahman at-Tarjumana and Ya'qub Johnson, book 30, no. 30.3.17, Center for Muslim-Jewish Engagement, http://www.cmje.org/religious-texts/hadith/muwatta/.

41 Ibid.

42 *Sahih Muslim* 3422.

43 *Sunan Ibn Majah*, vol. 3, book 9, hadith 1944. Sunnah.com, https://sunnah.com/urn/1262630.

44 Robert Spencer, "Al Azhar fatwa on adult suckling," *Jihad Watch*, May 18, 2007.

45 Robert Spencer, "Breastfeeding fatwa sheikh back at Al-Azhar," *Jihad Watch*, May 23, 2009.

46 Ibn Kathir, II, 422.

47 *Sahih Muslim* 3432.

48 *Reliance of the Traveller*, o9.13.

49 *Modern Muslim Societies* (New York: Marshall Cavendish, 2011), 52; P.K. Abdul Ghafoor, "Temporary Marriages with Indonesian Women on Rise," *Arab News*, April 18, 2009; "Sordid trade in the 'summer brides': Arab tourists are 'buying underage Egyptian sex slaves' to serve them for just a few months,'" *Daily Mail*, July 15, 2012.

50 *Sahih Muslim*, 3252.

51 *Sahih Muslim*, 3253.

52 *Sahih Muslim*, 3255.

53 *Al-Kafi (Fru al-Kafi)*, Muhammad Sarwar, trans. (New York: The Islamic Seminary 2015), V, 411.

54 Ibid.

55 Tisdall, "Shi'ah Additions to the Koran," 236.

56 Ibn Kathir, II, 424.

57 *Tafsir Anwarul Bayan*, I, 539-41.

58 *Tafsir Anwarul Bayan*, I, 541-2.

59 "Does the Qur'an Tolerate Domestic Abuse?," *BeliefNet*, July 2007.

60 Asad, 127.

61 *Tafsir Anwarul Bayan*, I, 550-551.

62 *Sahih Muslim*, 2127.

63 Bukhari, vol. 7, book 77, no. 5825.

64 Tisdall, "Shi'ah Additions to the Koran," 235. Translation modernized for clarity.

65 Ibn Kathir, II, 467.

66 *Sunan Abu Dawud*, book 40, no. 4484.

67 Ibn Kathir, II, 477.

68 Bell, I, 77.

69 Ibn Warraq, "Introduction," 42.

70 Tisdall, "Shi'ah Additions to the Koran," 235. Translation modernized for clarity.

71 Mawdudi, II, 49.

72 Sayyid Qutb, *In the Shade of the Qur'an (Fi Zilal al-Qur'an)*, Adil Salahi and Ashur Shamis, trans. (Leicester, England: The Islamic Foundation, 2001), III, 194.

73 *Tafsir Anwarul Bayan*, I, 579.

74 *Tafsir Anwarul Bayan*, I, 584.

75 Bukhari, vol. 9, book 93, no. 7142.

76 Tisdall, "Shi'ah Additions to the Koran," 235. Translation modernized for clarity.

77 Ibid.

78 Ibn Kathir, II, 507.

79 Maududi, EnglishTafsir.com, http://www.englishtafsir.com/Quran/4/index.html.

80 Ibn Kathir, II, 512.

81 "Full text: bin Laden's 'letter to America,'" *Observer*, November 24, 2002.

82 Al-Nawawi, *Riyad-us-Saliheen*, Muhammad Amin Abu Usamah Al-Arabi bin Razduq, trans. (Riyadh: Darussalam, 1999), book 11, ch. 16, no. 300.

83 Al-Wahidi, 96.

84 Bukhari, vol. 1, book 4, no. 233.

85 *Tafsir al-Jalalayn*, 206.

86 Smith, 84.

87 *Tafsir Anwarul Bayan*, I, 637.

88 Ibn Kathir, II, 581.

89 *Riyad-us-Saliheen*, book 17, ch. 36, no. 1646.

90 *Tafsir al-Jalalayn*, 217.

91 Ibn Kathir, II, 589.

92 Ibn Kathir, II, 600.

93 Ibid.

94 *Sunan an-Nasa'i*, vol. 3, book 24, no. 3040.

95 Ibn Kathir, II, 602.

96 Bukhari, vol. 4, book 56, no. 3017.

97 Ibn Hisham, 675.

98 Ibn Hisham, 676.

99 Ibid.

100 Bukhari, vol. 5, book 64, no. 4037.

101 Ibid.

102 Ibid.

103 Ibid.

104 Ibn Kathir, II, 615-6.

105 Ibn Kathir, III, 17-18.

106 "Quran - Comparing Hafs & Warsh"; Smith, 90.

107 "The Second Treatise of the Great Seth," Roger A. Bullard and Joseph A. Gibbons, trans., The Gnostic Society Library, http://gnosis.org/naghamm/2seth.html.

108 Ibn Kathir, III, 26.

109 Ibid.

110 Ibid.

111 Ibn Kathir, III, 26-7.

112 Ibn Kathir, III, 27.

113 *Tafsir Anwarul Bayan*, II, 8.

114 Bukhari, vol. 3, book 46, no. 2476.

115 Ibn Kathir, III, 32.

116 Tisdall, "Shi'ah Additions to the Koran," 236. Translation modernized for clarity.

117 Ibn Kathir, III, 59.

118 Bukhari, vol. 5, book 64, no. 4364.

SURA 5

1 Fischer, 446.

2 Ibn Kathir, III, 126-7.

3 *Tafsir al-Jalalayn*, 241.

4 Ibn Kathir, III, 129-30.

5 Ibn Kathir, III, 130.

6 Ibn Kathir, III, 159.

7 Tisdall, 239.

8 *Sahih Muslim*, 4185.

9 Ibn Kathir III, 183-4.

10 Ibn Kathir, III, 204.

11 Ibn Kathir, III, 221.

12 *Tafsir al-Jalalayn*, 259.

13 Stanley L. Jaki, *Chance or Reality and Other Essays* (Lanham, Maryland, and London: University Press of America; Bryn Mawr, Pa.: The Intercollegiate Studies Inc., 1986), 242.

14 Abu Hamid al-Ghazali, *The Incoherence of the Philosophers*, translated by Michael E. Marmura (Provo, Utah: Brigham Young University Press, 2000), 2.

15 Ibid., p. 8.

16 Tilman Nagel, *The History of Islamic Theology from Muhammad to the Present*, translated by Thomas Thornton (Princeton: Markus Wiener Publishers, 2000), 211.

17 Al-Ghazali, 226.

18 Stanley Jaki, *The Savior of Science* (Washington, DC: Regnery Gateway, 1988), 43.

19 Rodney Stark, *The Victory of Reason* (New York: Random House, 2005), 20-21.

20 Moses Maimonides, *The Guide for the Perplexed*, M. Friedländer, trans. (New York: Barnes & Noble, 2004).

21 *Tafsir al-Jalalayn*, 259.

22 *Tafsir Anwarul Bayan*, II, 98-9.

23 "Quran - Comparing Hafs & Warsh."

24 Tisdall, "Shi'ah Additions to the Koran," 236. Translation modernized for clarity.

25 Ibn Kathir, III, 231.

26 *Tafsir al-Jalalayn*, 264.

27 Ibn Kathir, III, 246.

28 *Tafsir Anwarul Bayan*, II, 110.

29 Ibn Kathir, III, 265.

30 Bukhari, vol. 6, book 65, no. 4623.

31 Smith, 84.

32 Christoph Luxenberg, "Christmas in the Koran," Ibn Warraq, trans. An abridged version of this article was first published in German in *Imprimatur* 1, March 2003, 13–17.

33 Samir Khalil Samir, "The Theological Christian Influence on the Qur'an," in Gabriel Said Reynolds, ed., *The Qur'an in Its Historical Context* (New York: Routledge, 2008), 149.

34 Samir, 149.

35 Luxenberg, "Christmas in the Koran."

36 Samir, 149–50.

37 Luxenberg, "Christmas in the Koran."

SURA 6

1 Ibn Kathir, III, 310.

2 Ibn Kathir, III, 313.

3 Sayyid Qutb, *In the Shade of the Qur'an (Fi Zilal al-Qur'an)*, Adil Salahi, trans. (Leicester, England: The Islamic Foundation, 2002), V, 49.

4 *Tafsir al-Jalalayn*, 281.

5 Barth, 426.

6 Ibn Kathir, III, 326.

7 *Tafsir al-Jalalayn*, 285.

8 "Shirk: the ultimate crime," *Invitation to Islam Newsletter*, Issue 2, July 1997.

9 *Tanwir al-Miqbas min Tafsir ibn Abbas*, 6:32, https://www.altafsir.com/Tafasir.asp?tMadhNo=0&tTafsirNo=73&tSoraNo=6&tAyahNo=35&tDisplay=yes&UserProfile=0&LanguageId=2.

10 Tisdall, "Shi'ah Additions to the Koran," 236. Translation modernized for clarity.

11 Bell, II, 447.

12 *Tafsir Anwarul Bayan*, II, 190.

13 Ibid.

14 Dan Gibson, *Early Islamic Qiblas: A Survey of Mosques Built between 1AH/622 C.E. and 263 AH/876 C.E.* (Vancouver: Independent Scholars Press, 2017), 73.

15 Daniel Alan Brubaker, *Corrections in Early Qur'an Manuscripts: Twenty Examples* (Lovettsville, Virginia: Think and Tell Press, 2019), 48.

16 Smith, 86.

17 "Protection from the Jinn," IslamQA.com, February 2, 2008, https://islamqa.info/en/answers/10513/protection-from-the-jinn.

18 Ibn Kathir, III, 427-8.

19 *Tafsir Anwarul Bayan*, II, 201.

20 Smith, 63.

21 Ibn Kathir, III, 454.

22 Smith, 85.

23 *Tafsir Anwarul Bayan*, II, 215.

24 Smith, 90.

25 *Tafsir Anwarul Bayan*, II, 221.

26 Ibn Kathir, III, 502.

27 Bukhari, vol. 9, book 87, no. 6878.

28 Ibn Majah, vol. 5, book 36, no. 4000.

SURA 7

1 Bell, I, 135.
2 Ibn Kathir, IV, 24.
3 Bukhari, vol. 4, book 60, no. 3326.
4 Bukhari, vol. 4, book 60, no. 3327.
5 *Tafsir al-Jalalayn*, 328.
6 Asad, 1135.
7 Zakir Naik, *Most Common Questions Asked by Non-Muslims Who Have Some Knowledge of Islam*, quoted in Sam Shamoun, "Is Satan an Angel or a Jinn? Analyzing the Quran's Confusing Statements," *Answering Islam*, http://www.answering-islam.org/Quran/Contra/iblis.html.
8 Bell, I, 7.
9 Ibn Kathir, IV, 29.
10 Ibn Kathir, IV, 32.
11 Barth, 425.
12 Ibid.
13 Smith, 64; "Quran - Comparing Hafs & Warsh."
14 *Sunan Abu Dawud*, 4447.
15 Ibn Kathir, IV, 133.
16 Smith, 65.
17 Alphonse Mingana and Agnes Smith Lewis, "Leaves from Three Ancient Qurans: Possibly Pre-Uthmanic with a List of Their Variants," in *Which Koran?*, 266.
18 Ibn Kathir, IV, 178.
19 Smith, 66.
20 *Sahih Muslim* 6426.
21 *Tafsir Anwarul Bayan*, II, 333.
22 Ibid.
23 Ibn Kathir, IV, 205.
24 Ibid.
25 Ibn Kathir, IV, 211.
26 Smith, 67.
27 Ibn Kathir, IV, 240.

SURA 8

1 Bukhari, vol. 1, book 8, no. 438.
2 Bukhari, vol. 4, book 56, no. 2977.
3 Ibn Kathir, IV, 273.
4 Ibn Kathir, IV, 274.
5 *Tafsir al-Jalalayn*, 379.
6 Ibn Hisham, 301.
7 Tisdall, "Shi'ah Additions to the Koran," 236. Translation modernized for clarity.
8 Ibn Kathir, IV, 314.
9 *Tafsir al-Jalalayn*, 385.
10 Abdur-Rahman Nasir as-Sadi, *Tafsir as-Sadi*, Nasiruddin al-Khattab, trans. (Riyadh: International Islamic Publishing House, 2018), III, 377.
11 Ibn Kathir, IV, 320.
12 Ibid.
13 Ibn Kathir, IV, 334.

14 Ibn Kathir, IV, 342.
15 Sayyid Qutb, *In the Shade of the Qur'an (Fi Zilal al-Qur'an)*, Adil Salahi, trans. (Leicester, England: The Islamic Foundation, 2003), VII, 190.
16 *Tafsir al-Jalalayn*, 393.
17 Ibid.
18 Ibn Kathir, IV, 356-7.

SURA 9

1 *Tafsir al-Jalalayn*, 397.
2 Ibid.
3 Ibn Kathir, IV, 375.
4 "Bin Laden's Sermon for the Feast of the Sacrifice," Middle East Media Research Institute (MEMRI), Special Dispatch No. 476, March 6, 2003.
5 "Surat at-Tawba: Repentance, Tafsir," http://bewley.virtualave.net/tawba1.html.
6 Ibid.
7 *Tafsir al-Jalalayn*, 398.
8 Ibn Kathir IV, 376.
9 Asad, 289.
10 Ibid.
11 *Tafsir al-Jalalayn*, 398.
12 Ibn Kathir, IV, 377.
13 Sayyid Qutb, *In the Shade of the Qur'an (Fi Zilal al-Qur'an)*, Adil Salahi, trans. (Leicester, England: The Islamic Foundation, 2003), VIII, 68.
14 "Surat at-Tawba: Repentance, Tafsir."
15 Ibn Kathir, IV, 377.
16 Ibn Kathir, IV, 379-80.
17 "Surat at-Tawba: Repentance, Tafsir."
18 Ibid.
19 Ibn Hisham, 504.
20 "Surat at-Tawba: Repentance, Tafsir."
21 *Tafsir al-Jalalayn*, 400.
22 "Surat at-Tawba: Repentance, Tafsir."
23 Ibid.
24 Ibn Kathir, IV, 394.
25 "Surat at-Tawba: Repentance, Tafsir."
26 Mingana and Lewis, 268.
27 "Surat at-Tawba: Repentance, Tafsir."
28 "Najis things » Impurities (najāsāt)," Sistani.org, http://www.sistani.org/english/book/48/2126/.
29 *Tafsir al-Jalalayn*, 404; "Surat at-Tawba: Repentance, Tafsir."
30 Ibid.
31 *Sahih Muslim*, 4366.
32 *Tafsir as-Sadi*, IV, 75.
33 Ibn Kathir, IV, 405.
34 "Surat at-Tawba: Repentance, Tafsir."
35 Ibid.
36 Ibid.
37 *Tafsir as-Sadi*, IV, 75.
38 *Sahih Muslim*, 30.
39 *Tafsir al-Jalalayn*, 404.

40 *Tafsir as-Sadi*, IV, 76.
41 Ibn Kathir, IV, 404-5.
42 *Tafsir as-Sadi*, IV, 75.
43 "Surat at-Tawba: Repentance, Tafsir."
44 Ibid.
45 Bat Ye'or, *The Decline of Eastern Christianity Under Islam: From Jihad to Dhimmitude* (Vancouver: Fairleigh Dickinson University Press, 1996), 271-2.
46 "Surat at-Tawba: Repentance, Tafsir."
47 Ibn Kathir, IV, 406.
48 "Surat at-Tawba: Repentance, Tafsir."
49 Ibid.
50 "Surat at-Tawba: Repentance, Tafsir."
51 Asad, 295.
52 Ibn Warraq, "Introduction to Sura IX.29," in *What the Koran Really Says*, 319.
53 Franz Rosenthal, "Some Minor Problems," in *What the Koran Really Says*, 324.
54 Ibn Kathir, IV, 406.
55 Ibid.
56 Ibid.
57 *Tafsir Anwarul Bayan*, IV, 441.
58 Qutb, VIII, 126.
59 Mawdudi, III, 202.
60 Ibid.
61 "Surat at-Tawba: Repentance, Tafsir."
62 Ibid.
63 Ibn Kathir, IV, 408.
64 *Jami at-Tirmidhi*, vol. 5, book 44, no. 3095, https://sunnah.com/urn/641040.
65 *Tafsir al-Jalalayn*, 406.
66 "Surat at-Tawba: Repentance, Tafsir."
67 *Mishkat al-Masabih* 42, https://sunnah.com/mishkat/1/38.
68 "Surat at-Tawba: Repentance, Tafsir."
69 Mingana and Lewis, 270.
70 Ibid.
71 Ibn Kathir, IV, 414.
72 Johannes J. G. Jansen, "The Gospel According to Ibn Ishaq (d. 773)," Conference paper, "Skepticism and Scripture" Conference, Center for Inquiry, Davis, California, January 2007.
73 Ibid.
74 Ibid.
75 Ibid.
76 Mingana and Lewis, 270.
77 Ibn Kathir, IV, 425.
78 Smith, 88.
79 Mingana and Lewis, 266.
80 "Surat at-Tawba: Repentance, Tafsir."
81 Mingana and Lewis, 270.
82 *Tafsir al-Jalalayn*, 407.
83 Ibn Kathir, IV, 430.
84 Ibn Kathir, IV, 434; *Tafsir al-Jalalayn*, 409; "Surat at-Tawba: Repentance, Tafsir."

85 Bukhari, vol. 4, book 56, no. 2785.
86 Mingana and Lewis, 266.
87 *Tafsir al-Jalalayn*, 410.
88 Ibn Hisham, 603.
89 *Tafsir Anwarul Bayan*, IV, 461.
90 Ibn Kathir, IV, 451.
91 Ibid.
92 *Tafsir al-Jalalayn*, 414.
93 *Tafsir al-Jalalayn*, 415.
94 Ibn Kathir, IV, 458.
95 "Surat at-Tawba: Repentance, Tafsir."
96 Ibid.
97 Smith, 68.
98 Smith, 90.
99 Ibid.
100 Ibn Kathir, IV, 475.
101 Ibid.
102 "Surat at-Tawba: Repentance, Tafsir."
103 Ibn Kathir, IV, 475.
104 Ibn Hisham, 242.
105 Ibid.
106 "Surat at-Tawba: Repentance, Tafsir."
107 Ibn Kathir, IV, 495-6.
108 Marco Schöller, "Medina," *Encyclopaedia of the Qur'an*, Vol. III, J—O, Jane Dammen McAuliffe, General Ed. (Leiden: Brill, 2003), 367.
109 Schöller, 368.
110 "Surat at-Tawba: Repentance, Tafsir."
111 Ibn Kathir, IV, 516.
112 Ibn Kathir, IV, 520.
113 "Surat at-Tawba: Repentance, Tafsir."
114 Ibid.
115 Ibid.
116 Ibid.
117 *Sahih Muslim* 6303.
118 Bell, I, 173.
119 Ibn Kathir, IV, 546.
120 Bukhari, vol. 6, book 65, no. 4679.
121 Ibn Abi Dawud, *Kitab al-Masahif*, 11, in John Gilchrist, *Jam' Al-Qur'an, The Codification of the Qur'an Text: A Comprehensive Study of the Original Collection of the Qur'an Text and the Early Surviving Qur'an Manuscripts* (Mondeor, South Africa: MERCSA, 1989), http://www.answering-islam.org/Gilchrist/Jam/index.html.

SURA 10

1 Ibn Kathir, IV, 558.
2 Al-Wahidi, 148.
3 Smith, 69.
4 Ibn Kathir, IV, 585.
5 Ibn Kathir, IV. 593.
6 Ibid.
7 Ibid.
8 Ibid.
9 "Quran - Comparing Hafs & Warsh"; Smith, 85.

10 Ibn Kathir, IV, 606.
11 Ibid.
12 Ibn Kathir, IV, 608.
13 "Quran - Comparing Hafs & Warsh"; Smith, 90.
14 *Tafsir al-Jalalayn*, 454.
15 Ibid.
16 Bell, I, 200.
17 Ibn Kathir, IV, 650.
18 *Sunan Ibn Majah*, vol. 5, book 36, no. 3992, https://sun-nah.com/ibnmajah/36/67.
19 *Tafsir al-Jalalayn*, 461.
20 Smith, 85.

SURA 11

1 Ibn Kathir, V, 18.
2 Ibn Kathir, V, 19.
3 Ibn Kathir, V, 22.
4 Bell, I, 206.
5 *Tafsir Anwarul Bayan*, III, 7.
6 Ibn Kathir, III, 356.
7 Ibid.
8 Mingana and Lewis, 268.
9 Ibid.
10 Barth, 420.
11 Ibn Kathir, V, 68.
12 Schub, 203.
13 Bell, I, 213.
14 Ibn Kathir, V, 120.
15 *Tafsir Anwarul Bayan*, III, 45.

SURA 12

1 Abu Ubayda, *Majaz*, i, 17-8, in Andrew Rippin, "Foreign Vocabulary," *Encyclopaedia of the Qur'an*, Vol. II, E—I, Jane Dammen McAuliffe, General Ed. (Leiden: Brill, 2002), 229.
2 Robert Kerr, "Aramaisms in the Qur'an and Their Significance," in *Christmas in the Koran*, 149.
3 Ibn Warraq, "In Search of Avocado," in *Christmas in the Koran*, 43.
4 Ibid; Christoph Luxenberg, "Syriac Liturgy and the 'Mysterious Letters' in the Qur'an: A Comparative Liturgical Study," in *Christmas in the Koran*, 510.
5 For a list, see Ibn Warraq, "Introduction," 52-6.
6 Pierre Larcher, "Language, Concept of," *Encyclopaedia of the Qur'an*, Vol. III, 108.
7 Larcher, 109.
8 Claude Gilliot and Pierre Larcher, "Language and Style of the Qur'an," *Encyclopaedia of the Qur'an*, Vol. III, 117.
9 Ibn Kathir, V, 134-5.
10 Maududi, IV, 144.
11 Ibn Kathir, V, 136.
12 Bukhari, vol. 9, book 91, no. 6995.
13 Maududi, IV, 153.
14 Maududi, IV, 144.
15 *Tafsir Anwarul Bayan*, III, 53.

16 Maududi, IV, 166.
17 Abraham Geiger, "What Did Muhammad Borrow From Judaism?," in Ibn Warraq, *The Origins of the Koran*, 202.
18 Ibn Kathir, V, 161.
19 Ibid.
20 Maududi, IV, 175.
21 Ibid.
22 Mawdudi, IV, 179.
23 Ibid.
24 Mawdudi, IV, 186.
25 Ibid.
26 Smith, 84.
27 Ibn Kathir, V, 188.
28 Mawdudi, IV, 195.
29 Barth, 421.
30 Ibid.
31 Barth, 420.
32 "Quran - Comparing Hafs & Warsh."

SURA 13

1 Ibn Kathir, V, 230.
2 Ibid.
3 *Tafsir al-Jalalayn*, 521.
4 Ibn Kathir, V, 232.
5 "Where is Allah?," compiled by Abu Abdullah from 'The Ever-Merciful Istawaa Upon the Throne' by Shaikh Abdullah As-Sabt, MissionIslam.com, http://www.missionislam.com/knowledge/whereallah.htm.
6 Ibid.
7 Ibid.
8 *Tafsir al-Jalalayn*, 522.
9 Ibn Kathir, V, 248.
10 *Tafsir al-Jalalayn*, 524.
11 G. F. Haddad, "The Qadariyya, Mu'tazila, and Shi'a," *Living Islam*, http://www.livingislam.org/n/qms_e.html.
12 "Quran - Comparing Hafs & Warsh"; Smith, 91.
13 Mingana and Lewis, 266.
14 *Tafsir al-Jalalayn*, 528, 530.
15 *Tafsir al-Jalalayn*, 532.
16 Smith, 85.

SURA 14

1 Ibn Kathir, V, 307.
2 Ibn Kathir, V, 308.
3 *Tafsir Anwarul Bayan*, III, 126.
4 Ibn Kathir, V, 316.
5 Mawdudi, IV, 249.
6 Smith, 85.
7 Ibn Kathir, V, 337.
8 Ibn Kathir, V, 335.
9 Bukhari, vol. 7, book 70, no. 5444.
10 Bukhari, vol. 7, book 70, no. 5445.
11 Bukhari, vol. 6, book 65, no. 4669.
12 Bukhari, vol. 6, book 65, no. 4700.
13 Ibn Kathir, V, 360.

14 Ibid.
15 Ibn Kathir, V, 361.
16 Ibid.
17 Keith E. Small, *Textual Criticism and Qur'an Manuscripts*, (Lanham, Maryland: Rowman & Littlefield), 2011, 116.
18 Small, 115.
19 Small, 117.

SURA 15

1 Ibn Kathir, V, 379.
2 Smith, 70.
3 *Tafsir al-Jalalayn*, 548.
4 Ibn Kathir, V, 382.
5 *Tafsir al-Jalalayn*, 552.
6 *Tafsir Anwarul Bayan*, III, 160.
7 Barth, 410.
8 Ibid.
9 Ibn Kathir, V, 410.
10 Ibn Kathir, V, 411.
11 Ibid.
12 Ibn Kathir, V, 417.
13 Ibn Kathir, V, 419.
14 Ibn Kathir, V, 420.

SURA 16

1 Ibn Kathir, V, 438.
2 *Tafsir Ibn Abbas*, https://www.altafsir.com/Tafasir. asp?tMadhNo=0&tTafsirNo=73&tSoraNo=16&tAyahNo=9&tDisplay=yes&UserProfile=0&LanguageId=2.
3 Smith, 91.
4 *Tafsir al-Jalalayn*, 563.
5 Mingana and Lewis, 266.
6 Ibn Kathir, V, 462.
7 Ibn Kathir, V, 463.
8 Ibn Kathir, V, 466.
9 *Tafsir al-Jalalayn*, 571.
10 *Tafsir al-Jalalayn*, 582.
11 Ibid.
12 Mingana and Lewis, 269.
13 Smith, 90.
14 Ibn Kathir, V, 527.
15 Bukhari, vol. 1, book, 1, no. 3.
16 Ibn Kathir, V, 530.
17 *Sahih Muslim*, 4294.

SURA 17

1 Tisdall, 279.
2 Tisdall, 280.
3 Mingana and Lewis, 268.
4 Ibn Kathir, V, 579.
5 Ibn Kathir, V, 580.
6 Ibid.
7 "Quran - Comparing Hafs & Warsh."
8 Luxenberg, *Syro-Aramaic*, 242-5.

9 *Tafsir Anwarul Bayan*, III, 295.
10 Tisdall, "Shi'ah Additions to the Koran," 237. Translation modernized for clarity.
11 Ibid.
12 *Tafsir Ibn Abbas*, https://www.altafsir. asp?tMadhNo=0&tTafsirNo=73&tSoraNo=17&tAyahNo=104&tDisplay=yes&UserProfile=0&LanguageId=2.
13 Ibn Kathir, VI, 104.

SURA 18

1 *Tafsir Anwarul Bayan*, III, 316.
2 Ibn Kathir, VI, 118.
3 Ibid.
4 Ibn Kathir, VI, 121.
5 Ibn Kathir, VI, 120.
6 Ibn Kathir, VI, 129.
7 Ibn Kathir, VI, 129-30.
8 Bukhari, vol. 4, book 59, no. 3225.
9 Ibn Kathir, VI, 130.
10 Tisdall, "Shi'ah Additions to the Koran," 238. Translation modernized for clarity.
11 Smith, 71.
12 Abdullah Yusuf Ali, *The Meaning of the Holy Qur'an* (Beltsville, Maryland: Amana Publications, 1999), 725.
13 Irfan Omar, "Khidr in the Islamic Tradition," *The Muslim World,* vol. LXXXIII, no. 3-4, July-October, 1993.
14 Ibn Saad, "Ibn Taymiyya says Khidr is Alive," *Seeking Ilm*, September 20, 2007.
15 *Sahih Muslim*, 4457.
16 Ibn Kathir, VI, 113.
17 Ibn Kathir, VI, 203.
18 Ibn Kathir, VI, 203-4.
19 *Tafsir al-Jalalayn*, 639.
20 Mawdudi, V, 127.
21 Muhammad al-Ghazali, *Journey Through the Qur'an: The Content and Context of the Suras*, Aisha Bewley, trans. (London: Dar Al-Taqwa, 1998), 207.
22 Ibn Kathir, VI, 205.
23 Ibn Kathir, VI, 206.
24 Ibn Kathir, VI, 205.
25 Smith, 71.
26 Khalid Jan, "Why Zul-Qarnain of the Qur'an is not Alexander the great," IslamAwareness.net, http://www.islamawareness.net/FAQ/zulqarnain.html.
27 Asad, 503.
28 Ibn Kathir, VI, 209.
29 Ibid.
30 Hafiz Salahuddin Yusuf, *Commentary on the Riyad-us-Salihin*, Muhammad Amin and Abu Usamah Al-Arabi bin Razduq, trans., (Riyadh: Darussalam, 1999), II, 1808.
31 Ibid.
32 Ibid.

33 *Jami at-Tirmidhi*, 2187, https://sunnah.com/tirmidhi/33/30.
34 Ibid.
35 Ibid.
36 Bukhari, vol. 8, book 81, no. 6530.
37 Bukhari, vol. 6, book 65, no. 4729.

SURA 19

1 Ibn Kathir, VI, 237.
2 Ibn Kathir, VI, 241.
3 "Question: In the Quran in 2:87, an excerpt: ...We gave Jesus the son of Mary clear (signs) and strengthened him with the holy spirit. What is the holy spirit?," Islam Question & Answer, https://islamqa.info/en/answers/14403/who-is-the-holy-spirit; Bukhari, vol. 8, book 78, no. 6152.
4 Ibn Kathir, VI, 244.
5 Luxenberg, *Syro-Aramaic*, 142.
6 Ibn Kathir, VI, 247.
7 Ibn Kathir, VI, 249.
8 Ibn Kathir, VI, 297.
9 Ibn Kathir, VI, 299.
10 Smith, 73.
11 Luxenberg, *Syro-Aramaic*, 123.
12 Ibid.
13 Luxenberg, *Syro-Aramaic*, 124.

SURA 20

1 Al-Ghazali, *Journey*, 217.
2 *Tafsir Anwarul Bayan*, III, 405.
3 Ibn Kathir, VI, 328.
4 Bell, I, 294.
5 Ibn Kathir, VI, 382.
6 *Tafsir al-Jalalayn*, 677.
7 Ibn Kathir, VI, 383.
8 Ibn Kathir, VI, 398.

SURA 21

1 Tisdall, "Shi'ah Additions to the Koran," 238. Translation modernized for clarity.
2 "Quran - Comparing Hafs & Warsh"; Smith, 93.
3 Ibn Kathir, VI, 425.
4 Ibn Kathir, VI, 427.
5 *Tafsir al-Jalalayn*, 688.
6 Ibid.
7 Ibn Kathir, VI, 435.
8 Barth, 414-5.
9 Bukhari, vol. 4, book 56, no. 2785.
10 Jeffery, *Foreign Vocabulary*.
11 Ibid.
12 Ibn Kathir, VI, 506.
13 Ibn Kathir, VI, 506–7.
14 Ibn Kathir, VI, 507.
15 Jeffery, *Foreign Vocabulary*.
16 Smith, 93.

SURA 22

1 Mawdudi, VI, 8.
2 Ibn Kathir, VI, 536.
3 *Tafsir Anwarul Bayan*, III, 490-1.
4 Bukhari, vol. 4, book 59, no. 3199.
5 Bukhari, vol. 4, book 60, no. 3448.
6 Ibid.
7 Ibid.
8 Mawdudi, VI, 20-1.
9 Mawdudi, VI, 2.
10 Ibn Kathir, VI, 582.
11 Mawdudi, VI, 2.
12 "Full text: bin Laden's 'letter to America,'" Observer, November 24, 2002.
13 Muhsin Khan and Hilali, V, 133.
14 Ibn Kathir, VI, 603.
15 Ibn Kathir, VI, 605.
16 Smith, 91.
17 Ibn Kathir, VI, 611.

SURA 23

1 *Tafsir al-Jalalayn*, 730.
2 Mawdudi, VI, 81.
3 *Sahih Muslim*, 3371.
4 Ibid.
5 Ibn Kathir, VI, 640.
6 *Tafsir Anwarul Bayan*, III, 530.
7 Brubaker, 55.
8 Ibn Kathir, VI, 685.
9 *Tafsir al-Jalalayn*, 744.

SURA 24

1 Bukhari, vol. 6, book 65, no. 4750.
2 Bukhari, vol. 5, book 64, no. 4141.
3 Ibid.
4 Ibid.
5 Ibid.
6 Bukhari, vol. 6, book 65, no. 4750.
7 Ibn Kathir, VII, 56.
8 Ibn Kathir, VII, 64.
9 Ibn Kathir, VII, 67.
10 *Tafsir al-Jalalayn*, 756.
11 *Sunan Abu Dawud*, 4104.
12 *Sunan Abu Dawud*, 2488.
13 Ibid.
14 Ibid.
15 Ibn Kathir, VII, 73.
16 Ibid.
17 Luxenberg, *Syro-Aramaic*, 210.
18 Luxenberg, *Syro-Aramaic*, 211.
19 Ibn Kathir, VII, 78.
20 Tisdall, "Shi'ah Additions to the Koran," 238. Translation modernized for clarity.
21 *Tafsir al-Jalalayn*, 764.
22 Ibn Kathir, VII, 111.

23 Ibid.
24 Ibn Kathir, VII, 113.
25 Ibn Kathir, VII, 114.

SURA 25

1 Heger, "Koran XXV.1," 388.
2 Bukhari, vol. 4, book 61, no. 3617.
3 Ibid.
4 Smith, 90.
5 Smith, 91.
6 Momen, 173.
7 Ibid.
8 Ibn Kathir, VII, 173.
9 Ibid.
10 Smith, 84.
11 *Tafsir Ibn Abbas*, https://www.altafsir.com/Tafasir. asp?tMadhNo=0&tTafsirNo=73&tSoraNo=25&tA-yahNo=52&tDisplay=yes&UserProfile=0&Lan-guageId=2.
12 Ibn Kathir, VII, 189.
13 Ibn Kathir, VII, 192.

SURA 26

1 Ibn Kathir, VII, 237.
2 Ibn Ishaq, 271.
3 Mawdudi, VII, 75.
4 Ibn Kathir, VII, 263.
5 *Jami at-Tirmidhi*, 1456.
6 Ibn Kathir, VII, 277.
7 Ibid.
8 Tisdall, "Shi'ah Additions to the Koran," 238. Translation modernized for clarity.
9 Ibid.

SURA 27

1 *Tafsir al-Jalalayn*, 809.
2 Tisdall, 245.
3 Bell, II, 365.
4 Ibid.
5 Tisdall, 245.
6 Tisdall, 246.
7 "Quran - Comparing Hafs & Warsh"; Smith, 91.
8 Ibn Kathir, VII, 320.
9 Ibid.
10 Ibn Kathir, VII, 321.
11 Bell, II, 367.
12 Ibn Kathir, VII, 327.
13 Tisdall, 246-7.
14 *Tafsir al-Jalalayn*, 818.
15 Ibid.
16 Smith, 91.

SURA 28

1 Mawdudi, VII, 192.
2 Ibid.

3 Ibn Kathir, VII, 411.
4 "Quran - Comparing Hafs & Warsh"; Smith, 84.
5 *Tafsir al-Jalalayn*, 841.
6 Ibn Kathir, VII, 425.
7 Ibn Kathir, VII, 454.
8 *Tafsir Ibn Abbas*, https://www.altafsir.com/Tafasir. asp?tMadhNo=0&tTafsirNo=73&tSoraNo=28&tA-yahNo=88&tDisplay=yes&UserProfile=0&Lan-guageId=2.

SURA 29

1 Ibn Kathir, VII, 462.
2 Ibn Kathir, VII, 476.
3 Maududi, EnglishTafsir.com, https://www.englishtafsir. com/Quran/29/index.html.
4 Smith, 91.
5 Ibn Kathir, VII, 492.
6 *Tafsir al-Jalalayn*, 861.
7 Bukhari, vol. 9, book 96, no. 7363.
8 *Tafsir al-Jalalayn*, 861.
9 Ibn Kathir, VII, 499.
10 *Tafsir al-Jalalayn*, 861.
11 Ibid.

SURA 30

1 *Tafsir al-Jalalayn*, 867.
2 *Jami at-Tirmidhi*, vol. 5, book. 44, no. 3194.
3 Ibid.
4 Ibid.
5 Ibid.
6 Ibid.
7 Ibid.
8 C. G. Pfander, *The Mizanu'l Haqq* (*Balance of Truth*), Thoroughly Revised and Enlarged by W. St. Clair Tisdall (New Delhi: Indo-Asiatic Publishers, 1910), 279, https:// www.answering-islam.org/Books/Pfander/Balance/p278. htm.
9 Ibid.
10 Brubaker, 45.
11 Ibn Kathir, VII, 528.
12 "'Islam is Peace' Says President: Remarks by the President at Islamic Center of Washington, D.C.," The White House, September 17, 2001, https://georgewbush-white-house.archives.gov/news/releases/2001/09/20010917-11. html.
13 Ibn Kathir, VII, 535.
14 Bukhari, vol. 2, book 23, no. 1358.
15 Ibn Kathir, VII, 547.
16 Ibid.

SURA 31

1 Ibn Kathir, VII, 571.
2 Maududi, EnglishTafsir.com, http://www.englishtafsir. com/Quran/31/index.html.
3 Ibn Kathir, VII, 578.

4 Bell, II, 401.
5 Ibn Kathir, VII, 579.
6 Ibn Kathir, VII, 581.
7 Smith, 91.
8 *Sahih Muslim*, 6985.
9 *Sunan Ibn Majah*, 4044.
10 Ibid.

SURA 32

1 Maududi, EnglishTafsir.com, http://www.englishtafsir.
   com/Quran/32/index.html.
2 *Sunan Ibn Majah*, vol. 5, book 36, no. 3973.
3 Ibid.
4 Ibn Kathir, VII, 621.
5 Maududi, EnglishTafsir.com, http://www.englishtafsir.
   com/Quran/32/index.html.

SURA 33

1 Ibn Kathir, VII, 634.
2 Bukhari, vol. 6, book 65, no. 4781.
3 Ibn Ishaq, 458.
4 Bukhari, vol. 4, book 56, no. 2813.
5 Ibn Ishaq, 461.
6 Ibid.
7 Ibn Ishaq, 464.
8 Ibid.
9 Ibn Sa'd, *Kitab al-Tabaqat al-Kabir*, S. Moinul Haq, trans.
   (New Delhi: Kitab Bhavan, n.d.), II, 93.
10 Ibn Kathir, VII, 694.
11 *Tafsir al-Jalalayn*, 904.
12 Ibid.
13 Bukhari, vol. 9, book 97, no. 7420.
14 Abu Ja'far Muhammad bin Jarir al-Tabari, *The History
   of al-Tabari*, Volume VIII, *The Victory of Islam*, Michael
   Fishbein, trans. (Albany, New York: State University of
   New York Press, 1997), 2.
15 Tabari, VIII, 3.
16 Ibid.
17 *Tafsir al-Jalalayn*, 904.
18 Tabari, VIII, 3.
19 Bukhari, vol. 9, book 97, no. 7420.
20 Ibn Kathir, VII, 702.
21 Powers, 9, 25.
22 Powers, 91.
23 *Tafsir al-Jalalayn*, 905.
24 Ibn Kathir, VII, 723.
25 Bukhari, vol. 6, book 65, no. 4788.
26 *Jami at-Tirmidhi*, vol. 5, book 39, no. 2685.
27 Ibn Kathir, VIII, 31.
28 "Quran - Comparing Hafs & Warsh"; Smith, 84.
29 Ibn Kathir, VIII, 51.
30 Ibid.
31 Ibid.

SURA 34

1 Ibn Kathir, VIII, 59-60.
2 Ibn Kathir, VIII, 68.
3 Bell, II, 423.
4 Ibn Kathir, VIII, 80.
5 Ibn Kathir, VIII, 90-91.
6 *Sahih Muslim*, 284.
7 Brubaker, 68-9.
8 Smith, 90.
9 "Quran - Comparing Hafs & Warsh."

SURA 35

1 Maududi, EnglishTafsir.com, http://www.englishtafsir.
   com/Quran/35/index.html.
2 Ibid.
3 Ibid.

SURA 36

1 Ibn Kathir, VIII, 169.
2 Ibid.
3 *Tafsir al-Jalalayn*, 941.
4 *Tafsir Ibn Abbas*, https://www.altafsir.com/Tafasir.
   asp?tMadhNo=0&tTafsirNo=73&tSoraNo=36&tA-
   yahNo=9&tDisplay=yes&UserProfile=0&LanguageId=2.
5 Ibn Kathir, VIII, 171.
6 Ibid.
7 Ibn Kathir, VIII, 172.
8 Ibn Kathir, 3/564, quoted in "Will men in Paradise
   have intercourse with al-hoor aliyn?," Islam Question
   & Answer, August 30, 2000, https://islamqa.info/en/
   answers/10053/will-men-in-paradise-have-intercourse-
   with-al-hoor-aliyn.
9 *Tafsir Ibn Abbas*, https://www.altafsir.com/Tafasir.
   asp?tMadhNo=0&tTafsirNo=73&tSoraNo=36&tA-
   yahNo=66&tDisplay=yes&UserProfile=0&Lan-
   guageId=2.
10 "Quran - Comparing Hafs & Warsh"; Smith, 91.

SURA 37

1 Ibn Kathir, VIII, 232.
2 Ibn Kathir, VIII, 235.
3 Ibn Kathir, VIII, 236.
4 Barth, 408.
5 *Tafsir al-Jalalayn*, 959.
6 Ibn Kathir, VIII, 249.
7 *Tafsir al-Jalalayn*, 959.
8 Ibid.
9 *Tafsir Anwarul Bayan*, IV, 347.
10 Ibn Kathir, VIII, 257.
11 Ibn Kathir, VIII, 258.
12 Ibid.
13 Bell, II, 556.
14 *Tafsir al-Jalalayn*, 962.
15 Barth, 409.
16 Ibn Kathir, VIII, 271.

17 Ibn Kathir, VIII, 271-2.
18 Smith, 74.
19 Ibn Warraq, "Introduction," 54.
20 Tafsir al-Jalalayn, 971.

SURA 38
1 Ibn Kathir, VIII, 312.
2 Maududi, EnglishTafsir.com, http://www.englishtafsir.
   com/Quran/38/index.html.
3 Ibn Kathir, VIII, 321.
4 Tafsir al-Jalalayn, 977.
5 Ibn Kathir, VIII, 328-9.
6 Ibn Kathir, VIII, 329.
7 Tafsir al-Jalalayn, 978, 980.
8 Ibn Kathir, VIII, 339.
9 Smith, 75.
10 Tafsir al-Jalalayn, 981.

SURA 39
1 Barth, 422.
2 Ibid.
3 Barth, 423.
4 Tafsir Anwarul Bayan, 408-9.
5 Barth, 423.
6 Ibn Kathir, VIII, 378.
7 Ibid.
8 Ibn Kathir, VIII, 381.
9 Tafsir al-Jalalayn, 993.
10 Ali, 1193.

SURA 40
1 Smith, 85.
2 Ibn Kathir, VIII, 449.
3 Tafsir al-Jalalayn, 1005.
4 Ibid.
5 Smith, 91.
6 Ibn Kathir, VIII, 474.
7 Ibn Kathir, VIII, 488.
8 Ibn Kathir, VIII, 488-9.
9 "Quran - Comparing Hafs & Warsh"; Smith, 91.

SURA 41
1 Maududi, EnglishTafsir.com, http://www.englishtafsir.
   com/Quran/41/index.html.
2 Ibn Kathir, VIII, 552.

SURA 42
1 Ibn Kathir, VIII, 568.
2 Tafsir al-Jalalayn, 1037.
3 Brubaker, 32.
4 "Quran - Comparing Hafs & Warsh"; Smith, 91.
5 Ibn Kathir, VIII, 593.
6 Smith, 85.

SURA 43
1 Maududi, EnglishTafsir.com, http://www.englishtafsir.
   com/Quran/43/index.html.
2 Tafsir al-Jalalayn, 1047.
3 Maududi, EnglishTafsir.com, http://www.englishtafsir.
   com/Quran/43/index.html.
4 Ibid.
5 Ibn Kathir, VIII, 616.
6 Smith, 85.
7 Ibn Kathir, VIII, 624.
8 Smith, 76.
9 Smith, 93.
10 Tisdall, "Shi'ah Additions to the Koran," 239. Translation
   modernized for clarity.
11 Tafsir al-Jalalayn, 1056.
12 Ibn Kathir, VIII, 651.
13 Tafsir Anwarul Bayan, IV, 525.
14 Ibn Kathir, VIII, 656.
15 "Quran - Comparing Hafs & Warsh."

SURA 44
1 Bukhari, vol. 2, book 15, no. 1007.
2 Ibn Kathir, VIII, 685.
3 Tafsir Ibn Abbas, https://www.altafsir.com/Tafsir.
   asp?tMadhNo=0&tTafsirNo=73&tSoraNo=44&tA-
   yahNo=32&tDisplay=yes&UserProfile=0&Lan-
   guageId=2.
4 Bell, II, 500; Gibson, Qur'anic Geography, 126.
5 Bukhari, vol. 4, book 59, no. 3254.
6 Luxenberg, Syro-Aramaic, 254.
7 Luxenberg, Syro-Aramaic, 259.
8 Tisdall, 281.

SURA 45
1 Ibn Kathir, IX, 23-4.
2 Bell, II, 504.
3 Ibn Kathir, IX, 26.
4 Mingana and Lewis, 265.
5 Mingana and Lewis, 266.
6 Tisdall, "Shi'ah Additions to the Koran," 240. Translation
   modernized for clarity.

SURA 46
1 Ibn Ishaq, 240-1; Bukhari, vol. 6, book 65, no. 4480.
2 Ibn Sa'd, I, 188.
3 Ibid.
4 Bell, II, 507.
5 Smith, 77.
6 Smith, 88.
7 Ibid.
8 Smith, 90.
9 Smith, 88.
10 Ibn Kathir, IX, 74.
11 Ibid.

12 Ibn Kathir, IX, 75.
13 Barth, 426.

SURA 47

1   *Tafsir Anwarul Bayan*, IV, 575.
2   Ibn Kathir, IX, 87.
3   *Tafsir al-Jalalayn*, 1088.
4   Ali, 1315.
5   Ahmed ibn Naqib al-Misri, *Reliance of the Traveller: A Classic Manual of Islamic Sacred Law*, Nuh Ha Mim Keller, trans. (Beltsville, Maryland: Amana Publications, 1999), xx; section o9.14.
6   Smith, 78.
7   *Sunan an-Nasai*, vol. 6, book 50, no. 5487.
8   Ibid.
9   Ibid.
10 Ibn Kathir, IX, 107.
11 Ibid.
12 Ibn Kathir, IX, 118.

SURA 48

1   Bukhari, vol. 4, book 58, no. 3182.
2   Smith, 90.
3   Ibid.
4   "Quran - Comparing Hafs & Warsh."
5   Ibn Kathir, IX, 148.
6   Ibn Kathir, IX, 149.
7   *Tafsir al-Jalalayn*, 1105.

SURA 49

1   Ibn Kathir, IX, 184.
2   Smith, 79.
3   Maududi, EnglishTafsir.com, http://www.englishtafsir.com/Quran/49/index.html.
4   *Sahih Muslim*, 2563a.
5   Daniel Pipes, "The FBI Fumbles," *New York Post*, March 14, 2003.
6   Ibn Kathir, IX, 206.
7   Ibid.

SURA 50

1   Ali, 1346.
2   *Tafsir al-Jalalayn*, 1115.
3   "Quran - Comparing Hafs & Warsh."

SURA 52

1   Ibn Kathir, IX, 288; *Tafsir al-Jalalayn*, 1130.
2   *Tafsir al-Jalalayn*, 1130.
3   Daniel Pipes, *Slave Soldiers and Islam: The Genesis of a Military System* (New Haven: Yale University Press, 1981), 35, 45.
4   Janet Afary, *Sexual Politics in Modern Iran* (Cambridge: Cambridge University Press, 2009).
5   Tisdall, "Shi'ah Additions to the Koran," 240. Translation modernized for clarity.

SURA 53

1   Ibn Ishaq, 165.
2   Ibid.
3   Abu Ja'far Muhammad bin Jarir al-Tabari, *The History of al-Tabari*, Volume VI, *Muhammad at Mecca*, W. Montgomery Watt and M. V. McDonald, trans. (Albany, New York: State University of New York Press, 1988), 107.
4   Ibn Ishaq, 166.
5   Ibid.
6   Tabari, VI, 111.
7   Ibn Ishaq, 166.
8   Ibn Sa'd, I, 236-9.
9   Ibn Kathir, IX, 338.
10 Ibn Kathir, IX, 339.

SURA 54

1   "Splitting of the moon," Quranaloneislam.org, https://www.quranaloneislam.org/splitting-of-the-moon.
2   Fischer, 446.
3   Ibid.
4   Ibn Rawandi, "On Pre-Islamic Christian Strophic Poetical Texts in the Koran: A Critical Look at the Work of Günter Lüling," in Ibn Warraq, ed., *What the Koran Really Says*, 681-2.
5   Ibn Kathir, IX, 373.
6   Ibid.

SURA 55

1   Ibn Kathir, IX, 383.
2   Maududi, EnglishTafsir.com, http://www.englishtafsir.com/Quran/55/index.html.
3   *Sunan Ibn Majah*, vol. 5, book 37, no. 4337.
4   *Jami at-Tirmidhi*, vol. 4, book 12, no. 2536.

SURA 56

1   *Riyad-us-Salihin*, I, 287.

SURA 57

1   Ibn Kathir, IX, 470.
2   Maududi, EnglishTafsir.com, http://www.englishtafsir.com/Quran/57/index.html.
3   Bukhari, vol. 7, book 77, no. 5815.
4   Ibid.
5   Bukhari, vol. 4, book 60, no. 3462.
6   *Tafsir al-Jalalayn*, 1174.
7   Ibn Kathir, IX, 503.
8   Ibid.
9   Ibn Kathir, IX, 504.
10 Ibid.
11 Ibid.
12 *Tafsir al-Jalalayn*, 1177.
13 Ibn Kathir, IX, 508.

SURA 58

1 *Sunan Ibn Majah*, vol. 1, book 1, no. 188.
2 Ibn Kathir, IX, 526.

SURA 59

1 Ibn Kathir, IX, 544.
2 Abu Ja'far Muhammad bin Jarir al-Tabari, *The History of al-Tabari*, Volume VII, *The Foundation of the Community*, M. V. McDonald, translator, State University of New York Press, 1987, 158.
3 Ibid.
4 *Sahih Muslim*, 4347.
5 Tabari, VII, 159.
6 Ibid.

SURA 60

1 Ibn Kathir, IX, 596.
2 Maududi, EnglishTafsir.com, http://www.englishtafsir.com/Quran/60/index.html.
3 Ibn Ishaq, 509.

SURA 61

1 Ibn Kathir, IX, 614-5.
2 Ibn Kathir, IX, 615.
3 Ibn Kathir, IX, 621.
4 *Tafsir al-Jalalayn*, 1201.
5 Ibn Kathir, IX, 626.
6 Ibid.

SURA 63

1 Ibn Ishaq, 363.
2 Ibid.
3 Ibid.
4 Ibid.
5 Maududi, EnglishTafsir.com, http://www.englishtafsir.com/Quran/63/index.html.

SURA 64

1 Smith, 90.
2 Ibn Kathir, X, 24.
3 Ibn Kathir, X, 28.

SURA 65

1 Bukhari, vol. 7, book 68, no. 5317.
2 Smith, 90.
3 Ibn Kathir, X, 55.
4 Ibn Kathir, X, 56.
5 Maududi, EnglishTafsir.com, http://www.englishtafsir.com/Quran/65/index.html.

SURA 66

1 Bukhari, vol. 3, book 46, no. 2468.
2 Maududi, EnglishTafsir.com, http://www.englishtafsir.com/Quran/66/index.html.
3 Bukhari, vol. 3, book 46, no. 2468.

4 Ibid.
5 Bukhari, vol. 7, book 68, no. 5267.
6 Ibn Kathir, X, 72.
7 Smith, 85.

SURA 68

1 Al-Adab al-Mufrad, 308, https://sunnah.com/urn/2303060.
2 *Tafsir al-Jalalayn*, 1232.
3 *Tafsir al-Jalalayn*, 1235.

SURA 69

1 Ibn Warraq, "Introduction," 42.
2 Ibn Kathir, X, 138.
3 Bukhari, vol. 5, book 64, no. 4428.

SURA 70

1 *Tafsir al-Jalalayn*, 1243.
2 Ibn Kathir, X, 156.
3 Fischer, 446.

SURA 71

1 Bukhari, vol. 6, book 65, no. 4920.

SURA 72

1 Ibn Kathir, X, 208.
2 Smith, 93.
3 Tisdall, "Shi'ah Additions to the Koran," 240. Translation modernized for clarity.

SURA 73

1 *Tafsir al-Jalalayn*, 1258.
2 Bell, II, 613.
3 Ibn Kathir, X, 236.

SURA 74

1 Ibn Kathir, X, 241.
2 Ibn Kathir, X, 251.
3 Günter Lüling, *A Challenge to Islam for Reformation* (Delhi: Motilal Banarsidass Publishers, 2003), 476.
4 Ibid.
5 Ibn Kathir, X, 253.
6 Smith, 91.

SURA 75

1 Ibn Kathir, X, 262.
2 *Tafsir al-Jalalayn*, 1270.
3 Ibn Kathir, X, 269.

SURA 76

1 Bell, II, 624.
2 Ibid.
3 Alphonse Mingana, "Syriac Influence on the Style of the Koran," in Ibn Warraq, ed., *What the Koran Really Says*, 181.

SURA 77

1 Bell, II, 626.
2 Ibn Kathir, X, 307-8.
3 Bell, II, 626.

SURA 78

1 Ibn Kathir, X, 333-4.

SURA 80

1 Ibn Warraq, "Introduction," 42.
2 Ibid.
3 Ibn Kathir, X, 366.

SURA 81

1 Ibn Kathir, X, 372.
2 Ibn Kathir, X, 376.
3 Ibid.
4 Ibn Kathir, X, 377.
5 *Tafsir al-Jalalayn*, 1300.
6 Ibid.

SURA 82

1 Bell, II, 640.
2 Ibn Kathir, X, 390.
3 *Tafsir al-Jalalayn*, 1303.

SURA 83

1 Ibn Warraq, "Introduction," 46–47.
2 Ibn Kathir, X, 407.
3 Bell, II, 643.

SURA 84

1 Bell, II, 645.
2 Bell, II, 644.

SURA 85

1 Ibn Kathir, X, 426.
2 Ibn Kathir, X, 436.

SURA 86

1 Ibn Kathir, X, 439.
2 Bukhari, vol. 4, book 60, no. 3334.
3 Ali, 1632.
4 Ibn Kathir, X, 442-3.

SURA 88

1 Bell, II, 653.

SURA 89

1 Bell, II, 654.
2 Ibn Warraq, "Introduction," 42.
3 Ibn Kathir, X, 471.
4 Gibson, *Qur'anic Geography*, 32.
5 Bell, II, 655.

6 Tisdall, "Shi'ah Additions to the Koran," 240. Translation modernized for clarity.

SURA 90

1 Ibn Kathir, X, 482.
2 Ibid.
3 Ibid.

SURA 91

1 Sayyid Abul A'la Mawdudi, *Towards Understanding the Qur'an*, translated and edited by Zafar Ishaq Ansari (Leicester: The Islamic Foundation, 2008), 955.
2 "Quran - Comparing Hafs & Warsh."

SURA 92

1 Ibn Kathir, X, 510.
2 Bell, II, 661.

SURA 93

1 Ibn Kathir, X, 517.
2 Ibn Kathir, X, 517-8.
3 Ibn Kathir, X, 520.

SURA 94

1 Ibn Kathir, X, 525.
2 *Tafsir al-Jalalayn*, 1340.

SURA 95

1 Ibn Kathir, X, 529.
2 Ibid.

SURA 96

1 Bukhari, vol. 1, book 1, no. 3.
2 Ibid.
3 Ibn Sa'd, I, 220.
4 Ibid.
5 Bukhari, vol. 6, book 65, no. 4953.
6 Ibn Ishaq, 106.
7 Ibn Rawandi, "Pre-Islamic Christian Strophic Poetical Texts," 673.
8 Luxenberg, "Christmas in the Koran."
9 Ibid.
10 Ibid.
11 Ibn Kathir, X, 537.
12 Bell, II, 667.
13 Bell, II, 668.
14 Ibn Kathir, X, 538.

SURA 97

1 Ibn Kathir, X, 541-2.
2 Ibn Kathir, X, 542.
3 Ibn Kathir, X, 543.
4 Tisdall, "Shi'ah Additions to the Koran," 240. Translation modernized for clarity.

SURA 98

1 *Tafsir al-Jalalayn*, 1346.
2 Smith, 80.

SURA 99

1 *Tafsir al-Jalalayn*, 1348.
2 Ibid.

SURA 100

1 Ibn Kathir, X, 566.
2 Ibid.

SURA 101

1 Bell, II, 674.
2 Fischer, 446.
3 Bell, II, 674.

SURA 102

1 Bukhari, vol. 8, book 81, no. 6438.

SURA 103

1 Ibn Kathir, X, 582.
2 Ibid.
3 Ibn Kathir, X, 582-3.
4 Ibn Kathir, X, 583.
5 Ibid.
6 Bell, II, 676.
7 Ibid.
8 Ibid.

SURA 104

1 Bell, II, 677.
2 Ibn Kathir, X, 586.
3 *Tafsir al-Jalalayn*, 1352.
4 Fischer, 446.

SURA 105

1 Ibn Warraq, "Introduction," 45.

SURA 106

1 Ibn Kathir, X, 600.

SURA 107

1 Bell, II, 680.
2 Ibn Kathir, X, 605.

SURA 108

1 Bell, II, 681.
2 Al-Mahalli and as-Suyuti, *Tafsir al-Jalalayn*, 1357.
3 Claude Gilliot, "Reconsidering the Authorship of the Qur'an," in Gabriel Said Reynolds, ed., *The Qur'an in Its Historical Context* (New York: Routledge, 2008), 98.
4 *Tafsir al-Jalalayn*, 1357.
5 Ibid.

SURA 109

1 *Tafsir al-Jalalayn*, 1359.
2 Al-Ghazali, 547.
3 *Sahih Muslim*, 31.

SURA 110

1 Ibn Kathir, X, 620.

SURA 111

1 Bukhari, vol. 6, book 65, no. 4770.
2 Ibid.
3 *Tafsir al-Jalalayn*, 1360.
4 Ibid.

SURA 112

1 Bell, II, 685.
2 Rosenthal, "Some Minor Problems," 332–34.
3 Rosenthal, 337.

SURA 113

1 Ibn Kathir, X, 645.
2 Ibid.

SURA 114

1 Ibn Kathir, X, 649.
2 Bell, II, 687.

Index